4425   9181   S0-AHB-148

POETRY
for Students

Advisors

POETRY
for Students

**Presenting Analysis, Context, and Criticism
on Commonly Studied Poetry**

VOLUME 32

GALE
CENGAGE Learning

Detroit • New York • San Francisco • New Haven, Conn • Waterville, Maine • London

GALE
CENGAGE Learning·

Poetry for Students, Volume 32

Project Editor: Sara Constantakis

Rights Acquisition and Management: Beth Beaufore, Barb McNeil, Tracie Richardson, Robyn Young

Composition: Evi Abou-El-Seoud

Manufacturing: Drew Kalasky

Imaging: John Watkins

Product Design: Pamela A. E. Galbreath, Jennifer Wahi

Content Conversion: Katrina Coach

Product Manager: Meggin Condino

For product information and technology assistance, contact us at
Gale Customer Support, 1-800-877-4253.
For permission to use material from this text or product,
submit all requests online at **www.cengage.com/permissions.**
Further permissions questions can be emailed to
permissionrequest@cengage.com

While every effort has been made to ensure the reliability of the information presented in this publication, Gale, a part of Cengage Learning, does not guarantee the accuracy of the data contained herein. Gale accepts no payment for listing; and inclusion in the publication of any organization, agency, institution, publication, service, or individual does not imply endorsement of the editors or publisher. Errors brought to the attention of the publisher and verified to the satisfaction of the publisher will be corrected in future editions.

Gale
27500 Drake Rd.
Farmington Hills, MI, 48331-3535

ISBN-13: 978-1-4144-4180-1
ISBN-10: 1-4144-4180-0

ISSN 1094-7019

This title is also available as an e-book.
ISBN-13: 978-1-4144-4953-1
ISBN-10: 1-4144-4953-4
Contact your Gale, a part of Cengage Learning sales representative for ordering information.

Printed in the United States of America
1 2 3 4 5 6 7 14 13 12 11 10

Table of Contents

Just a Few Lines on a Page

I have often thought that poets have the easiest job in the world. A poem, after all, is just a few lines on a page, usually not even extending margin to margin—how long would that take to write, about five minutes? Maybe ten at the most, if you wanted it to rhyme or have a repeating meter. Why, I could start in the morning and produce a book of poetry by dinnertime. But we all know that it isn't that easy. Anyone can come up with enough words, but the poet's job is about writing the *right* ones. The right words will change lives, making people see the world somewhat differently than they saw it just a few minutes earlier. The right words can make a reader who relies on the dictionary for meanings take a greater responsibility for his or her own personal understanding. A poem that is put on the page correctly can bear any amount of analysis, probing, defining, explaining, and interrogating, and something about it will still feel new the next time you read it.

It would be fine with me if I could talk about poetry without using the word "magical," because that word is overused these days to imply "a really good time," often with a certain sweetness about it, and a lot of poetry is neither of these. But if you stop and think about magic—whether it brings to mind sorcery, witchcraft, or bunnies pulled from top hats—it always seems to involve stretching reality to produce a result greater than the sum of its parts and pulling unexpected results out of thin air. This book provides ample cases where a few simple words conjure up whole worlds. We do not actually travel to different times and different cultures, but the poems get into our minds, they find what little we know about the places they are talking about, and then they make that little bit blossom into a bouquet of someone else's life. Poets make us think we are following simple, specific events, but then they leave ideas in our heads that cannot be found on the printed page. Abracadabra.

Sometimes when you finish a poem it doesn't feel as if it has left any supernatural effect on you, like it did not have any more to say beyond the actual words that it used. This happens to everybody, but most often to inexperienced readers: regardless of what is often said about young people's infinite capacity to be amazed, you have to understand what usually does happen, and what could have happened instead, if you are going to be moved by what someone has accomplished. In those cases in which you finish a poem with a "So what?" attitude, the information provided in *Poetry for Students* comes in handy. Readers can feel assured that the poems included here actually are potent magic, not just because a few (or a hundred or ten thousand) professors of literature say they are: they're significant because they can withstand close inspection and still amaze the very same people who have just finished taking them apart and seeing how they work. Turn them inside out, and they will still be able to come alive, again and again. *Poetry for Students* gives readers of any age good practice in feeling the ways poems relate to both the reality of the time and place the poet lived in and the reality of our emotions. Practice is just another word for being a student. The information given here helps you understand the way to read poetry; what to look for, what to expect.

With all of this in mind, I really don't think I would actually like to have a poet's job at all. There are too many skills involved, including precision, honesty, taste, courage, linguistics, passion, compassion, and the ability to keep all sorts of people entertained at once. And that is just what they do with one hand, while the other hand pulls some sort of trick that most of us will never fully understand. I can't even pack all that I need for a weekend into one suitcase, so what would be my chances of stuffing so much life into a few lines? With all that *Poetry for Students* tells us about each poem, I am impressed that any poet can finish three or four poems a year. Read the inside stories of these poems, and you won't be able to approach any poem in the same way you did before.

David J. Kelly
College of Lake County

Introduction

Purpose of the Book

The purpose of *Poetry for Students* (*PfS*) is to provide readers with a guide to understanding, enjoying, and studying poems by giving them easy access to information about the work. Part of Gale's "For Students" Literature line, *PfS* is specifically designed to meet the curricular needs of high school and undergraduate college students and their teachers, as well as the interests of general readers and researchers considering specific poems. While each volume contains entries on "classic" poems frequently studied in classrooms, there are also entries containing hard-to-find information on contemporary poems, including works by multicultural, international, and women poets.

The information covered in each entry includes an introduction to the poem and the poem's author; the actual poem text (if possible); a poem summary, to help readers unravel and understand the meaning of the poem; analysis of important themes in the poem; and an explanation of important literary techniques and movements as they are demonstrated in the poem.

In addition to this material, which helps the readers analyze the poem itself, students are also provided with important information on the literary and historical background informing each work. This includes a historical context essay, a box comparing the time or place the poem was written to modern Western culture, a critical overview essay, and excerpts from critical essays on the poem. A unique feature of *PfS* is a specially commissioned critical essay on each poem, targeted toward the student reader.

To further help today's student in studying and enjoying each poem, information on audio recordings and other media adaptations is provided (if available), as well as reading suggestions for works of fiction and nonfiction on similar themes and topics. Classroom aids include ideas for research papers and lists of critical and reference sources that provide additional material on the poem.

Selection Criteria

The titles for each volume of *PfS* are selected by surveying numerous sources on notable literary works and analyzing course curricula for various schools, school districts, and states. Some of the sources surveyed include: high school and undergraduate literature anthologies and textbooks; lists of award-winners, and recommended titles, including the Young Adult Library Services Association (YALSA) list of best books for young adults.

Input solicited from our expert advisory board—consisting of educators and librarians—guides us to maintain a mix of "classic" and contemporary literary works, a mix of challenging and engaging works (including genre titles that are commonly studied) appropriate for different age levels, and a mix of international, multicultural and women authors. These advisors also consult on each volume's entry list, advising on which titles are most studied, most appropriate, and meet the broadest interests across secondary (grades 7–12) curricula and undergraduate literature studies.

How Each Entry Is Organized

Each entry, or chapter, in *PfS* focuses on one poem. Each entry heading lists the full name of the poem, the author's name, and the date of the poem's publication. The following elements are contained in each entry:

Introduction: a brief overview of the poem which provides information about its first appearance, its literary standing, any controversies surrounding the work, and major conflicts or themes within the work.

Author Biography: this section includes basic facts about the poet's life, and focuses on events and times in the author's life that inspired the poem in question.

Poem Text: when permission has been granted, the poem is reprinted, allowing for quick reference when reading the explication of the following section.

Poem Summary: a description of the major events in the poem. Summaries are broken down with subheads that indicate the lines being discussed.

Themes: a thorough overview of how the major topics, themes, and issues are addressed within the poem. Each theme discussed appears in a separate subhead and is easily accessed through the boldface entries in the Subject/Theme Index.

Style: this section addresses important style elements of the poem, such as form, meter, and rhyme scheme; important literary devices used, such as imagery, foreshadowing, and symbolism; and, if applicable, genres to which the work might have belonged, such as Gothicism or Romanticism. Literary terms are explained within the entry, but can also be found in the Glossary.

Historical Context: this section outlines the social, political, and cultural climate in which the author lived and the poem was created. This section may include descriptions of related historical events, pertinent aspects of daily life in the culture, and the artistic and literary sensibilities of the time in which the work was written. If the poem is a historical work, information regarding the time in which the poem is set is also included. Each section is broken down with helpful subheads.

Critical Overview: this section provides background on the critical reputation of the poem, including bannings or any other public controversies surrounding the work. For older works, this section includes a history of how the poem was first received and how perceptions of it may have changed over the years; for more recent poems, direct quotes from early reviews may also be included.

Criticism: an essay commissioned by *PfS* which specifically deals with the poem and is written specifically for the student audience, as well as excerpts from previously published criticism on the work (if available).

Sources: an alphabetical list of critical material quoted in the entry, with full bibliographical information.

Further Reading: an alphabetical list of other critical sources which may prove useful for the student. Includes full bibliographical information and a brief annotation.

In addition, each entry contains the following highlighted sections, set apart from the main text as sidebars:

Media Adaptations: if available, a list of audio recordings as well as any film or television adaptations of the poem, including source information.

Topics for Further Study: a list of potential study questions or research topics dealing with the poem. This section includes questions related to other disciplines the student may be studying, such as American history, world history, science, math, government, business, geography, economics, psychology, etc.

Compare & Contrast: an "at-a-glance" comparison of the cultural and historical differences between the author's time and culture and late twentieth century or early twenty-first century Western culture. This box includes pertinent parallels between the major scientific, political, and cultural movements of the time or place the poem was written, the time or place the poem was set (if a historical work), and modern Western culture. Works written after 1990 may not have this box.

What Do I Read Next?: a list of works that might give a reader points of entry into a classic work (e.g., YA or multicultural titles) and/ or complement the featured poem or serve as a contrast to it. This includes works by the same author and others, works from various genres, YA works, and works from various cultures and eras.

Other Features

PfS includes "Just a Few Lines on a Page," a foreword by David J. Kelly, an adjunct professor of English, College of Lake County, Illinois. This essay provides a straightforward, unpretentious explanation of why poetry should be marveled at and how *Poetry for Students* can help teachers show students how to enrich their own reading experiences.

A Cumulative Author/Title Index lists the authors and titles covered in each volume of the *PfS* series.

A Cumulative Nationality/Ethnicity Index breaks down the authors and titles covered in each volume of the *PfS* series by nationality and ethnicity.

A Subject/Theme Index, specific to each volume, provides easy reference for users who may be studying a particular subject or theme rather than a single work. Significant subjects from events to broad themes are included.

A Cumulative Index of First Lines (beginning in Vol. 10) provides easy reference for users who may be familiar with the first line of a poem but may not remember the actual title.

A Cumulative Index of Last Lines (beginning in Vol. 10) provides easy reference for users who may be familiar with the last line of a poem but may not remember the actual title.

Each entry may include illustrations, including photo of the author and other graphics related to the poem.

Citing Poetry for Students

When writing papers, students who quote directly from any volume of *Poetry for Students* may use the following general forms. These examples are based on MLA style; teachers may request that students adhere to a different style, so the following examples may be adapted as needed.

When citing text from *PfS* that is not attributed to a particular author (i.e., the Themes,

Style, Historical Context sections, etc.), the following format should be used in the bibliography section:

"Angle of Geese." *Poetry for Students*. Ed. Marie Napierkowski and Mary Ruby. Vol. 2. Detroit: Gale, 1998. 8–9.

When quoting the specially commissioned essay from *PfS* (usually the first piece under the "Criticism" subhead), the following format should be used:

Velie, Alan. Critical Essay on "Angle of Geese." *Poetry for Students*. Ed. Marie Napierkowski and Mary Ruby. Vol. 2. Detroit: Gale, 1998. 7–10.

When quoting a journal or newspaper essay that is reprinted in a volume of *PfS*, the following form may be used:

Luscher, Robert M. "An Emersonian Context of Dickinson's 'The Soul Selects Her Own Society'." *ESQ: A Journal of American Renaissance* 30.2 (1984): 111–16. Excerpted and reprinted in *Poetry for Students*. Ed. Marie Napierkowski and Mary Ruby. Vol. 1 Detroit: Gale, 1998. 266–69.

When quoting material reprinted from a book that appears in a volume of *PfS*, the following form may be used:

Mootry, Maria K. "'Tell It Slant': Disguise and Discovery as Revisionist Poetic Discourse in 'The Bean Eaters'." *A Life Distilled: Gwendolyn Brooks, Her Poetry and Fiction*. Ed. Maria K. Mootry and Gary Smith. Urbana: University of Illinois Press, 1987. 177–80, 191. Excerpted and reprinted in *Poetry for Students*. Ed. Marie Napierkowski and Mary Ruby. Vol. 2. Detroit: Gale, 1998. 22–24.

We Welcome Your Suggestions

The editorial staff of *Poetry for Students* welcomes your comments and ideas. Readers who wish to suggest poems to appear in future volumes, or who have other suggestions, are cordially invited to contact the editor. You may contact the editor via E-mail at: **ForStudentsEditors@cengage.com**. Or write to the editor at:

Editor, *Poetry for Students*
Gale
27500 Drake Road
Farmington Hills, MI 48331-3535

Literary Chronology

712: Tu Fu is born in China.

757: Tu Fu writes "Jade Flower Palace."

770: Tu Fu dies in the Tan-chou region of China.

1552: Edmund Spenser is born in London, England.

1595: Edmund Spenser's "Sonnet 75" is published in *Amoretti and Epithalamion.*

1599: Edmund Spenser dies on January 13 in London, England.

Circa 1618: Richard Lovelace is born in Kent County, England.

1649: Richard Lovelace's "To Lucasta, Going to the War" is published in *Lucasta.*

1658: Richard Lovelace dies in England.

1792: Percy Bysshe Shelley is born on August 4 at Field Place, near Horsham, Sussex, England.

1795: John Keats is born on October 31 in Moorgate in London, England.

1817: John Keat's "On the Grasshopper and the Cricket" is published in his first collection *Poems.*

1820: Percy Bysshe Shelley's "To a Sky-Lark" is published in *Prometheus Unbound.*

1821: John Keats dies of tuberculosis contracted while nursing his brother, Thomas, through the same illness on February 23 in Rome, Italy.

1822: Percy Bysshe Shelley is drowned on July 8 in the Bay of Spezia, off the coast of Italy.

1830: Emily Elizabeth Dickinson is born on December 10 in Amherst, Massachusetts.

1874: Robert Frost is born March 26 in San Francisco, California.

1878: Emily Dickinson's "Success Is Counted Sweetest" is published in *A Masque of Poets.*

1886: Emily Dickinson dies of nephritis on May 15 in Amherst, Massachusetts.

1889: Anna Akhmatova is born on June 23 near Odessa, Russia.

1902: Arna (Arnaud) Wendell Bontemps is born on October 12 in Alexandria, Louisiana.

1914: Robert Frost's poem "After Apple Picking" is published in *North of Boston.*

1917: Gwendolyn Brooks is born on June 7 in Topeka, Kansas.

1922: Anna Akhmatova's "Everything Is Plundered" is published in the collection *Anno Domini MCMXXI.*

1924: Robert Frost is awarded the Pulitzer Prize for Poetry for *New Hampshire: A Poem with Notes and Grace Notes.*

1926: Arna Bontemps's "A Black Man Talks of Reaping" is published.

1930: Ted Hughes is born on August 17 in Mytholmroyd, in West Yorkshire, England.

1931: Robert Frost is awarded the Pulitzer Prize for Poetry for *Collected Poems*.

1932: Linda Pastan is born on May 27 in Bronx, New York.

1934: Audre Lorde is born Audrey Geraldine Lorde on February 18 in New York, New York.

1936: Robert Frost is awarded the Pulitzer Prize for Poetry for *A Further Range*.

1936: Marge Piercy is born on March 31 in Detroit, Michigan.

1943: Robert Frost is awarded the Pulitzer Prize for Poetry for *A Witness Tree*.

1950: Gwendolyn Brooks is awarded the Pulitzer Prize for Poetry for *Annie Allen*.

1951: Joy (Foster) Harjo is born on May 9 in Tulsa, Oklahoma.

1955: Dwight Okita is born on August 26 in Chicago, Illinois.

1957: Ted Hughes's "Horses" is published in his first published collection of poetry, *The Hawk in the Rain*.

1959: Gwendolyn Brooks's poem "The Explorer" is published in *Harper's* magazine.

1963: Robert Frost dies of complications following prostate surgery on January 29 in Boston, Massachusetts.

1966: Anna Akhmatova dies as a result of a heart attack on March 5 near Moscow, Russia.

1973: Arna Bontemps dies as a result of a heart attack on June 4 in Nashville, Tennessee.

1973: Marge Piercy's "To Be of Use" is published in *To Be of Use*.

1978: Audre Lorde's poem "Hanging Fire" is published in her book of poetry *The Black Unicorn*.

1983: Dwight Okita's "In Response to Executive Order 9066" is published in the anthology *Breaking Light*.

1983: Joy Harjo's poem "Remember" is published in *She Had Some Horses*.

1986: Linda Pastan's "Grudnow" is published in *Poetry* magazine.

1992: Audre Lorde dies of liver cancer on November 17 in Christiansted, St. Croix, U.S. Virgin Islands.

1998: Ted Hughes dies of cancer on October 28 at his home in North Tawton, England.

2000: Gwendolyn Brooks dies of cancer on December 3 in Chicago, Illinois.

Acknowledgments

The editors wish to thank the copyright holders of the excerpted criticism included in this volume and the permissions managers of many book and magazine publishing companies for assisting us in securing reproduction rights. We are also grateful to the staffs of the Detroit Public Library, the Library of Congress, the University of Detroit Mercy Library, Wayne State University Purdy/Kresge Library Complex, and the University of Michigan Libraries for making their resources available to us. Following is a list of the copyright holders who have granted us permission to reproduce material in this volume of *PfS*. Every effort has been made to trace copyright, but if omissions have been made, please let us know.

COPYRIGHTED EXCERPTS IN *PfS*, VOLUME 32, WERE REPRODUCED FROM THE FOLLOWING PERIODICALS:

American Notes & Queries, v. 10, May 1972; v. 21, January/February, 1983; v. 18, winter, 2005. Copyright © 1972, 1983, 2005 by Helen Dwight Reid Educational Foundation. All reproduced with permission of the Helen Dwight Reid Educational Foundation, published by Heldref Publications, 1319 18th Street, NW, Washington, DC 20036-1802.— *American Scholar*, v. 78, winter, 2009. Copyright © 2009 by Sudip Bose. Reprinted by permission of the *American Scholar*.—*Boston Globe*, August 30, 1998 for "Thirty Years of Linda Pastan's Work: From the Slight to the Extraordinary" by Liz Rosenberg. Reproduced by permission of the author.—*Chicago Tribune*, August 29, 1986; September 18, 1988. Copyright © 1986, 1988 Chicago Tribune Company. All rights reserved. Both reproduced by permission.— *College Literature*, v. 20, June 1993. Copyright © 1993 by West Chester University. Reproduced by permission.—*Emily Dickinson Journal*, v. 5, fall, 1996; v. 13, fall, 2004. Copyright © 1996, 2004 The Johns Hopkins University Press. Both reproduced by permission.—*Explicator*, v. 39, spring, 1981; v. 64, winter, 2006. Copyright © 1981, 2006 by Helen Dwight Reid Educational Foundation. Both reproduced with permission of the Helen Dwight Reid Educational Foundation, published by Heldref Publications, 1319 18th Street, NW, Washington, DC 20036-1802.— *Journal of Modern Literature*, v. 27, fall, 2003. Copyright © 2003 Indiana University Press. Reproduced by permission.—*Kenyon Review*, v. 15, summer, 1993 for "In Love and War and Music: An Interview with Joy Harjo" by Joy Harjo and Marilyn Kallett; v. 20, spring, 1998 for "A Harsh Day's Light: An Interview with Marge Piercy" by John Rodden and Marge Piercy. Both reproduced by permission of the respective authors.—*Lambda Book Report*, v. 3, July, 1993 for a review of Dwight Okita's "Crossing with the Light" by Jeffery Beam. Reproduced by permission of the author.—*London Magazine*, v. 10, January

1971. © *London Magazine*, 1971. Reproduced by permission.—*Los Angeles Times Book Review*, March 18, 1990. Reproduced by permission.—*MELUS*, v. 18, fall, 1993. Copyright *MELUS: The Society for the Study of Multi-Ethnic Literature of the United States*, 1993. Reproduced by permission.—*New Criterion*, v. 12, May 1994 for "Anna Akhmatova" by John Simon. Copyright © 1994 by the Foundation for Cultural Review. Reproduced by permission of the author.—*Poetry*, v. 173, February 1999 for a review of Linda Pastan's "Carnival Evening, New and Selected Poems: 1968-1998" by Leslie Ullman. Copyright © 1999 Modern Poetry Association. Reproduced by permission of the author.—*Progressive*, v. 55, January 1991. Copyright © 1991 by The Progressive, Inc. Reproduced by permission of *The Progressive*, 409 East Main Street, Madison, WI 53703, www.progressive.org.—*Publications of the Missouri Philological Association*, v. 10, 1985. Reproduced by permission.—*Romanticism*, v. 12, 2006. Copyright © Edinburgh University Press Ltd. 2006. Reproduced by permission.—*Studies in English Literature, 1500-1900*, v. 14, winter, 1974. Copyright © William Marsh Rice University, 1974. Reproduced by permission.—*Unesco Courier*, v. 43, April 1990. Reproduced by permission.—*Wicazo Sa Review: A Journal of Native American Studies*, v. 15, 2000 for "Joy Harjo and Her Poetics as Praxis: A 'Postcolonial' Political Economy of the Body, Land, Labor, and Language" by Azfar Hussain. Reproduced by permission of the author.—*Writer*, v. 105, October 1992 for "Yesterday's Noise: The Poetry of Childhood Memory" by Linda Pastan. Reproduced by permission of the author.

COPYRIGHTED EXCERPTS IN *PfS*, VOLUME 32, WERE REPRODUCED FROM THE FOLLOWING BOOKS:

Akhmatova, Anna. From "Everything Has Been Plundered," in *The Complete Poems of Anna Akhmatova*. Second Edition. Edited by Roberta Reeder. Translated by Judith Hemschemeyer. Zephyr Press, 2000. Translations of Akhmatova's poetry copyright © 1989, 1992, 1997 by Judith Hemschemeyer. Reproduced by permission.—Bontemps, Arna. From "A Black Man Talks of Reaping," in *Personals*. Paul Breman, 1963. Reproduced by permission of Harold Ober Associates Incorporated.—Frost, Robert. From *The Road Not Taken: A Selection of Robert Frost's Poems*. Henry Holt, 1985. Copyright © 1936, 1942, 1944, 1951, 1956, 1958, 1962 by Robert Frost. Reproduced by permission of Henry Holt and Company, LLC.—Harjo, Joy. From *How We Became Human: Selected Poems 1975-2001*. W. W. Norton, 2002. Copyright © 2002 by Joy Harjo. All rights reserved. Used by permission of W. W. Norton & Company, Inc.—Hinton, David. From *The Selected Poems of Tu Fu*. Translated by David Hinton. New Directions Publishing, 1989. Copyright © 1988, 1989 by David Hinton. All rights reserved. Reproduced by permission of The Advil Press Poetry Ltd. and New Directions Publishing Corp.—Keats, John. From "On the Grasshopper and the Cricket," in *Complete Poems*. Edited by Jack Stillinger. Belknap Press, 1982. Copyright © 1982 by the President and Fellows of Harvard College. All rights reserved. Reproduced by permission of Harvard University Press.—Kent, George E. From *A Life of Gwendolyn Brooks*. University Press of Kentucky, 1990. Copyright © 1990 by the estate of George E. Kent. Reproduced by permission of The University Press of Kentucky.—Lorde, Audre. From *The Collected Poems of Audre Lorde*. W.W. Norton, 1997. Copyright © 1997 by The Audre Lorde Estate. All rights reserved. Used by permission of W. W. Norton & Company, Inc.—Melhem, D. H. From *Gwendolyn Brooks: Poetry and the Heroic Voice*. University Press of Kentucky, 1987. Copyright © 1987 by The University Press of Kentucky. Reproduced by permission of The University Press of Kentucky.—Okita, Dwight. From *Crossing with the Light*. Tia Chucha Press, 1992. Copyright © 1992 by Dwight Okita. All rights reserved. Reproduced by permission of the auhtor.—Pastan, Linda. From *Carnival Evening: New and Selected Poems: 1968-1998*. W. W. Norton, 1998. Copyright © 1998 by Linda Pastan. All rights reserved. Used by permission of W. W. Norton & Company, Inc.—Shelley, Percy Bysshe. From "To a Sky-Lark," in *Shelley's Poetry and Prose*. Edited by Donald H. Reiman and Sharon B. Powers. W. W. Norton, 1977. Copyright © 1977 by Donald H. Reiman and Sharon B. Powers. All rights reserved. Used by permission of W. W. Norton & Company, Inc.—Tu Fu, From *The Selected Poems of Tu Fu*. Translated by David Hinton. New Directions, 1989. Copyright © 1988, 1989 by David Hinton. All rights reserved. Reproduced by permission of the Advil Press Poetry Ltd. and New Directions Publishing Corp.—Young, David. From *Five T'ang Poets*. Translated by David Young. Oberlin College Press, 1990. Copyright © 1990 by Oberlin College. Reproduced by permission.

Contributors

Susan K. Andersen: Andersen is an instructor of English literature and composition. Entry on "Remember." Original essay on "Remember."

Bryan Aubrey: Aubrey holds a Ph.D. in English. Entries on "The Explorer," "Grudnow," "Jade Flower Palace," and "To a Skylark." Original essays on "The Explorer," "Grudnow," "Jade Flower Palace," and "To a Skylark."

Jennifer Bussey: Bussey is an independent writer specializing in literature. Entry on "Success Is Counted Sweetest." Original essay on "Success Is Counted Sweetest."

Catherine Dominic: Dominic is a novelist and a freelance writer and editor. Entries on "Sonnet 75" and "To Be of Use." Original essays on "Sonnet 75" and "To Be of Use."

Sheldon Goldfarb: Goldfarb is a specialist in Victorian literature who has published nonfiction books as well as a novel for young adults set in Victorian times. Entry on "Hanging Fire." Original essay on "Hanging Fire."

Diane Andrews Henningfeld: Henningfeld is a professor emerita of literature and composition. Entries on "Everything is Plundered" and "In Response to Executive Order 9066: All Americans of Japanese Descent Must Report to Relocation Centers." Original essays on "Everything is Plundered" and "In Response to Executive Order 9066: All Americans of Japanese Descent Must Report to Relocation Centers."

Sheri Metzger Karmiol: Karmiol has a doctorate in English Renaissance literature. She teaches literature and drama at the University of New Mexico, where she is a lecturer in the university honors program. She is also a professional writer and the author of several reference texts on poetry and drama. Entry on "The Horses." Original essay on "The Horses."

David Kelly: Kelly is a writer and instructor of creative writing and literature. Entry on "A Black Man Talks of Reaping." Original essay on "A Black Man Talks of Reaping."

Bradley A. Skeen: Skeen is a classics professor. Entry on "On the Grasshopper and the Cricket." Original essay on "On the Grasshopper and the Cricket."

Leah Tieger: Tieger is a freelance writer and editor. Entries on "After Apple Picking" and "To Lucasta, Going to the Wars." Original essays on "After Apple Picking" and "To Lucasta, Going to the Wars."

After Apple Picking

ROBERT FROST

1914

Robert Frost's "After Apple Picking" was first published in 1914 in the poet's second collection, *North of Boston*. "After Apple Picking" has been continuously hailed as one of the finest poems by one of America's finest poets. Indeed, almost one hundred years after its publication, "After Apple Picking" is studied regularly in poetry classes throughout the United States. A descriptive poem that ostensibly relates the speaker's thoughts on picking apples in an orchard, "After Apple Picking" is a deceptively simple work. Its undertones reveal a deeply meditative poem on mortality and change. Some readings present the poem in light of a writing career coming to an impasse, of poems completed and yet to be written, and of those that will never be produced. In fact, while the poem is allusive, its exact allusions remain obscure, leaving it open to several interpretations.

These themes, among others, are presented through the extensive use of natural imagery. Written in a single stanza of forty-two lines, the poem is composed in a loose iambic pentameter (alternating stressed and unstressed syllables in a ten-syllable line). It is also written in rhyme, albeit loosely. The effect of this relaxed structure lends the poem a less formal and more conversational feel. Its descriptive language and underlying composition maintain a distinctively poetic tone. In this manner, "After Apple Picking" places itself squarely in the intersection between traditional and modern poetry, a style that would serve

Robert Frost (The Library of Congress)

Frost throughout his career. The poem can be found in *The Road Not Taken: A Selection of Robert Frost's Poems* (2001).

AUTHOR BIOGRAPHY

Robert Frost was born March 26, 1874, in San Francisco, California. His father, William Prescott Frost, was a teacher and editor of the *San Francisco Examiner*. He was also an alcoholic, and he died of tuberculosis on May 5, 1885. Following his death, Frost's mother, Isabelle Moodie, moved the family to Massachusetts to live with Frost's grandfather, William Frost. In 1892, Frost graduated from Lawrence High School, already determined to fulfill his ambition to become a great poet. Notably, he was covaledictorian with Elinor Miriam White, the woman who would ultimately become his wife. Frost went on to attend Dartmouth College, though he did not graduate. Instead, he began to teach and write, submitting and publishing poems in various periodicals. At the time,

Frost's style was considered quite innovative, and it served as a challenge to the decidedly Victorian aesthetic of the day. For this reason, his work was initially met with some resistance.

Soon after White graduated from St. Lawrence University in 1895, she and Frost were married, and they had several children in quick succession. While Frost had begun attending Harvard University, he was forced to leave before graduating in order to support his rapidly growing family. Frost's grandfather gave him a small annuity and a farm in Derry, New Hampshire, and the income from the annuity coupled with the income generated by the work on the farm was enough to keep Frost's family afloat. Notably, the nine years Frost spent on the farm were some of his most prolific, and he composed most of his best-known poems there. The rural content and natural imagery examined in Frost's poetry was also heavily influenced by his life on the farm. Frost, however, was not a farmer by choice, and in 1906 he returned to teaching. In 1907, Frost's sixth and final child was born.

By 1912, Frost's frustrated poetic ambitions led him to immigrate to England in the hopes of establishing his reputation there. Modernist poets such as Ezra Pound, William Butler Yeats, and T. S. Eliot had already had a great impact on poetry in England, and Frost was met with a far more receptive audience. His first book of poetry, *A Boy's Will*, was published there in 1913. It was followed a year later by the British release of *North of Boston* (which includes "After Apple Picking"). The book received international acclaim, and Frost returned to the United States with his reputation secured. In 1916, his collection *Mountain Interval* (including Frost's most famous poem "The Road Not Taken") was published, also to great acclaim.

Around the same time, Frost established the family homestead at a farm in Franconia, New Hampshire but he spent much of his time, teaching, lecturing, and writing. His work as a professor at Amherst College provided his family with a consistent income. His next collection, the 1923 *New Hampshire* (including the famed poems "Fire and Ice" and "Stopping by Woods on a Snowy Evening") garnered Frost a Pulitzer Prize the same year. He would later go on to receive three more Pulitzers throughout his life. Over the next few years, Frost published several poetry collections, all of which garnered praise. Frost's 1936 *A Further Range*, despite winning a Pulitzer

Prize, was largely criticized as too conservative, striking a tone discordant to the political and national mood during the Great Depression. By the 1940s, Frost had already long since produced the poems that would secure his renown as a legendary poet.

Frost was often considered the de facto poet laureate of the United States, and he was officially commended in a similar capacity by the U.S. Senate in 1950. Among his many congressional honors, Frost was selected to read his poetry at the inauguration of President John F. Kennedy in 1961. Frost was eighty-six at the time. He died of complications following prostate surgery on January 29, 1963, in Boston, Massachusetts. He is buried in the Old Bennington Cemetery in Bennington, Vermont. Despite his continued fame as a pioneer of American modernist poetry, Frost never achieved his greatest ambition, to earn the Nobel Prize for Literature.

POEM TEXT

My long two-pointed ladder's sticking through
   a tree
Toward heaven still,
And there's a barrel that I didn't fill
Beside it, and there may be two or three
Apples I didn't pick upon some bough.   5
But I am done with apple-picking now.
Essence of winter sleep is on the night,
The scent of apples: I am drowsing off.
I cannot rub the strangeness from my sight
I got from looking through a pane of glass   10
I skimmed this morning from the drinking
   trough
And held against the world of hoary grass.
It melted, and I let it fall and break.
But I was well
Upon my way to sleep before it fell,   15
And I could tell
What form my dreaming was about to take.
Magnified apples appear and disappear,
Stem end and blossom end,
And every fleck of russet showing clear.   20
My instep arch not only keeps the ache,
It keeps the pressure of a ladder-round.
I feel the ladder sway as the boughs bend.
And I keep hearing from the cellar bin
The rumbling sound   25
Of load on load of apples coming in.
For I have had too much
Of apple-picking: I am overtired
Of the great harvest I myself desired.
There were ten thousand thousand fruit to touch,   30

Cherish in hand, lift down, and not let fall.
For all
That struck the earth,
No matter if not bruised or spiked with stubble,
Went surely to the cider-apple heap   35
As of no worth.
One can see what will trouble
This sleep of mine, whatever sleep it is.
Were he not gone,
The woodchuck could say whether it's like his   40
Long sleep, as I describe its coming on,
Or just some human sleep.

POEM SUMMARY

"After Apple Picking" is told by an unidentified first-person narrator. It is written in a loose iambic pentameter, although several lines have varying feet (paired syllables with alternating stresses). The poem is also composed with end rhymes, though again not in any strict pattern. Notably, given that apples are picked in the fall, the onset of winter is fast approaching now that the orchard has been harvested. This onset is important because it seems to drive both the poem's tone and its content.

Lines 1–10
The speaker has just finished working in the orchard, and the opening lines describe the tools that now lay abandoned. The speaker's ladder still leans against the apple tree, and it is described as pointing toward heaven. An empty barrel that the speaker has not filled is also nearby, and there are a few apples left on the branch. However, despite these loose ends (signs of a chore half-completed), the speaker declares that he is done picking apples for the time being. Hints of the coming winter and its slumber can be felt in the burgeoning night. The smell of the apples also makes the speaker sleepy. He is unable to clear his eyes. His sight is distorted from his having looked through a sheet of glass.

Lines 11–20
In the eleventh line, the speaker reveals that the distorting glass was in fact a sheet of ice that he removed from the water trough in the morning. The speaker held the ice and looked at the frosted grass through it. As he held it, it began to thaw, and he let go of it, watching it fall and shatter. The speaker says, however, that he was beginning to fall asleep before the sheet of ice had fallen. He then states that as he was falling

MEDIA ADAPTATIONS

- A 1961 audio recording of "After Apple Picking" is read by Frost's daughter Lesley Frost in *Derry Down Derry: A Narrative Reading by Lesley Frost of Poems by Robert Frost*, produced by Folkways Records. The album was rereleased in 2004 and is also available as an MP3 download at *amazon.com*.

asleep he knew what his dreams would be before they had even begun. What follows is likely a description of the speaker's dreams: The apples loom larger than life, disappearing and reappearing as the top stemmed part of the apple and the bottom part, formed from the blossom, alternately reveal themselves. Each speck of reddish brown on the apples is immediately apparent.

Lines 21–30

Seemingly returning to the present, the speaker says that the arch of his foot is still dull with pain from standing on the ladder all day. However, it is also possible that the speaker is continuing to detail his dreams. The impression of the ladder on the speaker's feet leaves him feeling as if he can still sense the ladder moving beneath him, shifting in the branches as they bow under the ladder's weight. The echo of the sound of apples tumbling into the bin in the apple cellar still remains in the speaker's ears. They make a thundering noise as barrel upon barrel pours into the cellar. These ghosts of the experience stay with the speaker because, as he states, he has had more than his fill of picking apples. He is exceedingly exhausted by the large yield he wanted (and obtained). There were thousands upon thousands of apples to handle in the process.

Lines 31–42

Each apple had to be gently picked and laid in the barrel without being allowed to fall to the ground. This is because any apples that touch the earth, no matter how unscathed, must be set

aside for cider, presumably because they are no longer deemed fit to be taken to market. According to the speaker, it is as if by having touched the ground the apples have become worthless. Then, in a seeming change of subject, or perhaps finishing his description of his dreams, the speaker reiterates that he is aware of the thoughts that will disturb his slumber, whatever kind of slumber it might be. The speaker then says that if the woodchuck had not already left (presumably to begin its winter hibernation), then he could describe the feeling of his own coming slumber to it. Then, the woodchuck could tell the speaker whether his coming sleep is akin to the woodchuck's hibernation or if it is a slumber only experienced by human beings.

THEMES

Mortality

While "After Apple Picking" is open to numerous interpretations, almost all allow for the discussion of mortality. While the theme of mortality in this poem is not necessarily about death, it is about endings, and the things that are left unsaid and undone in the wake of those endings. In this sense, the poem could be about regret; there are, after all, a few ripe apples left unpicked on the bough. But the frost has come, and it has grown too late to harvest the remaining apples. There are also apples that the speaker has dropped and now must be relegated to the cider heap. These apples most clearly represent failed efforts, embodying unfinished projects or tasks. Notably, some critics interpret these defective apples as a reference to poems that will never be published.

Mortality, in its most basic form, is the end that comes to all living things. "After Apple Picking" seems largely concerned not so much with the end itself but with the shape that this end takes. One example of this notion can be seen in the tools (the ladder in the tree, the unfilled barrel) that are left scattered about; they represent the loose ends of a task that has come abruptly to a finish. The elusive shape of the end can also be traced in the speaker's exhaustion as he fades in and out of a dream. More than anywhere else in the poem, the closing lines wonder at the shape of the end that the speaker now faces. The speaker asks himself if he is to hibernate, as the woodchuck, in a seemingly ceaseless slumber. Will he

TOPICS FOR FURTHER STUDY

- "After Apple Picking" features a great deal of descriptive language, as it depicts an apple orchard after harvest. Taking the poem as your inspiration, use a digital camera to capture pictures that evoke the scene in the poem. Next, use a photo editing computer program to form a digital collage of your images. Present your collage to the class.

- In your opinion, what is the mood of the speaker in "After Apple Picking"? Furthermore, how would you describe the poem's tone? Write a brief essay in which you address these questions and be sure to use examples from the text to bolster your arguments.

- Research modernist poetry and write a persuasive essay on the subject. Do you think that Frost can be described as a modernist poet? Why or why not?

- Read several poems from *Talking Drums: A Selection of Poems from Africa South of the Sahara*, a poetry collection for young adults edited by Veronique Tadjo. Compare and contrast the descriptive language in the African poems with that of Frost's poetry. Present your findings to the class in a PowerPoint or oral presentation.

wake in a world transformed into spring? Or will he wake tomorrow morning, refreshed, as he normally would? This query, too, speaks to the uncertainty that mortality places upon all living beings. While one knows that the end is inevitable, one does not know when or how it will happen, or what it will be like.

Change

Mortality in and of itself is a change, an ending, and the poem also speaks to other changes. In particular, the change of the seasons is the most significant aspect of change in the poem. Apples are picked in the fall, but now the harvest is almost over, and the speaker skimmed ice from the water trough that very morning. The seasons are about to change, and winter is coming soon. It is a time for fields to lie fallow, animals to hibernate, and the world to sleep in an apparent death, a literal suspended animation. Unlike actual death, winter is temporary. Its very existence speaks of the spring that will follow. For this reason, the speaker's somewhat reflective approach is one that examines a year coming to a close, but it also allows for another to begin. Again, this interpretation can be justified by the speaker's final question. Is he to embark on a long sleep, or just a restful refreshing night? Is this the end or is it not? Regardless, there is a change on the horizon, but what it might be or mean remains unclear.

Aside from the passing of the seasons, change can also be seen in the apple harvesting itself. The harvest is a task completed, and yet some apples remain. There were thousands upon thousands of apples to be handled, picked, and carried, and each represents a possibility. Some will go to market, and some will be made into cider. This, too, is what change and mortality allow for; they open the door to possibility, perhaps success or failure. Nevertheless, at the beginning of the harvest, the speaker looked forward to reaping the literal fruits of his labor. However, now that the task is done, he is exhausted. This, even so, is also a sort of change.

Fatigue

Regardless of the many interpretations that can be applied to "After Apple Picking," the speaker's fatigue and exhaustion saturate the poem. The ladder and the barrel are left by the tree, a few apples remain on the branch, but the speaker decisively declares that he is finished picking apples. He then says that the hint of winter's sleep is coming on. In fact, sleep is mentioned six times in the poem, and it is also referred to in terms of tiredness, drowsiness, and dreaming on three additional occasions. Notably, of the six references to sleep, four occur in the final five lines of the poem. Indeed, this is a sleepy poem. Notably, the speaker mentions it and his tiredness when he is most awake, that is, at the beginning and end of the poem. Furthermore, the poem's midsection, where sleep is not mentioned, is largely comprised of a dream of apple picking. The poem's halting rhythm, established by the varying line lengths and almost randomly distributed end rhymes, also underscore the speaker's exhaustion.

Apples in an orchard (*Image copyright Tomo Jesenicnik, 2009. Used under license from Shutterstock.com*)

STYLE

Enjambment

Enjambment addresses how lines of poetry end and begin. The way that each line's ending is arranged changes how a poem is read and how it is interpreted. Each line break causes the eye to slow before it drops down and moves on to the next line. This changes the pace of the words as they are read, creating one aspect of a poem's rhythm. It can also change a poem's perceived meaning. For instance, if a poem read, "I went away / but only to the store," the reader would at first assume that the speaker has gone on a long journey. The next line reveals that the reader has made an error. This confusion would not have occurred if the line had read, "I went away, but only to the store." By removing the line break, the possibility for misinterpretation is also removed. This is why enjambment is so valuable in a poem; it allows for many changing impressions to exist within a single poem almost simultaneously. This

creates dual or even triple meanings in a single verse. In the case of "After Apple Picking," each line's enjambment is often used to create a seemingly independent statement that is then qualified or expanded upon in the following line.

Rhythm

Aside from the rhyme, the rhythm in this poem is its most remarkable technical aspect. It is written entirely in iambic meter, meaning that alternating syllables are in turn unstressed and stressed. The effect of this meter allows for a slightly elevated and poetic tone. Furthermore, the poem is largely written in iambic pentameter, meaning that most lines are composed of ten syllables (or five feet, with each foot containing the paired unstressed and stressed syllables that make the iamb). Twenty-six of the poem's forty-two lines are written in iambic pentameter. Were the entire poem written in pentameter, it would take on a more elevated and formal poetic tone. By breaking up this rhythm, the poem becomes somewhat more informal and conversational. The breaks in rhythm further indicate the narrator's fatigue. They also have a similar effect to the enjambment, changing and altering emphasis and meaning. For instance, aside from the opening couplet, the lines are most consistently structured at the beginning of the poem. They become less and less structured toward the poem's conclusion. One could interpret this to mean that the speaker is sure of himself at the poem's outset, and less so by its end. This is bolstered by the fact that the poem ends in literal uncertainty; the speaker does not know the type of sleep he is about to embark upon.

Rhyme

Like the rhythm in "After Apple Picking" the end rhymes simultaneously serve to alternately heighten and undermine poetic effect, as well as the poem's emphasis and meaning. The poem is formal, but it is not rigid. Also, much like the pentameter, the poem begins with a more reliable rhyming structure that deteriorates over the course of the poem. For example, the longest pause between end rhymes occurs at the end, with six lines separating the final line's rhyme from its preceding partner. In fact, for the most part, every six lines in the poem (up until the last twelve) contain a set of three rhymes. Additionally, directly repeating rhymes (a minimum of two consecutive rhymes in the same number of lines) appear four times in the first thirty-two lines of the poem. They do not occur at all in the last ten lines.

COMPARE & CONTRAST

- **1910s:** World War I begins in 1914, the same year that "After Apple Picking" is published.

  Today: The Iraq War, spearheaded by the United States, begins in 2003.

- **1910s:** Modernist poetry, a style in which poets challenge traditional poetic themes, language, and structures, is growing in popularity.

  Today: A prominent poetic movement is New Formalism. The movement entails a return to more traditional poetic forms and structures.

- **1910s:** The Industrial Revolution (which drives populations into urban centers and away from rural environs) is in full swing, having begun in the late 1800s. Though the rural lifestyle embodied in "After Apple Picking" is still common, it is becoming less so.

  Today: Rural life is much less common than it once was. According to the 2000 U.S. census, 79.2 percent of the population lives in urban centers. Projections for the 2010 census indicate that this percentage will continue to increase.

HISTORICAL CONTEXT

Modernism

Modernism is an artistic movement that began in the early twentieth century, just as Frost's career was beginning to take hold. Notably, the movement reached its peak during the 1920s and 1930s, Frost's most productive years. The style largely originated in Europe, although many of the poets at its forefront were American. The style was initially met with resistance in the United States, and many American poets, like Frost, found European critics and publishers to be more open-minded and receptive to the modernist style. They traveled there to do their work. Frost was unable to get a collection of his poetry published in the United States. His first two collections were published in England after he moved there, and he achieved fame in the United States only after establishing his reputation in England. While in England, Frost befriended other famous American expatriate modernist poets, including Pound and Eliot.

Modernists challenged traditional forms and themes, and the style was popular in both literature and the visual arts. Cultural changes at the turn of the twentieth century were largely responsible for the movement. For instance, new philosophies purported the importance of the individual as a singular being (as opposed to the importance of the individual as a part of society), which led to artists breaking with traditional forms and employing more personal or experimental forms of expression. Artists also questioned the meaning of life in an increasingly mechanized world. The advent of new technologies in the early twentieth century was changing the way people lived and how they interacted with one another. Writers and artists of the day sought to explore new forms and themes as a means of addressing the changing human experience. The movement was also fueled by the horrors of World War I. The first major war to be fought with advanced technologies, World War I accordingly led to a colossal number of deaths. The high number of casualties was shocking, and it caused artists to question the cost of patriotism, that is, of placing country before the individual.

Philosophical and psychological pioneers also explored changing ideas regarding the importance and complexity of individual experience. The work of psychologists Sigmund Freud and Carl Jung, as well philosophers Friedrich Nietzsche and Jean-Paul Sartre, had a great deal of influence on modernist writers and artists.

Modernism saw the emergence of the "I" as a predominant voice in poetry, a style that Frost became well known for. Furthermore, the idea of the subconscious mind, as set forward by Freud, led to an increased interest in dreams and surreal imagery. Both themes can be found in "After Apple Picking." Similar influences can also be found in the prose of the day by means of the stream-of-consciousness writing style made popular by such writers as Gertrude Stein and William Faulkner. Notably, while Frost is considered a modernist poet, his work tended to be more conservative and formal than that of his more experimental peers.

Impact of World War I

Although "After Apple Picking" was published the same year that World War I began, the poem's reading is enhanced when considered in light of the war. Notably, when *North of Boston* (the collection in which "After Apple Picking" first appeared) was released in England to great acclaim, Frost was finally able to secure his career as a poet. Soon afterwards, he was forced to return to the United States as World War I spread across Europe. Furthermore, the poem reflects on the end of a known era and the beginning of an unknown one. At the time, World War I functioned as just such a catalyst (agent of change). It was the first modern, mechanized war, and the first global conflict of the modern age. The war's impact on the twentieth century, politically and culturally, was undeniable. An estimated ten million soldiers were killed, and civilian casualties came to almost seven million. At the time, such numbers were inconceivable, and the losses forever changed the world's outlook on life and its meaning. These changes are more than evident in the modernist aesthetic of which "After Apple Picking" is part.

CRITICAL OVERVIEW

First published in *North of Boston* in 1914, Frost's "After Apple Picking" is one of the poet's best-known and best-loved poems. Notably, the collection in which it was published launched Frost's career. The book not only established his reputation but also shaped it, setting forth the stylistic and thematic hallmarks for which Frost would become renowned. David Sanders, in the *Journal of Modern Literature,* states,

Apple picking (*Image copyright Elena Elisseeva, 2009. Used under license from Shutterstock.com)*

North of Boston was Frost's second book of poems but the first to reveal his full dramatic power and moral awareness. It was also the first to explore the culture of rural New England in which these poetic powers had grown to maturity.

Sanders also explains that the collection

established Frost as a poet of people and place.... Even the volume's first-person lyrics—"Mending Wall,""After Apple-Picking," and "The Wood-Pile"—contain strong narrative and dramatic elements. Structuring the book through their strategic placement, they sound a keynote for the volume in their use of a conversational style, their exploration of character and motive, their emphasis on traditional skills and labor in a life in which winter is always near and survival never assured.

Commenting on the initial critical reception of the collection in the *Dictionary of Literary Biography*, Donald J. Greiner notes that "although today *North of Boston* is considered Frost's strongest overall collection, it is the book that puzzled early readers." Greiner explains that this is because it straddled the intersection between traditional and modernist forms. Nevertheless, Greiner praises "After Apple Picking," calling it "perhaps Frost's finest poem and a key lyric in his second book." Greiner declares this is true because "in the haunting 'After Apple-Picking,' [Frost] unifies technique and theme to illustrate how confusion confronts man despite his very best effort to contain it." Greiner adds: "*North of Boston* is full of such considerations." However, in a somewhat ambivalent review of the poem in the *Explicator*, Mike O'Connell remarks upon its volatility: "Up and down we go throughout the shambling poem, from heaven to the windfalls in the stubble, from sharp edges to softheadedness, from satiety to uncertainty, from hyperbole to humility." Furthermore, O'Connell praises the poem while simultaneously poking fun at the half-hearted attempts at farming that Frost made throughout his life, stating "The exhausted apple picker ... has plucked from the bough a great poem—one made possible by, for once, an honest day's work."

Applauding "After Apple Picking" in *American Literature*, Priscilla M. Paton finds that it "result[s] in oblique, graceful revelations of truth, knowledge, and love." Paton also states that the poem's final line "sounds ordinary as apples, though it may also hint at death. We could almost forget how the apple-picker's commitment, perception, and imagination have enriched the ordinary." Remarkably, while the poem does not appear to be affected by outside influences, *American Notes & Queries* contributor Kenneth T. Reed observes that "[Henry] Longfellow's sonnet 'Sleep' (1875) [is] a highly probable source for Frost's 'After Apple Picking.'" Reed comments, "So similar in theme, structure and tone are they that Frost's artistic conception for his poem could not have been merely coincidental."

CRITICISM

Leah Tieger

Tieger is a freelance writer and editor. In the following essay, she discusses the numerous possible interpretations of Frost's "After Apple Picking."

At first glance, Frost's "After Apple Picking" is a poem about a person who has just finished taking in the apple harvest. The winter is coming on and the speaker is exhausted by the completion of his great task. He is so tired, in fact, that he continues to feel and hear his labors as if they are still occurring. His foot retains the ghostly imprint of the ladder's rung as if he is still standing on it. He can imagine the thunderous sound of the apples as they tumble into the bin. The poem is entirely descriptive; it not only details the apple picking and its after effects, but it also addresses the late fall and the coming winter. The speaker uses the sheet of ice on the water trough to segue into his dream of apple picking. The poem is also highly allusive and metaphorical. Its genius, however, lies in the fact that the exact metaphor remains elusive (just out of reach), even upon multiple readings. The poem's refusal to align itself with any one concrete meaning leaves it open to multiple meanings and various interpretations. Among critics, there are three main interpretations, none of which are mutually exclusive. That is, all three interpretations can exist simultaneously in the poem without conflicting with one another.

The first and most apparent interpretation relates to themes addressing mortality. The poem as a meditation on mortality could also be simply described as resignation to the passing of time. The ladder is left lying out, the few apples remaining on the branch, the unfilled barrel—all are signs of a task half-complete. Yet the speaker declares that he is finished, and he then goes on to note that winter is in the air. The speaker appears to indicate that whether he wishes to finish or not is out of his hands; the coming winter has made the decision for him. The changing seasons are also a visible marker of the passage of time, a stark reminder of the speaker's mortality. Regardless, the speaker is exhausted, and he welcomes the excuse to cease his labors. He is drowsy, and just this morning he has taken a sheet of ice from the water trough. Looking through it has distorted his vision, and he has been unable to shake off the strangeness it inspired. The dream of apple picking that follows is a reflection of that which has already passed, moments of a life that will never be regained. The plentiful harvest he wished for has exhausted him. His exhaustion can also be seen in the poem's rhyme and rhythm, which deteriorates increasingly as the poem reaches its conclusion. This decline can also be seen as a sign of the sleep (perhaps a deathly sleep) as it approaches. Sleep is mentioned four times in the final five lines of "After Apple Picking." In these lines, the speaker wonders at the type of sleep

WHAT DO I READ NEXT?

- While "After Apple Picking" is one of the most famous poems by one of America's most famous poets, much can be gained by reading it as part of Frost's work as a whole. To this end, read *The Poetry of Robert Frost: The Collected Poems, Complete and Unabridged*, edited by Edward Connery Lathem. First published in 1969, the original edition remains in print, attesting to the lasting popularity of Frost's work.

- The Russian poet Anna Akhmatova lived and worked at the same time as Frost, and her fame in Russia is equal to Frost's fame in the United States. Her work also exhibits a clarity and simplicity of verse similar to that of Frost's. Her work has been widely translated in English, and the 2000 publication of *The Complete Poems of Anna Akhmatova*, edited by Roberta Reeder, is an excellent introduction to her work.

- For a concise, easy-to-read history of World War I, read Simon Adams's 2007 book *World War I*. The brief work is a history written specifically for young adults, and it is mainly comprised of photographs depicting battles, weapons, and soldiers. Each photograph is accompanied by explanatory captions and text.

- To learn more about modern poetry, read *100 Essential Modern Poems*, edited by

Joseph Parisi and published in 2005. Appropriate for high school literature students, the anthology includes work by modernist poets Yeats and Wallace Stevens, it also includes more contemporary poets, such as Rita Dove, Mark Strand, and Robert Pinsky. A biographical profile of each poet is also included in the volume, as well as introductions to each era and style of poetry over the twentieth century.

- Though Frost is best known as a poet, he also wrote numerous newspaper and magazine articles throughout his life. Never collected in his lifetime, these pieces have since been published in *The Collected Prose of Robert Frost*, edited by Mark Richardson. The 2008 volume features several previously unpublished writings as well as additional commentary by Richardson.

- Though the fatigue in "After Apple Picking" is largely mental, emotional, and spiritual, it is ostensibly triggered by the physical exhaustion brought on by the act of harvesting apples. For more information about life in an apple orchard, read Bruce Foxworthy's 2008 memoir *Making Do and Hanging On: Growing Up in Apple Country through the Great Depression*. The book details the hardships of rural life only fifteen years after the release of Frost's famed poem.

---

that awaits him. Will it be a lengthy slumber, or will he experience a more ordinary sleep? The former possibility carries connotations of death, emphasizing the interpretation of the poem as a mediation on mortality.

A second interpretation of "After Apple Picking" looks at the unfinished nature of the tasks at hand. Specifically, some critics observe that these unfinished tasks are incomplete, unworthy, or unpublished poems. They read "After Apple Picking" as a poem about writing, specifically about

the trials and travails and frustrations of writing. "In it are effort, loss," notes *American Literature* writer Priscilla M. Paton. The "effort" undertaken in the poem is clear (the harvest), and the "loss" can be viewed as the unpicked apples. Even more so, it can be seen as the apples that have fallen to the ground and have been subsequently relegated to the cider heap. Where the unpicked apples can be viewed as poems that have never been written, those that have been set aside after failing (or falling as the apples do so from the tree) can be seen as unsuccessful efforts. Given this interpretation, the successful harvest in the poem represents a flourishing or productive writing career. However, the speaker focuses least on that success. Instead, he devotes his attention to the effort he has set forth in making that achievement, and even more so to the fatigue that has followed. He also focuses a great deal on the poems that are unwritten and will remain so (the unpicked apples) and the failed efforts (the fallen apples). Where the speaker should feel satisfaction in the face of his accomplishments, he experiences only fatigue and dissatisfaction. This interpretation of "After Apple Picking" also makes the ending's uncertainty more intriguing. The speaker, having achieved his ends, does not know what will come next. Will he be refreshed and take up the pen again or not?

A sense of uncertainty seems to rule the poem. Its possible metaphorical meanings are as unsure as the speaker himself. This theory is underscored by the poem's dreamy imagery and halting rhythm, as well as its questioning conclusion. The speaker's peculiar vision, brought on by his looking through the ice in the water trough that morning, confirms a theme of uncertainty. The speaker's vision has been altered by the act, and he admits that it has not yet returned to normal by evening. This indecision, then, also extends to the third interpretation of "After Apple Picking," that of the poem as a song of exile from Eden. This interpretation is most often cited by critics; the apples are seen as a clear reference to the Garden of Eden and the fruit of the tree of knowledge in the Book of Genesis in the Bible. Although forbidden by God to eat from the tree of knowledge, Eve ate from it and gave some of the fruit to Adam. As punishment, God banished Adam and Eve from Eden. One image from the poem that is often mentioned in support of this interpretation is the ladder, which is described in "After Apple Picking" as pointing heavenward. By connecting the apples to Eden and the ladder to heaven, the metaphor becomes quite compelling. Kenneth Lincoln, writing in the *Southwest Review*, describes the poem as an exploration of "what happens to an aged Adam after apple-picking in the fall of the Fall, that is, post-Edenically when he begins to question eternity anew for real."

Dictionary of Literary Biography contributor Donald J. Greiner also discusses the Edenic allusions in "After Apple Picking." Greiner finds that

> "both speaker and reader are aware of the inviting association between apples and humanity's

expulsion from Eden, but one of the enduring pleasures of the poem is that neither speaker nor reader is certain how far the association should be pursued."

Frost's light touch in the poem, his creation of uncertainty, and his refusal to align himself with one meaning over another all serve to fill the poem with possibility. As Greiner points out, if the Edenic reference

> "is no more than decorative metaphor, then the speaker has successfully concluded a significant task—no matter what it literally is—and may reach for his rest in peace. But he cannot be sure; and if the mythological allusions to Eden carry meaning, then the speaker has finished a life's work only to be uncertain about whether finality or rebirth is at stake."

Source: Leah Tieger, Critical Essay on "After Apple Picking," in *Poetry for Students*, Gale, Cengage Learning, 2010.

Mike O'Connell

In the following review, O'Connell argues that what makes "After Apple Picking" unique is "its rare glimpse of Frost completing a full day's work, one that just about kills him."

When it came to early twentieth-century farm work, rugged New Englander Robert Frost was not afraid of it—in fact, he could lie down right next to it or run away from it. During the New England spring-mud season he was known to check his family into a New York hotel; during the hay feverish southern Vermont summers, Frost vacationed farther north in New Hampshire, leaving the garden weeding and haymaking and cow-milking to hired help, or to no one at all. After Christmas each winter, he hightailed it to Florida with his wife, and after her death, with his secretary Kathleen Morrison. "A man is rich in proportion to the number of things he can let go," wrote Thoreau, who in this regard had no truer disciple than Frost.

After being outed by Maine poet Edwin Arlington Robinson as something less than a real farmer, Frost insisted he had claimed to be no such thing. In his poems, we see him casually involved in some "outdoor fooling," working up a mild March sweat splitting wood, planting a few rows of beans and peas, swinging a scythe through the morning grass (someone else will have to follow later to make the hay). One of the things that sets "After Apple Picking" apart is its rare glimpse of Frost completing a full day's work, one that just about kills him.

As with his indoor scribbling, the chronically lazy Frost was occasionally capable of a reluctant, redemptive, outdoor stretch run. The poem begins with the early morning discovery of ice on the drinking trough; looking at the orchard grass through a broken sheet (or pane) of it sends the weary Frost into a reverie. Whatever symbolic meanings are to be skimmed here, the hard fact is that the October nights north of Boston have grown cold enough to make hard water, and to freeze—and thus damage—the unpicked apples: the end of the strenuous harvest season is mercifully at hand.

The "rumbling sound of load on load of apples coming in" tells us that the poet has had plenty of anonymous help, but his aching arches (the poem's most brilliant sensory cue) are convincing evidence that he has spent long hours ascending and descending the round rungs of the tall ladders himself. As usual, there is no "we" in the story: the word "I" is used fifteen times in forty-two lines. One who would attempt to separate the egocentric "speaker" in a Frost poem from the egocentric Robert Frost labors in vain.

Up and down we go throughout the shambling poem, from heaven to the windfalls in the stubble, from sharp edges to soft-headedness, from satiety to uncertainty, from hyperbole to humility. Although Frost magnifies his physical "lifting down" accomplishment, claiming an impossible personal harvest of "ten thousand thousand fruit," he admits to his characteristic laxity and fatigue: he may have overlooked a few apples, and likely dropped more than a few. His bushel basket runneth over; he is too tired to tidy up outside or to submit to the rigors of poetic form at his writing board in the house. As he drowses off, his line lengths vary widely, his rhyming is haphazard, his reader is confused and captivated.

"What wondrous life is this I lead / Ripe apples drop about my head" writes Andrew Marvell in "The Garden." But in Frost there is the sense of too many apples having fallen on his head. "Enough already," he seems to grumble at the gods who have given him the bumper crop he longed for. Marvell's immortal midsummer revelry is in contrast to Frost's autumnal sense of mortality—something like what he describes elsewhere as "winter and evening coming on together."

In some neighborhoods, the last day of the harvest might yield thoughts of a big evening meal or a cider and kitchen party for the orchard crew. At least a trip to the tavern. But all the

> WHILE FROST IS INCREASINGLY CANDID ABOUT THE HUMAN AND MORAL DIMENSION OF HIS POEMS AFTER HIS RETURN FROM ENGLAND, THESE CONCERNS REVEAL THEMSELVES EVEN BEFORE HIS EXIT FROM OBSCURITY."

bleary-eyed, konked-out Frost can think of (once he gets his poem put to bed) is to crash, perchance to dream. We need not equate sleep with death here. Old Man Frost lived another fifty-seven years after he stepped off the ladder to write this at the age of thirty. Even if the post-harvest nap turns out to be the "long sleep" of the woodchuck, that subterranean rodent will wake to chuck another day. And so will the exhausted apple picker, who has plucked from the bough a great poem—one made possible by, for once, an honest day's work.

Source: Mike O'Connell, Review of "After Apple Picking," in *Explicator*, Vol. 64, No. 2, Winter 2006, p. 91.

David Sanders

In the following excerpt, Sanders considers how the poems of North of Boston, *including "After Apple Picking," reflect the character of rural New England.*

North of Boston was Robert Frost's second book of poems but the first to reveal his full dramatic power and moral awareness. It was also the first to explore the culture of rural New England in which these poetic powers had grown to maturity. Published in May 1914 in London, fifteen months after *A Boy's Will, North of Boston* gained a warm reception in England and by September had made its way to Henry Holt in New York. Holt, buying the American rights from Frost's English publisher, David Nutt, reissued *North of Boston* in February of 1915, making it Frost's first American book and ending what had been, for him, two decades of obscurity at home. Reviewed by Amy Lowell in *The New Republic* the very week of Frost's return from England, the volume announced Frost to literary New York and Boston and revealed to America the poetic voice—vigorous and vernacular, yet subtle and complex—for which he would soon be widely known.

North of Boston also established Frost as a poet of people and place. Presenting earthy characters mainly in blank-verse narrative and dialogue, it takes us into the lives of working people in Frost's early twentieth-century New England. Even the volume's first-person lyrics— "Mending Wall," "After Apple-Picking," and "The Wood-Pile"—contain strong narrative and dramatic elements. Structuring the book through their strategic placement, they sound a keynote for the volume in their use of a conversational style, their exploration of character and motive, their emphasis on traditional skills and labor in a life in which winter is always near and survival never assured.

All of the sixteen poems that comprise *North of Boston* underwent final revision in England during the summer and fall of 1913, when the Frosts occupied a rented cottage in the London suburb of Beaconsfield. Yet the creative sources for these poems and their vernacular style go back to Frost's decade (1900–1909) on a small farm in Derry, New Hampshire. Frost, having left college a second time and suffering worrisome chest ailments, had, with money from his grandfather, turned away from the factory work and teaching that he already knew to try poultry farming, which promised to leave him time to write while supporting his family in a healthy rural environment. While the Derry years never quite made Frost either a farmer or a living, they shaped the poet he had determined to become, immersing him not only in the seasonal cycles and "country things" that would saturate his verse, but in the New England speech which he would make his poetic tongue. In doing so, the Derry years also made vivid and real the lives of the neighbors who would people *North of Boston* and, in wresting a living from hard climate and stony soil, would define a moral center for Frost's poetic world.

Considering his interest in its people, we might ask why Frost's comments on his verse in the year leading to the book's publication focus so thoroughly on matters of technique. The question is answered partly by Frost's immediate situation. The public response to *A Boy's Will* had raised doubts whether the artistry of his seemingly natural style would be understood by the audience, including the reviewers, of the volume in preparation, which Frost saw as pivotal to his career. In April 1913, for example, the *Times Literary Supplement* had described the

simplicity of *A Boy's Will* as "naively engaging." Ezra Pound's review in *Poetry* the following month had carried a greater sting. Although he had helped to promote Frost's name, Pound had made "the mistake," as Frost would soon complain to John Bartlett, "of assuming that my simplicity is that of the untutored child." Little as he had ever trusted Pound, Frost must still have felt betrayed by so cavalier an assessment from one who styled himself Frost's champion. He may also have worried that Pound had laid a path for others to follow. But perhaps more unsettling was Frost's own realization of how well-concealed his artistry could remain, even— or perhaps especially—to a cultivated audience. If such readers could miss so much in *A Boy's Will*, he feared what they would make of this next book, which took naturalness so much further, more obviously transgressing conventional boundaries between poetic language and ordinary speech.

The public response to *A Boy's Will* partly explains the vigorous discussion of poetic prosody that Frost developed over the following year with the English poets Frank Flint and T. E. Hulme and with Sidney Cox and John Bartlett back home. Frost hints at the value of this exchange when, early in July, a few days after the first of their specially arranged meetings, he thanks Flint, saying, "My ideas got just the rub they needed last week." In a letter to Bartlett three days later, Frost is more expansive. There, the dimensions of Frost's boast—"To be perfectly frank with you I am one of the most notable craftsmen of my time. That will transpire presently" (*Letters,* p. 79)—suggest how much is at stake for him and, thus, how important it was that he articulate principles at work in the poems. In fact, for much of the latter half of 1913, when he was shaping *North of Boston* as a book, Frost viewed his remarks on prosody as the dry run for "an essay or two I am going to write" (*Letters,* p. 113), even suggesting that Bartlett save his letters for that purpose. One can imagine something like Wordsworth's Preface to the *Lyrical Ballads* that would assert the method and sophistication behind his poetic experiments. In the end, Frost, who disliked writing prose, did not write the essay, perhaps trusting that the principles needed to appreciate his work were well enough understood by a few of the book's likely reviewers. Or perhaps he found that, in bolstering his own confidence, the important work was already done. But

Frost may also have felt that the poems, like the people in them and the language they spoke, would be diminished by any effort to explain them and could only distance him from a world of values that the poems had made his own.

Even in this pivotal year, then, Frost's reasons for stressing poetic technique are hard to disentangle from the moral aims embodied in his book. I stress the connection because, unlike his two most prominent models, Wordsworth and Emerson, Frost admits to these moral corollaries only rarely and obliquely. It is true that over the longer span of the book's development, roughly 1905–1913, Frost's most definite aim was to capture the sense of living speech within a metrical frame. Granted, too, that for an unproven poet measuring himself against both traditional and modernist rivals, technical mastery had a natural priority. And so, with an extravagance noted by William Pritchard and John Walsh, Frost announces himself to Bartlett as "possibly the only person going who works on any but a worn out ... principle ... of versification" (*Letters,* p. 79) and, a month afterwards, as "one of the few artists writing ... who have a theory of their own upon which all their work down to the least accent is done" (*Letters,* p. 88).

Still, there are many moments when Frost's pronouncements on prosody reveal something more than his pride of mastery and analytical insight. Consider, for example, his "new definition of a sentence," which he announces to Bartlett in February 1914 as "a sound in itself on which other sounds called words may be strung" (*Letters,* p. 110). With "a sound in itself" Frost puts grammar and logic aside for the moment to de-familiarize the written sentence. And, with these "other sounds called words," he even sneaks a backward glance toward the nature and origin of language itself—to the "expressiveness" that came "before words," the "brute tones of our human throat that may once have been all our meaning." At the same time, Frost engages us visually, asking us to imagine some fact on which these abstracted sounds "may be strung," only in the next moment showing us why: "You may string words together without a sentence hypersound to string them on just as you may tie clothes together ... and stretch them ... between two trees, but—it is bad for the clothes" (*Letters,* p. 111).

In this washday image, Frost—buoyed by Flint's response to his poetic theories and a

growing belief in his own poetic future—sets himself not only against the "worn out" prosodies of established contemporaries such as Robert Bridges, but also against the cultural pretensions that he felt in Pound and a whole aura of refinement that much of late nineteenth-century esthetics had cast over poetry. In this sense, just as Frost's concern with technique reveals itself as more than defensive, so it is more than technical. When he says that "An ear and an appetite for these sounds of sense is the first qualification of a writer" (*Letters,* p. 80) and that "The most original writer only catches them fresh from talk" (*Letters,* p. 111), Frost, like Wordsworth, is claiming a respect and an authority for the language of ordinary people from which poets, he felt, had too often set poetry apart. In doing so, he challenges an imbedded view of culture that gives precedence to the written word. Just a few years later, in distinguishing between "our everyday speech ... and a more literary, sophisticated, artificial, elegant language that belongs to books," Frost would claim that he "could get along very well without this bookish language altogether" (*Collected Poems,* p. 694). For Frost, who had found a touchstone for his craft in the talk of his Derry neighbors and who would always "say" rather than "read" his poems before audiences, ordinary speech was inseparable from those who spoke it, and the question of words not a question of words alone. When, for *North of Boston,* Frost avoided the singing harmonies of Tennyson and Swinburne that remained part of *A Boy's Will,* he was rejecting an estheticism largely English and upper-class in favor of a poetry that would speak to Americans, and for them, in a language that Americans spoke. It was a language of labor and use by which a literary culture could affirm the values of an oral, vernacular one, placing cultivation of the soil at least on a par with the cultivation of the drawing room.

Once back on American soil, where such populist strains might sound more sweetly, and with his poetic investment in England paying well, Frost is more direct about the human and social dimensions of his book. Finding *North of Boston* actively promoted by Henry Holt and himself courted by editors who had ignored his work for a decade, Frost may have felt less compelled to prove himself an artist and freer to claim the democracy of spirit central to his vision. After the painful experience of feeling unappreciated and misunderstood, he may also have been eager to expand or correct earlier statements of his artistic concerns. Thus he writes in March 1915 to William Stanley Braithwaite of the Boston *Evening Transcript,* giving him material for his weekly poetry column:

> It would seem absurd to say it (and you mustn't quote me as saying it) but I suppose ... that my conscious interest in people was at first no more than an almost technical interest in their speech—in what I used to call their sentence sounds—the sound of sense ... There came a day about ten years ago when I ... made the discovery in doing The Death of the Hired Man that I was interested in neighbors for more than merely their tones of speech—and always had been. (*Letters,* p. 158–59)

By placing this discovery in 1905, when he drafted the earliest *North of Boston* poems, Frost makes it a cornerstone of the volume itself. Later he would say that the realization that "I was after poetry that talked" had "changed the whole course of my writing" and would even call it "providential." Aided by so weighty a term, Frost implies that, since any vernacular is rooted in its culture, a poetry that "talked" could never be a purely technical achievement. A poetry that "talked" would not only sound like conversation. It would really say something—something human, basic, and significant. Seeking a poetry that talked in the accents of his Derry neighbors gave Frost a way both to test and to convey such realities. In addition to evoking a specific culture in which to ground the human conflicts which he wished to explore, the search gave Frost a language free of false refinements in which anything inauthentic would prove weak or untrue.

While Frost is increasingly candid about the human and moral dimension of his poems after his return from England, these concerns reveal themselves even before his exit from obscurity. Writing from England in July 1913, as he was shaping the book for publication, Frost conveys this interest to Thomas Mosher, an American collector and publisher, when he describes the "volume of blank verse . . . already well in hand" with "some character strokes I had to get in somewhere" (*Letters,* p. 83). Feigning apology for having "dropped into an everyday level of diction that even Wordsworth kept above," Frost tries at once to tweak and reassure, prompt and flatter the fastidious Mosher:

> I trust I don't terrify you. I think I have made poetry. The language is appropriate to the virtues I celebrate. At least I am sure that I can count on you to give me credit for knowing what I am about. (*Letters,* pp. 83–84)

"The language is appropriate to the virtues I celebrate": this unqualified assertion stands definite and tall amidst Frost's more calculated postures ("I trust ... I think ... At least I am sure") and underlines the importance which he attached to the human substance of these poems.

We see much the same emphasis in Frost's note to F. S. Flint written earlier that July, after their first discussion of "sentence sounds." Delighted as he is with Flint's response to his thoughts on prosody, Frost makes clear his greater concern with what his language is saying when he asks Flint, who had read eight of the longer narratives:

> Did I reach you with the poems[?] ... Did I give you the feeling of and for the independent-dependence of the kind of people I like to write about[?] ... The John Kline who lost his housekeeper and went down like a felled ox was just the person I have described and I never knew a man I liked better.... (*Writing,* p. 82)

A more pregnant comment on the kind of people whom Frost liked to write about—and on the way that character enacts itself through language—surfaces in the letter to Sidney Cox written in September 1913, after a family trip to Scotland. The passage is notable partly for Frost's first mention of the local stone walls that would soon prompt the writing of "Mending Wall." More remarkable still is the way it associates various facets of Frost's life—his experience of England and New England, his early exposure to Scots writers by his mother, his social and moral attitudes—with the volume in preparation and the hopes attached to it. He writes:

> The best of the adventure was the time in Kingsbarns where tourists and summer boarders never come. The common people in the south of England I don't like to have around me. They don't know how to meet you man to man. The people in the north are more like Americans. I wonder whether they made Burns' poems or Burns' poems made them. And there are stone walls (dry stone dykes) in the north: I liked those. My mother was from Edinburgh. I used to hear her speak of the Castle and Arthur's seat, more when I was young than in later years. I had some interest in seeing those places. (*Letters,* pp. 94–95)

This web of associations makes clear enough that the Americans whom Frost has in mind are those in the poems that he is readying for publication—another "common people" who "know how to meet you man to man" and have made their mark in stone across another northern landscape. Equally revealing is Frost's comment about Robert Burns, another poet of democratic and vernacular impulse whom Belle Frost had read to her son from early childhood and whose 1786 *Poems, Chiefly in the Scottish Dialect* had also asserted the worth of a rural people and their language. In the alchemy of Frost's memory and imagination—with thoughts of home stirred by the Scottish hills and people, and the whole process aided by his Scots mother and her literary legacy—Frost merges Burns's people with his own and, implicitly, himself with Burns. Perhaps most striking is Frost's surmise about the mutual act of making between one's poems and one's culture. When we realize how suddenly Burns's 1786 volume brought this farmer-poet to the attention of his nation's literary elite, we get a sense of the degree to which Frost's feelings of gratitude and obligation toward his Derry neighbors are entwined with his own poetic hopes: that their "making" of his poems would also "make" him as a poet, bringing him home to Boston and New York, just as Burns's second book had taken him to literary Edinburgh; that if they did so, these poems would impact the Derry neighbors to whose lives and speech they owed so much; that his book might bring their voices alive to readers who would not otherwise know them, gaining them a respect and recognition which they could never win for themselves, thus perhaps saving some part of their disappearing world. The poems might even show them some of their own substance and value, which Frost had seen and tried to capture in his poems.

Frost's concern for his human subjects and his wish to make them known is implicit in the book's dedication to Elinor—"to E.M.F. This Book of People"—and by the other titles that he considered for the volume: *New Englanders, New England Hill Folk,* or the one originally listed by his London publisher M. L. Nutt, *Farm Servants and Other People.* It may seem curious that, in the end, Frost chose a title that does not mention these people directly. Yet, as in so much of Frost's work, this reticence is eloquent. Like the book's language, the words "north of Boston" say something about its people not only by pointing to the region and culture that have shaped their lives, but by making clear what they are not. Posed against "Boston," with its history and urbanity, what lies "north" is simply out there, provincial and

exposed, somewhere between the capital and the pole, so that, even before we have read the book, *North of Boston* suggests the fortitude of its people by hinting at the cold and emptiness that they face. And, by the time we have finished its poems about failed and failing farms and the families who have left or will be leaving them, we see that their traditional way of life takes definition and value in opposition to the urban wealth and power to which it literally loses ground each year. With just a little the help from his dedication, Frost's title trusts the poems to bring his people to our notice, just as he has trusted their language to shape his poetic voice, and just as the poems, with their sparing narration, trust so largely to the speech of the characters themselves.

Source: David Sanders, "Frost's *North of Boston*, Its Language, Its People, Its Poet," in *Journal of Modern Literature*, Vol. 27, Nos. 1–2, Fall 2003, pp. 70–78.

Kenneth T. Reed

In the following article, Reed identifies Henry Wadsworth Longfellow's sonnet "Sleep" as a possible source for "After Apple Picking."

That Robert Frost admired the poetics of Henry Longfellow and was in some measure influenced by him is generally known, albeit the specific character of that influence is at best vaguely understood. As a contribution to that understanding, one might well begin by examining Longfellow's sonnet "Sleep" (1875) as a highly probable source for Frost's "After Apple-Picking". So similar in theme, structure and tone are they that Frost's artistic conception for his poem could not have been merely coincidental.

The themes of both poems center about the narrator's world-weariness, his physical and spiritual fatigue and his desire for sleep as the only balm for his lassitude. Each narrator suggests, moreover, that the sleep to which he refers is death. Longfellow makes that association in his last three lines: "Ah, with what subtle meaning did the Greek/ Call thee [sleep] the lesser mystery at the feast/ Whereof the greater mystery is death!"

Frost, with his dark "essence of winter sleep" and his "long sleep", unmistakably conveys the same impression, though in more suggestive and guarded terms. The falling apples and the conclusion of the autumn harvest both reinforce the death suggestion.

Although Frost's poem has precisely three times the number of lines that Longfellow's sonnet has, it unfolds in much the same way. Longfellow's narrator begins with a call for sleep ("lull me to sleep, ye winds") while Frost's declares that he is "drowsing off". Both speakers use eye and sight imagery. Longfellow cites the "hundred wakeful eyes of thought" and the "hundred wakeful eyes of Argus"; Frost has his narrator declare "I cannot rub the strangeness from my eyes". Both speakers refer to their physical pain. Longfellow's speaker wants his "pain released"; Frost's complains of the "ache" and "pressure of a ladder-round". As each poem moves toward its conclusion, the speaker cites some "authority" on sleep and death. In the Longfellow poem it is the "Greek", Frost's more rustic and less classical-minded speaker would consult only the humble woodchuck.

The tone of each poem is one of obvious fatigue and weathered spiritual resignation. Longfellow's "For I am weary and am overwrought/ With too much toil, with too much care distraught,/ And with the iron crown of anguish crowned." has a curious similarity to Frost's "For I have had too much/ Of apple-picking: I am overtired/ Of the great harvest I myself desired".

Frost's indebtedness to his predecessor is, I think, obvious enough. Still temperamentally different from one another, Frost's only major departure from Longfellow was to substitute a sage and mature rusticity for Longfellow's allusions to classical mythology.

Source: Kenneth T. Reed, "Longfellow's 'Sleep' and Frost's 'After Apple-Picking,'" in *American Notes & Queries*, Vol. 10, No. 9, May 1972, p. 134.

SOURCES

Armstrong, Tim, *Modernism: A Cultural History*, Polity, 2005.

Bradbury, Malcolm, and James McFarlane, *Modernism: A Guide to European Literature 1890-1930*, Penguin, 1978.

"Census 2000 Population Statistics: U.S. Population Living in Urban vs. Rural Areas," in *U.S. Census Bureau*, http://www.fhwa.dot.gov/planning/census/cps2k.htm (accessed May 7, 2009).

Frost, Robert, "After Apple Picking," in *The Road Not Taken: A Selection of Robert Frost's Poems*, edited by Louis Untermeyer, Henry Holt, 2001, pp. 244-45.

Greiner, Donald J., "Robert Frost," in *Dictionary of Literary Biography*, Vol. 54, *American Poets, 1880-1945*, 3rd ser., edited by Peter Quatermain, Gale Research, 1987, pp. 93-121.

Keegan, John, *The First World War*, Vintage, 2000.

Liebman, Sheldon W., "Robert Frost, Romantic," in *Twentieth Century Literature*, Vol. 42, No. 4, Winter 1996, p. 417.

Lincoln, Kenneth, "Quarreling Frost, Northeast of Eden," in the *Southwest Review*, Vol. 93, No. 1, Winter 2008, p. 93.

Link, Arthur Stanley, *The Impact of World War I*, HarperCollins, 1969.

Marshall, S. L. A., *World War I*, Mariner Books, 2001.

Marwick, Arthur, *The Impact of World War I: Total War and Social Change; Europe 1914-1945*, Open University Worldwide, 2001.

Muste, John M., "After Apple-Picking," in *Masterplots II: Poetry*, rev. ed., Salem Press, 2002.

O'Connell, Mike, "Frost's 'After-Picking,'" in the *Explicator*, Vol. 64, No. 2, Winter 2006, p. 91.

Parini, Jay, *Robert Frost: A Life*, reprint ed., Holt, 2000.

Paton, Priscilla M., "The Fact Is the Sweetest Dream that Labor Knows," in *American Literature*, Vol. 53, No. 1, March 1981, pp. 43-55.

Reed, Kenneth T., "Longfellow's 'Sleep' and Frost's 'After Apple-Picking,'" in *American Notes & Queries*, Vol. 10, No. 9, May 1972, pp. 134-35.

Sanders, David, "Frost's *North of Boston*, Its Language, Its People, and Its Poet," in *Journal of Modern Literature*, Vol. 27, Nos. 1-2, Fall 2003, pp. 70-78.

Stanlis, Peter, *Robert Frost: The Poet as Philosopher*, Intercollegiate Studies Institute, 2nd ed., 2008.

Whitworth, Michael, *Modernism*, Wiley-Blackwell, 2007.

FURTHER READING

Eliot, T. S., *Complete Poems and Plays: 1909-1950*, Harcourt, 1952.
> Eliot is perhaps America's foremost modernist writer, and his poetry and dramatic prose are collected in this 1952 edition, which remains in print as of 2009. Eliot's famous poems, such as "The Waste Land" and "Four Quarters," are included in the volume.

Faulkner, William, *As I Lay Dying*, new and corrected ed., Random House, 1964.
> For a look at modernist prose, this novel is exemplary. It is told from the points of view of several family members as they make a pilgrimage to bury the corpse of the family matriarch. The novel also features the stream-of-consciousness style that evolved as part of the modernist aesthetic.

Longfellow, Henry Wadsworth, *The Sonnets of Henry Wadsworth Longfellow*, Kessinger, 2007.

> Frost was a great fan of Longfellow's work, and a study of Frost is not complete without an understanding of Longfellow's work. This collection also includes the 1875 sonnet "Sleep," which some critics have identified as Frost's inspiration for "After Apple Picking."

Thompson, Lawrence Roger, *Robert Frost: The Years of Triumph, 1915-1938*, Henry Holt, 1970.

This literary biography of Frost looks at the poet's most prolific years. The volume is essential reading for all who wish to delve more deeply into Frost's life and work.

Visser, Thomas Durant, *Field Guide to New England Barns and Farm Buildings*, University Press of New England, 1997.

> For an in-depth look at the architecture and history of the milieu against which Frost's poem is set, Visser's guide book is an excellent reference.

A Black Man Talks of Reaping

When Arna Bontemps wrote "A Black Man Talks of Reaping" in 1926, America was a racially divided country. Many of the states that had belonged to the Confederacy during the Civil War sixty years earlier had laws that still reflected the slave-holding culture of the South, keeping races separated under a spurious "separate but equal" doctrine that did little to promote, much less enforce, equality. In the North, inequality between blacks and whites was not permitted by law, but social attitudes enabled an unofficial form of segregation to flourish. During the mid-1920s Bontemps lived in Harlem, a section of New York City that was famous worldwide as a center of black American culture. During the 1920s and 1930s it was also known as the meeting place of notable black intellectuals, artists, and writers who started a movement called the Harlem Renaissance. Bontemps and other Harlem artists became characterized as members of this group, also known as the New Negro Movement.

Among his Harlem Renaissance peers, such as Claude McKay, Countee Cullen, Langston Hughes, and Jean Toomer, Bontemps was known for writing about the conditions and attitudes facing black Americans in the South, which is certainly the case in "A Black Man Talks of Reaping." The poem uses a refined, graceful poetic cadence to capture the strong sense of tradition but ultimate sense of futility facing black Americans at a time when the accomplishments of their culture were frequently ignored. "A Black Man Talks of

ARNA BONTEMPS

1926

Arna Bontemps (AP Images)

Reaping," one of Bontemps's most famous and frequently anthologized poems, was published along with several of Bontemps's other poems from the 1920s in the 1963 collection *Personals*. The poem has been anthologized in several books, including the 1995 collection *The Columbia Anthology of American Poetry*, edited by Jay Parini.

AUTHOR BIOGRAPHY

Arnaud Wendell Bontemps was born October 12, 1902, in Alexandria, Louisiana. Three years later, his family moved to Los Angeles, California, to escape the racial prejudice that was common across the Deep South at that time. His mother, Maria Carolina Pembroke Bontemps, was a school teacher, and encouraged his love of books. After her death in 1915, Bontemps's father, Paul Bismark, a brick mason, sent his son to San Fernando Academy, a boarding school for predominantly white students. Bontemps attended the school from 1917 to 1920 and then went to Pacific Union College, graduating in 1923.

In 1924, Bontemps published his first poem in *Crisis*, the literary magazine of the NAACP

(National Association for the Advancement of Colored People). He moved to New York that year to teach at the Harlem Academy, a Seventh Day Adventist high school. In 1926 and 1927 he was awarded *Opportunity* magazine's Alexander Pushkin Poetry Prize. While teaching at the Harlem Academy, he became acquainted with writers and artists often associated with the Harlem Renaissance, such as poet and novelist Langston Hughes, with whom Bontemps formed a close, lifelong friendship, and the poet Countee Cullen, who later worked with him in adapting Bontemps's 1931 novel *God Sends Sunday* to a play. In Harlem, Bontemps met and married Alberta Johnson, with whom he would eventually raise six children.

In 1931 the Harlem Academy closed, and Bontemps returned to the South, where many of his literary works were set. He took a teaching position at Oakwood Junior College in Huntsville, Alabama. After moving to Alabama, he began writing children's literature, which he continued to write throughout his life. In addition to illustrated books like *You Can't Pet a Possum* and *Slappy Hooper, the Wonderful Sign Painter*, he began what would eventually become a multipart biography of antislavery crusader Frederick Douglass for young audiences. He left Oakwood Junior College in 1934 and taught in Chicago, Illinois, for three years. After the publication of his most famous work, the 1936 novel *Black Thunder*, Bontemps quit teaching. For a year, he worked for the Illinois Writers Project, and then he gave up teaching entirely, living briefly in the Caribbean, an experience that gave him material for his novel *Drums at Dusk*, published in 1939.

In 1943, Bontemps earned a master of library sciences degree from the University of Chicago. He became a librarian at Fisk University in Nashville, Tennessee, where he worked until 1965, expanding the school's collection of African American literature and collaborating on several anthologies of black literature. He died of a heart attack in Nashville on June 4, 1973, while working on his autobiography.

POEM TEXT

I have sown beside all waters in my day.
I planted deep, within my heart the fear
That wind or fowl would take the grain away.
I planted safe against this stark, lean year.

I scattered seed enough to plant the land   5
In rows from Canada to Mexico

But for my reaping only what the hand
Can hold at once is all that I can show.

Yet what I sowed and what the orchard yields
My brother's sons are gathering stalk and root,   10
Small wonder then my children glean in fields
They have not sown, and feed on bitter fruit.

POEM SUMMARY

Line 1

The first-person speaker who refers to himself as "I" at the start of "A Black Man Talks of Reaping" is not meant to be understood as an individual but instead as a composite of the cultural experiences that blacks have faced in the United States. The poem makes this clear in its opening line, where the speaker does not talk about working beside "some" or "many" waters, but instead refers to having been beside all of them. Although it would be impossible for any one person to have been everywhere in the world, it is conceivable that, over the course of history, members of any race may have been.

In addition to setting a mythical tone, the poem's first line also establishes its ongoing pattern of nature imagery. Water is a universal image, familiar to every culture. Combining it with the poem's main image of farming helps to make this poem relevant to people who might not understand specific cultural references.

Line 2

The second line continues the imagery of farming that began in the poem's title, referring to the planting of seeds that starts the process that ends with reaping. Line 2 ends with the mention of the speaker's fear, though the basis of the fear is not revealed to the reader until line 3.

Line 3

In line 3, the speaker refers to every farmer's constant fear of seeing the planted seeds swept away, either by birds or by wind, before they have a chance to take root. The wind is often used to represent the random elements of chance, as in the common expression "the winds of change," while the birds that are mentioned can be read broadly as representing a vast range of predators.

Line 4

In spite of the threats to the crops' growth, the speaker has taken steps to assure that his labor will not be done in vain. In a literal sense, planting the seeds deeply in the soil will ensure that they will

not be susceptible to wind or birds. On a symbolic level, Bontemps implies that black people have, over the years, learned to guard their accomplishments against elements in their surroundings that will do them harm. When the poem mentions that the current year is harsh, it refers to the changes in weather that are a constant concern for farmers. The reference is more applicable to the ever changing situation of farmers than to the constant oppression that black Americans had faced since the end of the Civil War in 1865.

Line 5

In this line the speaker refers to the farmer's need to plant an adequate amount of seeds, which in a way makes up for those that will inevitably be lost to wind or birds. The poem also reminds readers of how much of the constructive labor across the country was done by black Americans, using the planting metaphor to indicate all of the hard work should be expected to bring social growth.

Line 6

Line 6 expands on the point made in line 5. Although the poem started with a universal reference to all the waters in the world, these lines narrow the writer's scope down to the experience of the United States, focusing on events that occur in this country. Bontemps makes a point of mentioning that the seeds are planted methodically, in clear, distinct rows, indicating intelligence and care. The implication is that the black Americans have worked just as carefully as white Americans in order to ensure a better future.

Lines 7–8

In lines 7 and 8, the poet discusses the reaping announced in its title. Reaping of grain is generally done with a scythe (a farming tool with a long curved blade) or machine, cutting down wide columns of grain stalks with each pass. The fact that the reaping has been so limited here is indicative of the way black Americans were held back, so that the poem's speaker has only been able to mow his crops down one handful at a time. After laboring for decades to help build their country from one shore to the other, black Americans were only able to partake in minimal rewards. There was no law or organization that could act as the social equivalent of what the scythe or the harvester does for farming, expanding beyond the power of any one human being. Although the collective labor of black Americans was used to build the country, they had not been given the means to benefit from cultural and economic growth in the same way that white Americans were.

Line 9

In line 9, Bontemps returns to the idea of methodical patience stressed earlier in the poem. Throughout the previous lines, the speaker discusses his many accomplishments, especially the care that he has put into sowing the fields. There is a sense of futility in lines 7 and 8, however, as the poet shows, the hard work done has led to little reward for black Americans. In line 9, the speaker's work ethic is on display once again, as he talks about the balance between what he has sown in the field and what fruits the field has borne. Although the speaker does not derive that much benefit from his work, the poem's wording in line 9 betrays a true pride for what little he has gained.

Line 10

In line 10, the speaker refers to extended relations, not his direct descendents. Readers can assume that "brother" is meant in the broadest sense, as a reference to all of humanity. Referencing the title of the poem, it is likely that its suggestion might be limited to other black people. If this is so, "brother's children" can be read as meaning the subsequent generation that will follow those who have cultivated the soil so carefully.

The benefits that the next generation gains from the speaker's works will be meager. Instead

of harvesting the abundant crops that might be expected after hard work, they will only be able to gather the worst parts of the harvest. The stalks and roots of the plant are usually what is left over after the grain and fruit have been removed, but Bontemps says that this is all the next generation of black Americans will be able to collect.

Line 11

To "glean" means literally to gather what is left on the ground after reapers have taken away the important parts of the harvest. Figuratively, the word is often used to indicate that someone slowly comes to an awareness of a situation after lengthy observation of the available details. In the situation described here, the children of the speaker have access only to what is left on the ground after some unnamed force, presumably the might of more privileged races, has reaped the important parts of the crop. There is very little that is worthwhile left for the speaker's children and descendents, and that dilemma is slowly becoming undeniable to those affected by it.

Line 12

The poem ends with an ominous note. The up-and-coming generation of black Americans, the speaker says, will have to fend for themselves, giving up any pretense at social rights. The fields that they do not own and have not cultivated are symbolic of the way that black Americans were denied property ownership in the past. The way that American society refused to allow their participation made many of them bitter. Bontemps shows that those who have been given a bitter situation will often respond with bitterness, implying that the rage of the disenfranchised black Americans is likely to be reflected back toward mainstream American society.

THEMES

Black Identity

Bontemps tells of one individual's experiences in "A Black Man Talks of Reaping," but he also makes it clear that the situation described in the poem is meant to reflect the experiences of all black Americans. The first sign that he is describing more than just one person can be found in the phrasing of the poem's title. Using the words "a man" might have been open to interpretation about whether the poet was talking about one individual or all of humanity, including women, who according to standards of the time were often included within the general mention of "man" and "mankind." By specifying that the speaker is

TOPICS FOR FURTHER STUDY

- Read Walter B. Myers's novel *Monster* about a sixteen-year-old boy who goes to jail for murder. Myers's protagonist shows social injustice by turning his experience into a screenplay. Follow Myers's model and write a screenplay for a short film that captures the feelings of the speaker in the poem "A Black Man Talks of Reaping."

- The speaker of this poem talks about protecting his work from wind and birds by planting the seeds deep in the soil. Research modern agribusiness techniques to come up with five planting strategies that are used by large corporate farms, where hand-seeding is not used. Make a PowerPoint presentation incorporating a farming proposal and visual aids to persuade your class as to which of the five strategies is most effective and why.

- This poem adheres strictly to its rhythmic pattern. Set it to music in two styles. In one, use only percussion instruments, and in the other, use a melody of your own making. Have your classmates vote on which type of music they think is more appropriate

for the poem. Afterwards, lead a discussion about how the rhythm of the poem can be paired with music.

- Soon after this poem was published, Congress passed the Civil Rights Act of 1964. This act was seen as key to helping African Americans gain equal social footing. Review the provisions of the act and determine which would have been most relevant to a farmer like the one that Bontemps describes in the poem. Then determine which provisions would apply to something in your life currently. Use the results to write a letter to the speaker of "A Black Man Talks of Reaping," telling him what you two have in common.

- At the time when this poem was written, little was known about the culture of poor farmers. Read *When Rain Clouds Gather* by Bessie Head about farming in southern Africa. Select some instances when Head's descriptions sounds like the one Bontemps describes, and write an explanation that compares and contrasts the two situations.

---

a black man, though, Bontemps indicates that his character is a representative of characteristics that are common to all black people.

Another place where Bontemps reveals that this poem is about black identity is in the first line, when the speaker says that he has planted crops beside "all" waters. It would be impossible for any person to have been everywhere in one lifetime, of course. This statement makes perfect sense, though, if he is speaking as a representative for his race, which quite likely has had members in all areas of the world.

Most obvious, though, is the way that the poem's symbolism fits the experience of African Americans in general. Bontemps tells of a worker who has not been allowed to benefit from the hard work he has done, who has been left to survive on

the little that remains when almost everything useful has been consumed by others. The situation would be instantly familiar to any African American before the struggle for civil rights began to yield results in the 1950s and 1960s, whether that person was a farmer or not.

Fatalism

The speaker of this poem describes a grim and hopeless situation. He has worked hard, he says, using the metaphor of planting seeds to represent all of the hard work done by black people, who were then confined mostly to positions of manual labor. It is the course of nature that seeds will grow into beneficial crops, especially when they have been planted with the care that this speaker has used: he plants his seeds in straight rows, pushing them deep into the soil for protection. Despite the care

Plowing a field (© *Bettmann* / *Corbis*)

that he uses, he is allowed to have nothing substantial when the seeds have completed their growth cycle and are ready for reaping. In fact, he is the one who reaps the grain with his own hands, and yet he is still allowed nothing for his efforts. This is the way things have been all of his life, and he does not expect anything more. He is fatalistically resigned to the misery of his life, recognizing it as a terrible situation that may never end.

Anger

The only sign that this speaker has not entirely lost all hope in his life, that he is not completely bereft of spirit, appears at the end of the poem. He does not develop hope for a better life that pulls his worldview back from bleak fatalism; instead, he finds comfort in knowing that some time, probably not in his own lifetime, the oppression that his race has been forced to suffer will make people angry enough to fight. The poem's controlled tone does not show the speaker's anger, but it is hinted at

clearly in the last lines, when he explains that the coming generations will be left to struggle with even less and to feed off of the bitterness of inequality. Though the speaker clearly does not want the generation of his children to suffer, he does show a sense that someone in the future will eventually feel that they have suffered enough, and when that happens, he implies, there are bound to be consequences for the anger that has built up over the years.

Generations

In this poem, Bontemps mentions the coming generation twice, indicating two different sets of expectations about what will happen. In line 10 he mentions the sons of his brothers, who are related to him but not of direct lineage. Their lives are predicted to be the scrabble for survival by gathering whatever has been left on the ground, deemed useless after the harvest. These nephews appear to be of a different age than the speaker's children, since the situations facing the two groups are different: by the time the children of the speaker will have to fend for themselves, even the meager left from the harvest will not be available to them. The differences in the situations from the children of one brother to the children of another could be explained by reading Bontemps's reference to "my children" broadly. The speaker might not be referring to his own children in this phrase, but to his children's children, and all of his descendents, thereby implicating the future of all African Americans.

STYLE

Heroic Stanza

The form of this poem is a traditional one. Each line except the first one has ten syllables and is written in an *iambic* rhythm. An *iamb* consists of two syllables, the first one unstressed and the second stressed. Since there are five of these units per line, the meter is considered *iambic pentameter* ("penta-" is a prefix from the ancient Greek word for "five"). Although the first line has eleven syllables, the fact that the rest are written in clear iambic pentameter and that line 1 is so close to iambic pentameter, and would in fact fit the pattern perfectly if the first two words were contracted to "I've," identifies this poem as being predominantly iambic pentameter.

The rhyme scheme of this poem is a consistent *abab* pattern: the syllable ending the third line of each stanza sounds like the syllable ending the first line of that stanza, and the syllable ending the fourth line of each stanza resembles the syllable ending the second. Each stanza is a *quatrain*, which means that it has four lines. The designation for a quatrain written in iambic pentameter, with an *abab* rhyme scheme, is a *heroic stanza*, a term that derives from poetry composed with a dramatic mood, usually orally, to tell of the accomplishments of great warriors. In this case, the use of the heroic stanza helps to establish the talent and nobility of the speaker of the poem, even though he is socially considered a member of the lower class.

Extended Metaphor

A metaphor is a comparison that draws attention to similarities between two dissimilar entities without stating the comparison. It is, for example, metaphoric to refer to an airplane as a bird, since they both share the common element of flying with wings, though they are clearly two different items.

In "A Black Man Talks of Reaping," there are several elements that connect the agrarian image of growing and harvesting crops with the implied action of standing up for rights. For instance, the speaker in the poem is a black man; at the time, many black Americans were farm laborers, and they experienced oppression. Another similarity that links farming to coming vengeance is the image of sowing or planting, which may have originated in farm work but can easily be viewed as anything that will lead to its inevitable consequences in the way that crops are bound to grow into the plants that are sown. Finally, and most obviously, is the idea of reaping, which literally means the end result of farming but can easily be understood as the act of gathering up what one has earned; in this poem, it implies possible violence from those who have been oppressed. When one comparison between two situations is implied, it is a metaphor. When several comparisons between the same two situations are examined, it is an extended metaphor.

HISTORICAL CONTEXT

The Harlem Renaissance

The 1920s saw a boom in creativity for black intellectuals across the United States. Historians dubbed this period the Harlem Renaissance, after the area of New York City that was a prominent center for black artists.

Black Americans had been moving in great numbers from the formerly slave-holding southern states to the North for decades, with a steady migration that had begun at the end of slavery in 1865 and surging as black workers moved to follow the industrial jobs that became available during World War I, from 1914–1918. This migration led to growing populations in the large urban centers across the North, notably Chicago, Illinois; Detroit, Michigan; Pittsburgh, Pennsylvania; and Cleveland, Ohio. At the time, New York City was the intellectual and media center of the country, and many writers, poets, painters, and musicians settled in New York to have access to publishing houses, radio stations, and the most important theater district in the world.

Significant organizations dedicated to improving the conditions of black Americans were headquartered in New York City, too, including the National Urban League, the United Negro Improvement Association, and the National Association for the Advancement of Colored People.

COMPARE
&
CONTRAST

- **1920s:** Segregation is common and legal in the southern United States, with Jim Crow laws requiring that black Americans stay separated from white Americans in most social settings.

  1950s: Awareness of the inherent injustice of segregation is growing, with attention drawn to the treatment of black Americans by such notable events as the Montgomery Bus Boycott of 1955 in Montgomery, Alabama, and the violence surrounding the desegregation of schools in Little Rock, Arkansas, in 1957.

  Today: Although racial tension is often identified as one of the most serious social problems in the United States, segregation is illegal and prosecuted by law.

- **1920s:** The Great Migration of black Americans to the industrial North during the 1910s and 1920s has created a generation of urban African Americans with firsthand experience of rural life.

  1950s: A second wave of migration beginning during World War II leads to another influx of Southern black American workers relocating to Northern industrial cities, many trying to escape the segregationist laws in place in the South.

  Today: National laws regulating civil rights have led to a counter-migration of African Americans back to the American South, though people moving to the South tend to settle in urban areas such as Jackson, Mississippi; Atlanta, Georgia; and Birmingham, Alabama.

- **1920s:** During the Harlem Renaissance, black American artists converge in New York City, one of the largest black communities in the country and the acknowledged center of media activity.

  1950s: New York City retains its importance as a media center as the origin of the growing television field.

  Today: Advances in electronics allow artists to publish music online and produce recordings and videos on their personal computers, but New York City is still, with Los Angeles, California, one of the most important media centers in the country.

Magazines such as *Opportunity, Crisis,* and the *Messenger* focused on issues affecting black Americans and attracted black writers, who all lived, at least some of the time, in the relatively narrow confines of the Harlem neighborhood.

One milestone in the history of the Harlem arts boom was white writer Ridgely Torrence's *Three Plays for a Negro Theater*, produced in 1917, presenting for the first time black characters who were fully realized as human beings, countering the traditional stereotypes. This work opened the door to the 1921 musical *Shuffle Away*, a celebration of black creativity that was written by blacks for black performers, introducing many white audiences to black artistry for the first time. In 1922 James Weldon Johnson published the anthology *The*

Book of American Negro Poetry, providing a worldwide forum for some of the writers who had come to New York and encouraging more, like Arna Bontemps, to come to Harlem to work with their artistic and intellectual peers.

During the Harlem Renaissance, as with any intellectual movement, success and growth led people to align themselves with various schools of thought. For instance, older writers such as W. E. B. Du Bois, most famous for his 1903 work *The Souls of Black Folks*, openly questioned the morality in the works of the new guard, such as Jamaican immigrant Claude McKay. Other artists rejected the title "Harlem Renaissance" altogether and did what they could to assert their independence from any perceived movement. There was also

Sowing seeds (© *Andrew McConnell | Alamy*)

division about the importance of Africa to black Americans; Langston Hughes, for one, asserted that Africa was the wellspring of inspiration for the black artist, while poet Countee Cullen maintained that the history that connected black Americans to Africa should not be allowed to over-shadow acting in the present.

During the Great Depression, which began in 1929, all artistic movements in America suffered, and the Harlem Renaissance was no exception. Throughout the 1930s, artists and intellectuals still gathered in Harlem, but fewer of them, and for shorter stays. Some artists completed important works in the 1930s, such as Hughes's short-story collection *The Ways of White Folks* and the novels that Zora Neale Hurston produced at that time. In general, however, the concept of the Harlem Renaissance dissipated.

CRITICAL OVERVIEW

In the 1920s, when "A Black Man Talks of Reaping" was first published, Bontemps was considered a major poet of the Harlem Renaissance. He was awarded the Alexander Pushkin Poetry Prize by *Opportunity* magazine in 1926 and 1927. After the publication of his novel *God Sends Sunday* in 1931, though, he seldom wrote poetry, concentrating instead on fiction, plays, children's literature, and history. Today, he is mostly remembered for his fiction, in particular for the 1936 novel *Black Thunder*, which has remained his most celebrated work.

One of the few reviewers to directly address the merits of "A Black Man Talks of Reaping" was Arthur P. Davis, whose 1974 book *From the Dark Tower: Afro-American Writers 1900–1960* indicates just a faint sense of protest in Bontemps's words. Davis remarks that this poem has "the closest approach to direct protest" found in any of the poems Bontemps published. Social protest was implied obliquely rather than openly, which Davis states was "the kind of muted protest expected of a controlled poet like Bontemps." Davis also makes a distinction between Bontemps and other writers associated with the Harlem Renaissance:

> The poems of Arna Bontemps lack the clear, unambiguous statement of those of his contemporaries: McKay, Cullen, Hughes. There is a modern obscurity in these verses, and the so-called meaning often eludes the reader. Their craftsmanship, however, is impressive.

After Bontemps's death in 1973, white American writer Jack Conroy, who had collaborated with him during the 1930s, reminisced about reading the poems in Bontemps's collection *Personals*. In *American Libraries*, Conroy reflects:

> I thought as I read such selections as 'Southern Mansion,' 'To a Young Girl Leaving the Hill Country,' and 'A Black Man Talks of Reaping' that Arna had never lost that precious sense of wonder and discovery that flooded him when he first beheld Harlem. There is the elegiac and nostalgic note that pervades much of his later work, both in prose and verse, and makes it so appealing and heart-warming.

CRITICISM

David Kelly

Kelly is a writer and instructor of creative writing and literature. In this essay, he uses "A Black Man Talks of Reaping" to discuss the ways in which Bontemps establishes the injustice of his society and how he indicates that change is inevitable.

It is quite likely that the ultimate inspiration for Arna Bontemps's poem "A Black Man Talks of Reaping" is to be found in the New Testament of the Bible, in the letter of Paul to the Galatians. There, Paul admonishes a people who he sees as drifting away from their religious faith, telling them, "Do not be deceived; God is not mocked, for whatever a man sows, that he will also reap." The image Paul uses, whether originated by him or not, is so potent that the phrase "you reap what you sow" is still a commonly-used expression to this day, long after the United States completed the shift from a agriculture-based economy. When Bontemps's poem was written in the 1920s, the country was in the middle of the shift from an agrarian culture to an industrial society. Since then, the U.S. economy has gone ever further beyond that, to an economy based in information exchange.

As in the letter of Paul to the Galatians, the image of sowing and reaping carries a vague insinuation of danger in the way Bontemps uses it. However, there is a telling difference: Paul seems to be implying a more direct relationship between behaviors and consequences than Bontemps offers. While in "A Black Man Talks of Reaping" Bontemps warns readers that a particular behavior will bring specific results, he also adds an extra step, shrouded in mystery. The way this poem frames the situation, the disenfranchisement of black Americans from social advancement had

> **FOR A WRITER WORKING IN THE 1920'S, WHEN EVEN THE THREAT OF VIOLENCE WAS SOMETHING ANY BLACK AMERICAN KNEW COULD PUT HIM OR HER IN DANGER, IT IS QUITE UNDERSTANDABLE THAT BONTEMPS WOULD NOT SAY OPENLY THAT THERE WAS AN INEVITABLE CLASH OF CULTURES TO COME."**

yielded no observable consequences for white society at the time of Bontemps's writing, but the poem clearly indicates that consequences will be inevitable. Bontemps shows the pressure building for equality, and he also mentions the natural relationship between reaping and sowing, making it clear that black Americans were forbidden participation in the actual reaping of benefits of their work. Readers cannot help drawing the direct conclusion that the natural balance between reaping and sowing, which Paul in his letter to the Galatians attributes to God's will, is being violated in a way that must be corrected by any means, even if eventual confrontation might be the outcome.

The text of the poem subtly provides a persuasive argument against some of the most commonly-used justifications for racial inequality. For example, it states that the problems foisted onto the race of a people who originated in Africa cannot be ignored as a simply regional issue, as northern whites might have been inclined to do. Bontemps begins his poem by having his narrator note that he has sown seeds beside all waters, drawing attention to the universality of the black experience. This might not seem to be the most significant aspect about being black in the United States, but it is weighty enough for him to emphasize it in the poem's first words, to tell his audience that any urge to ignore this problem as some other region's issue is naive and intellectually dishonest. The inclusive "all" makes clear that segregation is not just a "southern" problem or even just an "American" problem, that racial injustice is bound to have global implications.

Once it has established that the situation faced by blacks is not just limited to the American South, the poem addresses two other excuses that were commonly used to justify unequal treatment. The first is the assumption that blacks were responsible for their own predicament because they were

WHAT DO I READ NEXT?

- Critics have noted the similarities of image in this poem with *Cane*, a 1923 novel by Jean Toomer, who was also considered one of the seminal figures of the Harlem Renaissance movement. *Cane* contains a collection of sketches from the segregated American South, as well as scenes set in urban Washington, D.C.

- Mildred Taylor's 1989 novel *Roll of Thunder, Hear My Cry*, published by Bantam Books, is the first in a series of young-adult novels about an African American family, based on her family's history. This volume concerns what it was like to live in a community of black sharecroppers in the 1800s, a situation that set the tone for Bontemps's poem.

- "Harlem (A Dream Deferred)," a poem by Bontemps's lifelong friend, writer Langston Hughes, contains the same theme that this poem implies: that suppression of generation after generation of African Americans is bound to result in explosive consequences. Hughes published the poem in 1951, as the civil rights movement was just starting to organize. The poem is available in *The Collected Poems of Langston Hughes*, published in an annotated edition by Vintage Press in 1995.

- The heroic tone of this poem reflects Bontemps's interest in the native folk wisdom of his people. This is reflected in many of the pieces that he and Hughes collected in *The Book of Negro Folklore*, published in 1958. Among the tall tales, superstitions, and traditional songs collected, there is a chapter titled "The Problem," in which the authors describe scattered examples of the troubles caused by segregation.

- The migration of African Americans within the United States is covered in-depth in *Anyplace but Here*, a book Bontemps wrote with Jack Conroy in 1945 as *They Seek a City* and then published in 1966 under the current title, with revisions to cover the Black Muslim movement and the violent racial turbulence of the mid-1960s. It was reprinted by the University of Missouri Press in 1997.

- Critics have pointed to the similarity between this poem and "From the Dark Tower," a poem by Countee Cullen, another key figure in the Harlem Renaissance, that also uses planting and reaping as its central metaphor. Both poems attempt to capture the suffering of African Americans who have been forced to hold their silence while being treated as inferiors. Cullen's poem is often anthologized and is available in *Caroling Dusk: An Anthology of Verse by Black Poets of the Twenties*, edited by Cullen and reprinted by Citadel in 1998, and also features Bontemps's "A Black Man Talks of Reaping."

- The stories compiled by Tim McKee and photographs of Anne Blackshaw in *No More Strangers Now: Young Voices from a New South Africa* (1998) provide a multicultural perspective of life under apartheid and beyond on twelve South African teenagers.

too lazy to take control of their own destiny. It would be difficult, if not outright impossible, for any reasonable reader of this poem to ignore the constant struggles that Bontemps depicts, of people fighting against a social engine that works to stymie them at every turn. Bontemps captures, in the poem's few lines, the work and care needed to nurture a growing plant from seed to maturity, a struggle played out across the country. Raising crops like this is not something that could be accomplished by people who were not diligent. Rather than argue against the "laziness" excuse, the poem simply sweeps it away with broad, solid evidence of the black workers' diligence.

The poem not only shows the workers' diligence, it also shows their intelligence, dispensing with the other commonly-used argument for having rules separating the races. Bontemps establishes the wit of the poem's narrator and his people by showing solid knowledge of successful farming procedures and skillful poetry. In this poem, black farmers provide smart responses to the troubles that nature throws at them, adapting to wind erosion and predators that want to feed off of their fresh-planted seeds by protecting the seeds with deeper layers of dirt. They plant their seeds in rows to counter the problems of soil erosion. These farmers may not be educated in the traditional sense, having been locked out of formal education by laws and social mores, but Bontemps steers past education as a measure of intelligence, putting the focus on forms of intelligence that are even more important for what they are trying to accomplish.

Intelligence is also established here by the poet's solid, understated skill. This poem is a tour de force for Bontemps, a showpiece for his talent that does not draw attention to its form. Bontemps works within a closed traditional form, squeezing his ideas into quatrains and iambic pentameter, following poetic standards that have been in place for centuries with such grace that readers might just take his technical mastery for granted. The poet's intelligence is present in every line, though, like the intelligence of the farmers who are the poem's subject. It is not talked about—it is simply there. The poem does not address the wisdom of the people it is discussing, instead taking the position that such intelligence must be obvious.

In the end, this poem uses a dual-edged meaning to explain the idea of reaping. When talking about reaping in agricultural terms, Bontemps is fairly direct in stating that reaping was forbidden to those who sowed the seeds. The black farmers presumably held the hope, while planting the seeds and tending the crops, that they might be able to prosper when the time for harvesting comes, but that never was the case. They were allowed to pick off the little that was left and considered unusable: the stalks and roots and gleanings left on the ground, just enough to sustain them and feed their hope. The people who have planted the crops are not allowed to reap what they have sown, which as the letter of Paul to the Galatians states is contrary to the laws of nature.

However, natural law and Biblical law should not be subverted. While Bontemps does not openly state it in "A Black Man Talks of Reaping," he does hint at a danger that a discerning reader can hardly ignore. The last few lines of the poem make it clear

that something is bound to happen, that the bitter fruit given to the coming generation to feed on will only lead to resentment, then resistance. Injustice can only be tolerated for so long before it boils over. For a writer working in the 1920s, when even the threat of violence was something any black American knew could put him or her in danger, it is quite understandable that Bontemps would not say openly that there was an inevitable clash of cultures to come. He could not speak as freely as, say, his friend Langston Hughes put it decades later in his 1951 poem "Harlem (A Dream Deferred)." Though Bontemps was not in a position to explicitly address the anger and frustration building up among black Americans, he was able to show social injustice powerfully enough to make all readers of all races empathetic to the situation forced on the title's black man. The implication is clear: such injustice, if left unaddressed for generation after generation, can only lead to a forced change.

The letter of Paul to the Galatians introduces the reaping/sowing metaphor, but it also addresses the situation that Bontemps gives readers, where sowing and reaping have been separated from one another. "And let us not grow weary in well-doing," Paul writes, "for in due season we shall reap, if we do not lose heart." "A Black Man Talks of Reaping" could have followed Paul's tone of gentleness and reiterated his faith in the future. Bontemps instead used the poem as a warning that something was bound to change, soon, once the patience of a generation raised with nothing of its own was exhausted. This poem is not a call to action; it is not telling its readers that the time for waiting is done, but only that there is inevitably going to be a time when waiting is no longer an option.

Source: David Kelly, Critical Essay on "A Black Man Talks of Reaping," in *Poetry for Students*, Gale, Cengage Learning, 2010.

SOURCES

Bloom, Harold, "Arna Bontemps," in *Black American Prose Writers of the Harlem Renaissance*, Chelsea House, 1994, pp. 1–2.

Conroy, Jack, "Memories of Arna Bontemps: Friend and Collaborator," in *American Libraries*, Vol. 5, No. 11, December, 1974, pp. 605–606, reprinted in *Black American Prose Writers of the Harlem Renaissance*, edited by Harold Bloom, Chelsea House, 1994, p. 8.

Davis, Arthur P., "First Fruits: Arna Bontemps," in *From the Dark Tower: Afro-American Writers 1900–1960*, Howard University Press, 1974, pp. 83–89.

"Heroic Poetry," in *Encyclopedia Britannica Online*, 2009, http://www.britannica.com/EBchecked/topic/263592/heroic-poetry (accessed May 5, 2009).

The Holy Bible, rev. standard ed., Thomas Nelson and Sons, 1952.

Parini, Jay, ed., *The Columbia Anthology of American Poetry*, Columbia University Press, 1995, p. 482.

FURTHER READING

Bontemps, Arna, "The Awakening: A Memoir," in *The Harlem Renaissance Remembered*, Dodd, Mead, 1972, pp. 1–26.
   This essay, included with Bontemps's essays about writers that he knew during that period, gives his impression of what it was like to be a participant in that literary movement during such a fertile intellectual time.

Bontemps, Arna, and Langston Hughes, *Arna Bontemps—Langston Hughes Letters, 1925–1967*, Charles H. Nichols, ed., Paragon House, 1990.
   Readers can witness the middle decades of the twentieth century, which were crucial years for the development of black social progress in America, reflected in the correspondences between two lifelong friends, both key figures in the Harlem Renaissance who held similar views of the world.

Price, Clement Alexander, "Race, Blackness, and Modernism During the Harlem Renaissance," in the *Encyclopedia of the Harlem Renaissance*, Facts On File, 2003, pp. xi–xiv.
   Price offers a clear synopsis of the period, analyzing the significance of notable events during the Harlem Renaissance.

Sitkoff, Harvard, *The Struggle for Black Equality, 1954–1992*, rev. ed., Hill and Wang, 1993.
   This book offers a comprehensive look at the reality of the situation that Bontemps's poem predicted in the 1920s, showing how the intolerable situation of segregation was eventually dismantled by the dedication of those involved in the social movement for equal rights.

Everything Is Plundered

ANNA AKHMATOVA

1922

"Everything Is Plundered," published in the collection *Anno Domini MCMXXI* (1922), is one of Russian poet Anna Akhmatova's most studied works. Akhmatova wrote the poem in 1921, during a time of tremendous social upheaval caused by the Russian Revolution of 1917 and the slightly later Russian Civil War.

The poem is short, only three stanzas long, but it is a powerful statement of hope in a time of great destruction and death. Akhmatova juxtaposes bleak images of despair with beautiful images of the natural world, suggesting that a mysterious "something" is about to happen, something that all people have wanted for many years. The poem achieves additional poignancy when the reader discovers that it was written just two months before Akhmatova's first husband was arrested and then shot as a counterrevolutionary. This event deeply marked Akhmatova's work and life.

Since Akhmatova's death in 1966, her stature as a poet has grown significantly. Poets such as Stanley Kunitz, Jane Kenyon, and Marilyn Hacker have translated her work and written tributes to Akhmatova. "Everything Is Plundered" appears as "Everything Has Been Plundered" in *The Complete Poems of Anna Akhmatova* (1997), translated by Judith Hemschemeyer and edited with an introduction by Roberta Reeder.

Anna Akhmatova (© *RIA Novosti / Alamy*)

AUTHOR BIOGRAPHY

Akhmatova was born Anna Andreyevna Gorenko on June 23, 1889, near Odessa, Russia. The third of five children, Akhmatova was the daughter of Andrey Gorenko, a naval engineer, and Inna Erazmovna Stogova, both aristocrats. Before Akhmatova reached her first birthday, the family moved to Tsarskoe Selo, a wealthy suburb of St. Petersburg, Russia. Amanda Haight reports in her book *Anna Akhmatova: A Poetic Pilgrimage* that Akhmatova attended school in Tsarskoe Selo briefly but became very ill when she was around ten years old and was not expected to live. After she recovered from her illness, she began to write poetry.

In 1905, several events had serious implications for young Akhmatova and her family. First, the Russian naval fleet was entirely destroyed by the Japanese. Second, according to Elaine Feinstein in *Anna of All the Russias*, workers across the country began uprisings and were met with great cruelty from the Tsar's forces. Also in 1905, her father retired from his job, and her sister Inna had to be hospitalized for tuberculosis. (In 1906, Inna became Akhmatova's second sister to die from the disease.) Finally, her parents separated in 1905, and Anna moved with her mother to Kiev, Ukraine, shortly thereafter. Akhmatova graduated from high school in Kiev in 1907 and then began to study law at the Kiev College for Women, according to Roberta Reeder in her essay, "Mirrors and Masks: The Life and Poetic Works of Anna Akhmatova."

Around this same time, Akhmatova's father told her not to shame the name of Gorenko with her poetry. From this point on, Akhmatova used the pseudonym Anna Akhmatova. The name was derived from that of her great-grandmother of Tatar (Turkic people mainly in the Tatar Republic of Russia, Siberia, and central Asia) heritage. In 1910, despite her earlier refusals of his advances, Akhmatova married the poet Nikolay Gumilyov. After their honeymoon in Paris, France, Akhmatova and Gumilyov returned to St. Petersburg, and Gumilyov soon left for a long trip to Abyssinia (now known as Ethiopia). While he was gone, Akhmatova began writing poetry in earnest, publishing in a number of journals. She also became active in the poetic scene in St. Petersburg, and she developed a friendship with the leader of the Russian Symbolist movement (late nineteenth and early twentieth century poetry and philosophy based on irrationality and mysticism), Alexander Blok, one of the most influential writers of the period. Gumilyov returned in 1911; he, along with Akhmatova and several other poets, founded the Acmeist Movement (poetry that reflected ideas about the world and culture) as a rejection of Symbolism.

In 1912, Akhmatova published her first volume of poetry, *Evening*. The book met with great popularity and critical acclaim. Later that year, Akhmatova gave birth to her son, Lev. However, as her marriage disintegrated, Lev was taken from her to be raised by his paternal grandmother, according to Reeder. *Rosary*, Akhmatova's second volume of poetry, was published in 1914, the same year Russia entered World War I after being attacked by Germany. Gumilyov enlisted in the army; Akhmatova endured the hardships of war on the home front. In 1917, Akhmatova published *White Flock*, a volume which Reeder states includes her most important war poetry. In the same year, the Russian tsar was deposed, and the provisional government was overthrown by the Bolsheviks in the Russian Revolution. It was a time of great social and political upheaval, particularly since the Revolution quickly devolved into the Russian Civil War, lasting until the end of 1921. The Soviet Union was established in 1922.

Akhmatova asked Gumilyov for a divorce in 1918, and she quickly married Vladimir Shileiko. This marriage proved disastrous, and in 1920, Akhmatova left Shileiko. While her personal life was troubled and the country was still enduring civil war, it was nonetheless a productive time for Akhmatova. Maria Rubins states in the *Dictionary of Literary Biography*, that for a brief period after the Revolution, writers had creative freedom. Akhmatova published two volumes very close together, *Plantain* (1921) and *Anno Domini MCMXXI* (1922), which includes the poem "Everything Is Plundered."

Her life, however, took a radical turn in August 1921. Reeder states that just two months after the composition of "Everything Is Plundered," Akhmatova's friend Blok died, and the ideals he created shattered. At Blok's funeral, Akhmatova learned that Gumilyov had been arrested as a counterrevolutionary. On September 1, 1921, she read in a newspaper that he had been executed by a firing squad. As a result of her association with Gumilyov and the growing tendency for her poetry to reflect lived experience contrary to the Communist ideal, Akhmatova's work was suppressed; her next book was not published until 1940. Despite the hardships she endured, Akhmatova did not leave the Soviet Union. After her divorce from Shileiko, she established a long-term relationship with art historian Nikolay Punin. During this time, she composed her long poem "Requiem" in secrecy. Rubins notes that Akhmatova's friends memorized the poem, line by line, so that she could burn the paper on which she wrote it. Discovery of the poem could have led to her imprisonment and execution. In the following years, she wrote and revised another masterpiece, *Poem without a Hero*.

Akhmatova's son, Lev, was imprisoned because of his parentage on and off between 1935 and 1956. In spite of extreme oppression, Akhmatova survived Joseph Stalin's rule, living to see her son released from prison in 1956 and the publication of several volumes of poetry in the 1950s and 1960s. She was allowed to leave the Soviet Union in 1964 to receive the Etna-Taormina Prize in Poetry in Italy, and again in 1965 to accept an honorary

doctorate from Oxford University. Akhmatova died on March 5, 1966, in Domodedovo, Russia. Although she was renowned throughout the world for her work, she did not live to receive acclaim in her native land. This did not occur until the 1980s. By the 2000s, Akhmatova was considered to be one of the greatest poets to have ever lived. As Reeder concludes, Akhmatova "made an indelible impression on many who knew her and on modern poetry itself."

POEM TEXT

Everything has been plundered, betrayed, sold out,
The wing of black death has flashed,
Everything has been devoured by starving anguish,
Why, then, is it so bright?

The fantastic woods near the town   5
Wafts the scent of cherry blossoms by day,
At night new constellations shine
In the transparent depths of the skies of July

And how near the miraculous draws
To the dirty, tumbledown huts ...   10
No one, no one knows what it is,
But for centuries we have longed for it.

POEM SUMMARY

Lines 1–4

The poem "Everything Is Plundered" was written in June 1921 and was dedicated to Akhmatova's friend, Natalya Rykova. The poem was originally written in Russian, and since its composition it has been translated into many languages, including English, most notably by the poet Stanley Kunitz and more recently by Judith Hemschemeyer. Examining the English translations, therefore, necessarily requires noting the decisions and devices used by the translators as well as those by Akhmatova herself. For the purposes of summarizing the poem here, Hemschemeyer's translation serves as the primary source material.

The poem is short, a mere twelve lines, divided into three quatrains, or stanzas of four lines each. Hemschemeyer's translation does not use a regular rhyme scheme, although in Russian, Akhmatova's lines rhyme *abab cdcd efef*. Hemschemeyer does, however, make use of alliteration (the repetition of initial consonants), assonance (the repetition of similar vowel sounds), and consonance (the repetition of similar consonant sounds) throughout her

MEDIA ADAPTATIONS

- *Inner Exile: The Poetry of Anna Akhmatova* is a 1971 documentary film about Akhmatova's poetry and her life in Stalin's Russia. The film is narrated by critic Faubion Bowers, and professors Samuel Driver and Irene Kirk provide commentary on Akhmatova's work. Written by Stephan Chodorov and produced by Camera Three Productions, the film was rereleased on DVD in 2007 by Creative Arts Television.

- *The File of Anna Akhmatova* is a black-and-white Russian DVD with English subtitles tracing Akhmatova's life. Originally released in 1989, Facets Studio rereleased the film on DVD in 2000.

- *Fear and the Muse* is a 2000 documentary film about Akhmatova's life, narrated by Christopher Reeve, directed by Jill Janows, and produced by the New York Center for Visual History. The documentary was released on videotape by Winstars.

- *A Film About Anna Akhmatova* is a 2008 film that explores Akhmatova's poetry and her experiences during the Russian Revolution and the Russian Civil War. In the film, poet Anatoly Naiman (Akhmatova's close friend) discusses Akhmatova's talent and life. Produced by Das Films, the film was directed by Helga Landauer and distributed by TurnstyleTV.

translation of the poem. The translation of this poem does not use a regular metrical scheme, either, although critics such as John Simon in his 2001 book *Dreamers of Dreams: Essays on Poets and Poetry* and Marjorie Perloff in her article "Anna Akhmatova in Translation," published in *PN Review* in 2006, speak of the importance of sound and rhythm in Akhmatova's poetry when read in Russian.

In the first line, the poet tells the reader that everything is ruined. Moreover, this ruin seems to be the result of human activity rather than natural disaster. The words chosen by various translators all carry the essence of desecration and betrayal. Indeed, the reader viewing this first line will form a picture of a vandalized, looted, and damaged scene. In the second line, Akhmatova introduces death into the picture. She paints death as a dark, flying creature that appears quickly and then is gone. In the third line, Akhmatova uses words of extreme pain and hunger. Hemschemeyer repeats the first three words of the first line as the first three words of the third line. The overall effect is to frame the second line concerning death with two lines of pain, hunger, sorrow, and plunder. The fourth line, then, comes as a surprise. Akhmatova poses a question: how is it that, in spite of the pain, darkness, despoliation, and death of the opening three lines, there is still light everywhere? Hemschemeyer also employs a sound device in this stanza. She ends lines 1, 2, and 4 with a stressed syllable that ends in the sound (but not the letter) "t," an example of consonance.

Lines 5–8

In the second stanza, Akhmatova turns to images from the natural world and away from the images of the human world of the first stanza. In the first line, she refers to a nearby forest that seems nearly supernatural in its beauty, particularly when compared to the scenes of devastation in the city from where the poet writes. In the second line, she uses an olfactory image, a description that engages the sense of smell. She writes that fruit trees in the forest are blooming, and their aroma reaches the city during the day. The third line contrasts the night with the day, but Akhmatova again employs an image of great beauty. She writes that the stars overhead form new shapes, and their light shines in the darkness. The final line of the stanza continues the description of the nighttime summer sky. Taken together, the lines of this stanza offer a contrast between the beauty of the day and the beauty of the night. In addition, this stanza stands in sharp contrast to the opening three lines of the poem. Thus, in spite of the devastation described early in the poem, the natural world is still able to produce beauty. In this stanza, the translation again provides consonance at the ends of lines 5 and 7. In addition, the words ending lines 6 and 8 both end in the letter "y," providing an "eye rhyme," that is, two words that look like they should rhyme when read, although they do not rhyme exactly when spoken.

Lines 9–12

In lines 9 and 10, Akhmatova once again invokes the supernatural. She juxtaposes the fantastical and the amazing in line 9 with the filthy devastation of broken-down houses in line 10. Just as the first stanza attempts to contrast darkness with light and the second stanza contrasts day and night, the third stanza contrasts miracles with reality. She does not try to name what that miracle is. In line 11, she tells the reader that nobody knows what causes this wonder and awe. Line 12, the concluding line of the poem, describes that although nobody knows what the miracle is, it is something that everyone has hoped for across many, many years. Hemschemeyer repeats the first two words of line 11 to emphasize both sound and sense; the echo of the sound reinforces the meaning of the words. In addition, the first word after the repetition is a homophone for the first and third words of the line. (A homophone is a word that sounds like another word, but is spelled differently and has a different meaning.) In the final line of the poem, the poet includes herself with the other inhabitants of the town. It is in this line that the first personal pronoun ("we") of the poem is used, and it has the effect of connecting the poet with those who have come before and those who will come in the future. All of these people have waited and ached for the amazing change that they sense is coming.

THEMES

Revolution

Akhmatova wrote "Everything Is Plundered" in 1921, publishing it in 1922, during a chaotic and tumultuous period in Russian history. After centuries of despotic, tyrannical rule by the Russian royal family, the populace rose up against the ruling classes in general and the Romanov dynasty in particular in 1917. However, the revolutionaries soon became embroiled in disputes amongst themselves, leading to civil war, a war that had just ended when Akhmatova wrote her poem. Thematically, then, Akhmatova is addressing "revolution" in several senses. In the first place, she dwells on the cost in human lives and possessions that the war has wrought. In this sense, she considers revolution as a dramatic upheaval of culture and values, as well as property. Moreover, not only is everything destroyed, there is also a sense of betrayal and greed created through her choice of words. By depicting the revolution in this way, she is clearly addressing the deliberate destruction of Russian land, people, and culture by the opposing forces. This destruction can be seen as a sort of betrayal of the very people the revolutionaries claim they represent.

The word revolution, however, has an additional meaning. The word is the noun form of the verb "to revolve," or go around in a circle. A revolution is not only an uprising against a form of government, it is also a circular movement, such as the path of the earth around the sun each year, or the turning of a wheel on a cart. In this sense, the word revolution suggests that all human life and history is circular. What has been destroyed will be recovered, and what has been lost will be found. It also suggests that such upheavals and recoveries take place repeatedly in human history. Such a view is not consistent with either Marxist (socialism based on the theories and principles of Karl Marx) or Christian interpretations of history, sharing more in common with eastern religions such as Hinduism or Buddhism. In "Everything Is Plundered," the wheel of revolution is clearly turning. Although there are scenes of great destruction and human evil in the poem, there are also images of renewal, rebirth, and recovery.

Hope

In "Everything Is Plundered," Akhmatova sets up two starkly contrasting ideas. On the one hand, she focuses on the hunger, death, and destruction caused by an upheaval in the social structure. Everywhere she looks, she sees burned buildings, people who are starving, and general desolation. At the same time, however, she notes the natural world in her descriptions of the forest and the cherry blossoms. The natural images infuse this poem about death and destruction with life and hope. Just as the forest recovers from winter, Akhmatova seems to be saying, Russia will recover from the civil war too.

In addition, there is an added sense that although the war has been terrible, the end results are something for which the people have longed for generations. It is a reminder of the dreadful conditions under which most people lived in Russia under the Romanovs. The royal family and the ruling class enjoyed extreme luxury and wealth at the expense of the poor, who were saddled with heavy taxation and grueling work. Thus, while there is darkness over the land caused by the warring factions, Akhmatova also sees light and hope for the future.

It is important to note that the hope Akhmatova seems to be addressing is not a religious hope.

TOPICS FOR FURTHER STUDY

- Akhmatova's poems have been translated by many different people, including Stanley Kunitz, Jane Kenyon, Walter Arndt, Judith Hemschemeyer, and D. M. Thomas. Find as many different translations of "Everything Is Plundered" as you can, using library and online resources. Write an essay in which you compare and contrast the choices made by the different translators, including words, rhymes, meter, and sounds. Using the information you have gathered, evaluate which translation seems the most accurate and defend your choice in an essay.

- With a small group of students, create a multimedia presentation of Akhmatova's life. To help all team members share the responsibility for the work, use a project management tool such as *www.teamness.com* to help you organize the project and make individual assignments. Focus on different aspects of Akhmatova's background, events that took place during her life, and how these aspects affected her poetry. Include at least three types of media, such as pictures, video clips, sound recordings, music, art, or historical documents, in your presentation. After presenting the project to your class, evaluate your successes and challenges working as a team in a brief report.

- Many contemporary poets have been fascinated and influenced by Akhmatova's work. Evidence of this is in the large number of poems dedicated to her or written about her. For example, Marilyn Hacker's poem "For Anna Akhmatova" was published in *Prairie Schooner* (2005). Collect as many such poems as you can find by authors from different countries or cultures by using computer databases located in your library and on the Internet. Afterwards, exercise your own creativity and write a poem to or about Akhmatova. Include your poem in a presentation with the other poems. Explain to your class how Akhmatova is represented in poems written about her (including your own).

- Take a series of photographs that evoke the same senses and images you find in "Everything Is Plundered." Prepare an exhibition of your photographs with titles for each photo and notes about their relevance to Akhmatova's poem. Select appropriate music (approved by your teacher or school administration) to play while others enjoy reading and viewing your work.

- With a group of your classmates, watch the documentary film *Fear and the Muse: The Story of Anna Akhmatova* (1997), narrated by Christopher Reeve, Claire Bloom, and poet Joseph Brodsky (one of Akhmatova's young friends). Using this information as well as additional research, write a one-act play about Akhmatova's life in 1921, the year that she wrote "Everything Is Plundered." Present the play to the rest of your class.

- Read *The Kitchen Boy: A Novel of the Last Tzar* (2004) by Robert Alexander, or one of his other young-adult novels set in the final days in the rule of Russian Tsar Nicholas II at the onset of the Russian Revolution. In addition, consult historical texts and documents to learn more about the revolution. Afterwards, write a short story or a poem cycle in which a young person finds him or herself living at a time of great civil unrest.

That is, she does not seem to be saying that people will be rewarded in heaven for their trials and tribulations on earth. Rather, her use of images of the natural world suggests that eventually people will find their dreams and hopes realized in this world, not the next. "Everything Is Plundered," then, is a poem more about hope and recovery than it is about death and destruction.

Constellations *(© Michael Siebert | zefa | Corbis)*

STYLE

Acmeist Poetry

In 1912, a small group of poets led by Nicolai Gumilyov reacted to what they saw as vagueness and affectation in the Russian Symbolist movement and formed a school of poetry called Acmeism. They insisted that poets should use the language exactly and precisely. Further, they wanted poetry that used clear and concrete imagery. This group, which included Akhmatova and Osip Mandelstam, was akin to the Anglo American Imagist movement led by poet Ezra Pound at about the same time in history, according to several scholars, including Elaine Rusinko in her 1982 article "Acmeism, Post-symbolism, and Henri Bergson," published in the *Slavic Review*. The Acmeists were noted for their economy of language, arguing that a clear and concise image could carry the weight of the poem, rather than obscure or elevated language. While the group was short-lived, due to the premature deaths of both Gumilyov and Mandelstam, its influence (largely through Akhmatova's work) was large. This is all the more remarkable as the Soviet government condemned the movement and its participants.

"Everything Is Plundered" is a fine example of the tenets of Acmeism. Akhmatova uses very few words in this poem, but she makes every word important. She relies on clear, concrete images to carry the weight of her poem. For example, she uses the image of a black bird or wing to evoke death. In addition, she uses a variety of different sensory images to deliver the poem's theme. In one instance

she uses olfactory imagery by referencing the scent of cherry blossoms. She also uses tactile imagery when she refers to the pain of starvation. Akhmatova also relies heavily on visual imagery, including stars and the night sky, to emphasize her thematic concern with hope.

Although it is not always completely clear in English translation, "Everything Is Plundered" can also be considered an Acmeist poem in its attention to form. In the Russian language, the poem has a rhyme scheme and rhythmic quality that is both precise and beautiful.

Thus, by utilizing the Acmeist project and standards, Akhmatova creates a poem that is at once very brief, highly charged, intense, and filled with images. As a result, "Everything Is Plundered" stands as a small masterpiece, offering hope in a war-torn world.

Lyric Poetry

A lyric poem is a brief, subjective poem that generally expresses emotional content seen from the narrator's point of view. In the distant past, lyric poetry was sung; although this is not the typical presentation of a lyric poem today, lyric poems continue to include a musical quality. In the case of "Everything Is Plundered," this is more evident in the original Russian verse with its sonorous sequences. On the other hand, the intensity of Akhmatova's emotional content in the poem certainly qualifies it as a lyric, even in English translation.

Lyric poetry is often contrasted with narrative poetry. The distinction is that lyric poetry reveals the subjective thoughts and feelings of the poet, rather than telling a story chronologically. While Akhmatova is clearly speaking about a historical situation in "Everything Is Plundered," she is not attempting to tell a story. Rather, she is sharing her contrasting feelings of despair and hope with the reader through the use of carefully selected images.

HISTORICAL CONTEXT

The Russian Revolution

For centuries, Russia was ruled by a leader called the Tsar and his family. By the beginning of the twentieth century, Tsar Nicholas II held tremendous power. Married to a granddaughter of the British Queen Victoria, Nicholas believed absolutely in his rights as sovereign. In a biography of Nicholas for the *St. Petersburg Times Online*

COMPARE
&
CONTRAST

- **1920s:** The Russian Civil War, which follows the Russian Revolution (an uprising that led to the fall of Tsar Nicholas and established Communism in Russia), continues until 1926, when Joseph Stalin becomes the absolute dictator of the Soviet Union, a post he will hold until 1958.

  Today: The Soviet Union no longer exists as a unified state, and the Communist Party, while still a viable political force in the Russian Federation, does not control Russia.

- **1920s:** Joseph Stalin emerges as the dictator of the Soviet Union after a long and violent struggle within the Central Committee of the Communist Party. By 1927, Stalin has solidified his control as the only leader of the U.S.S.R. by using the secret police to control the people.

  Today: Russia is a federated state under the leadership of a president and prime minister. The *Constitution of the Russian Federation* guarantees "the equality of rights and free-

doms of man and citizen.... All forms of limitation of human rights on social, racial, national, linguistic or religious grounds shall be banned." The Russian Federation also has issued a moratorium on the death penalty.

- **1920s:** Under Communist rule, the only art form acceptable to the state is "socialist realism," a form of art that is essentially propaganda and celebratory of the socialist state.

  Today: Artists and writers in Russia have greater freedom to express themselves and create imaginative works.

- **1920s:** According to all of her biographers, Akhmatova is censured by the Soviet government and is not permitted to publish her work.

  Today: Akhmatova is revered as one of the most important figures in Russian literature. In 2007, the government erects a statue in her memory in St. Petersburg, Russia.

(1999), Alexei K. Levykin writes that "despite growing pressure for revolution, he did not give way on a single issue, even when common sense and circumstances demanded it." Further, he quickly rescinded rights that had been granted to the people during a 1905 uprising.

Conditions in Russia during the years before World War I were not good; the country's treasury, however, was strained to the breaking point by Russia's entry into the war. Historian Philip E. Mosley states in his 2006 *History Channel* Web site article, "The Russian Revolution," that although Russia had plenty of men to serve in the army, "Russian industry... lacked the capacity to arm, equip, and supply the some 15 million men who were put in the field." As a result, Russia suffered extraordinarily high casualties in the field and severe food shortages at home. Also,

Tsar Nicholas ignored warnings from the Duma (an advisory legislative branch of the government) that societal conditions were ripe for a revolution.

On March 8, 1917, bread riots and worker strikes began in St. Petersburg. (The dates are according to the Gregorian calendar, adopted by the Soviet government in 1918.) Violence erupted, and by March 12, 1917, the military units garrisoned in St. Petersburg joined the revolutionaries. Political power was assumed by the Petrograd Soviet and a provisional committee of the Duma. On March 13, 1917, the Petrograd Soviet arrested Nicholas, his family, and his ministers. They were later executed, and the revolution quickly spread across Russia. However, the Soviet and provisional governments were quickly at odds as to whether Russia should continue its involvement in the war against Germany. In addition, there was a struggle for power going on within the Soviet government between two groups, the Bolsheviks and the Mensheviks.

The Russian Civil War and the Emergence of Joseph Stalin

Although the Russian Revolution was essentially completed by November 1917 with the deposition of the Tsar, the discord between the "red" faction (the Bolsheviks) and the "white" faction (the Mensheviks) continued. The Bolsheviks extricated Russia from World War I, but at great cost. Under the leadership of Vladimir Lenin, the Bolsheviks ultimately established control over the country by the end of 1920. Briefly, there was a great flowering of culture and art, following the tremendous social upheaval wrought by the Russian Revolution. Tellingly, it was during this period that Akhmatova achieved her fame as a poet in Russia.

The moment was short-lived. Even as early as 1921, the Bolsheviks were imposing aesthetic standards on artists. In addition, they arrested and executed those they considered enemies. In one such sweep, Akhmatova's first husband and the founder of the Acmeist Movement, Nicolai Gumilyov, was executed by a firing squad.

With Lenin's death in 1924, another power struggle emerged in what had become the ruling Communist Party. Ultimately, Joseph Stalin emerged the victor, establishing himself as the dictator of the country. A contributor to the *Geographia Web site* reports that "Stalin purged all opposition to himself within the party as well as all opposition to party policy in the country," including artistic opposition. Akhmatova's work came under negative scrutiny, and she was not permitted to publish any poetry between 1925 and 1940, when the ban was lifted briefly, according to Roberta Reeder in her article, "Mirrors and Masks: The Life and Poetic Works of Ann Akhmatova," published in *The Complete Poems of Anna Akhmatova: Expanded Edition.*

The hardships of World War I, the Russian Revolution, and the Russian Civil War form the backdrop to Akhmatova's collection *Anno Domini MCMXXI*, which includes "Everything Is Plundered." Akhmatova's biographers and critics state that her choice to remain in Russia rather than emigrating, as so many other artists did, came to be the single most important influence on her later work.

Cherry blossoms (Image copyright Jeremy Reynolds, 2009. Used under license from Shutterstock.com)

CRITICAL OVERVIEW

Akhmatova achieved fame as a poet at a very young age, and Russians of the period both lauded and emulated her work. Nonetheless, after the Russian Revolution, Akhmatova's work was banished by the government, with *Anno Domini MCMXXI* as the last book she was permitted to publish until the 1940s. In her book-length study of Akhmatova's later poetry, *In a Shattered Mirror: The Later Poetry of Anna Akhmatova*, Susan Amert notes that although Akhmatova was considered a "major new literary talent" after the publication of her first two books, the critical reception of her work published after the Russian Revolution "was mixed, ranging from admiring scholarly monographs to excoriating ideological attacks." Much of the negative criticism of Akhmatova, in other words, was the result of the political situation in Russia, where the new government did not approve of poems that were in opposition to its political agenda.

In recent years, however, Akhmatova's reputation has grown to such an extent that she is now considered one of the most important poets of her age, perhaps one of the best poets in history. For example, in an article for the *Antioch Review*, John Taylor summarizes the great critical respect given to Akhmatova, calling her both "legendary" and "one of the seminal poets of the twentieth century." Thus, Akhmatova is important not only for her own work but also for her influence on several generations of younger writers.

Critic and biographer Amanda Haight, in her book *Anna Akhmatova: A Poetic Pilgrimage,* comments that *Anno Domini MCMXXI* is not "just a haphazard collection of single lyrics, but a carefully compiled selection in which the order, the divisions, and the epigraphs were as important as the poems themselves." Thus, the collection that includes "Everything Is Plundered" continues to be considered one of Akhmatova's finest works. Mentioning "Everything Is Plundered" specifically, critic Constantin V. Ponomareff, writing in his book *One Less Hope: Essays on Twentieth-Century Russian Poets*, argues that Akhmatova demonstrates "movement away from her romantic self towards a more realistic awareness of life" in *Anno Domini MCMXXI*.

Contemporary critics find much to praise in Akhmatova's early poetry. For example, in his article "The Modified Modernism of Anna Akhmatova" (published in *Soundings: On Shakespeare, Modern Poetry, Plato, and Other Subjects*, 1991), Albert Spaulding Cook notes Akhmatova's "restrained simplicity" and "steady and composed understatement" in her early poems, comparing Akhmatova to the Russian writer Alexander Pushkin. In a review of *The Complete Poems of Anna Akhmatova*, critic Richard Eder called Akhmatova "the greatest woman poet in the Western World since Sappho."

The act of translating Akhmatova for English-speaking audiences troubled several critics. John Simon, in his book *Dreamers of Dreams: Essays on Poets and Poetry*, argues that Akhmatova's poetry is "virtually . . . untranslatable into English," using "Everything Is Plundered" as his prime example. On the other hand, noted poet and literary critic Stanley Kunitz was responsible for translating many of Akhmatova's poems into English. Discussing Akhmatova's work in his essay "On Translating Akhmatova" (published in *A Kind of Order, A Kind of Folly*, 1975), Kunitz remarks that Akhmatova's "poems exist in the purity and exactness of their diction, the authority of their tone, the subtlety of the rhythmic modulations, [and] the integrity of their form."

It is likely that the intense critical scrutiny directed at Akhmatova's poetry will continue, especially since new translations of her work continue to appear. In addition, many poets in the early years of the twenty-first century have registered their admiration for Akhmatova by writing tributes to her in their own poetry.

CRITICISM

Diane Andrews Henningfeld

Henningfeld is a professor emerita of literature and composition. In the following essay, she discusses the various English translations of Akhmatova's poetry, focusing on "Everything Is Plundered."

Poetry is a very special kind of language. In a few short lines and with very few words, a fine poet can paint a lasting word-picture, tell a story, or evoke an intense emotional response in the reader. The poet uses word choice, including connotative and denotative meanings, to insert additional meaning into the poem. The poet also depends on figurative language, such as metaphor (a figure of speech that expresses an idea through the image of another object) or simile (comparison, usually using "like" or "as," of two essentially dissimilar things), to help him or her make striking comparisons. The poet uses the sounds and rhythm of the words and rhyme to add dimension and tone to the poem. Thus, anyone who believes that poems just emerge directly from the poet's head to the paper does not truly understand the craft of poetry, one of the most difficult of all writing tasks.

Akhmatova, the great Russian poet of the early twentieth century, is an example in point. Along with the other members of the Acmeist Movement, Akhmatova believed that first and foremost, the poet is a craftsperson. It is clear when reading a poem like "Everything Is Plundered" that Akhmatova concentrated on exactly the right words, sounds, images, and metaphors in constructing her poem. Further, it is also clear in "Everything Is Plundered" that Akhmatova was inspired by the stark contrast between the ruined and plundered land, desecrated by her fellow citizens in their attempt to wrest control of Russia, and the bright luminescence of hope, symbolized by the cherry blossoms in the forest and the constellations in the dark night sky. Her poem attempts to bring readers into her world, to help them understand that even in the most difficult circumstances there exists an opportunity to start over.

Nevertheless, readers of Akhmatova must confront a difficult fact. The poet wrote only in Russian, and thus, another participant must enter into the relationship between the reader and the poet: the translator. Now, it is easy to think that translation of Akhmatova's poem is little more than substituting one word in English for its Russian equivalent. However, anyone who has studied a foreign language knows that each word

WHAT DO I READ NEXT?

- *The Complete Poems of Anna Akhmatova* (2000), translated by Judith Hemschemeyer, includes all of Akhmatova's poems. Also included in the book are biographical notes by Roberta Reeder and a memoir by the writer Isaiah Berlin.

- Stephen Dunn's *Walking Light* (2001) is a collection of essays designed to help students understand the role of poetry and poets within a culture. Dunn uses Akhmatova's "Everything Is Plundered" as an example when discussing the importance of historical context while reading a poem.

- George Orwell's *Animal Farm*, first published in 1945 and still widely available, is an allegory depicting the rise of Stalin to power in the Soviet Union, using farm animals as the characters.

- *Anna of All the Russias* (2005), by Elaine Feinstein, is an excellent biography of the Russian poet.

- Ying Chang Compestine's young-adult novel *Revolution Is Not a Dinner Party* (2007) is the story of a girl who experiences the horrors of the Chinese Cultural Revolution. The main character, the daughter of two surgeons, finds her life disrupted when members of the Communist Party move into the family home, and her father is arrested and jailed.

- Joseph Brodsky's *Collected Poems in English* (2002) offers a wide selection of Akhmatova's work. Brodsky was a famous Russian poet who was deeply influenced by his friendship with Akhmatova when she was elderly and he was a young poet. Brodsky later won the Nobel Prize and served as the U.S. poet laureate after being exiled from the Soviet Union.

- Marcus Sedgewick's young-adult novel *Blood Red, Snow White* (2008) is set at the time of the Russian Revolution. Based on a true story, the book traces the fall of the Romanov dynasty and the rise of Vladimir Lenin and Leon Trotsky, leaders of the Bolsheviks.

- *The Pillar of Fire* (1999, translated by Richard McKane) is a collection of poetry by Nicolai Gumilyov, the founder of the Acmeist Movement and Akhmatova's first husband.

- Robert Alexander's novel *The Kitchen Boy: A Novel of the Last Tzar* (2004) tells the story of a young kitchen boy working for the Romanov family, the last royal family of Russia, when they are captured by the Bolsheviks during the Russian Revolution.

- Stanley Kunitz's translation of Akhmatova's poems, *Poems of Akhmatova* (1973), remains one of the standard editions of the poet's work. In addition to a biographical sketch by Max Hayward, the volume features the original Russian verses alongside Kunitz's translations.

in a language has its own nuances that are only apparent in the native tongue. Therefore, translation is never transparent; it is never a mere restatement of the poet's words into another language. Rather, it is the careful working through of the poet's words, thoughts, poetic devices, and spirit that renders translation such a difficult task.

Poet Stanley Kunitz, one of Akhmatova's first translators, perhaps states it best in "On Translating Akhmatova" in his 1975 book *A Kind of Order, a Kind of Folly*: "The poet as translator lives with a paradox. His work must not read like a translation; conversely, it is not an exercise of the free imagination." Here, Kunitz identifies one of the key questions in translation: should the translator try to keep the translation of the poem as close to the literal meaning of the original as possible, or should the translator try to make a beautiful poem in the

> AKHMATOVA REMINDS THE READER THAT
> NO MATTER HOW HORRENDOUS THE LOSS, HOW
> DAMAGED THE LANDSCAPE, HOPE STILL FLUTTERS
> ON THE WIND LIKE THE SCENT OF CHERRY
> BLOSSOMS."

spirit of the original? Kunitz continues, "One voice enjoins him: 'Respect the text!' The other simultaneously pleads with him: 'Make it new!'" The task is particularly difficult with a poet such as Akhmatova who did not write long narrative verse, but rather very short, intense, and economical poems. She used not only the words to convey her theme and meaning but also the sound and rhythms of her native Russian.

Marjorie Perloff writes in her 2005 article "Anna Akhmatova in Translation," published in the *PN Review*, "Akhmatova's poems are almost always written in short rhyming stanzas, in which *melopoeia*, to use [poet Ezra] Pound's term for verse music, trumps not only *logopoeia* ('the dance of the intellect among words'), but also *phanopoeia* (the 'casting of images upon the visual imagination')." Although Perloff's description might seem difficult at first, considering it one section at a time makes it easier to understand. She argues that the music of Akhmatova's poems in Russian is the most important element, even more important than understanding the word choice or the construction of vivid images.

Likewise, Stephen Edgar, in his article "Translator's Note with Anna Akhmatova" in the April 2008 issue of *Poetry*, reveals, "Some poets have been served well by translation . . . but others seem to lose a lot of their magic in the process, Akhmatova among them. The intense singing quality of her verse seems not to come through." Clearly, then, readers approaching an English translation of Akhmatova's "Everything Is Plundered" are working at a distinct disadvantage. Or are they? In spite of the loss of sound quality, Akhmatova's work is of such importance that readers continue to find her work compelling. Perhaps the most useful way to approach the poem, then, is to first gather as many English translations as possible. There are many available, including those by Judith Hemschemeyer, Stanley Kunitz, Nancy K. Anderson, Jane Kenyon, and D. M. Thomas. In addition, Kunitz includes a facing page of Russian text of the poem, giving the reader the opportunity to compare the Russian original with Kunitz's English translation.

Next, the serious reader of Akhmatova should consider each of the translations individually, taking care to understand the choices each translator has made. For example, has the translator chosen to attempt rhyme or meter? Or has the translator chosen to render the poem in free verse? How clear are the images? The metaphors? At this point, the reader can identify some of the key words and phrases in the poem and compare how each of these is rendered in different translations. The reader has an opportunity here to evaluate the effectiveness of the translation and the poem, now that it is in the hands of a translator.

It becomes clear as one reads the varying translations of "Everything Is Plundered" that some translators take a more literal approach to the poem, while others take more license with the translation in order to make a beautiful, readable poem that remains true to Akhmatova's spirit. It should also be possible, even if one does not read Russian, to identify the differences in sound repetition and rhyme between the original and the translation, merely by looking at them side by side. Indeed, using the translations as a guide, an astute reader can try to imagine which of the Russian words match with the English ones. Why would one want to go to so much trouble to read one poem? The answer is both easy and complex. In the first place, Akhmatova has something important to say in "Everything Is Plundered." Akhmatova reminds the reader that no matter how horrendous the loss, how damaged the landscape, hope still flutters on the wind like the scent of cherry blossoms.

A second, more complicated reason why a reader ought to engage many translations of Akhmatova has to do with the unspoken contract between the reader and the writer of literature. Critics who practice a kind of literary theory known as reader response will argue that meaning in literature is a shared responsibility between the writer and the reader. That is, when a poet writes a poem, the poem does not have meaning in and of itself. Rather, it is when the reader engages with the poem that meaning arises. Meaning, for the reader-response critic, results from a collaborative effort between the poet and the reader, meeting together in the text of the poem. The reader brings his or her background and experience to the poem and connects with the poet's words.

Crow *(Image copyright Vladimir Prusakov, 2009. Used under license from Shutterstock.com)*

HER MOST CHERISHED POEMS COULD NOT BE PUBLISHED; HER EARLIER ONES SHE NO LONGER CARED FOR, AND COULDN'T UNDERSTAND WHY OTHER PEOPLE LIKED THEM."

Ultimately, it is this desire to make a poem meaningful that drives all translators and all readers. In the act of translation, the translator makes visible and explicit his or her engagement with the poem by actually placing his or her words, and language, within a poet's work. A translation is a collaborative effort, just as the best reading is collaborative as well. In this sense, it is little wonder then, that those who undertake translation are often poets in their own right, people who are intensely interested in the craft of writing. Kunitz concludes, "Poets are attracted to translation because it is a way of paying their debt to the tradition, of restoring life to shades.... It is also a means of self-renewal, of entering the skin and adventuring through the body of another's imagination."

Any poem worth reading must be read multiple times for its meaning to emerge. The advantage of reading many translations of "Everything Is Plundered" is that the reader has a rich opportunity to experience the poem from many different angles and perspectives. As a result, "Everything Is Plundered" takes on new meaning with each reading and each translation, growing in the process into a poem that touches the core of a reader's being, which fears destruction but also longs for hope. Surely this is worth the effort; surely this is worth the time.

Source: Diane Andrews Henningfeld, Critical Essay on "Everything Is Plundered," in *Poetry for Students*, Gale, Cengage Learning, 2010.

John Simon

In the following excerpt, Simon discusses the difficulties associated with translating Akhmatova's poems, including "Everything Is Plundered," and provides insight from Lydia Chukovskaya's The Akhmatova Journals.

"Poetry is what gets lost in translation," observed Robert Frost, and was only partly right. The thrust and sweep of epic poetry translates well enough: there is no dearth of decent translations of Homer, Virgil, Dante. Philosophical poetry also survives quite well: Eliot's *Four Quartets,* for example, has been successfully rendered into a number of languages. Lyric poetry is the one that has the most to lose.

There is, obviously, the problem of rhyme. Unrhymed poetry fares much better in translation: Walt Whitman reads just about as well (or poorly) in French or German. Even as delicate an unrhymed lyric as Leopardi's "L'infinito" has thrived in English. But rhyme is a killer. With elaborate rhyme schemes, tricky rhyming words, and short lines (dimeter, trimeter), the difficulty increases exponentially. Think of Byron's *Don Juan,* or this, from Heine: "Sie sassen und tranken am Teetisch, / Und sprachen von Liebe viel. / Die Herren, die waren ästhetisch, / Die Damen von zartem Gefühl." Verses 2 and 4, with their masculine rhymes, are no problem: "And talked about love and such" and "The ladies who felt so much." But 1 and 3 are impossible: the splendid joke lies in rhyming, femininely at that, *Teetisch* and *ästhetisch,* "tea table" and "aesthetic." Failing this, you've got nothing.

But there are poems untranslatable not because of their intricate rhyme scheme, rich rhymes, or fancy prosody. There exists something even more basic. In my doctoral dissertation, I quote from the journal of Jules Barbey d'Aurevilly for September 19, 1836: "[Maurice de] Guérin est venu. Causé de la poésie des langues, qui est toute autre chose que la poésie des poètes." I commented: "Languages have their intrinsic poetry, a poetry they yield to the proper touch with gracious forthrightness." This is the kind of *objet trouvé* that certain words or sequences of words offer up to the poet, as blocks of marble supposedly suggested to Michelangelo the figures he would hew from them.

Take the last lines of the beautiful "Járkálj csak, halálraitélt" (Keep walking, condemned man) by the great Hungarian poet Miklós Radnóti, which, after giving the contemporary poet various ways to live, concludes with "S oly keményen is, mint a sok / sebtöl vérzö, nagy farkasok." Literally: "And as toughly, too, as the from many / wounds bleeding, great wolves." (The Hungarian "s," by the way, is our "sh.") What is a translator to do, confronted with these darkly resonant sounds? Shoot the poem in the foot, or himself in the head? There is no way "great wolves" can render the mighty rumble of *nagy farkasok.* (*Nagy,* incidentally, is a monosyllable, not unlike our *nudge.*) This is the *poésie des langues,* the poetry inherent in the sounds of a language's words, and it is this more than anything that makes a poet such as Anna Akhmatova virtually (virtually? totally!) untranslatable into English.

Consider the opening quatrain of a three-stanza poem of 1921, which the poet dedicated to her friend Natalya Rykova. The "literal" prose translation in Dimitri Obolenski's *Penguin Book of Russian Verse* runs: "All has been looted, betrayed, sold; death's black wing flickered [before us]; all is gnawed by hungry anguish—why then does a light shine for us?" Peter Norman's translation reads: "Everything is ravaged, bartered, betrayed, / The black wing of death has hovered nearby, / Everything is gnawed through by hungry gloom, / Why then did we feel so light of heart?" Stanley Kunitz manages to get one rhyme into his translation: "Everything is plundered, betrayed, sold, / Death's great black wing scrapes the air, / Misery gnaws to the bone. / Why then do we not despair?" With all due respect, Kunitz would never have published such poetry under his own name. Finally, here is the version of Walter Arndt, one of our principal rhyming translators from the Russian: "All is looted, betrayed, past retrieving, / Death's black wing has been flickering near, / All is racked with a ravenous grieving, / How on earth did this splendor appear?"

This seems passable at first glance, but look now at the original: "Vsyo rashishchenyo, predano, prodano, / Chernoy smyerti mel'kalo krilo, / Vsyo golodnoy toskoyu izglodano, / Otchega zhe nam stalo svetlo?" There is no way the sonorities of that

very first line can be conveyed in English, especially the play on *predano, prodano.* And not even the supposedly literal version does justice to the simplicity of the last: "Why then did it become light for us?" with *stalo* and *svetlo* again creating an echo effect. Russian poetry is a poetry of sound effects *par excellence,* because Russian is a sonorous, declamatory language; this is what those latter-day stadium-filling poets—the Yevtushenkos, Voznesenskys, and Akhmadulinas—called "pop poets" by Akhmatova, were to exploit to her disgust.

And yet she, too, benefited from big public readings at various times in her life. For Russia is that rare country in which poetry is loved by the masses, a country where simple folk quote poetry at one another and discuss it as people here do a football game. Because they often declaim in huge auditoriums and stadiums, Russian poets have adopted a vatic mode of recitation: part hieratic, part histrionic, loud and singsongy. It was Mandelshtam who reproached one of the most stentorian perpetrators with, "Mayakovsky, stop reading your verse. You sound like a Romanian orchestra." But the vatic mode is still with us, and even such a Westernized poet as Joseph Brodsky, Akhmatova's dearest disciple and protégé, subscribes to it wholeheartedly. This vatic mode, in turn, battens on the "poetry of languages," as the Acmeists, the group of poets to which Akhmatova belonged, certainly did. The Poets' Guild, as the Acmeists called their splinter group from the Symbolists, believed, as Max Hayward puts it, that "language was like any other material, and in fashioning poetic artifacts from it, one had to take account of its natural qualities and limitations. . . ."

Her most cherished poems could not be published; her earlier ones she no longer cared for, and couldn't understand why other people liked them. I myself am more than a little puzzled by her own and other people's judgments on her poetry. In one of her autobiographical sketches, Akhmatova writes that of her entire first book, *Evening* (1912), "I now truly like only the lines: 'Intoxicated by a voice / That sounds exactly like yours. . . .'" With all allowances made for what gets lost in translation, it is impossible to understand what could make those two verses special. Even more mysterious, though, is the recollection of the poet Georgy Adamovich about the other great modern Russian poetess, Marina Tsvetayeva: "She [had] just read Akhmatova's 'Lullaby,' and praised it, saying that she would give everything she had written and would write in the future for a

single line from that poem: 'I am a bad mother.'"
Even if you allow for the context (a father is speaking), how can that line have such value? There is perhaps something even beyond the poetry that gets lost in translations from Akhmatova.

Amusingly, Anna discusses Pasternak's indifference to her work and goes on to comment with wonderful outspokenness: "Haven't you noticed that poets don't like the poetry of their contemporaries? A poet carries with him his own enormous world—why does he need someone else's poetry? When they're young, about 23 or 24, poets like the work of poets in their own group. Later though, they don't like anybody else's—only their own." Vyacheslav V. Ivanov confirms this: "Certainly Akhmatova was not inclined to listen to the praise of other literary figures of the first decade." Her attitude to Tsvetayeva was particularly ambivalent, even though Marina was much more generous: she called her rival "Anna Chrysostom of all the Russians," and her beautiful poem "To Anna Akhmatova" begins "O muza placha, prekrasneyshaya iz muz!" (O muse of weeping, loveliest of muses). This became a metonym for Akhmatova: Muse of Weeping—or, as Brodsky renders it, Keening Muse. Notice, again, the eloquent fanfare of *prekrasneyshaya;* how is an English translator to do justice to that?

Yet there were also times when the Russian language seemed to thwart Akhmatova. There is a droll page in the *Journals* where Anna agonizes to a couple of friends about something she had written: "One line has been vexing me all my life: 'Gde milomu muzhu detey rodila [Where she bore her dear husband children].' Do you hear: *Mumu?!* Can it be that neither of you, both such lovers of poetry, has noticed this mooing?" Whereupon she proceeds to recite Pushkin's "Monument" to her friends—only, as a footnote tells us, it wasn't that at all, but the epilogue to her own *Requiem*; she was trying to mislead those who, she claimed, were bugging her room. But the greater, metaphysical, risks of her profession haunted her most: "The word is much more difficult material than, for instance, paint. Think about it, really: for the poet works with the very same words that people use to invite each other to tea. . . ."

What is the poetry of Anna Akhmatova really like? Here is how Chukovskaya sees it:

> When you first apprehend it, it does not strike you by the novelty of its form as does, say, the poetry of Mayakovsky. You can hear Baratynsky and Tyutchev and Pushkin—sometimes,

more rarely, Blok—in the movement of the poem, in its rhythms, in the fullness of the line, in the precision of the rhymes. At first it seems like a narrow path, going alongside the wide road of Russian classical poetry. Mayakovsky is deafeningly novel, but at the same time he is unfruitful, barren: he brought Russian poetry to the edge of an abyss. . . Akhmatova's little path turns out to be a wide road in fact; her traditional style is purely external. . . within this she brings about earthquakes and upheavals.

Frankly, in struggling with her poems in Russian—never mind the translations—I cannot find the earthquakes. But I do see a poet with an original vision and a personal voice who manages to maintain her individual talent within the tradition. No wonder she admired T. S. Eliot. . . .

Source: John Simon, "Anna Akhmatova," in *New Criterion*, Vol. 12, No. 9, May 1994, pp. 29–39.

Richard Eder

In the following essay, Eder identifies Akhmatova as one of the greatest female poets in history and suggests that her "imperial largeness of spirit is catching."

The ship dwindles to the horizon and disappears; it is the watcher on the shore whose heart is shrunk by absence. The sailor, for better or worse, is where he is, life-size.

The night of Stalin's repression has been told in all kinds of ways, most famously by Alexander Solzhenitsyn's books about the prison camps and their inmates. But in the literature of Soviet suffering there may be no pages more powerful than the cycle of poems by Anna Akhmatova entitled *Requiem*.

Nothing inside the prison walls so fiercely expresses deprivation and injustice—with such a large intensity that it stands for an entire order of human loss—as her chronicle of the women who stood, year after year, outside those walls. After the death of both hope and despair, they waited for word of the fate of those within, and for the chance to hand a knitted cap through, or a pair of shoes. Like the mothers of Argentina's Plaza de Mayo, years later, who turned the "disappeared" into a visible presence, the Russian women, by standing outside the city's jails, jailed the entire city:

> That was when the ones who smiled
> Were the dead, glad to be at rest
>
> · · ·
>
> And like a useless appendage, Leningrad
> Swung from its prisons."

It is quite reasonable to think of Akhmatova, who died in 1966 at age 76, as the greatest woman poet in the Western World since Sappho. In a monumental endeavor, seemingly poised upon the frailest of underpinnings, the tiny Zephyr Press of Somerville, Mass., has brought out the first complete collection of her poems published anywhere in the world.

With original Russian versions and a supple translation that all but turns the facing pages warm to the touch, [*The Complete Poems of Anna Akhmatova*], more than 1,500 pages in length, includes more than 700 poems—some previously unprinted—copious notes, several introductions, prefaces and memoirs, and about 75 photographs and drawings.

Roberta Reeder, who edited the collection and the notes, contributes a monograph placing the poems in their historical and biographical context. Judith Hemschemeyer, the translator, provides additional commentary. Among her perceptive remarks is the point that Akhmatova's poetry, unlike that of many of her contemporaries, nearly always addresses a second person, explicitly or implicitly. The reader receives this burning gaze face to face.

Hemschemeyer's translations are not simply a work but a pilgrimage. A poet, she read a few of Akhmatova's poems in translation about 25 years ago. She then learned Russian so that, with the help of word-by-word literal versions, she could translate them all. "I became convinced that Akhmatova's poems should be translated in their entirety and by a woman, and that I was that person," she writes.

Akhmatova's imperial largeness of spirit is catching, clearly. So is a portion of her art. Hemschemeyer chose a very direct rendering, stressing clarity, intimacy and an unforced syntax over any effort to pursue the original's rhymes and sonorities. But she uses assonance and slant rhyme, and her seeming plain style is governed by a lyrical ear. In truth, her translations are not so much plain as transparent. If I did not know English, I would learn it to read them.

Akhmatova's life and her poetry were brutally cut in two by history. Born to a well-to-do family, living a privileged childhood, she became a glittering figure in the Bohemian literary world of pre-revolutionary St. Petersburg. She was a member of the Acmeist circle of poets—Osip Mandelstam, her lifelong brother in poetry and suffering, was another—and her first husband was a poet.

She was a flaming creature. Taking into account her bipolar candle-burning, and the long purgatory she underwent later on, one thinks of Edna St. Vincent Millay turned into Mother Courage. Except that the poetry of her youth, hugely successful, was also incomparably better. She wrote of childhood, of the countryside, of the city, and of all varieties of love from girlish to adult and adulterous.

She had a blinding sense of place and time. She fused the richness of things and passions with a premonition—and later, the memory—of their transience. Thus, an early poem evokes her sumptuous childhood garden together with a stone bust, toppled beside the water: "He has given his face to the waters of the lake / And he's listening to the green rustling. / And bright rainwater washes / His clotted wound . . . / Cold one, white one, wait, / I'll become marble too."

There is the young girl considering her new-found sexuality: "In my room lives a beautiful / Slow black snake; / It is like me, just as lazy, / Just as cold . . ."

The quick desolation of an early marriage: "The heart's memory of the sun grows faint. / The grass is yellower. / A few early snowflakes blow in the wind, / Barely, barely . . . / The willow spreads its transparent fan / Against the empty sky. / Perhaps I should not have become / Your wife . . ."

The excitement and insomnia of an affair: "Both sides of the pillow / Are already hot. / Now even the second candle / Is going out, and the cry of the crows / Gets louder and louder. / I haven't slept all night / And now it's too late to think of sleep . . . / How unendurably white / Is the blind on the white window. / Hello."

There was the pride of a woman and a poet in her prime, addressing a no doubt not imaginary lover: "Oh it was a cold day / In Peter's miraculous city. / Like a crimson fire the sunset lay, / And slowly the shadow thickened. / Let him not desire my eyes, / Prophetic and fixed. / He will get a whole lifetime of poems / The prayer of my arrogant lips."

The revolution came, and suddenly poverty gnawed away her life and, worse, her writing went out of favor. Poetry had to be hard and elevating. By 1925, the literary leaders were saying that she should have had the intelligence to be dead.

Hardship and the impossibility of publishing; expulsion from the Writers Union. Worse was to come. The purges of the mid-1930s spared her, but her only son, Lev, was arrested. For a year-and-a-half, she joined the lines outside the Leningrad prison. And, in *Requiem,* she found a voice again: harsh with knowledge, powerful with anger, yet with all the lovely particularity of her youth.

Source: Richard Eder, "The Greatest Woman Poet since Sappho," in *Los Angeles Times Book Review*, March 18, 1990, pp. 3, 7.

Yelena Byelyakova

In the following essay, Byelyakova explores the hardships that shaped Akhmatova's poetry, hardships evident in "Everything Is Plundered."

The life of Anna Akhmatova was a tragic one. Although she had her moments of glory she also experienced terrible humiliations.

She was born in 1889, and her youth coincided with an extraordinary literary flowering, the silver age of Russian poetry. Her first volume of verses, *Vecher* (*Evening*) was published in 1912. It was followed two years later by *Chyotki* (*Rosary*) which was reprinted eight times and made her name. The themes of most of her early poems are meetings and separations, love and solitude. Their style is rigorous, lucid, laconic.

Her poetry was read throughout Russia, and the critics predicted a brilliant future for this "Russian Sappho". She published regularly—*Belaya staya* (1917; *The White Flock*), *Podorozhnik* (1921; *Plantain*), and *Anno Domini MCMXXI* (1922).

Unlike many intellectuals in her circle, Akhmatova did not emigrate after the Revolution of October 1917. Yet in 1923 her work ceased to be published. The official view was that her lyrics were alien to the new generation of readers produced by the Revolution. Fame was followed by oblivion: for seventeen years her name vanished from literature.

Life had other trials in store for her. In 1921 her first husband, the poet Nikolay Gumilyov, was executed after being accused of taking part in a counter-revolutionary conspiracy. Her son, the orientalist Lev Gumilyov, was arrested in 1935 and eventually spent fourteen years in prison and exile in Siberia. Her third husband, the art historian Nikolay Punin, died in prison.

Yet Anna Akhmatova continued to write. The anguish she shared with thousands of other women who queued outside the prisons of Leningrad inspired the cycle *Rekviem* (1935–1940; *Requiem*), which tells the tragic story of a mother separated from her only son. She visited her friend the poet Osip Mandelstam, exiled in Voronezh, and wrote poems filled with foreboding about his imminent death. She denounced the illegal and arbitrary acts which were being committed in her country, and exposed the cruelty of Stalin and his entourage. Fearing arrest, she memorized her verses rather than write them down.

In 1940 several poems she had written before the Revolution were published. Later, patriotic lyrics she wrote during the war were published in several newspapers and magazines.

But in 1946 she became the main target of an ideological campaign launched against the artistic and literary intelligentsia by the Central Committee of the Communist Party, which passed a resolution condemning the literary reviews *Zvezda* ("The Star") and *Leningrad* for publishing her poetry, which was branded as "bourgeois and decadent", "devoid of an ideological message" and "alien to the Soviet people".

The entire printrun of her most recent collection of poems was destroyed and she was expelled from the Union of Soviet Writers. For ten years she was again ostracized. Not until the thaw which followed the death of Stalin was she reinstated in the Writers' Union and allowed to publish again. By now the interest in her poetry was immense.

In the 1960s Akhmatova became world famous. Her work was translated into English, French, German, Italian, Czech, Bulgarian and many other languages. Many articles, books and studies were published about her poetry. In 1964 she travelled to Italy where she was awarded the Etna-Taormina international poetry prize, and in the following year she received an honorary doctorate from Oxford University.

Anna Akhmatova died on 5 March 1966. As the years go by the interest in her work continues to grow. Her collections of poems are often reprinted, and unpublished works are coming to light, including some fine patriotic poems which were virtually unknown in the Soviet Union until recently. *Rekviem,* which had appeared in the West in the 1960s, was not published in the Soviet Union until 1987. In 1988, the Communist Party resolution against the reviews *Leningrad* and *Zvezda* was officially rescinded and in 1989 *Zvezda* devoted an entire issue to the centenary of Anna Akhmatova's birth.

The city of Leningrad, which played a major part in her life, was the centre of the centenary celebrations in June 1989. A memorial museum was opened on the Fontanka Embankment, where for over thirty years she had lived and composed some of her most tragic poems. Conferences were organized by the Russian Literature Institute of the USSR Academy of Sciences and the Leningrad Writers' Organization. At literary and musical evenings leading poets read her works and poems dedicated to her by contemporaries including Aleksandr Blok, Marina Tsvetayeva, Osip Mandelstam, and Boris Pasternak. Song cycles of her lyrics set to music by Prokofiev and Slonimsky were also performed.

The anniversary provided the opportunity to pay a fitting tribute to one of the greatest poets of the century.

Source: Yelena Byelyakova, "Anna Akhmatova: 'Mother Courage' of Poetry," in *Unesco Courier*, Vol. 43, April 1990, p. 48.

SOURCES

Akhmatova, Anna, "Everything Has Been Plundered," in *The Complete Poems of Anna Akhmatova: Expanded Edition*, translated by Judith Hemschemeyer, edited and introduced by Roberta Reeder, Zephyr Press, 2000, pp. 279–80.

Amert, Susan, *In a Shattered Mirror: The Later Poetry of Anna Akhmatova*, Stanford University Press, 1992, p. 3.

The Constitution of the Russian Federation, Chapter 2, Article 19, Section 2, http://www.constitution.ru/en/100 03000-03.htm (accessed April 15, 2009).

Cook, Albert Spaulding, "The Modified Modernism of Anna Akhmatova," in *Soundings: On Shakespeare, Modern Poetry, Plato, and Other Subjects*, Wayne State University Press, 1991, p. 82.

Dunn, Stephen, *Walking Light*, BOA Editions, 2001, pp. 169–70.

Eder, Richard, Review of *The Complete Poems of Anna Akhmatova*, in *Los Angeles Times Book Review*, March 18, 1990, p. 3.

Edgar, Stephen, "Translator's Note with Anna Akhmatova," in *Poetry*, Vol. 192, No. 1, April 2008, p. 9.

Feinstein, Elaine, *Anna of All the Russias*, Alfred A. Knopf, 2005, pp. 3–30.

Haight, Amanda, *Anna Akhmatova: A Poetic Pilgrimage*, Oxford University Press, 1976, pp. 3–40.

"Joseph Stalin," *Public Broadcasting Service Web site*, http://www.pbs.org/redfiles/bios/all_bio_joseph_stalin .htm (accessed April 25, 2009).

Kunitz, Stanley, "On Translating Akhmatova," in *A Kind of Order, A Kind of Folly*, Little, Brown and Company, 1975, pp. 39–46.

Laird, Sally, *Voices of Russian Literature: Interviews with Ten Contemporary Writers*, Oxford University Press, 1999.

Levykin, Alexi, "Nicholas II (Nikolai Alexandrovich)," in *St. Petersburg Times Online* (St. Petersburg, Russia), 1999, http://www.sptimes.ru (accessed April 15, 2009).

Mosley, Philip E., "Russian Revolution," *History Channel Web site*, 2006, http://www.history.com/encyclopedia .do?articleId = 221104 (accessed April 15, 2009).

Painter, Kirsten Blythe, "The Emergence of Tempered Modernism," in *Flint on a Bright Stone: A Revolution of Precision*, 2006, pp. 44–7.

Perloff, Marjorie, "Akhmatova in Translation," in *PN Review*, Vol. 31, No. 5, May 2005, pp. 28–35.

Ponomareff, Constantin V., "Conscience in Anna Akhmatova's Poetic Work," in *One Less Hope: Essays on Twentieth-Century Russian Poets*, Rodopi, 2006, p. 14.

Reeder, Roberta, "Mirrors and Masks: The Life and Poetic Works of Anna Akhmatova," in *The Complete Poems of Anna Akhmatova: Expanded Edition*, translated by Judith Hemschemeyer, edited and introduced by Roberta Reeder, Zephyr Press, 2000, pp. 1–34.

"Requiem to Anna," in *Russian Life*, Vol. 51, No. 2, March-April 2007, p. 16.

Rubins, Maria, "Anna Andreevna Akhmatova," in *Dictionary of Literary Biography*, Vol. 295, *Russian Writers of the Silver Age, 1890–1925*, edited by Judith E. Kalb and J. Alexander Ogden, Thomson Gale, 2004, pp. 3–20.

Rusinko, Elaine, "Acmeism, Post-symbolism, and Henri Bergson," in *Slavic Review*, Vol. 41, No. 3, Autumn 1982, pp. 494–510.

Simon, John, "Anna Akhmatova," in *Dreamer of Dreams: Essays on Poets and Poetry*, Ivan R. Dee, 2001, pp. 162–79.

"Socialist Realism," in *Merriam-Webster's Encyclopedia of Literature*, 1995, p. 1046.

Taylor, John, "Poetry Today," in *Antioch Review*, Vol. 64, No. 2, Spring 2006, p. 374.

"The Soviet Era," *Geographia Web site*, http://www.geo graphia.com/russia/rushis07.htm (accessed April 15, 2009).

"The Soviet Period," *Bucknell University Web site*, http:// www.bucknell.edu/x20139.xml (accessed April 15, 2009).

Waszink, Paul M., "Some Observations on Allegory in Akhmatova's Early Poetry," in *Slavic East European Journal*, Vol. 46, No. 4, Winter 2002, p. 745.

FURTHER READING

Akhmatova, Anna, *My Half Century: Collected Prose*, Ardis Publishers, 1992.
> This book is a collection of Akhmatova's essays, diary entries, historical accounts, and sketches of fellow artists.

Campling, Elizabeth, *The Russian Revolution*, "Living through History" series, Trafalgar Square Publishing, 1985.

This book, written for young adults, offers fifteen short biographies of Russians, Americans, and British citizens who witness or participated in the Russian Revolution and the Russian Civil War during the years that Akhmatova was writing.

Doherty, Justin, *The Acmeist Movement in Russian Poetry*, Oxford University Press, 1997.
This book offers a close look at the poetic movement founded by Nicolai Gumilyov, Osip Mandelstam, and Anna Akhmatova.

Driver, Sam N., *Anna Akhmatova*, Twayne Publishers, 1972.
This book offers an accessible introduction to Akhmatova's work and life and is especially suitable for students.

Gerstein, Emma, *Moscow Memoirs: Memories of Anna Akhmatova, Osip Mandelstam, and Literary Russia Under Stalin*, Overlook Hardcover, 2004.
This book contains the memoirs of a woman who lived in the Soviet Union between 1903 and 2002. She was close friends with Osip Mandelstam and his wife, Nadezhda, and their circle of friends, including Akhmatova.

Reeder, Roberta, *Anna Akhmatova: Poet and Prophet*, St. Martin's Press, 1994.
Reeder's book is a comprehensive critical biography of Akhmatova's life and work. The book includes a long and helpful bibliography.

The Explorer

"The Explorer" by the African American poet Gwendolyn Brooks, first appeared in *Harper's* magazine in September 1959 and was included as the first poem in Brooks's third collection of poems, *The Bean Eaters* (1960). It was not included in Brooks's *Selected Poems* (1963) but was reprinted in her collected poems, *The World of Gwendolyn Brooks*, published by Harper in 1971.

"The Explorer" is a short poem of fourteen lines divided into four irregular sections. It presents a restless, nameless man who is desperately seeking some peace and quiet in his life but is unable to find it. The poem might be understood in a universal way as an exploration of the pain of the human condition; it might also be interpreted in terms of the African American experience during the civil rights movement. The poem is valuable not only for its haunting depiction of a confused man but also as an example of the work of Brooks, one of the twentieth century's foremost African American poets, at a relatively early stage in her career, before her embrace of the militancy of the black arts movement in 1967.

GWENDOLYN BROOKS

1959

AUTHOR BIOGRAPHY

Brooks was born June 7, 1917, in Topeka, Kansas, to David and Keziah Brooks. One month after Brooks's birth, the family moved to Chicago, Illinois, where Brooks lived her entire life. Brooks began writing poetry as a child and always wanted

Gwendolyn Brooks (AP Images)

to be a poet. At the age of sixteen she met two established black poets, James Weldon Johnson and Langston Hughes, both of whom encouraged her in her writing. In 1934, the year she graduated from Englewood High School, Brooks was already contributing to a black newspaper, the Chicago *Defender*, which published nearly eighty of her poems. Four years later she married Henry Blakely, who also had ambitions of becoming a poet, and the couple moved to Chicago's South Side. They had two children, Henry, Jr., born in 1940, and Nora, born in 1951.

In 1943, Brooks won the Midwestern Writer's Conference Poetry Award in Chicago, and in 1945, her first collection of poetry, *A Street in Bronzeville*, was published by Harper and Row. The collection received a favorable review by well-known poet Paul Engle in the *Chicago Tribune*, and Brooks's career as a poet was launched. She was also named one of *Mademoiselle* magazine's "Ten Young Women of the Year." The following year she won a Guggenheim Fellowship and became a fellow of the American Academy of Arts and Letters. Brooks's second volume of poetry, *Annie Allen* (1949), won *Poetry* magazine's

Eunice Tietjens Prize, and in 1950, it won a Pulitzer Prize. Brooks was the first African American poet to receive this prestigious award. In 1953, Brooks published her only novel, *Maud Martha*, in part based on her life growing up in an all-black neighborhood. Her third poetry collection, *The Bean Eaters*, in which "The Explorer" appears, was published in 1960. By this time a well-established poet, Brooks was invited by President John F. Kennedy to read at a Library of Congress Poetry Festival in 1962, and her *Selected Poems* was published in 1963. She also began to teach, running a poetry workshop at Chicago's Columbia College in 1963. Later in the decade, she taught at Elmhurst College, Northeastern Illinois State College, Columbia University, City College of New York, and the University of Wisconsin as Rennebohm Professor of English.

In 1967, Brooks had a life-changing experience when she attended Fisk University's Second Black Writers' Conference in Nashville, Tennessee. She was astonished by the energy and self-confidence of the young members of the black arts movement she met there. As she wrote in her autobiography *Report from Part One* (1972), "*I had never been, before, in the general presence of such insouciance, such live firmness, such confident vigor, such determination to mold or carve something DEFINITE.*" From this point on Brooks became a member of the black arts movement and began directing her work at black audiences. After her 1968 poetry collection *In the Mecca*, she left her mainstream publisher for black publishers, including Broadside Press, which published *Riot* (1969), *Family Pictures* (1971), and *Beckonings* (1975). Brooks's later publications include *Black Love* (1982), *The Near-Johannesburg Boy, and Other Poems* (1987), and *Winnie* (1988). She received many honors in the 1980s and 1990s. In 1985, Brooks was appointed poetry consultant to the Library of Congress, and in 1988 she was inducted into the National Women's Hall of Fame. She received the National Book Foundation Medal for Lifetime Achievement in 1994 and earned approximately fifty honorary degrees from universities and colleges.

Brooks died of cancer on December 3, 2000, at her home in Chicago.

POEM SUMMARY

Stanza 1
"The Explorer" presents a nameless, restless man, referred to only as "he," who is seeking

MEDIA ADAPTATIONS

- *Essential Brooks* features Brooks reading twenty-seven of her poems. It was released on CD in 2006 by Caedmon Audio.

- The Web site *Poets.org*, maintained by the Academy of American Poets, features Brooks reading five of her poems. See http://www .poets.org/poet.php/prmPID/165.

but failing to find some peace and quiet in life. He feels overwhelmed by the cacophony of life as it goes on all around him. Line 2 makes it clear that he has hopes but they have been battered; he has desires, things he wants, but they have taken a beating too. One can guess that this is a frustrated, disappointed, dissatisfied man, who is driven by the need to change or improve his life, to satisfy some deep inner need. The poem is not specific about exactly what he seeks or what his goals are. The second line suggests that his hopes have led him on a circuitous path, and although they may be in ruins (stated in lines 2 and 3), they still exert a hold over him. He also still pursues them, although line 3 may imply that he is actually in despair and searching for some scrap of the hope he formerly had that will allow him to continue.

However, it appears that in spite of his efforts all he is really conscious of is the noise of life, which is a metaphor for the constant restless activity that he observes around him and in his own mind. The fact that he refers to it as noise suggests that he sees no pattern in it, no meaning. It is not the music of life but random, simultaneous sounds, which he finds oppressive. He is like a person seeking an oasis in a desert, something that would enable him to take pause, stop, and nourish his life again. Yet the very first word of the poem ("Somehow") suggests that this man has little or no idea of how to accomplish his goal. He does not know how to stop the perpetual noisy interference and end his restlessness. He just clings to the hope that somehow it will happen. In lines 4 and 5, he repeats his desire, hoping to find a peace that,

like a patch of satin on a garment, will be a bright presence in his life or, as is noted in line 5, a quiet space within his own mind. Also in line 5, the poet introduces a metaphor of life as a house or a building in which activity occurs. This metaphor continues in the next stanza.

Stanza 2

The man is walking down the halls of an unfamiliar large building. The description suggests that he may be walking lightly or even tiptoeing (as the sound of the word that begins the first line might suggest), perhaps trying not to make a sound or draw attention to himself. The halls are themselves disorderly in an unspecified way. He puts his hands on the door handles that would open into rooms, but he does so indecisively, as if he is not fully aware of what he is doing or not fully committed to it. The door handles vibrate in some way, possibly due to the loud noise coming from within the room. Behind the door is a babble of many voices, and it sounds as if everyone is in a high state of tension. The man may not turn the doorknob to enter the room, since he is not presented as doing so, or he may be about to turn it. The phrasing of the lines suggests an unobserved man silently listening to the turbulent push and pull of life—the sounds of distressed people bemoaning their myriad worries and concerns. The man in the poem is like a person standing at the edge of the deep end of a swimming pool, frightened and apprehensive, unsure of whether he has the courage to jump in. As lines 10 and 11 state, life seems completely tragic to him; everyone is babbling about their own sorrows, their own disappointments and failures. He also knows, as is noted in line 11, that if he turns the handle and enters this room—a metaphor for life—he will be forced not only to face grief but also to make choices.

Stanza 3

Line 12 stands by itself. In this line it is revealed that the existence of choices is what the man most fears. He does not trust himself to make decisions. So, it is implied, he hesitates. He does not want to do the hard work of making choices, which involves living with the consequences of those choices. Nonetheless, the need to make choices presses upon him; he knows that life somehow demands this of him. Life demands a decision with some urgency, and it scares him.

Stanza 4

The presence of choices may scare the man in the poem, but the last two lines make it clear that there is no escape for him. There are no boundaries,

TOPICS FOR FURTHER STUDY

- Pick one or two poems from Brooks's early work, up to and including the poems in *Selected Poems* (1963), and then compare them with some representative samples from her later work, written after she embraced the black arts movement in 1967. How do Brooks's themes and style change in the later poems? Write an essay in which you discuss the differences between her earlier and later poems.

- Brooks's most well-known poem, which appears often in anthologies, is "We Real Cool," first published in *The Bean Eaters* (1960). With a fellow student, practice reading this poem aloud. Then go to http://www.poets.org/poet.php/prmPID/165 and listen to a recording of Brooks reading it. How does her reading differ from your own? Why does she read it the way she does? What is unusual or unexpected about her reading? Give a class presentation in which you read and discuss this poem, and also play Brooks's reading of it. What is it about this poem that has made it popular? What does the poem say to you about the lives and attitudes of the young men it describes?

- Write a report in which you examine the relationship between the U.S. civil rights movement of the 1960s and the black arts movement. In what ways were they similar? Was the black arts movement most stimulated by the nonviolent movement headed by Dr. Martin Luther King, Jr., or the later black power movement? What were the achievements of the black arts movement and why was it controversial?

- Using for your research *Gwendolyn Brooks: "Poetry Is Life Distilled,"* a biography of the poet by Christine M. Hill (published by Enslow, 2005), give a class presentation in which you discuss how Brooks's life shaped her poetry. Organize your main points into a PowerPoint presentation to support your argument.

meaning that there are no places where he can find rest and peace. At least in his experience of it, life cannot be anything other than a dissonant, restless world of wants, desires, and discordant voices.

THEMES

The Search for Inner Peace

Although the persona of the poem is an individual man, the poem can be read as representing the universal human search for inner peace, for a restful state of mind far beyond the day-to-day noise and bustle of life. The search is presented as a difficult, perhaps impossible one because it seems to run counter to the basic conditions of human life. The man presented in the first stanza gives the impression of desperation. He is battered by the troubles of life and urgently seeks some kind of relief. The second stanza hints at the fact that human life is a perpetually discordant affair, no matter one's efforts. It is a stage on which, as lines 10 and 11 suggest, tragedies great and small are played out. The man tiptoeing down the corridors of life cannot find what he seeks, and the final line of the poem presents an unequivocal message that he is perhaps loathe to hear: life can offer him no peace, no rest, "no quiet rooms." At the universal level, this idea suggests that humans are ill-suited to the world they inhabit. They seek peace but find only turbulence, and that is the nature of things.

Life Philosophy

The poem presents human life as a restless sea. Like waves in the ocean, every moment something new comes up, an activity that needs to be performed, a desire that demands to be satisfied, or thoughts that disturb the tranquility of the mind. No prescription is given for how the innate human longing for peace, silence, and stillness can be attained. There appears to be only the vague hope that such qualities might be discovered somewhere, as line 5 states, by turning within, away from the sounds of distraught human activity that this man hears wherever he goes. In his own state of disquiet and restlessness, he suffers from fear and indecision. What life seems to be demanding of this reluctant actor is exactly what he appears unwilling or unable to perform: to engage fully in life, however difficult or unpleasant that might be. He must take some action, and every action demands a choice, as line 11 makes clear. Decisions must be made, and yet for every path in life taken as a result of a decision, there are many other paths that are automatically closed off. Perhaps this is what the man fears, and he therefore shrinks from making decisions that involve conscious choices. However, in doing so, he cuts himself off from the very thing that makes people human. Animals do not have choices, being propelled solely by their instincts, but humans have the gift of thought, reflection, and foresight, the ability to envision different consequences and different futures. The poem suggests a man who is avoiding life at the very time he is propelled toward taking a more active role in it. He is caught between two extremes, two poles of life: a much desired but never obtained tranquility and a restless turbulence that frightens him.

The reader comes away from the poem asking some questions to which the poem provides no answers: Is the man doomed forever to stalk the halls of life frightened, peering into each room, unwilling to thrust open the door and plunge into the hubbub of conflicting voices in which one person's desires and goals may well conflict with those of another? Or will he live up to the title of the poem? Will he become a true explorer, willing to enter into chaos and danger, shaping life as he goes, all the time taking responsibility for his own destiny, with nothing to guide him but his own conscience and his moral sense? As unsure as the man in the poem are the outcomes of his actions.

Old brass doorknob (*Image copyright James E. Knopf, 2009. Used under license from Shutterstock.com*)

STYLE

Free Verse
The poem is written in free verse rather than in a traditional poetic form. Free verse became popular after World War I, and by the 1950s and 1960s it was the most common type of poetry written in the United States. Free verse does not use traditional forms of meter or rhyme but allows the poet to create a variety of effects through other means. Free verse may use rhyme but more often it does not, or it may use it sparingly.

Rhyme
Rhyme refers to the use of words that sound identical or very similar in parallel positions in two or more lines in a poem. The poet uses rhyme several times in "The Explorer." In stanza 1, line 3 rhymes with line 5, the final line; in stanza 2, line 8 rhymes with line 11, the last line of the stanza. The last two lines of the poem contain

what is called imperfect or near rhyme, in which the vowel sounds may be close but not identical ("bourns" and "rooms"). The imperfect rhyme with which the poem ends reinforces the theme, suggesting the difficulty encountered by the persona of the poem in finding harmony and peace.

Stanza and Line Lengths

The poem is highly irregular in terms of the length of the stanzas (units of thought in a poem) and the lines. The line lengths vary considerably, both within each stanza and overall. Additionally, the number of metrical feet (the smallest units of rhythm in a line of poetry, typically combining one accented syllable with one or two unaccented syllables) in each line varies throughout the poem. The longest lines are line 2, which is a heptameter (a line of seven metrical feet) and line 12, which is a hexameter (a line of six metrical feet). The shortest line consists of only one metrical foot (line 11), and there are lines of almost all lengths in between.

The wide range in line length conveys the idea that the world of the man described in the poem is not smooth, easy, and regular, but jagged and discordant. This is also conveyed by the variation in the stanzas. The first stanza has five lines, the second stanza has six. After that the poem departs from any stanzaic structure, the remainder consisting of a single line, then a space, followed by two short lines. Thus the poem, like the character described, has no resting place in terms of a regular form. This irregularity conveys well the disturbed state of mind of the person being described.

Alliteration

Brooks is known for her frequent use of alliteration, the repetition of words or syllables with the same initial consonants. Examples can be found in lines 1 and 2 and lines 8 and 11.

Run-on and End-stopped Lines

The poet uses both end-stopped and run-on lines. An end-stopped line occurs when the end of the line coincides with the conclusion of a clause or sentence, often indicated by a comma or period. In contrast, a run-on line occurs when the syntax and meaning of the line is not complete in itself but carries over into the following line. Lines 6 and 7 are run-on lines; lines 12, 13, and 14 are end-stopped lines. The run-on line often has a caesura, or pause, somewhere in the following line, to complete the grammatical unit that began in the preceding line. This occurs in line 7, for example. The presence of the caesura, in this case a period, in

the short line that concludes the second stanza (line 11) is another striking example of the irregularity of the poem. It is as if the poem itself, in its surprising variety, is indicating that there are many choices that can be made—for a poet as she creates the form of her poem, as well as for the character in the poem, who is daunted by the many choices available to him.

HISTORICAL CONTEXT

The Civil Rights Movement in the 1950s

The poems in *The Bean Eaters*, many of which deal with issues of race, were written during the 1950s, when the civil rights movement began. Over the next twenty years, the civil rights movement would fundamentally change race relations in the United States, giving African Americans far greater equality of opportunity in employment, education, and housing than they had ever known before. One of the early landmarks in the civil rights movement was the 1954 U.S. Supreme Court ruling in *Brown v. Board of Education* that separate schools for black and white students were inherently unequal and therefore unconstitutional. This ruling paved the way for desegregation in public schools. The following year in Montgomery, Alabama, an African American woman named Rosa Parks refused to move to the back of the bus as segregation policies required. This led to a bus boycott by African Americans led by Dr. Martin Luther King, Jr., which resulted in the end of segregation in public transportation in that city. In the same year, a shocking murder of an African American boy named Emmett Till in Money, Mississippi, caused a national uproar. Till was a fourteen-year-old boy from Chicago who was visiting relatives in the South. He allegedly tried to flirt with a young white woman in a grocery store. A few days later Till was abducted and brutally killed by the woman's husband and another man. The killers were tried and acquitted but later confessed to the crime. Brooks's poem in *The Bean Eaters*, "The Last Quatrain of the Ballad of Emmett Till," presents a picture of Till's mother after the murder and funeral of her son. Another significant event in the civil rights movement came in September 1957, in Little Rock, Arkansas. Nine African American students who had enrolled in the all-white Little Rock High School were prevented from attending

COMPARE
&
CONTRAST

- **1960:** Racial discrimination against African Americans, especially in the South, is deeply entrenched, but change is taking place rapidly. In Raleigh, North Carolina, the Student Non-violent Coordinating Committee (SNCC) is founded. Over the next decade, SNCC plays a major role in involving students in the civil rights movement.

  Today: Although discrimination against African Americans has decreased, according to *The State of Black America 2009*, a report by the National Urban League edited by Stephanie J. Jones, African Americans still lag behind whites in key areas such as economics, education, health, social justice, and civic engagement. This is in spite of success in the political realm with the election of Barack Obama, the first African American to become president of the United States.

- **1960:** Black writers who are published in the mainstream press write for a predominantly white audience. However, during the black arts movement in the 1960s, African American writers inspired by the civil rights movement appeal to black audiences as they continue to explore issues of racial discrimination and cultivate racial pride. Publishing houses and magazines are established for the distribution of work by African Americans.

  Today: Although African American literature does exist as an independent category in literary studies, many African American writers transcend this classification. Novelists such as Alice Walker and Toni Morrison are part of the mainstream literary culture of America, as are poets such as Maya Angelou, Rita Dove, Sonia Sanchez, and Nikki Giovanni.

- **1960:** African Americans are grossly under-represented in Congress. Only four members of Congress are African Americans. They are all Democrats, and they all represent Northern states. In 1967, Edward William Brooke, III (Republican, MA) becomes the first African American member of the U.S. Senate since the Reconstruction era.

  Today: When the 111th Congress convenes in January 2009, there are forty-one African American members of the House of Representatives, all members of the Democratic Party. One member of the U.S. Senate is African American.

by National Guard troops acting on an order from Arkansas governor Orval Faubus. President Dwight Eisenhower sent federal troops to Little Rock to ensure that the students were allowed to attend the school. Brooks's poem "The Chicago *Defender* Sends a Man to Little Rock," also published in *The Bean Eaters*, is a reference to this incident. It describes the conflicting feelings of a reporter from a Chicago newspaper who has been sent to Little Rock to report on the furor. Surprisingly, although he is aware of the riots and the hatred directed at black people, he discovers that people in Little Rock are for the most part just like people everywhere, and he loses the hatred he had formerly felt for them.

The civil rights movement continued to gather strength as the decade ended. In 1960, in another incident that would become famous, four black college students in Greensboro, North Carolina, began sit-ins at the lunch counter of a restaurant that refused to serve blacks. The number of demonstrators quickly grew, and four days later, three hundred people turned up to protest restaurant policy. The protest drew huge publicity and soon spread to other parts of the South. Protests such as these fueled the civil rights movement, laying the groundwork for the achievements of the 1960s, including the Civil Rights Act of 1964, which outlawed racial segregation in schools, employment, and public places, and the Voting

Rights Act of 1965, which outlawed discriminatory voting practices.

African American Poetry, 1940–1960

Brooks belongs to a generation of poets sometimes referred to as the "middle generation." Mostly born around the time of World War I, they were too young to participate in the Harlem Renaissance of the 1920s but came to maturity in the 1940s before the next renaissance of African American literature, the black arts movement, began in the 1960s. "Middle generation" poets include Melvin B. Tolson, Robert Hayden, Margaret Walker, Margaret Esse Danner, and Dudley Randall. Tolson's work is known for its stand against social injustice from a Marxist and Christian point of view. His first published book was *Rendezvous with America* (1944). He was named poet laureate of Liberia in 1947 and published a long ode, *Libretto for the Republic of Liberia*, celebrating that nation, in 1953. Hayden's poems are notable for his exploration of African American history. He published his first collection, *Heart-Shape in the Dust* in 1940, followed by *Figure of Time: Poems* in 1955. Walker's *For My People* (1942) won the Yale Series of Younger Poets Award. At the age of twenty-seven, Walker was the first black woman to receive a prestigious national poetry award. Danner's background is very similar to that of Brooks. Two years older than Brooks, Danner also came from Chicago and graduated from Englewood High School. Danner won an award at the Midwestern Writers Conference at Northwestern University in 1945, which was the same conference where Brooks won four awards. In 1951, the prestigious *Poetry* magazine published "Far From Africa," a series of four poems by Danner. She became known for writing about Africa; and in 1960 her first collection, *Impressions of African Art Forms*, was published by the Contemporary Studies of Miles Poetry Association of Wayne State University in Detroit, Michigan. Randall, a poet and librarian, had to wait until the black arts movement arrived in the 1960s before his poetry found its way into print. Randall founded Broadside Press in 1965, which in the late 1960s became Brooks's publisher. Randall also published *Poem-Counterpoint* (1966), a collection of ten poems by him and Danner. The most well known poem in the collection is Randall's "Ballad of Birmingham," based on an incident in 1963 when a Baptist church in Birmingham, Alabama, was bombed by white supremacists, killing four young black girls. With the exception of Hayden, who stood apart, these poets became

Dark corridor (*Image copyright Fernando Blanco Calzada, 2009. Used under license from Shutterstock.com*)

influential figures in the black arts movement of 1960 to 1970, in which African American poetry became vitally engaged in the struggle for civil rights and embraced a political militancy in keeping with that turbulent decade.

CRITICAL OVERVIEW

Brooks's third collection of poems, *The Bean Eaters*, in which "The Explorer" appears, was in general not as well received as Brooks's two previous collections. Some of the criticism of her work was harsh. Robert Patrick Dana, in *Prairie Schooner*, censures what he calls Brooks's poor use of language, as well as "breakdowns of syntax, strained use of nouns as verbs, and cliché." Some critics objected to the social element in the poems, by which they meant Brooks's treatment of contemporary issues of race, although others saw this as one of the best aspects of her poetry. Reviewing all three of Brooks's collections in the *Nation* (1962; published in *On Gwendolyn Brooks: Reliant Contemplation*, 1996), Harvey Curtis

Webster declares *The Bean Eaters* to be the best of her volumes and stated of her work as a whole that "her bitter and sympathetic poems make the Negro a problem in the heart of every American." Webster concludes that "compared not to other Negro poets or other women poets, but to the best of modern poets, she ranks high."

"The Explorer" was little mentioned in reviews; critics preferred to comment on the political poems in which racial themes are explored through flesh-and-blood characters and situations, rather than the somewhat abstract nature of "The Explorer." Omitted from Brooks's *Selected Poems* three years later and rarely reprinted, "The Explorer" might be considered one of Brooks's neglected poems. However, later critics have given some attention to the poem.

In *Gwendolyn Brooks: Poetry & the Heroic Voice*, D. H. Melhem comments, "Irregularly rhymed and metered, its tone recalls [T. S.] Eliot." In the quest to find a moment of stillness in a noisy world, Melhem finds echoes of Eliot's poem "Burnt Norton," and also of William Wordsworth's sonnet "The World Is Too Much with Us." Overall, however, Melhem does not assess the poem highly, concluding, "Considering the volume's dynamic political character, this piece inadequately serves as introduction." Harry B. Shaw, in *Gwendolyn Brooks*, views "The Explorer" in terms of the metaphor of the labyrinth, which is "characterized by myriad pitfalls, dead ends, endless wrong choices, and other hazards" that present themselves to black people as they attempt to negotiate their way through white-dominated society, always seeking what Brooks elsewhere calls a "way back home." Shaw continues, "The effort to run the maze is interrupted only by the quest for rest which becomes part of the labyrinth itself." In *A Life of Gwendolyn Brooks*, George E. Kent notes, "The powerful expressionistic imagery marks the inner human condition," and he connects the poem as an introduction to the poems that follow: "It is difficult not to feel the poem's tremendous weight within the book, which presents several scenarios that bear out the explorer's discoveries. It is also difficult not to read 'The Explorer' as a symbol of the discoveries of the poet."

CRITICISM

Bryan Aubrey

Aubrey holds a Ph.D. in English. In this essay he interprets "The Explorer" in terms of the civil rights movement of the 1950s and 1960s.

> 'THE EXPLORER' EMPHASIZES NOISE, THE DISCORDANT DIN THAT IS LIFE, REFLECTING THE TURBULENT EXPERIENCE OF AFRICAN AMERICANS DURING THE 1950S AND 1960S AND THEIR CALL TO ORGANIZE AND PROTEST AGAINST LONG-STANDING INJUSTICE."

Simply in terms of the words on the page, there is nothing in "The Explorer" to suggest that it might be interpreted in terms of race or historical events. However, poems also take their meaning from the contexts in which they appear. Brooks was an African American poet, and when this poem was first published in 1959 in *Harper's* magazine, the civil rights movement was shaking the American political and social landscape. The poem was reprinted as the first poem in Brooks's *The Bean Eaters*, in which a number of the poems refer to events important in the civil rights movement. It therefore seems reasonable to suppose that the "he" in the poem might well refer collectively to African Americans at a particular point in U.S. history. In his book, *Gwendolyn Brooks*, Harry B. Shaw takes exactly this view. He interprets the poem as depicting what he calls the "labyrinth," which represents "an elaborate system that has evolved in the United States which makes black people's movement in the direction of dignity and freedom overwhelmingly perilous and bewildering." Shaw also notes that Brooks's poetry is full of images such as "apartment buildings, halls, doors, rooms, streets, alleys, paths, stairways, and many others that represent the mad wandering in the black ghetto."

This is indeed a useful way of approaching "The Explorer," which is one of Brooks's poems featuring halls, rooms, and a man wandering, confused, through them. However, the poem might be read in a more positive light than Shaw suggests. One may suppose that "The Explorer" depicts a typical African American man and his experience at this critical juncture—the late 1950s—in his own life and that of his fellow African Americans. Perhaps Brooks had

WHAT
DO I READ
NEXT?

- *The Essential Gwendolyn Brooks* (2005), edited by Elizabeth Alexander, is the most representative selection of the range of Brooks's work. It contains poems from nearly all her books, from *A Street in Bronzeville* (1945) to *Children Coming Home* (1991), and the posthumously published *In Montgomery and Other Poems* (2003). The selections clearly show her development as a poet.

- *Shake Loose My Skin: New and Selected Poems* (2005), by Sonia Sanchez, is an excellent selection from six of Sanchez's previous books, as well as several new poems. The work contains much evidence for why Sanchez is considered one of America's finest contemporary poets. Sanchez was one of the leading voices in the black arts movement, and her work is notable for its ability to capture the rhythms and language of black speech.

- *Gwendolyn Brooks: Poet from Chicago* (2003), by Martha E. Rhynes, is a biography of the poet for young readers. Rhynes describes Brooks's life and work in the context of black history and culture, and she shows how the poet's views changed as a result of her encounter with the black arts movement in 1967. The book includes photographs, a time line, and a bibliography.

- *The Oxford Anthology of African-American Poetry* (2005), edited by Arnold Rampersad and Hilary Herbold, is a wide-ranging anthology organized by theme rather than author. Well-known poets such as Brooks,

Langston Hughes, Rita Dove, Maya Angelou, Sonia Sanchez, and Amiri Baraka are well represented, but many less familiar voices are included as well. The collection includes dozens of themes and topics, from the American South to Africa, from civil rights and protest to issues of family and faith.

- Langston Hughes was the leading poet of the Harlem Renaissance and a great influence on Brooks and many other poets. Hughes also wrote for children and young adults; his work for younger readers is available in *Works for Children and Young Adults: Poetry, Fiction, and Other Writing* (2003), Volume 11 of *The Collected Works of Langston Hughes*. This volume, edited by Dianne Johnson, contains short stories and poetry, many of which are delightful and appealing to all ages.

- *Eyes on the Prize: America's Civil Rights Years, 1954–1965* (1988), by Juan Williams, is based on the Public Broadcasting Service television series of the same name, but it stands alone as one of the best, most readable accounts of the civil rights movement. Williams begins with the *Brown v. Board of Education* Supreme Court ruling in 1954 and ends with the passage of the Voting Rights Act of 1965. The book includes many photographs and interviews with participants in the civil rights movement.

- The alternate theme of exploration in the poem can be more extensively studied from a multicultural perspective in Bobbi Katz's *Trailblazers: Poems of Exploration* (2007).

---

her own neighborhood in mind, the historically black area in Chicago's South Side called Bronzeville. Even so, the exact location does not matter, since none is depicted. Indeed, the poem gains from its lack of a specific geographic area, since it can more readily be seen in terms of a symbolic, archetypal situation relevant to an entire people.

The man in the poem looks out at the world from historically deprived eyes. He and his people, all fellow African Americans, have been oppressed since the beginning of the republic, originally as slaves but still bound and unfree now, in the 1950s, in spite of the fact that the Emancipation Proclamation (declaring the freedom of all slaves) had been issued almost a hundred years before. And yet the pressure for radical change is building, and this man is feeling it; he cannot escape it. As Brooks said about the civil rights movement in an interview with Paul Angle in 1967 (published in *Conversations with Gwendolyn Brooks*, 2003), "it was bound to *evolve* sooner or later...there was bound to be an accelerated press for civil rights. I am surprised it did not happen before it did. The impatient seeds, of course, were always about." Here in "The Explorer," then, is one of those "impatient seeds," a man on the threshold of...of what? It is as if this representative man sees prophetically what is in store for his people, a great struggle, with noble and just goals but also presenting great danger. Understandably, he wants to shrink from the task but also knows that he cannot. He has to make the hard choice, to ignore the illusory lure of a quiet life, to emerge from his private comfort zone and engage with the larger social issues of his time that vitally concern him and his people. He is called to be, exactly as the title of the poem states, an explorer, a man who journeys into unknown territory to help achieve justice. Is it any wonder that he should want to draw back, find a quiet place somewhere, and not face this difficult fight?

"The Explorer" emphasizes noise, the discordant din that is life, reflecting the turbulent experience of African Americans during the 1950s and 1960s and their call to organize and protest against long-standing injustice. The civil rights movement was characterized by marches and demonstrations, which are not quiet events, especially when they take place in a hostile environment, as anyone who has ever participated in one will know. Even so, thousands of black people made a choice to participate in them. As the poem states, life is all about choices, and many people, impelled by the pressure of the time and their own moral convictions, chose to become involved. In the poem, choices are what the man fears. He knows what may await him. The choice to become an activist in those dangerous, prejudice-filled days was a brave one. In many cases, it put a person's life in danger, and a number of people paid a high price for their involvement in the civil rights movement. Medgar Evers, a black World War II veteran from Jackson, Mississippi, was a civil rights leader who in June 1963 was shot to death in his own driveway by a white supremacist. He was thirty-seven years old when he died. (Brooks later wrote a poem about him.) Black demonstrators in Birmingham, Alabama, in May 1963, were first drenched with fire hoses and then

placed at the mercy of police dogs. As Taylor Branch writes in *Parting the Waters: America in the King Years, 1954–1963*: "Where the crowd was too tightly massed to flee cleanly, the growling German shepherds lunged toward stumbling, cowering stragglers. They bit three teenagers severely enough to require hospital treatment." There were no quiet places for hundreds of marchers in the vanguard of the planned march from Selma, Alabama, to Montgomery in March 1965, a day that became known as Bloody Sunday. As they crossed the Edmund Pettus Bridge in Selma, they were confronted by state and local police firing tear gas and wielding nightsticks. Between seventy and eighty people were injured, with wounds including broken teeth, gashed heads, and broken wrists and ribs. Activist Dr. Martin Luther King, Jr., faced constant threats on his life yet told his supporters in his "I Have a Dream" speech that they "must rise to the majestic heights of meeting physical force with soul force."

Does the diffident explorer in the poem yet know the meaning of "soul force"? Probably not, because he is still nervous about what he will meet in those rooms that he fears to enter and the consequences of those choices he fears to make. As a legacy of so many years of discrimination, he does not yet know his own power or how to move purposefully forward even in the midst of the pain of life. As those early African American protesters learned, nonviolence takes great self-discipline and courage because it involves facing adversaries who do not share a nonviolent philosophy. The nonviolent protesters of the civil rights movement had to be prepared to subject their own bodies to the possibility of pain and injury in order to uphold a moral cause that they knew in their hearts would eventually prove stronger than any physical force used to stop it. There were no quiet places for King and his followers, nor did they seek them. On the last night of his life, King, pointing to the Parable of the Good Samaritan in the New Testament of the Bible, called for a "dangerous unselfishness" that would allow people to reach out to help those who were suffering from injustice, even if doing so meant exposing themselves to many perils. When King was killed by an assassin's bullet the next day, April 4, 1968, he met the fate that had been waiting for him since he made that bold choice, in 1955, to step to the front and lead the Montgomery bus boycott that ignited the mass civil rights movement. Many were inspired by his example and were transformed from passive victims, fearful, like the man in the poem, of becoming involved in something so fraught with difficulty and danger, into determined activists who learned how to make a difference. King made explorers out of ordinary people—men and women who entered those unquiet rooms described in the poem, who joined the furious argument, the hubbub of voices, and came out victorious. It is the achievement of Brooks's poem, "The Explorer," to make it plain to readers just how much courage these actions must have taken.

Source: Bryan Aubrey, Critical Essay on "The Explorer," in *Poetry for Students*, Gale, Cengage Learning, 2010.

George E. Kent

In the following excerpt, Kent identifies the "small victories" in the poems of The Bean Eaters, *arguing that "The Explorer" anchors the volume.*

In *The Bean Eaters,* Gwendolyn's movement beyond the autobiographical territory seems, at first examination, to create a universe in which significant gestures are rarely possible. Earlier works, of course, had presented numerous instances in which the triumph of human gesture was sustained primarily by illusion, but they carried more than images of futility. On closer examination, there are similar small victories in *The Bean Eaters.* Mrs. Small seems somehow to triumph in the poem of that name, though her role is confined to homemaking and dealing with the pandemonium of children, by her insistence upon carrying out her part of the world's business in defiance of its power to confuse. In "A Lovely Love," the couple seems to defy the lack of social and cosmic symbols for expressing their emotion. Other characters exhaust the moment or make something out of what little is at hand. In the desperate and heroic defense of home and family made by Rudolph Reed, however, it must be admitted that the universe itself seems to have no promise, and the human spirit is sustained only by its will not to fall.

In "The Explorer," the opening poem, the speaker, his hopes disintegrating, seeks not some far-away Eldorado but "A satin peace somewhere. / A room of wily hush somewhere within."

> So tipping down the scrambled halls he set
> Vague hands on throbbing knobs. There were behind
> Only spiraling, high human voices,
> The scream of nervous affairs,
> Wee griefs,
> Grand griefs. And choices.

Of these, the explorer fears most "the choices, that cried to be taken." The "choices,"

> *IT IS DIFFICULT NOT TO FEEL THE POEM'S TREMENDOUS WEIGHT WITHIN THE BOOK, WHICH PRESENTS SEVERAL SCENARIOS THAT BEAR OUT THE EXPLORER'S DISCOVERIES."*

if taken, might lead to the grandly significant, but our overwhelming tendency to seek "satin" peace will prevent that or any other discovery. The powerful expressionistic imagery marks the inner human condition; the rhymes are scattered, sometimes conventional and sometimes the kind of neat-rhymes that signal disharmony. The lines are irregular, well-paced to comport with the nervous uncertainty of the poem's speaker. It is difficult not to feel the poem's tremendous weight within the book, which presents several scenarios that bear out the explorer's discoveries. It is also difficult not to read "The Explorer" as a symbol of the discoveries of the poet.

"The Contemplation of Suicide: The Temptation of Timothy," had been submitted earlier, for inclusion in *Annie Allen.* Although it was thus written much earlier than most of the other poems in *The Bean Eaters,* it underlines the philosophy of "The Explorer," and since it comes late in the book it helps to complete an explicit philosophical framework. In it, one contemplates suicide after having come through confusions ("mazes"), touches of beauty ("robins"), and unfulfilled strivings and attempts to tear away that in existence which blinds (fog), only to observe one's foolish end. Those "downtown" not contemplating suicide are the "sluggish" who are shrugging their shoulders, slinking, talking. But even this awake and questioning observer clings ignominiously to life:

> Then, though one can think of no fact, no path, no ground,
> Some little thing, remarkless and daily, relates
> Its common cliché. One lunges or lags on, prates.—
> Too selfish to be nothing while beams break, surf's epileptic chicken reeks or squalls.

The clinging would seem to be not quite ignominious but based on Maud Martha's suggestion that somehow the fact of life itself is good, though one surrounded with considerable disappointment. One thus keeps going in a universe that readily surrounds one with terror.

Yet if go back to the explicit findings of Maud Martha, a work admittedly heavily infused with autobiography, we find a universe that rarely provides "tragedy." "The truth was," Maud Martha says in the chapter "on Thirty-fourth Street," "if you got a good Tragedy out of a lifetime, one good, ripping tragedy, thorough, unridiculous, bottom-scraping, *not* the issue of human stupidity, you were doing, she thought, very well, you were doing well." One was more likely to be caught up in a comedy and to find oneself either laughable or ridiculous. Yet the universe seemed also basically strange, its strangeness compounded by human stupidity and other unlovely human qualities, a fact which made the act of laughter necessary as a bulwark against insanity. One also needed something to lean upon which was constantly available, but human things were inconstant, and the behavior of the Creator seemed not to be useful to one in this life. In "Tim" we read: "Maud Martha saw people, after having all but knocked themselves out below, climbing up the golden, golden stairs, to a throne where sat Jesus, or the Almighty God; who promptly opened a Book, similar to the arithmetic book she had had in grammar school, turned to the back, and pointed out—the Answers! And the people, poor little things, nodding and cackling among themselves—So that was it all the time! that is what I should have done!' 'But—so simple! so *easy!* I should just have turned here! instead of there!' How wonderful! Was it true? Were people to get the Answers in the sky? Were people really going to understand It better by and by! When it was too late?"

Maud Martha and Annie Allen also counted upon extracting from moments what was at hand. Paradoxically, it is all the more necessary, in the face of the social and metaphysical discouragements afforded by this universe, to confront existence with the resilience of spirit—to retain, as Annie Allen's parents did not, the light that "bites and terrifies." The poem "the parents—" seems to suggest that there is an outside chance of retaining in one's life the qualities of swans and swallows, or that the struggle to retain such qualities is itself worthwhile.

The Bean Eaters seems to endorse the adventurous life as the rewarding one, regardless. "Naomi," without assuming that tangible rewards are inevitable, emphasizes this theme.

Naomi herself is too vigorously searching out the density of existence to make a blueprint for her brother or to warn her "dull mother" that life is richer than her domesticity evidences, or to urge her "small father" not to become static among his small commercial treasures. She could not etch out what she hoped to get from her "hunt" or state what it was not. Hope existed only if one diligently cared to find out what life was for. "For certainly what it was not for was forbearing."

A recognition of the possibilities of the human spirit in this somewhat ambiguous universe, as seen in the foregoing poems, enables us to see both human errors in approaching it and the complexity with which Gwendolyn imaged the situation. In "My Little 'Bout-town Gal," a rather slight poem, the human spirit defeats itself by cultivating its own corruptness. "Strong Men, Riding Horses" is more challenging. In it Lester uses the illusion cast by a "Western" movie to measure his own smallness. Ironically, the example of courage afforded by the movie is so simply drawn that it offers nothing to the complexity of Lester's situation in the city, where he must deal with "illegible landlords" and robbers and must pay rent for the small space he is allowed to claim for his intimate needs. The images of the movie run an allegory before him: Strong men in vast spaces, always ready to confront Rough Man, as the Challenger, an image giving full scope to physical manliness and the natural entitlement to space. Lester cannot make the Walter Mitty escapist identification with a fictitious model and cringes in self-recognition.

> I am not like that, I pay rent, am addled
> By illegible landlords, run, if robbers call.
> What mannerisms I present, employ,
> Are camouflage, and what my mouths remark
> To word-wall off that broadness of the dark
> Is pitiful.
> I am not brave at all.

"The Bean Eaters," "Old Mary," and "A Sunset of the City," are representative of those whom time has reduced by its erosions. The title poem, "The Bean Eaters," has its source in Gwendolyn's familiarity with the life and environment of a poor, elderly aunt and uncle who "could make a pound of beans go further than a pound of potatoes." The title itself was inspired by Van Gogh's "The Potato Eaters." The old couple of "The Bean Eaters," though merely good people who have had their day and exist now as time-markers, have still their memories of both pleasures and defeats ("Remembering, with twinklings and twinges"). Presumably, Old Mary, who now can think of experiences she will not have without being pained, has nonetheless had enjoyable ones. In "A Sunset of the City," Kathleen Eileen seems to be a complete loser whose former lovers, husband, and children afford no rich memories. She is pictured thinking of suicide. The poem is one of those somewhat marred by lines and postures too reminiscent of T. S. Eliot:

> I am cold in this cold house this house
> Whose washed echoes are tremulous down
>   lost halls.
> I am a woman, and dusty, standing among
>   new affairs.
> I am a woman who hurries through her
>   prayers.

The Eliot echoes occur also in poems dealing with sterility, such as "A Man of the Middle Class," "The Chicago *Defender* Sends a Man to Little Rock," and, less importantly, "The Lovers of the Poor." But such poems also represent the terror of the universe compounded by human deficiencies. The lighter poems, "The Crazy Woman" and "Pete at the Zoo," represent what seems to be a terror simply endemic to the universe. The crazy woman will sing terribly in November, a month foreshadowing death, instead of in May. Pete wonders simply whether the deserted elephant at the zoo experiences loneliness in the same way he does.

Other poems, as earlier suggested, represent the dangers of the universe compounded with individual error and social stupidity. In "We Real Cool," the naive confrontations of youth with the ills of life will lead to their doom, and the situation is presented with pathos by the suggestions of self-doubt and baffled pride in the youths' halting and emphatic boasts. The reader will also see a social basis for the youths' situation, although Gwendolyn confines herself to their statements of their intentions.

Among poems reflecting the stupidity of man's social arrangements, the least effective are "A Bronzeville Mother Loiters in Mississippi. Meanwhile, a Mississippi Mother Burns Bacon" and "The Chicago *Defender* Sends a Man to Little Rock." Elizabeth had felt that Gwendolyn stopped being an artist when a white character showed up in her literary creations and that when Gwendolyn could laugh at and pity whites in the way she could laugh at and pity blacks, she "would command the show." It is clear, of course, that in actual life Gwendolyn did and does sympathize with all

humanity, but in "Bronzeville Mother ... Mississippi Mother" she seems determined to present the reader with unmistakable evidence of this. The poem is obviously inspired by the lynching of Emmett "Bobo" Till, a fourteen-year-old Chicago black boy who was brutally killed and dumped into a Mississippi river because he allegedly made "advances" to a young white woman in a Mississippi crossroads store during the summer of 1955. The local Mississippi courts tried and, with some dispatch, acquitted the husband and his massive friend of the deed.

Gwendolyn thought of the situation in terms of the common denominator Mother. How, on both sides, would a mother feel in such a situation? The young white woman of the poem is seen through the concept of motherhood and the chilvaric tradition of the ballad—the framework through which she herself looks at the crime. She is the "maid mild / Of the ballad" who must be worth the killing performed in her behalf by the Fine Prince. After a feeling of temporary exaltation at seeing herself in this storybook role, it occurs to her that the Dark Villain really lacked the matured evil to validate the ritual: the fun was all but destroyed when the villain was not the murderer of many "eaten knights and princesses" but "a blackish child / Of fourteen, with eyes still too young to be dirty, / And a mouth too young to have lost every reminder / Of its infant softness."

There are interesting but very obvious dramatic devices. At breakfast, the husband is concerned with his hands as the instrument of the boy's murder, though he spews contempt for northern newspapers, the northern black mother, and outsiders in general. His proneness to violence overtakes him when the younger baby throws molasses in his brother's face and the Fine Prince learns across the table and slaps him. The hand now becomes the Hand and is seen by the young white wife in association with blood as the husband deals with the children and approaches her for the night's intimacies. "She heard no hoof-beat of the horse and saw no flash of the shining steel." When he kisses her his red mouth also becomes associated with blood. The movement of the poem is thus one in which hard realities break through the universe of romance in which the sensitive woman had heretofore found her worth. Thus a deep hatred for her husband forms within her.

Gwendolyn had certainly operated as creative artist and had boldly entered the consciousness of a white character, a risk rarely taken by William

Faulkner in his portrayal of blacks and one taken, with disastrous consequences, by William Styron in his portrayal of Nat Turner. Unfortunately, Gwendolyn's portrait also seems psychologically false. The pressure of public and historical knowledge of such lynching situations made them rituals through which white southern women of almost any "moral" condition were instantly transformed into Miss Southern White Woman, and the rhythms of southern culture and tradition arose to absorb their "conscience" in the "conscience of the community." Where cultural and historical circumstances press a counter image upon the mind, the artist has more to do to show great strain and struggle before the simple universal woman's heart emerges. It is a matter of charging artistic illusion with sufficient power.

Basically, the same judgment is called for regarding "The Chicago *Defender* Sends a Man to Little Rock," a poem inspired by the very bitter outbreak of violence against young black boys and girls when mobs in Little Rock attempted to prevent desegregation of schools. As in the preceding poem, there are brilliant lines and mastery of the homely detail. The poem contains a kind of truth—but one not sufficiently dramatized against the city's cultural context. Little Rock arrives at the universal by a quick strip-tease of its cultural clothing and by immediate emphasis upon what it shares in common with others. Thus we light upon the universal: "They are like people everywhere."

"The Lovers of the Poor" and "Bronzeville Woman in a Red Hat" hold as tightly to the historical as the two preceding poems do to the universal. They form sharp contrasts and make no bones about offering offenders against decency the powerful satirical purge. The women of "The Lovers of the Poor" represent those who would give without charity and prescribe all the conditions of giving. Gwendolyn represents them as too repelled by the conditions of people in a slum building to be able to offer the gifts they have brought. At the climax of their encounter with humanity, the women recoil.

> Tin can, blocked fire escape and chitterling
> And swaggering seeking youth and the
>   puzzled wreckage
> Of the middle passage, and urine and stale
>   shames
> And, again, the porridges of the underslung
> And children children children. Heavens!
>   That

Was a rat, surely, off there, in the shadows?
    Long
And long-tailed? Gray?

The ladies from the Ladies' Betterment League make a comical exit:

> Keeping their scented bodies in the center
> Of the hall as they walk down the hysterical
>   hall,
> They allow their lovely skirts to graze no
>   wall.
> Are off at what they manage of a canter,
> And, resuming all the clues of what they
>   were,
> Try to avoid inhaling the laden air.

The ladies conceive themselves as having no kinship with the rest of mankind—a pharisaic disease.

In "Bronzeville Woman in a Red Hat," Gwendolyn administers the purge for pretentiousness with still greater forthrightness. Mrs. Miles, a haughty woman, treats domestics as her slaves. Since she offends against both an Irishwoman servant (Patsy Houlihan) and the black woman in the red hat, Gwendolyn sees her as basically an offender against the poor, although she makes it clear that whereas Mrs. Miles considers the Irishwoman in slave terms, she goes a step further with the black woman and considers her no better than an animal. Mrs. Miles is emotionally sterile. Her responses to her child are based upon the studied guides for rearing children, on which she is entirely dependent.

> —This was the way to put it, this the relief.
> This sprayed a honey upon marvelous
>   grime.
> This told it possible to postpone the reef.
> Fashioned a huggable darling out of crime.
> Made monster personable in personal sight
> By cracking mirrors down the personal
>   night.

Thus, like the ladies from the Ladies' Betterment Society, she can love the child only by re-creating for herself its image so that its features are pleasant and undisturbing. Therefore, she loses the affections of her child to the maid, who responds to it spontaneously and offends by caressing the child: "Her creamy child kissed by the black maid! square on the mouth!"

Whereas the lovers of the poor were shown to be ridiculous by being placed in undignified postures, Mrs. Miles is undermined by being described in stylized and set verse, which implies that she is common and easily defined.

> She, quite supposing purity despoiled,
> Committed to sourness, disordered, soiled,
> Went in to pry the ordure from the cream.
> Cooing, "Come." (Come out of the cannibal
>   wilderness,
> Dirt, dark, into the sun and bloomful air.)

Stylized verse is used also to give emphasis to the simple and natural responses of the child: "Conscious of kindness, easy creature bond. / Love had been handy and rapid to respond."

Obviously, such poems reveal the extent to which man compounds the difficulties endemic to his cramped universe. In contrast to the poems that indict the white middle class, in particular, for narrowness, sterility, and racism, "Bessie of Bronzeville Visits Mary and Norman at a Beachhouse in New Buffalo" tells of a black woman who enjoys herself with the white couple she visits.

> And I was hurt by cider in the air.
> And what the lake-wash did was dizzying.
> I thought of England, as I watched you
>   bring
> The speckled pebbles,
> The smooth quartz; I thought of Italy.
> Italy and England come.
> A sea sits up and starts to sing to me.

Gwendolyn had in mind Mary and Norman Springer, a couple involved in liberal politics and academia. They had come to a party she had given for Langston Hughes, and she and Henry had accepted an invitation to visit them and had had a lovely time. Once when Norman had taken Gwendolyn on public transportation to visit his writing group on the North Side of Chicago, other passengers had stared at the apparently interracial couple, making Gwendolyn self-conscious and embarrassed. It was difficult in America to escape the impact of racism, even in the company of a liberal white. . . .

Source: George E. Kent, "Reachings," in *A Life of Gwendolyn Brooks*, University Press of Kentucky, 1990, pp. 117–52.

D. H. Melhem

In the following excerpt, Melhem explores the poems of The Bean Eaters *and contends that, "considering the volume's dynamic, political character,"* "The Explorer" *does not adequately introduce it.*

The title poem, "The Bean Eaters," irregularly metered and rhymed, describes an "old yellow pair" who are "Mostly Good." They continue the

> " CIRCUMSPECT, THE PHILOSOPHICAL POEMS REFLECT METAPHYSICAL AND MORAL CONCERNS OF DAILY LIFE."

routines of their lives, strong in mutual affection and shared memories. Because they are indigent, their conventional lives have neither troubled nor impressed the world. In subdued tone, they echo the endurance of Mrs. Small. Their reward for a "good" life is an old age of poverty, symbolized by the beans they can afford. Their fate implicitly rebukes a youth-obsessed society that neither esteems nor intelligently employs its elderly.

"Old Mary," a cameo portrait of fortitude, declares, "My last defense / Is the present tense." The verb proclaims that her limited present gives her a kind of immortality. Complementing Old Mary's vigor, "The Crazy Woman" chooses to sing in November "a song of gray," recurrent hue of death and decay. Singing her ballad, flaunting conventional censure, she will not submit to an ageist pattern. "Crazy Woman" is capitalized as concept and person. Through her persona, the poet rejoices in a determined spirit that will praise life to the end.

"A Sunset of the City" compassionately depicts an aging woman alone. Emotionally dependent, facing empty later years, suicide enters her thoughts. Her monologue laments that children, husband, lovers, all view her as a relic of the past. "My daughters and sons have put me away with marbles and dolls" suggests the urban erosion of family life. "Indrying" flowers of "summer-gone" illustrates Brooks's compounding technique.

"On the Occasion of the Open-Air Formation / of the Olde Tymers' Walking and Nature Club" observes, with gentle amusement, the attempt of old people to recapture their childhood closeness to nature. Stately iambic pentameter and the title's antiquated spelling wryly comment on the proposed romp in the woods. The poet identifies with the old people ("we merry girls and men"), who may falter.

A lively strand of continuity from earlier volumes explores the romantic terrain. "My Little 'Bout-town Gal" is an amusing ballad in Calypso rhythm about two lovers who cheat on each other. "A Lovely Love," its antithesis, crafts a lyrical Petrarchan/Shakespearean sonnet variation of deep feeling. The birth of love in shabby surroundings is imaged in the Nativity. The lovers must hide in alleys and halls. There is no proper place for them, just as there was no proper place at the inn for Mary and Joseph, who stayed in the barn. The poem begins, "Let it be alleys. Let it be a hall / Whose janitor javelins epithet and thought." The javelin image fits the chronology of reference. An elegant diction and stately meter, together with the Nativity allusions, elevate the action. The last line, "Definitionless in this strict atmosphere," its first word connoting the ineffable mystery, completes the Nativity reference. "Definitionless," also limitless, is literally down or away from the finite, paradoxically restricted by physical location and, pertinently, the confines of the sonnet form. Thus the infinite within the finite is expressed through love.

Turning from sincerity to fatuousness, Brooks chides, "For Clarice It Is Terrible Because with This He Takes Away All the Popular Songs and the Moonlights and Still Night Hushes and the Movies with Star-eyed Girls and Simpering Males." This little editorial on false sentiment and values recalls the mock-heroic approach to Annie Allen's early romanticizing. The poet's impatience also etches "Callie Ford." More intelligent than Clarice and equipped with Annie Allen's defensive irony, Callie imagines both the experience of love and its ending. Her name wryly suggests, among other meanings, the call of natural beauty and the house plant "calla." ("Calla" and "Calliope" derive from the Greek *kallos,* beauty.) "Ford" produces an image of shallow waters, representing Callie's somewhat shallow feelings in the poem.

"Priscilla Assails the Sepulchre of Love," a finely wrought ballad, studies the self-restraint that may "assail" the death of love. "Priscilla," the name of a ruffled curtain, also refers to a prophet associated with Montanus, who claimed inspiration by the Holy Spirit or Paraclete. Later followers, their sect proscribed by Justinian, locked themselves in their churches and set them afire. Priscilla dares not "unlock" her eyes (in Christian symbolism, the windows of the soul), which would reveal her passion. Since her lover wants "no sort of gift outright," an allusion to Robert Frost's "The Gift Outright," where the gift to the country is one's whole life, she defends against rejection by suiting his restricted needs. Negatives, especially mounted in stanza 2, deftly express emotional barriers in the relationship.

Circumspect, the philosophical poems reflect metaphysical and moral concerns of daily life. "The Explorer" follows the dedication. Irregularly rhymed and metered, its tone recalls Eliot. "Somehow to find a still spot in the noise" renews the quest for "the still point of the turning world" in *Burnt Norton* or the Wordsworthian lament that "the world is too much with us." The "spiraling" human voices are those Prufrock fears will drown us. The Explorer "feared most of all the choices." "There were no bourns. / There were no quiet rooms." "Bourns" invokes the "bourne" in Hamlet's soliloquy. Considering the volume's dynamic, political character, this piece inadequately serves as introduction.

"Strong Men, Riding Horses," male companion piece to "For Clarice," looks ahead to the later style of capitalization ("Strong Men," "Rough Man," "Challenger"), epithet ("Desert-eyed")—used here for Romantic irony—and compounding ("To word-wall off"). Again chiding the fictive movie ideal, the poem explores interactions of myth and reality. Although the speaker, like "The Explorer," is fearful, he is more self-aware ("I am not brave at all") and less apologetic. Appraising his life gives him a kind of strength the "Strong Men" cannot achieve.

"The Artists' and Models' Ball," a sestet in a blank verse with some slant rhyme, notes the wonder of the commonplace and its mutability. As a costume ball, its marvels are visible. But daily matters and, by inference, the humans conducting them, are even more extraordinary in their transience. The theme of wonder in everyday existence complements Brooks's concept of the heroic potential in the Bronzeville Everyman. The poem is dedicated to Frank Shepherd, a Chicago photographer who was director of the South Side Community Art Center at the time.

"The Contemplation of Suicide: / The Temptation of Timothy" is the only poem on suicide among Brooks's published works, excepting mention in "A Sunset of the City" and "A Man of the Middle Class." Rejected for the *Annie Allen* volume, where it would have had companion poems about death, here it is unique. Brooks begins at a distance with the indefinite third person, then closes in with first person quotation. The poem quietly inverts the theme from meditation on death to acceptance of life. The name "Timothy" means "honoring God," in Greek. For the poet, honoring God means respecting the life force in daily existence.

Widely varying verse length (increased by justified margins) and irregular rhyme express the mood of the poem. The urgent sweep of the verses allows, in their several rhythms, a fluid restlessness of thought. The long, stress-packed lines expand the conceptual space and time (cf. Milton's *Paradise Lost,* Book II, l. 621). Alliteration and assonance propel the imagery. Beginning, "One poises, poses, at track, or range, or river," the poem finds Timothy examining his life and deeming it worthless; he has come to a "foppish end." The first stanza presents his despair; the second begins "Then," as if following a hypothetical "if," and concludes with life as a given, a natural value that "relates / Its common cliché." The chicken ("chicken reeks or squalls") recurs as the image of innocent sacrifice.

"The Egg Boiler," a Shakespearean sonnet, ironically glorifies the aesthetics of utility, "the mudane," as described in Brooks's comments on the poem (*RPO,* 186). The man presents a narrowly utilitarian view of life and art. "Being you, you cut your poetry from wood. / The boiling of an egg is heavy art." The poem begins ingenuously and contrasts the other poets ("We fools") who cut their poetry from air. The latter recall Yeats who, when asked how he had written his poetry, replied that he had made it "out of a mouthful of air." Air signifies a "weightlessness" or lightness so heavy with meaning (as opposed to the "heavy art" of egg boiling) that it sometimes is "much to bear."

Yet there is respect for the matter of existence. The egg carries a potential for life, and so pertains both to the making of art and to its content. Wood has a potential to boil the egg, as well as a sturdiness and a utility that can also relate to the making of a poem. It is the conventional, ethereal "poetic" images, "Night color, wind soprano and such stuff," however, that Brooks wafts here through the deprecating sensibility of the subject. "You watch us, eat your egg, and laugh aloud," she concludes. The egg, instead of hatching ideas and life, is consumed. The Egg Boiler has transformed latent life, and therefore art, into an object useful to himself. For him the creative act is primarily self-nourishing. In "We fools" we again encounter Brooks's ironic extravagance. The Egg Boiler, as prototype, marks the obverse of "the young Dante" in Pound's "The Study in Aesthetics," who admires, for its own sake, the beauty of sardines being packed for market.

The three poems on children represent diverse strands in the poet's development. "Pete at the Zoo," a ballad, mirrors Brooks's deep sensitivity to children, their needs for security, imagination, and freedom, and their ability to identify with other creatures. "Naomi" shows the adolescent impatience with unimaginative grownups that nagged Annie Allen's childhood. She would seek the meaning of life outside the material setting of her conventional existence. Naomi, in Hebrew, means "my sweetness," and implies here a search for the speaker's own self or "sweetness." The biblical Naomi (from the Book of Ruth) was the mother-in-law whom Ruth would not abandon. In the poem, Naomi's alienation promotes her developing selfhood.

One of the most interesting pieces technically is probably the most widely known of Brooks's works: "We Real Cool." Along with "the preacher: ruminates behind the sermon," it was banned in a 1974 West Virginia public school dispute and in Nebraska, allegedly for use of the word "jazz." Erroneously interpreted as a sexual reference, which it has acquired, the word has an obscure etymology, possibly African via French. Brooks's usage pertains to "having fun."

In both the Stavros interview and her notes to the poems (*RPO*) she describes the soft reading of the line-terminal *Wes,* "tiny, wispy, weakly argumentative 'Kilroy-is-here' announcements." The pause at the end of the line, she explains, signifies the reflection upon *"validity,* the self-questioning and uncertainty of the speakers" (155–56, 185). Hearing Brooks read the verses, however, reveals them as breath pauses which incur a syncopation, reinforced by alliteration and epistrophe. This is the peculiar and subtle brilliance of the poem. The subhead "The Pool Players, Seven at the Golden Shovel," implies the jazzy or modish pre-dilections of the protagonists. Seven, a number favored in gambling, connotes the element of chance in their lives, the lack of planning. Gold is the recurrent image of illusion; "the Golden Shovel" is clarified by the last line. The poem's eight lines are these:

> We real cool. We
> Left school. We
> Lurk late. We
> Strike straight. We
> Sing sin. We
> Thin gin. We
> Jazz June. We
> Die soon.

Typographically, Brooks handles the diminished and tentative status of the boys in two ways; by enjambment, which truncates the thought (at "we"), and by linear brevity, the narrow field of vision and short breath required by the lines. The capitalized *Wes* are also balanced by the capitalization at line initial. The eye is trapped between the capitals just as the pool players are trapped in their lives. Pairing of the short lines, in addition to the paired stresses, rhymes, and *Wes,* conveys both the closeness and the narrowness of the group. The eye hops down from couplet to couplet without going far left or right horizontally. The hopping itself suggests the pronounced rhythm in the poem's diction. Verbal as well as phonic repetition at the end of each line impedes any sense of continuity or development in the teenagers' lives. The only line that does not end in "We" is the last line, referring to death. While the poem abounds in rhyme, internal and terminal, the *Wes* rhyme only with each other, just as the adolescents relate only among themselves. The trail of *Wes* faintly suggests the nursery rhyme "This little piggy went to market." The fourth piggy, one remembers, had no roast beef, and the fifth cried "Wee, wee, wee, wee, wee" all the way home.

Indeed, these are children who have no roast beef or much of anything else except their peer-group sense of stylish behavior. The coolness of the players is the crux of their personalities, the key to their lives and to the poem. Despite presentation, in the voice of the gang, this is a maternal poem, gently scolding yet deeply sorrowing for the hopelessness of the boys. While "Old Mary" vigorously defends herself by immersion in the vital present, the pool players defend themselves against defeat, despair, and indifference by rejecting social norms. Their "coolness" of alienation responds by dropping out, drinking, debauching, dying. It is this wasteful aggression against the self, this fragile wall of bravado that the poet mourns.

The three remaining poems are slight in relation to Brooks's other works, but they serve to widen her lens. One subject, fame, is new; faith, prominent in *A Street in Bronzeville* and *Annie Allen,* is restricted to one poem here although religion, subordinate to politics, appears elsewhere in the volume; nature, never a strong interest, is attended in one poem and noted in "The Olde Tymers." Fame, a part of the poet's life for years, filters through a social consciousness. Faith in God recedes as Brooks turns to the individual's faith in self, her people's selfhood merging into racial pride. Concern with nature, often minimal for an urban poet whose landscapes are human, is complicated by the black

experience in the United States. In 1969, acknowledging the controversy among black poets over the propriety of nature as a subject, Brooks observed that all subjects merited poetic attention. However, "A black poet may be involved in a concern for trees, if only because when he looks at one he thinks of how his ancestors have been lynched thereon" (*RPO,* 166). Such equivocal reference shapes the black experience into a naturally complex vision, a synthesis of opposites and contrasts. Blacks pay a terrible price for this enrichment, this ground of serious literature.

The title, "Kid Bruin" and the subhead, "Arranges Another Title Defense," announce the subject as a young black (or "brown," in Danish; also a bear) pugilist, embattled like his people. He must use the weapons literally at hand, his fists (bare) as compared with the dapper "Bronzeville Man with a Belt in the Back." The first lines, "I rode into the golden yell / Of the hollow land of fame," with their faintly equestrian image, summon a major figure in Brooks: the gallant, romantic hero (or mock hero, like the "paladin" of "The Anniad") and his role as fighter in the struggle of everyday life. (See also "Riders to the Blood-red Wrath," chapter 6.) The trial is social as well as economic and political. The poem criticizes indirectly the society that offers a poor man this brutal, destructive channel for success ("Bruin" aurally yokes "brutal" and "ruin"). The youth pursues the rainbow into the "hollow land," morally empty, like fame itself, and presumably populated by hollow men, more deceitful than Eliotic. Conversely, the rainbow is a biblical symbol of hope ("God gave Noah the rainbow sign," in the words of the Negro spiritual). In the hollow land, it is supposedly unknown, evanescent, possibly mythical. Integration, anticipated like colors coexisting in the rainbow (before Jesse Jackson's "Rainbow Coalition"), proves chimerical as the permanence of fame.

Gold as illusion attaches to the rainbow, conventionally imagined with a pot of gold at the end. Gold also appears as a pejorative symbol in Hughes. (His poem "Revolution," for example, exhorts the "Mob" to "split his golden throat," referring to the enslaving white capitalist "of iron and steel and gold" [*GMR,* 6].) The ballad form reinforces the sense of a mythic fold figure. Kid Bruin's lament holds special meaning for common people who similarly aspire and who, usually on lesser levels, are also disappointed.

"Jack" represents a significant reduction of concern with religious belief per se in Brook's poetry, as her religious motives become increasingly politicized. The skepticism of earlier volumes was an engaged skepticism, a wrestling with conscience about something that deeply mattered. Here attention shrinks to a man who "is not a spendthrift of faith." His belief—divine or humanistic—is lean, contingent, pragmatic. "He spends a wariness of faith." Like a cautious investor, Jack will commit himself only to the degree of profitable return. Minimal expectations that insure him against disappointments also contract feelings and spirit into his "skinny eye" and "store" of belief. The name "Jack" denotes of the common people, Everyman; it also denotes the game of jacks, where a number of objects are picked up from a progressively diminishing store; it is a coarse, cheap, medieval garment worn for defense; and, in the vernacular, it can mean money. All of these meaning apply.

"Bessie of Bronzeville Visits Mary and Norman at a Beach-house in New Buffalo" is the only poem in the volume that celebrates nature for its own sake. Its additional interest lies in oblique class confrontation and the psychic metamorphosis of Bessie, for whom the lake changes into a sea. She romanticizes in the style of "Big Bessie" and Annie Allen. Despite skillful formal structure (mainly iambic pentameter), the direction toward irony seems uncertain.

The *Bean Eaters* marks Brooks's ascent to the foothills of her grand heroic style. From the new level, we see the power of skill and commitment combining with her narrative gift. We note the inclusion of more types of characters, white as well as black; the use of satire along with irony; and projection into white consciousness. We observe the precision that extends to titles, the increasing freedom of linear length, the adaptations of conventional form, and the artistry of joining random, slant, internal, and full rhyme. While romantic love crumples with a wry, post-Annie Allen disenchantment, passion centers on ethics, politics, and politicized religion. The topical poem surges dominant, sounding the righteous thunder of the Civil Rights Movement.

Source: D. H. Melhem, "Chapter 6: *The Bean Eaters*," in *Gwendolyn Brooks: Poetry and the Heroic Voice*, University Press of Kentucky, 1987, pp. 100–31.

SOURCES

Angle, Paul, "An Interview with Gwendolyn Brooks," in *Conversations with Gwendolyn Brooks*, edited by Gloria Wade Gayles, University Press of Mississippi, 2003, p. 17.

Black Americans in Congress, http://baic.house.gov (accessed April 6, 2009).

Branch, Taylor, *Parting the Waters: America in the King Years, 1954–1963*, Simon and Schuster, 1988, p. 760.

Brooks, Gwendolyn, "The Explorer," in *The Bean Eaters*, Harper & Brothers, 1960, p. 13.

———, *Report from Part One*, Broadside Press, 1971, p. 85.

Dana, Robert Patrick, "Double Martini and Broken Crankshaft," in *Prairie Schooner*, Vol. 35, No. 4, Winter 1961–62, p. 362.

Garrow, David J., *Bearing the Cross: Martin Luther King, Jr., and the Southern Christian Leadership Conference*, Vintage Books, 1988.

Hill, Christine M., *Gwendolyn Brooks: "Poetry Is Life Distilled,"* Enslow, 2005.

Jones, Stephanie J., ed., *The State of Black America 2009: Message to the President*, National Urban League, 2009.

Kent, George E., *A Life of Gwendolyn Brooks*, University Press of Kentucky, 1990, p. 137.

King, Martin Luther, Jr., "I Have a Dream," in *U.S. Constitution Online*, http://www.usconstitution.net/dream.html (accessed April 9, 2009).

———, "I've Been to the Mountaintop," in *American Federation of State, County and Municipal Employees*, http://afscme.org/about/1549.cfm (accessed April 9, 2009).

Melhem, D. H., *Gwendolyn Brooks: Poetry & the Heroic Voice*, University Press of Kentucky, 1987, p. 125.

Miller, R. Baxter, ed., *Black American Poets Between Worlds, 1940–1960*, University of Tennessee Press, 1988.

Prince, Zenitha, "Black America 2009—Unchanged and Slightly Worse," in *BlackPressUSA.com*, http://www.blackpressusa.com/News/Article.asp?SID=3&Title=Hot+Stories&NewsID=18338 (accessed April 6, 2009).

Samuel, Manohar, "Deferred Dreams: The Voice of African American Women's Poetry Since the 1970s," in *American Studies Today Online*, http://www.americansc.org.uk/online/samuel.htm (accessed April 6, 2009).

Shaw, Harry B., *Gwendolyn Brooks*, Twayne's United States Authors Series, No. 395, Twayne Publishers, 1980, pp. 94, 111.

Webster, Harvey Curtis, "Pity the Giants," in *On Gwendolyn Brooks: Reliant Contemplation*, edited by Stephen Caldwell Wright, University of Michigan Press, 1996, pp. 19, 22; originally published in *Nation*, September 1, 1962.

FURTHER READING

Baldwin, James, *Collected Essays*, Library of America, 1998.
   Many of the essays in this volume by African American writer Baldwin were written in the 1950s and 1960s. Baldwin was one of the leading writers from whom white America learned what black Americans were thinking and feeling about

racial issues. Baldwin rejected the separatism of the Black Muslims and favored an integrationist approach to race relations based on an ethic of love.

Bryant, Jacqueline, ed., *Gwendolyn Brooks and Working Writers*, Third World Press, 2007.

Seventeen contributors, including writers, educators, and friends of the poet discuss the extent to which their own work was influenced by Brooks's poetry, and they reveal their respect and affection for her as a person. The book also contains some of Brooks's most well-known poems.

Mootry, Maria, K., and Gary Smith, eds., *A Life Distilled: Gwendolyn Brooks, Her Poetry and Fiction*, University of Illinois Press, 1987.

This collection of eighteen critical essays examines all aspects of Brooks's work from her early publications up to the mid-1980s. It also includes a biographical chronology and an extensive bibliography.

Stewart, Jeffrey C., *1001 Things Everyone Should Know about African American History*, Main Street Books, 1998.

Stewart is a historian, and this books consists of short, entertaining essays about the most significant people and events in African American history. It is organized in six sections: great migrations; civil rights and politics; science, inventions, and medicine; sports; military; and culture and religion.

Grudnow

LINDA PASTAN

1986

"Grudnow," by American poet Linda Pastan, first appeared in *Poetry* magazine in October 1986; it was reprinted in Pastan's volume of poetry *The Imperfect Paradise* in 1988. The poem can also be found in Pastan's *Carnival Evening: New and Selected Poems: 1968–1998* (1998), and in two anthologies: *American Identities: Contemporary Multicultural Voices* (1996), edited by Robert Pack and Jay Parini, and *Great Writing: A Reader for Writers* (2001), edited by Harvey S. Wiener and Nora Eisenberg. The poem describes an old man through the eyes of his granddaughter. The old man is Jewish, and he immigrated many years ago to the United States from a town called Grudnow (usually spelled Grodno), which was then part of Russia and is now in Belarus. The granddaughter looks back on what she learned about her grandfather, both from his words and by observation of his actions and mannerisms. She imagines what life must have been like in those long-ago days in Grudnow. "Grudnow" is a typical poem by Pastan, a leading contemporary poet. The work is short and well-crafted, and it focuses on a number of important topics, including the history of the Jews, Jewish immigration to the United States, and cultural assimilation.

AUTHOR BIOGRAPHY

Pastan was born May 27, 1932, in the Bronx, New York, to Jacob L. and Bess Olenik. She was raised in a traditional Jewish extended family. As the only

Linda Pastan *(Photograph by Thomas Victor. Reproduced by permission of the Estate of Thomas Victor)*

surviving child of her family, Pastan recalls in her article, "Yesterday's Noise: The Poetry of Childhood Memory" (published in *The Writer's Handbook*, 1993) that her childhood was lonely and she had difficulty making friends. In sixth grade, she writes, none of the other children wanted to play with her. She believes that what she calls her "failure at childhood" had some effect on her poetry. As a child who was often solitary she developed a love of reading and writing, and at the age of twelve she submitted one of her poems to the *New Yorker* magazine.

Pastan attended Radcliffe College in Cambridge, Massachusetts, where she wrote poems, she recalls, mainly about aging and death. She received national attention when, as a senior at Radcliffe, she won a Dylan Thomas Poetry Award from the magazine *Mademoiselle*. After graduation in 1954, she went on to graduate study at Brandeis University and received an M.A. in English in 1957.

In 1953, when she was still in college, Pastan married Ira Pastan, who had just graduated and

who would become a molecular biologist and one of the leading scientific researchers in the United States. Pastan put her career on hold as she raised the couple's three children (two boys and a girl). In an interview with Jeffrey Brown for the Public Broadcasting Service's *Online Newshour* in 2003, Pastan stated that she was a typical young wife of the 1950s. She called it "the perfectly polished floor syndrome. I had to have a homemade dessert on the table for my husband every night." She felt she could not be an excellent wife and mother and commit herself to poetry at the same time, so for nearly ten years she stopped writing. However, she never lost the desire to write, and, as she told Brown, "my husband finally said he was tired of hearing what a good poet I would have been if I hadn't gotten married. Let's do something about it." So at about the age of thirty she began seriously to write poetry again. Her first collection of poetry, *A Perfect Circle of Sun*, was published in 1971, when she was thirty-nine years old.

From that point on, Pastan has written many volumes of poetry. Her books include *The Five Stages of Grief* (1978); *PM/AM: New and Selected Poems* (1982), which was nominated for the National Book Award; *The Imperfect Paradise* (1988), which included the poem "Grudnow" and was a nominee for the *Los Angeles Times* Book Prize; *Heroes in Disguise* (1991); *An Early Afterlife* (1995); *Carnival Evening: New and Selected Poems 1968–1998* (1998), which was nominated for the National Book Award; *The Last Uncle* (2002); and *Queen of a Rainy Country* (2006).

Throughout her career, Pastan has received many awards, including the De Castagnola Award from the Poetry Society of America in 1978 for *The Five Stages of Grief*; the Bess Hokin Prize, 1985; the Maurice English Award, 1986; and the 2003 Ruth Lilly Poetry Prize given for lifetime achievement, which included a cash award of $100,000. From 1991 to 1995, Pastan was the poet laureate of Maryland.

POEM TEXT

When he spoke of where he came from,
my grandfather could have been
clearing his throat
of that name, that town
sometimes Poland, sometimes Russia,   5
the borders pencilled in
with a hand as shaky as his.
He left, I heard him say,
because there was nothing there.

I understood what he meant   10
when I saw the photograph
of his people standing
against a landscape emptied
of crops and trees, scraped raw
by winter. Everything   15
was in sepia, as if the brown earth
had stained the faces,
stained even the air.

I would have died there, I think
in childhood maybe   20
of some fever,
my face pressed for warmth
against a cow with flanks
like those of the great aunts
in the picture. Or later   25
I would have died of history
like the others, who dug

their stubborn heels into that earth,
heels as hard as the heels
of the bread my grandfather tore   30
from the loaf at supper. He always
sipped his tea through a cube of sugar
clenched in his teeth, the way
he sipped his life here, noisily,
through all he remembered   35
that might have been sweet in Grudnow.

MEDIA ADAPTATIONS

- An audio book version of *Mosaic: 35 Poems* features Pastan reading her own work. It was released on audio cassette in 1987 by the Watershed Foundation.

- The Web site *Poets.org*, maintained by the Academy of American Poets, features Pastan reading her poem "The Cossacks." See http://www.poets.org/viewmedia.php/prmMID/16381.

- The Library of Congress Webcast features a twenty-six-minute video of Pastan reading her poems at the National Book Festival, 2004. See http://www.loc.gov/today/cyberlc/feature_wdesc.php?rec = 3622.

POEM SUMMARY

Stanza 1

In "Grudnow," the speaker recalls how her grandfather spoke about the country from which he immigrated to the United States. Line 3 suggests the difficulty of pronouncing the name of the town he speaks of, or at least it is difficult for the speaker who was, presumably, born and raised in the United States. In line 5, the speaker reveals that the town her grandfather spoke of was either in Poland or Russia. It seems that the town was on the border between these countries and was sometimes part of Russia and at other times a part of Poland as borders shifted. Lines 6 and 7 compare the changing identity of the town with the unsteadiness of the old man's hands, an image that suggests his great age. In line 8, the poet reports something her grandfather said about his homeland, that he left it because it offered him nothing. Grudnow was obviously in a very poor region of the country.

Stanza 2

In this stanza the poet reports that she has seen an old photograph of her grandfather with his family and perhaps others in Grudnow. When she saw the photograph she understood more of what her grandfather had told her about the place. The photograph, taken outside, depicted a dismal winter scene. Everything looked barren. Like many very old photos, it was in sepia, a shade of brown, and gave the impression that everything was brown: the faces of the people as well as the landscape.

Stanza 3

Stanza 3 switches the focus of the poem from the speaker's description of her grandfather and the photograph to her own reactions. She thinks that had she lived in Grudnow, she would never have been able to survive such a harsh environment. She would have died of some illness. She thinks of herself clinging to the flank of a cow for warmth, an image suggested to her by the ample hips of the female relatives in the photograph. Had she managed to survive childhood, she speculates that some other thing would have caused her death, something related to the long history of deprivation that seemed to attach itself to the town of Grudnow. She would have been just like others who had lived and died in that inhospitable place.

Stanza 4

This stanza continues the ideas of stanza 3, with the speaker reflecting on the resilience of those who

TOPICS FOR FURTHER STUDY

- An old family photograph forms part of "Grudnow." Find some old photographs from your family album. Write a short free verse poem in which you reflect on your feelings as you look closely at those photographs. What strikes you about them? The old-fashioned clothes? The expressions on the people's faces? The backgrounds? Try to capture in the poem the difference between your life now and what you imagine life to have been like during the time the photographs were taken. Scan your family photographs into a computer and create a PowerPoint presentation incorporating your photos and your poem.

- Talk with a grandparent, or an older person you know, about their lives when they were young. Where did he or she live? What was his or her family life like? How different was his or her life from your own? Give a class presentation in which you describe your discussion. What were the elements of the life of the older person that you found hard to relate to? What were your own feelings as you learned more about how life was during his or her childhood?

- Read "Grandmother," a poem by Valzhyna Mort. Mort is a poet from Belarus, the country in which Grudnow is now located. Write an essay in which you compare this poem to "Grudnow." What themes do the two poems have in common? How do they differ? You can find the poem in Mort's collection, *Factory of Tears* (2008), or online at the Web site maintained by UniVerse: http://www.universe ofpoetry.org/belarus.shtml.

- Consult the young-adult book *Jews in America*, a survey of over three hundred years of Jewish life in America by Hasia R. Diner (Oxford University Press, 1998). Write an essay in which you explain the challenges that would have been faced by a man such as the grandfather depicted in "Grudnow" immigrating to America around 1900. What obstacles would such an immigrant have to overcome, in terms of language, culture, employment, and other vital elements of life?

managed to persevere in Grudnow. Then she turns her thoughts back to her grandfather, picturing him tearing off a piece of bread from the loaf at supper. She also comments on how he used to keep a sugar cube in his mouth as he drank his tea. Then she makes a comparison: there is something about how her grandfather sips his tea that makes her think of how he lived his life in America, tinged with his memories of home, and some of those memories, the speaker speculates, may have been pleasant.

THEMES

The Immigrant Experience

By presenting two characters from the same family, widely separated by years and life experience, the poem suggests the large cultural differences between the Eastern European country from which the speaker's grandfather immigrated and the American life known by the much younger speaker. The grandfather experienced hardship and want. He left his country because he could no longer envision having a life there, the prospects were so bleak. For the speaker, born in America, the land of plenty, it is as if her grandfather had lived on another planet, so remote is his experience from her own.

In presenting this contrast, the poem reflects the typical experience of immigrants who came to the United States at the end of the nineteenth or the beginning of the twentieth century. The grandfather in the poem is Jewish and emigrated from Eastern Europe, but the experience was much the same for countless immigrants who came to the United States. Many had experienced poverty, deprivation, and persecution. They settled in the United States and worked hard to establish themselves. Their children, sometimes born in America, sometimes arriving as very young children, often fared better than their parents, managing to climb higher on the socioeconomic ladder. The immigrants' grandchildren were fully American, American society and culture being the only thing they had known. Their grandparents would tell them tales from the "old country," and the children, like the speaker in the poem, simply could not imagine being able to live under those harsh circumstances.

The Distance between Generations

The poem says nothing directly about the relationship between the speaker and her grandfather, but much is implied. For the speaker, her grandfather is a rather remote figure. She has heard him speak about his homeland, but she does not say that he told her about it directly. It is as if she has overheard him telling someone else, perhaps as a child when she sat at the dinner table. She also says that she saw the photograph of her grandfather's family (or perhaps it was just a group of unrelated Jewish people in Grudnow) but does not specify that it was her grandfather who showed it to her. Because their experience of life is so different, the gap between them is vast. However, the speaker tries to bridge that gap. She observes her grandfather—his manner at supper, for example—and tries to understand him, to get into his mind, by imagining the reservoir of memories he must have from his life in Grudnow.

Reminiscence, Memory, and Imagination

"Grudnow" is a poem about looking back. It does not take place in the present; the speaker is recalling the past. The poem uses the past tense in reference to the grandfather, implying that he is no longer alive. It is a poem of reminiscence in two senses: the speaker is an adult looking back on what her grandfather said and did at earlier times in his life (perhaps including when she was a child), as he himself looked back at his own past and origins. Memory is an important theme because the speaker, in herself remembering, imagines the memories that her grandfather must have had. Although he seems, from the glimpse the speaker gives, to have been something of an austere figure who said little, she has the ability to humanize him by imagining the memories of his homeland that he still possessed, both of loss and pleasure. In doing this, the speaker shows the interaction of fact, memory, and imagination that constitutes the poem. Fact includes the photograph and her

Cup of tea (*Image copyright Marylooo, 2009. Used under license from Shutterstock.com*)

grandfather's origins; memories include her own and those of her grandfather; imagination refers to the ideas and images that the brief facts and reminiscences stimulate in her. These imaginings include her own fate had she lived in Grudnow and her envisioning of the lives of the people there, how they clung to the land, even though it yielded little for them.

STYLE

Imagery

One notable aspect of the imagery (figurative language) of the poem is how it connects the human body to the earth and the remembered landscape. In the first verse, for example, the drawing of the map of Poland and Russia is linked to the shakiness of an old man's hands. In the second stanza the sepia color of the faces in the old photograph is connected to the brown color of the earth. In stanza 3, the flanks of the cows the speaker imagines in Grudnow are linked by a simile (a comparison between two apparently dissimilar things that brings out a connection between them) to legs of the aunts in the photograph. This imagery brings out the theme that the body, with all the memories it contains, is inextricably linked to the earth and the land from which it comes.

Free Verse

The poem is written in free verse rather than in a traditional poetic form. Free verse does not employ traditional poetic elements such as meter and rhyme. For example, this poem uses mainly short, unrhymed lines. However, a sense of order and pattern is created by the fact that each of the four stanzas contains nine lines. The general pattern is for each stanza to consist of two sentences, a longer one followed by a shorter one, although the pattern is varied by the presence of the run-on line that ends the third stanza.

Run-on and End-stopped Lines

In this free-verse poem, the poet uses many run-on lines. A run-on line occurs when the syntax and meaning of the line is not complete in itself but carries over into the following line. The reader is, so to speak, pulled along onto the next line in order to get the meaning. In this poem, the run-on lines occur because most of the lines are short but the sentences themselves are quite long, so the meaning carries over from one line to the next. The most striking example of a run-on line occurs at the end of the third stanza. Whereas the first two stanzas conclude with end-stopped lines (in which the end of the line coincides with the conclusion of a clause or sentence), the third stanza ends in mid-sentence and continues into the first line of the final stanza.

In stanzas 2, 3, and 4, the first sentence ends in the middle of a line, which means that the period acts as a caesura, or pause, within the line. The presence of a caesura in the middle of or at some other position in the line is a way of varying the rhythm in a free-verse poem.

Diction

The poet uses simple diction (word choice) and a conversational rather than formal tone, as if she is just speaking her thoughts naturally. The poem succeeds in part because of very careful word choice on the part of the poet. In stanza 1, for example, when the speaker hears her grandfather pronounce the name of the town he comes from, the unfamiliar, foreign sound reminds her of the old man clearing his throat. The way the speaker hears the sound suggests to her a metaphor: it is as if, in the act of clearing his throat, her grandfather is expelling or getting rid of the painful memory of his hometown. Similarly, the choice of the word *tears* to describe the way the grandfather breaks off a piece of bread suggests urgency, and it brings to mind the possibility that he is unconsciously continuing a habit he might have acquired in childhood, when food was not plentiful and he often went hungry.

Pun

A pun is a play on words created by using two words that sound the same or similar but have different meanings. Pastan uses a pun in stanza 4, with the word *heel*, meaning both the back of the foot and the crusty end of a loaf of bread. The purpose of the pun is to link the image of the imagined world of the grandfather's homeland to the image of eating a meal at the family table.

HISTORICAL CONTEXT

The History of Grudnow (Grodno)

The town that the poem refers to as Grudnow is more commonly known as Grodno, which is also the name of the surrounding region. Grudnow is an old city that dates back to the twelfth century; it has had a substantial Jewish population since the fourteenth century. The city was originally part of the Grand Duchy of Lithuania; it later became associated with Poland due to the sixteenth-century union of Lithuania and Poland. In 1795, following the Third Partition of Poland, the city and region was annexed by Russia, and in 1801, Grudnow became the main city of a Russian province. This explains the reference in the poem to the shifting border between Russia and Poland; sometimes the city was in Poland, sometimes in Russia. According to one estimate, in 1887, the population of the city was 39,826, of which 27,343 (68.7 percent) were Jews. Ten years later, in 1897, with the population increasing to 46,919, the number of Jews dropped to 22,684 (48.3 percent). This indicates the large-scale emigration of Jews that took place during this period. For centuries, the Jews in Grudnow had suffered bouts of persecution. In the early nineteenth century there were several cases of blood libel (accusations that Jews murdered Christian children). Despite this, the Jews for the most part flourished economically. In 1886, Jews owned two-thirds of the real estate in the city, and the majority of business owners and merchants were Jews.

Persecution of the Jews in Russia

In Russia during the late nineteenth century, the Jews were persecuted. This occurred especially during the reign of Tsar Alexander III, who succeeded the assassinated Alexander II in 1881. As explained by C. D. M. Ketelbey in *A History of Modern Times*

COMPARE
&
CONTRAST

- **1900s:** Thousands of Jews from Eastern Europe flee persecution, immigrating mostly to the United States and England. They face discrimination and prejudice but nothing on the scale of the pogroms (organized killing of a minority group) that scar their lives in Eastern Europe.

  1980s: Russian Jews, facing anti-Semitism in the Soviet Union, continue to immigrate to the United States. However, anti-Semitism (discrimination against or hostility toward Jews) exists in the United States, too. The Anti-Defamation League (ADL) reports that during the 1980s, more than 9,500 anti-Semitic incidents take place, including vandalism, arson, bombings, and cemetery desecrations.

  Today: According to a 2005 survey by ADL, 14 percent of Americans hold anti-Semitic beliefs. ADL also reports that in 2004, anti-Semitic incidents reach their highest level since 1995, reporting 1,821 such incidents. The high level of anti-Semitic acts is attributed to increased activity by neo-Nazi groups and increased anti-Semitism in U.S. public schools.

- **1900s:** Grudnow is under Russian rule. In 1904, the Jewish population of Grudnow is 27,874, amounting to 64.1 percent of the total population of the city. The Jewish labor movement is active in the city, especially in the tobacco factory, where working conditions are very poor. Grudnow is also noted for its creation of institutions for the teaching of Hebrew and the training of teachers of Hebrew. However, the Jewish community still faces anti-Semitism, and in 1903 and 1907, the Jews of Grudnow organize for self-defense against persecution.

  1980s: Grudnow (now more commonly spelled "Grodno") is part of the Soviet Union, and its citizens live under a communist system of government. As a result of the Holocaust, there are few Jews left living in Grudnow. During World War II, 44,049 Jews from Grudnow were sent to Nazi concentration camps. This included 20,577 from the city itself and 23,472 from surrounding hamlets (villages). After the war, only 180 Jews remained in Grudnow, although two thousand later resettled there. In the 1960s there was not a single synagogue in Grudnow, and in the 1980s the Great Synagogue of Grudnow remains closed by the Soviet authorities.

  Today: Grudnow is in Belarus, following the dissolution of the Soviet Union in 1991 and the creation of the independent nation of Belarus in the same year. Grudnow has a population of about 350,000, and Grudnow province has a population of about 1,123,000. Of the latter figure, Jews make up only 0.4 percent of the population. The Great Synagogue of Grudnow is reopened and once more controlled by the Jewish population.

- **1900s:** Large-scale Jewish immigration makes the United States home to one of the world's largest population of Jews. In 1900, New York City—where half of the Jewish immigrants live—contains more Jews than any other city in the world.

  1980s: As the second largest Jewish community in the world (after Israel) the American Jewish population is highly influential. However, some Jewish American leaders are concerned that the process of assimilation, which is partly responsible for why many Jews have become very successful in America, will be detrimental to the long-term survival of the Jewish community. For example, statistics show that more Jews marry outside their religion than within it.

  Today: Jews make up 2.2 percent of the population of the United States, less than the percentage in 1930. In 2006, the most concentrated Jewish populations are on the East Coast, in New York (1,618,320, which amounts to 8.4 percent of the total population), New Jersey (480,000, or 5.5 percent), Massachusetts (275,030, or 4.3 percent), and Maryland (235,350, or 4.2 percent).

Old man (*Image copyright Igor Burchenkov, 2009. Used under license from Shutterstock.com*)

from 1789, Alexander III wanted to create an auto-cratic, nationalistic state that adhered to Orthodox Christianity and he initiated a policy of repression against those groups that did not conform to the ideal. The Jews were the group that suffered most. They were forced to live in certain towns and were not permitted to join local governments. They faced limitations on their educational opportunities and property restrictions. They also had to endure attacks by mobs that would invade their homes, and rob, beat, and kill them, while the authorities turned a blind eye. These attacks were called pogroms. The result of the anti-Semitic policies of the Russian government was the creation of impoverished Jewish ghettos in the towns, the growth of Zionism (a movement to create a Jewish state in Palestine and later to support the state of Israel), and widespread emigration.

After Alexander III died in 1894 and was suc-ceeded by Nicholas II, the position of the Jews deteriorated further; attacks on them became more frequent. One of the most notorious pogroms occurred in Kishinev, in the province of Bessarabia, in 1903. It followed the murder of a Christian boy, which was blamed on the Jews. (It was later

established that the boy was killed by a relative.) In carefully planned attacks, mobs roamed the streets attacking Jewish homes and shops and kill-ing any Jews they could find. Max Margolis and Alexander Marx, in *A History of the Jewish People*, describe the massacre in detail:

> The drunken mob invaded the synagogues; the sacred scrolls were torn into shreds, trampled underfoot and defiled. In one sanctuary, the aged beadle, wrapped in his prayer shawl, defended with his body the holy Ark until he was struck down.

The massacre went on for several days. Forty-five Jews were killed and nearly six hundred were injured. Three years later, in 1906, there was another pogrom, this time in Bialystok, which is less than one hundred miles from Grudnow. Bialystok is now in northeast Poland but at the time it was under Russian rule. In three days of mob attacks, from June 1 to June 3, 1906, seventy Jews were killed and ninety were seriously injured.

Russian Jewish Immigration to the United States

As a result of the persecution they faced in Russia, Jews emigrated in large numbers. According to

Ketelbey, between 1880 and 1900, over a million and a half Jews emigrated from Russia. Most went to the United States, settling predominantly in New York City and New Jersey. (This is likely the period that the speaker's grandfather in the poem left Grudnow for the United States.) The rapid influx of Jews into a new country, living in crowded conditions, resulted in changes in Jewish life. As Margolis and Marx explain, "The newcomers adjusted themselves to the strange language and customs—the children quite rapidly, the elders more slowly." The immigrants produced their own large-circulation newspapers, and in some areas continued to speak their own language (mostly Yiddish), but there was also a process of assimilation that created an interesting mix of perspectives: "The native Jews strove to speed the process of . . . 'Americanizing' the foreigner, while the latter brought into the community at large an intenser Jewish atmosphere."

During this period, and continuing into the early twentieth century, there was a struggle in the United States between those who wished to restrict immigration and advocates of a more liberal policy, such as the American Jewish Committee, formed in 1906. Anti-immigration sentiment resulted in a bill requiring a literacy test for immigrants that passed the U.S. House of Representatives and Senate. However, the bill was vetoed by President Howard Taft in 1913, and it was vetoed again by President Woodrow Wilson in 1914. The wave of Jewish immigration to the United States continued until 1924 when the Immigration Act placed restrictions on immigration.

CRITICAL OVERVIEW

Pastan is a highly regarded poet, her work generously assessed by reviewers. However, she has not attracted the attention given by critics to other leading contemporary poets. There is, for example, no book on Pastan's work and few scholarly articles. "Grudnow," however, has attracted the attention of at least one critic. In an overview of Pastan's work in *Contemporary Poets*, Jay S. Paul sees the poem as an example of what he calls "the miracle of renewal" that he observes in a number of Pastan's poems. Referring to the last stanza of the poem, Paul writes that "Pastan depicts her immigrant grandfather as having willed such optimism." Peter Stitt, reviewing Pastan's book *The Five*

Stages of Grief in the *Georgia Review* (1979), makes a comment that could well apply to "Grudnow":

> Pastan is a master of the well-made poem. Her use of technique is so precise, so careful, that it seems she would be a perfect example to use in teaching young poets how to control their material. Her best poems are specimens, admirable for the telling way in which their point is made.

Ellen Kaufman, reviewing *Carnival Evening: New and Selected Poems, 1968–1998* (in which "Grudnow," appears), for *Library Journal*, notes that Pastan "is a poet of small gestures and great vision" with a "steady popular appeal." In the *Dictionary of Literary Biography*, Benjamin Franklin V reaches a similarly positive conclusion about the quality of Pastan's work: "Pastan deserves serious attention for her finely wrought dark comments on the human condition. Not spectacular, she is a solid poet whose work speaks to all of mankind."

CRITICISM

Bryan Aubrey

Aubrey holds a Ph.D. in English. In this essay, he discusses "Grudnow" as a series of word-pictures that evoke the experience of the immigrant grandfather and how his granddaughter tries to comprehend what lies beyond her own experience.

Pastan is noted for the straightforward nature of her poetry. Her poems are generally not too difficult to read or understand, however they express deep thoughts. She is a poet who reflects on her life experience in a sensitive and uncompromising manner. Sometimes her poems give the impression of being almost artless, the words flowing with apparent naturalness and ease, but as far as the craft of the poet is concerned, this impression may be deceptive. Pastan commented in an interview with Jeffrey Brown for the Public Broadcasting Service's *Online Newshour* that "there is no ease in writing. The job is to make it by the end feel as if it flows easily. But each poem of mine goes through something like 100 revisions." Pastan elaborated on her comment, explaining that she wants "every word to have to be there. I want a certain kind of impact on the reader . . . the sort of condensed energy that can then go out."

"Grudnow" is one of Pastan's poems that reads very easily and may seem at first to be slight, but the choice of words and images is so exact, so economical, that the poem achieves the kind of

WHAT DO I READ NEXT?

- In Isaac Bashevis Singer's short story "The Son from America," an old Jewish man and his wife who live in a village in Poland are visited by their son, who immigrated to America forty years before. The son has become wealthy and arrives with big plans to help the village. However, he finds that the villagers, rooted in their traditional Jewish culture, need nothing from him. The story can be found in *The Collected Stories of Isaac Bashevis Singer* (1983).

- In Pastan's most recent book of poems, *Queen of a Rainy Country* (2006), she shows once again how she can make poetry out of everyday incidents, as well as childhood memories. These are well-crafted, deceptively simple poems.

- *New World Waiting* (2006), a novel for young adults by Anne G. Faigen, is set in Pittsburgh, Pennsylvania, in 1900. It tells the story of Molly Klein, a fifteen-year-old Jewish immigrant to the United States who must deal with all the challenges facing her in the "New World." Faigen writes a compelling story of Molly's adventures and her relationships with her family members.

- *Telling and Remembering: A Century of American Jewish Poetry* (1997), edited by Steven J. Rubin, contains over two hundred poems by fifty-six Jewish American authors. Poets represented include Pastan, Stanley Kunitz,

Howard Nemerov, Carl Shapiro, Anthony Hecht, Maxine Kumin, Louis Gluck, Philip Levine, Allen Ginsberg, Adrienne Rich, and Robert Pinsky. Subjects include anti-Semitism, the Holocaust, Israel, and many aspects of Jewish language, culture, and faith.

- "Fish Cheeks," by Chinese American author Amy Tan, is an essay about how at the age of fourteen Tan fell in love with an American boy. However, she had to deal with the cultural differences between them when her mother invited the boy and his family to Christmas Eve dinner. The tale shows the misunderstandings that can arise when people from two different cultures interact, and how immigrants often need to maintain a dual cultural identity. The essay can be found in Tan's *The Opposite of Fate: A Book of Musings* (2003).

- "Theme for English B" is a poem by Langston Hughes, one of the great African American poets and the leading voice of the Harlem Renaissance in the 1920s. In this poem, Hughes reflects on being asked to write a short paper in an English class that will express who he is. He acknowledges that what he writes will be different from what a white student might write, but nonetheless there will be some common elements. The poem can be found in *The Collected Poems of Langston Hughes* (1995).

---

impact to which Pastan refers. That it may have been through one hundred revisions suggests the kind of hard, painstaking work that creating a poem of such quality requires.

When it was first published in Pastan's volume, *The Imperfect Paradise* in 1988, the poem appeared in the first section, which was titled "In the Rearview Mirror," a visual image which suggests looking back through a kind of picture frame at a past that is quickly vanishing. "Grudnow" in a sense, reclaims at least some of the past. Indeed, the

poem might be seen as a series of word-pictures that open up with exactly the kind of "condensed energy" that Pastan mentioned in her interview with Brown. These word-pictures, one of them literally a photograph, transform into rich evocations of the experience of the immigrant grandfather and how that long-ago life appears to his granddaughter as she struggles to comprehend something that lies so far beyond her own experience.

Writing a poem about a grandparent is a risky enterprise for any poet, who must avoid the danger

> **THE MAN PRONOUNCES THE NAME OF THE TOWN AS ONLY HE CAN; IT IS PROBABLY A GUTTURAL SOUND FROM THE BACK OF HIS THROAT. ALTHOUGH ONLY ONE WORD, IT STRONGLY SUGGESTS ANOTHER TIME AND CULTURE, BEFORE THE FAMILY MOVED TO THE UNITED STATES AND ASSIMILATED TO MAINSTREAM AMERICAN LIFE."**

of sentimentality (excessively emotional) or triteness (boring and unoriginal). Indeed, the editor of the poetry journal *Response* once announced that he would no longer accept poems on such popular topics for Jewish poets as "the Holocaust, grandparents, Friday night candle lighting, . . . Jerusalem at dusk," to which a defiant Pastan wrote a succinct poem in which she mentioned all these topics. The poem is called "Response" and appears in Pastan's collection, *Waiting for My Life*, published in 1971. The words of the editor of *Response* are quoted in Pastan's headnote to the poem and also by Sanford Pinsker, in his essay, "Family Values and the Jewishness of Linda Pastan's Poetic Vision," published in *Women Poets of the Americas: Toward a Pan-American Gathering* (1999).

In "Grudnow," Pastan avoids the traps of sentimentality and triteness. What, then, are these word-pictures that she creates in the poem? There is one in each stanza. The first stanza presents a picture of the old man talking about his homeland, uttering the name of his hometown in Russia. He must have mentioned too that the city was sometimes a part of Russia and sometimes within Polish borders. Grudnow, or Grodno as it is usually spelled, must have been under Russian rule when the old man left it for the United States, but the city was returned to Polish rule in 1919 after World War I. Grudnow was transferred once more to Russian authority after World War II as part of the Soviet Union. This information accounts for the comment in lines 5 and 6 about the shifting borders in the region.

What is most arresting about the image of the old man is his pronunciation of Grudnow, which the speaker (no doubt U.S. born and fluent in only English) hears as similar to the sound of her grandfather clearing his throat. The picture is a homey one—the grandfather telling of his early life while his granddaughter listens—but the pronunciation of the name of the city by one who used to live there and who speaks the language introduces a foreign, alien element into the picture. The man pronounces the name of the town as only he can; it is probably a guttural sound from the back of his throat. Although only one word, it strongly suggests another time and culture, before the family moved to the United States and assimilated to mainstream American life. To the speaker, the pronunciation almost suggests that her grandfather is trying to cough up the memory of his hometown, perhaps to free himself of it. The stanza suggests one element in the grandfather's memory of Grudnow, that of deprivation and want. It had nothing to offer him.

The second stanza reinforces this bleak picture in its description of a photograph that the speaker comes across, perhaps in a family photo album. The landscape described is barren and desolate, which reinforces in the speaker's mind the negative idea she has received, from her grandfather himself, of his original home. Everything in the sepia photograph described, including the people and the landscape, is a dull brown color, as if there is no variety in this scene of people enduring in an inhospitable environment. What stands out in this stanza also is the word the speaker uses to describe the people in the scene. They are not described as the grandfather's family (although some of them may be). They are described with a word that suggests a wider shared identity, implying the solidarity of an entire people. It calls to mind the Jewish sense of a shared identity that has endured thousands of years or persecution.

The third stanza takes the focus away from the grandfather and places it on the speaker and her dire imaginings of what a life in Grudnow would have been like for her. The speaker imagines a life of disease, cold, and lack of shelter, the only comfort being the warmth of a cow's flank that she envisions rubbing up against for body heat. She is sure that such an environment would have killed her as a child; had she by some miracle survived into adulthood, she would have been worn down by the oppressiveness of life in that region, amongst those people; the sheer weight of their troubled history would eventually have ended her life.

In the final stanza the speaker leaves her imaginings in a past she did not in fact have to live and returns to the subject of her grandfather.

Winter in a small village *(Image copright Katarzyna Mazurowska, 2009. Used under license from Shutterstock.com)*

This stanza presents perhaps the most vivid picture in the entire poem, and it also provides a hint of a change in thought toward something more optimistic. The scene is once again homey—a family table at supper time. The granddaughter shows herself to be a close observer of her grandfather's habits and idiosyncrasies. She notices how he breaks and eats his bread and sips his tea. As he drinks, he holds a sugar cube between his teeth. This becomes a key image of the entire poem. The poet states that the way her grandfather drank his tea, with the sugar cube between his teeth, suggests two things to her. First, it signifies that some of his memories of Grudnow may not have been so bitter. Second, it also indicates the way her grandfather lived his life in America, suggesting that he cultivated optimism, determined to find something sweet in life, however sour it might appear on the surface or had been in the past. This final image, then, suggests the opposite of the utter bleakness of Grudnow that is evoked in the first three stanzas. Life may still be sweet to those who are determined to make it so.

"Grudnow" is thus an evocative poem. Without ever mentioning it directly, Pastan explores her Jewish heritage, and in doing so she gives little snapshots of Jewish American history. These snapshots range from one of the many inhospitable regions in late-nineteenth-century Russia to the United States and the culturally assimilated Jewish American generation born there during the decade before World War II—American through and through but still learning about and bearing traces of their Jewish forbears.

Source: Bryan Aubrey, Critical Essay on "Grudnow," in *Poetry for Students*, Gale, Cengage Learning, 2010.

Leslie Ullman

In the following review, Ullman contends that Pastan's poems have "a particular endurance, an ongoing ability to hold ambivalences in suspension."

This substantial collection, which includes selections from nine previous volumes plus twenty-seven new poems, spans the poet's adult life to reveal at every stage a voluptuous awareness of loss. Motifs such as the passing of parents, the changes of seasons, and the self as it is subtly ambushed by aging recur in a circular fashion, giving the volume the sinuousness and unity of a fugue.

As a backdrop to personal experience, Pastan includes numerous poems that reflect upon and sometimes reinterpret figures from Greek mythology and the Bible, especially Eve, revealing the origins not so much of sin as a kind of grace under fire. Eve's frequent appearances at once mirror and enlarge the persona of a speaker who also looks beyond the safety of gardens and seeks, however steep the price, "the fully lived life."

Elegiac as her poems tend to be, many of them contain considerable wit and playfulness, and even the poems most focused on loss do not bog down in lamentation. Pastan is too objective for that, positioning herself to simply take everything in, including the changes the future will undoubtedly bring, and holding it in a suspension that becomes the atmosphere of heightened awareness from which her vision arises: "On the small, imaginary / kitchen scales, / I place on one side ... / my mother's suede glove—/ that emptied udder; // on the other the mitten / my grandson just dropped—/ a woolen signpost he'll soon outgrow.... / Equilibrium is simply / that moment when the present / is as real as the past / or the future."

Although Pastan has worked successfully with forms and has included several fine sonnets from a sequence titled "The Imperfect Paradise," most of the poems collected here are free-verse lyrics that use the short line to isolate moments of perception and guide the reader deftly through layers of implication. They are unadorned, sure of their moments, and weightier than they first appear amid the ample white space they leave on the page. Often they seem to arise as songs, perhaps arias, playing out the tensile strength of a spirit willing to celebrate the connections implicit in "ordinary" life and then bear witness to the nuances as well as to the conventional gestures of relinquishment.

In the process, these poems offer moments of consolation and pleasure which paradoxically arise from the succinct articulation of painful truths. Pastan does this especially well in poems that touch upon the dark undercurrents of durable marriage and also in poems such as "The Death of a Parent," which begins, "Move to the front / of the line / a voice says, and suddenly / there is nobody / left standing between you / and the world, to take / the first blows / on their shoulders. / This is the place in books / where part one ends, and / part two begins, / and there is no part three."

Such a large collection of Pastan's work reveals a particular endurance, an ongoing ability to hold ambivalencies in suspension to the point where one wonders how she can live her life relationally, as the daughter, mother and long-married wife she evidently has been, and at the same time observe it so intensely, with the keenness and irony of one living in the margins. Pastan admits to being "a tourist / in my own life" and to a preference for living in "those spaces neither here // nor there, like the crack / between my parents' pushed-together beds / where I used to lie," but clearly her poems arise also from a woman immersed in the community of family. "Who is it accuses us of safety," she asks, going beyond irony into the realm of the sinister, "as if the family were soldiers / instead of hostages...? / Consider the pale necks of the children / under their colored head scarves, / the skin around the husbands' eyes, flayed / by guilt and promises... I tell you household gods / are jealous gods... they will poison your secret wells / with longing."

Beyond the shadows underscoring daily life, however, Pastan remains continually aware of the death's greater shadow. Many of her poems envision her world after she has passed from it, but she seems to anticipate her death as an echo rather than an absence, like the absence of her own forbears which resonates as something alive within her. This vision gives the best sort of purpose and authority to an ongoing poetic endeavor whose spirit is revealed succinctly at the end of one of her new poems, "This Enchanted Forest": "I know most endings / are unhappy, and the time / for my own fiery one / is approaching so fast / all I can try to do / is set it to music."

Source: Leslie Ullman, Review of *Carnival Evening, New and Selected Poems: 1968–1998*, in *Poetry*, Vol. 173, No. 4, February 1999, pp. 308–309.

Liz Rosenberg

In the following review of Carnival Evening, *Rosenberg argues that Pastan "must be one of the most underrated poets currently writing in America."*

What a strange, clenched pleasure it is to write about a book beyond one's power of praise. Linda Pastan must be one of the most underrated poets currently writing in America. Certainly I have read her for years, and admired her, without understanding what I was seeing. But her large and eclectic new collection, *Carnival Evening: New and Selected Poems, 1968–1998*, reveals 30 years of work between two covers, and it is a dazzling display, fireworks and more. The book is wide, wise, various, sly, sexy, quiet, heartbreaking. The effect of reading this collection reminded me of only a few other modern poets: Robert Frost, in his virtuosity and beauty, and the great Russian poet Anna Akhmatova, in her passion and straightforward honesty.

This is not to say there are not a few small, more minor poems in among the brave beauties—perhaps these have tricked us into underestimating Pastan over the years. But they are vastly outweighed by poems of great depth and delicacy. In the poem, "Pain":

> ... you are pulled down by the weight
> of your own hair.
> And if your life should disappear ahead of
> you
> you would not run after it.

Or on love: "loving, being loved / the panicking / of the pulse." Pastan understands understatement, juxtaposition, and contraction. Her poems can come like gasps, or move beautifully among open spaces, as in "Consolations":

> the dog whines
> and in the changeling trees
> late bees mumble, vague
> as voices
> barely heard
> from the next room ...
>
> You touch me——
> another language. Our griefs
> are almost one;
> we swing them between us
> like the child lent us awhile
> who holds one hand of yours
> and one of mine
> hurrying us home
> as streetlights
> start to flower
> down the dark stem
> of evening.

Alas, she is schooled in the language of grief and loss, but her work strikes every possible tone: comical ("In the English, where I spent my girlhood, / I used to think chillblains were a kind of biscuit"), coiled ("But underground, / their banner still furled, / whole armies of flowers wait"), gaudy ("the pale flowers / of the shamrock fold / their fragile wings"), sexy ("desire and need / become the same animal / in the silken / dark"), and often, full of wisdom, by which I mean many wisdoms—there is no fixity here.

> I had even forgotten how married love
> is a territory more mysterious

> the more it is explored, like one of those
> terrains
> you read about, a garden in the desert
> where you stoop to drink, never knowing
> if your mouth will fill with water or sand.

Much has been made of Pastan's "domesticity," but I find that her attention to homely detail resembles the Nobel Prize-winning Polish poet, Wislawa Szymborska, unmasking the seeming simplicity of complex things. There is nothing contrained or domestic about Pastan's subjects. She writes about everything from science to history, memory, poetics, geology, art, dreams, myths.

One review does not allow space to show Pastan's narrative abilities, but she is a wonderfully inventive storyteller. Her mind moves elegantly through a poem, feeling and thought together:

> Russia ... I thought, Russia ... a country
> my grandfather thought he had escaped
> from
> but which he wore always, like the heavy
> overcoat
> in the story by Gogol, or the overcoat he
> wrapped me in
> one night when the grown-ups kept on
> talking,
> and I shivered and yawned in an ecstasy
> or boredom that made my childhood
> seem a vast continent I could only escape
> from
> hidden in a coat, in steerage, and at great
> risk.

Pastan is a Jewish poet, an urban poet who both remembers the subways and buses of the Bronx, and has lived in rural Maryland long enough to observe "the garbled / secrets / of the waterfall / about to be stunned / on rock" or "these blossoms, sprinkled / like salt through the dark woods." She is also in fundamental ways a female poet, writing about women in all their strengths, weaknesses, guises, and disguises:

> And I have been Niobe,
> all mother, all tears,
> but myself somewhere hidden
> in the essential stone.
> You say I write
> like a man
> and expect me
> to smile.

Her phrases often have an oracular, aphoristic quality, perception sharpened to a point: "How much of memory / is imagination? And if loss / is an absence, why does it grow / so heavy?" Or, on childbirth: "But this work / this forcing / of one life from another / is something I signed for / at a moment when I would have signed anything." It is impossible to choose from the many pleasures of *Carnival Evening*: dogeared reviewer's copy looks like origami. The selection of poems is abundant and strong, showing a poet at the height of her powers. The difficulty here is to take pieces from poems that work as wholes, like hundreds of suns and moons. And Pastan is a poet of wholeness—a sane poet, who expresses a full range of the possibilities and potencies of the human, feminine voice. In the collection's title poem—based on a painting by Henri Rousseau:

> the two small figures
> at the bottom of this picture glow
> bravely in their carnival clothes,
> as if the whole darkening world
> were dimming its lights for a party.

Here in one image is the poet's hopefulness, her anxiety, her palette and celebration. One may love and remember small moments, but the accomplishment of *Carnival Evening* is large, large. We can only be grateful for Pastan's sharp eye, her tenderness.

Source: Liz Rosenberg, "Thirty Years of Linda Pastan's Work: From the Slight to the Extraordinary," in *Boston Globe*, August 30, 1998, p. F1.

Linda Pastan

In the following essay, Pastan discusses the importance of writing poems that unearth difficult childhood memories, an exercise arguably accomplished in "Grudnow."

> How sweet the past is, no matter
> how wrong, or how sad.
> How sweet is yesterday's noise.
> —Charles Wright, "The Southern Cross"

I wrote an essay ten years ago called "Memory As Muse," and looking back at it today I am struck by the fact that in the poems I write about childhood now the mood has changed from one of a rather happy nostalgia ("Memory as Muse") to a more realistic, or at least a gloomier, assessment of my own childhood and how it affects me as a writer ("Yesterday's Noise"). Let me illustrate with a poem called "An Old Song," from my most recent book.

> An Old Song
> How loyal our childhood demons are,
> growing old with us in the same house
> like servants who season the meat

> "

> **I ADMIT THAT AT FIRST GLANCE JUNIOR HIGH DOESN'T SEEM THE MOST FERTILE TERRITORY FOR POEMS TO GROW IN. ON THE OTHER HAND, INSECURITY, AWAKENING SEXUALITY, FEAR OF FAILURE—MANY OF THE GREAT SUBJECTS DO EXIST THERE."**

> with bitterness, like jailers
> who rattle the keys
> that lock us in or lock us out.

> Though we go on with our lives,
> though the years pile up
> like snow against the door,
> still our demons stare at us
> from the depths of mirrors
> or from the new faces across a table.

> And no matter what voice they choose,
> what language they speak,
> the message is always the same.
> They ask "Why can't you do
> anything right?"
> They say "We just don't love you anymore."

As A. S. Byatt said about herself in an interview: "I was no good at being a child." My mother told me that even as a baby I would lie screaming in the crib, clearly terrified of the dust motes that could be seen circling in the sun, as if they were a cloud of insects that were about to swarm and bite me. By the time I was five or six, I had a series of facial tics so virulent that I still can't do the mouth exercises my dentist recommends for fear I won't be able to stop doing them. I'm afraid they'll take hold like the compulsive habits of childhood that led my second-grade teacher to send me from the room until I could, as she put it, control my own face. There was the isolating year (sixth grade) of being the one child nobody would play with, the appointed victim, and there was the even more isolating year (fourth grade) of being, alas, one of the victimizers. There was my shadowy room at bedtime, at the end of a dark hallway, and, until some worried psychologist intervened, no night light allowed.

I thought about calling my last book *Only Child* because something about that condition seemed to define not only me, but possibly writers in general who sit at their desks, necessarily alone, for much of the time. In some ways, of course, it defines all of us, born alone, dying alone, alone in our skins no matter how close we seem to be to others. I tried to capture my particular loneliness as a child, my difficulty in making friends, my search for approval, in what I thought would be the title poem of that book:

Only Child
Sister to no one,
I watched
the children next door
quarrel and make up
in a code
I never learned to break.

Go Play!
my mother told me.
Play! said the aunts,
their heads all nodding
on their stems,
a family of rampant
flowers

and I a single shoot.
At night I dreamed
I was a twin
the way my two hands,
my eyes,
my feet were twinned.
I married young.

In the fractured light
of memory—that place
of blinding sun or shade,
I stand waiting
on the concrete stoop
for my own children
to find me.

At a reading I gave before a group of Maryland PEN women last year, someone who had clearly not read beyond the tables of contents of my books introduced me as a writer of light verse. I remember thinking in a panic that I hardly had a single light poem to read to those expectant faces, waiting to be amused. Did I have such an unhappy life, then—wife, mother, grandmother, with woods to walk in, books to read, good friends, even a supportive editor?

I am, in fact, a more or less happy adult, suffering, thank God, from no more than the usual griefs age brings. But I think my poems are colored not only by a possibly somber genetic temperament, but also by my failure at childhood, even

when I am not writing about childhood per se. And more and more, as I grow older, those memories themselves insist upon inserting themselves into my work. Perhaps it is the very way our childhoods change in what I called "the fractured light of memory" that make them such an inexhaustible source of poetry. For me, it is like the inexhaustible subject of the seasons that can be seen in the changeable light of the sun, or the versatile light of the imagination, as benign or malevolent or indifferent, depending upon a particular poet's vision at a particular moment.

I want to reflect a little then on those poems we fish up from the depths of our childhoods. And for any teachers reading this, I want to suggest that assigning poems to student writers that grow out of their childhoods can produce unusually good results, opening up those frozen ponds with what Kafka called the axe of poetry.

Baudelaire says that "genius is childhood recalled at will." I had a 19-year-old student once who was not a genius but who complained that he couldn't write about anything except his childhood. Unfortunately, his memory was short, and as a result, all of his poems were set in junior high school. He had taken my course, he told me, in order to find new subjects. I admit that at first glance junior high doesn't seem the most fertile territory for poems to grow in. On the other hand, insecurity, awakening sexuality, fear of failure—many of the great subjects do exist there. It occurred to me that when I was 19, what I usually wrote about were old age and death. Only in my middle years did I start looking back into my own past for the subjects of poems. This started me wondering about the poetry of memory in general. Did other poets, unlike my young student, come to this subject relatively late, as I had? As I looked rather casually and unscientifically through the books on my shelves, it did seem to me that when poets in their twenties and thirties wrote about children, it was usually their own children that concerned them, but when they were in their late forties or fifties or sixties, the children they wrote about tended to be themselves.

Donald Justice, in an interview with *The Missouri Review,* gave as good an explanation of this as anyone. He said, "In the poems I have been thinking of and writing the last few years, I have grown aware that childhood is a subject somehow available to me all over again. The perspective of time and distance alter substance somewhat, and so it is possible to think freshly of things that were once familiar and ordinary, as if they had become strange again. I don't know whether this is true of everybody's experience, but at a certain point childhood seems mythical once more. It did to start with, and it does suddenly again."

There are, first of all, what I call "Poems of the Happy Childhood," Donald Justice's own poem "The Poet At Seven" among them. But for poets less skilled than Justice, there is a danger to such poems, for they can stray across the unmarked but mined border into sentimentality and become dishonest, wishful sort of recollections. When they are working well, however, these "Poems of the Happy Childhood" reflect the Wordsworthian idea that we are born "trailing clouds of glory" and that as we grow older we are progressively despiritualized. Even earlier than Wordsworth, in the mid-17th century, Henry Vaughan anticipated these ideas in his poem, "The Retreat."

I mention Wordsworth and Vaughan because in looking back over the centuries at the work of earlier poets, I find more rarely than I expected poems that deal with childhood at all. Their poems are the exceptions, as are Shakespeare's 30th Sonnet and Tennyson's "Tears, Idle Tears." Perhaps it wasn't until after Freud that people started to delve routinely into their own pasts. But nostalgia per se was not so rare, and in a book called *The Uses Of Nostalgia: Studies in Pastoral Poetry*, the English critic Laurence Lerner comes up with an interesting theory. After examining pastoral poetry from classical antiquity on, he concludes that pastoral poems express the longing of the poets to return to a childhood arcadia, and that in fact what they longed to return to was childhood itself. He then takes his theory a step further and postulates that the reason poets longed for childhood is simply that they had lost it. He writes, "The list is varied of those who learned to sing of what they loved by losing it. . . . Is that what singing is? Is nostalgia the basis not only of pastoral but of other art too?" Or as Bob Hass puts it in his poem "Meditation at Lagunitas," "All the new thinking is about loss. / In this it resembles all the old thinking."

But though there are some left who think of childhood as a lost arcadia, for the most part Freud changed all of that.

We have in more recent times the idea of poetry as a revelation of the self to the self, or as Marge Perloff put it when describing the poems of Seamus Heaney, "Poetry as a dig."

The sort of poems this kind of digging often provides are almost the opposite of "Poems of the Happy Childhood," and they reflect a viewpoint that is closer to the childhood poems I seem to be writing lately. In fact, a poem like "Autobiographia Literaria" by Frank O'Hara actually consoles the adult by making him remember, albeit with irony in O'Hara's case, how much more unpleasant it was to be a child. If the poetry of memory can console, it can also expiate. In his well-known poem, "Those Winter Sundays," Robert Hayden not only recreates the past but reexamines his behavior there and finds it wanting. The poem itself becomes an apology for his behavior as a boy, and the act of writing becomes an act of repentance.

If you can't expiate the past, however, you can always revise it—and in various, and occasionally unorthodox, ways. Donald Justice in the poem "childhood" runs a list of footnotes opposite his poem, explaining and clarifying. Mark Strand in "The Untelling" reenters the childhood scene as an adult and warns the participants of what is to occur in the future.

Probably the most ambitious thing a poem of childhood memory can accomplish is the Proustian task of somehow freeing us from time itself. Proust is perfectly happy to use random, seemingly unimportant memory sensations as long as they have the power to transport him backwards. When he tastes his madeleine, moments of the past come rushing back, and he is transported to a plane of being on which a kind of immortality is granted. We can grasp for a moment what we can never normally get hold of—a bit of time in its pure state. It is not just that this somehow lasts forever, the way we hope the printed word will last, but that it can free us from the fear of death. To quote Proust: "A minute emancipated from the temporal order had recreated in us for its apprehension the man emancipated from the temporal order." Proust accomplished his journey to the past via the sense of taste, but any sense or combination of senses will do. In my poem "PM/AM," I used the sense of hearing in the first stanza and a combination of sight and touch in the second. Here is the second:

> AM
> The child gets up
> on the wrong side of the bed.
> There are splinters
> of cold light on the floor,
> and when she frowns
> the frown freezes on her face
> as her mother has warned her it would.

When she puts her elbows roughly
on the table her father says:
you got up on the wrong side of the bed;
and there is suddenly
a cold river
of spilled milk.
These gestures are merely formal,
small stitches in the tapestry
of a childhood she will remember
as nearly happy. Outside
the snow begins again,
ordinary weather
blurring the landscape
between that time and this,
as she swings her cold legs
over the side of the bed.

But did I really say: "A childhood she will remember as nearly happy"? Whom are you to believe, the poet who wrote that poem years ago or the poet who wrote "An Old Song"? As you see, the past can be reinterpreted, the past can be revised, and the past can also be invented. Sometimes, in fact, one invents memories without even meaning to. In a poem of mine called "The One-Way Mirror Back," I acknowledge this by admitting: "What I remember hardly happened; what they say happened I hardly remember." Or as Bill Matthews put it in his poem "Our Strange and Lovable Weather"—

> ...any place lies about its weather, just as we
> lie about our childhoods, and for the same
> reason: we can't say surely what we've under-
> gone and need to know, and need to know.

This "need to know" runs very deep and is one of the things that fuels the poems we write about our childhoods.

But the simplest, the most basic thing such poems provide are the memories themselves, the memories for their own sakes. Here is the third stanza of Charles Simic's poem "Ballad": "Screendoor screeching in the wind / Mother hobble-gobble baking apples / Wooden spoons dancing, ah the idyllic life of wooden spoons / I need a table to spread these memories on." The poem itself, then, can become such a table, a table to simply spread our memories on.

Looking back at some of my own memories, I sometimes think I was never a child at all, but a lonely woman camouflaged in a child's body. I am probably more childlike now. At least I hope so.

Source: Linda Pastan, "Yesterday's Noise: The Poetry of Childhood Memory," in *Writer*, Vol. 105, No. 10, October 1992, pp. 15–18.

SOURCES

"ADL Audit: Anti-Semitic Incidents at Highest Level in Nine Years," in *Anti-Defamation League*, April 4, 2005, http://www.adl.org/PresRele/ASUS_12/4671_12.htm (accessed April 25, 2009).

"ADL Survey: Anti-Semitism Declines Slightly in America; 14 Percent of Americans Hold 'Strong' Anti-Semitic Beliefs," in *Anti-Defamation League*, April 4, 2005, http://www.adl.org/PresRele/ASUS_12/4680_12.htm (accessed April 25, 2009).

Brown, Jeffrey, "Conversation: Pastan," in *Online Newshour*, July 7, 2003, http://www.pbs.org/newshour/bb/entertainment/july-dec03/pastan_07-07.html (accessed April 24, 2009).

Franklin, Benjamin, V, "Linda Pastan," in *Dictionary of Literary Biography*, Volume 5 *American Poets Since World War II*, 1st ser., edited by Donald J. Greiner, Gale Research, 1980, pp. 158–63.

Kaufman, Ellen, Review of *Carnival Evening: New and Selected Poems, 1968–1998*, in *Library Journal*, Vol. 123, No. 7, April 15, 1998, p. 84.

Ketelbey, C. D. M., *A History of Modern Times from 1789*, 4th ed., George G. Harrap, 1966, p. 378.

"Lost Jewish Worlds: Grodno," in *Yad Vashem: The Holocaust Martyrs' and Heroes' Remembrance Authority*, http://www1.yadvashem.org/about_holocaust/lost_worlds/grodno/grodno_history_and_geography.html#top (accessed April 25, 2009).

Margolis, Max L., and Alexander Marx, *A History of the Jewish People*, Temple, 1975, pp. 710, 721.

Pastan, Linda, "Grudnow," in *Carnival Evening: New and Selected Poems: 1968–1998*, W. W. Norton, 1998, pp. 194–95.

———, "Yesterday's Noise: The Poetry of Childhood Memory," in *The Writer's Handbook*, edited by Sylvia K. Burack, The Writer, 1993, p. 410.

Paul, Jay S., "Linda Pastan," in *Contemporary Poets*, 5th ed., edited by Tracy Chevalier, St. James Press, 1991, pp. 743–44.

Pinsker, Sanford, "Family Values and the Jewishness of Linda Pastan's Poetic Vision," in *Women Poets of the Americas: Toward a Pan-American Gathering*, edited by Jacqueline Vaught Brogan and Cordelia Chávez Candelaria, University of Notre Dame Press, 1999, pp. 203–204.

Rabin, Dov, "Grodno," in *Encyclopaedia Judaica*, Vol. 7, Keter, 1972, pp. 923–27.

Renck, Ellen Sadove, "History of Grodno," in *Belarus-SIG*, http://www.jewishgen.org/belarus/info_history_of_grodno.htm (accessed April 25, 2009).

Sarna, Jonathan D., and Jonathan Golden, "The American Jewish Experience in the Twentieth Century: Antisemitism and Assimilation," in *National Humanities Center*, http://nationalhumanitiescenter.org/tserve/twenty/tkeyinfo/jewishexp.htm (accessed April 27, 2009).

Sheskin, Ira M., and Arnold Dashefsky, "Jewish Population of the United States, 2006," in *American Jewish Year Book 2006*, Vol. 106, edited by David Singer and Lawrence Grossman, American Jewish Committee, 2006.

Stitt, Peter, "Violence, Imagery, and Introspection," in *Georgia Review*, Vol. 33, No. 4, Winter, 1979, pp. 927–32.

FURTHER READING

Adelman, Ken, "Word Perfect: For Linda Pastan, Revision Is the Purest Form of Love," in *Washingtonian*, Vol. 31, No. 8, May 1996, pp. 29–31.

In this interview, Pastan discusses her writing habits, what led her to write, why she chose to write poetry rather than novels, and many other aspects of her work.

Finkelstein, Norman, *Not One of Them in Place: Modern Poetry & Jewish American Identity*, State University of New York Press, 2001.

Finkelstein examines how Jewish beliefs and culture have been expressed in American poetry over the last century.

Hertzberg, Arthur, *The Jews in America*, Columbia University Press, 2001.

Hertzberg describes the anti-Semitism that Jews encountered in the United States and how they overcame it. He argues that by assimilating to the dominant culture, Jews have abandoned their spiritual roots.

Rubin, Stan Sanvel, "'Whatever Is at Hand': A Conversation with Linda Pastan," in *The Post-Confessionals: Conversations with American Poets of the Eighties*, Fairleigh Dickinson University Press, 1989, pp. 135–49.

In this interview, Pastan talks about all aspects of her work.

Hanging Fire

AUDRE LORDE
1978

"Hanging Fire," a poem about teenage angst by Audre Lorde, first appeared in her poetry collection *The Black Unicorn* in 1978. The poem has been reprinted in several literary anthologies, such as the *Norton Introduction to Literature* (9th edition, 2005) and the 1997 edition of *The Collected Poems of Audre Lorde*.

In *Conversations with Audre Lorde* (2004) Joan Hall reports that Lorde was a self-described "Black lesbian feminist poet warrior mother" who liked to focus on "differences" while disputing notions of universality, and the book in which "Hanging Fire" first appeared is noted for its evocation of African spirituality. Yet "Hanging Fire" is not overtly about the African American experience, and its one apparent reference to romance seems to be heterosexual. It is true that there is a feminist suggestion in the poem's closing stanza, but for the most part the poem speaks in a broad way to the anguish and anxiety of adolescent life generally; some readers even mistake the speaker for male.

The poem coincides with Lorde's usual concerns in its depiction of the speaker as a lonely, unhappy outsider and in its suggestion of a difficult mother-daughter relationship. However, its evocation of the adolescent condition has a universal quality not usually associated with Lorde, though it is this quality that no doubt accounts for the poem's inclusion in anthologies and classroom discussions.

Audre Lorde (*The Library of Congress*)

AUTHOR BIOGRAPHY

Audre Lorde was born Audrey Geraldine Lorde in the Harlem district of New York City on February 18, 1934, the daughter of immigrants from the West Indies. While still quite young she decided she disliked the look of the "y" at the end of her first name and so began spelling it as Audre. As recounted in her autobiographical work, *Zami: A New Spelling of My Name*, from an early age Lorde felt like an outsider: a black girl in white schools with very poor vision, causing her to be clumsy, and a self-image as fat and ugly. She also felt unloved by her parents, having an especially difficult relationship with her strict but distant mother. One redeeming quality in her adolescent life was her writing, which she began when she was twelve. At Hunter High School, Lorde worked for the school literary magazine and was part of a literary circle. However, even this involved alienation, for she was the only African American in the circle and was turned down when she sought the editorship of the magazine. The magazine also turned down one of her poems, which she was able to get published in a commercial publication, *Seventeen* magazine, in April 1951.

After high school, Lorde studied off and on at Hunter College, eventually graduating with an arts degree in 1959. Afterwards, she completed a degree in library science at Columbia University and worked as a librarian and later as an English and creative writing teacher, eventually becoming an English professor at Hunter College in 1980. In 1962 she married Edwin Rollins, by whom she had two children. Lorde and Rollins separated in 1970, after which Lorde moved to Staten Island, New York with her long-term partner Frances Clayton. She later moved to St. Croix, U.S. Virgin Islands, where she lived with Gloria Joseph.

Beginning in 1968, Lorde published eleven books of poetry and her "biomythography," *Zami* (1982), an exploration of her racial and sexual identity, which some regard as her masterpiece. "Hanging Fire" appeared in her seventh book of poetry, *The Black Unicorn* (1978), the second of her books to be published by a mainstream publisher (W. W. Norton), as opposed to the smaller presses that published her earlier work.

In 1977, Lorde was diagnosed with breast cancer, an experience she wrote about in *The Cancer Journals* (1980). She also published two essay collections, *Sister Outsider* (1984) and *A Burst of Light* (1988), putting forward her hard-hitting and sometimes controversial views on politics and the various liberation movements with which she was associated. Though she achieved iconic status within these movements, she continued to be something of an outsider, at odds with the feminist movement over racism and in opposition with the black liberation movement over the treatment of women and gays. "Something about me troubles everyone," she said in a 1986 interview with Dorothee Nolte, reprinted in *Conversations with Audre Lorde* (edited by Joan Wylie Hall), "be it that I am black, that I am lesbian, poet, feminist, mother, warrior—I have always been an outsider."

In the mid-1980s, Lorde was diagnosed with a recurrence of cancer, which had spread to her liver. She continued to write, however, and published a tenth book of poetry the year of her death, 1992. She died on November 17, 1992, in St. Croix. An eleventh collection was published the following year. The year before she died, Lorde was named New York State's poet laureate.

POEM TEXT

I am fourteen
and my skin has betrayed me
the boy I cannot live without
still sucks his thumb
in secret   5
how come my knees are
always so ashy
what if I die
before morning
and momma's in the bedroom   10
with the door closed.

I have to learn how to dance
in time for the next party
my room is too small for me
suppose I die before graduation   15
they will sing sad melodies
but finally
tell the truth about me
There is nothing I want to do
and too much   20
that has to be done
and momma's in the bedroom
with the door closed.

Nobody even stops to think
about my side of it   25
I should have been on Math Team
my marks were better than his
why do I have to be
the one
wearing braces   30
I have nothing to wear tomorrow
will I live long enough
to grow up
and momma's in the bedroom
with the door closed.   35

POEM SUMMARY

Title

The title "Hanging Fire," according to the *Oxford English Dictionary*, literally means a "delay in the explosion of the charge of a gun or of a blasting charge." *Webster's New World Dictionary of the American Language* similarly defines the phrase to mean "to be slow in firing" and by extension to mean to be slow in anything or "to be unsettled or undecided." The notion of being unsettled certainly fits Lorde's poem, and the notion of delay may fit as well; there is a sense in the poem that the speaker is suspended, not knowing what to do. A definition of "hanging fire" from *Brewer's Dictionary of Phrase & Fable* is somewhat different: "To fail in an expected result," derived from guns that fail to go off. This definition would make the poem seem more negative, suggesting that it is

not only about being unsettled and delayed but also about failure.

First Stanza

The speaker announces her age (fourteen) and begins listing the problems in her life. The first concerns her skin, which she says has let her down, presumably meaning that she is suffering from acne. The speaker then refers to a boy she states she needs, presumably a boyfriend. However, this boy sucks his thumb in private—not the most appealing or socially acceptable behavior for a teenager—suggesting that the speaker feels less than desirable because she associates with someone with this undesirable trait. The speaker then returns to her skin, complaining that her knees are ashy, the one point in the poem that suggests she is African American, as "ashy" is a relatively common slang term used in the African American community to describe dry skin.

The stanza ends by moving from specific complaints to a sudden concern of the speaker's that she might die before the morning, suggesting great unhappiness. The last two lines of the stanza then refer to the speaker's mother, who has apparently shut herself away in her bedroom. This could be seen as just another problem for the speaker, but as Jerome Brooks states in his article on Lorde's poetry (in *Black Women Writers (1950-1980): A Critical Evaluation*, edited by Mari Evans, 1984), it seems to be more than that. These two lines end each stanza, suggesting they are especially important, and the importance would seem to be that the one person the speaker wants to turn to for help with her other problems has made herself unavailable. That is, not only does the speaker have problems but she also seems to have no one to help her with them; even the person one usually expects to be the giver of help, one's mother, is not there for her.

Second Stanza

The second stanza plunges into additional problems. The speaker needs to learn how to dance in time for an upcoming party, and she thinks her room is too small for her to do so. In this stanza, though, after just two complaints over three lines, the speaker quickly moves to thoughts of death, more quickly than in the first stanza, where she first outlined three problems and did not introduce the motif of dying until the eighth line.

The second stanza's introduction of the fear of death is tied to graduation. Now instead of fearing death before the morning, the speaker is afraid that she will die before she graduates. The fear thus seems to be attached in this case to a feeling that she will fail to accomplish what she is supposed to do. She also appears to worry that though people will sing sad songs when she dies, they will then tell the truth about her, as if the truth is something negative.

The last part of the second stanza begins with a capitalized word, as if beginning a new sentence. This is the only time in the poem that this happens in the middle of a stanza, suggesting that the sentence is of some importance, and the sentence proves to have large implications. On the surface it is just a statement that the speaker has nothing she wants to do while at the same time she has too much she has to do. It could be a common teenager's complaint about having to do unwanted chores while at the same time feeling bored and aimless, but it seems a moment when the poem is emphasizing a more widespread human condition, about restlessness and dissatisfaction with one's goals combined with a sense of being overwhelmed by responsibilities. The second stanza then ends with the repetition of the speaker's mother being in the bedroom behind a closed door.

Third Stanza

Whereas the second stanza moves quickly from particular complaints to a more generalized expression of despair, the third stanza begins with a general statement that no one thinks about the speaker, but then moves back to particulars: that the speaker should have been the one named to the math team because her grades were better than those of the boy who was chosen, that she is unhappy to be wearing braces, and that she has nothing to wear.

Like the previous two stanzas, the third stanza references death; the speaker wonders if she will live long enough to grow up. As in the second stanza, the implied fear is of not accomplishing goals or fulfilling one's destiny. The third stanza ends as the other two do with the chorus about the speaker's mother being closed off from her. By ending the poem with this repetitive statement, Lorde seems to reinforce the feeling of despair, reminding the reader that the speaker sees no way out or feels there is no one to help her with her many problems in her state of despair.

THEMES

Adolescence

The opening line of the poem reveals that the speaker is a teenager, framing everything that follows and putting it into the context of early adolescence, a time that in modern Western society is usually marked by physical and social anxieties. The poem aptly captures the discrepancy between apparently trivial problems (acne-ridden skin, having to wear braces, feeling one has nothing to wear) and the dramatic notions about death accompanying them. However, to the adolescent undergoing these issues, even trivial problems can loom large. The poem expertly captures the sense of this from the inside; the reader is plunged into the mind of a suffering teenager who jumbles together concerns over acne with larger, existential questions about death and growing up.

Misfortunes

"Hanging Fire" involves a long litany of complaints about the speaker's life, unrelieved by anything positive, with the possible exception of a line in the second stanza—it states that if the speaker dies, people will sing sad songs for her, but even after the singing there will be truth-telling, an apparently ominous prospect. The list of complaints is somewhat reminiscent of the Book of Job from the Bible, in which Job suffers one misfortune after another. In the Bible story, though the misfortunes are in themselves more serious, there is an explanation of their cause—the will of God. This is comforting, because it is explanatory and indicates that misfortunes can be reversed through the power of God.

In this poem, in contrast, there is no explanation of the suffering and no sense of God or an external force able to reverse the present conditions of the speaker's life. On the contrary, the one external force that is referred to, the speaker's mother, has closed her door on her daughter, leaving the latter alone to cope with what seem like inexplicable misfortunes afflicting her all at once.

Mother-child Relationships

Mother-daughter relations preoccupied Lorde. Her autobiographical book *Zami*, for instance, discusses the difficulties she had with her mother as someone who was both strict and distant. Her poem "Black Mother Woman" depicts the harshness of a mother. In "Hanging Fire," in contrast, the mother's apparent distance and lack of involvement in her daughter's life are problematic. In part, the poem focuses on the refusal of a mother to help her daughter, or at least on the daughter's perception that the mother is unavailable to her.

Sexism

In the final stanza of the poem, the speaker complains that she should have been on the math team instead of a boy whose grades were lower

TOPICS FOR FURTHER STUDY

- Organize a classroom debate about teenage suffering. Is the sort of suffering described in "Hanging Fire" widespread? Are most teenagers actually better adjusted than the speaker in the poem, or are the feelings she describes common?

- Compare the poem with the young-adult novel *A Brief History of My Impossible Life* (2006) by Dana Reinhardt. Write an essay comparing the speaker in the poem with the protagonist in the novel. To what extent are they similar or different? Does the novel portray a more hopeful outlook than the poem? Also, discuss the different mother-daughter relationships in the novel and the poem.

- Listen to the song "Welcome to My Life" (2004) by Simple Plan. Song lyrics are available at *A-Z Lyrics Universe* (http://www.azlyrics.com/lyrics/simpleplan/welcometomylife.html). Write an essay discussing to what extent the situation in the song resembles that in the poem.

- Prepare a research paper on the Book of Job from the Christian Bible. Describe the various afflictions of Job and recount what happens to him. Find some commentaries on the Job story, and present an account of the various interpretations of it. In your presentation, compare and contrast Job's tribulations with that of the poem's speaker.

- Organize a debate about women's rights. Could it still happen that a boy would get on the Math Team or win a similar privilege even if a girl was more deserving? Does it ever happen the other way around now? Is either situation fair?

- Work in groups to produce a music video about teenage life in a culture different than your own. Combine original material with links to relevant photographs, videos, and songs.

- Watch the documentary film *A Litany for Survival: The Life and Work of Audre Lorde*. Write a report on the film in which you comment on Lorde's life and views. Explain to what extent they illuminate the poem.

---

than hers. The suggestion is that the boy was chosen precisely because he is male, as if there was some sexist preference at work in favor of a male over a more deserving female. Lorde describes a somewhat similar situation in *Zami*, in which the election for a school presidency is guaranteed to the male candidate.

This is the only complaint in the poem that seems directly connected to larger sociopolitical issues. Elsewhere the speaker complains about physical problems (acne and ashy knees) or interpersonal issues (having a thumb-sucking boyfriend and learning to dance). One could argue that having a small room and nothing to wear might be references to poverty, but the speaker also complains about having to wear braces, which suggests her family is not poor. The problem of having nothing to wear seems more a personal issue, a subjective statement that there is nothing in her closet that she likes. Similarly, her comment regarding the size of her bedroom may be merely subjective; if objectively true, the statement may reflect more so the interactions within the family than any economic issues.

That most of the problems in the poem do not stem from systemic, political situations is striking in a work by a poet who is known for her focus on such situations, for instance, racism and the sexism that is indeed touched on here. However, Lorde's writing often included a less political and more personal and introspective stance (and she argued in her works that the personal is political in any case).

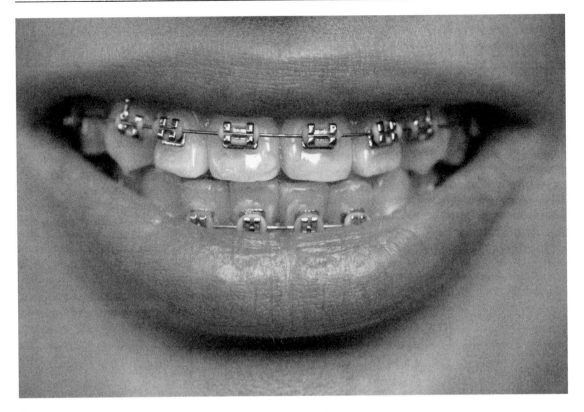

Braces (Image copyright John Leung, 2009. Used under license from Shutterstock.com)

STYLE

Free Verse

The poem is in free verse, that is, verse without a regular meter or rhyme scheme, a quite common form for twentieth-century poetry. Here, free verse seems an appropriately free-flowing vehicle for the rush of the speaker's thoughts, as she jumps from skin problems to her thumb-sucking boyfriend to other skin problems, then on to worries about death.

On the other hand, sometimes the free flow of words and thoughts slows as Lorde introduces an unusually short line, the first time to say in two words that the boyfriend does his thumb-sucking in secret; secrecy is emphasized this way. Similarly, in the second stanza, Lorde uses a two-word line to stop the flow and focus on the fact that the speaker is worried that people will speak the truth about her. Also, in the third stanza a two-word line is used, this time forcing the reader to pause on the notion that the speaker is the only one wearing braces; the pause suggests that the speaker is singled out in a more generalized sense—the center of a hostile universe, the only one afflicted by misfortune.

Capitalization

As with many free-verse poems, there is very little capitalization in "Hanging Fire." Basically only the first word of each stanza and the word "I" are capitalized. There are two exceptions, one for the math team, perhaps just to denote that it is the name of the team. Also, capitalization is used in the line stating there is nothing the speaker wants to do and yet so many things she has to do, an important thematic point in the poem.

Repetition

The most obvious repetition in the poem is the concluding refrain of each stanza, in which the speaker says, three times over, that her mother is in the bedroom with the door closed. The repetition accentuates the force of this statement, which is an important one for the abandonment the speaker feels. Repetition is also relevant in the sense that the speaker lists complaint after complaint, eight particular ones, which again emphasizes a sense that the speaker's life is one long grievance. A fear of dying is also a repeating theme in the poem, indicating the larger existential issue afflicting the speaker.

COMPARE
&
CONTRAST

- **1970s:** In the early years of the women's movement there is still discrimination preventing women from obtaining positions for which they are qualified. Congress proposes an Equal Rights Amendment to the U.S. Constitution in 1972, but it is withdrawn in 1982 because not enough states ratified it.

  Today: After several decades of campaigning, the introduction of antidiscriminatory laws, and changes in attitudes, more areas of employment are open to women and overt discrimination is rare. In 2008 New York senator Hillary Clinton comes close to gaining the Democratic nomination for U.S. President in the same year that Alaska governor Sarah Palin is the Republican vice-presidential candidate.

- **1970s:** Lesbian and gay rights are just beginning to be talked about openly. On October 14, 1979, the first gay-rights march on Washington, DC, takes place.

  Today: Gay rights remain a controversial topic, but there is much greater acceptance of homosexuality, and laws in some jurisdictions permit gay marriages.

- **1970s:** Teenagers, including teenage girls, often feel miserable over large and small problems in their lives.

  Today: Teenage angst remains a real concern, prompting books on how to deal with it. Some observers suggest that there has been an increase in bullying, especially bullying (often by electronic means) among girls.

Diction

Diction, or word choice, in the poem is fairly simple, reflecting the fact that the speaker is fourteen years old. It is partly through the level of diction that readers can picture themselves in the mind of a fourteen-year-old girl. The simplicity of the diction and the use of the term "momma" for the speaker's mother also conveys the notion that the speaker is childlike; she does not analyze her situation; in a very elemental way, she is simply uttering her pain and angst.

HISTORICAL CONTEXT

The Women's Movement

The speaker's complaint about discrimination based on sex (that she should have been on the math team rather than the boy with lower grades) can be seen as a microcosm of sexism in the 1960s and 1970s in the United States. The struggle for women's equal rights has stretched over decades and centuries, and it came to the forefront in U.S. society in the 1960s and 1970s

as the women's liberation movement, of which Lorde was an uneasy part. As an African American conscious of the history of racism in the United States, Lorde often found herself at odds with the white leaders of the American feminist movement, for instance the editors of the feminist magazine *Chrysalis*. At the same time, Lorde struggled for recognition of women's rights within African American groups and in society at large.

Gay Rights

Although the reference to romance in "Hanging Fire" is to a girl's interest in a boy, Lorde often portrayed lesbian relationships in her poetry, and she was active in the struggle for gay and lesbian rights. In 1979, a year after "Hanging Fire" was published, she took part in the first National March for Gay and Lesbian Rights in Washington, D.C. In the 1980s she also helped found a publishing house for lesbian women of color called Kitchen Table. In general, her activism on behalf of lesbian women played a role in the advancement of gay rights that began in the 1970s and has continued into the twenty-first century.

Teenage girl (*Image copyright Mika Heittola, 2009. Used under license from Shutterstock.com*)

Black Arts Movement

In the 1960s and 1970s, paralleling the rise of black political movements, the Black Arts Movement began in an attempt to promote African American culture. Led by LeRoi Jones and Nikki Giovanni, the movement attracted such notable writers as Gwendolyn Brooks and led to the founding of independent African American publishing houses. One of these publishing houses, Broadside Press published two of Lorde's early poetry collections. Even so, Lorde had difficulty with Broadside Press, because they initially refused to include one of her love poems about lesbian women.

Harlem and Caribbean Immigration

Lorde's parents were not unusual in leaving the Caribbean and immigrating to Harlem, New York. In the early years of the twentieth century, Harlem was a vibrant district of New York City, attracting African Americans from the South as well as immigrants from the West Indies and elsewhere. During the first three decades of the twentieth century, approximately forty thousand immigrants came to Harlem from the Caribbean. Such immigrants brought with them a caste system based on color; Lorde's mother was fairly light-skinned and maintained relatively negative views of those darker than herself. Lorde herself was darker-skinned than her mother, one of the elements of estrangement between the two women.

Lorde had moved away from Harlem, but she returned in the 1950s to attend sessions of the Harlem Writers Guild, an organization founded in the previous decade to assist young black writers. She was involved with the guild only temporarily, but it led to the publication of a poem in one of the guild's magazines and helped her create literary connections at an early stage of her career.

CRITICAL OVERVIEW

Although "Hanging Fire" has appeared in a number of anthologies and, to judge from browsing the Internet, is frequently assigned for classroom discussion, there has been little or no commentary on it in academic publications. The book it first appeared in, *The Black Unicorn*, has received a fair amount of attention, but the focus of the commentaries has been on its connection to African spirituality.

Since her early works appeared in relatively unknown magazines or books published by small presses, Lorde did not receive much attention at first. Even so, Dudley Randall, the publisher of Broadside Press, praised her first work and published several of her subsequent books. As reported by Alexis de Veaux in *Warrior Poet: A Biography of Audre Lorde* (2004), Randall praised Lorde's use of imagery and found her to be quiet and introspective, traits atypical of Lorde's later work. For instance, a critical reviewer of *The Black Unicorn*, as noted in de Veaux's biography, calls it "not-too-gentle." Rochelle Ratner, also quoted by de Veaux, praises the same book for being "hard-edged."

Lorde's previous book, *Coal* (1976), was her first work published by a mainstream publisher. *Coal* marked her emergence from the small presses, which de Veaux states, made her "the first out black lesbian to crash the gates of the literary mainstream." Some critics, however, did not like this "crashing"; in a 1982 reviewer of a later volume, an anonymous contributor quoted in de Veaux's biography criticizes Lorde as belonging to a school of poetry that was too much like jazz in being full of "raw emotional energy" but without craft. This review prompted protests against what was perceived as racial stereotyping of African American poetry.

More typical are reviews like one by Sally Jo Sorensen, also quoted in de Veaux's biography, praising Lorde for such things as her "astonishing range and complexity." That Lorde is wider ranging than some commentators suggest is a point made by Jerome Brooks, who says her poems about fathers are ones "her vast feminist following is likely to overlook." So it is perhaps a mistake to be surprised that Lorde wrote a generalized poem about teenage angst; she adopted a number of voices in her career.

Still, Lorde is remembered mostly for her writings about mothers, her exploration of homosexual relationships, and her evocation of African spirituality. In *Women's Stories of the Looking Glass: Autobiographical Reflections and Self-Representations in the Poetry of Sylvia Plath, Adrienne Rich, and Audre Lorde* (1996), Carmen Birkle describes Lorde as "a poet of difference." Birkle also quotes Lorde's fellow poet Adrienne Rich, stating that she was "a great poet" because she could write both of "beauty" and "the harsh materials of human struggle."

CRITICISM

Sheldon Goldfarb

Goldfarb is a specialist in Victorian literature who has published nonfiction books as well as a novel for young adults set in Victorian times. In this essay, he explores the nature of teenage suffering in "Hanging Fire" and its relevance to adult readers.

"Hanging Fire" is about teenage suffering; that much is clear. In great detail, and in a convincing recreation of the voice of a teenager, Audre Lorde presents all the horrors of being fourteen years old.

It is possible to look at these horrors and think that the poem is one of utter despair. When reading the poem, one may think of other sufferers, like Job in the Bible, who similarly suffered a variety of afflictions. It is possible to compare the speaker in "Hanging Fire" to Job. One may even argue that the speaker is in a worse situation than Job, because Job at least learns that there is an explanation for his suffering and thus there is a chance that it may cease. The speaker in "Hanging Fire," in contrast, seems to live in a hostile universe with no sign of a power that could help her. The only such power is her mother, who is in her bedroom with the door closed, locking herself away from the speaker.

In the Book of Job, though the response Job receives from God is not entirely satisfactory—it consists largely of God saying he is all-powerful and can do anything—at least he receives a response. As a rewriting of the Book of Job, "Hanging Fire" can be seen as part of the Modernist tradition, in which God is absent from the universe. If not absent, then God as represented by momma in the poem has turned his back on sufferers and will not even answer them.

It is not clear from the poem whether the speaker has actually tried to approach her mother about her problems. Perhaps the God in this poem is simply unaware. In any case, the speaker seems to feel there is no help or even response of any sort to come from that quarter. It is a large part of her despair, as is indicated by the threefold repetition of the lines about her mother in the bedroom, that her mother is unavailable to help her cope with her long list of problems. Also if the poem is stating that people live in a hostile universe without the hope of help, it is possible to read it as even more despairing than the Book of Job. This can be said even though Job's afflictions are about the death of children and the destruction of property, while the afflictions in "Hanging Fire" are about acne and not having anything good to wear. To state the

WHAT DO I READ NEXT?

- *Sister Outsider*, published in 1984, is Lorde's first collection of essays. In the volume she deals with sexism, racism, and homophobia, and she emphasizes the importance of difference.

- For a classic novel of teenage angst, see J. D. Salinger's *The Catcher in the Rye*, published in 1951. Narrated by an alienated teenager (Holden Caulfield), the novel recounts Holden's adventures as he rebels against the phoniness he sees around him.

- Franz Kafka's *The Castle*, first published in 1926, is an earlier novel about frustrations, delay, and stagnancy. In this dark novel, the almost nameless protagonist seeks fruitlessly to enter a distant and forbidding castle.

- For a nineteenth-century novel about alienation, see Fyodor Dostoevsky's *Notes from Underground*, first published in 1864. In this novel Dostoevsky presents a bitter, unnamed narrator who criticizes both society and himself.

- *The Outsiders*, a coming-of-age novel written by S. E. Hinton when she was a teenage girl, was published in 1967, and features two rival groups of characters from broken homes.

- Sharon M. Draper's *Copper Sun* (2006) is an award-winning young-adult novel focusing on the African American experience about a teenage African girl sold into slavery in colonial America.

- For a collection of poems for and about girls, see *I Wouldn't Promise You a Valentine: Poems for Young Feminists*, edited by Carol Ann Duffy (1997). The volume includes "Hanging Fire."

- Inexplicable suffering is depicted in *When Bad Things Happen to Good People* by Harold Kushner (1981). The book is a guide for coping with the difficulties of life.

> IN THIS SENSE, THE READER CAN FEEL SIMULTANEOUSLY SWEPT UP IN THE PROBLEMS OF ADOLESCENCE AND YET ALSO STAND APART ENOUGH TO KNOW THAT THE POEM'S ULTIMATE MEANING IS THAT THE PROBLEMS DEPICTED WILL PASS."

nature of the afflictions in both cases does, however, make those in "Hanging Fire" seem much less horrible. How can one really see utter despair in a poem about having to wear braces or not having a big enough room? At least the speaker has a room. Apparently her family has enough money to pay for her braces, and the acne she complains of will go away (as will the braces).

To compare the sufferings of the speaker with those of Job thus makes one believe that the speaker is overreacting and dramatizing her situation, which is perhaps merely another way of saying she is only fourteen. It is true that the speaker feels her problems are serious—so serious, indeed, that they lead to thoughts of death. Fear of death is stated in each of the poem's three stanzas; it is something the speaker worries about, though it is not entirely clear why.

Acne and ashy knees will not cause death, nor will having to wear braces. Perhaps it is just a sign of overdramatization in the speaker that her thoughts jump to death. However, the thoughts of death do seem heartfelt. It is one of Lorde's achievements to make her readers feel like this teenager and accept her worries about mortality, which are possibly not entirely about literally dying. At one point, the speaker fears that if she dies, people will tell the truth about her. This is less a fear of death, actually, than of being exposed, presumably as some sort of failure. It is also significant that these thoughts come when she fears dying before graduation, that is, before successfully completing school. If this is a poem about failure of that sort, then perhaps the title should be interpreted to mean failure rather than delay. The final reference to death also involves failure; in the final stanza the speaker wonders whether she will live long enough to grow up and become an adult. One can thus see the poem as being about failure in a hostile world, something akin to the writings of Franz Kafka, in which characters are constantly trying to achieve something but never do. Therefore, the poem could be categorized with the despairing works of some twentieth-century modernists.

Certainly, the poem's meaning involves more than teenage angst. The haunting lines in the middle of the second stanza (about there being nothing the speaker wants to do while there is yet so much that has to be done) could be seen as a general comment on the human condition. Such an idea is applicable to both teenagers and adults. It is not just teenagers who sometimes feel that they have lost their purpose and no longer have anything they truly want to do while being weighed down by responsibilities. Yet "Hanging Fire" is primarily a poem about teenagers. To a large extent Lorde is able to put herself into the mind of a teenager and thus makes the reader feel that the speaker's problems are devastating and ominous. And there are echoes that speak to adult experience. It is terrible that the speaker feels that her mother is not there for her as well. Even so, at least for an adult reader, the opening statement that the speaker is fourteen colors all that follows and must surely provoke a slight smile as the poem unfolds. Adults know that acne passes, that there are greater tragedies than not knowing how to dance, and that most teenagers do not die before graduation.

Some teenagers do die before graduation, however. As a teenager, Lorde had a friend who committed suicide. There is some truth to the darker possibilities of the speaker's complaints. It is also true that even adults may fear that they will die before they grow up—they may die without learning what they should have or achieving all they could. This notion is perhaps Lorde's greatest triumph in "Hanging Fire." It is not just that she captures the teenage experience so that adults can read it and identify with the speaker. She also creates a haunting poem about ultimate failure, or fear of failure, even for adults, who may sometimes wish they had a mother nearby offering assistance and comfort.

One may describe this poem as a litany of foolish complaints by a self-centered teenager who asks plaintively why she has to "suffer" so much. The poem allows readers, in other words, to look at the speaker from a distance and smile at her overdramatizations. However, it also draws readers in and makes them share in the melodrama. It touches all readers in a vulnerable place. When the speaker fears that truth will be told about her, she expresses a sort of insecurity with which many may be able to identify. Why should she fear the truth? Does she think she is so bad or inadequate? In part, this poem is about secrecy. The thumb-sucking boyfriend hides his taboo habit. The speaker feels that she has hidden negative truths that will be revealed when she dies. Yet in general "Hanging Fire" examines an individual dealing with a difficult universe, whatever that universe may be. The problems may change, but there are always problems, and there may be no God or mother to help with them. However, the fact that problems change also suggests that they can be overcome. Acne goes away; braces are removed.

Near death from cancer, Lorde kept writing poetry. In one poem about death, Lorde recognizes that death has not come yet, not on this particular day. It is a poem about soldiering on despite problems. "Hanging Fire" also incorporates this message in a way. It is written both from inside and outside the mind of a teenager, because an adult poet captures how a teenager thinks and feels. In this sense, the reader can feel simultaneously swept up in the problems of adolescence and yet also stand apart enough to know that the poem's ultimate meaning is that the problems depicted will pass. It is a delicate balancing act Lorde performs in "Hanging Fire," weighing giving in to despair and recognizing that the despair is overblown.

In the end, the title of the poem must surely mean the more common meaning of "hanging fire," that is, a delay. "Hanging Fire" is about the frustrating situation of a teenager who cannot seem to move on with her life, but it is written from an adult point of view, which possesses the insight of someone older who knows that life will eventually progress. This is a point of view applicable to adults as well as teenagers. Thus, the poem may seem to speak only to and about the adolescent experience, establishing the difference of adolescents from adults. However, in the end it speaks across this difference to adults who may remember what it was like to be fourteen years old and who know that some of the feelings of adolescence never go away.

Source: Sheldon Goldfarb, Critical Essay on "Hanging Fire," in *Poetry for Students*, Gale, Cengage Learning, 2010.

Door *(Image copyright Bruno Ferrari, 2009. Used under license from Shutterstock.com)*

Brenda Carr

In the following excerpt, Carr examines the importance of gender, race, audience, and repetition—all prominent aspects of "Hanging Fire"—in Lorde's work.

. . . Audre Lorde's primary venue for coming to voice is poetry. While socialist feminists often critique cultural feminists' emphasis on aesthetic productions as being divorced from the material conditions of women's lives, Lorde asserts the opposite in her essay "Poetry is Not a Luxury":

> For women, then, poetry is not a luxury. It is a vital necessity of our existence. It forms the quality of light within which we predicate our hopes and dreams toward survival and change, first made into language, then into idea, then into more tangible action. Poetry is the way we help give name to the nameless so it can be thought.

Here, Lorde speaks in the name of women, brings gender to the fore as the basis of the coalition she envisions. For her, coming to voice in poetry provides women with "illumination," a "spawning ground for the most radical and daring of ideas."

Challenging the formalist binarism (evidenced in the Sontag essay) between the aesthetic and the historical/political, Lorde also reminds us of how the visionary is integral to liberation struggles. Alternative sociocultural realities are birthed in the realm of the imagination as Martin Luther King's "I have a dream" speech indicates. While the word "visionary" is often used negatively to mean idealistic and unpractical, it also means to have discernment and wisdom. Visionary thought, as Lorde suggests, is theory at its best, formulating future possibility, opening up the questions that can be asked.

Lorde implements her theory of visionary activism in a literary context in *The Black Unicorn.* Throughout the volume, she equates the pain of "having to live a difference that has no name" with voicelessness: "the pain of voiceless mornings / voiceless kitchens I remember / cornflakes shrieking like banshees in my throat." The volume is redolent with instances of the poet/speaker in the acts of vocalizing, laughing, singing, drumming, screaming—in short, making sounds that mark her responses to the specific conditions of her life.

VISIONARY THOUGHT, AS LORDE SUGGESTS,
IS THEORY AT ITS BEST, FORMULATING FUTURE
POSSIBILITY, OPENING UP THE QUESTIONS THAT CAN
BE ASKED."

Frequently, Lorde invokes musical or oratorical forms such as the litany, dirge, eulogy, ballad, and lullaby with such title as "A Litany for Survival" and "Woman/Dirge for Wasted Children." These signal her affiliation with African expressive culture. For instance, "A Litany for Survival" makes use of the African call-and-response pattern to give poetic shape to Lorde's theorizing of the relationship between fear, silence, and invisibility in contrast to courage, coming to voice, and visibility. This poem occupies an intersection of Western and African traditions, so that the Western liturgical form of the litany or antiphonal prayer is resonant with the African call and response structure. By repeating the lines "for those of us" at the beginning of stanzas one and two with the variant "for all of us" at the end of stanza two, the poet/speaker establishes the litany framework:

> For those of us who live at the shoreline
> standing upon the constant edges of decision
> crucial and alone
> for those of us who cannot indulge the
>   passing dreams of choice
> who love in doorways coming and going
> in the hours between dawns
> looking inward and outward
>
> . . . .
> For those of us
> who were imprinted with fear
> like a faint line in the middle of our
>   foreheads
> learning to be afraid with our mother's milk

Through phrasal repetition, the speaker signals her inclusion in a community, marked by the collective pronouns "us" and "we"; but uncharacteristically for Lorde, the communal identity is not distinctively specified. Because of this, the poem seems to gesture toward the universal. There are, however, several indicators that the members of this community affiliate around determinately intersecting oppressions. When the poet/speaker equates a future with bread in the children's mouths in

stanza one, she signals that this community is not economically privileged. Further, "heavy-footed" in stanza two, with its military and masculinist associations, suggests gender oppression. Lorde also invokes figures of liminal or in-between spaces in the opening stanza with the phrases "at the shoreline," "upon the constant edges of decision," "in doorways," "looking inward and outward." These signify the community's peripheral status. Such a spatial construction may also signal heterosexist oppression of lesbians, "who cannot indulge / the passing dreams of choice / who love in doorways coming and going."

However, such readings of the indicators of this communal subject positioning are somewhat speculative unless "A Litany for Survival" is read intertextually with other poems from *The Black Unicorn* and essays from the same period. A purely formalist reading of such a poem in isolation from its contexts is an abdication of the responsibility that attends reading across different subject positionings, although this is an issue I can only gesture toward here. Because an ethically responsible contextualized reading accounts for the particular communities invoked in the poem, it uncloses the notion of the lyric as a bounded text, a private voice speaking in a closed frame. Phrases and concepts circulate between the poem and a resonant essay (one of many possible sociodiscursive contexts). "The Transformation of Silence into Language and Action" was originally delivered at the 1977 MLA "Lesbian and Literature Panel" and originally published in *The Cancer Journals,* written during Lorde's experience with breast cancer. Her near death caused her to realize that safety in silence is a false illusion. In "A Litany for Survival," by cataloging and ultimately playing a reversal on a litany of fears that block speech-acts of resistance, she enjoins other black women to come to voice despite silencing fears:

> when we are loved we are afraid
> love will vanish
> when we are alone we are afraid
> love will never return
> and when we speak we are afraid
> our words will not be heard
> nor welcomed
> but when we are silent
> we are still afraid.
> So it is better to speak
> remembering
> we were never meant to survive.

A moving intertext from "The Transformation of Silence into Language and Action" marks the specific communities signaled by the ambiguously unmarked pronoun "we" in the poem:

> In the cause of silence, each of us draws the face of her own fear—fear of contempt, of censure, or some judgment, or recognition, of challenge, of annihilation. But most of all, I think, we fear the visibility without which we cannot truly live. Within this country where racial difference creates a constant, if unspoken, distortion of vision, Black women have on one hand always been highly visible, and so, on the other hand, have been rendered invisible through the depersonalization of racism. Even within the women's movement, we have had to fight and still do, for that very visibility which also renders us most vulnerable, our Blackness. For to survive in the mouth of this dragon we call America, we have had to learn this first and most vital lesson—that we were never meant to survive. Not as human beings. And neither were most of you here today, Black or not. And that visibility which makes us most vulnerable is that which also is the source of our greatest strength. Because the machine will try to grind you into dust anyway, whether or not you speak. We can sit in our corners mute forever while our sisters and our selves are wasted, while our children are distorted and destroyed, while our earth is poisoned; we can sit in our safe corners mute as bottles, and we will still be no less afraid.

In this excerpt, which explicitly equates coming to voice with cultural visibility, Lorde seems to speak first in the name of generic woman: "each of us draws the face of her own fear." However, it soon becomes clear that she is speaking specifically in the name of black women, to and for them from within their shared experience of racism. In this way, she problematizes the notion of a generic "woman" for the women's movement by reminding us that sexual difference can never be the only explanation for unequal power relations. Similarly, when she ends her poem "A Woman Speaks" with the declaration "I am woman and not white," Lorde brings the black woman to what bell hooks calls the "speaking center," while shifting a white academic woman such as myself to the rearground.

Survival is defined in terms of race as well as gender. However, as soon as Lorde invokes the nominal essentialism of her racial identity as it intersects with gender in the essay, she undercuts this as a stable point of location by gesturing back toward the universal to include her audience members at large in the group who were never meant to survive. In this way, Lorde speaks in "diverse known tongues" (Henderson

> **"** I WAS ONE OF THE EDITORS OF OUR HIGH-SCHOOL MAGAZINE AND WROTE A LOVE SONNET FOR THE MAGAZINE. BUT A TEACHER SAID, 'NO, NO,' THAT IT COULDN'T BE PUBLISHED. SO I SUBMITTED IT TO *SEVENTEEN* MAGAZINE AND IT WAS PUBLISHED.**"**

1989, 22), negotiates multiple axes of community affiliation, in a manner that suggests the possibility of a provisionalized universal around which coalitions of "corresponding differences" may be formed (Marlatt 1990, 189)....

Source: Brenda Carr, "'A Woman Speaks...I am Woman and Not White': Politics of Voice, Tactical Essentialism, and Cultural Intervention in Audre Lorde's Activist Poetics and Practice," in *Race-ing Representation: Voice, History, & Sexuality*, edited by Kostas Myrsiades and Linda Myrsiades, Roman & Littlefield, 1998, pp. 119–40.

William Steif

In the following excerpt from an interview with Steif, Lorde reflects on her life, politics, and motivations for writing.

Audre Lorde, fifty-six, describes herself as "a black-lesbian-feminist-warrior-poet-mother." She is all of those things and more: Author of a dozen books, teacher, lecturer, cancer patient, exemplar of courage, exponent of unvarnished truth. She has championed the rights of women, lesbians, blacks, and Third World people, and she has pioneered the writing of political poetry. Her works include *ZAMI: A New Spelling of My Name*, *Sister Outsider*, *The Cancer Journals*, *The Black Unicorn*, *Chosen Poems—Old and New*, and *Our Dead Behind Us*.

Lorde now lives in St. Croix in the U.S. Virgin Islands in a pleasant house not far from the sea. It was there I first encountered her after she'd returned from addressing a conference in Boston.

Q: As the daughter of Grenadian parents and as a socialist, what did you—and what do you—think of the U.S. "intervention" in Grenada in 1983?

Audre Lorde: I feel right now exactly the same way I felt in 1983. The Pentagon was spoiling for a fight for a long time, the same as in Panama. There were many lies then and these are still lies. Grenada hasn't been broken but it's been terribly attacked. The United States isn't concerned now, but unemployment in Grenada today is far higher than it was under the New Jewel Movement. There are many social ills. The magnificent U.S. promises didn't materialize. I believe now that if the United States were remotely interested in democracy in the Caribbean, it wouldn't be supporting Haiti and the Dominican Republic.

Q: Despite your Caribbean background, you're a New Yorker, born and bred. How come?

Lorde: My father, originally from Barbados, moved with my mother to Grenada in 1924. That was part of a large migration because of a drought in Barbados. My mother was from Grenville [Grenada's east-coast town]. My mother had sisters working in New York. The dream in those days was to make some money in New York and return to the islands to open a little store or business. My parents came to New York and then came the Depression and babies—I was born in 1934.

Q: Where did you live in New York?

Lorde: In the middle of Manhattan, 142nd Street and Lenox Avenue. My mother was Catholic and I went to a Catholic neighborhood school. I sat for the Hunter High School entrance exam and passed. While in high school, I also worked at what was then Beth David Hospital, a private hospital.

Q: When did you start writing?

Lorde: I've always written. I was—am—an avid reader. I wrote poetry in the seventh or eighth grade and loved music. Some teachers encouraged me and I expressed a lot of things about how I felt. I was one of the editors of our high-school magazine and wrote a love sonnet for the magazine. But a teacher said, "no, no," that it couldn't be published. So I submitted it to *Seventeen* magazine and it was published.

Q: You continued writing then?

Lorde: Yes, I developed from there. I came to writing early. I got out of Hunter High in 1951 and entered Hunter College. I left home right after high school and became self-supporting, but I didn't get out of Hunter College until 1959–1960. After a year at college I went to Mexico, taught, wrote, traveled. In Mexico I saw something different: It was the first time I'd seen dark-skinned people,

people of color, everywhere. I'd always had the feeling I was strange, different, that there was something wrong with me. In Mexico I learned to walk upright, to say the things I felt. I became conscious that I hadn't the courage to speak up.

Q: This changed your life?

Lorde: Like all of us, I'd started as a coward, inarticulate, very shy. I have to put a political context into this—it was the height of the McCarthy era. Those of us who called ourselves progressives, who sought an alternative way, were perceived to be under threat. We thought about the Rosenbergs and said this is not right. I was driven by a sense of moral outrage.

Q: How did you come to socialism?

Lorde: When you're engaged in the world, you try to see what is best for yourself and for others. I extrapolate what's best for me and others and come to socialism as the only real way to make sense of life.

Q: You chose to marry a white man in the early 1960s. How did that happen?

Lorde: Nothing in our lives just happens. I married a legal-aid attorney in Brooklyn in 1962. He's now in private practice. We were divorced in 1970. It was a difficult time for a black woman and a white man to be married. Our children are very important. Our daughter, twenty-seven, is now in her second year of medical school. Our son, twenty-six, is an intelligence officer in the U.S. Navy. He's a very good person. I trust him, though I have very strong feelings against the U.S. military opposing liberation movements around the world.

Q: How can the racism and sexism that seem so endemic to U.S. society be overcome?

Lorde: More and more I feel that racism, sexism, and homophobia have become more articulated in the last ten years. The Reagan-Bush Administrations have legitimized these positions with financial pressures. There's a sense of doom here. To overcome these positions I—or anyone—must work in the service of what we believe. The first step is recognition—recognizing that none of us is untouched by anything in this country or in the world. Then we have to recognize the force of what we believe in. You speak up to the racist cab driver or you speak about what is excluded from the school curriculum.

You are who you are. You take what you are and learn to use it. This happened in [Eastern] Europe and has to happen here. We talk about what the American dream offers, but there are too many people in the United States who are set apart from the American dream. Look at the American Indians, for example. There are going to be periods of upheaval. I think it'll be worse before it's better. But it is going to get better.

Q: You were nearly refused entry into the British Virgin Islands last year because you wear your hair in dreadlocks style. What happened?

Lorde: Yes, and I wouldn't have been able to go to Virgin Gorda for Christmas as planned. I was asked if I was a Rastafarian. I wanted to say, "What does it matter if I am a Rasta or not?" But I saw our bags sitting out in the sun, the pilot walking slowly to his plane. Deep in my heart I thought, "It is always the same question, where do we begin to take a stand?" But I turned away. "No, I am not a Rastafarian," I said, and I am not. But deep inside me I felt I was being asked to deny some piece of myself, and I felt a solidarity with my Rastafarian brothers and sisters I had never been conscious of before. Later I used my words to spread the story around.

Q: Why have you come to live in St. Croix?

Lorde: I had my first bout with cancer—that was breast cancer—in 1978 and my second bout, liver cancer, in 1984. It was then I came here to Gloria Joseph's house to avoid the increasingly difficult winters. I had my third bout—with ovarian cancer—in 1987, and thought it would be easier living in St. Croix, which is so much warmer and smaller than New York. In addition, I always felt a pull back to the Caribbean.

Q: When you write you always lower-case the A in america and the C in christian. Why?

Lorde: I do it because I'm angry about the pretenses of america—lower-case a. It's on the wrong side of every liberation struggle on Earth. When I travel abroad I say I'm an African Caribbean-american and I am registering my protest at the american refusal to give up power. I feel pretty much the same way about christianity.

Q: You were raised by a Catholic mother and attended Catholic schools. Do you belong to or attend any church?

Lorde: I considered myself a Quaker. The gap between what Catholics say and do is too great. I raised my children to give them a sense of the divine. But now I consider myself an animist.

Q: Your poetry sometimes is extremely specific, as in references to a ten-year-old black boy

murdered in Brooklyn and his white killer acquitted. Is the specificity done primarily to vent your own feelings or do you want to impress others with the crime's monstrousness?

Lorde: I was teaching at John Jay College of Criminal Justice in New York when that particular acquittal came through. I was driving crosstown when I heard about it [on the radio] and I felt a rush of rage. I wanted to run down the first white person I saw. Instead, I pulled over on 77th Street and wrote in my journal, making a piece of truth inescapable. Poetry is the conflict in the lives we lead. Poetry as an art intensifies ourselves, alters and underlines our feelings. It is most subversive because it is in the business of encouraging change.

Q: Living in the Caribbean, do you pay much attention to what's happening in such places as Haiti or Cuba?

Lorde: I try to be conscious of what's happening in the Caribbean. One of the salvations of the Virgin Islands is the recognition of these islands' connection to Caribbean life. At the same time, the Virgin Islands are in a very anomalous position. They are a colony receiving manna from the United States, but on the other hand the United States puts us down. We are neither fish nor fowl.

Actually, that is a favorite position of mine, the outsider—there is strength in that, you can see both directions at once. But the position of the United States in the Caribbean is so retrograde...

Source: Audre Lorde and William Steif, "Interview with Audre Lorde," in *Progressive,* Vol. 55, No. 1, January 1991, pp. 32–33.

SOURCES

Birkle, Carmen, *Women's Stories of the Looking Glass: Autobiographical Reflections and Self-Representations in the Poetry of Sylvia Plath, Adrienne Rich, and Audre Lorde,* Fink, 1996, pp. 179, 212.

Brewer's Dictionary of Phrase & Fable, 9th ed., Cassell, 1965.

Brooks, Jerome, "In the Name of the Father: The Poetry of Audre Lorde," in *Black Women Writers (1950-1980): A Critical Evaluation,* edited by Mari Evans, Anchor Press/Doubleday, 1984, pp. 274–75.

De Veaux, Alexis, *Warrior Poet: A Biography of Audre Lorde,* W. W. Norton, 2004, pp. 5–13, 38–39, 91–93, 99–100, 163, 214, 217, 312, 313.

Lorde, Audre, "Hanging Fire," in *The Collected Poems of Audre Lorde*, W. W. Norton, 1997, p. 308.

———, *Zami: A New Spelling of My Name*, Crossing Press, 1982, p. 62.

Nolte, Dorothee, "The Law Is Male and White: Meeting with the Black Author, Audre Lorde," in *Conversations with Audre Lorde*, edited by Joan Wylie Hall, University Press of Mississippi, 2004, pp. vii, 143.

Oxford English Dictionary, online edition, Oxford University Press, 2009, http://dictionary.oed.com/cgi/entry/50102326, entry “hang-fire” (accessed June 9, 2009).

Webster's New World Dictionary of the American Language, 2nd college ed., Simon & Schuster, 1984.

FURTHER READING

Evans, Sara M., *Born for Liberty: A History of Women in America*, rev. ed., Free Press, 1997.
    This historical study traces the role of women in the United States from the seventeenth century to the late twentieth century.

Gabbin, Joanne V., ed., *The Furious Flowering of African American Poetry*, University Press of Virginia, 1999.
    In this collection of essays and interviews from the 1994 Furious Flower Conference on African American Poetry, Gabbin presents discussions of the various issues connected to African American poetry.

Smith, Barbara, ed., *Home Girls: A Black Feminist Anthology*, Rutgers University Press, 2000.
    First published in 1983, this revised edition contains poetry and other writings by black feminist and lesbian writers, including a poem by Lorde.

Straus, Martha B., *Adolescent Girls in Crisis: Intervention and Hope*, W. W. Norton, 2007.
    Straus discusses the rage and despair felt by many adolescent girls and discusses what to do to help.

The Horses

TED HUGHES

1957

Ted Hughes's poem "The Horses" appears in his first published collection of poetry, *The Hawk in the Rain* (1957). Hughes's wife, Sylvia Plath, encouraged him to enter his poetry manuscript in a book publishing contest sponsored by the American publisher Harper & Brothers Publishers. The manuscript won first prize. Published in England later that same year, *The Hawk in the Rain* helped to make Hughes a well-known poet in both the United States and England. The book also won the Guinness Poetry Award in 1958. Many of the poems this collection focus on nature, which would become a continuing theme in much in Hughes's work throughout his career. "The Horses" is thirty-seven lines of free verse, mostly divided into two-line stanzas. The poem tells of the narrator's vision of ten horses silhouetted against the predawn sky. Although many of Hughes's poems about animals focus on the violence of nature, "The Horses" emphasizes the beauty and strength of nature. The poem also captures the isolation of nature and reflects the poet's love of the countryside and animals, which he first experienced as a young boy growing up in Mytholmroyd, England. "The Horses" is included in the 2003 volume, *The Collected Poems of Ted Hughes*, published posthumously.

Ted Hughes (*AP Images*)

AUTHOR BIOGRAPHY

Hughes was born Edward James Hughes on August 17, 1930, in Mytholmroyd, a small mill town in West Yorkshire, in northern England. Hughes was the youngest of three children and was known throughout his life by his nickname, "Ted." His mother, Edith, was a homemaker; and his father, Henry, was a carpenter who built portable wooden buildings. Hughes loved the English countryside and the animals he encountered there. In 1937 the family moved to Mexborough, a coal-mining town, where Hughes's father bought a small newspaper store. Hughes attended local grammar schools and after graduation from high school spent two years in the Royal Air Force. Upon completion of his military service, Hughes enrolled at Pembroke College at Cambridge University in Cambridge, England, where he studied English and anthropology. Also at Pembroke College, he began to write poetry. He graduated with a B.A. in 1954. In 1956, Hughes cofounded *St. Botolph's Review*, literary magazine. Around the same time, he met the American poet Sylvia Plath, who was studying at Cambridge on a Fulbright scholarship. They married only a few months later. Hughes's first collection of poetry,

The Hawk in the Rain (1957) won first prize in a book publishing contest promoted by Harper & Brothers Publishers and the 1958 Guinness Poetry Award.

For a brief period after they married, Hughes and Plath lived in Massachusetts, where he taught at Amherst College. However, in 1959 they returned to England where their first child, Frieda, was born in 1960. That same year, Hughes's published his second collection of poetry, *Lupercal*, for which he was awarded a Guggenheim fellowship and a Somerset Maugham Award. A second child, Nicholas, was born to Hughes and Plath in 1962. During these early years of fatherhood, Hughes began writing books for children, including a collection of poetry for children *Meet My Folks*, published in 1961.

In 1962 Hughes fell in love with Assia Gutmann Wevill, a married woman who rented Hughes's apartment, and he began an affair with her. Hughes and Plath separated, but before they could divorce, Plath committed suicide the following year by asphyxiation from the gas oven in their kitchen. Hughes refused to discuss Plath's suicide and was often blamed for it by Plath's admirers. In 1965, Hughes and Wevill had a daughter together, Shura. In 1967, two additional collections of Hughes's poems were published—*Animal Poems* and *Gravestones*. In 1969, Wevill murdered four-year-old Shura and committed suicide in the same manner as Plath.

Some of Hughes's best-known poetry focuses on animals, including one of his most famous collections, *Crow: From the Life and Songs of the Crow*, published in 1970. Hughes married Carol Orchard in 1970, and the two lived on her father's Devonshire farm, where Hughes would write about his experiences as a farmer in a collection of poems, *Moortown* (1979). Hughes was appointed poet laureate of England in 1984, for which he was paid a small stipend and a case of wine every year. Hughes never spoke of Plath, but in 1998 a collection of poems that he wrote about their love for one another and their marriage was published as *The Birthday Letters*. The work won the T. S. Eliot Prize for Poetry, South Bank Award for Literature, Whitbread Prize for Poetry, and Whitbread Book of the Year award.

Hughes was a prolific writer who had at least thirty collections of poetry published. He wrote many plays, including drama for adults and children, and many works of prose. Hughes also edited and translated many other works. In all, he published more than one hundred works over the course of his life. He was awarded the Order of Merit by Queen Elizabeth II in October 1998. On October 28, 1998, Hughes died of a heart attack while undergoing treatment for colon cancer at his home in North Tawton, England, and was buried at Westminster Abbey in London, England. Hughes and Plath's son, Nicholas, committed suicide by hanging himself on March 16, 2009 after a long struggle with depression.

POEM SUMMARY

Stanzas 1–2
"The Horses" opens with the narrator explaining that he is walking through the woods in the early morning hour. He uses the word climbing to suggest that there is exertion involved and that he is moving uphill. It is still night, not yet dawn, the narrator explains, and so readers understand that the narrator walks in the darkness. Strangely the poet describes the night air as evil air. The use of evil suggests air with the potential to be harmful, or perhaps just miserable in its isolation and coldness. It is cold enough that the speaker sees his breath in the chill air. The darkness and cold make the walk seem particularly difficult. Nothing is moving in the cold. There is no breeze to stir the leaves on the trees, nor are there any birds to welcome the narrator on his lonely morning walk. The narrator climbs through the woods and emerges above the tree line. The world is frozen, still without sound or movement. This is fitting, given the early morning cold and the white frost visible on the surface of the world. The image in these first two stanzas is a world defined as inhospitable, frigid, and isolating.

Stanzas 3–4
In stanza 3, the reader learns that the air is so cold that the narrator's breath freezes, instead of evaporating into the air. He describes the shape of his frozen breath as twisted or winding. It is still not dawn, but there is some impenetrable light, the color of iron, a gray that is not quite black. However, that faint light penetrates only the top of the hill, where the narrator stands. In the moors (countryside) below the woods, the sun has not yet reached into the darkness. The moors are open land, often marshy and sometimes covered with heather. The moors are sometimes thought of as wasteland, even uninhabitable, although both

MEDIA ADAPTATIONS

- *Ted Hughes: Poetry in the Making*, published in January 2008 by the British Library, is a two-CD set of Hughes reading his poetry and explaining how he composes his poems. The recordings on this CD set were made for schools and were designed to inspire students to write poetry.

- *Ted Hughes: Poems and Short Stories*, published in January 2008 by the British Library, is a two-CD set of recordings in which Hughes reads many of his poems. This set also includes interviews with Hughes and discussions about his feelings about being appointed poet laureate of England.

- *Ted Hughes Reading His Poetry*, published in May 1996 by HarperCollins, is an audio book of Hughes reading many of his poems.

- *Saving the American Wild Horse* is a 2008 documentary by filmmaker James Kleinert. This documentary captures the beauty of horses, as depicted in Hughes's poem "The Horses."

- *El Caballo* is a 2001 documentary film by High Plains Films about the wild Spanish horses, much like those described in Hughes's poem that were brought to North America in the 1500s.

humans and animals live there. On the moors, the higher hills block the light, and so the valley seems to siphon off the darkness of the night, holding on to it, long after the faintness of dawn has begun to cast some light on the tops of the hills. This is the moment when there is a line separating dark from dawn, black from gray. It is as if the sky has been cut in half, with one side gray and the other still enveloped in black. This is the moment when the narrator tells readers that he sees horses. These are "the" horses, not his horses or the farmer's horses. The use of "the" signifies that the horses are not owned. They simply exist; they are free. This line ends with a colon, which signals the reader to pay special attention to the first line of the next stanza.

Stanzas 5–6

Stanza 5 begins with a description of the horses. It is their sheer size that is first noticed. They are huge, barely seen against the gray sky. There are ten horses. They stand so still that the poet compares them to megaliths, a term that refers to the huge Neolithic monuments that were built by ancient people. This description suggests something akin to Stonehenge—impressively large. They breathe, but except for the movement of their chests, they stand still, accepting that they are objects of admiration and fascination. The narrator described the draped manes of the horses, suggesting that their manes have been carefully arranged and are not just the result of chance. The horses remain still, their hind hooves tilted, as though posed in wait for the morning rains to begin. This tilting of hind hooves is the pose of horses who must stand and endure the cold rains. The horses fit perfectly with the descriptions of the woods in the cold morning. Like the woods and the hill above, the horses emit no sound. They are perfectly silent.

Stanzas 7–8

In stanza 7, the poet writes that he walks past the horses but they do not acknowledge his presence. It is as if he does not exist to them. There is no movement to flee, nor any movement to suggest that the horses are aware of the narrator passing. The horses are motionless entities, standing silently in the gray morning light. Hughes refers to the horses as gray fragments to suggest their isolation. They are detached from the world in which the narrator stands. The horses are a piece of nature, a fragment of the world, a seemingly incomplete part of the gray world of the narrator's experience. It is as if the horses exist in a separate physical dimension from that of the narrator.

Stanzas 9–10

In stanza 9, the poet stands on the moor ridge listening to the silence. The quiet of the moment mirrors the seeming emptiness of his world. The narrator suggests his own emptiness in line 16 when he describes how he listens "in emptiness," implying that the emptiness is within him. His life is as barren as the moment in which he emerged from the woods to the darkness above the tree line. When the narrator feels most alone, he hears the sound of the curlew (a large marsh-dwelling bird with a curved bill that is almost one-third its body length), shrieking at the narrator's intrusion. It is

as if the bird's call is an order for nature to release the sun and clear away the darkness. For a few moments, the narrator can pick out small details still partially hidden by the predawn darkness, but then suddenly the sun bursts through to eliminate the darkness. Hughes refers to this moment as the sun erupting. The world in which he stands is suddenly and almost violently changed.

Stanzas 11–12

The eruption of the sunrise has been without sound, except of course for the curlew's shrieking. The violence of the sunrise is emphasized in the poet's description of the moment when the sun lights the sky with vivid colors. The shadows just before sunrise have been replaced with all of the colors illuminated by the sun. The sun breaks through the gray of early morning, revealing the blueness of sky. This is not a gradual illumination though. The sunrise is a violent upheaval, where the night sky is torn open and the sun forces itself through to escape the darkness. Hughes captures what happens in the early morning, when it seems that in the distant sky there is a flicker of gray, and within the briefest moment, it appears that the sun is thrust out into the open. The suddenness of the sunrise is too fast for the night sky. The stars of night and the planets that are seen as only small stars do not have time to hide. Instead, they are left hanging there for just a moment, exposed in daylight, as sometimes happens to the moon, when it shares the sky with the sun, as if it had forgotten that it should only be seen at night. At this moment, the narrator turns and begins to move once again.

Stanzas 13–14

In stanza 13, the shock of the sunrise leads the narrator to stumble as if barely awake. He walks down the hill, as if in a dream, toward the woods and the trees below him. He moves toward the shelter of the woods, where he is protected from the light that threatens to expose him to what he does not wish to see. He stumbles back toward the horses. They are standing as they did earlier, but now the sun shines on them, clarifying all that the poet struggled to see when they stood in the darkness of early dawn. They remain quiet and still, as if they are indeed the megaliths of an ancient people. Although they do not move, the horses emit their own heat in the early morning cold. Their breath is like steam in the air and their coats shine, reflecting the sun's rays. Where they stand, the world is alive.

Stanzas 15–17

As they were in stanza 6, the manes of the horses are once again draped, artfully arranged. The horses stand ready to move, with hooves tilted, as if once again ready for the rain so common to the English countryside. They appear to move, stirring in the dawn, and yet they remain still. The horses are living things, to which nature responds by coming alive in the morning sun. The frost of early dawn succumbs to the heat of the sun. There is movement as the frost thaws, but not from the horses, which continue to stand quietly. This stillness is noted in the first lines of the poem, emphasized again in line 5 in the narrator's breath, and in line 10 when the horses are described as huge stones. The horses do not snort, as they might in an attempt to get the scent of the man who intrudes upon their world. There is no moving of their heads in an effort to see the man who walks toward them. Nor do they stamp their feet, as might be expected as they prepare to flee. Instead, the horses continue to be an image of complete stillness. They are as unchanging as the world in which they live. In this small part of Hughes's world, the landscape remains stagnant. The horses hang their heads in much the same way as the sun hangs in the sky. The image is one of constancy—a world in which the sun rises in the sky each morning to illuminate the valley below.

Stanzas 18–19

In the final two stanzas, the narrator takes the memory of the horses and the stillness of that dawn with him. Although Hughes no longer lives in the Calder Valley of his childhood, the home of his childhood continues to haunt his life and his poetry. This feeling is transferred to the narrator. Whether he lives in a busy city amongst strangers and seeing faces he does not recognize, recalling the horses brings him back to the quiet and isolation of that moment when he stood above the trees, looking down, and first saw the horses. The poet can still find his memory in that place, where the sunrise did more than lighten the day; it revealed his own loneliness and isolation. Although he stumbled toward the safe darkness of the woods that morning, the image of the horses and their quiet strength left the narrator with a sense of resilience and power that he had previously lacked. The freedom of the horses and the connection they make with the narrator reminds him of his own struggle toward freedom. The scream of the curlew woke the narrator to the world that had been hidden by the gray-black of night and revealed to him his own strength.

THEMES

Color

The world that Hughes creates in the opening lines of "The Horses" is painted in shades of gray and black. The woods are dark, and even when the narrator emerges from the woods, he is able to hide in a world still hidden by the night sky, disappearing into the gray of early dawn. The gray of this world suggests a world of emptiness, but it seems to offer safety for the narrator. The horses, when he can see them, appear as if they are huge rocks and not living beings. Where the blackness had initially seemed empty, the gray of early morning reveals the horses, just waiting to be discovered. The narrator marvels that the horses blend into the gray of early dawn. They fit into their world perfectly, which is something the narrator strives to do but cannot manage completely. He does not fit in, which becomes evident when the sun begins to rise in the sky. At the first glimmer of the sun, described in vivid terms of reds and oranges and blues, the narrator seeks to flee, stumbling in his rush to escape being illuminated. He wants to hide in the nothingness of gray and black.

The blackness of night is also sometimes thought of as evil, which is a term that the narrator uses in line 2 to describe the air of the woods as he walks through them. The color black is also associated with sorrow and suffering and with the loss of hope. As the dawn approaches and the sky turns to gray, the meaning associated with that color is one of dreariness. Although black is often referred to as a color, in fact, black is caused by the absorption of all light rays and so technically is the absence of color. Gray is the imperfect absorption of light rays, and so it is the flawed absence of color. The brilliant primary colors revealed by the sunrise force the narrator to face the world, which in the final stanzas has brought healing to his life.

Horses

The setting for "The Horses" is the natural world, but the horses appear to be more than representative of nature. They are almost magical. The horses are depicted as perfect beings, the creation of a

TOPICS FOR
FURTHER
STUDY

- Imitate Hughes's poetic style of free verse, repetition, and line breaks. Using his poem as a guide, write at least two poems that imitate his style, language use, and content. When you have completed your poems, write a brief evaluation of your work, comparing it to Hughes's poem. In your critique, consider what you learned about the difficulty of writing poetry about animals and nature.

- Poetry can create images in the reader's mind. Imagist poetry uses brevity and conciseness of language to create images that the poem's reader can visualize while reading the poem. Draw or illustrate in some way one of the images that Hughes's poem creates in your mind as you read it. Present this drawing to your class and explain its relevance to the poem.

- Hughes also wrote stories for children. Like his poetry, his stories are very autobiographical, in some cases, like poetry transformed into prose. Stories can also be transformed into poetry. Instead of writing a research paper, write a research poem from the perspective of either a woman or a man. Choose a famous person from history and use at least one or two important events from his or her life to create a narrative poem. Remember that poetry does not have to rhyme. Instead, try to use free verse to capture the emotion and intensity of this person's life. Write a brief description of your poem, explaining how it evokes the historical figure's life experiences.

- An excellent way to understand poetry is to read it aloud, and yet very few readers make an effort to do so. Read Hughes's poem aloud to yourself, and then read it to an audience of friends or classmates. Ask two or three of your peers to read the poem aloud and listen to their voices, noting the inflections of tone as he or she reads it. What do you discover about the poem in each of these readings? Consider if the poem changes with these subsequent readings and what you learn about poetry. Record the readings and share them with your class, presenting your observations.

- Artists are often inspired to create their works by poets. Spend some time looking through art books in the library and try to select a picture or illustration that you feel best illustrates Hughes's poem. Then, in an essay, compare the art that you have selected to "The Horses," noting similarities and differences in the portrayals of wild horses.

- Hughes's poem captures an image that is often described in Native American stories and poetry: the isolation, majesty, and beauty of horses as they run freely across the landscape. Research Native American legends about horses and write an essay in which you compare the legend that you have chosen to Hughes's poem.

- Research the life of one of the following twentieth-century British poets who were contemporaries of Hughes: Geoffrey Hill, Basil Bunting, Lee Harwood, David G. Jones, and Tom Raworth. Write a research paper in which you discuss how this person's life, history, and experiences are reflected in at least two of his poems. Use images, collected online or from books, to supplement your paper.

perfect nature. They appear in the gray dawn as if they have always been standing there, waiting to be discovered by the narrator. They stand as magical creatures, as large as huge rocks or statues created by an ancient people to honor their perfection. There is absolutely no movement in the early gray sky of dawn, and yet, the horses are alive. They stand as if posed by a sculptor. Their manes

Horse *(Image copyright Jaimie Duplass, 2009. Used under license from Shutterstock.com)*

are perfectly draped by nature's hand, and they stand with their hind hooves slightly tilted. The horses are nature at its best, completely independent of human intervention. They exist without the narrator, and in fact, they do not acknowledge his presence. The impression is that the horses have always existed as they do that morning when the narrator sees them and will exist long after he has left. Their perfection has a healing effect upon the narrator, who uses the memory of that early morning encounter to combat the noise of the city and fill him with a spirituality that the memory of the horses brings into his life.

Sound

Although the only sound is of the curlew's shriek, "The Horses" illuminates the importance of simply listening. This is a world in which the absence of sound reveals much of the poet's meaning. In the first stanza the emphasis is on the stillness of the predawn world. The horses are the first living beings that the narrator sees on his journey, and yet they are completely silent. They do not move in any way. Even their breathing is without sound. As the world comes to life around them, the horses reveal the quiet strength of survival. This calm offers an important lesson for the narrator. By the end of the poem, the narrator wants to hear again the sound of the horizon, the sound of quiet. The busy streets are not unlike the cry of the curlew, filled with shrieks and noises that disrupt the quiet of the narrator's thoughts, but when he recalls that morning when he stood and looked at the horses and the valley below him, he is able to recall the stillness of that earlier world and the healing power of silence.

STYLE

End-stopped Lines

End-stopped lines occur when a phrase or sentence is marked at the end of a line with a mark of punctuation. In a few cases, such as at the end of lines 3, 7, and 9, Hughes uses a long dash to signal a pause for the reader. In addition to the long dash, there are several sentences with no punctuation, in which Hughes instead uses enjambment (the continuation of a thought through to the next line of poetry).

Free Verse

Free verse is verse with no discernible structure, rhyme scheme, or meter. Free verse allows the poet to fit the poetic line to the content of the poem. The poet is not restricted by the need to shape the poem to a particular meter but can instead create complex rhythm and syntax. Free verse is not the same as blank verse, which also does not use a rhyme scheme. Blank verse almost always adheres to iambic pentameter, while free verse relies on line breaks to create a rhythm. Free verse is most often associated with modern poetry, such as Hughes's poem. There is no pattern of rhyme or meter to "The Horses;" instead, the irregular line breaks give the poem a musical rhythm that is best appreciated by reading it aloud.

Line Breaks

Line breaks are a defining element of poetry. They are one characteristic that is used to impart meaning or to focus the reader's emphasis on an idea, to create a rhyme or rhythm, or to lend a specific appearance to the poem on the page. Hughes uses line breaks to create a brief pause and to emphasize ideas. The use of a line break at line 14 emphasizes the importance of the phrase that follows at line 15 and the repetition of the gray silent world. Line breaks are not the same as the use of the long dash at line 22, where Hughes wants to create more tension and put more emphasis on his having turned to flee. The line breaks force the reader's attention on those words, whose meaning emphasizes the words that precede and follow.

Modern Poetry

The label "modern poetry," like modern novels and other forms of modern literature, refers to the poet's strong and conscious effort to break away from tradition. Modern poetry attempts to create a new world by changing perceptions of the old world. Modern literary works identify the individual as more important than either society or social conventions and privileges the mind and the poet's inward thoughts. The imagination of the poet often prefers the unconscious actions of the individual. Hughes's poetry suggests that poets can be free of conventional ideas about nature. His poem moves beyond typical definitions of what is pretty to privilege strength over fragility, just as modern poetry values the freedom to challenge traditions.

Repetition

Repetition of a word, sound, or phrase is useful in emphasizing ideas in a poem. This stylistic device is one way to express several ideas of similar importance in a similar manner or to establish the importance of a particular idea. Hughes uses repetition to emphasize ideas and create tension. For example, repetition is used when the speaker states that he climbed (structurally repeated in lines 13, 16, and 23) and as he states that he passed, listened, and turned. Another example occurs with the use of the phrase "grey silent" in lines 14 and 15, in which Hughes demands that the reader visualize these horses as representative of the world in which they live, a world in which they fit quite perfectly into nature. This use of repetition focuses the reader's attention on these words and actions and signifies their importance in the poem.

Symbolism

Symbolism is the use of one object to represent another idea. During the nineteenth century, American writers used symbolism as a way to infuse images of nature as representative of ideas, rather than actual objects or beings. In late nineteenth-century France, writers used symbolism as a way to represent unique emotional responses, often in very complex ways. "The Horses" provides several examples of symbolism in poetry. For instance, the shriek of the curlew is a symbol of the intrusiveness of sound that interrupts the silence of the morning. Later, back in the city, the narrator recalls the sound of the curlew and connects it to the noisiness of city life. However, the horses are probably the most important symbol in Hughes's poem. The horses symbolize the perfection of nature certainly, but they also symbolize freedom and create an emotional response in the narrator, which is one of strength and endurance. Like the megaliths to which they are compared, the horses endure, standing silently in the valley below. Later, when he is living in the city, the narrator identifies with the freedom, endurance, and strength of horses, which now represents a world far different than the chaotic world of his life in the city.

HISTORICAL CONTEXT

Rural Life in Yorkshire

The world that Hughes captures in "The Horses" is an idyllic oasis in the country, presumably in Yorkshire, England, Hughes's childhood home and the location for many of his poems. Historically, Yorkshire was an agricultural area, but more importantly, it was the center of the wool industry in England, from as early as the fifteenth century. Although Yorkshire continued to be recognized for its wool industry and cloth trade, it also became known for its mineral waters and spas, which drew many visitors. Industry became important to the economy in Yorkshire as well, especially coal mining and steel. In Mexborough, England, the small town where Hughes grew up, the economy was based on industry, especially coal mining, brickwork, stone quarrying, and rail transportation.

As industry grew, illness and mortality also increased. By the early twentieth century, overcrowding in many areas of Yorkshire became a problem, as did unemployment, which was on the rise by the 1930s. Prior to World War II, farming had declined in the rural towns of Yorkshire, which was true of many rural areas in England where industry had assumed a greater importance in rural life. However, in the first year of the war, it is estimated that more than four hundred merchant ships were lost to German attack. As a result, the rural communities of England started a program

COMPARE
&
CONTRAST

- **1950s:** Prior to World War II, an estimated 50 percent to 70 percent of the food consumed in England is imported from other countries. German submarine attacks severely halt food imports, resulting in a policy of strict food rationing. Rationing during World War II leads to the consumption of horse meat in Great Britain and the United States. The rationing of meat in England does not end until 1954, and thus the consumption of horse meat continues in Great Britain until that time. In Yorkshire, where Hughes grew up, horse meat is eaten until the late 1940s.

  Today: In 2007, when celebrity chef Gordon Ramsay publicizes his plan to serve horse meat at his London restaurant, he is met with many protests. Although Ramsay argues that horse meat is high in protein, low in fat, and high in omega-3, which is good for heart health, British horse lovers are not swayed. Protestors from the People for the Ethical Treatment of Animals (PETA) Europe dress as horses, picket his restaurant, and dump a ton of horse manure on the pavement outside Ramsay's restaurant.

- **1950s:** Great Britain develops their own atomic bomb in 1952. The post–World War II world is one of tension and the threat of war. The development of atomic weapons is considered by many people to increase the risk of destroying the earth. Poets, such as Hughes, use poetry as a way to emphasize the natural beauty of the world and counteract the threat of war.

  Today: Since Great Britain developed their own atomic bomb in 1952, France (1960) and China (1964) have joined the official internationally recognized list of countries with nuclear weapons now participating in the Nuclear Non-Proliferation Treaty. The United States (1945) and Russia (1949) were the first two countries to develop the atomic bomb. India (1974), Pakistan (1998), and North Korea (2006) have also tested nuclear weapons, but they are not participants in the treaty. Several of these countries have been the site of political dissension and unrest, and so the risk of war has not changed significantly since Hughes wrote "The Horses."

- **1950s:** Beginning in 1926, there was a movement to protect the English countryside and maintain rural life. By the mid-1950s, there is increasing pressure on the government to create national parks. The Yorkshire Dales National Park is established in 1954. The following year, the government acknowledges the need to protect more green areas around cities and towns. There is also a strong movement to protect wooded areas from new roads and to eliminate billboards in the countryside.

  Today: After more than eighty years, the effort to protect England's rural countryside is only partially successful. It is estimated that another twenty-one square miles of countryside is replaced with concrete and asphalt each year. Airport construction, new roads, and urban sprawl combine to create more noise and less of the tranquility that the narrator found so healing in Hughes's poem.

---

to increase subsistence farming and decrease the country's reliance on imported food. With the emphasis placed back on farming rather than industry, the countryside returned to the agricultural beauty of earlier centuries. Farmers were not just growing more potatoes. They were also turning fields into acres of wheat, barley, and oats. Many more acres were turned into grazing grasses for large animals, such as sheep, cows, and horses. Farming also provided employment for people who were not part of the war effort. In short, Yorkshire was returning to the rural setting that Hughes captures in his poem, "The Horses." By the mid-1950s, farming and country life had become even more valued after the many years of deprivation and bombings endured during World War II.

Horses in England

Horses have existed in England since ancient times, probably for more than ten thousand years. Horses played a significant role in the Roman invasions of Britain two thousand years ago, which brought larger, more powerful horses into the British breeding pool. Horses also had an important role in the Viking invasions of Britain twelve hundred years ago, when the Vikings captured British horses, seriously depleting the horse population. Later, Norman cavalry forces secured the victory at the Battle of Hastings in 1066 (completing the Norman Conquest of England). Eventually horses were bred to be larger and heavier, so that they could carry the weight of an armored knight, both during battle and during competitive jousts. As the population of London grew, horses became the primary means of transportation in the city, but they were equally useful pulling carts on farms, where they were so effective that they eventually replaced oxen for this duty. During the sixteenth century, there was an increased interest in using horses for hunting and racing. Careful breeding of horses resulted in the English thoroughbred, the most celebrated of all English horses. During the early nineteenth century, the so-called Golden Age of Coaching, it is estimated that 150,000 horses pulled mail coaches and stagecoaches throughout Britain. Horses also pulled barges along the rivers and canals, and when harnessed to a treadmill, horses provided the power needed to run coal mines. By the twentieth century, although horses were no longer being used for power, they still pulled wagons. At the start of the twentieth-first century, it is estimated that there are more than a million horses in Great Britain. Although horses are no longer used for warfare or work, their presence suggests that the horse is still an essential part of the English countryside. In "The Horses," Hughes's narrator is held captive by the beauty and majesty of the ten horses that he sees in the valley below. As the history of horses in Britain suggests, such a scene is timeless and infinitely soothing, and it is the everlasting nature of the moment that offers solace and comfort to the narrator.

The Movement

The Movement was a term given to a group of poets and critics in the 1950s who rejected modernism and the romanticism of 1940s poetry. The term

Horses *(Image copyright Jeanne Hatch, 2009. Used under license from Shutterstock.com)*

was coined in 1954 and was applied to several British poets, including Hughes, Philip Larkin, and Thom Gunn. The Movement promoted realism, common sense, and clarity. Although a short-lived critical approach to poetry, the focus of this poetry was practicality, stoicism (emotional indifference), and an embracing of middle-class values. The poetry of this literary movement focused on tradition. Hughes's poem, "The Horses," fits this style well. Hughes emphasizes traditional values, particularly nature, and a love of the land. He also embraces practical traditions, such as the ability of nature to heal the isolation of the narrator.

CRITICAL OVERVIEW

When Hughes's first book of poetry, *The Hawk in the Rain*, was published in 1957, it was reviewed in the *New York Times Book Review*. In writing about this first-time poet's work, critic, W. S. Merwin, writes that the opportunity to review Hughes's book "gives reviewers an opportunity to do what they are always saying they want to do: acclaim an exciting new writer." Merwin claims that Hughes's poems are so good that there is no need to provide a polite, though wary, endorsement of his work. The poems in *The Hawk in the Rain*, Merwin states, are uniquely original, while still reflecting contemporary poetic traditions. Merwin remarks the poems in the volume reveal a talent that the poet was "born with," rather than carefully developed through undergraduate study at Cambridge University. Merwin sees Hughes as a poet with a gift for composition and a talent for the use of form and development that results in poems that can be appreciated for each individual stanza. In other words, Hughes's poems are so carefully crafted that it is not necessary to read the entire poem to appreciate each single line.

In Merwin's review, he wonders about the future Hughes, the mature poet, and the poetry that this talented young poet might someday create. When Hughes died forty years later, Merwin's questions about Hughes's future as a poet would be answered in a series of obituaries that honored the poet's life and work. In Sarah Lyall's obituary of the poet, published in the *New York Times*, Lyall writes that Hughes was known for his "powerful, evocative poetry, replete with symbolism and bursting with dark images of the Devonshire countryside in which he lived." Also celebrating Hughes's poetry is Marjorie Miller, who in a *Los Angeles Times* obituary of Hughes refers to the poet as "an enormously successful author who made poetry popular." Miller also notes that Hughes was often "ranked . . . alongside such 20th-century greats as T. S. Eliot and W. H. Auden." As might be expected, Hughes was remembered most passionately in England, where he lived and wrote and was honored as England's poet laureate from 1984 until his death. Writing for the London *Independent*, poet Ruth Padel says that "with his first four books Hughes changed British poetry, shooting into it a new charge of energy, risk, and an extraordinary, impacted power, revealing myth in all kinds of unnoticed physical things." Of course Hughes's talent did not end with his first four books, as Padel reminds readers. She predicts that in the future, "poets will honour him most for that burning vitality of imagination and language, [and for] the unique mix of delicacy and brute strength" that was an identifying feature of Hughes's poetry. By the end of his life, Hughes had received various awards and royal honors. Although he sometimes felt overshadowed by his brief marriage to Sylvia Plath and her subsequent suicide, the obituaries published at his death remind readers that Hughes was far more than just Sylvia Plath's husband. He was an accomplished poet in his own right.

CRITICISM

Sheri Metzger Karmiol

Karmiol has a doctorate in English Renaissance literature. She teaches literature and drama at the University of New Mexico, where she is a lecturer

WHAT DO I READ NEXT?

- *Collected Poems* by Ted Hughes was reissued in 2005 by Farrar, Straus, and Giroux. This book of more than thirteen hundred pages is a collection of all of Hughes's poems, from the earliest, which were only published previously in journals, to the poems that he wrote as England's poet laureate.

- Hughes wrote many poems for children, 250 of which are included in *Collected Poems for Children* (2008). This collection begins with poems for very young children and progresses to more complex poems for adolescents and young adults.

- *Ted Hughes: The Life of a Poet* (2001), by Elaine Feinstein, is a biography of Hughes's life.

- Joanny Molin's *Ted Hughes Alternative Horizons* (2005) is a collection of scholarly essays about Hughes's writings, including his poetry.

- *Ted Hughes: A Literary Life* (2007), by Neil Roberts, is a critical examination of Hughes's poetry using his own letters as a way to situate his poetry within the influences of his life.

- *Footprints on the Roof: Poems about the Earth* (2002), by Marilyn Singer, is a collection of poetry for children that focuses on the natural beauty of the earth. This book also includes detailed illustrations.

- *River of Words: Young Poets and Artists on the Nature of Things* (2008), edited by Pamela Michael, is a collection of poetry about water and nature written by children and teens. The focus of the book is environmentalism.

- *The Circle of Thanks: Native American Poems and Songs of Thanksgiving* (2003) is a collection of songs and poems by Native American poets that honor nature.

> THE NARRATOR'S RELATIONSHIP WITH THE HORSES IN 'THE HORSES' REPRESENTS THE UNBREAKABLE CONNECTION BETWEEN ANIMAL AND MAN AND REMINDS READERS THAT SUCH A CONNECTION CAN BE A HEALING FORCE."

in the university honors program. She is also a professional writer and the author of several reference texts on poetry and drama. In this essay, she discusses the symbolism of horses and their depiction in Hughes's poem, "The Horses."

Quite often, poems are read and then quickly put aside. That is not the case with Ted Hughes's poem "The Horses." Instead, Hughes creates a poem in which readers can immerse themselves and from which they can draw strength, long after having read it. Many possibilities lie within the poem. Readers can hear the quiet of the horses, feel their immobility, and sense their movements; all are images held tightly in place by the poet's careful narration. Even the positioning of the horse's mane invites the reader's touch. Although the final lines of the poem make clear that the narrator is recalling an event from the past, the vivid descriptions make it appear as if the narrator is still standing on the moors of England at dawn, captivated by the peaceful beauty of the horses. This ability to pull the reader into the poem and to make the horses come alive on the page is one of the strengths of Hughes's poetry. He accomplishes this through his imaginative recreation of the English countryside of his youth, in which man and animal relate to one another in an unspoken bond.

Hughes's depiction of the horses in his poem "The Horses," is designed to draw the reader into the world of the poet's childhood on the moors of the Yorkshire countryside. In the part of Yorkshire where Hughes was born, the countryside is composed of mountains and moors. This is Emily Brontë's countryside as well, the area in which she situates *Wuthering Heights*. In this part of England, it is cold, wet, windy, and practically uninhabitable for humans and animals in almost all seasons. Even so, it is home to both. This is not the countryside of romantic, idyllic pastoral poetry, of flowers, grasses, and gentle shepherds. Hughes's English countryside is one of real flesh and blood. This is a landscape without form, where the land and the sky blend into one another in shades of gray. In this static world, nothing moves, and nothing is seen or heard. The narrator describes this world as one in which he moves quietly without disturbing the horses, for whom the narrator does not exist. Yet as he walks among them, he draws from their strength. When the narrator is part of the natural world among the horses, he is strong; but later, when he returns to the city, he must try to recall the horses's serenity, the quiet landscape, and the nature of the moors in order to find his inner peace and strength once again.

The horses are the heart of Hughes's poem. The poet focuses on the narrator's response to the appearance of the horses, as he emerges from the woods and onto the moors. These horses are ready for whatever occurs. They stand perfectly still, posed for an event that has not yet begun. In his short story, "The Rain Horse," Hughes notes that when it rains, horses hang their heads, tilt a hind hoof, and half-close their eyes to shelter themselves from the moisture. In "The Horses," these horses stand perfectly still, like huge stones capable of withstanding the worst weather that England's notorious wet countryside experiences. In his short story, Hughes creates a picture of the horses that is almost identical to that described in "The Horses." The observations about the horses are those of a man who has lived in the country and who has watched horses stand like lonely sentinels against the onslaught of rain. In Sarah Lyall's obituary of Hughes for the *New York Times*, she mentions that Hughes "developed a lifelong passion for the countryside, for animals, and for hunting, a passion that would inform his poetry in the years to come." The dark moors of Yorkshire are the landscape of Hughes's childhood and his early poems, including "The Horses." This is a region where gray and sodden land meets equally gray and sodden skies and where horses find shelter from harsh cold rains. At the same time, this is the landscape where men and women draw their strength from the land and the animals.

The horses represent the kind of quiet endurance that is common to the Yorkshire countryside. To watch the horses endure the cold, damp weather helps the man, who must also withstand the environment. Lyall quotes Thomas Nye's obituary in the London *Times*, in which Nye writes that Hughes "wanted to capture not just live animals, but the aliveness of animals in their natural state." It is the horses' "aliveness" that Hughes captures in his poem. They do not move; they only endure. The narrator watches the horses with what can only be called envy. He envies their strength, endurance, and ability to patiently wait for whatever is to come. When the narrator has returned to the city, he recalls the strength and patience of the horses and uses that memory to soothe his soul and make him more tolerant of the conflicts he faces in the city.

In "Ted Hughes's Crying Horizons: 'Wind' & the Poetics of Sublimity," published in *Ted Hughes: Alternative Horizons* (2004), Christian La Cassagnère suggests that the purpose of "The Horses" is to force the reader "into hearing the silence behind the text, a silence where the meeting may take place at long last." The meeting between the narrator and the horses is one of near silence, but as the narrator describes in the poem, he can hear the horizons of that day long after it has passed. In "The Horses," a few lines condense the events of a brief period of time, a few minutes at the morning's dawn, transforming the grays and darks of night into the brilliant light of day. Grays and blacks become reds and oranges, and the world is transformed. This is a daily event, and yet Hughes transforms it into sensations of vision and sound. When the sun erupts in vivid shades of red and orange and the gray disappears, it is as if the dark never existed. The quiet sounds of the horses' easy breathing is mixed with the curlew's shriek; the sounds and colors are recorded in the poet's memory to be recalled in time of need.

The representation of the horses becomes the dominant image that readers take away from Hughes's poem. In the essay, "Spirit and Animal Images in Hughes' Two Short Stories: 'The Harvesting' and 'The Rain Horse,'" published in *Selçuk Üniversitesi Sosyal Bilimler Enstitüsü Dergisi*, Gülbün Onur and Dilek Zerenler claim that Hughes uses animal imagery as a way to confront human suffering and survival. Thus, animal imagery is one way to access "the inner world of the characters" in his short stories. This is equally true of Hughes's poetry. In "The Horses," the narrator finds healing through his interaction with the horses. Midway through the poem at lines 24 and 25, when the narrator first emerges from the woods, he is so tormented and afraid of

the light of dawn that he runs toward the darkness and safe haven of the woods. However, by the end of the poem, he draws strength from the horses and their quiet presence on the moors. Onur and Zerenler suggest that animal images reflect Hughes's "reaction to the rationalistic demand of society." Thus, Onur and Zerenler state, the narrator is able to use the horses' patient endurance to revitalize his own "spiritual and instinctual energies." The horses, then, are healers who "give access to the power habitually held in check by society," Onur and Zerenler remark. Animals live a natural life that proceeds without much planning. They lack the social manifestations that hold back the narrator. The horses' existence in the countryside offers limitless possibilities to roam freely, save any artificial confines created by mankind. In contrast, the narrator is restricted by the written and implied rules of a society that, while supposedly in place to bring order from chaos, serve to replace creativity with rationality. The animal imagery in Hughes's poem frees the narrator to find his own way in a chaotic world.

The narrator's ability to connect to the horses is an important feature of "The Horses." In their study of Hughes and his work, *Ted Hughes: A Critical Study* (1981), Terry Gifford and Neil Roberts explain that an important theme for Hughes is his effort to "articulate the continuities between the human self and the animal world." The animals, while different from humans, provide Hughes with a means to stimulate his imagination. As animals lack the rational confines of a human, their freedom can challenge the poet to find his own intellectual and emotional freedom. Guilford and Roberts suggest that "Hughes's animals are unmistakably 'other' in that they present a shock and a challenge to the poet." In this respect, the horses of Hughes's poem awaken in him an awareness of both the strength of the horses and the challenge that they present to the narrator to find his own inner strength. In watching the horses, the narrator imagines his own freedom, and by imagining it, he finds a way to create freedom in his own life.

Keith Sagar argues in his book *Literature and the Crime Against Nature* (2005) that imagination is one way in which people can understand the world in which they live. Sagar states that the poet uses the imagination to make connections, in a sense to "unify the subjective and the objective, inner and outer" worlds, or the worlds of man and animal in the case of "The Horses." Sagar argues that imagination is the language of metaphor and symbol. Therefore, Hughes's poem symbolizes the healing that man finds in nature. What the narrator sees that morning on the moors is the healing force of nature. The narrator's relationship with the horses in "The Horses" represents the unbreakable connection between animal and man and reminds readers that such a connection can be a healing force. The horses symbolize the possibility of change and escape from the rational world—they are a metaphor for freedom. More importantly for Hughes, the horses embody nature, imagination, and the enduring connection between man and animal.

Source: Sheri Metzger Karmiol, Critical Essay on "The Horses," in *Poetry for Students*, Gale, Cengage Learning, 2010.

Sudip Bose

In the following excerpt, Bose traces the development of Hughes's poetic career and relationship with Sylvia Plath, identifying "The Horses" as "a cosmically beautiful lyric."

Few other tragedies have given rise to as much rumor and gossip as the suicide of Sylvia Plath on February 11, 1963. Perhaps it was the particularly gruesome nature of her death—she killed herself using the gas oven in her kitchen while her two children, Nicholas and Frieda, lay sleeping—that gripped the popular imagination. But as Plath became a martyr to legions of readers who seized upon her brilliant canon as if the writings were holy texts, her husband, the English poet Ted Hughes, was increasingly portrayed as the villain in a sensational plot, the person mainly responsible for his wife's psychic distress. Every prying eye in the literary world was cast upon Hughes and the children just when they should have been left alone to grieve.

Hughes remained silent on the matter for much of his life, and it is for this reason, more than any other, that his letters are essential reading. As literature, they are magnificent pieces of prose—intense, beautiful, lyrical, passionate, wise. What makes them all the more striking, however, is how nakedly they confess, how honestly they lay bare the writer's soul—how utterly different they are from most of his verse. Like Yeats, Hughes believed that confession alone does not constitute art, that one must shine personal experience through a prism of metaphor and symbol for it to be transformed into something meaningful.

HUGHES'S POETIC SENSIBILITIES EMANATED FROM A RESONANT PERSONAL MYTHOLOGY GROUNDED IN NATURE, FOLKLORE, AND SHAMANISM."

Hughes's poetic sensibilities emanated from a resonant personal mythology grounded in nature, folklore, and shamanism. His superb early poems, collected in *The Hawk in the Rain* and *Lupercal*, drew frequently upon the animal kingdom (foxes, hawks, horses, fishes, and bulls)—as well as the west Yorkshire hillsides of his boyhood, an unforgiving landscape of immensity and grandeur—in order to render a complex inner world. In a letter to Plath, sent shortly after their marriage in 1956, Hughes memorably described a solitary foray made while his wife had been away:

> At dusk the sky was pure washed stretched green, still wet and runny, with brilliant illumination on the landscape. Then from the north, covering the whole breadth of the sky, came a lid of black cloud, and under it the land black. It drew slowly over the whole sky. At one stage a great advance of it overhung the green west sky, and hanging from it, black against the green were great trailing swaths of falling rain, like a long black fine mane. Or like many manes hanging down between the side by side pressed bellies of cloud.... Anyway I'd just got fairly down into the wood when it began to hail. I stood under a leaning tree and watched the hail, for an hour, filling the valley up. Leaves were coming off, the wood was sodden and seeping.

The passage calls to mind several of Hughes's early poems: "Wind," which begins by describing a house seemingly adrift in a torrential storm; "The Hawk in the Rain," whose opening lines depict the speaker struggling across a stretch of waterlogged farmland; and "The Horses," a cosmically beautiful lyric in which a man, climbing through file woods on an unbearably chilly morning, encounters 10 statuesque horses, perfectly still.

Almost from the beginning, Hughes was a famous poet, and though Plath herself successfully placed several poems in prominent magazines, she seemed to play the part of the pupil, and he the wiser teacher. Plath's many insecurities, including those about her poetry, have been well documented, but Hughes was always encouraging and a close, careful critic of her work. In letter after letter (to Plath and to others), he championed her visionary talent, her "startling poetic gift," with not the slightest hint of rivalry or jealousy.

Although the early days of their relationship seem heady and blissful, the marriage would eventually crack as Plath became more volatile and as Hughes gravitated toward other women. In 1962, Hughes met and fell in love with Assia Wevill, and the two began an affair, deepening Plath's paranoia. "Marriage," Hughes wrote, to his friend Daniel Weissbort, "is a nest of small scorpions, but it kills the big dragons." Only temporarily was it so, for Hughes soon abandoned his wife, explaining his reasons to his brother, Gerald:

> The one factor that nobody but quite close friends can comprehend, is Sylvia's particular death-ray quality. In many of the most important ways, she's the most gifted and capable & admirable woman I've ever met—but, finally, impossible for me to live married to.... The main grief for me is that a life that had all the circumstances for perfection, should have been so intolerable, and that little Frieda loses a father & I lose little Frieda. She's been my playmate for 2 years & become absolutely a necessary piece of my life.

Within a year, Plath would be dead, and a disconsolate Hughes was left to blame himself for not perceiving the signs of trouble. "She asked me for help, as she so often has," he wrote to his sister, Olwyn. "I was the only person who could have helped her, and the only person so jaded by her states & demands that I could not recognise when she really needed it." To Plath's mother, Aurelia, he bathed himself in an even harsher light, taking responsibility for his own part in his wife's unhappiness: "I don't want ever to be forgiven. I don't mean that I shall become a public shrine of mourning and remorse, I would sooner become the opposite. But if there is an eternity, I am damned in it."

From then on, the literary public descended upon Ted Hughes's private life and a distinct change in tone can be felt in his letters: they became more guarded, more self-conscious. "Do you know what oppresses me?" Hughes wrote to Wevill in 1965. "[T]he thought that you save my letters.... Assia, I'm foolishly oppressed enough as it is with bloody eavesdroppers & filchers & greedy curiosity.... As it is I'm always expecting my notes to get intercepted so I don't write a fraction of what I would."

The scrutiny only increased after Wevill—who had ended her own marriage to be with Hughes—killed herself and her daughter, Shura, in 1969. Frayed and fragile, Hughes recoiled from the world, especially the world of critics, biographers, and graduate students, whom he viewed as his chief antagonists. "What an insane chance," he wrote despairingly to fellow poet Richard Murphy, "to have private family struggles turned into best-selling literature of despair & martyrdom."

To give his own account of their relationship was asking far too much of a man still very much in agony. Writing about Plath, he explained to Robert Lowell, "dragged me into a morass of feelings I simply could not deal with in words." But Hughes's public silence had just as much to do with protecting his children and, later, his second wife, Carol Orchard, whom he married in August of 1971. When Amelia Plath began compiling a collection of her daughter's correspondence, Hughes urged her to leave out the most personal letters. "Frieda & Nick are already living in a mausoleum—I just want to cut down the furnishings & the tourist visitors & the general mess of publicity," Hughes wrote. "I certainly don't want my private life with Sylvia exposed. Carol feels enough like an also-ran, & I feel quite enough of a second-hand relic husband, as it is."

In 1971, the critic A. Alvarez published *The Savage God: A Study of Suicide,* which speculated on various motives for Plath's death. Hughes felt betrayed. His letter to Alvarez, who had been a friend, is the most passionate outcry in this collection. Literary criticism, Hughes furiously wrote upon seeing Alvarez's book serialized in the *Observer,*

> cannot be bothered to distinguish between remarks made on paper and their consequences in real life.... Whatever Sylvia may be for your readers & for you, for her mother & me & her children she is something different, she is an atmosphere we breathe.... What makes you think you can use our lives like the text of a novel—something on the syllabus—for facile interpretations to keep your audience of schoolteachers up on the latest culture?

In the end, for Hughes, there would be only one way out of the morass—to finally tell the story that had simmered within him for too long. "Sometimes I think I ought really to try and write it all out," Hughes admitted to his friend Daniel Huws. "What's certainly wrong is staggering along year after year, neither dealing with it nor letting it go, just getting older." The publication of Hughes's much-celebrated *Birthday Letters* in 1998 ended his long and painful silence. For many years, he had been writing poems—spare, unadorned, and haunting—about his relationship with Plath, in the confessional style that, ironically, he so detested. In *Birthday Letters,* Hughes lifted the metrical, metaphorical, and mythological scrim, revealing the story of his love for Plath on a bare, unadorned stage. The resulting poems were "so raw, so vulnerable, so unprocessed, so naive, so self-exposing & unguarded, so without any of the niceties that any poetry workshop student could have helped me to," as he wrote to the scholar Keith Sagar. "And so dead against my near-inborn conviction that you never talk about yourself in this way—in poetry."

The poems were nothing short of a catharsis, achieved at a time when their author was dying of cancer. In a beautiful and heartfelt letter sent to his son, Nicholas, in 1998, Hughes compared the decades of silence to a logjam, and he explained the startling effect the book's publication had had on him:

> It was when I realised that my only chance of getting past 1963 was to blow up that logjam, and assemble whatever I had written about your mother and me, and simply make it public—like a confession—that I decided to publish those *Birthday Letters* as I've called them.... And the effect on me, Nicky, the sense of gigantic, upheaval transformation in my mind, is quite bewildering. It's as though I have completely new different brains. I can think thoughts I never could think. I have a freedom of imagination I've not felt since 1962. Just to have got rid of all that.

Or, as Hughes wrote to Marie and Seamus Heaney not long before he died, "Strange business, confession."

One finishes the *Letters of Ted Hughes* as if emerging from a great watery depth, exhausted, almost gasping for air. The tragedies of his life were so acute, the heartbreak and guilt and defiance so overwhelming, the personality so towering, that one gets the feeling at times that the world did not extend much beyond the poet and his immediate circle of friends and loved ones....

Source: Sudip Bose, "Cal & Liz & Ted & Sylvia," in *American Scholar*, Vol. 78, No. 1, Winter 2009, pp. 126–31.

Egbert Faas

In the following excerpt from an interview with Faas, Hughes discusses his status as an outsider and other poets who have influenced his work.

> I FANCY IF THERE IS A JURY OF CRITICS SITTING OVER WHAT I WRITE, AND I IMAGINE EVERY WRITER HAS SOMETHING OF THE SORT, THEN YEATS IS THE JUDGE."

...From the very beginning of your poetic career you have been considered an outsider. And although this has changed in recent years mainly through your already far-ranging influence on other poets you still don't fall into what Robert Conquest would consider the mainstream of the English poetic tradition. Now what is your attitude towards this tradition which you once referred to as "the terrible, suffocating, maternal octopus of ancient English poetic tradition"?

I imagine I wouldn't have said that if I hadn't burdened myself with a good deal of it. I should think my idea of the mainstream is pretty close to Robert Conquest's. What I meant by the octopus was the terrific magnetic power of the tradition to grip poets and hold them. Helped by our infatuation with our English past in general. The archetypes are always there waiting... swashbuckling Elizabethan, earthy bawdy Merrie Englander, devastatingly witty Restoration blade and so on. And some of the great poets are such powerful magnetic fields they remake us in their own image before we're aware. Shakespeare in particular of course.

As you suggested in our previous interview you try to escape this influence by drawing on your own native dialect and its mediaeval literature. From Sir Gawain and the Green Knight, *for example, you derived the title and motto of* Wodwo.

I grew up in West Yorkshire. They have a very distinctive dialect there. Whatever other speech you grow into, presumably your dialect stays alive in a sort of inner freedom, a separate little self. It makes some things more difficult... since it's your childhood self there inside the dialect and that is possibly your real self or the core of it. Some things it makes easier. Without it, I doubt if I would ever have written verse. And in the case of the West Yorkshire dialect, of course, it connects you directly and in your most intimate self to middle English poetry.

The main poets who are mentioned in the criticism of your poetry are Hopkins, Donne, Dylan Thomas and D. H. Lawrence. Would you agree that these poets exerted the greatest influence on your work? Also what is your relation to Yeats and Blake whose work and development seems to show an increasing resemblance to your own poetry and especially to your development from a poet of nature to a "sophisticated philosopher" and a "primitive, gnomic spellmaker"?

Well, in the way of influences I imagine everything goes into the stew. But to be specific about those names. Donne . . . I once learned as many of his poems as I could and I greatly admired his satires and epistles. More than his lyrics even. As for Thomas, *Deaths and Entrances* was a holy book with me for quite a time when it first came out. Lawrence I read entire in my teens . . . except for all but a few of the poems. His writings coloured a whole period of my life. Blake I connect inwardly to Beethoven, and if I could dig to the bottom of my strata maybe their names and works would be the deepest traces. Yeats spellbound me for about six years. I got to him not so much through his verse as through his other interests, folklore, and magic in particular. Then that strange atmosphere laid hold of me. I fancy if there is a jury of critics sitting over what I write, and I imagine every writer has something of the sort, then Yeats is the judge. There are all sorts of things I could well do but because of him and principles I absorbed from him I cannot. They are principles that I've found confirmed in other sources . . . but he stamped them into me. But these are just the names you mentioned. There are others. One poet I have read more than any of these is Chaucer. And the poet I read more than all other literature put together is Shakespeare. More than all other fiction or drama or poetry that is.

In one of your essays you speak of Shakespeare's utility general-purpose style. I think it is in one of your essays on Keith Douglas.

Maybe that's an ideal notion, and yet maybe not. It's connected to the dream of an ideal vernacular. I suppose Shakespeare does have it. I remember the point in Lear where I suddenly recognized this. It was very early in my reading, we were going through *Lear* in School and *Lear* as you know is the most extraordinary jumble of styles. I can't remember what I thought of Shakespeare before that but at one particular mutilated and mistaken looking phrase I suddenly recognized what Shakespearean

language was . . . it was not super-difficult language at all . . . it was super-easy. It wasn't a super-processed super-removed super-arcane language like Milton . . . it was super-crude. It was backyard improvization. It was dialect taken to the limit. That was it . . . it was inspired dialect. The whole crush and cramming throwaway expressiveness of it was right at the heart of it dialect. So immediately I felt he was much closer to me than to all those scholars and commentators at the bottom of the page who I assumed hadn't grown up in some dialect. It enabled me to see all sorts of virtues in him. I saw all his knotted up complexities and piled up obscurities suddenly as nothing of the sort . . . they were just the result of his taking short cuts through walls and ceilings and floors. He goes direct from centre to centre but you never see him on the stairs or the corridors. It's a sort of inspired idleness. Wherever he turns his attention, his whole body rematerializes at that point. It's as if he were too idle to be anything but utterly direct, and utterly simple. And too idle to stop everything happening at the speed of light. So those knots of complexity are traffic jams of what are really utterly simple confrontations. His poetic virtue is hitting the nail on the head and he eventually became so expert that by hitting one nail he made fifty others jump in of their own accord. Wherever a nail exists he can hit it on the head.

When did you first get interested in poetry?

When I was about fifteen. My first subjects were Zulus and the Wild West. I had sagas of involved warfare among African tribes, for some reason. All in imitation of Kipling.

From what you're saying, I gather that the influence of Hopkins, Thomas and Lawrence is not really as great as often claimed.

I read Lawrence and Thomas at an impressionable age. I also read Hopkins very closely. But there are superficial influences that show and deep influences that maybe are not so visible. It's a mystery how a writer's imagination is influenced and altered. Up to the age of twenty-five I read no contemporary poetry whatsoever except Eliot, Thomas and some Auden. Then I read a Penguin of American poets that came out in about 1955 and that started me writing. After writing nothing for about six years. The poems that set me off were odd pieces by Shapiro, Lowell, Merwin, Wilbur and Crowe Ransom. Crowe Ransom was the one who gave me a model I felt I could use. He helped me get my words into focus. That put me into production. But this whole business of influences is mysterious. Sometimes it's just a few words that open up a whole prospect. They may occur anywhere. Then again the influences that really count are most likely not literary at all. Maybe it would be best of all to have no influences. Impossible of course. But what good are they as a rule? You spend a lifetime learning how to write verse when it's been clear from your earliest days that the greatest poetry in English is in the prose of the Bible. And after all the campaigns to make it new you're stuck with the fact that some of the Scots ballads still cut a deeper groove than anything written in the last forty years. Influences just seem to make it more and more unlikely that a poet will write what he alone could write.

In fact there is an increasing use of mythological and biblical material in your poetry, in particular since Wodwo. T. S. Eliot once described the use of myth in James Joyce's Ulysses *(and indirectly in his own* Waste Land*) as a means of 'manipulating a continuous parallel between contemporaneity and antiquity ... [and as] a way of controlling, or ordering, or giving a shape and a significance to the immense panorama of futility and anarchy which is contemporary history'. How does your own use of mythological and biblical material differ from this?*

He speaks specifically of contemporary history which was his own red herring I imagine. Somewhere else he speaks of the *Waste Land* as the chart of his own condition, and of history, if at all, just by extension and parallel.

But you speak about the disintegration of Western civilization as well. Might not T. S. Eliot have attempted something similar?

I can't believe that he took the disintegration of Western civilization as a theme which he then found imagery and a general plan for. His sickness told him the cause. Surely that was it. He cleaned his wounds and found all the shrapnel. Every writer if he develops at all develops either outwards into society and history, using wider and more material of that sort, or he develops inwards into imagination and beyond that into spirit, using perhaps no more external material than before and maybe even less but deepening it and making it operate in the many different inner dimensions until it opens up perhaps the religious or holy basis of the whole thing. Or he can develop both ways simultaneously. Developing inwardly, of course, means organizing the inner world or at least searching out the patterns there and that is a mythology. It may be an original mythology. Or you may uncover the

Cross—as Eliot did. The ideal aspect of Yeats' development is that he managed to develop his poetry both outwardly into history and the common imagery of everyday life at the same time as he developed it inwardly in a sort of close parallel ... so that he could speak of both simultaneously. His mythology is history, pretty well, and his history is as he said 'the story of a soul'.

So, when you use biblical and mythological material, these really represent, as it were, the aim in themselves, and are not merely a kind of device as in Eliot to give order, as he says, to something else?

You choose a subject because it serves, because you need it. We go on writing poems because one poem never gets the whole account right. There is always something missed. At the end of the ritual up comes a goblin. Anyway within a week the whole thing has changed, one needs a fresh bulletin. And works go dead, fishing has to be abandoned, the shoal has moved on. While we struggle with a fragmentary Orestes some complete Bacchae moves past too deep down to hear. We get news of it later ... too late. In the end, one's poems are ragged dirty undated letters from remote battles and weddings and one thing and another.

May we for a moment come back to The Waste Land *and its difference from* Wodwo, *the main theme of which you described to me as a "descent into destruction of some sort". Even in* Wodwo, *anticipating* Crow, *you seem to go beyond portraying the disintegration of our Western civilization.*

What Eliot and Joyce and I suppose Beckett are portraying is the state of belonging spiritually to the last phase of Christian civilization, they suffer its disintegration. But there are now quite a few writers about who do not seem to belong spiritually to the Christian civilization at all. In their world Christianity is just another provisional myth of man's relationship with the creator and the world of spirit. Their world is a continuation or a re-emergence of the pre-Christian world ... it is the world of the little pagan religions and cults, the primitive religions from which of course Christianity itself grew.

Which writers are you referring to? Are you thinking of Schopenhauer and Nietzsche whose thought seems to show a striking resemblance to yours?

The only philosophy I have ever really read was Schopenhauer. He impressed me all right. You see very well where Nietzsche got his Dionysus. It was a genuine vision of something on its way back to the surface. The rough beast in Yeats's poems. Each nation sees it through different spectacles.

Like Schopenhauer you had to look towards the east in quest of a new philosophy. When did you first read the Tibetan Book of the Dead?

I can't say I ever quested deliberately for a philosophy. Whatever scrappy knowledge of Indian and Chinese philosophy and religious writings I have picked up on the way . . . tied up with the mythology and the folklore which was what I was mainly interested in. And it's the sort of thing you absorb out of pure curiosity. The *Bardo Thodol,* that's the *Tibetan Book of the Dead,* was a special case. In 1960 I had met the Chinese composer Chou Wenchung in the States, and he invited me to do a libretto of this thing. He had the most wonderful plans for the musical results. Gigantic orchestra, massed choirs, projected illuminated mandalas, soul-dancers and the rest.

Did you ever write this libretto?

Yes, I rewrote it a good deal. I don't think I ever came near what was needed. I got to know the *Bardo Thodol* pretty well. Unfortunately the hoped-for cash evaporated, we lost contact for about nine years, and now of course we've lost the whole idea to the psychedelics. We had no idea we were riding the Zeitgeist so closely. We had one or two other schemes . . . and maybe we'll do them some day.

The Bardo Thodol *must have brought you a confirmation of many ideas which are already latent in your earliest work, even in The Hawk in the Rain. How far and in which way can one speak of its influence on Crow? An expression like "womb door" seems to be lifted straight out of the* Tibetan Book of the Dead *and besides such obvious direct parallels one could easily point to several more general metaphorical, thematic, and philosophical resemblances.*

From one point of view, the *Bardo Thodol* is basically a shamanistic flight and return. Tibetan Buddhism was enormously influenced by Tibetan primitive shamanism. And in fact the special weirdness and power of all things Tibetan in occult and magical circles springs direct from the shamanism, not the Buddhism.

What exactly is Shamanism?

Basically, it's the whole procedure and practice of becoming and performing as a witch-doctor, a medicine man, among primitive peoples. The individual is summoned by certain dreams. The

same dreams all over the world. A spirit summons him . . . usually an animal or a woman. If he refuses, he dies . . . or somebody near him dies. If he accepts, he then prepares himself for the job . . . it may take years. Usually he apprentices himself to some other Shaman, but the spirit may well teach him direct. Once fully-fledged he can enter trance at will and go to the spirit world . . . he goes to get something badly needed, a cure, an answer, some sort of divine intervention in the community's affairs. Now this flight to the spirit world he experiences as a dream . . . and that dream is the basis of the hero story. It is the same basic outline pretty well all over the world, same events, same figures, same situations. It is the skeleton of thousands of folktales and myths. And of many narrative poems. *The Odyssey,* the *Divine Comedy, Faust,* etc. Most narrative poems recount only those other dreams . . . the dream of the call. Poets usually refuse the call. How are they to accept it? How can a poet become a medicine man and fly to the source and come back and heal or pronounce oracles? Everything among us is against it. The American healer and prophet Edgar Cayce is an example of one man who dreamed the dreams and accepted the task, who was not a poet. He described the dreams and the flight. And of course he returned with the goods. . . .

Source: Ted Hughes and Egbert Faas, "Interview with Ted Hughes," in *London Magazine,* Vol. 10, No. 10, January 1971, pp. 5–20.

SOURCES

Burnett, John, "The Second World War," in *Plenty and Want: A Social History of Food in England from 1815 to the Present Day,* 3rd ed., Routledge, 1989, pp. 289–91.

"Fair Shares: Rationing and Shortages," in *History in Focus Online,* http://www.history.ac.uk/ihr/Focus/War/londonRation.html (accessed March 17, 2009).

Gifford, Terry, and Neil Roberts, *Ted Hughes: A Critical Study,* Faber and Faber, 1981, pp. 62–63, 80.

Goodall, Armitage C., "Masborough, Mexborough," in *Place-Names of South-West Yorkshire,* Cambridge University Press, 1913, p. 209.

Hamilton, Ian, ed., "Ted Hughes," in *The Oxford Companion to Twentieth-century Poetry in English,* Oxford University Press, 1994, pp. 241–42.

Harmon, William, and Hugh Holman, *A Handbook to Literature,* 11th ed., Prentice Hall, 2008, pp. 286–87, 356, 339–40.

"The Horse in British History," in *Kentucky Horse Park,* http://www.imh.org/pdf/4%20HorseHistory.pdf (accessed April 2, 2009).

Hughes, Ted, "The Horses," in *The Hawk in the Rain*, Faber and Faber, 1957, pp. 15–16.

La Cassagnère, Christian, "Ted Hughes's Crying Horizons: 'Wind' & the Poetics of Sublimity," in *Ted Hughes: Alternative Horizons*, edited by Joanny Moline, Routledge, 2004, p. 53.

Lambert, Tim, "A Brief History of Yorkshire," in *Local and National Histories*, http://www.localhistories.org/yorkshire.html (accessed March 19, 2009).

Lyall, Sarah, "Ted Hughes, 68, a Symbolic Poet and Sylvia Plath's Husband, Died," in the *New York Times*, October 30, 1998, p. 1.

Merwin, W. S., "Something of His Own to Say," in *New York Times Book Review*, October 6, 1957, p. 43.

Miller, Marjorie, "Britain Loses Poet Laureate Ted Hughes, 68, to Cancer," in *Los Angeles Times*, October 30, 1998, pp. A1–2.

"The Movement," in *Encarta Online*, http://au.encarta.msn.com/encyclopedia_781534699/movement_the.html (accessed March 16, 2009).

"Nuclear Weapons: Who Has What at a Glance," *Arms Control Association Web site*, http://www.armscontrol.org/factsheets/Nuclearweaponswhohaswhat (accessed March 19, 2009).

Onur, Gülbün, and Dilek Zerenler, "Spirit and Animal Images in Hughes' Two Short Stories: 'The Harvesting' and 'The Rain Horse,'" in *Selçuk Üniversitesi Sosyal Bilimler Enstitüsü Dergisi*, No. 10, 2003, pp. 331–32.

Padel, Ruth, "The Hawk Who Held 'Creation in a Weightless Quiet,'" in *Independent* (London, England), October 30, 1998, p. 4.

"Ramsay Restaurant Covered in Manure," *Metro.co.uk*, http://www.metro.co.uk/news/article.html?in_article_id = 49127&in_page_id = 34 (accessed March 16, 2009).

"Rationing," in *Channel 4*, http://www.channel4.com/history/microsites/0-9/1940house/ref/food/rat.htm (accessed March 16, 2009).

Sagar, Keith, *Literature and the Crime Against Nature*, Chaucer Press, 2005, p. xiv.

Sonnenberg, Ben, "Ted's Spell," *Raritan*, No. 4, Spring 2002, pp. 240–44.

"What We've Achieved," in *Campaign to Protect Rural England*, http://www.cpre.org.uk/about/achievements (accessed March 20, 2009).

FURTHER READING

Bowden, Charles, *The Last Horsemen: Life on Britain's Only Horse-Powered Farm*, Andre Deutsch, 2001.
> This illustrated book is the true story of a year in the life of a family whose ancestors have lived on the same horse farm in Great Britain for more than 150 years. This family works the last horse farm to survive in England. The story and illustrations in this book provide readers with a chance to see what farming with horses used to be like before mechanized farming became the standard.

Howkins, Alum, *The Death of Rural England*, Routledge, 2003.
> This book provides a social history of rural England during the twentieth century. Howkins also considers the impact of war on the countryside, as well as urban growth and development.

Hunt, Roger, and Simon Jerkins, *Rural Britain Then & Now: A Celebration of the British Countryside Featuring Photographs from the Francis Frith Collection*, Cassell, 2004.
> This book is a collection of fifty years of photographs of rural England, from the late nineteenth and early twentieth century. The author pairs the earlier photos with contemporary photos showing the changes that have occurred in the English countryside over a period of one hundred years.

Rackham, Olive, *The History of the Countryside: The Classic History of Britain's Landscape, Flora and Fauna*, Phoenix Press, 2001.
> This book is both a social and biological study of England's rural countryside and how it has changed over the previous one hundred years. The author focuses on the interactions of humans, animals, and plant life and how these components have shaped the English rural landscape.

Shepheard, Chris, *Images of Rural Life: The Lost Countryside*, Breedon, 2001.
> This book is an illustrated history of the way life used to be in the English countryside more than one hundred years ago.

Stillman, Deanne, *Mustang: The Saga of the Wild Horse in the American West*, Houghton Mifflin Harcourt, 2008.
> Although Hughes writes of horses in the English countryside, this book allows readers the opportunity to consider the role of horses in the American West over the past four hundred years.

Titchmarsh, Alan, *The Nature of Britain: A Celebration of Our Landscape*, British Broadcasting Corporation (BBC), 2007.
> This book is the companion book to a BBC series of the same name that examines the animals and plants of Britain. It includes essays about each of the many differing habitats of Britain, mountains, fields, valleys, and woodlands. Each essay is accompanied by many photographs.

In Response to Executive Order 9066: All Americans of Japanese Descent Must Report to Relocation Centers

DWIGHT OKITA

1983

Dwight Okita's poem "In Response to Executive Order 9066: All Americans of Japanese Descent Must Report to Relocation Centers" briefly tells the story of a young Japanese American girl in the days shortly after the bombing of Pearl Harbor on December 7, 1941. At this time, an order signed by President Franklin D. Roosevelt stipulated that all Japanese Americans must report to relocation camps to be interned for the duration of the war. Also known as internment camps, the facilities were in reality prison camps where Japanese Americans were detained without cause. Okita's poem, written in the form of a letter from the narrator to the U.S. government, makes clear the absurdity of Order 9066 and the underlying fear and racism that allowed it to be enforced. Okita states that he was inspired to write the poem because of his mother's experience during her teenage years as an internee at a relocation camp. The poem, first published in 1983, has enjoyed significant popularity in the ensuing years and has been widely anthologized. Okita's 1992 poetry collection *Crossing with the Light* includes "In Response to Executive Order 9066" and is easily available in libraries and bookstores.

AUTHOR BIOGRAPHY

Okita was born August 26, 1958, in Chicago, Illinois, to Fred Yoshio Okita and Patsy Takeyo Arase. His father was from Seattle, Washington, and his mother from Fresno, California. When the United States entered World War II after the Japanese bombing of Pearl Harbor, many Japanese Americans living on the West Coast were placed in internment camps by order of the U.S. government. Fred Okita, according to Claudia Milstead, writing in the *The Greenwood Encyclopedia of Multiethnic Literature*, was only at the camp briefly because he soon joined the 442 Battalion, an army unit made up of Japanese Americans. Okita's mother, however, spent four of her teenage years in the camp.

Okita's parents met after their respective families moved to Chicago following their release from relocation camps; they married and had two sons. Okita reports on his official Web page (http://www.dwightland.homestead.com) that he began writing poetry as early as the first grade because he had trouble producing a straightforward narrative. Okita attended public schools in Chicago and continued to write poetry throughout his school years.

When Okita was sixteen, he told his parents he was gay. To his surprise, according to Christina Chiu, writing in *Lives of Notable Asian Americans: Literature and Education*, his parents were both accepting and supportive of his announcement.

Okita graduated from high school in 1976, and he enrolled at the University of Illinois at Chicago. At the university, he majored in theater. He graduated in 1983 with a degree in creative writing. In 1982 while still an undergraduate student, Okita wrote "In Response to Executive Order 9066." The poem was selected for publication in the anthology *Breaking Light*, published in 1983. Since this publication, the poem has been widely anthologized. The Illinois Art Council awarded Okita a fellowship for achievement in poetry in 1988. In 1992, Okita published his first volume of poetry, *Crossing with the Light*, which included "In Response to Executive Order 9066." The book was nominated as the best Asian American literature book of 1993 by the Association for Asian American Studies.

Okita turned from writing poetry to drama during the 1990s, composing plays such as *Richard Speck* (1991) and *The Salad Bowl Dance* (1993). In 1995, Okita collaborated with Anne V. McGravie, Nicholas A. Patricca, and David Zak to produce *The Radiance of a Thousand Suns: The Hiroshima Project: A Drama with Music. The Prospect of My Arrival*, Okita's first full-length novel, was named an Amazon Breakthrough Award semifinalist in 2009.

Okita continues to grow as a writer and take on new themes, genres, and styles. As Milstead writes in *Voces de América*, "As long as his writing remains rooted in the personal, however, it will be flavored by both his ethnicity and his sexual orientation."

POEM TEXT

Dear Sirs:
Of course I'll come. I've packed my galoshes
and three packets of tomato seeds. Denise calls them
love apples. My father says where we're going
they won't grow.   5

I am a fourteen-year-old girl with bad spelling
and a messy room. If it helps any, I will tell you
I have always felt funny using chopsticks
and my favorite food is hot dogs.
My best friend is a white girl named Denise—   10
we look at boys together. She sat in front of me
all through grade school because of our names:
O'Connor, Ozawa. I know the back of Denise's head very well.

I tell her she's going bald. She tells me I copy on tests.
We're best friends.   15

I saw Denise today in Geography class.
She was sitting on the other side of the room.
"You're trying to start a war," she said, "giving secrets
away to the Enemy, Why can't you keep your big
mouth shut?"   20

I didn't know what to say.
I gave her a packet of tomato seeds
and asked her to plant them for me, told her
when the first tomato ripened
she'd miss me.   25

POEM SUMMARY

Stanza 1

The complete title of Okita's poem is "In Response to Executive Order 9066: All Americans of Japanese Descent Must Report to Relocation Centers." From the title, the reader learns that what he or she is about to read is some kind of answer to the governmental order requiring all Japanese Americans to leave their homes and go to a place where they will be kept under guard. The poem is written in free verse, that is, without a regular rhyme or meter. It is twenty-five lines long, unevenly divided

MEDIA ADAPTATIONS

- An audio recording of *Holt Elements of Literature*, edited by G. Kylene Beers and including "In Response to Executive Order 9066," was released on compact disc in 2004 by Recordings for the Blind and Dyslexic.

into five stanzas. The first stanza reveals that the response will be in the form of formal letter. The opening line is a standard opening for a business letter, and the colon after the word "sirs" further emphasizes that this a formal response.

The speaker writing the letter is polite. She tells the government officials that she has already begun to pack, selecting overshoes to keep her feet dry in the rain and vegetable seeds for planting. Two additional characters make their presence known in the opening stanza: a girl named Denise and the narrator's father. Denise comments on the vegetable seeds, giving them another name. The narrator's father is pessimistic and tells his daughter that the seeds are unlikely to thrive where they are being required to go. The contrast between the name that Denise gives the vegetable and the father's pessimism presents verbal irony; the place where the narrator and her family will be going is not a place where love will thrive.

Stanza 2
In the second stanza, the narrator reveals more about herself. The reader discovers that she is a typical young teenager. Like other teenagers, sometimes she has trouble with her spelling, and she does not always keep her bedroom tidy. However, in the next line, the narrator tells the government official that she does not easily manage the traditional eating instrument of Asian peoples (chopsticks), and her preferred food is the all-American frankfurter. She gives the official this information in the hope that it will make a difference as to whether she is going to be considered an American or a Japanese person.

The narrator then offers some information about Denise, saying that she is Caucasian and is the narrator's closest companion. Together the two girls do what typical American girls do: they talk about young men. The narrator also reveals that the two girls have been in the same class from the time they started school. Denise's last name is O'Connor, while the narrator's name is Ozawa, a Japanese surname. This, too, presents irony, since O'Connor is an Irish name. It is likely that Denise's family came to the United States from Ireland several generations earlier, just as the narrator's family came from Japan several generations back. Since Denise's seat is in front of the narrator in their classes, the narrator reveals that she is very familiar with the back of her friend's head.

Stanza 3
The third stanza is only two lines long. Structurally, the short stanza divides the poem in two. In the first line of the stanza, the girls tease each other in short phrases. The second line of the stanza is a restatement of the closeness of their friendship.

Stanza 4
The poem takes a turn immediately after the narrator affirms that she and Denise are close friends who spend all their time together. In addition, in the fourth stanza, the narrator introduces the chronology, or time frame, of the poem. Throughout the beginning of the poem, she has talked about the way things have always been between the two girls. In the fourth stanza, however, the speaker specifies that the events happen on the current day. The narrator reports that she has seen Denise in a class in which they study the countries of the world. Instead of sitting in her usual place right in front of the narrator, Denise has moved to the other side of the room. Denise turns to the narrator and cruelly accuses her of beginning the hostilities between the United States and Japan. She also accuses the narrator of leaking important information to the Japanese. She concludes by asking the narrator why she just will not shut up. Clearly, Denise has been influenced by the fear and racism of her elders who believe that all Japanese Americans, born in the United States or not, will be loyal to Japan.

Stanza 5
The narrator is stunned into silence by the accusations of a girl she thought was her best friend. Okita seems to be saying that there are no words to respond to such cruelty. However, the

narrator reveals much about herself in the final four lines. She gives her friend a package of the vegetable seeds that her father says will not grow in the camp. She asks her friend to sow them and tells her that by the time the vegetables are ready to be picked, Denise will mourn the loss of her friend.

These closing lines lend a somber, empty tone to the entire poem. They demonstrate in microcosm (a small representation of a larger idea or community) what is happening to the entire country. That is, Okita uses a very small example to stand in for the large issue of what it means to imprison an entire population of U.S. citizens for no other reason than their heritage.

THEMES

Racism

In his poem "In Response to Executive Order 9066," Okita subtly yet effectively focuses on the impact of racism and fear on a friendship between two teenage girls. Racism can be defined as the irrational hatred and fear of one racial group for another. Racism also supports the belief that the social and moral development of a person is solely determined by the biological fact of the person's racial or ethnic background.

In the first lines of the poem, Okita establishes that the narrator is a teenager, just like any other teenager, with problems in school and a tendency toward untidiness at home. There is no indication of the race or ethnic origin of the narrator until line 8, when the narrator expresses her discomfort using the traditional eating utensils of Asian peoples. This oblique reference causes the reader to wonder why the narrator would even mention this trait. The statement suggests, therefore, that the speaker must be an American of Asian descent, but one who considers herself fully American. In order to fully develop this thought, Okita refers to the narrator's love of all-American food at the same time he mentions her uneasiness using chopsticks.

The first direct reference to race occurs in line 10, when the narrator identifies her best friend Denise as a Caucasian teenager, implying that the narrator herself is not Caucasian, since it would be unusual for one white girl to stipulate that her friend is another white girl. In this line, then, the racial differences between the two friends are established. However, Okita immediately returns to demonstrating the similarities, rather than the differences, between the two girls: they have been

in the same schools and classes for a long time, they like to talk about boys, and they know each other well. In line 13, Okita once again indirectly refers to their different ethnic backgrounds: Denise's last name is Irish, while the narrator's is Japanese.

The division between the two girls and the evidence of fear and racism happens suddenly. In line 17, when the narrator comes into her classroom, she sees her friend sitting far away from her usual seat. This is a symbolic image, demonstrating that as close as the two girls have been most of their lives, something powerful is proving divisive. When Denise accuses the narrator of essentially being a spy and helping the Japanese war effort, the effects of racism are clear. Denise's response to her fear of war is to irrationally blame the narrator. Rather than continuing to see her friend as someone just like her, Denise has labeled the narrator as a dangerous "other," someone who cannot be trusted, simply because she is of different racial background.

The moment is fraught with emotion for the narrator, who is rendered speechless. Facing physical separation from her friend and emotional displacement from her entire life because of Executive Order 9066, the narrator must also unexpectedly face both fear and racism in the one person she would have counted on for support. Okita poignantly illustrates the damage that fear and racism can do to human relationships by making it personal. Instead of talking about fear and racism in abstract, global terms, he instead uses the concrete example of two young girls to represent an event deserving of national shame.

Friendship

"In Response to Executive Order 9066" explores the limits of friendship. As the poem is narrated by a young Japanese American girl, the reader only has insight into her understanding of the friendship between her and Denise. The reader has no reason to doubt the narrator's account of their friendship, until suddenly, Denise turns on her friend essentially accusing her of treason.

It is difficult to assess why Denise verbally attacks the narrator, although it would appear that Okita uses Denise as a parrot; that is, she is merely repeating the propaganda being broadcast in the media and, in all likelihood, what she is hearing at home. One cannot help but wonder if these attitudes were simmering beneath the surface all along, and that the friendship was more sincere

TOPICS FOR FURTHER STUDY

- Locate the full text of Executive Order 9066, available at the *National Archives and Records Administration* at www.archives.gov/histori cal-docs/todays-doc/index.html?dod-date = 219/. Read the document carefully and analyze it, using the "Written Document Analysis Worksheet" developed by the staff of the National Archives in Washington, D.C., and located at www.archives.gov/education/lessons/worksheets/document.html. Use the information from your worksheet to structure an essay discussing how and why the internment of over 100,000 Japanese Americans took place.

- Working collaboratively with a small group, gather as much primary source information as you can from credible Internet sites and your local library about the internment of Japanese Americans during World War II. (Possible Web sites include the *Harry S. Truman Memorial Library and Museum* Web site at www.trumanlibrary.org/, and the *National Archives and Records Administration* at www.archives.gov/.) In addition, research what life was like on the West Coast in 1941. Now, imagine that you and your classmates are living in California in 1941. Divide your small group in half and hold a debate for the rest of your class about the legality of imprisoning American citizens for the duration of World War II. Be sure to articulate your thoughts clearly and effectively.

- Gather as many photographs as you can find online and in books that represent the relocation camps. Try to imagine life in the camps by first noting particular details in the images you have found. Choose one of the people you see in the photographs and make him or her the main character in a short story you write by imaginatively entering the world of the relocation camps. In your short story, demonstrate your originality and inventiveness and your ability to respond to diverse perspectives.

- With a small group of your classmates, view the Public Broadcasting Corporation (PBS) documentary *Children of the Camps*, available at http://www.pbs.org/childofcamp/documentary/index.html/. Discuss the stories of the various children, and then write several diary entries that express the thoughts of one of the children at various points during their internment.

- Gather a selection of images from the Internet and books of anti-Japanese propaganda during World War II in the United States. What messages do these visual images suggest? Do the images change across time? How do you think this propaganda affected the decision to place Japanese Americans in internment camps? Prepare a PowerPoint presentation for your classmates in which you present your findings.

- Read the novel *Two Suns in the Sky* (1999) by Miriam Bat-Ami about the only camp for Holocaust survivors in the United States. Write an essay that compares and contrasts the Japanese internment camp experience with that of the experiences of the fictional characters in the novel.

---

on the part of the narrator than on the part of Denise.

If Denise's attitude reveals the limits of friendship, the narrator's response illustrates the boundless forgiveness that is possible among friends.

Although she is initially speechless, her later response to her friend is not to fight back or protest, but rather give her a package of tomato seeds. As Denise's name for tomatoes is love apples, the implication is that if Denise plants the seeds and

Japanese American citizens on their way to an internment camp (© *Historical Premium / Corbis*)

nurtures them, the love between the two friends might someday come to life again. However, there is also the sad note at the end poem, that although Denise might one day regret her hasty rejection of a valuable friendship and want to make amends, the narrator will be gone. Denise will then realize how much her friend's absence pains her.

STYLE

Epistle

The word "epistle" means letter. Generally, however, the word applies to a formal or artistic letter for public consumption; usually an epistle will have a strong thematic message for those who read it. Examples of well-known epistles include those written by Paul in the Christian Bible and verse epistles written by the seventeenth-century English writer Ben Jonson.

"In Response to Executive Order 9066" is written in the epistle format. The situation of the poem is that a Japanese family has received word they must relocate to an internment camp shortly after the bombing of Pearl Harbor. The poem itself is ostensibly a letter from a teenage girl to the U.S. Government in response to the receipt of Executive Order 9066, an order signed by President Franklin D. Roosevelt restricting all Japanese Americans to such camps.

By choosing the epistle format, Okita is able to write the poem in the voice of a teenage girl. He can also make the poem more poignant as it pits the voice of one individual child against the

entire establishment of the U.S. Government. As the reader is well aware that any such letter is likely to be ignored, in spite of its eloquence, the reader also internalizes how devastating Executive Order 9066 must have been to those people affected by it.

Persona

In a poem, the speaker through whom the writer presents his or her work is sometimes called the persona. At times, the persona seems to merge with the poet's self. In other cases, such as in "In Response to Executive Order 9066," the writer establishes a very different persona to tell the story.

Okita has mentioned in several interviews and on his Web site that the persona of "In Response to Executive Order 9066" is based on his mother's experience, who was restricted to an internment camp for four years during World War II. Okita does not claim that his mother wrote any letters to the government; rather, he uses his mother's situation as the jumping off point for his fictional accounting of one girl's experience.

The voice Okita gives his persona in this poem is young, trusting, and naive. She clearly does not see herself as any different from other Americans. She and her friend Denise speak the same language, and until line 17, they are best friends. Ironically, the persona's voice is fully revealed in her silence, after she is attacked by Denise. She does not retort in anger or protest; rather, she remains quiet. Indeed, Okita gives no indication that she ever responds directly to the ridiculous accusations that she is passing important information to the Japanese war machine.

Finally, by using a young woman persona as the focal point of the poem, Okita is able to demonstrate that Executive Order 9066 is a reactionary and racist piece of legislation born out of fear and hatred against a visually identifiable group of Americans. The speaker in this poem is clearly not a spy; rather she is a teenager just like any other American adolescent. Her impending punishment has no other cause than her racial background.

HISTORICAL CONTEXT

The Bombing of Pearl Harbor

On December 7, 1941, Japanese aircraft attacked Pearl Harbor, Hawaii. Although Hawaii was not a U.S. state at that time, it was an American territory, and the Naval Base at Pearl Harbor was the home of the U.S. Pacific fleet.

COMPARE
&
CONTRAST

- **1940s:** Citizens of the United States fear Japanese attack, such as that launched against Pearl Harbor, Hawaii, on December 7, 1941.

  1980s: Citizens of the United States feel threatened by a perceived military threat from the Soviet Union. President Ronald Reagan responds by proposing the Strategic Defense Initiative, a space-based nuclear missile system that would destroy incoming enemy missiles.

  Today: Citizens of the United States feel threatened by terrorist attacks, such as those launched against the World Trade Towers in New York City and the Pentagon in Washington, D.C., on September 11, 2001, by radical Islamic terrorists.

- **1940s:** The U.S. government publishes propaganda posters depicting Japanese soldiers as physically ugly, subhuman rapists and murderers. Such propaganda influences the way that some Americans think about all people of Japanese descent.

  1980s: President Ronald Reagan delivers a speech to the National Association of Evangelicals uplifting the moral superiority of Americans over Russians, calling the Soviet Union "the focus of evil in the modern world" and "the evil empire." This rhetoric influences the way some Americans think about Russians.

  Today: In the article "Smearcasting: How Islamophobes Spread Fear, Bigotry and Misinformation," writer Steve Rendell and his colleagues argue that some members of the media exhibit hostility that "tends to dehumanize an entire faith . . . attributing to it an inherent, essential set of negative traits such as irrationality, intolerance and violence." Such media hostility influences the way some Americans think about people of Middle Eastern descent.

- **1940s:** By order of Executive Order 9066, most areas on the West Coast of the United States are considered "exclusion zones" where Japanese Americans are no longer permitted to live. They are forced to report to relocation, or internment, camps by order of the federal government, in what is later recognized as a serious infringement of their civil liberties.

  1980s: In 1988, Congress passes the Civil Liberties Act of 1988, "Restitution for World War II Internment of Japanese Americans and Aleuts." The purpose of the act is to offer an apology to those interned and to order restitution be paid to them in token of the losses they sustained because of their internment.

  Today: Debate continues over the civil liberties of those whom the government suspects of terrorist action. One of the hotly debated topics is the closing of the U.S. military base in Guantanamo Bay, Cuba. After the September 11, 2001 attacks, suspected terrorists are held there indefinitely.

In the months before the attack, diplomatic relations between the Japanese and U.S. governments deteriorated dramatically. In 1940, the United States outlawed shipments of scrap iron, steel, and airplane fuel. They did so in protest of Japan's expansion into Indochina, an area held under French and Dutch colonial control. Japan believed that with the German defeat of France and the Netherlands, it was a good time to take over their colonial holdings.

As Japanese expansion continued, the United States, Britain, and the Netherlands froze all Japanese assets in their country, making it very difficult for Japan to buy oil, something it needed for its military machine. Although both Japan and the United States were working at a diplomatic solution, Japan was also formulating a military solution to its problem. Japan decided that it would attack the U.S. Pacific fleet without warning in order to cripple the U.S. Navy and allow them to capture lands throughout Southeast Asia.

On a beautiful Sunday morning, shortly before 8:00 a.m., Japanese aircraft began bombing Pearl Harbor. Within two hours, more than 3,500 Americans were dead and 18 ships were sunk, including all of the battleships of the U.S. Pacific Fleet. In addition, hundreds of airplanes were destroyed. The people of the United States were horrified by this action. The attack led to the United States entry into war with Japan and also into war with the Axis powers, led by Germany. The conflagration came to be known as World War II.

The swiftness and surprise of the attack frightened everyone in the United States, but none more so than those living on the West Coast. Many feared an attack on mainland United States was imminent. This, along with growing resentment and racism directed at Japanese Americans living on the West Coast, contributed to the signing of Executive Order 9066.

Executive Order 9066

On February 19, 1942, President Franklin D. Roosevelt signed into law Executive Order 9066. This order allowed the military to designate "exclusion zones," places where any people or groups of people could be excluded. In this case, the military designated nearly all of the West Coast as an exclusion zone and stipulated that all persons of Japanese descent be removed from the area. By May 3, 1942, all people of Japanese descent in the exclusion zones were required to report to assembly centers where they would be relocated to camps set up in various parts of the United States. By the time the relocation was completed, over 110,000 people were interned. Two-thirds of these were American citizens, and over one-half were children. The internees were only allowed to take with them what they could carry and were forced to leave behind (or sell for pennies on the dollar) the rest of their possessions. For many, this also meant leaving behind businesses, farms, and jobs. Many people also had their financial assets frozen. When the war was over, many internees discovered that their personal and financial possessions had been stolen or lost. The internment was economically devastating to most families.

Japanese children wave American flags (© Horace Bristol / Corbis)

The reason given for the internment of the Japanese Americans is that many in the United States government believed that they posed a risk to national security. This made government officials believe that the Japanese Americans would offer help and aid to the enemy. However, there is evidence, as reported by the Commission on Wartime Relocation and Internment of Civilians in 1982, that the action was largely the result of racism and antagonism toward people of Asian descent, particularly on the West Coast. As legal scholar and law professor Anupam Chander states in his article "Legalized Racism: The Internment of Japanese Americans" (available at *Anupam Chander.com*): "The internment of Japanese Americans in the West Coast during World War II grew out of rampant anti-Asian sentiment in the pre-war period.... the internment flouted nearly every provision of the Bill of Rights of the U.S. Constitution."

CRITICAL OVERVIEW

Although Okita's poem "In Response to Executive Order 9066" has been widely anthologized and read by students across the country, there has been little critical attention to his poetry by literary scholars. Moreover, Okita's decision to focus on writing drama and novels has meant that his most recent (and only) volume of poetry, *Crossing with the Light*, is now nearly two decades old. Thus, the body of his poetic output is small.

In a brief 1995 *Horn Book* magazine review of *Celebrate America: Poetry and Art*, an illustrated poetry anthology for young people, Rudine Sims Bishop notes that Okita's work is included in the book. She writes that the anthology is "tempered by the inclusion of voices usually relegated to the margins of this society and by reminders that the nation has not always lived up to its promises."

Christina Chiu, writing about Okita in her book *Lives of Notable Asian Americans: Literature and Education*, reveals that Okita has been influenced by poets such as Philip Levine and playwrights such as Tony Kushner. Perhaps the most frequent commentator on Okita's work is Claudia Milstead, who has studied Okita's work closely for a number of years. In a chapter in the book *Voces de América: American Voices*, she includes an interview with the poet and discusses the inspiration for Okita's poetry. She writes, "Many of Okita's poems and plays reflect experiences that are uniquely Asian American, rooted principally in the events of World War II."

Perhaps the best critique of Okita's poetry comes from the poet himself. Okita offers analysis and insight into his own poetry, both in interviews and on his self-maintained Web site. He reveals that "In Response to Executive Order 9066" was inspired by his mother's experience of being sent to the internment camps as a girl. He imagines what the word "camp" would mean to a child: a place where someone goes in the summer to have fun. Thus, Okita writes on his Web page, he "wrote the poem in the form of a kind thank-you letter which [he] imagined she might've written to the American government." Okita also makes it clear that although the inspiration came from his mother's experience, the details of the poem are fictional, placed in the poem for artistic and thematic reasons. The widespread inclusion of Okita's poetry, and particularly "In Response to Executive Order 9066," in well-respected anthologies suggests that critical interest in his work will build in coming years.

CRITICISM

Diane Andrews Henningfeld

Henningfeld is a professor emerita of literature and a literary critic who writes widely for

> THE POETIC DEVICE OF IRONY, SUBTLY AND SKILLFULLY APPLIED, ALLOWS OKITA TO BOTH TELL THE STORY OF THE EVENT, AND AT THE SAME TIME, MAKE A PUBLIC STATEMENT OF PROTEST."

educational publishers. In the following essay, she examines the use of irony in "In Response to Executive Order 9066."

Dwight Okita's poem "In Response to Executive Order 9066: All Americans of Japanese Descent Must Report to Relocation Centers" is a moving document, imaginatively recounting the experience of a young Japanese American who has just discovered that she and her family will be removed from their homes and relocated in camps. By choosing the experience of just one child, in this case, a girl based on his own mother, Okita focuses the reader's attention on the utter absurdity of the order. At the same time, he also offers a poignant statement about friendship and racism: the seeds of racism can destroy even the closest of friendships. Okita accomplishes much in the brief poem. The poetic device of irony, subtly and skillfully applied, allows Okita to both tell the story of the event, and at the same time, make a public statement of protest.

Irony can take many forms in a work of literature. Quite simply, irony is a contradiction or incongruity between expectation and reality. In addition, irony can occur when there is an incongruity between the knowledge and belief of a narrator in a work of literature and the knowledge and belief of the writer or the reader. An additional form of irony, irony of situation, is at work when the situation itself is incongruous with what the reader expects.

The irony displayed in "In Response to Executive Order 9066" is very quiet and subtle, but at close examination, it reveals itself. In the first place, the poem is written in the form of a letter from the narrator to the government. She is writing in response to Executive Order 9066. Her expectation is that she might be able to change the order if those giving the order can understand that she is truly an American, not a Japanese spy. However, readers understand that her belief is naive; she is just one young girl

WHAT
DO I READ
NEXT?

- *The Radiance of a Thousand Suns: The Hiroshima Project*, a drama written by Anne V. McGravie, Dwight Okita, Nicholas A. Patricca, and David Zak, with music by Chick Larkin, was published in script form in 1998 by Dramatic Publishing. The play was written to memorialize the fiftieth anniversary of the atomic bombing of Hiroshima and portrays many of the events and people surrounding the development and use of nuclear weapons. The foreword to the play, written by Martin Harwit, former director of the National Air and Space Museum, provides an important historical overview.

- Okita maintains his own Web site where students can read messages from the writer, biographical information, notes about "In Response to Executive Order 9066" and other poems, a bibliography, and updates about Okita's current work. The Web site is located at http://www.dwightland.homestead.com.

- The *Harry S. Truman Library and Museum* Web site includes a large section titled "The War Relocation Authority and the Incarceration of Japanese Americans During WWII." The collection includes 14 photographs, 62 documents comprising 911 pages, a chronology of events from 1941–1998, and a selection of oral histories. The Web site can be accessed at http://www.trumanlibrary.org/.

- *Farewell to Manzanar*, written by James A. Houston, Jeanne Wakatsuki Houston, and James D. Houston, is a nonfiction memoir about the Wakatsuki internment at the Manzanar War Relocation Camp. The book was published by Houghton Mifflin Books for Children in 2002.

- Jane Wehrey's 2008 publication, *Manzanar*, is a selection from Arcadia Publishing's "Images of America" series. Wehrey's book is a pictorial history of the site of one of the major relocation camps, and it includes images from photographer Ansel Adams, Dorothea Lange, and Toyo Miyatake, a former resident of the camp. Historian Wehrey has been a park ranger at the Manzar National Historic Site.

- Michael Cooper's *Remembering Manzanar*, published by Clarion Books in 2002, is an illustrated description of daily life in a relocation camp, written for younger readers. The book includes photographs and statements from former internees.

- Ken Mochizuki's *Baseball Saved Us* (1995), published by Lee and Low Books, is the story of a young Japanese American boy who must go to an internment camp with his parents. While there, he excels at baseball, and the game gives him and the other internees purpose and direction while they are held captive. The book is also available as an audio CD, read by the author. Although written for a young audience, *Baseball Saved Us* is a moving fictional account for all ages to enjoy.

- Lois Lowry's Newberry Award-winning *Number the Stars* (1989) chronicles the mission of a Danish girl to save her Jewish best friend from Nazi-German invaders in this fictionalized true-story account.

---

writing to a vast military and governmental machine. The reader knows that no matter what the narrator writes, it will not make a difference in the outcome. Thus, Okita establishes an incongruity between what the narrator expects and what the reader knows.

Further, the opening lines of the poem provide an example of irony. The narrator writes that she will come to the camp, as if there is no question. The first line of her letter reads as if she is answering an invitation to a party, almost as if she is responding to an RSVP. Again, her expectations of what a camp will be are very different from what readers of the poem know. It appears that she almost imagines it will be like summer camp. Readers, however, understand that the narrator and her family are actually being sent to something much more like a prison camp, a place from which they will not be permitted to leave and with armed guards to keep them in.

The narrator also reports in her letter what she has packed for her trip to the camp. Readers know that interned Japanese Americans were only allowed to take with them what they could carry to the internment camps, and so the narrator's choice of taking overshoes and tomato seeds seems poignant and sad. Moreover, there is irony in the fact that her best friend Denise calls tomatoes by another name, love apples. The narrator's father responds to this name by telling his daughter that her seeds will not grow into tomato plants at the camp. Essentially, he states that anything with the word "love" cannot exist in the place where they are going. Further, given what the reader learns about Denise in the coming lines, it is even more ironic that she should use the term love apples for the tomatoes the narrator plans on sowing. Denise does not treat her friend with anything like love.

The second stanza addresses another form of irony. The incongruity here is between what people stereotypically might think about a young woman who looks Asian and the reality of the young woman's life. In this case, the narrator is truly an American: she acts like an American teenager, she enjoys American food, and she does not know how to use chopsticks. With this passage, Okita reminds the reader that most of the 110,000 people interned during the war were American citizens, some of them third- and fourth-generation. In fact, two-thirds of all Japanese Americans interned were American citizens, and over half of them were children, according to a contributor to the National Asian American Telecommunications Association Web site. The notion that such people are in direct communication with the Japanese military is ludicrous, and by placing the words in the mouth of a teenage girl, Okita epitomizes this absurdity.

A second irony, one that begins to hint at the racism involved in Executive Order 9066, arises at the end of the second stanza. The narrator tells the reader that Denise's last name is O'Connor while hers is Ozawa. Both names begin with the letter "O," emphasizing the similarity between the two girls. The real similarity is in the ethnic origins of their names. O'Connor is an Irish name, and it is likely that Denise's family came to the United States from Ireland, perhaps in the nineteenth century. Likewise, the narrator's family, if based on Okita's family, has been in the United States for three generations at least. Thus, both girls are the offspring of immigrants. However, because the narrator is visibly Asian, as opposed to European, it is easier for the mainstream white culture to single out her and others like her. Across the nation, although Japanese Americans were interned, German Americans were not, yet the history of their immigration to the United States was quite similar. It is likely that this was because German Americans were Caucasian as opposed to Japanese Americans who were Asian.

In the second line of the third stanza, the narrator tells the reader that she and Denise are best friends. This statement quickly becomes ironic in the next stanza. The narrator and the reader both have an understanding of what a best friend should be and do. The two girls have grown up together and have what is obviously a close and playful relationship. However, the fourth stanza of the poem shatters that expectation. Apparently listening to war propaganda and messages of hatred and racism discussed at home, Denise chooses to separate herself from the narrator. That they are in geography class at the time makes the moment even more ironic; one of the reasons that students study geography in school is so that they can reach a better understanding of the countries and people of the world, even those at a long distance from the United States. Denise's choice to sit at the opposite side of the classroom suggests that the distance between her and the narrator is as great as the expanse between the United States and Japan.

In addition, Denise's accusations that the narrator is attempting to start World War II and that she is an enemy spy are incongruous with what the reader knows about the narrator. Everything in the poem thus far suggests that the narrator is a polite and thoroughly American teenager. Since this is the case, the reader must see Denise's words as irrational and the product of hatred, not what the reader would expect from a best friend.

Interestingly for a poem full of irony, the final stanza does not seem to exhibit this literary device. In this stanza, the narrator's actions are

Patriotic Japanese girl *(Image copyright Avava, 2009. Used under license from Shutterstock.com)*

completely in keeping with what the reader has learned of her up until this point. The narrator, by offering a gift of what Denise calls love apples, demonstrates both her kindness and sadness. She knows that someday her friend will be sorry for what she has said, and she will discover that she is lonely for her best friend. In some ways, it is as if the narrator forgives Denise before she even endures four long years in the internment camp. The final stanza focuses on the pain of one young girl, and by extension addresses the pain of the 110,000 men, women, and children ripped from their lives and placed behind the wire fences of relocation camps. Most of these people lost everything they had in their lives from before the war; for the narrator, however, the most painful loss is that of her best friend.

Okita's poem, then, reveals a personal dimension of the Japanese American internment. He shows through subtle irony that Executive Order 9066, while ostensibly about national security, was in fact the product of hysteria, racial hatred, and fear of difference. The effectiveness of the poem is in Okita's ability to present in the microcosm of one teenager's experience the total shameful event that was the response to Executive Order 9066.

Source: Diane Andrews Henningfeld, Critical Essay on "In Response to Executive Order 9066: All Americans of Japanese Descent Must Report to Relocation Centers," in *Poetry for Students*, Gale, Cengage Learning, 2010.

Jeffrey Beam

In the following excerpt, Beam offers a mixed review of Crossing with the Light, *singling out "Executive Order 9066" for its realism.*

...Dwight Okita's *Crossing with the Light* reads like a diary. If it had been in prose form, with its easy prosaic sentences, its frequent use of "I," and the accumulation of everyday objects, hopes, fears and experiences, I can imagine a document affecting in its rain of human secretes. Rather what one perceives is a catalog of poetic truisms. Okita's poems are too self-obsessed for my taste, even slightly maudlin, as expressed in this poem, "I have wanted to tell you how nice it is": "How some nights I have a bowl of cereal/and dream and the cornflakes wilt/and I go on dreaming and my future/is as certain as the knife cutting through/the banana." One can write such observations in one's diary and not look too trivial.

Some poems, however, remind us of how poetry, as Richard Blackmur demanded, "adds to the stock of available reality." In Okita's well-anthologized poem "In Response to Executive Order 9066: All Americans of Japanese Descent Must Report to Relocation Centers," the 14 year old girl's letter to the "executive" captures in its first person declarative lines the wrenching horror she feels as her life-long friend turns on her: "My best friend is a white girl named Denise—/we look at boys together/.... "You're trying to start a war," she said, "giving secrets/away to the Enemy, Why can't you keep your big/mouth shut?"

I admit my bias toward poetry more lyrical in approach, less full of shopping malls and bottles of Perrier. I prefer poetry in which the world reveals more than it seems, more than just what I want it to reveal, more than the obvious correspondences....

Source: Jeffrey Beam, Review of *Crossing with the Light*, in *Lambda Book Report*, Vol. 3, No. 11, July 1993, p. 44.

June Sawyers

In the following article, Sawyers discusses with Okita his development of the poetry video form, including his video "Crossing with the Light."

Dwight Okita is a Chicago poet—sort of a soft-spoken rebel with a cause. His dream is to reach as wide an audience as possible by whisking poetry off the printed page and onto, of all things, the small screen. And he thinks he has found the answer. Poetry video.

"It's such a new form," he says. "There are no guidelines. You can't do something wrong because there's no right yet. That's the exciting part."

His first poetry video, "Crossing with the Light," premieres on cable television's Ch. 19 on the Chicago Access Network at 9 p.m. Monday. A 5-minute reverie that combines imagery, poetry and music the video uses the street as a metaphor for love, the land of myriad possibilities. Crossing the street, Okita suggests, is just as dangerous as falling in love.

It opens with a still black-and-white photo of the poet staring pensively through the window of the Days Inn across Clark and Diversey. In the background is a billboard for Kirin beer. "Mysteriously Satisfying," it says.

Paul Winter's evocative music complements the wistfulness of Okita's voice-over. The camera then does a slow 360-degree pan of the corner: the faces, the subtle danger, the unpredictability, the promise of a city night.

It ends with a close-up freeze of Okita once again crossing the street, continuing his life journey.

Though he has been talking about making a poetry video for several years, Okita admits that everything just fell into place recently. Armed with a $5,000 grant from the Illinois Arts Council, Okita secured the services of producer and director Marsha V. Morgan and photographer Jennifer Girard. He had no difficulty receiving permission to use Winter's "Grand Canyon Sunrise," while a friend's apartment in the Days Inn offered a perfect birds-eye view of the street below.

"A lot of fortunate things happened that shouldn't have. It was a series of doors opening," he says. As a practicing Buddhist, he views these occurrences as more than mere coincidence.

Okita is currently considering other outlets for "Crossing with the Light"—WTTW's "Image Union," the local club circuit, even MTV and David Letterman.

Poetry on Letterman?

Okita certainly hopes so: "Who says art can't be entertaining?"

Source: June Sawyers, "Poetry Video Comes to the Small Screen," in *Chicago Tribune*, September 18, 1988, p. 2.

June Sawyers

In the following article, Sawyers examines the revitalization of the poetic community in Chicago through active poets like Okita.

There are two popular images of the poet. One is of the snooty academic looking down from his ivory tower; the other, of the hip genius wise to the street but dictated to only by the rhythms in his head.

Both images are hopelessly outdated.

Between the scholar and the beatnik lies a modern world where the emphasis is on building bridges, not creating barriers. Small presses, literary magazines and offbeat newsletters provide a forum for divergent cultures and various opinions.

The first great wave of poetic activity in Illinois occurred during the early years of the 20th Century when Carl Sandburg, Edgar Lee Masters and Vachel Lindsay put the Prairie State firmly on the poetic map. Arising from the Midwestern heartland, this trinity of poets celebrated a deeply felt sense of place and served as role models for future generations of American writers.

Poetry Magazine played a major role in fostering Chicago's reputation as a literary center. Founded in 1912 by Harriet Monroe, *Poetry* gained an international following by publishing the work of Ezra Pound, T.S. Eliot, William Butler Yeats, Padraic Colum and Edna St. Vincent Millay.

Poetry in Chicago is now witnessing a resurgence of activity not seen since the days of the Body Politic Theatre and Banyan Press readings of the mid-'70s. Readings take place in bookstores, libraries, museums, cabaret settings, bars, art galleries, universities and the traditional coffeehouses. Most critics agree there is no clearly defined Chicago school of poetry, although some, like *Poetry* editor Joseph Parisi, see a pronounced trend toward narrative, more formal verse and a growing appreciation of craftsmanship and technique.

The breadth and variety of the city's small presses and literary magazines are impressive, from the firmly established (*TriQuarterly, Chicago Review*) to the familiar yet unpredictable (*Another Chicago Magazine, Oink*) to the highly specialized (*Primavera*) and the up-and-coming (*Black & White*).

Paul Hoover, editor of *Oink*, calls Chicago one of the top poetry towns in the U.S., while Marc Smith, poet and editor of the *Open Mike* newsletter, places the city on a par with New York and San Francisco. "Exploding" is the term used by Michael Zerang, an experimental musician and one of the men behind the success of Link's Hall, an avant-garde venue and local watering hole that since November, 1985, has presented a wide-ranging series of inventive new music and cutting-edge poetry.

"The audience is there," says Zerang. Although originally he had not intended to book poets ("I tacked them on Thursday nights because I like them"), the response has been so good that Zerang, beginning in September, will honor the small press and little magazine heritage of Chicago and the Midwest with readings from representative poets on 15 consecutive Thursdays through December at Link's Hall.

Some cite the renewed literary ferment as proof that a new generation of poets is seeking to court fresh, untried audiences. Performance poetry, a theatrical variation of the traditional poetry reading, has especially caught on with those who might be intimidated by the word "poetry."

"People in the past just got up and read their poems," says Smith. "In performance poetry, you use all the other trappings of theater and visual art. It's trying to enhance the word whenever possible, because you have only that one chance to get it across."

Other poets stress collaboration among the arts; such a cross-fertilization of music, words and movement has already spawned at least one new artistic medium, the poetry video. Dwight Okita, who has staged a number of poetry events around town, believes strongly in "incorporating other art forms people are already comfortable with." Unlike most poets who read straight from the page, Okita memorizes his lines. "That way I see the real show, which is seeing the expression on the faces of the people. Something happens when you look at people's eyes."

The most influential effect performance poetry may have is "to break down the bias of poetry," says Smith. "The general public thinks of poetry as some intellectual exercise (which they are not qualified to decipher). They confuse the poet's ineffectiveness in getting his message across with their own intelligence."

"There is a literary junta that tries to dictate what poetry is," says poet-musician David Hernandez. "Poets belong to everybody."

But others don't believe it's simply a matter of the literary establishment forcing its effete tastes on the people.

"The ordinary man doesn't give a damn about poetry," says Barry Silesky, editor of *Another Chicago Magazine.* "Poetry—whether we like it or not—has a small, rarefied audience. The dream of a huge democratic audience is just unrealistic,

mainly because there are so many competing entertainments."

Mass market "poetry," such as popular song lyrics or the work of Rod McKuen, may reach a larger audience, but "it has nothing to do with poetry," says Joseph Parisi. Colleague Paul Hoover adds: "The idealistic poet would like to think anybody could walk in (on a reading) and the work would be clear enough to communicate on some level. But we know that's not always true."

Despite the difference in philosophy, Chicago appears remarkably free of the petty internecine disputes that plague other cities. Factions may exist—performance poets, published poets, college students, scholars, street poets, feminists, Latinos and blacks—but disagreements rarely escalate into full-fledged battles. "It's a source of liveliness. It's not destructive in any way," Silesky says.

A large portion of the audience is "a community of poets who go to each other's readings," notes Debbie Pintonelli, editor of *Letter eX,* a monthly poetry newsletter. Writer and teacher Michael Anania believes these mutual admiration societies serve a purpose. "Poets need a sense that their work is being attended to—and if it's by a small circle of friends, that's fine."

The poetry network may not be as cohesive as some wish, but that doesn't necessarily mean the sense of caring and commitment has been lost. The black community throughout the 1960s, for example, stressed spiritual and ethnic solidarity during an era of great political and social upheaval. Now, tempered by time, blacks' need for cultural belonging is not as strong.

There still exists "a sense of tradition and a sense of analyzing what has happened," says Sterling Plumpp, professor of Afro-American studies at the University of Illinois at Chicago and past winner of the Carl Sandburg award for poetry. "The sense of poetic brotherhood and sisterhood and nationhood is still very much there, but on an individual level."

Source: June Sawyers, "Poetry in Chicago: The New Wave Muse Is Back in Sandburg's Town," in *Chicago Tribune,* August 29, 1986, p. 5.

SOURCES

Bishop, Rudine Sims, "Books from Parallel Cultures: Celebrating the Americas," in *Horn Book,* Vol. 71, No. 3, May-June 1995, pp. 313–18.

Chander, Anupam, "Legalized Racism: The Internment of Japanese Americans," in *Anupam Chander.com*, April 2001, http://www.chander.com/docs/internment.pdf (accessed May 10, 2009).

Chiu, Christina, "Dwight Okita," in *Lives of Notable Asian Americans: Literature and Education*, Chelsea House Publishers, 1996, pp. 111–19.

"Exploring the Japanese American Internment Through Film and the Internet," in *National Asian American Telecommunication Association*, 2002, http://www.asianamericanmedia.org/jainternment/ww2/index.html (accessed May 12, 2009).

Han, John Jae-Nam, "Dwight Okita," in *Asian American Playwrights: A Bio-Bibliographical Sourcebook*, edited by Miles Xian Liu, Greenwood Press, 2002, pp. 263–67.

Milstead, Claudia, "Dwight Okita," in *The Greenwood Encyclopedia of Multiethnic American Literature*, edited by Emmanuel S. Nelson, Greenwood Publishing, 2005, pp. 1663–664.

———, "A Net of Images," in *Voces de América: American Voices*, edited by Laura P. Alonso Gallo, Aduana Vieja, 2004, pp. 583–603.

Okita, Dwight, "In Response to Executive Order 9066," in *Crossing with the Light*, Tia Chucha Press, 1992, p. 22.

———, "Writer Info," in *Dwight Okita: Official Web site*, http://dwightland.homestead.com/WRITERPAGE.html (accessed May 2, 2009).

Pach, Chester, "Ronald Reagan's Evil Empire Speech (1983)," in *Milestone Documents.com*, 2009, http://www.milestonedocuments.com/document_detail.php?id = 81&more = fulltext (accessed May 10, 2009).

"Pearl Harbor History: Why Did Japan Attack?," in *Pearl Harbor.org*, http://www.pearlharbor.org/history-of-pearl-harbor.asp (accessed May 11, 2009).

"Personal Justice Denied: Report of the Commission on Wartime Relocation and Internment of Citizens," in *National Park Service*, 1982, http://www.nps.gov/history/history/online_books/personal_justice_denied/intro.htm (accessed May 12, 2009).

"Posters from World War II," Japanese American Internment Curriculum, in *San Francisco State University*, http://bss.sfsu.edu/internment/posters.html (accessed May 10, 2009).

Rendell, Steve, et. al., "Smearcasting: How Islamophobes Spread Fear, Bigotry and Misinformation," in *Smearcasting.com: FAIR: Fairness and Accuracy in Reporting*, 2008, http://www.smearcasting.com/pdf/FAIR_Smearcasting_Final.pdf (accessed May 10, 2009).

Sullivan, Robert, "Pearl Harbor—What Really Happened," in *Time.com*, May 25, 2001, http://www.time.com/sampler/article/0,8599,128065,00.html (accessed May 11, 2009).

FURTHER READING

Benti, Wynne, ed., *Born Free and Equal: The Story of Loyal Japanese Americans*, Spotted Dog Press, 2002.
This is an impressive book of text and photographs based on the 1944 book *Born Free and Equal: The Story of Loyal Japanese Americans*, published by *U.S. Camera*; the book includes photographs and texts by Ansel Adams.

Kadohata, Cynthia, *Weedflower*, Atheneum, 2006.
Kadohata's young-adult novel is based on her family's experience, and features the story of a young girl interned at a relocation camp in Arizona.

Ling, Amy, ed., *Yellow Light: The Flowering of Asian American Arts*, Temple University Press, 1999.
This exceptional collection gathers the work and thoughts of a wide variety of Asian American writers, musicians, dancers, and artists, providing insight into the field of Asian American arts. Ling's introduction is particularly useful for an overview of Asian American art and culture.

Schumacher, Julie A., Rebecca Christian, and Rebecca Burke, eds., *A Multicultural Reader: Collection Two*, Perfection Learning, 2002.
This book is an anthology of excellent contemporary literature that includes selections from many different cultures, including a poem by Okita.

Stanley, Jerry, *I Am an American: A True Story of Japanese Internment*, Scholastic, 1998.
This nonfiction book for young adults covers the historical details of the internment period and uses the experiences of high-school senior Shi Nomura to give a personal account of the event.

Jade Flower Palace

"Jade Flower Palace" was written by the Chinese poet Tu Fu (sometimes called Du Fu) in 757. The poet was traveling on a two-hundred mile journey home when he came across a palace that had fallen into ruins. He was struck by the sight, and he used it to meditate on the transience of life, the passing of all things, and the vanity of all worldly riches and power. Everything ends in death. Nothing is immortal. The theme is a common one amongst Chinese poets, and for Western poets, too.

Tu Fu is usually regarded as the greatest of Chinese poets, although he is still little known in the West. Over fourteen hundred of his poems survive, and "Jade Flower Palace" has been translated into English at least five times. William Hung, in his 1952 biography of the poet (now out of print), made a prose translation. In 1971, the poem appeared in Kenneth Rexroth's *One Hundred Poems from the Chinese*, which is out of print, but Rexroth's translation is available in Holt's *Elements of Literature Sixth Course, British Literature* (2008). David Hinton has translated the poem under the title "Jade-Blossom Palace." Burton Watson's translation appears in his *The Selected Poems of Du Fu* (2002), and David Young includes the poem in his translations, *Du Fu: A Life in Poetry* (2008).

With its note of melancholy and its sharp imagery drawn from nature, "Jade Flower Palace" serves as a small but pleasing introduction to the work of a poet declared by his translator Rexroth,

TU FU

757

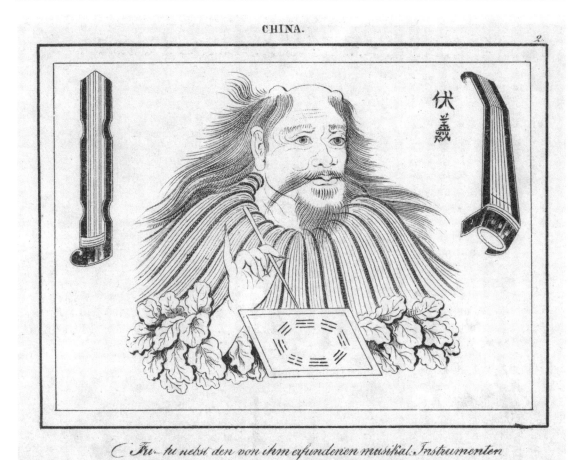

CHINA.

伏羲

Fu-hi nebst den von ihm erfundenen musikal. Instrumenten

Tu Fu *(© Mary Evans Picture Library / Alamy)*

in his notes to his volume mentioned above, "the greatest non-epic, non dramatic poet who has survived in any language."

AUTHOR BIOGRAPHY

Tu Fu was born in China in 712 CE, birthplace unknown, at the beginning of the reign of the emperor Hsüan-tsung, in the T'ang Dynasty, during a time of peace and prosperity. This period is considered the high point of Chinese civilization, in which arts and culture flourished. Tu Fu came from a distinguished family. His grandfather had been a famous poet, his father was a district magistrate, and his mother a direct descendent of the founder of the T'ang Dynasty Tu Fu had an early love of poetry, and received an excellent education. By his early twenties he had traveled extensively, and in 735 he arrived in Ch'ang-an, the capital city, to take the examination that would lead to a government position. Unexpectedly, he failed the exam. He left the capital, and after a few years in the countryside he settled with his wife and two sons in Lo-yang, the eastern capital. In about 744 Tu Fu met another great poet, Li Po, and they became friends.

Tu Fu returned to Ch'ang-an, and in 747 he again took the government examination, and again failed. This appears not to have been his fault, however, since that year, the Machiavellian chief minister Li Lin-fu ensured that all the candidates failed. Tu Fu remained for some years in the capital and was highly regarded in literary circles because of his poetry, but it was not until 755 that he was appointed to a political position. He was not able to enjoy this, however, because late that same year a rebellion broke out, led by a military governor, An Lu-Shan. Tu Fu fled from the capital with his wife, two sons, and two daughters, and settled in Fu-chou, north of Ch'ang-an.

Tu Fu later returned to the rebel-occupied capital but then escaped in early 757 and joined the emperor's court in exile at Fenghsiang, where he received an official appointment. But he angered the emperor by defending the imperial general who had suffered heavy military defeats, and he was sent home to join his family. It was on this journey of over two hundred miles, the first seventy miles or so on foot and the remainder on horseback, that Tu Fu came across the ruined palace that is the subject of "Jade Flower Palace" (757). Later that year he returned to Chang'an, which had been retaken by the emperor's forces, and his family soon joined him. After a few months he was sent to Hua-chou, east of the capital, where he was given a minor administrative position. He was forced to leave because of famine, and he spent much of the next few years on the move. No longer involved in public life, Tu Fu devoted himself to writing, a decision that caused economic difficulties for him and his family. However, most of his finest poetry was written during this period, which took up the last twelve years of his life. He was in poor health for some years, and he died traveling north on a boat in the Tan-chou region in the winter of 770. After his death his reputation as a poet grew, and he became known as China's greatest poet, a reputation he still holds today.

POEM TEXT

Below long pine winds, a stream twists.
Gray rats scuttle across spent rooftiles.
Bequeathed now beneath cliffs to ruin—who
knows which prince's palace this once was?

Azure ghostflames flood shadow-filled rooms.   5
Erosion guts manicured paths. Earth's
ten thousand airs are the enduring music,
autumn colors the height of indifference.

All brown earth now—the exquisite women
gracing his golden carriage have all become   10
their rouge and mascara sham. Of those
stately affairs, one stone horse remains.

Sitting grief-stricken in the grasses,
I sing wildly, wiping away tears for life
scarcely passes into old age, and no one   15
ever finds anything more of immortality.

POEM SUMMARY

Stanza 1

"Jade Flower Palace" records the impression made on a traveler in medieval China when he comes upon a ruined palace. In the translation by David Hinton, the poem is split up into four four-line stanzas (also known as quatrains), although other translators present the poem as one verse paragraph with a varying number of lines. The first lines describe where the palace is located. Above it are pine woods through which the wind blows. It is near a stream and below some cliffs. But its state of decay is indicated in line 2, in which rats scuttle across the ruined roof. In the last line the traveler/poet comments that he does not know which ruler or prince once owned this palace, and he suggests that probably no one knows.

Stanza 2

In the second stanza, the poet describes the ruin further. The otherwise dark rooms are lit up by an eerie kind of light; the paths around the palace, once so carefully tended, are becoming eroded by time. Beginning at the end of line 6, the poet contrasts the decaying palace with the permanence of the music-like sounds that emanate from the earth. The poet does not explain what he means by this, but perhaps part of the music is the rustling of the leaves in the autumnal wind, since the last line of this stanza refers to the colors taken on by autumn, which are dull and uninteresting, the poet says, perhaps by comparison with the brightness of spring and summer.

Stanza 3

In this stanza the poet brings to mind the contrast between the present and former state of the palace. Everything that once made the palace lively has disappeared into the earth. The beautiful women who were part of the prince's entourage when he rode in his carriage are gone. The poet comments that much of their beauty was false anyway, since most of it was supplied by facial makeup. Beginning in line 11, the poet comments that of all the pomp and splendor that surrounded the owner of the palace during his lifetime, only one stone sculpture of a horse remains.

Stanza 4

The poet devotes the final stanza to his own mournful reflections on the sight he has witnessed.

He sits down sorrowfully on the grass and weeps and then sings because he is so moved by the sense of the transience of all life. Life moves on swiftly, and for humans, old age soon comes. Nothing in the world is immortal. In Kenneth Rexroth's translation, rather than singing, the poet starts to write a poem, but he is overcome by sadness and is unable to complete it. The translation by Burton Watson is notable because in these last four lines, instead of the poet relating his own feelings and response to the ruin, the translator has the poet address the reader directly, giving him instruction about what to do when sadness comes upon him (sing and weep at the same time). The effect is to make the poem less personal and make the poet seem more detached from the scene, less affected by it, more willing just to give out advice for the benefit of others.

THEMES

The Transience of All Life

"Jade Flower Palace" is a lament for the impermanence of life. Everything in the world is transient; nothing lasts forever; the passage of time destroys even the finest products of human civilization. The point is made forcefully because the ruined building was not a modest dwelling; it was a palace, the home of the first emperor of the T'ang Dynasty. The poet does not indicate this directly in the poem, but scholars affirm that as an educated man, Tu Fu must have known that the palace had been built in 647, west of the capital city, Ch'ang-an, by the emperor T'ai-tsung. While the palace was occupied, it exhibited all the splendor that earthly riches can bestow. This is indicated by the many rooms, the formerly cultivated paths, and the luxurious carriages that the poet imagines must have come and gone in the old days, as well as the beautiful, well-adorned women who must have been frequent visitors and residents at the palace. But even this seat of power cannot withstand the vicissitude of time; the nature of life is change; nothing ever remains the same, and now the glory of this human creation has vanished.

This theme leaves the reader contemplating the fact that even the rich and powerful in this world are subject to the same laws as everyone else. Palaces come and go, as do people, rich or poor. There is also a feeling that the poet is disillusioned, even bitter, about the beauties of the world, not only because they fade but also

TOPICS FOR FURTHER STUDY

- Read the poem "Ozymandias," by Percy Bysshe Shelley and write an essay in which you compare and contrast it to "Jade Flower Palace." What theme do these two poems have in common, and how does each poet treat that theme?

- Write a short poem in which you reflect on the fact that something in your life is gone and will never return. The subject could be the death of a relative or a pet, the departure of a friend, or any other topic that encourages you to reflect on the passage of time and the passing of things. Read your poem aloud to the class.

- Write a short story in which two American teens on a vacation in China stumble upon ancient or medieval ruins. What do they find there? What do they learn from the experience? Consult *Exploring Cultural History: Living in Imperial China*, edited by Jann Einfeld (Greenhaven Press, 2004), to lend authenticity to your story.

- With two other students, use the Internet to research ancient ruins in the United States. In what states are ruins found? What culture are they from? What would a visitor see if he or she went to one of these sites? Give a class presentation, if possible using slides assembled in PowerPoint or a similar program to illustrate your presentation.

- Read *The Remarkable Journey of Prince Jen* (1991) by Lloyd Alexander. Write a poem in the style of Tu Fu to describe how Prince Jen grows as a result of his experiences and travels.

because they may not always be quite what they seem. The women who occupied the palace, for example, may have appeared beautiful, but the poet says this was only because of the makeup they wore. The beauty on which they no doubt prided themselves was an illusion, created by artificial means.

Tu Fu's cottage (© *John T. Young* / *Corbis*)

Eternal Cycles of Nature

The poet sets up a contrast between the decay of the structures built by humans, which are always subject to decay over time, and the eternal cycles of nature, which is time presenting itself in ever-renewing, recurring patterns. The wind still blows, the pine wood still stands, the river still twists and turns. Even more important in this respect is the poet's statement that the only thing that endures is the music that emanates from the earth itself. As the translator David Hinton explains in a note to the poem, this music of the earth contrasts with the music that was produced within the palace during its glory days. Hinton quotes a passage from an ancient Chinese text by the philosopher Chuang Tzu to show what the poet had in mind when he wrote of the earth's music. The wind, he says, is the breath of the earth, and when it is active the trees pipe up with their own voices, which make up a chorus: "They roar like waves, whistle like arrows, screech, gasp, cry, wail, moan, and howl.... In a gentle breeze they answer faintly, but in a full gale the chorus is gigantic."

Sorrow and Affirmation

From his observation of the ruins, the poet is led to grieve at the transience of human life. People become old almost before they know it, and then they die. All that is of the earth must return to the earth, and this causes sorrow because it conflicts with the human desire for permanence. Whatever troubles a person might have in life, very few people welcome death. It is life that is to be enjoyed, but all life is only for a time. However, it is also human to defy the passage of time, to affirm life in all the ways that humans can, in spite of the fact that it will not last for long. This is what the poet appears to do in the final stanza, when he sings with abandon. He acknowledges his grief but he also sings in spite of it, as an affirmation of life.

STYLE

Imagery

The poem gains much of its effect through sharp, concrete images that create in the reader's mind the scene witnessed by the poet. It is the images that create the contrast between ever-present nature and the vanished human world on which the meaning of the poem rests. Nature, in the form of wind, woods, water, cliffs, grass, and earth, is real in its immediate impact on the senses; it cannot be ignored. The silent palace with the vibrant life of its former inhabitants has to be conjured up by the imagination of the poet. The live rats that scamper in the ruins provide a contrast to the immovable sculptured horse that is all that remains of the great processions that once passed in and out of the palace. Another contrast is between the brown earth as it is now and the imagined bright colors of the court women and the carriages in which they rode.

Syntax, Line Breaks, and Diction in Translation

Rexroth noted in his translation of the poem that "almost every line . . . has more than one possible translation," so it is perhaps not surprising that each of three translations renders the poem in a different form. Hinton creates a sixteen-line poem divided into four four-line stanzas. Rexroth's version is one verse paragraph of twenty lines, while Burton Watson renders it in one verse paragraph of sixteen lines. Rexroth's version is notable for its frequent use of run-on lines. A run-on line (also known as enjambment) is when the syntax and meaning of the line carries over into the following line. The reader must read the following line as well to understand the meaning. No less than thirteen of the twenty lines in Rexroth's version are run-ons. In contrast, Hinton, at least in the first part of the poem, uses predominantly end-stopped lines, which means that the end of the line coincides with the conclusion of a syntactical unit. The first two lines in Hinton's version, for example, as well as the first line of the second stanza, both end with periods; the meaning is self-contained within each line.

Hinton notes that in its Chinese original, the poem is end-stopped in keeping with Chinese poetic tradition. However, this does not mean that a translation into English must follow this form. Hinton notes that his purpose in translating was to "recreate Tu Fu as a compelling poetic voice in English." Therefore Hinton "freely used the resources available to contemporary English, though these resources share rather little with those of the High T'ang poetic language." It is for this reason that Tu Fu's frequent use of

rhyme, alliteration (the repetition of initial consonants), and assonance (the repetition of similar vowel sounds) are reflected in the English translations to markedly different degrees. The translator who makes most use of alliteration is Hinton, the device being particularly noticeable in the first stanza and the first line of the second stanza.

HISTORICAL CONTEXT

Founding of the T'ang Dynasty

Tu Fu lived during the middle of the three-hundred-year T'ang Dynasty. The T'ang Dynasty was founded in 618 by Li Yüan, who established the capital at Ch'ang-an. In 627, Li Yüan abdicated in favor of his son, T'ang T'ai-tsung, who reigned until his death in 649. It was this emperor who built the palace that Tu Fu would come upon over a century later on his journey home. It is especially ironic that the poet would use T'ai-tsung's creation as a symbol of the transience of all human achievement, because T'ai-tsung's reign is considered, in the words of historian Kenneth Scott Latourette, "one of the most brilliant reigns in China's long history." T'ai-tsung defeated the Turks in central Asia and compelled Korea and Tibet to become vassals of the Chinese empire. Latourette notes that T'ai-tsung "succeeded in thoroughly unifying the country, in stimulating its culture and increasing its prosperity, and in placing it on a new pinnacle of power." During this period China was the greatest empire and the most advanced civilization in the world. Its emperor was known as the "Son of Heaven." After T'ai-tsung's death, his son Kao-tsung reigned until 683. Under this emperor, Chinese power was for a period again extended, incorporating much of Korea and Manchuria.

Height of the T'ang Dynasty

When Hsüan-tsung became emperor in 712, the same year in which Tu Fu was born, the T'ang Dynasty entered its most glorious phase. Hsüan-tsung was known as the "Brilliant Emperor," and he set about strengthening and enlivening China in every aspect of life. According to William Hung, in his biography of Tu Fu, Hsüan-tsung chose excellent generals to secure China's borders, establishing eight military outposts with forces of nearly half a million men and

COMPARE
&
CONTRAST

- **700s:** Poetry occupies an honored place in T'ang culture. Poets are drawn from the aristocracy and are respected figures at the imperial court. New, very demanding forms of poetry develop, such as the *lü-shih*, of which Tu Fu becomes a master.

  Today: With the growth of a more visually oriented culture, fewer people in China read poetry than a generation before. However, unlike in the 1980s, there is little government interference in what poets write and how they organize themselves. In 2006, one of China's most famous exiled poets, Bei Dao, is allowed to return to China. There are now few domestic or foreign travel restrictions on most of the poets who went into exile in the late 1980s. Chinese poetry also flourishes on the Internet, with hundreds of Web sites and forums devoted to it. The Internet facilitates the transcendence of geographical borders, allowing communication between Chinese poets around the world.

- **700s:** Chang'an is the capital city of the T'ang Dynasty. It is laid out in the form of a rectangular grid, based on the belief that the universe is also rectangular. The idea is to create a city that reflects the divine. Chang'an extends six miles east to west and five miles north to south and contains numerous large and impressive buildings, including the

emperor's palace, the homes of the aristocracy, and Buddhist and Taoist monasteries.

  Today: Chang'an is now known as Xi'an. It is a thriving city of over four million people and a tourist destination because of the many historical monuments and ruins. Some of these historical sites are from the T'ang Dynasty, including the Big and Small Wild Goose Pagodas, which were built in the eighth century CE.

- **700s:** In the first part of the century, China enjoys a golden period under the Emperor Hsüan-tsung. Expanding its territories west and north, China is the largest and most prosperous empire in the world. By mid-century, however, rebellion and civil war weaken the T'ang Dynasty.

  Today: China is the most populous nation in the world and is emerging as a formidable global economic power. Living standards are rising, although they do not yet match Western standards on a per capita basis. In 2008, China is the second-largest economy in the world after the United States. The estimated growth rate of China's gross domestic product for 2008 is 9.8 percent. Although the adoption of free-market principles has allowed the economy to grow, China remains a one-party communist country in which the central government exerts firm political control.

eighty thousand horses. This was to defend a nation that in 742 totaled nearly forty-nine million people. As a result of this successful strategy for national defense, China under Hsüan-tsung experienced great prosperity. Hung states that "the distribution of land was generous, the taxation light. Commodities were plentiful, and prices low. No one needed to find it difficult to make a living.... Communications were well maintained.... There was no banditry.... Crime was rare." During Hsüan-tsung's reign, Ch'ang-an, the capital city, located in the northwest part

of the country, became one of the wonders of the medieval world. It was home to a million people, including, according to David R. McCraw in *Du Fu's Laments from the South*, "envoys, clerics, and merchants from all over Asia. Tribute poured in from the entire known world. Vendors brought wine, spices, and gems from Persia and Syria. Minstrels sang psalms of India and strummed lutes of Kucha."

During Hsüan-tsung's reign there were considerable cultural achievements. The emperor founded schools for the study of music and

Xinchang county, China (© Tan Jin / XinHua / Xinhua Press / Corbis)

dancing, and he kept a company of actors. He was himself an accomplished musician. He also developed the imperial library and founded an institution to encourage the writing of books. He encouraged the study of literature, including the texts of Taoism, and opened his court to poets such as Tu Fu and Li Po (701–762). Indeed, this period is known as the golden age of Chinese poetry, according to McGraw, who also notes that writing various forms of poetry became "an integral part of civil service exams." In addition to his patronage of poets, the Brilliant Emperor invited noted painters to attend the court. These included Wu Tao-hsüan, who drew the human form; Han Kan, who excelled in the depiction of horses; and Wang Wei, who painted landscapes. Hsüan-tsung's reign also produced technological achievements, including the construction of an iron suspension bridge over the Yellow River and a water-powered astronomical clock. The emperor was by all appearances the ideal monarch: a humane, cultivated, civilized man who did his best to ensure the welfare of the people.

However, Hsüan-tsung also initiated wars that impoverished his people, and later in his reign his popularity waned. The rebellion led by An Lu-shan that began in 755 signaled a turning point in the T'ang Dynasty, after which it went into a slow decline. Interestingly, Tu Fu was somewhat prophetic when he used the over one-hundred-year-old ruined palace as a symbol of the transience of wealth and power, because at that time, whether he was aware of it or not, he was living during the beginning of a major transition in the dynasty from prosperity and strength to relative weakness and then to final decline. As a result of the An Lu-shan rebellion, Hsüan-tsung abdicated in 756 in favor of one of his sons, and he died in 762. The rebellion, as Latourette states, "became a major dividing point in Chinese history." Economic, political, and ideological factors all combined to produce the decline. The dynasty would still last for nearly 150 years, with brief revivals at various points, but its greatest days were behind it. However, despite its inglorious last days, the T'ang Dynasty is still known as China's greatest age.

CRITICAL OVERVIEW

Tu Fu was little recognized as a poet in his lifetime, partly because he made innovations in form, language, and subject-matter that took time to be understood and appreciated. But according to A. R. Davis, in *Tu Fu*, "By the Sung period of the tenth to the thirteenth centuries, Tu Fu had come to rest on his pinnacle of unquestioned eminence." In the medieval period in China, more commentaries were written about his work than that of any other Chinese poet. Today he is universally regarded as China's greatest poet. His biographer William Hung comments that Tu Fu embodies "the highest achievements in loftiness of aspirations, in depth of pathos, in variety, in metrical technique, in the meticulous patness of literary allusions, and in the revolutionary daring of appropriating some colloquial terms."

In the West, Tu Fu has been little known, and it was not until the early twentieth century that the first English translations of his work were made. These were in Florence Ayscough's *Tu Fu: The Autobiography of a Chinese Poet*, a two-volume biography published in 1929 and 1934, constructed from Tu Fu's own poems that contain biographical information. Ayscough did not translate "Jade Flower Palace," but Hung did so in a prose version published in his biography of the poet in 1952. Between 1971 and 2008, four different translations of the poem have appeared, a sign perhaps of the esteem in which it is held by modern poets and scholars.

In spite of this recent attention, Tu Fu remains relatively unknown in the West. But those who have understood his greatness have introduced him to their readers with the highest of praise, referring to him variously, as Hung points out, as the Chinese Virgil, Horace, Ovid, William Shakespeare, John Milton, Victor Hugo, or Charles Baudelaire, among others. Hung argues that although Tu Fu may be as great as many of these poets, he is not like any of them, because he is unique.

CRITICISM

Bryan Aubrey

Aubrey holds a Ph.D. in English. In this essay he discusses "Jade Flower Palace" first as a possible response by the poet to the Taoist quest for physical immortality and then in terms of the fascination that ruins exert on the human imagination.

The theme of the transience of all human life was not a new one, even when Chinese poet Tu Fu wrote "Jade Flower Palace" in 757. It had long

> IT SEEMS THAT THERE IS SOMETHING ABOUT A RUIN THAT STIMULATES THE IMAGINATION TO CONJURE UP A LOST AGE, A GLORY NOW VANISHED, AN EMPIRE TURNED TO DUST, AND TO MEDITATE ON THE FRAGILITY OF THE THINGS HUMANS MOST TREASURE."

been a common theme in Chinese poetry, found also in one of the other great poets of the T'ang Dynasty, Li Po. Tu Fu himself addressed the same theme in another poem, titled "Lung-men" (presented in its entirety in A. R. Davis's book, *Tu Fu*), in which he describes a city that he visits in different seasons and notes that the routes by land or water will always be there, but the people whom he meets on the way he will likely never see again. As in "Jade Flower Palace," there is a contrast between the eternal cycles of nature and the ephemeral nature of human existence. Nor was Chinese culture alone in producing observations of this kind. A thousand years before Tu Fu, the Hebrew author of the book of Ecclesiastes, which now forms part of the Old Testament, bemoans the fact that human life is so fleeting and declares all life to be "Vanity of vanities! All is vanity" (ch. 1, verse 2). Taking a pessimistic and skeptical attitude, the author claims to see no point in life, since nothing lasts, and like Tu Fu he contrasts the short duration of human life with the eternal presence of nature: "A generation goes, and a generation comes, but the earth remains for ever" (ch. 1, verse 4).

The observation that no one is immortal might seem an unremarkable one, obvious to anyone who spends even a moment contemplating human life. The reality of death is perhaps the one inescapable fact of human existence. However, in the case of "Jade Flower Palace" there may be a more complex and unusual story lurking beneath the surface of the poet's thematic assertions. As one digs deeper into the background of the time and place in which Tu Fu lived, one discovers that right in the heart of the T'ang Dynasty was a very serious quest, conducted by some of the finest and best

WHAT DO I READ NEXT?

- *Du Fu: A Life in Poetry* (2008) is the newest collection of Tu Fu's poems in English, translated by David Young, himself a poet and a well-known translator of Chinese poetry. This volume, which contains 170 poems, including a translation of "Jade Flower Palace," is one of the largest collections of Tu Fu's poems to appear in one volume in English.

- *Wang Wei, Li Po, Tu Fu, Li Ho, Li Shang-yin: Five T'ang Poets* (1990), translated and introduced by David Young, is a concise introduction to the work of five of the finest poets of the T'ang Dynasty. The anthology contains sixty-nine poems, with an introduction to each of the five poets.

- *The New Directions Anthology of Classical Chinese Poetry* (2003), edited by Eliot Weinberger, includes the work of thirty-seven Chinese poets, dating from the earliest poets up through the thirteenth century, translated by American poets William Carlos Williams, Ezra Pound, Kenneth Rexroth, Gary Snyder, and David Hinton. This is not only an introduction to Chinese poetry but also an illuminating study of the art of translation, because the anthology contains different versions of some of the poems by various translators. It also contains several essays on Chinese poetry by the translators.

- *Chinese Life* (2006) by Jonathan Clements is an account of Chinese civilization from its beginnings in the Shang Dynasty, nearly four thousand years ago. The book is written for readers age ten and older.

- *Maples in the Mist: Poems for Children from the Tang Dynasty* (1996), edited by Minfong Ho and illustrated by Jean Tseng and Mou-Sien Tseng, contains sixteen poems from the T'ang Dynasty that were traditionally taught to children in China. While some of the poems are aimed at younger children, some contain images and ideas suitable for contemplation by older readers.

- *The Dragon King's Daughter: Ten Tang Dynasty Stories*, translated by Gladys Yang and Xianyi Yang (2008), contains ten stories covering a wide range of themes and styles. Some are stories of the supernatural, others have political or romantic themes, and some are adventures.

- *The Heart of Jade* (1944) by Salvador de Madariaga is an young-adult historical novel about the impact and consequences of the Spanish invasion on the Aztec empire in Mexico.

---

educated minds, for physical immortality. Whereas the immortality of the soul was not a concept that appeared in Confucianism or Taoism, the two indigenous systems of Chinese thought, or in the imported religion of Buddhism, in Taoism there did emerge a body of thought and practice dedicated to achieving an immortality of the body. As Trevor Ling explains in *A History of Religion East and West*, "the quest for physical immortality became one of the major concerns or even obsessions of Taoist religion." In order to achieve this, the Taoists believed that they had to unite themselves with the Tao, understood as the eternal origin of all existence and the essence of all being. This involved not only meditative practices aimed at ridding the mind of all desires but also a "preoccupation with alchemy, in the search for the elixir of life, and to various kinds of crude rituals and practices of a quasi-magical kind." Such practices had been increasingly supported by the seventh and eighth century T'ang emperors, who no doubt felt that if anyone could become immortal, it should surely be themselves. The reality was a little different, however. As Ling wryly observes, one emperor in the late T'ang period took to quaffing an elixir that supposedly would confer, or help to confer, immortality, but which "appears, as in most other cases, to have a deleterious effect upon his health, and shortly ... he lost the power of speech and was deposed in favor of his uncle."

A century earlier than this unfortunate emperor, in the so-called golden age of the mid-T'ang period, no less a figure than the emperor Hsüan-tsung himself, Tu Fu's contemporary, was a Taoist devotee who invested considerable energy and resources to the development of Taoism and its esoteric practices. Indeed, the collapse of his forty-four year reign is often attributed by historians, at least in part, to his enthusiasm for Taoism. This is mentioned by Tu Fu's biographer William Hung, who notes the emperor's interest in Taoist "superstition" and comments, "The selfish desire for longevity by the practice of alchemy and Taoistic rites would distract him from the duties of government."

Not surprisingly, since Tu Fu lived in the midst of this culture, he was familiar with the Taoist quest for immortality. His friend the poet Li Po was deeply immersed in Taoism and in the search for such an elixir. Tu Fu wrote a poem addressed to Li Po in which he clearly alludes to his friend's esoteric Taoist interest in longevity and immortality, perhaps indicating some passing interest of his own. (This poem appears in Hung's translation, under the title of "Presented to Li Po.") According to Hung, Tu Fu visited a famous temple to Lao Tze, the founder of Taoism, when he was in his late twenties. He also, according to A. R. Davis, once tried to visit a Taoist master, only to find out that the man had died. Hung concedes that Tu Fu may indeed have been drawn to Taoism at one point in his life, but that the esoteric practices ran counter to the general temper of his mind. Indeed, anyone who peruses a representative selection of Tu Fu's work will get the impression of a down-to-earth man, honest in the acknowledgement of his feelings and with a realistic appraisal of life. He was neither romantic nor mystic nor a seeker after fantastic, unobtainable goals.

Seen in this light, is it perhaps possible that when, at the very time the An Lush-an rebellion was spelling the end of the Taoist emperor's reign, Tu Fu wrote in "Jade Flower Palace" that no one achieves immortality, he was staking out an opposition, in the name of common sense and rational understanding, to the futile Taoist quest for immortality. He even suggests, in the Hung prose translation of the last line of the poem, that it does not matter how long anyone lives.

Leaving aside the question of whether this was indeed a rejection of Taoist quackery (since the answer can never be known for sure), it must also be pointed out that if Tu Fu was not the first person to lament the transience of all life, nor was he alone in having his imagination seized by the sight of a formerly splendid palace now in ruins. The capital city of the T'ang Dynasty, Ch'ang-an, had been a ruin before, after the collapse of the Han Dynasty in the third century CE, and it would become ruins again after the fall of the T'ang Dynasty in 904. As Edward H. Schafer notes in his book, *Ancient China*, "For generations afterward, the site of the great capital provided a theme for melancholy reflection by poets on the transience of human glory." Indeed, such sentiments had flourished even before the final fall of T'ang. In its last years, according to Schafer, the theme of transience and melancholy became even more pronounced for the dynasty's poets: "All beautiful things seemed illusory, all human values decaying."

It is not only Chinese poets who have reflected on such things. In the West, travelers for hundreds of years, including many artists and poets, have been fascinated, as Tu Fu was by the ruined palace, by the ruins of ancient Rome. The most impressive of these ruins is the Colosseum, the huge amphitheater completed in 80 CE in which the Romans held gladiatorial contests and other spectacles. As Christopher Woodward notes in his fascinating book, *In Ruins*, writers including Henry James, Nathaniel Hawthorne, Edgar Allan Poe (although Poe went to Rome only in his imagination), and Charles Dickens have all recorded their impressions of the Colosseum in fiction or nonfiction. Woodward quotes Dickens's *Letters from Italy*, published in 1846, in which Dickens observed this "ghost of old Rome," with "its walls and arches overgrown with green; its corridors open to the day; the long grass growing in its porches," and was deeply moved by it:

> It is the most impressive, the most stately, the most solemn, grand, majestic, mournful sight, conceivable. Never, in its bloodiest prime, can the sight of the gigantic Coliseum, full and running over with the lustiest life, have moved one heart, as it must move all who look upon it now, a ruin: GOD be thanked: a ruin!

It seems that there is something about a ruin that stimulates the imagination to conjure up a lost age, a glory now vanished, an empire turned

*Lighted lantern display devoted to Tu Fu at
the Chinese mid-autumn festival in Hong Kong*

(© Paul Yeung / Reuters / Corbis)

to dust, and to meditate on the fragility of the things humans most treasure. The result is often a sober, melancholy feeling that is also oddly pleasurable, like the pleasure derived from watching a tragic play. There may even be something ennobling about such thoughts. Ruins remind us of what may happen to our own civilization; they give us a vision of the long stretch of time, they lift us out of ourselves and the smallness of our daily concerns. Contemplating a ruin, we may weep and sing at the same time, like the poet Tu Fu did when he looked upon the emperor's ruined palace, all those long years ago in medieval China.

Source: Bryan Aubrey, Critical Essay on "Jade Flower Palace," in *Poetry for Students*, Gale, Cengage Learning, 2010.

David Young

In the following essay, Young provides an overview of Tu Fu's life and legacy, arguing the "adversity was certainly one source of [his] greatness."

> HIS POETRY IS MORE AUTOBIOGRAPHICAL, AND MORE HONEST ABOUT HIS FAILINGS AND FEELINGS, THAN ANY POET'S HAD MANAGED TO BE BEFORE."

The widely held view that Tu Fu is China's greatest poet is partly based on admiration for his technical brilliance, a fluent mastery of traditional forms combined with an originality that gives rise to apparently effortless innovation; Yeats in our own time provides an analogy, and Keats is a similar instance among the Romantics. These qualities will not be apparent in translations, and neither in my versions nor in others I have seen does Tu Fu's formal excellence distinguish him significantly from other Chinese poets. But a poet's greatness, especially the kind of ultimate tribute accorded to Tu Fu, is never founded solely on craft and technique; ultimately, the poet's vision of existence is what wins readers, and if the refinements of expression and form associated with his own language and tradition are apt to be lost in the change from one language to another, the fundamental means of his poetry—the images and their relationships and the world they serve to create—can, fortunately, be reflected, so that a large portion of his essential genius is recreated and preserved. Tu Fu is a great-minded, great-hearted poet with a commanding imagination, qualities a translator can still hope to capture.

Adversity was certainly one source of the greatness. Until his middle years Tu Fu was a poet of undeniable talent, but, on the evidence of his work, a somewhat boastful and querulous man, concerned mainly about his career and lack of advancement, and rather given to feeling sorry for himself. He received some patronage and official recognition, but never enough to satisfy him. His bitterness began to take the form of social criticism and a new concern for the sufferings of others. (His own woes were not after all very significant in comparison.) This growing tendency toward compassion and widening sense of the tragic features of the human condition were then given a tremendous impetus by the historical events in which he was suddenly caught up. His little son starved to death in a famine before Tu Fu was able to get to his family and help them. The An Lu-shan rebellion broke out, and the poet fled with his wife and two children to a safer place. Tu Fu fell into the hands of the rebels and was held for some time in the captured capital. Eventually he escaped and rejoined the exile court, but it was some time before he was reunited with his family. These experiences, in the midst of social chaos that affected everyone he saw, gave him enormous compassion for the sufferings of poor people, soldiers, and scattered families. He became a great poet, transcending self-pity and setting even his poems about pleasure in an implicit frame of pain.

That we know enough to say all this about Tu Fu is due to the fact that he was a man of extraordinary candor. His poetry is more auto-biographical, and more honest about his failings and feelings, than any poet's had managed to be before. He documented his own life in great detail, placing it in the contexts of both historical change and day-to-day life, in the capital and in provincial villages throughout the empire, so that we have in his total output (the largest corpus of any of the four poets in this collection, something around 1,400 poems) a remarkably complete portrait not only of the man but of his time and place as well. It is, we feel, an unvarnished and vividly observed account; listening to Tu Fu narrate some circumstance of his life, such as his flight with his family from the rebel troops, we feel that experience is being transcribed effortlessly and candidly; it is as though we were in the presence of the man himself, as he tells his story, or, often, as though the experiences were our own and we were living through them. Part of that great technical accomplishment was a naturalness of manner and style that wins readers and creates a special bond with them. It is art so magical that we have to stop to remind ourselves that it is art, compounded of contrivance and calculation. Yeats's ideal comes to mind: "A line will take us hours maybe; / Yet if it does not seem a moment's thought, / Our stitching and unstitching has been naught." That would have appealed to Tu Fu, who strove always for an overall effect of spontaneity.

The end of the rebellion saw Tu Fu back in the capital for a brief period of royal favor and government office, but he was soon exiled to an outlying province, and the post he held there did not suit him; within a few years he had abandoned it and begun another period of moving his family around in search of food, shelter, and peace of mind. For a few years he lived rather happily in a thatched hut, writing poetry of a bucolic sort, but further rebellions and disruptions kept him on the move and living hand to mouth for most of the rest of his life. From his own point of view, Tu Fu was a failed and disappointed man; from ours, he was enjoying years of incredible poetic productivity and development. We who see literature as an end in itself find it difficult to understand why Tu Fu would think of himself as a failed writer because his life had included no significant public service. But the Confucian ideals that associated the two things were so strong in his mind that he could never rid himself of them.

His response to this situation, if it was partly disappointment, was a sense of artistic independence; he could write to please himself and express his feelings, and it probably made a greater and more individual poet of him. "Poetry," as A. R. Davis puts it, "became the central preoccupation of his life, and he became more nearly a professional poet." Had Tu Fu realized his ambition to be a high government official in the capital, he would not have traveled as he did, and thus would not have written the marvelous body of travel poetry that portrays the China of his time so effectively; he would have associated far less with ordinary people, peasants, artisans, and soldiers, and thus been far less able to reflect their lives and speak to their suffering; and, as he would have been a more conventional man, he would probably have remained a more conventional writer. It's both hindsight and speculation to say that we owe this great poet to the woes that beset him and his country in the middle of the eighth century, but something of that kind does seem to be the case.

Almost all commentators remark on the range of Tu Fu's poetry. His subjects are those of other poets, but unlike other poets, he seems to cover them all. The same can be said of the range of his themes and his tones. He is a comprehensive poet whose imagination seems capable of taking on almost anything. We value him, quite rightly, for his realism, directness, and candor. But we should also recognize his artfulness, the cunning management of the medium and of the reader's response that must characterize the work of any great writer. Most of all, I suppose, we associate Tu Fu with a vigorous poetry that manages to transcend unhappiness and melancholy by its enormous range and immense humanity.

Tu Fu has been blessed with a wealth of translators and commentators. I have already mentioned Arthur Cooper's *Li Po and Tu Fu* (Penguin, 1973). Some of Tu Fu's later work is to be found in A. C. Graham's *Poems of Late T'ang*. He is also represented in Kenneth Rexroth's memorable *One Hundred Poems from the Chinese* (New Directions, 1956). Among the books entirely devoted to Tu Fu, my own favorites are David Hawkes's *A Little Primer of Tu Fu* (Oxford, 1967), which gives poems in transliteration, character-by-character translation, and prose paraphrase with accompanying notes and comments—a translator's delight; A. R. Davis's biography, *Tu Fu* (Twayne, 1971); William Hung's two volume *Tu Fu, China's Greatest Poet* (Harvard, 1952), a biography with very extensive prose translations of the poetry; and Erwin von Zach's *Tu Fu's Gedichte* (Harvard, 1952), which contains *all* the poems in German translations. Other studies include Underwood and Chu, *Tu Fu, Wanderer and Minstrel under Moons of Cathay* (Mosher, 1929); Florence Ayscough's *Tu Fu, the Autobiography of a Chinese Poet* (Jonathan Cape and Houghton Mifflin, 1929, 1934, 2 vols.); and Alley and Chih, *Tu Fu, Selected Poems* (Peking Foreign Language Press, 1964).

Source: David Young, "Tu Fu: Introduction," in *Five T'ang Poets*, translated by David Young, Oberlin College Press, 1990, pp. 77–83.

David Hinton

In the following excerpt, Hinton discusses the objective realism, subjectivism, despair, and ultimate detachment that characterize Tu Fu's poetry.

. . . The poet's transformation from craftsman to artist was perhaps the most fundamental of many High T'ang innovations in poetry. Singular artistic personalities emerged, culminating in the "banished immortal" Li Po made of himself, and in Tu Fu, the first complete poetic sensibility in Chinese literature. Suffused from the beginning with Confucian humanism, the Chinese poetic tradition is essentially lyric and secular. It is a poetry of entirely vulnerable and human dimensions, and Tu Fu remains its great exemplar. He explored the full range of experience, and from this abundance

shaped the monumental proportions of being merely human.

Tu Fu's inquiry was so comprehensive and original, in fact, that it produced the poetic possibilities which came to define the tradition. Although the radical innovations of his poetry denied him recognition during his own lifetime, his work soon inspired such dissimilar poetics as Po Chü-yi's plain-spoken social realism and Meng Chiao's black, quasi-surreal introspection. And after the T'ang fell, the Sung's poetry of things at hand, with its composed simplicity, also found its source in Tu Fu. Indeed, his influence is so pervasive that China's poetic tradition can be located in terms of his work almost as readily as his work can be located in terms of it.

One dimension of Tu Fu's range is an objective realism unheard of in earlier poetry. He brought every aspect of public and private experience into the domain of poetry, including life's more unpleasant aspects, which traditional decorum had frowned upon. And the spirit of Tu's engagement with this unexplored terrain was profound in its implications: he conceived experience in the precise terms of concrete detail. As a result, the very texture of his poetry is an act of praise for existence itself.

Certain stereotyped hardships of the common people had long been treated indirectly in *yüeh-fu* ballads, but Tu Fu was the first poet to write extensively about real, immediate social concerns. The devastating An Lu-shan rebellion, about which Tu Fu wrote relentlessly, was scarcely mentioned by Wang Wei, though he had a broader range than any poet before him and was as deeply affected by the rebellion as Tu Fu. And in his private poems, Tu found poetry in the most pedestrian experience. Such things as a poet's family and the small beauties and trials of ordinary life had scarcely appeared in Chinese poetry, and never in such a comprehensive, naturalistic way. But there is rarely such a clear distinction between the public and private in Tu Fu's poetry. Tu, who is known as the "poet-historian," lived at a particularly turbulent period in Chinese history, and few of his private poems are without social concerns. At the same time, his public poems rarely lack a private dimension. This dovetailing, in and of itself, was a substantial innovation in Chinese poetics, which traditionally required thematic unity.

Even during the High T'ang, poems were expected to address one topic while maintaining a single setting, mood, and tone. As these restrictions precluded the density his poetry required, Tu Fu routinely shifted between thematic concerns while combining discontinuous moods, tones, images, perspectives, etc. Indeed, he often juxtaposed these disparate elements within a single couplet, the fundamental unit of Chinese poetry, radically altering its traditional poise. Another strategy Tu Fu invented to increase the complexity of his poems was the lyric sequence: a series of lyrics not just grouped together, but closely interwoven to form a single long and complex poem. His comprehensive sensibility also seems to explain Tu's relative lack of distinction in the 4-line quatrain form, and why his most significant contributions to that form are three integrated sequences.

In addition to a new world of objective clarities, Tu Fu's realism opened up new depths of subjectivity, not only in terms of subject matter, but formally as well. During his later years of wandering, Tu's writing focused more and more on the solitary self cast against the elemental sweep of the universe, and that new subject matter was reflected in Tu's innovative language. While the discontinuous organization continued to give his poems a kind of intuitive complexity, Tu Fu's highly refined language extended richness to the extreme, and beyond. It became so distilled and distorted as to be nearly unintelligible at times, while his imagery often approached the surreal. And in his K'uei-chou poems, Tu also became the first Chinese poet to exploit syntactic ambiguity in a calculated, generative way, often with quite dissonant effects.

At first glance, Tu Fu's ceaseless worry over political affairs may seem familiar to us, though extreme. As citizens of a democratic state, we live with the promise that we determine the government's policy, and we each suffer a peculiar grief of personal responsibility for the abuses of "our" government. A scholar-official in the Confucian order lived with a much greater promise and responsibility because he belonged to the class whose very *raison d'être* was to administer the government. And in Tu Fu's case, the grief of implication was compounded by an almost metaphysical sense of displacement which is quite foreign to us. While a scholar-official's one proper place in the Confucian universe was helping the emperor care for the people, Tu briefly held only two governmental positions in his lifetime.

But a much deeper despair can be heard in the background of Tu Fu's poetry: the despair of a Confucian loss of faith. The human community was itself sacred and absolute in the Confucian order (its "religious" structure was manifest in a system of myth and ritual). By the end of his life, Tu had precious little reason for faith in that order. And without it, without civilization which was its full embodiment, nothing remained for him but an abyss—a metaphysical abyss come to life in the form of barbarian armies threatening to destroy China.

Nevertheless, there is at the heart of Tu Fu's sensibility a profound detachment from things, himself included. Rather than offering freedom from the mundane world, Tu's detachment is hopelessly complicated by a deep love for all things. While it allows his empathy to surpass the bounds of personal response, it also graces him with an exquisite sense of humor, one capable of subtly bringing a geologic perspective to even the most trying of his own circumstances.

In his later years, Tu Fu forged an identity of his life and art. His wandering in a decimated and increasingly foreign world became not just his predicament, but the human predicament. And the myriad details of his daily life became correlatives for the bones of exile which shape our spirit. He was a man of great wisdom speaking of an encounter with the extremes of our human experience, and in the measure of his voice even those extremes find repose....

Tu Fu's years of wandering did not end with his death. Because of the poverty and dislocation of his family, he was not finally buried in the family graveyard near Lo-yang until his grandson managed to arrange it in 813, forty-three years after his death. Although Tu's work had aroused relatively little interest during his lifetime, the praise in Yüan Chen's tomb inscription indicates that his poems had begun to startle and move readers. Thus, he satisfied the terms of his famous statement on poetics: "If my words aren't startling, death itself is without rest." My hope for these translations is that they might deepen Tu's millennial repose.

Source: David Hinton, "Introduction," in *The Selected Poems of Tu Fu*, translated by David Hinton, New Directions Publishing, 1989, pp. vii–xvi.

SOURCES

Ayscough, Florence, *Tu Fu: The Autobiography of a Chinese Poet, Volume I, A.D. 712–759*, Houghton Mifflin, 1929.

———, *Travels of a Chinese Poet: Tu Fu, Guest of Rivers and Lake, Volume II, A.D. 759–770*, Houghton Mifflin, 1934.

Central Intelligence Agency, "China," in *CIA World Factbook*, https://www.cia.gov/library/publications/the-world-factbook/geos/ch.html (accessed March 11, 2009).

Davis, A. R., *Tu Fu*, Twayne's World Authors Series, No. 110, Twayne Publishers, 1971, p. 154.

Du Fu, *The Selected Poems of Du Fu*, translated by Burton Watson, Columbia University Press, 2002, p. 40.

The Holy Bible, Revised Standard Version, Oxford University Press, 1952, p. 709.

Hung, William, *Tu Fu: China's Greatest Poet*, Russell & Russell, 1952, pp. 27, 42, 43–44, 45.

Latourette, Kenneth Scott, *The Chinese: Their History and Culture*, 4th ed., Macmillan, 1972, pp. 142–43, 149.

Ling, Trevor, *A History of Religion East and West*, Macmillan, 1968, pp. 105, 234.

McCraw, David R., *Du Fu's Laments from the South*, University of Hawaii Press, 1992, pp. 6, 8.

Rexroth, Kenneth, *One Hundred Poems from the Chinese*, New Directions, 1971, pp. 9, 135, 138.

Schafer, Edward H., *Ancient China*, Time-Life Books, 1967, pp. 108, 148.

Tu Fu, *The Selected Poems of Tu Fu*, translated by David Hinton, New Directions, 1989, pp. xiv, 30, 140.

Woodward, Christopher, *In Ruins*, Pantheon Books, 2001, p. 13.

"Xi'an," in *MSN Encarta Online Encyclopedia*, http://encarta.msn.com/encyclopedia_761572407/Xi%E2%80%99an.html (accessed March 11, 2009).

Yeh, Michelle, "Anxiety and Liberation: Notes on the Recent Chinese Poetry Scene," in *World Literature Today*, July 1, 2007.

FURTHER READING

Benn, Charles, *China's Golden Age: Everyday Life in the Tang Dynasty*, Oxford University Press, 2004.

Benn provides a lively portrait of how people lived in the T'ang Dynasty. He covers topics such as entertainment, fashion, marriage, food, hygiene, dwellings, and transportation. He also provides a history of the rise and fall of the T'ang Dynasty as well as its social structure. The author also provides his own illustrations.

Chou, Eva Shan, *Reconsidering Tu Fu: Literary Greatness and Cultural Context*, Cambridge University Press, 1995.

Chou discusses the development and nature of Tu Fu's reputation and its effect on how his poetry is interpreted. She also considers his poetry in terms of subject matter, style, and other elements, discussing and translating many poems. Much of this book is for advanced students only, but the first two chapters, which cover Tu Fu's life, his poetic and cultural legacy, and his social conscience, are accessible for the general reader.

Cooper, Arthur, trans., *Li Po and Tu Fu*, Penguin, 1973. This includes generous selections of the poetry of Li Po and Tu Fu translated into English. The translator includes a guide to the pronunciation of Chinese words and names and an introduction in which he discusses the times in which the poets lived and the background to T'ang poetry. Some of the poems are also provided in Chinese calligraphy alongside the English translations.

Hucker, Charles O., *China's Imperial Past: An Introduction to Chinese History and Culture*, Stanford University Press, 1995. Writing for the general reader, Hucker traces Chinese history from the earliest times to 1850. He divides Chinese history into three major epochs, the T'ang Dynasty forming the end of the second epoch. Each major epoch is discussed in terms of its history, political institutions, socioeconomic factors, religion and philosophy, and literature and the arts.

On the Grasshopper and the Cricket

JOHN KEATS

1817

John Keats's sonnet "On the Grasshopper and the Cricket" was written on December 30, 1816, in friendly competition with the poet and editor Leigh Hunt. It was one of the first flowers of a genius that within two years would produce master-pieces among the greatest in world literature, such as *Endymion* and *Lamia, Isabella, The Eve of St. Agnes, and Other Poems*. Although his talent is universally acclaimed today, Keats failed to attain great literary success or recognition in his lifetime. "On the Grasshopper and the Cricket" was origi-nally published in his 1817 collection *Poems* and later that year was republished in one of Hunt's newspapers to promote the book. Keats was only twenty-one years old at the time. However, political and class considerations doomed the work to fail-ure, together with Keats's later publications. Only the most discerning of Keats's contemporaries, such as the poet Percy Bysshe Shelley, recognized his genius in his lifetime. Following Keats's crush-ing literary failure, his life was tragically cut short at the age of twenty-five by tuberculosis. "On the Grasshopper and the Cricket" is included in most anthologies of Keats's poetry and is available in *Complete Poems*, Jack Stillinger's edition of Keats's complete works.

"On the Grasshopper and the Cricket" is a celebration of the Romantic conception of nature. Following its immortal opening line, it deals in simple and beautiful metaphors with the most profound experiences of the human condition.

John Keats (*The Library of Congress*)

On one level, the poem is an evocation of the life of the English countryside; yet its insect characters also symbolize the larger spheres of life and death.

AUTHOR BIOGRAPHY

Keats was born on October 31, 1795, in London, England. His father, Thomas Keats, ran a successful stable with an attached pub. Thomas died in 1804 in a riding accident, leaving behind his wife, Frances, and their four children: Keats, his two brothers Tom and George, and his sister Fanny. Thomas's estate was sufficient to support his family and to pay for Keats to study at Enfield school, and then as an apothecary (a position comparable to a pharmacist today). Nevertheless, Keats developed an intense love of poetry at school and abandoned his medical studies when they were near completion in order to become a professional poet.

Keats debuted in the poetical world of Regency London (period in the early 1800s in England marked by elegance and achievement in the arts) under the auspices of Leigh Hunt, an influential editor, journalist, and poet. While this relationship granted Keats personal introductions to

writers like William Wordsworth and Percy Bysshe Shelley and quick publication in journals edited by Hunt or his friends, it also associated Keats with Hunt's liberal politics. Overall his association with Hunt had a disastrous affect on the critical and popular acceptance of Keats's poetry. Nevertheless, at the beginning of Keats's career, on December 30, 1816, Keats wrote "On the Grasshopper and the Cricket" in an informal poetry writing competition with Hunt, who produced a sonnet with the same title. The poem was published the next year in Keats's first collection, *Poems*, and reprinted on September 21, 1817, in Hunt's newspaper, the *Examiner*.

Keats devoted the years 1817–1819 to writing poetry full time. He also began courting his eventual fiancée, Fanny Brawne. In 1818 he published a second volume of poetry, *Endymion*, and the next year he completed the composition of a third, *Lamia, Isabella, The Eve of St. Agnes, and Other Poems*, published in 1820. This volume included what were to become his best-known works: "Ode to a Nightingale" and "Ode on a Grecian Urn."

Throughout most of 1818 Keats nursed his brother Tom through the final stage of tuberculosis, a highly contagious and at the time incurable disease. Tom died on December 1, 1818, and in less than a year it was clear that Keats had caught the disease as well. Knowing from his medical training what was in store for him, Keats realized that *Lamia, Isabella, The Eve of St. Agnes, and Other Poems* would be his last important published work (though he left a large number of fragmentary texts). At this time, he also cut off all contact with Fanny, fearing lest he infect her, though their letters continued to show their passionate regard for each other. In 1820 Keats traveled to Rome, Italy, following medical opinion of the time that tuberculosis might improve in a warmer climate. Nevertheless, he died on February 23, 1821, in an apartment overlooking the Spanish Steps which is now known as the Keats-Shelley House.

Keats might well have been forgotten had his reputation not been championed by the poet Shelley in his poem written on hearing news of Keats's death, "Adonais." Keats's reputation grew throughout the nineteenth century due to his influence on poets like Alfred, Lord Tennyson and Oscar Wilde. In the modern age, though he died at the age of twenty-five, Keats is highly regarded not only among the English poets, as he had hoped, but as one of the greatest poets of any time or culture.

POEM TEXT

The poetry of earth is never dead:
When all the birds are faint with the hot sun,
And hide in cooling trees, a voice will run
From hedge to hedge about the new-mown
    mead;
That is the Grasshopper's—he takes the lead   5
In summer luxury,—he has never done
With his delights; for when tired out with fun
He rests at ease beneath some pleasant weed.
The poetry of earth is ceasing never:
On a lone winter evening, when the frost   10
Has wrought a silence, from the stove there
    shrills
The Cricket's song, in warmth increasing ever,
And seems to one in drowsiness half lost,
The Grasshopper's among some grassy hills.

POEM SUMMARY

"On the Grasshopper and the Cricket" is a Petrarchan sonnet (also known as the Italian sonnet, developed by Italian poet Francesco Petrarch). In terms of the poem's meaning and structure, the poem is divided into two unequal parts. The first eight lines or octave form one unit, and the last six lines or sestet form a second unit. Although the two parts of the sonnet are connected, each part also has its own distinct function and meaning.

Lines 1–8

The octave (or first eight lines) of the poem deals with the grasshopper. At the most basic level of meaning, the famous first line refers to the "song" of the grasshopper—its familiar buzzing, humming call—as if this sound of the natural world is directly comparable to human poetry. This natural music lives on throughout every hour of the day and throughout the year because, even when the grasshopper's song is silenced by the time of day or the season, other natural sounds take its place. Taken on its own, however, the first line might as well describe human poetry (as opposed to, for instance, the divine), an interpretation that begins to suggest a larger meaning for the poem.

The remainder of the octave elaborates on the special role of the grasshopper in this continuous natural song. The second and third lines state that birdsong is one of the most familiar and pleasant natural sounds. However, it is also associated with the cool of the morning. Accordingly, birds cannot sound the song of nature in the heat of a summer afternoon. Instead, they shade themselves in trees during the hottest time of the day. Even so, this does not mean there is merely silence. There is another voice—the grasshopper's—that sings.

The fourth line of the sonnet establishes very precisely the location of the scene being described. It is in the English countryside, a landscape that is often romanticized as the epitome of naturalness but is in fact wholly artificial. The natural forests of Britain had mostly been cleared from the arable land (suitable for growing crops) in Britain during pre-Roman times and the landscape of the island had been entirely shaped by human beings to use in agriculture for many centuries. The actual land in Britain consisted mostly of fields. Every area of forty or eighty acres is surrounded by an earthen embankment topped by a row of trees and hedges making a nearly impenetrable barrier. This system was used beginning in medieval times to control the division and allotment of farmer's fields throughout the English countryside. The grasshopper is driven to these hedgerows because the field it has been occupying is a meadow used to grow hay, which has just been harvested. So the scene of Keats's poem is bucolic or pastoral, associated with the countryside developed as farmland, rather than purely natural in the sense of wild, untamed nature.

The fifth through eighth lines describe the grasshopper's role in the natural chorus more directly. It sings in the heat of summer when other animals are silent. Even when the grasshopper becomes fatigued and must cease singing, it constantly renews and replenishes itself by resting in the shade to gain strength to continue its song. These lines also emphasize the rich abundance of summer that creates enough natural wealth to allow even animals time to rest and play.

Lines 9–14

The last six lines (or sestet) of the poem continue the themes of the octave but deal with the cricket rather than the grasshopper. The ninth line of the poem repeats and rephrases the first line. The immediate impression of this act is that the song goes on, always the same yet also different. This continuation is suggested also by the apparent relationship of the cricket and the grasshopper. The two insects are seemingly closely related variants of the same form, particularly because of their similar jumping ability. (In fact the cricket and grasshopper are only distantly related, and their bodily similarities are more a matter of chance than kinship, though this was not known in Keats's time.)

Lines 10 through 12 of the sonnet give another example of how the song of nature is continued out of season. In winter, insects either died off for the year or hibernate. However, often enough, because of humanity's intervention in nature, chopped wood that has been cured outside for some time to use as firewood will be brought into the house. It is not unusual for a cricket which hid in such a piece of wood to hibernate for the winter to come onto the hearth and begin to chirp once it has warmed up from the heat of the fire. Yet the sense of the poem seems to go beyond this simple fact, using the cricket as a symbol of the hospitality and cheer of sitting near a fire on a cold winter night.

The last two lines of the sonnet take a different and quite unexpected direction. For the first time, a human being appears in the poem. This person is sitting before the fire and falling asleep. It is important to note that the individual is neither fully asleep nor fully awake, but in a state in between, which psychologists refer to as a hypnagogic state. In this state, in which a person has mixed sensations of waking experience and dreaming, Keats and other Romantic poets believed that the mind could discover meaningful inspiration. In the poem, the person who is falling asleep hears the cricket on the hearth on a night in winter and imagines instead hearing a grasshopper singing outside during a summer's day. While the whole structure of the poem leads to the two insects as contrasting with each other, Keats in the end also suggests an essential and meaningful identification between them.

THEMES

Nature

Keats was part of the Romantic movement. The Romantics were dissatisfied with the modern, increasingly industrial world in which they lived, so they often looked for ideals in times and places they considered the opposite of modern. Evoking past times in contrast to the contemporary world was a common Romantic theme, and Keats's long narrative poems are always set in the Middle Ages or classical antiquity. These eras are made to stand as an antithesis (direct contrast) to the modern world of the Romantic poets. Another contrast to the human world of factories and squalid cities could be found in the pristine beauty of the natural world. "On the Grasshopper and the Cricket" presents an idyllic pastoral world as a refuge from the unnamed conflicts of modernity, and in its final couplet, it seeks to synthesize the

TOPICS FOR FURTHER STUDY

- Read Keats's "On the Grasshopper and the Cricket" and the companion poem of the same title by Leigh Hunt. Lead a class discussion concerning the differences and similarities of the two sonnets.

- Read through several poems by Keats and write a sonnet in reaction to his ideas and language. Write an analysis of your sonnet, explaining Keats's influences on your work.

- Make an artistic representation of a significant scene from "On the Grasshopper and the Cricket." Present your creation to your class and explain your interpretation in relation to the sonnet.

- Read one or more versions of the popular Aesop fable "The Grasshopper and the Ant." Write a brief play to perform for your class. Make cutout figures of the characters together with backdrops and a small frame to act as a stage and perform the play as puppet theater.

- Research the taxonomy of grasshoppers and crickets. Try to determine which species Keats would have had in mind in southern England. Are the animals as closely related as Keats seems to imagine? Create a Power-Point presentation with images of the grasshopper and cricket you choose and report on this topic to your class.

- *Wisdom from Africa: African Fables* (2005) by Dianne Stewart devotes an entire chapter to insect fables. Using this book or a similar one, write a poem about an insect that represents African folklore beliefs about life and death.

opposites represented by the grasshopper and the cricket.

"On the Grasshopper and the Cricket" first compares and contrasts the two types of insects in its title on a literal level. The grasshopper sings during the heat of the summer afternoon in the fields of the countryside, while the cricket sings

Grasshopper *(Image copyright Peter Wey, 2009. Used under license from Shutterstock.com)*

on a winter night when people stay indoors and doze by the fireplace. Keats uses this imagery as the basis of a larger symbolic meaning in which the associations of each insect come to describe two opposite aspects of human life. The use of this kind of symbolism, rather than just spelling out the meaning, forces readers to come to their own understanding of Keats's poem through a meditative and introspective process that has far greater impact than any plain assertion could.

"On the Grasshopper and the Cricket" is a beautiful evocation of the countryside and country life. The nature it celebrates, however, is the natural world created by tradition, the countryside of fields and farms. Wild nature and virgin forest, so often sentimentalized in the modern age, were unknown in the British experience. The island of Great Britain had been deforested in pre-Roman times (although there were wilder areas in hills and mountains where forest had to a degree regrown). Completely untamed and uninhabited wilderness would have seemed threatening to nineteenth-century Europeans, including the Romantics.

Hypnagogia

A hypnagogic state (from the Greek words *hypnos* or sleep and *agoge* or leading) exists between wakefulness and sleep, experienced when falling asleep or awakening, but also in a light sleep when the wandering of the imagination is neither truly dreaming nor fully directed by conscious will. In Greek philosophy, for example in *On the Mysteries of the Egyptians* by Iamblichus, hypnagogia is said to be the condition of mind when true inspiration from the gods is communicated to human beings, resulting either in prophetic dreams or the infusion of poetic talent in a poet. In fact, during this condition, the mind is more open to hallucinations and other unreal sensations than in waking life, but it is free of the more systematic experience of the dreams associated with deep sleep. It was a mental condition of great interest to the Romantics and especially to Keats. For instance, his 1818 poem "Dear Reynolds, as Last Night I Lay in Bed," (unpublished in his lifetime), Keats attempts to record all of the mental imagery that occurred to him one night as he fell asleep, some of which was later reused in "Ode to a Grecian Urn." The mystical imagery in "Ode on a Nightingale" also comes while falling asleep (or symbolically while passing from life to death) and leaves the speaker unable to tell if he is awake or asleep. "On the Grasshopper and the Cricket" is Keats's earliest exploration of the hypnagogic state. Toward the end of the poem, he suggests that for someone falling asleep, the song, and hence the symbolic value, of the two insects might become indistinguishable.

STYLE

Romanticism

In addition to Keats, the Romantic movement included poets such as William Blake; William Wordsworth; Samuel Taylor Coleridge; Gordon, Lord Byron; and Percy Bysshe Shelley; and novelists including Shelley's wife, Mary. Leigh Hunt, though an important editor and a great influence in shaping Keats's career, is generally thought of as a poet of secondary significance. German Romantics such as Friedrich Schiller and Johann Wolfgang von Goethe are no less important as poets and are most often seen as the leaders of the ideological construction of Romanticism (which is not to deny original thought to the English Romantics, especially Keats). The name Romanticism and the perceived unity of Romantic work was only applied to these writers by critics of the Victorian period a generation or so later.

The Romantics were the first generation to come of age after the full effect of the Enlightenment (eighteenth-century philosophy emphasizing rationalism, especially advanced by Thomas Locke, Jean-Jacques Rousseau, and Thomas Paine) and the Scientific Revolution (a period of great advances in scientific disciplines, advanced by such scientists as Robert Boyle and Sir Isaac Newton). Also, during the period of Romanticism, the social transformations of the Industrial Revolution had an effect on Romantic thought. The Romantics therefore came into possession of two inheritances. On the one hand, they were educated in the tradition of Western culture that had developed in Europe from Roman times through the Middle Ages. (Although Keats was certainly the least educated Romantic—he did not, for example, read ancient Greek and never had the opportunity to attend a liberal arts university.) This education included the Greek and

Latin literature of antiquity with its mythology and philosophy and the Christian religion. On the other hand, they inherited the philosophy of the Enlightenment which seemed to cancel out many aspects of tradition. The modern scientific method had falsified the ancient conception of the natural world found in the works of Greek writers like Aristotle and Ptolemy as well as the creation narrative of the Bible. The new religion of Deism held that the Jewish and Christian scriptures had no special significance except as books of moral instruction and that the god who had created the universe was an impersonal and withdrawn figure. In this sense, God did not intervene in history or the physical world to perform the miracles supposedly carried out by the saints, to perform ritual miracles such as the transubstantiation (the transformation of the substance of bread and wine into the body and blood of Jesus Christ) of the Catholic and Anglican masses, or to interfere in matters such as human salvation. The new political thought of the Enlightenment and the new realities of industrialization seemed also to undercut the validity of traditional social institutions such as monarchy and feudalism as well as the basic class system. While the Enlightenment answer to this dichotomy had been for the most part to simply reject tradition, the matter was not so easily resolved for the Romantics.

The Romantic answer was to treat the problem of modernity dialectically, according to the philosophy of G. W. F. Hegel. They were not so ready to simply reject tradition where they still found a great deal of value, especially value to the inner condition and development of man, which the Enlightenment was not interested in and often sought to deny. According to this view, tradition and enlightenment were a thesis and antithesis that, while both being essentially true, seemed to falsify each other but could be logically resolved into a synthesis that would create something greater than either concept. Whatever forms this new synthesis might take, it would function at a higher level, reconciling any apparent contradictions in a new and more insightful understanding of truth. However, this project was never completed and remained an unfulfilled dream of Romanticism. What the Romantics accomplished was to shed light on unresolved conflicts that still exist in modern culture.

Though hardly an ideological thinker, Keats participated fully and enthusiastically in the project of Romanticism. His doctrines of negative capability (the ability of the poet to draw on the higher aesthetic synthesis to create art representing truths not otherwise accessible) and soul-making (that salvation may be achieved by the interaction of feeling and intelligence within individuals struggling in the world) certainly sought practical solutions to the creation of a new Romantic consciousness. Much of Keats's mature poetry lamented the impossibility of the human condition finding a higher synthesis while enmeshed in the world ("Ode to a Nightingale"), or sought escape to a perfection that can exist only in art ("Ode on a Grecian Urn"). "On the Grasshopper and the Cricket," as simplistic as it might at first seem, addresses many of the same issues.

Sonnet

The sonnet (which means "little song") is a form of poetry invented by the medieval troubadours of the Mediterranean coasts of Spain, France, and northern Italy. It became especially important and influential in the works of the fourteenth-century poet Francesco Petrarch. The original subject of the sonnet was the love of the poet for a woman, usually a love that was unrequited or impossible to consummate. It became an important form in English verse in the sixteenth and early seventeenth centuries among such poets as Sir Philip Sydney, William Shakespeare, and John Milton. The sonnet's typical English form was established by Edmund Spenser and is called the Spenserian sonnet. The Petrarchan or Italian sonnet consists of a problem established in the first eight lines (octave) followed by a resolution in the last six lines (sestet). The tradition of romantic subject matter continued strong in English sonnets, but English poets also adapted the form to poems on religious and meditative subjects. Many early English sonnets followed the Petrarchan form. The Spenserian sonnet consists of three groups of four lines (quatrains) whose meaning is self-contained, followed by a final couplet (pair of rhymed lines). Each line of the sonnet is an iambic pentameter, that is, consists of five iambs or groups of feet (the smallest unit of rhythm in a line of poetry), each consisting of an unstressed followed by a stressed syllable. Rhyme is the property of poetry wherein the endings of different lines share the same stress and sound. For example if the first and third lines of a poem end in 'we' and 'thee' and the second and fourth lines end in 'die' and 'fly' these lines would be said to rhyme and the poem to follow the rhyme scheme *abab*. A Spenserian sonnet generally followed the rhyme scheme: *abab bccb cdcd ee*. However,

considerable substitution and variation in meter and rhyme scheme were allowed in Spenserian sonnets.

In Keats's "On the Grasshopper and the Cricket," the sensible division of the material follows the structure of the Petrarchan sonnet with the octave devoted to the grasshopper and the sestet to the cricket; indeed the first line is restated in the ninth. However, the final couplet takes off in a new direction. Its meter, though well executed, is not exceptional. Its inventive rhyme scheme follows an *abba acca defdef* pattern.

Anthropomorphism

Anthropomorphism is the assigning of human characteristics to nonhuman entities, especially animals. This technique is familiar from, for example, Aesop's fables and cartoon characters such as Bugs Bunny or Mickey Mouse. In "On the Grasshopper and the Cricket" the grasshopper takes on the human desire for enjoyment. This stands in sharp contrast to Leigh Hunt's sonnet in competition with which Keats's poem was composed. Hunt's poem relies mostly on a very extensive anthropomorphism of its insect subject and partly for that reason achieves a more trivial effect.

Alliteration

Alliteration is the repetition of sounds (practically speaking, letters) within a poem for dramatic effect. Keats uses this sparingly in "On the Grasshopper and the Cricket," but in the fourth line, the repetition of the letters "W" and "M" suggests restfulness of a summer afternoon too hot for work.

Enjambment

Enjambment occurs when the grammatical structure of a sentence or clause begun in one line of verse does not end with the metrical line, but continues over into the next line. In "On the Grasshopper and the Cricket," the octave and sestet are both single sentences, and enjambment occurs frequently: between lines 3 and 4, lines 5 and 6, lines 6 and 7, lines 7 and 8; and in the sestet, between lines 10 and 11, and lines 11 and 12. The overall effect is to support that idea that the song that is the subject of the poem is continuous.

HISTORICAL CONTEXT

Poetry Competition

It was common in the early nineteenth century for well-known poets to enter into competition

COMPARE & CONTRAST

- **1810s:** The Spenserian and Petrarchan sonnets are a common form of poetry.

  Today: Traditional forms, especially those involving rhyme and meter, are rejected by many poets as naive. However, the new formalism movement initiates a return to metrical and rhymed poetry.

- **1810s:** The hearth or fireplace is the center of life throughout much of the year because it is a necessary device to provide warmth.

  Today: Fireplaces are for the most part used to recall past ways of life and are not central to everyday life. It seems to some that the television is now the center of domestic life.

- **1810s:** Authors often have to pay for the publication of their own books.

  Today: Although the circumstances of publication are changing rapidly and unpredictably because of the Internet and electronic and self-publishing, traditional publishing houses pay authors advances for their work. Books whose publication is financed by the author are often dismissed by critics.

- **1810s:** Though the balance of population between country and city is rapidly shifting, most people still live on farms in intimate contact with the land, and agricultural labor, such as mowing hay (with a scythe), is done by hand.

  Today: A small fraction of the population in England, as in most industrialized nations, is employed in agricultural labor, which is mostly carried out by specialized machinery and on large corporate farms.

with each other and each write a poem (often but not always a sonnet) on a given theme within a specified time limit (often as little as fifteen minutes). This practice may have developed from the techniques used in teaching sonnet composition in schools of that era. Such competition usually occurred among an informal gathering of friends and colleagues. While one of the writers might be deemed the winner by the audience who would hear or read the poems at the conclusion, the real purpose of the contest was less about competitiveness than a chance for the poets to have their poems read and critiqued by others. The speed and spontaneity with which the poems had to be produced also related to Romantic ideas of inspiration. The poems consisted of the immediate thoughts and impressions of the poet, not something crafted by long arduous labor. Perhaps the most famous poem produced in this way is Shelley's "Ozymandias."

Leigh Hunt was especially fond of poetry competitions of this kind. On December 30, 1816, Keats and their mutual friend Cowden Clarke (who described the event in his memoirs) were visiting Hunt at his home. They read together the thirty-fourth "Ode of Anacreon," which concerns a grasshopper, translated from the ancient Greek by Thomas Moore. Later, Hunt noticed a cricket on his hearth, and he challenged Keats that the two of them should immediately write sonnets "on the grasshopper and the cricket." They proceeded to do so in short order, and Keats finished his sonnet first. Perhaps out of politeness or affection, both poets insisted the other had produced the better poem. However, Hunt's Spenserian sonnet is a sentimental depiction of the insects in anthropomorphic (assigning of human characteristics to nonhuman entities) terms. Walter Jackson Bate points out in his biography *John Keats* (1963), "Keats, on the other hand, typically focuses on a psychological process," producing a more symbolic poem with much greater depth of meaning.

Cockney Poets

Keats is increasingly grouped by scholars with a group referred to as the Cockney Poets. *Cockney* refers to the local accent of English spoken in London, which was noticeably distinct to the standard English of Oxford and Cambridge that marked the upper classes of British society.

Although schools like Enfield taught standard English, Keats was embarrassed throughout his adult life by his slight but noticeable Cockney accent. However, in this case, Cockney goes beyond linguistic designations to mark a class of bourgeois (social middle class) Londoners who might command considerable wealth but make their money by industry rather than from land ownership in the traditional aristocratic manner. Most bourgeois Londoners were politically and economically opposed to the aristocratic government of England in the early nineteenth century. In general, this group supported liberal politics that favored the strengthening of democratic institutions and the encouragement of business. They considered, for instance, that the prince regent (a prince who rules during the minority, disability, or absence of a monarch) was a ridiculous figure, uninterested in governing the country, and they resented their tax dollars going to support his luxurious lifestyle. The Prince Regent at the time was the eldest son of George III, who suffered from mental illness, causing the Parliament (council of state) to empower his son to rule in his place. (He eventually ruled in his own right as George IV.) Although Keats was of liberal political sympathies, his work did not possess much of a political nature. However, Keats's association with Leigh Hunt linked him to the Cockney school. Hunt had risen to prominence as a political martyr when he had served two years in jail for the crime of publically criticizing the Prince Regent. This association meant that reviewers aligned with the ruling aristocratic faction mercilessly attacked the publications of Hunt's protégé Keats, ensuring that he would never be able to make a living from his writing.

Publishing Industry in the Eighteenth and Early Nineteenth Centuries

In eighteenth-century England, writing was not a profession; it was ideally an occupation for the free time of the aristocratic classes. Writing was an ornament to the careers of professors and clergy for whom it could speed professional advancement. The number of writers who actually lived from the proceeds of their work was quite small, and their incomes were usually small compared to other professionals. The decision, or the necessity, to live by writing was often allied with radical political positions as in the case of Mary Wollstonecraft (British writer, feminist, and philosopher) or Leigh Hunt. Keats, however, had no such strong political views of his own; he merely wished to live as a poet. Nevertheless, the very fact that Keats desired to gain an income from writing is a marked break from earlier periods in which he might more naturally seek the support of a wealthy patron.

Keats's intentions seemed extraordinarily foolish to the trustee of his inheritance. Upon taking over his fortune on his twenty-first birthday, Keats informed his trustee that he was leaving the equivalent of a modern medical residency to make his living as a poet, based on his faith in his own genius. Keats made this decision in October 1816, and he moved with great rapidity to publish his first volume of verse, *Poems*, by the second week of March 1817. "On the Grasshopper and the Cricket," composed on December 30, 1816, was the last work to be added to the publication, causing the proofs of the book to be hastily rearranged. The publishers of the book were the Ollier brothers, who were also Hunt's protégés and who had, until sometime in 1816, worked as bank clerks. However, when the bank that employed them collapsed, they decided, with Hunt's encouragement, to become publishers. Keats's volume was the Ollier brothers' first book. During this time period, it was not unusual for authors, especially unknown authors, to pay for their works to be published. No stigma of using a vanity press attached to such an arrangement as it would in the modern age. (For instance, Jane Austen published her novels and Shelley his poems and essays in this way.) Keats himself almost certainly paid the approximately £50 cost of the five hundred copy print run. This fee was exactly equivalent to Keats's annual salary as a surgical assistant and was certainly a relatively large sum of money. Nevertheless, owing to the complete lack of reputation and utter inexperience of both publishers and author, the publication was a failure. Of the five hundred copies, Keats distributed seventeen as presentation copies among his relatives and Hunt's circle, while about a further dozen were sold in all of 1817. Hunt's republication of "On the Grasshopper and the Cricket" in his newspaper the *Examiner* that September did nothing to help. The Ollier brothers were out of the publishing business by 1823. However, even with a disastrous publication, Keats believed strongly in his talents and managed to convince the more prestigious publishers Taylor and Hessey to take over his future work. From Taylor and Hessey, he secured a large advance (£200), and the publication of his two other books *Endymion* (1818) and *Lamia, Isabella, The Eve of St. Agnes, and Other Poems* (1820).

Cricket *(Image copyright Orionmystery@flickr, 2009. Used under license from Shutterstock.com)*

CRITICAL OVERVIEW

"On the Grasshopper and the Cricket" is one of Keats's early works that has not received the scholarly attention devoted to his mature poetry. There is general agreement that the first line of the poem is remarkably beautiful and meaningful, and when the work is introduced into the classroom curriculum it is usually for the sake of that line. *John Keats*, Bate's 1963 biography of the poet, quotes Leigh Hunt's immediate reaction to reading the first line of the sonnet moments after Keats wrote it: "Such a prosperous opening!" Interest in the poem is usually based on this exceptional line. Bate also recounts in full the contest during which the poem was produced, while Alan Osler, in "Keats and a Classical Grasshopper," published in the *Keats-Shelley Memorial Bulletin* (1973), establishes the indebtedness of Keats to Thomas Moore's translation of a grasshopper ode by the ancient Greek poet Anacreon. Lillie Jugurtha, in *Keats and Nature* (1985), reads Keats's sonnet only in connection with her interest in the Romantic's depiction of nature. Jugurtha states that the poem implies "that nature is varied, that the life

of a solitary entity is brief, but that the life of the genus is continuous." In his 1997 biography *Keats*, Andrew Motion views much of the poem as merely decorative in a style heavily influenced by Hunt. Motion concludes that the sonnet's final identification of the cricket and grasshopper "commemorates a conventionally Romantic ideal of mutuality." Duncan Wu, in his article "Keats and the 'Cockney School'" in the *Cambridge Companion to Keats* (2001), acknowledges the heavy influence of Hunt that Keats labored under still at the end of 1816. However, Wu treats "On the Grasshopper and the Cricket" as evidence of a more profound influence on Keats from the more poetical William Wadsworth. Keats's interest in appearance over reality and in inspiration already move him away from Hunt and toward his accomplishments in "Ode to a Nightingale."

CRITICISM

Bradley A. Skeen

Skeen is a classics professor. In this essay, he interprets the grasshopper and the cricket in

WHAT DO I READ NEXT?

- A recent biography of Keats is John Walsh's 1999 *Darkling I Listen: The Last Days and Death of John Keats*, which focuses on the events of the last year of his life but treats earlier periods retrospectively.

- In 2000 Penelope Hughes-Hallett published *The Immortal Dinner: A Famous Evening of Genius and Laughter in Literary London, 1817*, an account of a famous dinner party attended by Keats, William Wadsworth, and other leading poets and artists who played an important role in Keats's later career.

- *The Persistence of Poetry: Bicentennial Essays on Keats*, edited by Robert M. Ryan and Ronald A. Sharp in 1998, offers a variety of scholarly essays on various aspect of Keats and his work.

- Valerie Porter's 2006 *Yesterday's Countryside: Country Life as it Really Was* gives an account of traditional English country life by an author who has written extensively on the subject for young people and who has devoted herself to preserving those traditions as much as possible in the modern world.

- For an eastern perspective on the subject of life and death, read this young-adult biography *Buddha* (1996) by Ed Demi to learn about the path to enlightenment through understanding the cycle of life and death.

- *Insect Mythology*, Gene Kritsky's 2000 collection of insect myths from around the world, provides a context for comparing Keats's use of insects as metaphors with similar traditional stories.

- The second edition of the Norton Critical Edition of *Shelley's Poetry and Prose* (2002) presents a selection of work by the Romantic writer closest to Keats in style and themes, along with critical studies of the texts.

- *The Poetical Works of Leigh Hunt* (1884), a collections of texts by Keats's patron and competitor in the contest that led to "On the Grasshopper and the Cricket," has not been reprinted since 1923 when it was edited by H. S. Milford. Since this book is out of copyright, its complete text is available online at http://books.google.com.

Keats's sonnet "On the Grasshopper and the Cricket" as symbols of the psychological principles of the life instinct and death instinct, and of life and death themselves.

A simple reading of "On the Grasshopper and the Cricket" reveals that it is a celebration of the life and beauty of the English countryside. It makes as much an explicit contrast between summer and winter as it does an implicit one between the traditional ideal life of the natural countryside and the conditions of modern life in the growing cities that cut off the population from rural traditions. The octave, or first eight lines of the sonnet, is devoted to the grasshopper; while the sestet, or final six lines, is devoted to the cricket. The two insects are described in terms of opposite seasons, times of day, and

moods. In many ways, the grasshopper and the cricket stand for opposite poles, but in the final couplet of the sonnet the two insects are nevertheless identified with each other. Similarly, both insects are resolved in rest, even if one is associated with respite after a morning's work in summer and the other with a calm evening by the warmth of a winter fire. In the final couplet, the cricket essentially becomes the grasshopper. An examination of the two fields of symbolism that define and join the two insects reveals the deeper meaning of Keats's youthful poetic exercise.

The first line of the sonnet, "The poetry of earth is never dead," indicates that the sounds of the natural world never cease; they form an endless poem. Literally this means that when one goes outside in the country, nature will always be singing some song, whether it is the chirruping of insects or

> THE DROWSING PERSON IS DREAMING THE CRICKET INTO THE GRASSHOPPER AS A KIND OF PROPHECY."

the babbling of a stream. Though true, the surface level of meaning is not in and of itself very significant. The opening line also suggests that there is a larger and continuing life to the natural world, compared to a human life, which ends in death. It also suggests that the poem is going to concern larger issues of life and death. In the octave, the grasshopper comes into his own in summer when the natural world is most full of life and the agricultural world is also in full swing. The grasshopper is associated with leisure after hard labor, for example, relaxation after the harvest of a hay field when the day has become too hot for work. However, it is not an idle leisure of sleep or mere rest; it is one in which as much energy is put into pleasure as was consumed by work. This act of relaxation would be familiar to Keats, as traditional rustic festivals of singing, dancing, and religious celebrations dominate his later works such as "Ode on a Grecian Urn." It is only when the grasshopper becomes entirely exhausted by the expenditure of energy on both work and play that it is forced to rest.

The first quatrain of the sestet begins to examine the two insects as the two halves of an equation or unity. From the sleep of the grasshopper, the cricket emerges in an entirely different realm. It is now midwinter when, with the shortening of the days and the cold weather of the northern hemisphere, tradition holds that the sun is dying only to be reborn in the new year. The scene is at night; the natural time of rest, and Keats's description emphasizes the cold weather of winter. The cricket is not described visually, but its call from within the wood box by the hearth is the only music of the earth, which was so lively in the summer, that remains.

Comparing the two insects, the grasshopper is associated with life, energy, and activity, while the cricket is linked to rest and even death. There is hardly a more natural contrast imaginable than between life and death. As life and death are the boundaries of human existence, the psychologist Sigmund Freud, writing a century after Keats, envisions life and death as the goals of two instincts that dominate and control animal and human

behavior. Freud saw the life of animals, and therefore the elementary basis of human life, as dominated by two instincts, which he describes in *Beyond the Pleasure Principle* (1920). First, it is in the interest of an animal to conserve its energy so that it needs as little food as possible and its activity exposes it as little as possible to predators. This instinct to rest and conserve energy lies behind survival strategies in nature such as sleep and hibernation. At the same time, other instincts drive animals to expend energy wastefully, including hunger, which drives the search for food. Yet even more important to Freud, the drive to reproduce also causes an animal to waste large amounts of energy in activities such as display and aggression against other members of its own species in competition for mates. None of these acts sustain or lengthen the life of an organism (often it does exactly the opposite), but individuals are compelled to propagate themselves by the strongest instinctual urges that have evolved to perpetuate a species as a whole. The life instinct, another tendency of living beings, not only sustains and propagates life but also leads to an animal's most intense experience of life through releasing the highest levels of energy. The opposite instance, the need to conserve energy, is the death instinct, because death is logically an animal's lowest energy state; if the death instinct was the only operative factor in life, it would lead to the organism's death and extinction. Freud states that in comparison to the life instinct, the death instinct is comprised "of tendencies more primitive than it and independent of it," so that, paradoxically, "the aim of all life is death." Freud adds that an organism's behavior is always a balance "between life instincts and death instincts," with each dominating in turn.

Freud was keenly interested in literary criticism, and his work is the foundation of much modern interpretation of literature. However, he did not apply his theory of the death and life instincts to the analysis of literature in his own writings. Even so, "On the Grasshopper and the Cricket" seems to be a significant translation of Freud's theory about the ultimate meanings of life in the form of poetry. Freud often said that many of his insights had been anticipated by poets. The grasshopper expends his energy on living life to the fullest in every sense and only then collapses into rest ("rest" is often a euphemism [a substitution of a less offensive or unpleasant term for the intended word] for death). The cricket, on the other hand, symbolizes the ebb of the year when there is nothing left do but rest by a pleasant fire, which gives warmth to a frigid world. If poetry and

Single tree on grassy hill (*Image copyright Mark Aplet, 2009. Used under license from Shutterstock.com*)

song are how Keats describes what Freud calls instinctual energy, then the cricket and his human companion have nothing left to do except build their wasted energy back up, expressed in the cricket's shrill singing.

This interpretation of the grasshopper and the cricket as symbols of human energy devoted to the life instinct and death instinct illuminates the final couplet of the sonnet. Here, the only human character in the poem, an exhausted person falling asleep, imagines or dreams that the cricket is the grasshopper. If the two insects symbolize the two instincts that constantly alternate in their influence over human life and activity, then it may truly be said that one transforms into the other. The drowsing person is dreaming the cricket into the grasshopper as a kind of prophecy. In time, as energy is recovered, the death instinct will indeed give way to the life instinct once again.

This pattern of rest and the renewal of energy giving way to its extravagant expenditure and then back to more rest in a cycle is seen not only in the life and death instincts that dominate animal and human life. All of nature goes through the same

round in the cycle of the seasons. The same pattern is seen in the mythical representation of life, death, and resurrection, which underlays the ancient Greek Eleusinian mysteries as much as it does the hope of reincarnation in Hinduism or eternal life in Christianity. The dreamer is indeed dreaming prophecy: he sees the cricket reborn as the grasshopper—death reborn as life. By linking the trivial lives of insects to this greater realm of life and death, Keats not only creates a simple poem about nature. He also supports the expansion of its symbolic structure to encompass many of humanity's most profound beliefs and ideals. A task such as this is a grand achievement for a twenty-one-year-old writer.

Source: Bradley Skeen, Critical Essay on "On the Grasshopper and the Cricket," in *Poetry for Students*, Gale, Cengage Learning, 2010.

John Barnard

In the following excerpt, Barnard details the circumstances of the publication of Keats's first volume of poetry, which included "On the Grasshopper and the Cricket," providing a timeline of the book's production.

"KEATS WAS AN ALTOGETHER MORE DRIVEN MAN THAN PREVIOUSLY REALIZED, ONE PREPARED TO BORROW AGAINST HIS FUTURE EXPECTATIONS TO GAMBLE ON A SUCCESSFUL ENTRY INTO THE LITERARY WORLD."

. . . Keats must have finished 'I stood tip-toe upon a little hill', which he had evidently put to one side, 'in one more attack' shortly after 17 December. There are three manuscript versions of the poem, all of which are dated December 1816, and a fourth, now lost, was made for the printer. Stillinger places these, according to the evidence provided by the textual variants, in the following sequence:

(1) Keats's draft given to Charles Cowden Clarke (who over the years cut it up to give away: it is now scattered through various collections).

(2) Keats's fair copy given to Haydon (Harvard).

(3) Tom Keats's transcript based on a lost manuscript later than the preceding (Harvard).

(4) The lost manuscript from which *Poems* (1817) was printed, possibly the one from which Tom made his transcript.

This sequence indicates that the first two versions were both made prior to the one sent to the printer. The draft contains deletions and changes made later: unusually, Keats numbered the lines. Exactly when Keats gave Clarke and Haydon their copies is not known, though Haydon, who told Wordsworth on 31 December 1816 '[Keats] is now writing a longer sort of poem of "Diana and Endymion" to publish with his smaller productions', had evidently not received his copy by then.

In the latter part of the month Keats was copying out his other poems for the printer. By 25 December he had transcribed 66 pages of his poems for the press, as far as Sonnet XIV, the second Elgin Marbles sonnet, 'Great spirits now on earth are sojourning'. Stillinger reports that '66' is written in the upper right hand corner. This cannot be the printer's numbering (the sonnet

occurs on p. 92 of the printed volume). Stillinger further records that one of the Harvard holograph copies of Sonnet I, 'To My Brother George', was used as copy for *Poems* (1817), and has '53' in the upper right hand corner. Keats, that is, was using only the recto of each leaf. As the 'Poems' (less 'I stood tip-toe upon a little hill') take up 35 printed pages and the 'Epistles' 23 printed pages (excluding half titles and blanks), the total number of pages, 58, is close to the '53' Keats wrote on the holograph of Sonnet I. Hence, by 25 December Keats had probably copied all the 'Poems' section (excluding 'I stood tip-toe') and fourteen of the sonnets into a separately numbered section of the copy which went to the printer. ('I stood tip-toe upon a little hill' must have been sent as a separate manuscript, and the same may have been true of 'Sleep and Poetry' for which there is no manuscript evidence.)

In the same month, Tom Keats transcribed fourteen of Keats's poems into a notebook, now at Harvard. These are not arranged in order of their composition, but approximate the order found in *Poems* (1817), and Tom Keats added a note after 'Calidore', 'marked by Leigh Hunt—1816'. The latest poem with a known date included in Tom's notebook is the sonnet 'Written in Disgust of Vulgar Superstition', which was composed on Sunday evening, 22 December but not printed in *Poems* (1817). The notebook is evidently in some way related to Keats's preparation of his poems for the printer because his transcripts of those printed in *Poems* (1817) are textually very closely related.

It is clear that Keats, with his brother Tom, gave a great deal of time and energy to transcribing his poetry this month. There is no clear evidence of the precise sequence in which of these holograph copies, drafts and transcripts were made in December 1816, nor is it clear why Tom Keats transcribed the whole of 'I stood tip-toe upon a little hill', though it suggests he was in some way supporting his brother's work in the volume's final stages. Between 17 December, when Keats told Clarke he was about to finish 'I stood tip-toe upon a little hill' and 30 December when he wrote 'On the Grasshopper and the Cricket' in competition with Leigh Hunt at Hampstead, an occasion witnessed by Cowden Clarke, there are only two days on which there is any record of Keats's social life. On 18 December, as noted above, he visited Hunt in

Hampstead and probably saw Cowden Clarke in Clerkenwell, and on 22 December Cowden Clarke visited the brothers in Cheapside, the day Keats composed 'Written in Disgust of Vulgar Superstition'. Keats had plenty of time in which to transcribe his poems for the press, and since 'I stood tip-toe upon a little hill' was not completed until after 17 or 18 December, the numbered section of 'Poems' may have been started before that date.

When Keats told Cowden Clarke on 17 December he 'had done little on Endymion lately' and hoped to finish it 'in one attack' how much more work on the poem was left to do? It is certain that he was referring to 'I stood tip-toe upon a little hill' because Tom Keats's transcript (intermediate between the fair copy for Haydon and the manuscript given to the printer) is headed 'Endymion'. The story of Diana and Endymion takes up the final fifty lines of the 242 lines of 'I stood tip-toe upon a little hill', which means that he must have already composed enough of these fifty closing lines to know how he intended to conclude the poem, and was sufficiently excited by what he had written for the ending to colour the whole poem, whose other two hundred lines and more have nothing to do with Diana or Endymion. (Keats's decision to print the poem without a title, as all his biographers note, shows that as he finished 'I stood tip-toe upon a little hill' he realized the myth would provide the framework for his ambitious long poem, the 'Poetic Romance',*Endymion*.) The changes made to this part of the poem in Keats's draft are relatively limited in fact, so Keats's 'final attack' on the draft did not involve any major re-writing of its conclusion (ll. 193–242). Making the fair copies from the draft probably interrupted progress on Keats's preparation of the numbered section of poems he was preparing for the press. The fair copies, in particular that for Haydon, demonstrate the measure of his satisfaction with the newly completed poem.

Keats had probably completed his manuscript for the printer before his visit to Hunt's on 30 December. On that occasion Keats wrote the sonnet, 'On the Grasshopper and the Cricket' (it is so dated in the holograph and the printed text) in competition with Hunt, before walking home that night with Cowden Clarke. The sonnet was added to the copy for *Poems* (1817) at the last moment.

It was perhaps on this occasion that Hunt marked up approvingly Tom Keats's transcription of 'Specimen of an Induction to a Poem' and 'Calidore', because the notebook into which it was copied contains 'Written in Disgust of Vulgar Superstition', composed on 22 December. However, it is possible that Hunt saw Tom's notebook earlier since his marking are restricted to 'Specimen of an Induction to a Poem' and 'Calidore', which are written on its first nine pages. If so, Keats was seeking Hunt's advice about these poems and the volume he was putting together. In either case, the marginal markings suggest that Hunt had not been previously shown either poem. The annotations include an alteration, possibly by Hunt, which Keats adopted in *Poems* (1817), and pick out two passages which Hunt was to quote later in his *Examiner* review of Keats's poems. This shows the extraordinarily closeness of Keats's and Hunt's poetic taste at this time, and is further evidence of the influence of *The Story of Rimini* on both poems.

The striking thing about this timetable for Keats's preparation of copy for his printer is its extreme concentration. Although some of the details above are speculative, three facts are incontrovertible. The Olliers, we now know, only decided to become publishers around 11 December 1816; by 25 December Keats had copied a substantial number of poems for the press; and, at the same time, Tom Keats was busy transcribing his brother's poems. (Keats's overnight stay with Thomas Richards on 14 December, a visit Keats believed Cowden Clarke knew about beforehand, is also firmly documented—could Thomas's brother, Charles, have been present?) Everything confirms the speed with which Keats set about readying his poems for the press from mid-December.

The likely reason for this haste was that Keats's had duties to fulfil at Guy's in January and February. He still had to complete his year's term as a dresser, and must have been due to spend at least one more week on hospital duty in these months. Between 31 December 1816 and 20 January 1817, when Keats was present at the fierce debate between Shelley and Haydon over dinner at Horace Smith's, a period of almost three weeks, there is no record of Keats either writing anything or meeting anyone in his circle. In February there are similar gaps in the record of Keats's social life outside the hospital.

Keats's copy went to the printer at some point after 30 December 1816. The setting and printing of Keats's volume's eight and a quarter sheets, if Charles Richards employed a journeyman and the two of them worked side by side, cannot have taken more than a week. The sheets would then need to be revised and corrected. Charles Richards had some six or seven weeks in which to set, proof, and correct Keats's volume before sending it to the binders. He must have printed *Poems* (1817) concurrently with other jobs, or he not would have had the successful business he did (it ran until at least 1849, by which time he had added lithographic printing to his activities).

There is no firm evidence of when Keats received his final proofs. It is possible that Keats took his proofs, in one form or another, to Hampstead when he visited Hunt on Saturday, 15 February, since the following evening Hunt 'showed' Keats's poems to his dinner guests, the Shelleys, the Godwins, the Hazlitts and Basil Montagu. Among the poems, which Hunt's guests 'pronounced as extraordinary', was the Chapman sonnet. The gathering at the brothers' Cheapside lodgings during which Keats received the final proofs and hastily composed the dedicatory sonnet to Hunt in the presence of Charles Ollier, Cowden Clarke and others, must have taken place shortly before or shortly after Hunt's dinner party.

After Charles Richards had completed printing off the edition of *Poems* (1817), Keats asked him to change the title-page. The replacement title-page almost certainly added, as Wise surmised, the vignette head of Shakespeare. This image of Shakespeare, based on the bust in Holy Trinity church, Stratford, reproduced and sold by George Bullock from 1814, was thought to be based on a life mask, and was popular among Hunt and his circle. Wise thought the vignette 'an ordinary conventional' one, 'doubtless found by the printer among his stock of book-ornaments, and employed as being suitable to the occasion'. That may be so, though Richards could have obtained it from another printer. The important point, however, is that the alteration was made at Keats's request. (As Keats knew artists through Haydon and Severn, he may even have had it specially made.) The symbolic statement made by his title-page clearly mattered to Keats. Its epigraph from Spenser's *Muiopotmos*, 'What more felicity can fall to creature, / Than to enjoy delight with liberty', is included in the *Times* advertisement on 10 March. In the penultimate stages of preparing

'I stood tip-toe upon a little hill' for the press Keats had considered using the epigraph to head that poem but, before sending his (lost) manuscript to the printer, he replaced it with a line from Hunt's *The Story of Rimini*. He evidently decided instead to save the quotation from Spenser for his title-page. This was in the very final stages of preparing his manuscript for the printer. The epigraph, therefore, was almost certainly on the title-page Keats received in proof from Richards. This greatly strengthens the assumption that the replacement title-page added the vignette of Shakespeare.

Although Leigh Hunt delayed reviewing *Poems* (1817) until June and early July, he promoted Keats's work in the spring issues of the *Examiner*. In spite of the fact that he had little space for original poetry, Hunt followed up his 'Young Poets' article of December 1816 by publishing 'To Kosciusko' (shortly to appear as Sonnet XVI in *Poems* (1817)) on Sunday, 16 February, over Keats's initials. The following Sunday, 23 February, he printed, 'After dark vapours have oppress'd our plains', written as recently as 31 January 1817, also signed 'J. K.'. Hunt intended to publish a third poem in the issue for 2 March, only days before *Poems* (1817) was published, but the Examiner told his readers (and Keats), 'J. K.'s Lines are delayed, owing to the great pressure of temporary matter.' (The 'lines' in question must have been the very recently composed sonnet which Hunt entitled 'Written on a Blank Space at the End of Chaucer's Tale of "The Floure and the Lefe"'.)

By that same Sunday, 2 March, Keats had received his pre-publication copies, a date we can establish by two facts. Thomas Richards (not Charles Ollier as is normally said) dated the sonnet he wrote to Keats in his presentation copy 2 March 1817, and Leigh Hunt dated the holograph of his two sonnets 'On receiving an Ivy Crown' from Keats, 1 March. That must have been the date on which Keats gave, or showed him, a copy of his newly printed volume.

At some point in the same weekend Keats composed his two sonnets to Haydon following their visit to see the Elgin Marbles at the British Museum. The visit and these sonnets have an inferred dating of Saturday or Sunday, 1 or 2 March. Since Saturday was a day for general 'cleansing' of the Museum, which was closed to the public on both days, their visit could have taken place on the Friday. More likely, given

Haydon's standing with the Museum as a result of his campaign for the purchase of the Marbles, it took place, by special permission, on the Sunday.

The presentation copy of *Poems* (1817) which Keats gave to John Hamilton Reynolds, now at Harvard, confirms what some biographers doubted, that the exchange of laurel and ivy crowns by Keats and Hunt took place at this time. Further, an examination of Reynolds's copy, together with other evidence, allows for a more detailed account of the sequence of these events than has previously been given.

Keats had been sent a number of pre-publication copies of *Poems* (1817) in publisher's boards by Saturday, 1 March. That day, which was cloudy but warm for the time of year, he took one of these to Hampstead as a presentation copy for Leigh Hunt. Since Keats knew Hunt's weekly routine, which involved spending Saturdays in his Covent Garden office, completing the following day's issue of the *Examiner* for the press, he probably reached Hunt's cottage in the late afternoon. However, Hunt had not yet returned, so Keats walked back down Millfield Lane, meeting Hunt on his way home, and gave him his copy of *Poems* (1817).

Hunt invited Keats to stay for dinner; after dinner they celebrated by drinking wine. Keats then wrote his sonnet on Hunt's giving him a laurel crown, and Hunt wrote two sonnets commemorating his own crowning with an ivy wreath. Since Keats copied his sonnet, 'To the Ladies Who Saw Me Crown'd', into the presentation copy he gave to Reynolds one or two days later, this was probably composed, also extemporaneously, on this occasion when Reynolds's sisters unexpectedly joined the two men. By the time Keats went home the sky had cleared, since he later recalled that the 'Pleiades were up' that evening.

(The whole occasion quickly came to embarrass Keats as presumptuous, but others in his circle took Hunt's gesture as a tribute worth recording. Thomas Richards planned to copy Hunt's two sonnets into his presentation copy of *Poems* (1817) and George Keats copied both poems into his own copy of the volume.)

The following day, Sunday, Haydon took Keats to the British Museum for his first view of the Elgin Marbles. They were almost certainly accompanied by Reynolds. Keats wrote the two sonnets on the Marbles when he returned home, and sent them to Haydon, who received them the following morning, and promptly sent back an effusive reply, even reopening his letter to add a postscript thanking Keats again for praising him.

That evening, on Monday, 3 March, Keats, Reynolds and Cowden Clarke met, as previously arranged, at Haydon's studio. Keats's forthcoming volume must have been celebrated by all four men, and, given Haydon's impetuous enthusiasm, Keats was very likely called upon to read out his two latest sonnets. This was a doubly significant day. In the morning, *Poems* (1817), financed by Keats himself, had been advertised in the *Morning Chronicle* for publication the following Monday. And 3 March was exactly a year to the day since Keats had registered himself as William Lucas's dresser. The celebrations in Haydon's studio marked the end of Keats's formal commitment to medicine and Guy's Hospital and the beginning of his life as a published author.

It is not clear exactly when Keats sent his gift copy to Reynolds, but he is unlikely to have given it to him on that evening at Haydon's studio because he could not have done so openly without also giving copies at the same time to Haydon and Cowden Clarke, neither of whom seem to have received their presentation copies until later. Keats personalized his gift copy for Reynolds, which was in publishers' boards, by copying both the sonnet he wrote 'On Receiving a Laurel Crown from Leigh Hunt' and that to the ladies who were present. In addition, Keats copied out the two sonnets to Haydon, as a memorial of their joint visit to see the Marbles with Haydon, and perhaps with the hope that Reynolds might print them. When Reynolds published his glowing review of the volume in the *Champion* on Sunday, 9 March, he included both the Elgin Marbles sonnets as further proofs of Keats's genius based on the text Keats had given him. Since the text of 'To Haydon, with a Sonnet Written on Seeing the Elgin Marbles' which Keats copied out for Reynolds differs substantively from that which Haydon received on the morning of 3 March, the text published in the *Champion* is probably a later version, and may have been copied out after the evening in Haydon's studio. If so, Keats had already sent a copy of the sonnets to Hunt for publication in the *Examiner* since the text of 'To Haydon' published there follows the one Keats sent to Haydon.

On 7 or 10 March *Poems* (1817) was finally published, closely coinciding with Reynolds's review and the simultaneous appearance of the

Elgin marble sonnets in slightly different versions in the *Champion* and the *Examiner*. Hunt evidently printed the two sonnets in preference to Keats's much inferior lines on Chaucer's 'The Floure and the Lefe', which he held back to the next issue of the *Examiner* on 16 March. There Hunt added an introductory note referring back to his 'Young Poets' article, and, unusually, identified Keats by name:

> [The following exquisite Sonnet, as well as one or two others that have lately appeared under the same signature, is from the pen of the young poet (KEATS), who was mentioned not long since in this paper, and who may already lay claim to that title:—
>
> The youngest he,
> That sits in shadow of Apollo's tree.]

Hunt's double association of Keats with Apollo and, through the quotation from Ben Jonson, with the great age of Elizabethan and Jacobean poetry and drama exactly mirrored Keats's own ambitions and reflected both men's tastes. But Hunt's efforts on Keats's behalf, and his premature claims on behalf of the young poet, had little effect beyond their immediate circle.

The seventeen presentation copies Keats is known to have given his family and friends, and to members of the Hunt network, proves that Keats exaggerated only slightly when he said that *Poems* (1817) 'was read by some dozen of my friends who lik'd it; and some dozen who I was unacquainted with who did not'. While Keats's biographers have made clear the powerful effect of the failure of *Poems* (1817) on Keats, they do not note that if he had paid for its production, with George's eager encouragement, his disappointment would have been doubly sharp, and would have had a direct effect upon his own finances, already a cause for serious anxiety. Keats was an altogether more driven man than previously realized, one prepared to borrow against his future expectations to gamble on a successful entry into the literary world....

Source: John Barnard, "First Fruits or 'First Blights': A New Account of the Publishing History of Keats's *Poems* (1817)," in *Romanticism*, Vol. 12, No. 2, 2006, pp. 71–101.

Sidney Colvin

In the following excerpt, Colvin discusses Keats's friendship with Leigh Hunt and describes the circumstances in which "On the Grasshopper and the Cricket" was composed.

...Hunt was a confirmed Voltairian and sceptic as to revealed religion, and supplied its place with a private gospel of cheerfulness, or

> HENCE, AS THIS PROFOUND AND PASSIONATE YOUNG GENIUS GREW, HE COULD NOT BUT BE AWARE OF WHAT WAS SHALLOW IN THE TALENT OF HIS SENIOR AND CLOYING AND DISTASTEFUL IN HIS EVER-VOLUBLE GENIALITY."

system of sentimental optimism, inspired partly by his own invincibly sunny temperament and partly by the hopeful doctrines of eighteenth-century philosophy in France. Keats shared the natural sympathy of generous youth for Hunt's liberal and kindhearted view of things, and he had a mind naturally unapt for dogma: ready to entertain and appreciate any set of ideas according as his imagination recognised their beauty or power, he could never wed himself to any as representing ultimate truth. In matters of poetic feeling and fancy the two men had up to a certain point not a little in common. Like Hunt, Keats at this time was given to 'luxuriating' too effusively and fondly over the 'deliciousness' of whatever he liked in art, books, or nature. To the everyday pleasures of summer and the English fields Hunt brought in a lower degree the same alertness of perception and acuteness of enjoyment which in Keats were intense beyond parallel. In his lighter and shallower way Hunt also truly felt with Keats the perennial charm and vitality of classic fable, and was scholar enough to produce about this time some agreeable translations of the Sicilian pastorals, and some, less adequate, of Homer. But behind such pleasant faculties in Hunt nothing deeper or more potent lay hidden. Whereas with Keats, as time went on, delighted sensation became more and more surely and instantaneously transmuted and spiritualised into imaginative emotion; his words and cadences came every day from deeper sources within him and more fully charged with the power of far-reaching and symbolic suggestion. Hence, as this profound and passionate young genius grew, he could not but be aware of what was shallow in the talent of his senior and cloying and distasteful in his ever-voluble geniality. But for many months the harmony of their relations was complete.

The 'little cottage' in the Vale of Health must have been fairly overcrowded, one would suppose, with Hunt's fast-growing family of young children, but a bed was made up for Keats on a sofa, 'in a parlour no bigger than an old mansion's closet,' says Hunt, which nevertheless served him for a library and had prints after Stothard hung on the walls and casts of the heads of poets and heroes crowning the bookshelves. Here the young poet was made always welcome. The sonnet beginning 'Keen, fitful gusts are whispering here and there' records a night of October or November 1816, when, instead of staying to sleep, he preferred to walk home under the stars, his head full of talk about Petrarch and the youth of Milton, to the city lodgings where he lived with his brothers the life affectionately described in that other pleasant sonnet written on Tom's birthday, November 18, beginning 'Small, busy flames play through the fresh-laid coals.' The well-known fifty lines at the end of 'Sleep and Poetry,' a poem on which Keats put forth the best of his half-fledged strength this winter, give the fullest and most engaging account of the pleasure and inspiration he drew from Hunt's hospitality:—

> The chimes
> Of friendly voices had just given place
> To as sweet a silence, when I 'gan retrace
> The pleasant day, upon a couch at ease.
> It was a poet's house who keeps the keys
> Of pleasure's temple. Round about were
>   hung
> The glorious features of the bards who sung
> In other ages—cold and sacred busts
> Smiled at each other. Happy he who trusts
> To clear Futurity his darling fame!
> Then there were fauns and satyrs taking aim
> At swelling apples with a frisky leap
> And reaching fingers, 'mid a luscious heap
> Of vine-leaves. Then there rose to view a
>   fane
> Of liny marble, and thereto a train
> Of nymphs approaching fairly o'er the
>   sward:
> One, loveliest, holding her white hand
>   toward
> The dazzling sun-rise: two sisters sweet
> Bending their graceful figures till they meet
> Over the trippings of a little child:
> And some are hearing, eagerly, the wild
> Thrilling liquidity of dewy piping.
> See, in another picture, nymphs are wiping
> Cherishingly Diana's timorous limbs;—
> A fold of lawny mantle dabbling swims

> At the bath's edge, and keeps a gentle
>   motion
> With the subsiding crystal: as when ocean
> Heaves calmly its broads swelling smooth-
>   ness o'er
> Its rocky marge, and balances once more
> The patient weeds; that now unshent by
>   foam
> Feel all about their undulating home …
> Petrarch, outstepping from the shady green,
> Starts at the sight of Laura; nor can wean
> His eyes from her sweet face. Most happy
>   they!
> For over them was seen a free display
> Of out-spread wings, and from between
>   them shone
> The face of Poesy: from off her throne
> She overlook'd things that I scarce could
>   tell.

It is easy from the above and from some of Keats's later work to guess at most of the prints which had caught his attention on Hunt's walls and in his portfolios and worked on his imagination afterwards:—Poussin's 'Empire of Flora' for certain: several, probably, of his various 'Bacchanals,' with the god and his leopard-drawn car, and groups of nymphs dancing with fauns or strewn upon the foreground to right or left: the same artist's 'Venus and Adonis': Stothard's 'Bathers' and 'Vintage,' his small print of Petrarch as a youth first meeting Laura and her friend; Raphael 'Poetry' from the Vatican; and so forth. These things are not without importance in the study of Keats, for he was quicker and more apt than any of our other poets to draw inspiration from works of art,—prints, pictures, or marbles,—that came under his notice, and it is not for nothing that he alludes in this same poem to

> —the pleasant flow
> Of words on opening a portfolio.

A whole treatise might be written on matters which I shall have to mention briefly or not at all,—how such and such a descriptive phrase in Keats has been suggested by this or that figure in a picture; how pictures by or prints after old masters have been partly responsible for his vision alike of the Indian maiden and the blind Orion; what various originals, paintings or antiques or both, we can recognize as blending themselves into his evocation of the triumph of Bacchus or his creation of the Grecian Urn.

On December the 1st, 1816, Hunt, as has been said, did Keats the new service of printing the Chapman sonnet as a specimen of his work in an essay in the *Examiner* on 'Young Poets,' in which the names of Shelley and Reynolds were bracketed with his as poetical beginners of high promise. With reference to the custom mentioned by Hunt of Keats and himself sitting down of an evening to write verses on a given subject, Cowden Clarke pleasantly describes one such occasion on December 30 of the same year, when the chosen theme was 'The Grasshopper and the Cricket:'—'The event of the after scrutiny was one of many such occurrences which have riveted the memory of Leigh Hunt in my affectionate regard and admiration for unaffected generosity and perfectly unpretentious encouragement. His sincere look of pleasure at the first line:—

The poetry of earth is never dead.

"Such a prosperous opening!" he said; and when he came to the tenth and eleventh lines:—

On a lone winter morning, when the frost
Hath wrought a silence—

"Ah that's perfect! Bravo Keats!" And then he went on in a dilatation on the dumbness of Nature during the season's suspension and torpidity.' The affectionate enthusiasm of the younger and the older man (himself, be it remembered, little over thirty) for one another's company and verses sometimes took forms which to the mind of the younger and wiser of the two soon came to seem ridiculous. One day in early spring (1817) the whim seized them over their wine to crown themselves 'after the manner of the elder bards.' Keats crowned Hunt with a wreath of ivy, Hunt crowned Keats with a wreath of laurel, and each while sitting so adorned wrote a pair of sonnets expressive of his feelings. While they were in the act of composition, it seems, three lady callers came in— conceivably the three Misses Reynolds, of whom we shall hear more anon, Jane, afterwards Mrs Thomas Hood, Mariane, and their young sister Charlotte. When visitors were announced Hunt took off his wreath and suggested that Keats should do the same: he, however, 'in his enthusiastic way, declared he would not take off his crown for any human being,' and accordingly wore it as long as the visit lasted. Here are Hunt's pair of sonnets, which are about as good as any he ever wrote, and which he not long afterwards printed:—

A crown of ivy! I submit my head
To the young hand that gives it,—young, 'tis true,

But with a right, for 'tis a poet's too.
How pleasant the leaves feel! and how they spread
With their broad angles, like a nodding shed
Over both eyes! and how complete and new,
As on my hand I lean, to feel them strew
My sense with freshness,—Fancy's rustling bed!
Tress-tossing girls, with smell of flowers and grapes
Come dancing by, and downward piping cheeks,
And up-thrown cymbals, and Silenus old
Lumpishly borne, and many trampling shapes,—
And lastly, with his bright eyes on her bent,
Bacchus,—whose bride has of his hand fast hold.

It is a lofty feeling, yet a kind,
Thus to be topped with leaves;—to have a sense
Of honour-shaded thought,—an influence
As from great Nature's fingers, and be twined
With her old, sacred, verdurous ivy-bind,
As though she hallowed with that sylvan fence
A head that bows to her benevolence,
Midst pomp of fancied trumpets in the wind.
'Tis what's within us crowned. And kind and great
Are all the conquering wishes it inspires,—
Love of things lasting, love of the tall woods,
Love of love's self, and ardour for a state
Of natural good befitting such desires,
Towns without gain, and haunted solitudes.

Keats had the good sense not to print his efforts of the day; they are of slight account poetically, but have a real biographical interest:—

'On Receiving a Laurel Crown from Leigh Hunt'

Minutes are flying swiftly, and as yet
Nothing unearthly has enticed my brain
Into a delphic labyrinth—I would fain
Catch an immortal thought to pay the debt
I owe to the kind poet who has set
Upon my ambitious head a glorious gain.
Two bending laurel sprigs—'tis nearly pain
To be conscious of such a coronet.
Still time is fleeting, and no dream arises
Gorgeous as I would have it—only I see
A trampling down of what the world most prizes,

Turbans and crowns and blank regality;
And then I run into most wild surmises
Of all the many glories that may be.

'To the Ladies Who Saw Me Crowned'
What is there in the universal earth
More lovely than a wreath from the bay
     tree?
Haply a halo round the moon—a glee
Circling from three sweet pair of lips in
     mirth;
And haply you will say the dewy birth
Of morning roses—ripplings tenderly
Spread by the halcyon's breast upon the
     sea—
But these comparisons are nothing worth.
Then there is nothing in the world so fair?
The silvery tears of April? Youth of May?
Or June that breathes out life for butterflies?
No none of these can from my favourite
     bear
Away the palm—yet shall it ever pay
Due reverence to your most sovereign eyes.

Here we have expressed in the first sonnet the same mood as in some of the holiday rimes of the previous summer, the mood of ardent expectancy for an inspiration that declines (and no wonder considering the circumstances) to come. It was natural that the call for an impromptu should bring up phrases already lying formed or half formed in Keats's mind, and the sestet of this sonnet is interesting as containing in its first four lines the germs of the well-known passage at the beginning of the third book of *Endymion,*—

There are who lord it o'er their fellow-men
With most prevailing tinsel—

and in its fifth a repetition of the 'wild surmise' phrase of the Chapman sonnet. The second sonnet has a happy line or two in its list of delights, and its opening is noticeable as repeating the interrogative formula of the opening lines of *Sleep and Poetry,* Keats's chief venture in verse this winter.

Very soon after the date of this scene of intercoronation (the word is Hunt's, used on a different occasion) Keats became heartily ashamed of it, and expressed his penitence in a strain of ranting verse (his own name for compositions in this vein) under the form of a hymn or palinode to Apollo:—

God of the golden bow,
And of the golden lyre,

And of the golden hair,
And of the golden fire,
Charioteer
Of the patient year,
Where—where slept thine ire,
When like a blank idiot I put on thy wreath,
Thy laurel, thy glory,
The light of thy story,
Or was I a worm—too low crawling, for
     death?
O Delphic Apollo!

And so forth: the same half-amused spirit of penitence is expressed in a letter of a few weeks later to his brother George: and later still he came to look back, with a smile of manly self-derision, on those days as a time when he had been content to play the part of 'A pet-lamb in a sentimental farce.'

Source: Sidney Colvin, "October 1815–March 1817: Hospital Studies: Poetical Ambitions: Leigh Hunt," in *John Keats: His Life and Poetry, His Friends, Critics, and After-Fame,* Scribner's, 1917, pp. 27–58.

Arthur Symons

In the following excerpt, noted critic and poet Symons explores the role of imagination in Keats's work, commenting that the poet's happy nature results in an "accidental sadness" in his poetry.

The poetry of Keats is an aspiration towards happiness, towards the deliciousness of life, towards the restfulness of beauty, towards the delightful sharpness of sensations not too sharp to be painful. He accepted life in the spirit of art, asking only the simple pleasures, which he seemed to be among the few who could not share, of physical health, the capacity to enjoy sensation without being over come by it. He was not troubled about his soul, the meaning of the universe, or any other metaphysical questions, to which he shows a happy indifference, or rather, a placid unconsciousness. "I scarcely remember counting upon any happiness," he notes. "I look not for it if it be not in the present hour. Nothing startles me beyond the moment. The setting sun will always set me to rights, or if a sparrow were before my window, I take part in its existence, and pick about the gravel." It is here, perhaps, that he is what people choose to call pagan; though it would be both simpler and truer to say that he is the natural animal, to whom the sense of sin has never whispered itself. Only a cloud makes him uneasy in the sunshine. "Happy days, or else to die," he asks for, not

> YOU HAVE TO GET AT SHELLEY'S OR WORDSWORTH'S POINT OF VIEW; BUT KEATS HAS ONLY THE POINT OF VIEW OF THE SUNLIGHT. HE CANNOT WRITE WITHOUT MAKING PICTURES WITH HIS WORDS, AND EVERY PICTURE HAS ITS OWN ATMOSPHERE."

aware of any reason why he should not easily be happy under flawless weather. He knows that

All charms fly
At the mere touch of cold philosophy,

and he is not cursed with that spirit of analysis which tears our pleasures to pieces, as in a child's hands, to find out, what can never be found out, the secret of their making. In a profound passage on Shakespeare he notes how

Several things dove-tailed in my mind, and at once it struck me what quality went to form a man of achievement, especially in literature, and which Shakespeare possessed so enormously—I mean *negative capability,* that is, when a man is capable of being in uncertainties, mysteries, doubts, without any irritable reaching after fact and reason. Coleridge, for instance, would let go by a fine isolated verisimilitude, caught from the penetralium of Mystery, from being incapable of remaining content with half measures.

And so he is willing to linger among imaginative happiness, satisfyingly, rather than to wander in uneasy search after perhaps troubling certainties. He had a nature to which happiness was natural, until nerves and disease came to disturb it. And so his poetry has only a sort of accidental sadness, reflected back upon it from our consciousness of the shortness of the time he himself had had to enjoy delight.

And they shall be accounted poet-kings
Who simply tell the most heart-easing things,

he says in "Sleep and Poetry," and, while he notes with admiration that Milton "devoted himself rather to the ardours than the pleasures of song, solacing himself at intervals with cups of old wine," he adds that "those are, with some exceptions, the finest parts of the poem." To him, poetry was always those "cups of old wine," a rest in some "leafy luxury" by the way....

Keats, at a time when the phrase had not yet been invented, practised the theory of art for art's sake. He is the type, not of the poet, but of the artist. He was not a great personality; his work comes to us as a greater thing than his personality. When we read his verse, we think of the verse, not of John Keats. When we read the verse of Byron, of Coleridge, of Shelley, of Wordsworth, we are conscious, in different degrees, of the work being a personal utterance, and it obtains much of its power over us by our consciousness of that fact. But when we read the verse of Keats, we are conscious only of an enchantment which seems to have invented itself. If we think of the writer, we think of him as of a flattering mirror, in which the face of beauty becomes more beautiful; not as of the creator of beauty. We cannot distinguish him from that which he reflects.

Keats has a firm common sense of the imagination, seeming to be at home in it, as if it were literally this world, and not the dream of another. Thus, in his most serious moments, he can jest with it, as men do with those they live with and love most....

"Man should not dispute or assert, but whisper results to his neighbour," he affirms; "let us open our leaves like a flower, and be passive and receptive, budding patiently under the eye of Apollo, and taking hints from every noble insect that favours us with a visit." That passive and receptive mood was always his own attitude towards the visitings of the imagination; he was always "looking on the sun, the moon, the stars, the earth and its contents, as materials to form greater things"; always waiting, now "all of a tremble from not having written anything of late," now vainly longing to "compose without fever," now reminding a friend: "If you should have any reason to regret this state of excitement in me, I will turn the tide of your feelings in the right channel by mentioning that it is the only state for the best kind of poetry—that is all I care for, all I live for." Perhaps it is this waiting mood, a kind of electrically charged expectancy which draws its own desire to itself out of the universe, that Mr. Bridges means when he speaks of Keats' "unbroken and unflagging earnestness, which is so utterly unconscious and unobservant of itself as to be almost unmatched." In its dependence on a kind of direct inspiration, the fidelity to first thoughts, it accounts, perhaps, for much of what is technically deficient in his poetry.

When Keats gave his famous counsel to Shelley, urging him to "load every rift with ore," he expressed a significant criticism, both of his own and of Shelley's work. With Shelley, even though he may at times seem to become vague in thought, there is always an intellectual structure; Keats, definite in every word, in every image, lacks intellectual structure. He saw words as things, and he saw them one at a time. "I look upon fine phrases like a lover," he confessed, but with him the fine phrase was but the translation of a thing actually seen by the imagination. He was conscious of the need there is for the poet to be something more than a creature of sensations, but even his consciousness of this necessity is that of one to whom knowledge is merely an aid to flight. "The difference," he says, in a splendid sentence, "of high sensations, with and without knowledge, appears to me this: in the latter case we are continually falling ten thousand fathoms deep, and being blown up again, without wings, and with all the horror of a bare-shouldered creature; in the former case our shoulders are fledged, and we go through the same air and space without fear." When Keats wrote poetry he knew that he was writing poetry; naturally as it came to him, he never fancied that he was but expressing himself, or putting down something which his own mind had realised for its own sake. "The imagination," he tells us, in a phrase which has become famous, "may be compared to Adam's dream—he awoke and found it truth." Only Keats, unlike most other poets, never slept, or, it may be, never awoke. Poetry was literally almost everything to him, and he could deal with it so objectively, as with a thing outside himself, precisely because it was an almost bodily part of him, like the hand he wrote with. "If poetry," he said, in an axiom sent to his publisher, "comes not as naturally as the leaves to a tree, it had better not come at all." ...

"To load every rift with ore" that, to Keats, was the essential thing; and it meant to pack the verse with poetry, with the stuff of the imagination, so that every line should be heavy with it. For the rest, the poem is to come as best it may; only once, in *Lamia,* with any real skill in narrative, or any care for that skill. There, doubtless, it was the passing influence of Dryden which set him upon a kind of experiment, which he may

have done largely for the experiment's sake; doing it, of course, consummately. *Hyperion* was another kind of experiment; and this time, for all its splendour, less personal to his own style, or way of feeling. "I have given up *Hyperion,*" he writes; "there were too many Miltonic inversions in it—Miltonic verse cannot be written but in an artful, or, rather, artist's humour. I wish to give myself up to other sensations." ... It was just because Keats was so much, so exclusively, possessed by his own imagination, so exclusively concerned with the shaping of it into poetry, that all his poems seem to have been written for the sake of something else than their story, or thought, or indeed emotion. Even the odes are mental picture added to mental picture, separate stanza added to separate stanza, rather than the development of a thought which must express itself, creating its own form. Meditation brings to him no inner vision, no rapture of the soul; but seems to germinate upon the page in actual flowers and corn and fruit.

Keats' sense of form, if by form is meant perfection rather of outline than of detail, was by no means certain. Most poets work only in outline: Keats worked on every inch of his surface. Perhaps no poet has ever packed so much poetic detail into so small a space, or been so satisfied with having done so. Metrically, he is often slipshod; with all his genius for words, he often uses them incorrectly, or with but a vague sense of their meaning; even in the "Ode to a Nightingale" he will leave lines in which the inspiration seems suddenly to flag; such lines as

Though the dull brain perplexes and retards, which is nerveless; or
In ancient days by emperor and clown,

where the antithesis, logically justifiable, has the sound of an antithesis brought in for the sake of rhyme. In the "Ode on a Grecian Urn," two lines near the end seem to halt by the way, are not firm and direct in movement:

Thou shalt remain, in midst of other woe
Than ours, a friend to man, to whom thou
say'st.

That is slipshod writing, both as intellectual and as metrical structure; and it occurs in a poem which is one of the greatest lyrical poems in the language. We have only to look closely enough to see numberless faults of this kind in Keats; and yet, if we do not look very closely, we shall not see them; and, however closely we may look, and however many faults we may find, we shall end, as we began, by realising that they do not essentially matter. Why is this?

Wordsworth, who at his best may seem to be the supreme master of poetical style, is often out of key; Shelley, who at his best may seem to be almost the supreme singer, is often prosaic: Keats is never prosaic and never out of key. To read Wordsworth or Shelley, you must get in touch with their ideas, at least apprehend them; to read Keats you have only to surrender your senses to their natural happiness. You have to get at Shelley's or Wordsworth's point of view; but Keats has only the point of view of the sunlight. He cannot write without making pictures with his words, and every picture has its own atmosphere. Tennyson, who learnt so much from Keats, learnt from him something of his skill in making pictures; but Tennyson's pictures are chill, conscious of themselves, almost colourless. The pictures of Keats are all aglow with colour, not always very accurate painter's colour, but colour which captivates or overwhelms the senses.... That is why he can call up atmosphere by the mere bewitchment of a verse which seems to make a casual statement; because nothing, with him, can be a casual statement, nothing can be prosaic, or conceived of coldly, apart from that "principle of beauty in all things" which he tells us that he had always loved, and which to him was the principle of life itself.

Source: Arthur Symons, "John Keats," in *Monthly Review*, Vol. 5, No. 13, October 1901, pp. 139–55.

SOURCES

Barnard, John, "First Fruits or 'First Blights': A New Account of the Publishing History of Keats's *Poems* (1817)," *Romanticism*, Vol. 12, No. 2, 2006, pp. 71–101.

Bate, Walter Jackson, *John Keats*, Belknap, 1963, pp. 120–22.

Freud, Sigmund, *Beyond the Pleasure Principle*, in *The Standard Edition of the Complete Psychological Works of Sigmund Freud*, Hogarth, 1955, Vol. 18, pp. 7–64.

Iamblichus, *On the Mysteries*, translated by Emma C. Clark, John M. Dillon, and Jackson P. Hershbell, Society of Biblical Literature, 2003, pp. 120–29.

Jugurtha, Lillie, "Keats and Nature," in *English Language and Literature* Vol. 18, American University Studies, Fourth Series, Peter Lang, 1985, pp. 49–50.

Keats, John, *Complete Poems*, edited by Jack Stillinger, Belknap Press, 1978, pp. xvi–xvii, 54.

Moore, Thomas, *Odes of Anacreon Translated into English Verse with Notes* Vol. II, 10th ed., James Carpenter, 1820, pp. 168–171.

Motion, Andrew, *Keats*, Farrar, Straus & Giroux, 1997, pp. 132–33.

Osler, Alan, "Keats and a Classical Grasshopper," *Keats-Shelley Memorial Bulletin*, Vol. 24, 1973, pp. 25–26.

Wu, Duncan, "Keats and the 'Cockney School,'" *The Cambridge Companion to Keats*, edited by Susan J. Wolfson, Cambridge University Press, 2001, pp. 37–51.

FURTHER READING

Chandler, James, *England in 1819: The Politics of Literary Culture and the Case of Romantic Historicism*, University of Chicago Press, 1998.

This work places Keats and the Romantic movement in its political and historical framework.

Keats, John, *The Letters of John Keats*, 2 vols., edited by Hyder Edward Rollins, Cambridge University Press, 1958.

This collection includes all of Keats surviving personal correspondence and is the principle source for his biographical information and many of his aesthetic ideas.

Moffett, H. Y., "Applied Tactics in Teaching Literature: 'On the Grasshopper and the Cricket,'" in *English Journal*, Vol. 16, 1927, pp. 515–18.

Moffett presents a lesson plan for teaching sonnet composition that relies on, surprisingly not Keats's, but Hunt's poem as its example.

Ward, Aileen, *John Keats: The Making of a Poet*, rev. ed., Farrar, Strauss, and Giroux, 1986.

This biography of Keats focuses on the psychological aspects of Keats's life and work.

Remember

JOY HARJO

1983

Joy Harjo belongs to the second generation of the Native American Renaissance, a literary movement arising in the 1960s that includes distinguished writers such as Leslie Marmon Silko, N. Scott Momaday, and Simon Ortiz. Of Muskogee-Creek heritage as well as Cherokee, Irish, and French, Harjo is familiar with both Native American and white cultures. Raised in U.S. cities, with university degrees and an academic career, Harjo has nevertheless been nurtured primarily by her Muskogee tradition, which she fully embraces. She combines her knowledge of the visual arts, music, and language to depict the Native American perception of life as relevant to the present time. Her experimental poems fold the landscape of city nightlife, poverty, violence, and the bloody history of her people into the larger mythic presence of the natural landscape with its cycles, beauty, and forgiveness. She speaks of the spiritual journey to wholeness that everyone, not only Native Americans, must make.

Memory is a key theme in her work and is the main theme of the poem "Remember," from her third collection of poems, *She Had Some Horses* (1983). For Harjo, memory is a dynamic and passionate process that brings together past, present, and future. It links all life together, and all peoples. To lose the memory of the way individuals are connected is to lose one's humanity.

As a poet, Harjo is noted for her direct, deep emotion and lack of irony. She does not describe as much as she evokes, with words and images

Joy Harjo *(© Carlo Allegri | Getty Images)*

that derive from a sense of ceremony. A poet of attachment to place, her work is grounded in the American Southwest where she was born, yet Harjo is a traveler as well. Her poems view the mythic overlay of cities like Washington, D.C.; Albuquerque, New Mexico; and New Orleans, Louisiana; with the same magical perception she has of nature. Besides her own prolific artistic output in stories, poems, music, and film writing, Harjo has contributed much work to promoting native cultures through her organizational work, editing, and anthologizing of other Native women writers. A copy of the poem "Remember" can be found in Harjo's collection of her poems *How We Became Human: New and Selected Poems: 1975-2001*, published by W. W. Norton in 2002.

AUTHOR BIOGRAPHY

Harjo was born Joy Foster on May 9, 1951, in Tulsa, Oklahoma, to Allen and Wynema Foster. Her father was a full-blooded Muskogee (Creek), a construction worker who died of asbestos-related lung disease. Her mother was Cherokee, French,

and Irish, and served and cooked in truck stops. In 1970, Harjo took the surname of her Muskogee grandmother, Naomi Harjo, and became enrolled as a member of the Muskogee tribe. Harjo credits her great-aunt, Lois Harjo Ball, to whom she dedicated *She Had Some Horses*, with teaching her about her Indian identity.

Having won prizes in school for her visual art, at sixteen Harjo enrolled in the Institute of American Indian Arts in Santa Fe, New Mexico, hoping to be a painter, like her Muskogee aunt and grandmother. Harjo raised two children, Phil and Rainy Dawn, and worked as a waitress and nursing assistant while she pursued her education.

Harjo graduated from the University of New Mexico in 1976 with a B.A. in poetry after she decided to switch from art to writing. She received her M.F.A. in creative writing from the University of Iowa in 1978 and has held teaching positions at the Institute of American Indian Arts, Santa Fe Community College, Arizona State University, University of Colorado, University of New Mexico, and University of California, Los Angeles. Important influences on her poetry are Leslie Marmon Silko, Simon Ortiz, Galway Kinnell, Maridel Le Sueur, Audre Lorde, and Pablo Neruda.

Books of her poetry and stories include *The Last Song* (1975), *What Moon Drove Me to This?* (1979), *She Had Some Horses* (1983), *In Mad Love and War* (1990), *The Woman Who Fell from the Sky* (1994), *A Map to the Next World: Poems and Tales* (2000), and *How We Became Human: New and Selected Poems: 1975-2001* (2002). With Gloria Bird, she edited an important anthology called *Reinventing the Enemy's Language: Contemporary Native Women's Writings of North America* (1997). Harjo contributed poetic prose to photographs by Stephen Strom in *Secrets from the Center of the World* (1989) and wrote a children's book titled *The Good Luck Cat* (2000). She has been an editor for literary journals and a member of the Native American Public Broadcasting Consortium Board of Directors as well as a narrator and scriptwriter for educational television.

Harjo plays tenor and soprano saxophone to accompany readings of her poems on her first music CD, *Letter from the End of the 20th Century* (1997), with her band, Poetic Justice. Other CDs include *Native Joy for Real* (2004), *She Had Some Horses* (2006), and *Winding Through the Milky Way* (2008).

Selected awards include the American Book Award from the Before Columbus Foundation; the William Carlos Williams Award; the American Indian Distinguished Achievement in the Arts Award; and the Lifetime Achievement Award from the Native Writers Circle of the Americas.

POEM TEXT

Remember the sky you were born under,
know each of the star's stories.
Remember the moon, know who she is.
Remember the sun's birth at dawn, that is the
strongest point of time. Remember sundown   5
and the giving away to night.
Remember your birth, how your mother
struggled
to give you form and breath. You are evidence
of
her life, and her mother's, and hers.
Remember your father. He is your life, also.   10
Remember the earth whose skin you are:
red earth, black earth, yellow earth, white earth
brown earth, we are earth.
Remember the plants, trees, animal life who all
have their
tribes, their families, their histories, too. Talk
to them,   15
listen to them. They are alive poems.
Remember the wind. Remember her voice. She
knows the
origin of this universe.
Remember you are all people and all people
are you.   20
Remember you are this universe and this
universe is you.
Remember all is in motion, is growing, is you.
Remember language comes from this.
Remember the dance language is, that life is.   25
Remember.

POEM SUMMARY

Line 1

The poem repeats the title word sixteen times. The repetition becomes a chant and a ceremony, reconnecting the individual to the cosmos. It seems to be addressed by a Native American speaker who remembers her heritage, telling her story to another person who may have forgotten this shared identity. The second person point of view is used throughout as a direct address from the speaker of the poem to the listener.

Remembering who one is in relation to the universe is a key concept in Native American tradition. One does not exist apart or cut off from the forces of nature. The place where one was born is particularly important. The place of birth is not only a particular geographical location but is also the earth itself, indicated by the reference to the sky overhead.

Line 2

The stars or constellations for Native Americans, as for many cultures, are spiritual beings. They bring a spiritual influence to the lives of the people on the earth. The speaker exhorts the listener to be aware of the personalities of these sacred beings and know how to relate to them.

Line 3

The moon is referred to as a female that must be remembered. In tribal traditions, the moon is a deity and her cycles govern planting times, harvest, hunting, and especially ceremonies. Time in Native American cultures is reckoned by the sun, moon, and stars.

Line 4

Dawn is the most powerful time of day when the sun rises for a new day. It is when traditional peoples pray, worship, and perform ceremonies. The sun is the life-giver and has particular meaning for native peoples as it is the symbol for the Great Spirit.

Line 5

Equally important is the sunset, a time when another transition takes place. Sunset also has a special feeling to it. The line break at the end makes the listener wait to hear what that feeling is.

Line 6

Line 6 completes the thought of line 5. One must let go of the day at the end and let the night begin. The poem helps the reader to remember the rhythms of nature, to be in tune with all things.

Line 7

The speaker says to remember the moment of birth and the mother who gave birth through effort. In the same way, the earth is the mother who gives birth to all humans and feeds and shelters them. This implies a sacrifice on the part of the mother, and therefore, the children owe her honor and gratitude. To emphasize the role of mothers in Native American society, the poet herself changed her last name to her grandmother's.

MEDIA ADAPTATIONS

- *She Had Some Horses*, an audio recording for compact disc (Mekko Productions, 2006), features Joy Harjo reading the poems from her book of the same name, including "Remember." Three additional tracks on the CD provide musical versions of poems, including "She Had Some Horses." It is also available as an MP3 download at *PayPlay.FM*.

- *Letter From the End of the Twentieth Century* (1997) is a CD audio recording of Harjo reading a selection of poems from various collections to the musical accompaniment of Poetic Justice, her all Native American band, produced by Mekko Productions (re-released in 2006). She also plays tenor and soprano saxophone on the recording. The recording is also available as an audio cassette or MP3 download.

- *Native Joy for Real* is Harjo's experimental CD produced by Mekko Productions in 2004, with the poet debuting as a singer using her poems and jazz and folk accompaniment. It is also available as an MP3 download.

- *Eagle Song*, is Harjo's music video of her reading of the poem by the same name to images of Native Americans today. It was produced by Mekko Productions in 2002 and is available at http://www.youtube.com.

- *The Nearly Unbearable Grace of the Poetry of Joy Harjo* is a music video of Harjo performing her poetry, recorded by the University of California Television, 1997. It is available at http://www.youtube.com.

Line 8

This line continues the thought about the mother and what she gives to the child: her essence, gifts, and traits. The child is a testimony to her. The human mother or Mother Earth gives one the body to live in and breathe in.

Line 9

Line 9 refers again to the matrilineal (maternal) descent of a human being. The mother, grandmother, and great-grandmother are remembered and honored as the bestowers of life, tradition, and place in the world.

Line 10

Line 10 includes the father, who also gave the listener life. Parents receive great respect in tribal life, for they are the roots of family, the teachers of the next generation. They must remember what happened before them and pass it on to the child.

Line 11

Line 11 implies the intimate relationship of human beings and earth. We are merely the outer covering of Mother Earth. The image implies that we can feel earth's joy and pain, and she can feel ours. We are her outer membrane.

Line 12

The people of earth are one, no matter their skin color, just as the earth holds different colors. We must remember the unity instead of the differences.

Line 13

Line 13 again asserts that people everywhere are the same. Native American religions stress the equality of all life and the consequences of forgetting that we are all children of the earth.

Line 14

We must remember the animal and plant kingdoms for they also share the earth and are the children of earth. The line break at the end of line 14 creates suspense about the animal and plant kingdoms, giving the reader time to remember why they deserves respect.

Line 15

The thought of line 14 is completed as the speaker brings up the idea that other species also have families, tribes, and stories. This idea of communicating to other species and nature is part of Native American ceremony and religion. All life on earth is sacred.

Line 16

The speaker instructs the listener to not only speak to nature but also listen to it. Other creatures are like poems that we can learn from. They are our teachers.

Line 17

We should remember the wind, who is female, a mother who wants to give us not only sustenance but also wisdom. The secret she has to tell is saved for the next line through a line break.

Line 18

This line explains what kind of secrets the wind carries. She knows how the universe began. The wind knows what a person really needs to know; that is, where we came from and where we are going. Nature is the most valuable school, our teacher about the essence of life.

Line 19

The speaker proclaims another remembrance: we are everyone. This point reinforces lines 12 and 13. There is a commonality among all people as children of the earth.

Line 20

Line 20 completes the meaning of line 19 but repeats and emphasizes through direct address to the listener to remember that he or she is one with everyone else; we all belong to one another.

Line 21

We must remember that we are also identical to the total universe. Each person is a microcosm, or a replica of the whole cosmos. The unity of the universe is apparent at every scale, from atomic to galactic.

Line 22

The entire cosmos is likewise identical with the individual. This interconnectivity and identity implies that each part must be respected as representing and containing the whole.

Line 23

The speaker reminds us that nothing is static. Everything is constantly changing and evolving. This alludes to the idea of cycles and change. Everything has its purpose, its moment, and must be honored and accepted.

Line 24

The speaker says that language itself comes from this constant motion and evolution.

Line 25

Language is the dance of life. The speaker does not think of language as separate from nature. In regard to the nature of language, lines 24 and 25 refer to lines 15–18, insisting that all living things have voices and that humans need to listen to the language of other beings and species. Language has a unifying and creative purpose among all species.

Line 26

The last line is the repeated title. It is a command; the speaker has performed a ceremony to renew life by remembering, as the listener should now go forth and do so as well.

THEMES

Memory

Remembering is an important act for Native Americans for connecting to their own lives and traditions. The voice in the poem is that of an elder or teacher. One imagines a grandmother passing on her wisdom. She does not refer to the way things are in the white world or in modern civilization where humans have a seeming amnesia about who they are and what they are doing on earth. Yet this Native American speaker could be a mother or grandmother to the entire human race at the present time, telling it something vital it has forgotten.

The poem gently shakes the listener, repeating over and over to wake up and remember who he or she is. She does not say to remember a particular set of rules or facts. The reader must perform a more important act of remembering, such as knowing the sky (line 1), the stars (line 2), the moon and sun (lines 3–4), his or her mother and father (lines 7–10), the earth (line 11), people of all races (lines 12 and 13), and animals and plants (lines 14 and 15). One is told to do this to fulfill one's place in the scheme of things and one's duty to each other and the earth. One must remember how to communicate with all these beings (lines 13–14).

The poem does not set up a tension between remembrance and forgetfulness. Neither does it state what happens when we do not remember who we are. The speaker's view is seemingly naive, as though spoken from an earlier or simpler time where what she speaks is the obvious truth. Most readers of this poem, including many Native Americans, live in a complex urban world that has forgotten the earth and sky. One cannot remember oneself in such a setting. The poem refers instead to the slower and eternal cycles of nature, the only proper context for memory.

TOPICS FOR FURTHER STUDY

- Prepare an oral report explaining the parallels between the values of Native American cultures and the main tenets of the science of ecology. How do both view human relationships to the land? How does scientific study of ecology validate the Native American worldview? Give specific examples and use PowerPoint slides, displays, or other visual aids to make the parallels easy to follow.

- Research one Native American tribe using both Internet and library resources. Explain the history of the tribe, mention any famous leaders, and summarize their cultural values. Follow-up with information about this tribe today and record your findings in a research paper.

- Create a presentation on the biography of one historical Native American hero or heroine (such as Sacajawea or Geronimo). Use visual aids like a photograph or drawing of the person, pictures of the location, or photographs of the life of that tribe. Also, use any written documents, such as speeches or letters. Find out if there are any documentaries or films on this figure, and use clips of the film as an aid to discuss in class. Has the person's life been romanticized or distorted? Are the facts known? Have new facts come to light about the individual's life? How was this person viewed in his or her own time? How is he or she viewed today?

- Read the young-adult appropriate *Grandmothers of the Light: A Medicine Woman's Sourcebook* (1991) by Paula Gunn Allen. Write a paper or give a presentation that discusses the memories from this poem that can be found to be important in the myths and legends of the book.

- Read the Native American novel *House Made of Dawn* by N. Scott Momaday (1968). View the 1972 film of the book scripted by Momaday, using a distinctly Native American point of view. Discuss how both novel and film use images and language differently than European American stories. Which version is more effective as an introduction for non-natives? In a brief presentation, discuss your conclusions, giving examples from the film and book.

- Read poems aloud in a group from Harjo's *She Had Some Horses*, including "Remember." Then play Harjo's CD *She Had Some Horses* with her reading and accompaniment. Lead a class discussion focusing on how the CD changes your experience of the poems.

- View Harjo's performance of her poetry, "The Nearly Unbearable Grace of the Poetry of Joy Harjo," recorded by the University of California Television, 1997, available at http://www.youtube.com. Write a research paper on the oral tradition of poetry and record your impressions of how Harjo uses the power of that tradition in her live performances.

The purpose of this poem is not to have readers remember their mistakes or feel guilty for their present way of life, but to remember the way it is supposed to be. The speaker is the authoritative teacher, and yet she does not impose a certain doctrine on readers. She tells them to remember for themselves the way things naturally are, as for instance, at dawn, or at one's birth, the absolute beginning of existence.

The truth can be lost in the hurry of the modern age. However, the truth can be heard from anyplace or anyone, for everything and everyone has a common origin. The wind can tell us, the animals and the moon, or people of different races and traditions. The speaker emphasizes that everything has a voice to remind us, but we have to listen. Everything is a poem like the author's poem, a sort of ceremony of remembrance. By

Earth *(Image copyright MaxFX, 2009. Used under license from Shutterstock.com)*

participating in the poem, the reader begins to remember.

Earth as Mother

For Native Americans, the earth is sacred and treated as one's own mother. In the poem, the audience is reminded to respect one's mother for giving birth, which is a sacrifice (lines 7 and 8). The line of mothers goes back as a heritage and tradition (lines 8 and 9). In the same way, earth should be regarded as a mother and remembered as part of the human tradition. The wind, for instance, has a female voice that will tell us the secret of the universe if we listen to her. Earth has all the knowledge and help that we need, and the various species on the planet each tells their story and gives their medicine or gifts (lines 14–16).

A mother loves all her children, and the speaker is clear that all the skin colors of human races are a part of the mother's own skin (lines 11–13). The plants and animals also belong to her as her tribes (line 15). Everything is in motion and growing, and the mother principle is that which integrates everything harmoniously (line 23). Mother is the unifying force (lines 19–22), represented by the voice of the speaker who is reminding the listener of the equality of every species. Mother, in both human guise and the guise of the earth, is the one who gives the child its breath and form of the body in the womb (lines 7 and 8). Though the father is naturally part of this process, the mother's role is highlighted as primal. This insistence of a loving mother taking care of all life makes the listener secure in the orderly structure of things, confident in knowing one's place.

Interconnection of All Living Things

The unity of all life is a major theme of the poem, stated in many different ways. First, individuals are supposed to remember their relation to the sky, stars, sun, and moon. Then, they are reminded to go back to the beginning, where they were originally connected—to mother and father, the earth, plants, and animals. They are told that they are able to speak and listen, not only to other races of people but also to other species and creatures (lines 14–16). The anxiety prevalent in modern literature with its cry for knowledge about the human condition is thus answered by the speaker in terms of nature. Nature has the answers, if one knows how to be still and listen. The wind, for instance, is alive, and could tell one the origin of the universe (lines 17 and 18). This is not strange, for if every individual is the universe in small (lines 21 and 22), then one can easily find out the meaning of life, because it is within. The truth of life is never far away. By being simple and going back to the beginning, by looking and listening, one can remember and reconnect. The speaker asserts that interconnection is the true state of life, not something difficult to experience.

Native American View of Life

The poem presents a complete and condensed wisdom of life in a simple format, like a chant, which is easy to remember. The repetition brings the listener constantly back to the main point of remembering who one is. Harjo honors the contribution of Native American traditions by stating them directly and succinctly in a sort of formula. The poem does not refute, deny, denounce, or become ironic about the history between whites and Native Americans or modern life. It simply asserts in an authoritative way the simple truths of native teachings.

The Native American beliefs stated in the poem are as follows. First, parents are honored, especially mothers and Mother Earth, for giving the gift of life and the body. Second, the poem posits a democratic view in that all beings on earth are equal in terms of deserving respect. Third, all life is interrelated and interdependent—an ecological point of view. Fourth, communication is important between people and species for maintaining the health and unity of life. Fifth, every creature in nature is a teacher, giving its gifts and wisdom. Sixth, life is unified, which can be known by experiencing and remembering that the universe is not a stranger—it is within all individuals. Seventh, language is as sacred as the earth, for it is the essence of ceremony. The poem, then, becomes like a nature's poem, a way to give back, to celebrate and unify.

STYLE

Native American Chant

Native American ceremony is the basis of most modern Native American poetry, either directly or indirectly, because it embraces a certain perception of the world. Native American tribal ceremonies use formal structures of incantation, song, dance, prayer, visual symbols, and gestures to restore wholeness to the land and community. These oral traditions were intended to integrate the community with the cosmic forces. The ceremonies, such as the "Navajo Night Chant" used for healing, were sacred and performed at specific times and places. Paula Gunn Allen's poem, "The Turning Point," for instance, creates a ceremonial moment where she learns to turn within to find her place in the world.

The ceremonial chant is an underlying structure in "Remember," which is constructed as though it could be used in a ceremony to urge listeners to remember their spiritual tradition. Like ceremonies, it uses repetition to create a hypnotic sense of union with nature, naming the stars, sun, moon, and wind as divine personalities rather than images. The lines are emphatic, like drumbeats or heartbeats, moving rhythmically along like a dance to the end. There is not so much a sense of development of thought as a circular shape, like a wheel, giving all the statements equal value. The oral forms are appropriate for reflecting the Native American way of knowing or remembering life as sacred and interconnected. The structure of Native American literature thus does not rely on conflict and resolution or linear movement. It depicts and fosters relationship and celebrates the eternal cycles.

Native American Myth

Traditional tribal stories of creation and the interaction of gods, humans, animals, and plants are often fused with modern storytelling in Native American fiction and poetry. Harjo does this in her poetic short story "The Woman Who Fell From the Sky," where she melds a city love story (Johnny and Lila meet in a Safeway parking lot) with an Iroquois creation myth. A myth is a story that uses symbols as poems do. It gives meaning to the ordinary world by viewing it in an eternal dimension. Lila is thus seen not as a woman, but as the creator of the world coming down from the sky, bringing salvation to Johnny.

A myth demands the emotional or spiritual participation of the listener rather than intellectual understanding. In "Remember," there is a mythic feel of returning to origins, to the beginning of creation. One must know the stories of the creation, and the stories of stars, the sun, the moon, where one was born, mother earth, and the secret the wind knows about the beginning. As in mythic storytelling, the poem is direct and innocent in perspective. It is not trying to be ironic or personal. It asks the listener to remember what is always true rather than what is only accidental, partial, or temporary. In this way, one remembers the important connections of life, beyond the daily confusions. Like myths, the poem places the listener in relationship to cosmic forces. The speaker assumes a communal memory of nature when she brings up the tradition of mothers (lines 8 and 9) and language (lines 24 and 25).

Native American Tribal Poetry

Traditional tribal songs assume the interconnectedness of all life, using their language, music, and rhythm to preserve unity and harmony. They are chanted or sung, usually suggestive and economical, with few words and images, thus short in length. There are songs for all occasions—religious songs, love songs, hunting songs, lullabies, healing songs, social songs, and songs for spirits or deities. The language is used in a magical or incantatory way to communicate with supernatural forces and bring about change. The songs are rhythmic and hypnotic with a lot of repetition. They generally begin without introduction and thus assume communal understanding. Musical instruments are often used to accompany the song, such as drums, rattles, and whistles. An example is the Nez Perce song, "The Bear Hunter," sung when a bear is killed, to propitiate (appease) its spirit.

"Remember" has characteristics of the tribal song. It is short, suggestive, and uses its language economically in a communal way to remember the way life is. One can feel the dancing in the poem and imagine musical accompaniment. The words are meant to be a magical command, transforming the listener who participates in the act of remembering with the community. Though a modern poem, it is given a traditional feel by not revealing the specifics of a particular time period. It is the voice of an elder to the people.

Contemporary Native American Poetry

Harjo graduated with an M.F.A. in creative writing, so "Remember" appears to be a modern poem with its free verse, dramatic line breaks, and carefully crafted details—the color of the earth, the mother birthing, and the animals and plants. Many of Harjo's poems do include the challenging contemporary conditions of Native Americans, such as her poem "The Woman Hanging From the Thirteenth Floor Window," a poem written about the hard life of Native Americans in Chicago, Illinois. Other Native American poets, such as the Acoma Pueblo poet Simon Ortiz, in "What Is a Poem?," also blend details of life today with a characteristic Native American point of view.

"Remember" does not speak directly of Native American dispossession. Instead, it tries to reconnect with the positive and ongoing native perception of life, explaining it to a new generation. The fact that the poet speaks this song in English to a wider audience than just her Muskogee people places the poem within contemporary poetry rather than traditional poetry. "Remember" is contemporary because the act of remembering is ongoing. It is not about the past so much as the present survival of her people and their way of life.

Native American literature in English before the 1970s was often imitative of Western genres and points of view (such as the sentimental poems of Cherokee John Rollin Ridge's *Poems*, 1868). The aim of Native American poets in the last forty years has been to reassert their roots, beliefs, and customs, bringing out their unique perspective on modern American life. In spite of the fact that Native American authors are writing in English and are educated in English-speaking universities, their poetry retains the traditional context of language used for ritual rather than intellectual purposes. In other words, language remains magical and mythic in its core. Many Native American writers also retain the performance aspect of oral tribal poetry by performing their poems with music, like Harjo and Ortiz do. "Remember" is like the poems of other Native American writers today who render experience directly without the ironic filters and distancing personae of modernist poets. Figures in Native American poetry often have a mythic quality, such as Harjo's character, Noni Daylight, in "Someone Talking."

HISTORICAL CONTEXT

The Native Americans before European Colonization of the Americas

According to some theories, the indigenous people living in the Americas had migrated there some

COMPARE
&
CONTRAST

- **1980s:** Native American authors write in English because tribal languages are lost to them through the one hundred year suppression of native language learning in U.S. schools.

  Today: After the passage of the Native American Languages Act of 1990, native languages cannot legally be suppressed. They are taught in schools and universities, and writers and performers return to their native tongues for self-expression and ceremony.

- **1980s:** Kenneth Lincoln's book, *Native American Renaissance*, announces the beginning of a rebirth of Native American culture and art in modern America.

  Today: Native American artists, such as Momaday, Silko, and Harjo, are sought after for their books and views that weave together tradition and the contemporary scene, bringing a healing perspective to modern problems.

- **1980s:** Native American women struggle with poverty and anonymity on reservations or in cities.

  Today: Native American women's voices are being heard in public—in literature anthologies, organizational work, the media, universities and schools, politics, and on the reservations, as in some traditional tribal councils.

- **1980s:** Native Americans are the most economically disadvantaged group in the United States. Some tribes open casinos on reservations to earn tribal money, though this is controversial and causes legal battles.

  Today: New efforts are made to help Native Americans achieve greater economic independence, such as through the Northwest Area Foundation, organized in 2004, to provide funding and training for Native American businesses and organizations.

---

twelve thousand years ago from Europe and Asia on a land bridge across the Bering Strait. The indigenous people themselves have other versions of their origins in their oral traditions. When the Europeans came to the Americas, they found hundreds of ethnic groups there, each with their own nation, language, and culture.

European Exploration and Colonization of the Americas

Early Spanish explorers in the fifteenth and sixteenth centuries such as Christopher Columbus, Juan Ponce de Léon, and Hernando de Soto, brought back tales of the wealth of the Americas to Europe, prompting many European expeditions for plunder or settlement. There seemed room for all at first. Early contacts between Europeans and natives were friendly, with Native Americans helping Europeans through the hard winters by giving them food and teaching them how to plant crops.

From the sixteenth to the nineteenth century, more and more Europeans (English, Dutch, Spanish, French, and Portuguese) came to claim the land, and the natives were seen as a threat or a problem that had to be exterminated so white settlers could civilize the continent. The indigenous people were largely treated as heathens who had no right to the land. The Europeans not only warred on the indigenous Americans with guns, against which the natives could not protect themselves, but they also took their lands by force or guile (treaties that were not honored). The indigenous populations also suffered from contagious European diseases such as small pox, measles, and bubonic plague, for which they had no immunity. Europeans took advantage of intertribal rivalries to enslave Indians and to use them in their own wars. The dramatic decline of native populations during this time from disease alone caused many tribes to move or reorganize.

The Europeans brought horses and guns, thus changing tribal life, especially on the plains where tribes could move around quickly while hunting buffalo. Though there was some fruitful trade among indigenous Americans and Europeans, the influence of the whites, such as the introduction of alcohol, was largely negative and destructive to the native cultures. There is some evidence that the U.S. founders borrowed democratic ideas from the tribal cultures where freedom was prized. The democratic model of government of the Iroquois Confederation of Nations was known to the founding fathers of the United States.

The Wild West

In the nineteenth century, as the settlers from Europe were pushing the indigenous people from the American east coast into the interior of the country, Native Americans began to be romanticized by European and American writers as a noble but vanishing people (as in James Fenimore Cooper's *The Last of the Mohicans*). In this view, Native Americans were not seen so much as subhuman heathens but as noble savages, close to nature. They were vanishing, but their innocent ways could teach Europeans something about the new continent, which, in the march of progress, would inevitably be taken over by the colonizing races. This sentimental view of Native Americans did as much harm as the previous view, for it denied their existence, culture, and right to the land.

This was the tragic time of the treaties that were broken or falsely negotiated between the U.S. government's Bureau of Indian Affairs and various tribes. When settlers wanted to move onto land that had been reserved for indigenous people, the Indians were essentially betrayed. Westward expansion and the passage of the Indian Removal Act in 1830, which relocated 100,000 Native Americans from eastern to western lands, led to Indian Resistance, or the Indian Wars. Native Americans were portrayed as warlike in the press, but many tribes sought peace. If they fought, it was for survival. Harjo's great-great-grandfather, Monahwee, led the Red Stick War of the Creeks against President Andrew Jackson. Harjo's people, the Muskogee-Creek, were one of the five southern tribes forced to leave their homeland. The Creeks were removed from Alabama to Oklahoma in 1832. An image of her ancestors walking to Oklahoma occurs in Harjo's poem, "Protocol." Similarly, thousands of Cherokees perished on the shameful Trail of Tears in 1838, a thousand-mile relocation and movement of Native Americans from their homelands to Indian Territory (present-day Oklahoma). On the march, many Native Americans died of exposure, disease, and starvation.

Assimilation

The reservations of the 1800s were not the sole government solution to what was known as the Indian Problem. Assimilation was a policy meant to force Native Americans into mainstream culture. After the Civil War, boarding schools run by Christian missionaries were set up to educate Native American children and convert them to Christianity. Children were taken from their parents on the reservations. They were not allowed to speak their native language nor practice their religion. Native Americans began to be granted U.S. citizenship in the nineteenth century, and it was made universal by the Indian Citizenship Act of 1924, though they were not allowed to vote in local elections.

In 1894 all Indian religion was banned by the Bureau of Indian Affairs, even on the reservations, and Indians were prosecuted for singing or performing religious dances. The final attempt to assimilate the native population came with the Indian termination policy in the 1950s and 1960s. The policy was an attempt to move all natives off the reservation and relocate them to cities, thus disbanding their tribal groups and taking their land and control of its natural resources. Therefore, the U.S. government no longer recognized tribal sovereignty. With the example of the black civil rights movement of the 1960s, Native American activist groups were formed and fought the Indian termination policy. In 1975 the Indian Self-Determination and Education Assistance Act allowed Native Americans to form their own governing bodies and remain on reservations. In 1978 the American Indian Freedom of Religion Act was passed. Even so, the United States still does not recognize Indian nations as sovereign nations, and Native American land is manages by the Bureau of Indian Affairs.

Modern-day Native Americans

Although they once constituted 100 percent of the population of the Americas, Native Americans are only one half of one percent of the modern U.S. population. In the twenty-first

Ballet dancer *(Image copyright AYAKOVLEVdotCOM, 2009. Used under license from Shutterstock.com)*

century, many indigenous peoples are located primarily as groups in California, Arizona, and Oklahoma, due to the Indian removal policies. Modern-day Native Americans are usually of mixed blood, and many live urban lives, so it is difficult to establish legal identity as a tribe with the government in order to obtain tribal rights. The high rate of alcoholism, poverty, mental illness, heart disease, and drug addiction among Native Americans testifies to the ongoing hardship they face to preserve their traditions and identity. Some states are still attempting to pass laws of termination to take the land of Native Americans. Today, different tribes have their own rules for formally enlisting members. However, U.S. federal law requires that an individual claiming Native American heritage must have one-quarter native blood, which must be registered by a Certificate of Degree of Indian Blood for Bureau of Indian Affairs scholarship eligibility and other benefits.

The Native American Literary Renaissance in the 1970s and 1980s, in which Harjo was involved, made Americans more aware of Native American history and contributions. Despite attempts to eradicate Indian language and culture, original Native American languages are still spoken in the United States, and the oral tradition still exists. Though many Native Americans feel they are struggling to survive, they are proud that their culture has not died. Some tribes have built museums and cultural centers to share their culture and traditions.

CRITICAL OVERVIEW

Harjo's third book of poems, *She Had Some Horses*, containing her poem "Remember," was published in 1983. Kenneth Lincoln's book *Native American Renaissance*, was published that same year, bringing attention to the promising new generation of Native American writers arising after N. Scott Momaday's 1968 Pulitzer Prize winning novel, *House Made of Dawn*, was published. This new generation included Harjo, Paula Gunn Allen, James Welch, Simon Ortiz, Leslie Marmon Silko, Linda Hogan, Wendy Rose, Joseph Bruchac, Barney Bush, and Louise Erdrich.

These writers established the foundation for Native American Studies in universities, contributing their fine creative work and criticism. Harjo's writing was brought to attention with her first book of collected poems, *The Last Song*, in 1975. From the publication of *What Moon Drove Me to This?* in 1979, Harjo's poetry received acclaim from critics. Her fame grew with each volume, and *She Had Some Horses*, her third book, sealed her place as a leader in this new movement.

In a review of *She Had Some Horses* for *Library Journal*, Brian Swann states that Harjo "possesses a great lyric gift and a religious nature.... The result is a book of much beauty and power." G. E. Murray, in a review for *Chicago*, describes the book saying, "This is a haunting poetry of body, blood, and being ... loaded with intriguing and brilliant sparks that ignite both heart and mind." Rayna Green, in a contribution to *Ms.* magazine, admires Harjo for "an intense passion for survival.... This is a book for reclaiming power, for awakening." Jan Clausen shares similar views as other critics in her lengthy review for *Women's Review of Books*, but finds *She Had Some Horses* uneven.

Clausen states that she is "puzzled by the way the poems are organized" and objects to the love poems set among the "superb incantatory selections" like "I Give You Back." Clausen praises "the structural rigor and mythic intensity" of the best poems, such as, "She Had Some Horses." Overall Clausen marvels at Harjo's spirituality that does not sacrifice the political and material world. In a review of *She Had Some Horses* and Harjo's other works, *Village Voice* contributor Dan Bellm asserts, "Joy Harjo is now writing a visionary poetry that is among the very best we have," noting an "occasional diffuseness" and "a way of stating connections in a poem."

In July 1990, Margaret Randall in the *Women's Review of Books* notes that Harjo's poetry is being widely anthologized and that she is a popular performer at public readings. Randall, like Bellm, praises *In Mad Love and War* as surpassing the promise of *She Had Some Horses.* Even more enthusiasm met *The Woman Who Fell From the Sky*, as Pat Monaghan reviewed it for *Booklist* (November, 1994) saying: "Harjo fulfills her earlier promise in a stunning, mature, wholehearted, musical series of poems." Harjo's reputation continued to build with *A Map to the Next World*, reviewed by William Pitt Root in *Whole Earth* (Fall 2000). He says it is "the best collection yet" and says Harjo "never raised a shield of irony or cynicism to prevent a direct hit to the heart."

CRITICISM

Susan K. Andersen

Andersen is an instructor of English literature and composition. In this essay she considers the way Joy Harjo's poetry, including "Remember," can be read as a healing ceremony.

Native American poets, no matter their tribal affiliation, come from a collective awareness that is fundamentally different from the heritage of European American poets. Their assumptions about life and art are reflected in their work and scholarship. American Indian poetry arises from an oral tradition in which nature is perceived as fully alive, and language is used as a means to communicate with all beings, even the nonhuman landscape. Language is not descriptive but evocative and charged with energy. Harjo's poems, songs, and stories, like the works of other Native Americans

THIS RELATIONSHIP OF LAND, LIFE, AND PEOPLE IS REENACTED IN HARJO'S POEMS, SO THAT THE LISTENER MAY PARTICIPATE IN CEREMONIES OF RESTORATION AND WHOLENESS."

authors, are ceremonial in structure and purpose. She believes her poetry has the power to heal and change.

In an interview for the Public Broadcasting Service with Bill Moyers for the radio program *Power of the Word*, Harjo describes her poetic language as coming from a different place than the language she hears around her, calling the source a "mythic place." Jim Ruppert, in *American Indian Quarterly*, identifies mythic space as "an older, more eternal world where spirit, physical reality, and the individual merge." Myth refers to the creation stories and hero stories of ancient peoples that tell the place of humans in the universe. They are stories of a magical time when gods, humans, and all nature could communicate with each other. Harjo explains that for the Native American, this mythic space and time is not in the past, but is an ongoing perception of the world as sacred.

Native American poets find a lack of mythic space in American culture, a lack of understanding in public awareness of the sacredness of all beings. As Ruppert explains, for these poets, "The mythic realm is always present—masked by the mundane world, ready to be pierced by the artist or visionary." Harjo sees the mythic dimension of the ordinary world, as for instance, in her poem "Moonlight." The moon is seen in a city setting, but it is not an invented symbol for something else. It is perceived as a presence, a living and sacred woman, whom she sees coming out of a bar in Albuquerque, New Mexico. In *The Sacred Hoop: Recovering the Feminine in American Indian Traditions*, Paula Gunn Allen comments on the mythic personification of the moon in this poem: "the intelligent consciousness of all things, is the identifying characteristic of American Indian tribal poetry."

In an interview published in *Joy Harjo: The Spiral of Memory: Interviews* with Angels Carabi,

WHAT DO I READ NEXT?

- *Code Talker* by Joseph Bruchac (2005) is a widely recommended young-adult novel with exciting drama by an Abenaki writer. It tells the story of a Navajo boy, raised in a school where his native tongue was forbidden, as he joins the Marines in World War II and becomes one of the Code Talkers, the Indian team that invented a Navajo code the Nazis and Japanese could not crack.

- *Dark Dude* (2008) by Pulitzer Prize winning author Oscar Hijuelos is a young-adult novel about Rico, a Cuban teen who runs away from a drug life in Harlem, New York, to a farm in Wisconsin to discover his Latino identity.

- *Native American Almanac: A Portrait of Native America Today* (1998) by Arlene Hirschfelder and Martha Kreipe de Montano, presents an overview of past history and present Native American life, including facts on reservations, laws, treaties, demographics, language, education, religion, sports, and media. Hirschfelder is a Native American scholar, and de Montano is a Native American manager at the Smithsonian's Museum of the American Indian.

- *Spirits of the Earth: A Guide to Native American Nature Symbols, Stories, and Ceremonies* by Bobby Lake-Thom, published by Plume in 1997, is an illustrated guide by a Native healer with a Karuk, Seneca, and Cherokee descent. He explains the symbolic significance of animals, the medicine wheel, native rituals and dreams, and retells popular traditional stories. The book will appeal to readers of any age.

- *The People Shall Continue*, by Simon Ortiz, originally published by Children's Book Press in 1977 and reprinted in paperback in 1988, is a history poetically told in Native American voice for young readers, from creation to the present day. Ortiz is an Acoma Pueblo poet, and this book is a perfect complement to Harjo's poem "Remember."

- *The Woman Who Fell From the Sky* (1996) includes Harjo's reinvented myth of the Iroquois creation story set in the city, along with pieces that she often performs, including "The Myth of Blackbirds," "Letter from the End of the Twentieth Century," and "Reconciliation."

- Chickasaw poet Linda Hogan's *The Book of Medicines* (1993) focuses on the theme of healing. These poems use the image of skin as the site of both pain and healing, reconciling Native American knowledge with contemporary life.

Harjo explains, "A common belief to all tribal people is that the world is alive; absolutely everything is connected.... The supernatural world is ingrained in our culture and it is another way of knowing." This view is common in the sacred stories of every mythology, for instance, Greek or Norse, though today such stories are seen as primitive. Scorned as juvenile or superstitious, the mythical and magical perception of the world eroded with the rise of the scientific paradigm in western civilization. This is a tragic loss according to Harjo; she believes it is part of her responsibility as a Native woman to keep the sacred memory alive, not only for her own people, but for everyone. In an interview for the *North Dakota Quarterly* with Abenaki poet Joseph Bruchac, she asserts "All people are originally tribal, but Europeans seem to feel like they're separated from that, or they've forgotten it." She exhorts the listener in "Remember" to understand the connection and unity of all life. She tells Bruchac that remembering means "not just going back, but occurring right now, and also future occurrence."

Memory is especially the province of women. American tribal women had great responsibility. They were storytellers and artists, keeping the traditions alive for the next generation. They were the clan mothers, the councilors who advised in major decisions. They were the direct representatives of Mother Earth and the female Creator who was known as Thought Woman, Spider Woman, or Corn Maiden. Identity was counted in many tribes from the female descent. Harjo tells Laura Coltelli in "The Circular Dream: Interview with Joy Harjo" in *Joy Harjo: The Spiral of Memory: Interviews* that she did not chose to be the memory of her people; it was chosen for her. The ancestors live in her: "when I write there is an old Creek within me that often participates." Her visions, however, often contain "the larger tribal continental memory and the larger human memory, global." Her memory is not of the past alone: "There are seeds of dreams I hold, and responsibility."

Harjo's dreams and visions guide her writing. She told Carabi: "I remember my dreams since childhood, and I have been in many places in them.... I always wear the mythical world around or inside and feel things directly out of it." Harjo's poem "Skeleton of Winter" asserts her place in the living web of memory of her people through her vision. As Allen states in *The Sacred Hoop*, visionary experience is the source of power and religion in Native American culture. It is considered a gift and is used to guide the people. Harjo uses her mythic insight to see the current stories of her people as well as the past stories, as for instance, in the poem, "The Woman Hanging From the Thirteenth Floor Window," inspired by the plight of Native American women she met in Chicago. What Harjo wants to preserve is not the horror of the memory of the destruction of her people, but the memory of who they truly are. Her poems describe a mythic pattern of the circular journey: union, separation, journey, and reunion. The movement of her work is from psychic fragmentation to wholeness.

The tribe participated with all the life in a physical location through ceremony. Allen describes ceremony as an act that restores wholeness to people and the land through songs, chants, dances, and music. It acknowledges all beings as equals; all animals, people, and creatures are the children of Mother Earth. Ceremony is the basic model of literary expression for Native Americans. Ceremony unites all the beings of a place together in spiritual harmony. "'Remember' was written out of a definite

acknowledgement of ceremony," Harjo tells Sharyn Stever in an interview published in *Joy Harjo: The Spiral of Memory: Interviews*.

This relationship of land, life, and people is reenacted in Harjo's poems, so that the listener may participate in ceremonies of restoration and wholeness. Myth or sacred space, opened up by the poem, becomes a place where the listener enters and experiences the healing available there. In another interview published in *Joy Harjo: The Spiral of Memory: Interviews*, Harjo tells Donelle R. Ruwe, "I understand myth to be at the root of all event. It's the shimmering framework for all else to occur." Harjo does not rewrite old myths but creates them anew as ceremonies of transformation. For instance, in the poem "She Had Some Horses," she names irreconcilable parts of herself as types of mythic horses (some who lie, some who tell the truth), accepting all of the ritual horses within her, thus, creating a model of forgiveness for everyone.

The surreal quality of the images in Harjo's poems is not so much a literary technique as it is a reflection of the Native American perception of reality. Allen states in *The Sacred Hoop* that tribal peoples "view space as spherical and time as cyclical, whereas the non-Indian tends to view space as linear and time as sequential." In the spherical or mythic space, worlds overlap and time comes full circle. Healing can thus take place, for whatever harm has occurred can be transformed into something healing. Harjo tells Bruchac that she was influenced by a statement of Mahatma Gandhi's, that rage toward the colonizing oppressor could be conserved and "transmitted into power which can move the world." The mythic space in her poems allows suffering to be rewritten into positive power. In "Grace," for example, she describes how her people are able to swallow unthinkable tragedy and still emerge whole. Rhythm and repetition are techniques for transmitting the healing power of Harjo's poems. As in a ceremony where drumbeats aid in putting the participants into a trance-like state where they can let go, so a poem like "Remember" uses the same kind of rhythm and repetition to create a chant, a suggestion to the deeper mind for how things should be.

Harjo was unable to speak out in her childhood and became a visual artist at an early age as a way to express herself. She was not inspired by conventional poetry, but by Native American writers like Simon Ortiz and Leslie Silko, African American writers Alice Walker and James Wright, and by Chilean poet Pablo Neruda. The anthology edited by Gloria Bird and Joy Harjo, *Reinventing the Enemy's Language: Contemporary Native Women's Writings of North America*, is an example of transforming anger into healing. Acknowledging the suppression of their voices by the government policy of forbidding Indian schoolchildren from speaking their mother tongues, the writers turn victimization into empowerment by creating literature in the enemy's language.

Harjo does not speak her native Creek tongue but does speak some Navajo, which has influenced her poems. She expresses irritation with the limitations of English to Joseph Bruchac, commenting that English is "very materialistic," while native languages convey "a more spiritual sense of the world." Yet, the form of poetry allows her in some measure to correct for this lack by giving "a new dimension, a new depth to English," as Bruchac notes.

Language itself is a kind of magic prayer that can make things happen, Harjo discusses with Bruchac: "certain words or certain things make particular events happen ... writing can help change the world." In *Studies in American Indian Literature: Critical Essays and Course Designs*, Linda Hogan explains the difference between Native American language and Western use of language. Hogan describes a healing chant as creating "a form of internal energy" in the listener. Tribal language carries the sense of its own power to create or destroy, while in Western civilization, language has lost this sense through its commercial use. Also in a contribution to *Studies in American Indian Literature*, Larry Evers suggests that students studying Native American literature should speak it aloud to recapture some of the performative power of the oral tradition.

Source: Susan K. Andersen, Critical Essay on "Remember," in *Poetry for Students*, Gale, Cengage Learning, 2010.

Azfar Hussain

In the following excerpt, Hussain examines how land, the body, labor, and language intersect in the poems of She Had Some Horses, *including* "Remember," *as part of an anticolonial national struggle.*

Thunderclouds (Image copyright Andre Helbig, 2009. Used under license from Shutterstock.com)

... Harjo's profound sense of land-based struggle invites immediate comparisons with a number of Third World poet-activists. A former member of the Israeli Communist Party and an ardent supporter of the ongoing Palestinian struggle for a national homeland and the right-of-nations-to-self-determination, Tawfiq Zayyad pointedly pronounces the imperatives of land-based struggle in his work. At the very beginning of his poem "On the Trunk of an Olive Tree," Zayyad in fact zeroes in on his usurped land, suggesting that he would reclaim it by decisively carving each of his deeds in that very land. The Palestinian poet Mahmud Darwish, noted for his extremely powerful land-based poems, finds no alternatives whatsoever to the struggle for the land. In his by-now-famous poem "Identity Card," Darwish raises his voice with full force and intensity, speaking of the need for turning hunger into anger—the kind of anger that would reclaim the very land that has been usurped. Puhui Pataxó, a vice-cacique and Indian activist,

> 'REMEMBER' EMPHASIZES THE POETICS,
> POLITICS, AND PRAXIS OF REMEMBRANCE IN WAYS
> IN WHICH THE POEM ITSELF BECOMES A CALL FOR
> WAGING A TOTAL WAR ON THE VIOLENT
> TECHNOLOGIES OF COLONIALISM—TECHNOLOGIES
> CHARACTERISTICALLY DEPLOYED TO DESTROY
> NATIONAL AND COLLECTIVE MEMORY."

issues an explicit battle cry, while underlining the desideratum of an organized and united movement for the land against the colonizer.

Insofar as one form of oppression remains linked or even leads to another, and insofar as, thus, one struggle "here" also relates to another struggle "there" (to apply Harjo's own event-based "here/there" dialectic), poets such as Tawfiq Zayyad, Mahmud Darwish, Puhui Pataxó, and Joy Harjo—despite their different histories, different locations, and different problems—can forge counterhegemonic links as oppositional forces against territorial colonialism-capitalism-patriarchy-racism, all of which have today targeted the land as the site of both exploitation and value in their various meanings and inflections.

The horizons of the land's meanings are, I think, most complexly and intersectionally negotiated in Harjo's collection of poems *She Had Some Horses*—a collection that follows *What Moon Drove Me to This?* I would therefore like to dwell—at some length—on a few selected but significant textual sites in *She Had Some Horses*. But, first, a few words on the general framework of the book. Rhonda Pettit observes:

> Harjo develops an individual voice not only by dealing with Native American subjects and experience but by echoing the sound of Native American chants and rituals through her use of repetition. She also more successfully transforms her story-telling technique to produce a poetry of witness that moves beyond mere victimization. If her characters and speakers are at times still driven by an outside force or condition, they are now more likely to seek the spiritual guide or vision that will grant them a sense of agency. Two poems about fear—one that faces it, and one that denies its power over the speaker—provide a frame for the book.

The question of agency Pettit raises in the above passage is, however, not at all absent in Harjo's earlier poetry, as I have argued. But I also argue that in *She Had Some Horses* the mode of resistance gets articulated in different but profoundly intertwined sites. The land certainly continues to constitute a decisively important site of struggle, but its historical and topographical logics as well as its production/value-logics cannot be dissociated from the nexus of other significant sites like language, labor, and the body. I will argue that in *She Had Some Horses* Harjo focuses on all those four sites almost at once—for the first time— in such a way that enables one to articulate a political economy of the body, land, labor, and language as they keep intersecting and interacting with one another.

One exemplary poem attesting to my above argument is "For Alva Benson, And for Those Who Have Learned to Speak." In this poem Harjo begins by enunciating and enacting a dialectic of the land and language, suggesting that language emanates from the land and that to reclaim the land is to reclaim the language itself. To follow Harjo's suggestion, then, the production of language dialectically and even directly corresponds to the production of the land itself, insofar as the latter is also a function of people's interventions in terms of the realization of labor-power in the land and its exploitation by the capitalist colonizer. Harjo therefore explores—as a mode of resistance to territorial colonialism and territorial capitalism—what she herself calls "land-based" language in consonance with the Native perspective that the Navajo language remains profoundly linked to the earth or to the land in the very act of giving birth itself. The first six lines of the poem "For Alva Benson"—its first stanza—bring out this point with full force. In those lines, Harjo mobilizes the image of the ground that speaks at the time of giving birth to the child, while Harjo also speaks of the mother who can hear and answer in Navajo and thus establish a conversation with the ground itself, enacting the very continuity of both this conversation and the act of giving birth itself:

> And the ground spoke when she was born. Her mother heard it. In Navajo she answered as she squatted down against the earth to give birth. It was now when it happened, now giving birth to itself again and again between the legs of women.

Indeed a myth-oriented interpretation of the above lines is likely to dwell upon the trajectories of the mythical-historical (un)conscious of Joy Harjo, intertextualizing her work by exploring its possible links to many Native American myths of creation, emergence, and the Earth itself. Such intertextualist explorations are surely politically important insofar as they help recuperate and resurrect certain linkages destroyed through what Fanon calls "the perverted logic" of colonialism, and thus such acts may even turn out to be a weapon in the anticolonial native nationalist struggle in the Cabralian sense.

But the kind of political-economic interpretation I am attempting here would begin by pointing out that a certain feminist rewriting of the traditional male-centered political economy seems to mark the very poetic conjuncture of Harjo that I have described above. In the conjuncture captured at the very beginning of the poem "For Alva Benson," it is not at all difficult to see that the production of speech or language (as opposed to the written word, of course, the written word being the tool of colonization and the tool of what Benedict Anderson, on another register, calls "print-capitalism") is a function of the production-relations obtaining and operating between the earth and the birth. Certainly language here does not simply fall from the skies, nor does it always already obtain in some static and universal form. In fact, language gets produced in the very space called the earth. So a question arises: What is it that produces this land-based language? One answer is, of course, the land. But Harjo's textual conjuncture also seems to suggest that it is labor that constitutes the basis of this production, generating value—if not the kind of exchange-value that Marx enunciates and theorizes in connection with the production of commodities.

Labor involved in the very act of giving birth seems emphasized by Harjo. This labor is not necessarily the kind of traditional male proletariat labor-power that is "recognizably" realized in industries, factories, and mills as such—male-dominated spaces in which, however, woman's labor-power again constitutes a driving factor in the production-processes. Labor, in Harjo's poem, is woman's or mother's pain. And this labor seems to constitute not only the basis of production as such but also the basis of the entire cycle of production and re(-)production. This point is brought out with particular force in Harjo's own single line toward the end of the first stanza of "For Alva Benson" in which Harjo calls attention to the very continuity of giving birth itself.

Given the above interpretation that I have advanced, I cannot but see an instructive point of contact between Harjo's own poetic political economy of labor and that of Judy Grahn. Grahn's collection of poems *She Who* (1972) continuously nuances the notion of labor and women's work in an attempt to rewrite the male-dominated political economy in distinctly feminist terms. In her poems Grahn introduces the notion of what she calls "first labor," characterized as it is by the otherwise unheeded cycle of activities that make living possible, bearing and rearing children.

One can certainly stretch the implications of Grahn's notion of first labor and argue that under the capitalist mode of production, which is characteristically as sexist as it is racist, women's labor is never recognized as even labor, let alone "first labor," and thus such labor is continuously exploited by both men and capital. Also, the classical mode-of-production remains indifferent to what might be called "the domestic mode of production," characterized as it is by the continuous process of the proletarianization of women. In fact, taking cues and clues from both Grahn and Harjo's poetically articulated political economy that rewrites and nuances labor, I would argue that, under the very racist-sexist-territorial-colonialist-capitalist mode of production, women are always subject to the processes of multiple proletarianization and multiple colonization. First, women are laborers in the act of giving birth. Second, women are laborers under the domestic mode of production in which their labor remains invisible and unpaid. Third, women are certainly laborers under the larger global mode of production in which women's labor is always already inserted into—as Gayatri Chakravorty Spivak so eloquently argues—"the most labor intensive stages of production." In each instance, of course, the law of value does not wither away, while global exploitation remains a systemic constant. Now working-class and landless peasant-class women of color located in Third World countries—such as Bangladesh or Kenya—certainly add more levels and layers to the kind of political economy of labor and exploitation that both Grahn and Harjo seem to be suggesting in their works.

But there is another material site implied in the poem "For Alva Benson, And for Those Who Have Learned to Speak"—the very site from which labor itself emanates or the very site on which pain itself is inflicted. This is the site of the body—the female body—which is rendered more explicit in the second stanza of the poem. In fact, to follow Harjo's own implications, labor cannot be separated from the female body itself, and the exploitation of labor thus amounts to the exploitation of the body. The female body also thus turns out to be the site and the source of the production of value. In this connection it is indeed significant and revealing to recall the Bengali short story "Standayini" (Breast-Giver) by the Indian novelist-activist Mahasweta Devi based in Calcutta. Her story is now available in Gayatri Spivak's translation. "Standayini" indeed most exemplarily *sites* and *cites* the political economy of the subaltern female body. In Mahasweta's story, Jashoda—the central female subaltern character—is compelled by her poverty to sell her bodily labor-power in the form of selling her "surplus-milk" (Mahasweta directly uses the English word "surplus" in her Bengali text) to a wealthy family that has an acute demand for such milk for its children. In Mahasweta's superb politico-economic treatment of the production-processes in her story, Jashoda's body turns out to be a site of reification and alienation on the one hand and certainly a site of the production of values ranging from use-value through exchange-value down to surplus-value on the other. Can we then advance *a body theory of value*? I will turn to Harjo's specific engagements with the issue of the body soon, but let me make the point that in the very first stanza of "For Alva Benson," Harjo for the first time brings together the four sites of the body, land, labor, and language, as they keep intersecting and interacting with one another.

Now an even more effective interweaving—an organic orchestration—of those four crucial sites of the body, land, labor, and language is tellingly exemplified in the second stanza of "For Alva Benson," where we have a citing and a siting of an Indian hospital in Gallup—the site of labor—followed by the return of the speaking-ground or land-based image in which of course lies embedded the very signifier of the body—the body shown to be tied and reacting and expressive all at once:

> maybe it was the Indian Hospital in Gallup.
> The ground still spoke beneath mortar and
> concrete. She strained against the metal stir-
> rups, and they tied her hands down because
> she still spoke with them when they muffled
> her screams. But her body went on talking
> and a child was born.

This stanza thus turns out to be a charged activist textual site in which a dialectic of oppression and opposition is enacted with full force. But this dialectic is also enacted in such a way that the body, land, labor, and language come together coalitionally and even inseparably against contemporary technological capitalism, represented synecdochically as it is by the images of mortar, concrete, and metal in the stanza in question. Apparently, Harjo seems to capture a particular conjuncture when a woman gives birth to a child. Birth in this reckoning, however, is not a noun but a verb. It accounts for the relentless *energeia* of opposition under the very capitalist mode of production itself. This *energeia* is particularly exemplified in the image of the continuously speaking body that Harjo employs with a certain force. In fact, the images mobilized in "For Alva Benson" are significantly interlinked, and they tend to produce some kind of activist coalition-effect.

Harjo's image of the ground that continues to speak stages the return of the notion of the land-based language, as I have already indicated. Then this image suggests that land itself is language and that language in turn is the land. However, the land does not talk alone; the land alone is not language. The body talks, too. This rather unrelenting speaking body—giving birth to a child—seems to suggest that the site of both labor and language is the body itself. And the body in turn becomes the land in the sense that both the land and the body keep talking to each other, sharing and even being the same language. The very birth of this language—a language that is decidedly oral and corporeal at once—thus marks the birth of oppositions to the silencing and colonizing logos or language of concrete and mortar and metal. Such images of concrete, mortar, and metal—in the way they are deployed by Harjo—seem to point to the semiology, genealogy, and the materiality of colonialism and capitalism all at once.

Given the kind of reading I have advanced so far, it is possible to conclude—at least tentatively here—that in Harjo's "For Alva Benson," a dialogic political economy of the body, land, labor, and language gets articulated as a charged space of oppositional, coalitional, counterhegemonic linkages in the service of movements against territorial colonialism (colonization of *land*), linguistic colonialism (colonization of *language*), glocal capitalism (local and global exploitation of *labor*), and racialized-gendered international division of labor (colonization and exploitation of the female subaltern *body* of color, this body being inserted by capital into the circuit of the most labor-intensive phases of production in the Third World). All such categories of power and production, against which Harjo enables us to articulate a political economy as a space of struggle, certainly appear somewhat separate in the way that I have put them above. But I must again emphasize the point that those categories profoundly overlap in the sense that—as I have demonstrated earlier—the logic of capitalism is also the logic of colonialism, that the logic of colonialism is also the logic of patriarchy and racism, and that the logic of patriarchal racism or racist patriarchy is also the logic of colonialist capitalism.

Now the kind of political economy of the body, land, labor, and language that I have tried to map out through my selective reading of Harjo so far also finds support from many other poems or textual sites Harjo has produced from *She Had Some Horses* onward. My purpose here is not to close-read them all, nor is my purpose to offer a complete and accurate inventory of all those sites. However, I will try to point up more symptoms—again selectively—of the political economy of the body, land, labor, and language that seems to be variously inhabiting Harjo's textual spaces.

In fact, in the title poem "She Had Some Horses," Harjo's deployment of the horse symbol does not merely forge intertextual linkages to Native American mythology and religious ceremony as such but also produces and reproduces a symbolic space—and a powerful contestatory space—in which horses and humans themselves struggle anaphorically over the questions of the *land* (as particularly, if not exclusively, indicated in the image of the blood-drawn map that Harjo uses in the poem); *language* (as indicated in the image of the horses who were stripped of their voices because they told the truth); *labor* (as particularly indicated in the image of horses licking razor blades), and the *body* (as indicated in the image of the very bodies of the horses that Harjo pointedly foregrounds in the poem). Also, all such sites remain interconnected in the poem because Harjo's "horses" both evoke differences and forge links. Equally significantly, this performance-oriented, anaphoric, chant-like poem enacts a dialectic of both oppression and opposition because Harjo writes of horses who waited for both destruction and resurrection.

In another poem, "Remember," included in *She Had Some Horses,* Harjo's preoccupations with the questions of the body, land, labor, and language are rendered explicit in terms of the repeatedly deployed imperative "remember." But what shall we remember? Harjo says: Remember your *land* (she wants us to remember the earth whose skin we are made of); remember your *language* (she wants us to remember the language of dance with which she equates life itself); remember your *labor* (again she wants us to remember the very moment of our birth, which can only be attributed to the bodily struggle of the mother), and remember your *body* (Harjo returns to the image of the earth-skin to account for the corporeal raison d'être of our continued interactions on earth). My own reading of Joy Harjo is then a response to her own call for remembering the body, land, labor, and language.

"Remember" emphasizes the poetics, politics, and praxis of remembrance in ways in which the poem itself becomes a call for waging a total war on the violent technologies of colonialism—technologies characteristically deployed to destroy national and collective memory. Indeed, colonialism—through its production/power/knowledge networks—attempts to destroy indigenous people's myths, folklore, stories, tales, histories, sagas, and languages (the body cultural, that is), including the body biologic, the body politic, the body economic, and the body politico-economic of the colonized. Thus when Fanon maintains that "decolonization is always a violent phenomenon," he actually suggests that colonialism itself is a violent phenomenon to begin with. The very act of remembering, therefore, turns out to be a particularly important weapon against the epistemic violence of colonialism.

The Colombian novelist Gabriel García Márquez, in his novel *One Hundred Years of Solitude*, instructively illustrates the collective need for remembering. He does it with an unforgettable episode in his novel that concerns the plague of insomnia, accompanied by an invasion of amnesia, in the fictional town of Macondo. This invasion of amnesia—as García Márquez treats it—turns out to be a signal-metaphor for the subsequent invasion of colonialism itself. And with the advent of colonialism—synecdochically suggested as it is by banana company and railroad in the García Márquez novel—the colonizer's attack is seen to be launched on, among others, the people's collective memory as history in the form of imposing *official history* on the original inhabitants of Macondo. The conflicts between colonially imposed official history and the people's *unwritten history*—and for that matter their struggle for remembering—considerably shape the anticolonial content and character of the García Márquez novel. It is in this tradition that Harjo's characteristic acts of historicizing, storytelling, narrativizing, and myth recovering in her poetry and prose become politically significant in terms of an anticolonial national struggle—a struggle as crucial to contemporary Native Americans as it is to many other Third World people at a time when globalization has become a violent phenomenon, perpetrating all kinds of violences on the economies, histories, and cultures of Third World nations today. The kind of political economy of land-language-labor-and-the-body I am trying to emphasize in my reading of Harjo remains intimately linked to the kind of national struggle that confronts and contests various forms and forces of colonialism and imperialism at every turn. . . .

Source: Azfar Hussain, "Joy Harjo and Her Poetics as Praxis: A 'Postcolonial' Political Economy of the Body, Land, Labor, and Language," in *wicazo sa review: A Journal of Native American Studies*, Vol. 15, No. 2, 2000, pp. 27–61.

Marilyn Kallet

In the following excerpt from an interview with Kallet, Harjo discusses how she began writing, as well as her family background, culture, teachers, and influences.

MK: What were your beginnings as a writer?

JH: I could look at this in a couple of ways. One is to look at the myths and stories of the people who formed me in the place where I entered the world. . . . Another way is to look at when I first consciously called myself a writer. I started writing poetry when I was pretty old, actually—I was about twenty-two. I committed to poetry the day I went in to my painting teacher who mentored me and expected a fine career in painting for me, and told him I was switching my major to poetry. I made the decision to learn what poetry could teach me. It was a painful choice. I come from a family of Muscogee painters. My grandmother and my great-aunt both got their B.F.A.'s in Art in the early 1900s. And from the time I was very small you could always find me drawing, whether it was in the dirt or on paper. That was one thing that

> CULTURE JUST IS. CERTAINLY I'M ALWAYS ASKING MYSELF QUESTIONS ABOUT HOW WE CAME TO BE, AND HOW WE'RE BECOMING, AND WHO WE ARE IN THIS WORLD. . . ."

made me happy. . . . . I always said that when I grow up I am going to be a painter, I am going to be an artist. Then I made the decision to work with words and the power of words, to work with language, yet I approach the art as a visual artist. From childhood my perceptions were through the eye of a painter. I feel any writer serves many aspects of culture, including language, but you also serve history, you serve the mythic structure that you're part of, the people, the earth, and so on—and none of these are separate.

MK: It seems like almost any question we ask about your writing, about your cultural background, is going to lead us in the same paths of discussion about your family life, your tribal life, and your life as a writer.

JH: Well, they are not separate, really. Though the way I've come to things is very different from say, Beth Cuthand, who is a Cree writer from Saskatchewan, or Leslie Silko from Laguna. There's a tendency in this country to find one writer of a particular ethnicity and expect her to speak for everyone and expect her experience to be representative of all Native women and all Native people. My experience is very different from Silko's and Cuthand's, although it's similar in the sense of a generational thing, of certain influences on us and influences we have on each other. But my experience has been predominantly urban. I did not grow up on a reservation—we don't even have a reservation. There are more rural areas where the people are. I'm not a full-blood, and yet I am a full member of my (Muscogee) tribe, and I have been a full member of my tribe since my birth into the tribe. I find some people have preconceived ideas—I was talking to this guy on the plane and he says, "Well, you don't fit my idea of an Indian." What does that mean? I think for most people in this country, it means to be a Hollywood version of a Plains tribe, as falsely-imagined 100 or 150 years ago. Most people in this country have learned all they know about Indian people from movies and television. . . .

MK: Certain books have helped to popularize Plains culture. Black Elk Speaks *is taught most often at the university. . . .*

JH: And even then it's a perversion of what it means to be an Indian in this country—how do you translate context? Within my tribe you have people who are very grounded in the traditions, and are very close to the land. Then you have people who are heavily involved in church; some are involved in both; some live in Tulsa, which is where I grew up; others live all over but are still close to that place which is home. It is more than land—but of the land—a tradition of mythologies, of ongoing history . . . it forms us.

MK: What is there specifically in the Muscogee culture that lends itself to poetry?

JH: That's like asking what is it in life that lends itself to poetry . . . it's the collective myth balanced with history.

MK: When you talk about particulars of individuals and tribes, you are continually breaking down conventions and stereotypes. Does that become tiresome for you?

JH: Yes, it does. I find that wherever I speak I always get asked more questions having to do with culture than with writing.

MK: You must feel like a cultural missionary sometimes. . . .

JH: Right. I feel like I'm having to explain something that's not really easily explainable.

MK: Among your friends, and among the other writers you mentioned, surely you don't have to keep explaining.

JH: No. There's no need. Culture just is. Certainly I'm always asking myself questions about how we came to be, and how we're becoming, and who we are in this world. . . .

MK: In terms of your own background, were there people in your family who loved words? Where does your love of language come from?

JH: Probably from both sides. I have a grandfather, my father's grandfather, who is a full-blooded Creek Baptist minister. I often feel him and I know much of what I am comes from him (including my stubbornness!) I know that he had a love for words and he spoke both Muscogee and

English. My mother used to compose songs on an old typewriter. I think she loved the music more than the words, she wasn't particularly a wordsmith, but could translate heartache. From her I learned Patsy Cline, and other "heartbreak country."

MK: Do you remember what made you write that first poetry in your twenties?

JH: Yes, very distinctly. The urge was the same urge I had to make music. Around that time was the first time I heard music in poetry, heard Native writers like Leslie Silko, and Simon Ortiz read their work. I also heard Galway Kinnell for the first time, his was one of the first poetry readings I ever attended. I became friends with Leo Romero whose dedication to poetry impressed me. He was always writing and reading his work to me. I witnessed process and began writing my own pieces. Of course, the first attempts were rather weak. Like newborn colts trying to stand just after birth. . . .

MK: You attended the M.F.A. Program in Creative Writing at the University of Iowa. Was that helpful to you?

JH: Well, I have to take into consideration my age when I went—I was in my mid-twenties. I was a single mother. I arrived at this strange country with two small children—my daughter was three years old. I knew no one, did not know the place, or the people. About the university setting—I felt like I had walked into a strange land in which I had to learn another language. This comes from being of Native background, from the West, but it also comes from being a woman in that institution. I heard the Director say once to a group of possible funders—I was one of the people they chose to perform for them in the workshop—he told them that the place was actually geared for teaching male writers, which is honest; it was true, but I was shocked. I remember Jayne Ann Phillips and I looking at each other, like "can you believe this? Then why are we sitting here?" Certainly I think I learned a lot about technique. I also learned that what was most important in a poem had nothing to do in some ways with what I thought was most important. I felt like the art of poetry had broken down into sterile exercises. And yet, I know I admire some of the work of those people who taught me. But the system had separated itself from the community, from myth, from humanhood.

MK: But you saw it through?

JH: I did see it through. I wanted to walk away. One way I made it through was through the help of people like Sandra Cisneros—through close ties to the Indian and Chicano communities, to the African-American community, to women's groups.

MK: Have you been able to bring back some of the technical skill you learned to what you consider fundamental?

JH: Yes. You can have the commitment to writing, the fire, but you can write crummy poems. Certainly you need technique. I guess what I'm saying is that I felt values were out of balance.

MK: What was missing?

JH: Heart. And yet some of the poets who taught me there had heart in their poems. But sometimes I felt like what was more important was the facade of being a poet. It became more of an academic pursuit than a pursuit of what it means to live. Granted I was young and I had a lot of misconceptions to work through.

MK: Could you say more about your true teachers of poetry, those who have influenced your work?

JH: I feel like Galway Kinnell has been a teacher, even though I have never met him. I love his work. I think that what he has is a beautiful balance between technique and music. He is such a poet. He's a poet's poet with the music . . . and that's important to me. Of course James Wright. Richard Hugo. Adrienne Rich. I admire her sheer audacity. In the face of everything she learned from the fathers, given the time when she grew up and her own father's admonitions, still she became herself.

MK: I see that in your work, too. I don't know if you are aware of how daring your work is, and how dangerous!

JH: I'd better be! I love the work of Audre Lorde; she has also been one of my teachers. . . .

MK: Are there other writers who have been important to you that we should know about?

JH: Yes. I can think of a lot of writers who are important to me—Leslie Silko, for instance, whom I met shortly after I started writing. I actually took a fiction class from her at UNM as an undergraduate. . . . I especially liked our wine breaks in our office, the stories as we listened to Fleetwood Mac, watched for rain. . . . There are a lot of people . . . Beth Brant, Louis Oliver, June Jordan. . . .

MK: You dedicated the poem "Hieroglyphics" (from In Mad Love and War) to June Jordan. Why did she get that one?

JH: Well, it's a long story.

MK: It's a wonderful poem. It moves across time and space, defying boundaries. Maybe June Jordan has a mythic imagination that can comprehend those leaps?

JH: Yeah. I mean she is somebody you can talk to like that and you can't talk to everyone that way. Sometimes in a poem you assume you can.

MK: Maybe you assume that because you need to make the poems accessible. You want people to feel like you are talking to them. In Mad Love and War is a breakthrough in terms of form and content. How do you feel about being formally inventive?

JH: I don't know. I don't really know what I'm doing.

MK: You lean into the unknown in those lines and see what happens?

JH: Yes, I do. I don't analyze. I mean certainly analysis is also part of the process of writing poetry, but it's not primary. It comes later in the process.

MK: In part it's probably discipline that lets you explore. Discipline from the habit of years of writing. Do you write daily?

JH: I don't. I try to! (laughter) Well, do you?

MK: No, of course not! We were talking before about having families and having lives, and here you are in Knoxville. I mean, how are you supposed to write every day? Though William Stafford writes every day, even when he's traveling.

JH: Writing is a craft and there's something to doing it or you lose it. I used to paint and draw, and was quite a good artist, but I can't do it at the same level anymore. It's not that I've lost it but I'd have to get my chops together, so to speak, practice.

MK: Do you regret the decision to give up painting?

JH: I don't know that I regret it, but I certainly miss painting. That particular language was more familiar to me than the literary world. . . .

MK: What can you do in poetry that painting could not achieve?

JH: Speak directly in a language that was meant to destroy us.

MK: You have focused on your writing and on your music.

JH: Yes. If I'm not writing I'm thinking about it, or looking at things—I feel this infuses my vision. I'm listening for stories and listening to how words are put together and so on.

MK: Living a "writer's life"?

JH: Yes.

MK: The theme of music gets into your poetry when you dedicate poems to Billie Holiday or make reference to Coltrane. But I also sense the influence of jazz on your forms.

JH: Well, that wasn't conscious. I think it's coming out of playing the saxophone. I realized recently that I took it up exactly when I entered academe. I don't feel like I've become an academic but if you're going to be in that place, certainly it's going to rub off on you. (laughter)

MK: So you needed some way back to the body?

JH: Yes. Anyway, it was a time when I started teaching at the University of Colorado, Boulder. I had run from teaching in universities. I remember applying once years ago for the University of Texas, El Paso, and then I couldn't make it to MLA because I had no money. I preferred to keep my own hours, worked free lance, doing screenplay writing and readings and workshops—somehow the money always came in—but it's a tough existence, you have to have a lot of faith. I got a position as Assistant Professor at the University of Colorado, Boulder. I wrote "We Must Call a Meeting" right after I started teaching there because I was afraid that in that atmosphere, in that place, I was going to lose my poetry. That was around the time I started playing tenor sax. I play tenor and soprano now, but I realize that in a way it was a way to keep that poetry and keep that place.

MK: Keep your sanity, keep your juice!

JH: Yeah. I mean you pick up the saxophone again, I suppose it's like writing poetry, you are picking up the history of that. Playing saxophone is like honoring a succession of myths. . . . I never thought of this before but: the myth of saxophone and here comes Billie Holiday and there's Coltrane. I love his work dearly, especially "A Love Supreme." That song has fed me. And all of that

becomes. When you play you're a part of that, you have to recognize those people.

MK: There's a very strong sense of community in your work, community of musicians you address; community of other writers, community of women. . . . I want to ask you about your great-aunt, to whom you dedicated She Had Some Horses.

JH: She's the relative I was closest to, and my life in some ways has uncannily paralleled hers. I miss her dearly. I always felt like I dropped into an alien family almost—maybe most people do—but when she and I got together, then I felt akin. She was very interested in art—she was a painter and was very supportive of the Creek Nation Museum in Okmulgee, and donated most of her paintings to them. She traveled. We followed the same routes. Like her, I left Oklahoma for New Mexico—I was sent to an Indian boarding school in Santa Fe. It was a school for the arts, very innovative in its time, sort of like an Indian *Fame* school. When I left Oklahoma to go to high school there, in a way it saved my life. . . . In my travels I often met relatives of people that she knew. I have a necklace that Maria Martinez gave her—Maria, the potter from San Ildefonso. (My great-aunt) was someone who was married for six months and didn't like it and got a divorce, and spent a lot of time driving—she liked traveling Indian country—and also opened a jewelry shop.

MK: So there's movement, dynamism, in your family, and that restlessness. . . .

JH: Yes. Through her and her life I understand myself more clearly, and I love her dearly and miss her. . . .

MK: I want to ask you whether there is a connection between poetry and politics, and poetry and prayer? Are these intermingled?

JH: Of course.

MK: In the back of In Mad Love and War, there's a poem based on a Native traditional form. . . .

JH: Which comes out of the Beauty Way Chant. I used to speak Navajo fairly well. I know that it's influenced my writing.

MK: I've been told that it's a very difficult language.

JH: It's a beautiful language. I love the way that you can say things in that language. So that's been a powerful influence.

MK: How did you learn Navajo?

JH: When I was a student at UNM I took Navajo Language for a year and a half. I had a wonderful teacher the first year, Roseanne Willink, a Navajo from western New Mexico. We had a great time in there. I remember making up jokes and then starting dreaming in Navajo. I don't know my own language, and wish to learn.

MK: Was your family bilingual?

JH: No, my father's mother had died when he was young. His father married a white woman. He had a lot of difficulties as a child. He was beaten a lot by his dad, and sent to a military school in Ponca City, Oklahoma. I think being Creek—which he was proud of—became a very painful thing for him.

MK: No wonder he had such a hard time coping. You spoke earlier about his alcoholism. He had so much to contend with as such a young person.

JH: Yes, he did. But anyway, back to your earlier question—for me there's always a definite link between poetry and prayer. I think that you can say that a poem is always a prayer for whomever you're speaking of. "Eagle Poem" at the end (of *In Mad Love and War*) is most obviously a prayer. You could look at all poems as being a prayer for our continuance. I mean even the act of writing, to be creative, has everything to do with our continuance as peoples.

Source: Joy Harjo and Marilyn Kallett, "In Love and War and Music: An Interview with Joy Harjo," in *Kenyon Review*, Vol. 15, No. 3, Summer 1993, p. 57.

Nancy Lang

In the following essay, Lang describes the patterns of memory within the narratives of Harjo's poems.

Contemporary Native American poet Joy Harjo expresses and reflects patterns of ongoing, multilayered and multivocal memories within the narratives of her poems. These memories flow and interweave on a continuum within a metaphysical world that begins deep within her personal psyche and simultaneously moves back into past memories of her Creek (Muskogee) heritage, as well as forward into current pan-tribal experiences and the assimilationist, Anglo-dominated world of much contemporary Native American life. Harjo's poetic memories may be personal stories, family and tribal histories, myths, recent pan-tribal experiences, or spiritual icons of an ancient culture and history.

> AS HARJO EXPLAINS MEMORY, ONE HAS NO AUTHENTIC VOICE WITHOUT MEMORY; AND WITHOUT AN AUTHENTIC VOICE, ONE IS SPEECHLESS, HARDLY HUMAN, AND UNABLE TO SURVIVE FOR VERY LONG."

And, while Harjo writes using both an "alien" language, English, and within expected structural and narrative formats of contemporary poetry, her poems also frequently resonate with the distinctive chanting rhythms and pause breaks associated with traditional Native American oralities. As with other contemporary Native American women poets such as Paula Gunn Allen (Laguna Pueblo/Sioux), Linda Hogan (Chickasaw), and Wendy Rose (Hopi/Chowchilla Miwok), Harjo's past memories and present experiences seamlessly fuse together within individual poems; and when read together as a group, her poems construct in the reader's mind a single consistent, cohesive, and unified poetic utterance.

The importance of memory to Harjo's poetry best reveals itself through a survey and examination of one of her most important ongoing tropes, the contemporary American city. Within her varied urban landscapes, Harjo's poetry most clearly illustrates the multi-voiced nature of any marginalized poetry, and of Native American women's poetry in particular. On the one hand, after a first reading Harjo may seem to be writing out of the city-as-subject tradition of American poets like Walt Whitman, Carl Sandburg, Hart Crane, and William Carlos Williams. On the other hand, her city landscapes do not reflect promise and optimistic excitement, as do many urban settings of earlier white male American poets. Rather, Harjo's cities resonate with Native American memories of an endless and ongoing history of Eurocentric and genocidal social and political policies: war, forced removal, imposed education, racism, and assimilationism.

While Allen, Hogan, and Rose often use the contemporary city as negative physical setting in a variety of ways, Harjo especially foregrounds the psychological and spiritual impacts, and the resulting personal chaos, of urban life on the Native American survivor. As Patricia Clark Smith and Paula Gunn Allen note, Harjo's "particular poetic turf is cities" (193), perhaps because she grew up in Tulsa, Oklahoma, and has spent much of her adult life in cities. In any case, the speakers within her urban narratives roam freely throughout the United States on a life's journey reflecting simultaneously Harjo's own current travels on the urban/academic lecture-powwow-poetry reading circuit, as well as the age-old, traditional wanderings of her Creek ancestors.

What sustains Harjo's contemporary speakers in such an alien environment are memories—memories of ancestral lands, family and tribal life, traditional spirituality, and a pan-tribal heritage. In Harjo's poems the multi-voiced city experiences of Native Americans living within indifferent and often hostile urban landscapes offer a strikingly different reading from contemporary Anglo experience of the American city, and thus they make an important statement about current American societies. Moreover, we can also trace a distinct growth in the richness, complexity, and tone of Harjo's city trope from her earliest to her most recent poetic texts.

Even in her first chapbook collection, *The Last Song* (1975), Harjo begins to develop a clear but subtle city-as-negative motif, as her speaker wistfully looks out from the streets of Albuquerque, off toward the distant natural world. In "Watching Crow, Looking South Towards the Manzano Mountains," the speaker yearns for the freedom of a crow "dancing" with a New Mexico winter wind; and in "3AM," she seeks both a physical and a spiritual escape from Albuquerque's airport, back to the Hopis' Third Mesa. This pattern of wanting to leave cities continues in *What Moon Drove Me To This?* (1979), where Chicago, Kansas City, Gallup, Albuquerque, and nameless bars in Oklahoma towns serve as meeting grounds for often negative and superficial social encounters between men and women. Here also, in "The First Noni Daylight," appears the first statement of Harjo's early poetic "otherself," Noni Daylight, a beautiful young Native American urban woman caught in the assimilationist trap of contemporary life, while trying to hold on to her man by faking a suicide and thus tying him to her by guilt.

In his article "Nightriding with Noni Daylight: The Many Horse Songs of Joy Harjo," Andrew Wiget focuses on the specific "otherself" persona of Noni Daylight as an important clue into understanding Harjo's early poetry. Concentrating as he does on the growth in Harjo's poetic voice from *What Moon Drove Me To This?* (1979) to *She Had Some Horses* (1983), Wiget examines the developing complexities of Harjo's poetic voice by looking at several of her characteristic images. Noting that the otherself motif grows out of early descriptions of social and psychological alienation, especially of bar life and of troubled love relationships in *What Moon Drove Me To This?*, Wiget sees Harjo's more complex *She Had Some Horses* as developing a self/otherself dialogue that begins to build a "cyclic quest of a voice looking for a home" (186). While he foregrounds the importance of Harjo's using natural landscapes and the moon as recurring identifications with the earth and sky, Wiget also sees Noni Daylight as an early Harjo expression of the suffering individual who longs for the total ecstasy that might be found in a past of eternal comfort, "the womb-worn memory of her mother's heartbeat" (188).

Wiget's ideas help to give clarity to much of Noni Daylight's seemingly erratic behavior. For example, because of the psychological and spiritual hopelessness of her life, Noni Daylight often turns at night to high-speed interstate driving, which for her becomes a perfect form of escape into a soothing, rhythmic mindlessness. In *What Moon Drove Me To This?*, "Origin" describes her driving west, toward Flagstaff, into a mysterious darkness, "where stars have come down into rocks" (33) and into memories of old Native American stories that tell of mythic origins as Noni tries to construct a pan-tribal map leading back into an understanding of herself and her mixed-blood heritage. But her efforts bring her no answers, and Noni's unnamed and unstated fears increase as she continues the journey of her life. In "heartbeat" she drives through a silent nighttime city, obediently waiting for red lights to change at empty intersections, and toying with the trigger of the pistol cradled in her lap. In the "Evidence" of *She Had Some Horses,* her nighttime flirting with the highway's yellow line becomes more than just a veiled hint pointing toward Noni's dimly-formulated thoughts of suicide. Still, while the lure of complete oblivion tempts her, Noni Daylight also "needs / the feel of danger, / for life" (46). Unlike the bilingual little girl of "For Alva Benson, and For Those Who Have Learned to Speak," Noni Daylight freezes into an inarticulation far surpassing that of words and language.

Wiget sees Harjo's ongoing and often contradictory dialogues of and with the poetic self as best reflected in the more mature, seemingly paradoxical language and imagery of "She Had Some Horses," one of Harjo's most powerful poems, and also a poem that illustrates Wiget's idea of "crossing over to apocalypse" (192). Through its often paradoxical juxtapositions, "She Had Some Horses" also foregrounds the important truths of borders and living on the borders, or what Gloria Anzaldúa in her "Preface" to *Borderlands: La Frontera* defines as that place where "two or more cultures edge each other, where people of different races occupy the same territory, where under, lower, middle and upper classes touch" (np). The interwoven and often violently clashing images in "She Had Some Horses"—"She had horses who threw rocks at glass houses. / She had horses who licked razor blades."—also offer a broader, more all-encompassing statement of those fears and silences which so wracked Noni Daylight's unhappy, cramped life.

It is with the poems of *She Had Some Horses* (1983), and especially with one of her most powerful poems, "The Woman Hanging From the Thirteenth Floor," that Harjo fully articulates the interlocked problems of unnamed fears and the resulting speechlessness of an oppressed and dispossessed woman. Told in the flat, seemingly unemotional voice of a dispassionate observer, this highly rhythmic prose poems tells the story of a young Native American mother caught in the trap of her life and trying to find some way, any way, out of her nightmare. Memories of her own traditionally-oriented childhood, her family, her children, and her lovers no longer sustain her, as "her mind chatters like neon and northside bars." Hanging in space, thirteen floors up from the city streets of an East Chicago ghetto, she hears some people screaming that she should jump, while others try to help her with their prayers. At the end of the poem "she would speak," but *will* she take charge of her own life? Or, is she doomed to death and oblivion?

In an interview with Laura Coltelli, Harjo tells the story of how "The Woman Hanging From the Thirteenth Floor" came to be written. Growing out of a private experience she had at the Chicago Indian Center, the poem reflects Harjo's invented persona and voice, yet people continue to come up to her at readings and say they know a woman like that; or they have read such a story in the newspaper, but the incident occurred somewhere else. Whether by accident or by design, Harjo has constructed a folkloric, urban Native American example of every woman's ultimate fear, the fear of being totally and absolutely frozen and helpless, without the power to speak, unable to function, and therefore not able to choose either life or death for herself.

Harjo writes a deliberately incomplete ending to the unnamed woman's story, because the woman considers letting go and falling, as well as trying again by climbing back through her apartment window. In this way, Harjo gives her readers the freedom to become writers, since the unnamed woman's story has the potential to become every woman's multi-voiced yet muted struggle against fear, depression, death, and oblivion. Much the same pattern of quiet personal struggle appears in Linda Hogan's *Savings* (1988), where several poems underscore the unrelenting stresses of being one of the urban poor and oppressed. In particular, Hogan's ironically-titled "The New Apartment: Minneapolis," describes shabby, worn-out living spaces, dangerous neighborhoods, and memories of blatant racism: "last spring white merchants hung an elder / / on a meathook and beat him / and he was one of The People" (9).

These same urban stresses and fears also echo in Harjo's final development of Noni Daylight's ongoing life story. In "Kansas City," now a much older and no longer beautiful woman with many children by many fathers, Noni watches the trains roll by, remembers her past life, and vows that she still would choose to live her life as she always has. Yet her bravado seems hollow and pathetic, since she, too, is still spiritually and psychologically inarticulate, trapped in unnamed and unresolved fears, and still watching the trains roll out of a city where she is destined to live out her life.

In "Anchorage," a poem dedicated to Audre Lorde, Harjo's speaker, now seemingly free from fear, strides purposefully through this Alaska city "of stone, of blood, and fish." Speaking in a powerfully articulate voice, and sustained by memories of a once-strong, now lost and buried Native American heritage echoing along the streets and lying under the earth, Harjo's central figure also knows that the spirit world still lives.

While on the surface the Anchorage of Harjo's poem appears to be a city of mountains, ancestral Athabascan voices, and creatures of the air and ocean, the speaker also knows that lying "underneath the concrete / is the cooking earth," or the earth of suppressed volcanic forces barely held in check by the thin concrete skin of the modern city. Like the unarticulated stories of "someone's Athabascan / grandmother," the smothered earth and native peoples of Alaska are muted for now. Yet even so, sometimes a story breaks through, and someone pays homage to life. Within the 6th Avenue jail a man named Henry tells his story of surviving eight shots aimed at him outside an L. A. liquor store, and the other inmates laugh at the impossible truths in his tale. Like the earth itself, Anchorage's poor and oppressed native people somehow continue to survive by creating bridges of ongoing dialogue with each other and the land.

In the same vein, but now within the radically different Deep South world of New Orleans, Harjo continues her travels. Unlike Hopi poet Wendy Rose's "Searching for Indians in New Orleans," a poem that comments on the unfamiliar "silence of petroglyphs, / stiff birds and stick women" (*What Happened When the Hopi Hit New York* 21), Harjo's poem returns to its spiritual Creek home through memory. Moving through an ancestrally familiar landscape, her memory "swims deep in blood, / a delta in the skin," as the speaker moves from Oklahoma into the French Quarter, looking for Creek voices echoing along the streets of the present-day city. As she searches for historical or spiritual echoes of her Creek ancestors, she discovers a Spanish horse, frozen speechless as a statue, juxtaposed against a man in a rock shop selling magic stones and unaware of their power. Over and over again, Harjo refers to careless Anglo supremacist behavior, like the contemporary rock shop salesman and the historic Spanish explorer DeSoto, both of whom exert a strong but superficial power over deeper, more private native Creek and natural world powers. And always lying just under the surface of Harjo's New Orleans are those ancestral Creek "stories here made of memory," waiting once again to be told.

Especially in "She Had Some Horses," "Anchorage," and "New Orleans," Harjo's ongoing circularities of memory, story, history, and ancestral voices all work together to create and explain natural cycles underlying human existence, and thus to define the interconnectedness of life itself.

Out of the earth and ancestral lands and peoples comes memory, out of memory comes the present, and the resulting interplay of tensions fuses together into story and life. Throughout the poems of *She Had Some Horses,* landscape and story often merge into an individual voice tied simultaneously to memories of a traditional past, as well as to the life of the present; and it is this voice that helps one to survive in the city.

While one may survive in the city, Harjo believes that one truly lives only on the land, or within memories of the lands. In *Secrets from the Center of the World* (1989), she and photographer Stephen Strom together create an interlocked picture celebrating the fundamental importance of landscape and story within the Native American world view. Harjo begins, her prose poems by remarking that while New York, Paris, or Tokyo may operate as the center of the earth for some people, for her "my house is the red earth; it could be the center of the world"; and even more important, "words cannot construct it, for there are some sounds left to sacred wordless form." This inherent spirituality of place, this cosmic spiritual link with a sentient being that is greater and more powerful than humanity (and indeed *is* the source of all humanity), serves to explain Harjo's deep reverence for specific landscapes in the Navajo Nation. While signs of an alien and dominating Anglo world may intrude—telephone and electricity poles, power plant smoke, and concrete highways— nonetheless "the landscape forms the mind," and "stories are our wealth." Thus, Harjo's memory fuses together dinosaur tracks, an individual lifespan, and linear time into an ongoing spiritual dance of life.

With her most recent book, *In Mad Love and War* (1990), Harjo leaves her home once again and returns to the city as significant setting; and the sheer mass of those urban centers that she names underscores her vision of herself as wanderer in an alien Anglo land. From "Climbing the Streets of Worcester, Mass." to New York City, Denver, Anchorage, New Orleans, and especially Albuquerque and Santa Fe, Harjo is constantly moving through cities and almost never settling into them, but always aware of where the earth is, how the people are feeling, and what the spirit world is doing.

In "We Encounter Nat King Cole as We Invent the Future" Harjo speaks of an old friend, Camme, and the experiences they share of music, love, and old times. Within these seemingly rather ordinary shared memories, Harjo suddenly juxtaposes a dramatically heart-lifting, precisely described personal vision:

> Yesterday I turned north on Greasewood
> the long way home and was shocked to see a
>   double rainbow
> two-stepping across the valley. Suddenly
> there were twin gods bending over to plant
>   something like
> themselves in the wet earth, a song
> larger than all our cheap hopes, our small-
>   town radios,
> whipping everything back
> into the geometry of dreams...

What to non-Native Americans might be just a beautiful sight here speaks in a multi-voiced, spiritual discourse to Harjo. As she sees the double-arched rainbow dancing across the sky, the speaker simultaneously remembers stories describing the eternal Navajo *yei* bending down to the earth in rainbow curves, planting themselves as seeds and thereby fulfilling the sacred promise of life and renewal. Much the same sudden flash of spiritual insight also appears in "Fury Of Rain," where in an unnamed city thunder-as-gods, "naked to their electric skeletons," dance in the streets and shake their rattles of memory during a violent summer rainstorm.

Experiencing such sights and memories as these through a pan-tribal vision often leads, in turn, to Harjo's increasing awareness of time and space, as well as to ongoing dialogic patterns of latent and shared strength among oppressed peoples. In "Hieroglyphic," a poem addressed to African American poet and activist June Jordan, Harjo describes a flash of personal insight that she experienced within the Egyptian Room of New York's Metropolitan Museum. As her memory connects stories of ancient Egypt, her own childhood in Oklahoma, and her present life, she recognizes the ironic surrealism of an interlocking human pattern—while *who* holds power over others may change, oppression remains. Sometimes the clownish humor of "Anchorage's" Henry may temporarily relieve this surreal tension, but such humor is not the Eurocentric, Bakhtinian-related carnivalization of explosive laughter leading to release and relaxation. Rather, Native American clownish humor may often deliberately play the Fool in order to mask and subvert rising hysteria. For example, in "The Book of Myths," the speaker

sees the traditional Creek Trickster "Rabbit sobbing and laughing / as he shook his dangerous bag of tricks / into the mutiny world on that street outside Hunter [College]." Trapped on the "stolen island of Manhattan," both the speaker and Rabbit struggle to stay alive and hang on to their self-control in a dangerous place; and foolish behavior and stories help to keep terror at bay.

This postmodern humor of Harjo's "Anchorage" and "The Book of Myths" varies from Rose's angry, sardonic humor in "Stopover in Denver." Here Rose's speaker, embarking from a plane flight, sees herself caught in the tacky world of Plastic Kachina. Running the gauntlet of tourists, who "scrape my skin with / a camera lens" (*What Happened When the Hopi Hit New York* 10), she remembers childhood tricks of making and selling fake prayersticks, as the pain of ongoing cultural exploitation and personal alienation continues unabated in her life. Like Harjo's clownish Fool, Rose's sardonic poetic voice chooses the release of active laughter rather than passive tears.

When underlying and often unstated personal anger and fears link up with the shocks of urban socio-cultural experience, a highly distinctive, intensely personal poetic statement often results. The rich complexities of Harjo's most recent postmodernist voice are particularly evident in "Santa Fe," a surreal and sensuous prose poem juxtaposing memories of lilacs, Saint Francis Cathedral, the De Vargas Hotel, a cocaine-addicted fox-woman, and a man riding a Harley-Davidson, all swirling in and out of a spiral dance through the speaker's memory, as time "is here...is there," and "space curves, walks over and taps me on the shoulder" (*In Mad*). Whereas Harjo's early city poems are usually set physically in bars, apartments, or automobiles and often describe aimless and alienated drifting, her later poems tend to be set in the mind and its memories of an urban experience, and to describe both a clear-eyed acceptance of life as it is and a quiet but fiercely unwavering commitment to the Native American belief in the inherent spirituality within all life forms.

Thus memory, what Paula Gunn Allen refers to as "that undying arabesque" (*Shadow Country,* 9), underlies all of Harjo's poetry. While all Native American cultures value the powers of memory, the contemporary urban pulse-beats and incidents recorded in Joy Harjo's poems bring memory most fully and dramatically into the non-Native

American reader's awareness and understanding. When she juxtaposes her Native American memories of the earth against present-day urban life experiences, Harjo creates a uniquely surreal, yet frighteningly accurate and familiar picture of modern American cities and their alienated citizenry. As Harjo explains memory, one has no authentic voice without memory; and without an authentic voice, one is speechless, hardly human, and unable to survive for very long. Thus, Harjo's braided strands of multilayered memory and poetic voice intertwine into the very warp and woof of her poetic creation.

Source: Nancy Lang, "'Twin Gods Bending Over': Joy Harjo and Poetic Memory," in *MELUS*, Vol. 18, No. 3, Fall 1993, p. 41.

SOURCES

Allen, Paula Gunn, *The Sacred Hoop: Recovering the Feminine in American Indian Traditions*, Beacon Press, 1986, pp. 59, 60–63, 107, 167, 194.

———, "Introduction," in *Song of the Turtle: American Indian Literature 1974–1994*, edited by Paula Gunn Allen, One World Ballantine Books, 1996, pp. 3–17.

Aull, Bill, James McGowan, et al., "The Spectrum of Other Languages: Interview with Joy Harjo," in *Joy Harjo: The Spiral of Memory: Interviews*, edited by Laura Coltelli, University of Michigan Press, 1996, pp. 106–107, originally published in *Tamaqua* Vol. 3, No. 1, Spring 1992.

Bellm, Dan, "Ode to Joy: In Dreamtime Begin Responsibilities," in *Village Voice*, Vol. 36, April 2, 1991, p. 78.

Bruchac, Joseph, "Interview with Joy Harjo," in *North Dakota Quarterly*, Vol. 53, 1985, pp. 222–24, 226, 229.

———, *Lasting Echoes: An Oral History of Native American People*, Harcourt Brace, 1997, pp. 25–26, 46–47, 102–103, 118, 127, 129.

Carabi, Angels, "A Laughter of Absolute Sanity: Interview with Joy Harjo," in *Joy Harjo: The Spiral of Memory: Interviews*, edited by Laura Coltelli, University of Michigan Press, 1996, pp. 136–37, originally published in *Belles Lettres: A Review of Books by Women* Vol. 9, No. 4, Summer 1994.

Clausen, Jan, "American in the Singular," in *Women's Review of Books*, Vol. 2, No. 1, October, 1984, p. 7.

Coltelli, Laura, "The Circular Dream: Interview with Joy Harjo," in *Joy Harjo: The Spiral of Memory: Interviews*, edited by Laura Coltelli, University of Michigan Press, 1996, pp. 61–62, 65, originally published in Coltelli, Laura, *Winged Words: American Indian Writers Speak*, University of Nebraska Press, 1990.

———, "Introduction: The Transforming Power of Joy Harjo's Poetry," in *Joy Harjo: The Spiral of Memory: Interviews*, edited by Laura Coltelli, University of Michigan Press, 1996, pp. 5–6.

Evers, Larry, "Cycles of Appreciation," in *Studies in American Indian Literature: Critical Essays and Course Designs*, edited by Paula Gunn Allen, Modern Language Association of America, 1983, p. 30.

Green, Rayna, Review of *She Had Some Horses*, in *Ms.*, Vol. 12, July, 1983, p. 21.

Harjo, Joy, *How We Became Human: New and Selected Poems 1975–2001*, W. W. Norton, 2002.

——— and Gloria Bird, eds., "Introduction," in *Reinventing the Enemy's Language: Contemporary Native Women's Writings of North America*, W. W. Norton, 1997, pp. 19–31.

Hogan, Linda, "Who Puts Together," in *Studies in American Indian Literature: Critical Essays and Course Designs*, edited by Paula Gunn Allen, Modern Language Association of America, 1983, p. 169.

Howard, Helen Addison, "The Style of Indian Poetry," in *American Indian Poetry*, Twayne's United States Authors Series, No. 334, Twayne Publishers, 1979, pp. 21–41.

Jaskoski, Helen, "MELUS Interview with Joy Harjo," in *MELUS*, Vol. 16, No. 1, 1989, pp. 5–13.

Kallet, Marilyn, "In Love and War and Music: Interview with Joy Harjo," in *Joy Harjo: The Spiral of Memory: Interviews*, edited by Laura Coltelli, University of Michigan Press, 1996, p. 123, originally published in *Kenyon Review*, Vol. 9, No. 3, Summer 1993.

Lincoln, Kenneth, *Native American Renaissance*, University of California Press, 1983, pp. 8, 12, 76.

Monaghan, Pat, Review of *The Woman Who Fell from the Sky*, in *Booklist*, Vol. 91, No. 6, November 15, 1994, p. 573.

Moyers, Bill, "Ancestral Voices: Interview with Joy Harjo," in *Joy Harjo: The Spiral of Memory: Interviews*, edited by Laura Coltelli, University of Michigan Press, 1996, p. 36, originally from the "Power of the Word" series, Public Broadcasting Service (PBS), 1989.

Murray, G. E., Review of *She Had Some Horses*, in *Chicago*, Vol. 32, May, 1983, p. 132.

Nies, Judith, *Native American History: A Chronology of a Culture's Vast Achievements and Their Links to World Events*, Random House, 1996, p. 249.

Randall, Margaret, Review of *In Mad Love and War* and *Secrets from the Center of the World*, in *Women's Review of Books*, Vol. 7, Nos. 10–11, July, 1990, pp. 17–18.

Review of *She Had Some Horses*, in *Choice: Current Reviews for Academic Libraries*, Vol. 23, June, 1986, p. 1509.

Root, William Pitt, Review of *A Map to the Next World*, in *Whole Earth*, Fall 2000, p. 99.

Ruoff, LaVonne Brown, "Old Traditions and New Forms," in *Studies in American Indian Literature: Critical Essays and Course Designs*, edited by Paula Gunn Allen, Modern Language Association of America, 1983, p. 147–68.

Ruppert, Jim, "Paula Gunn Allen and Joy Harjo: Closing the Distance Between Personal and Mythic Space," in *American Indian Quarterly*, Vol. 7, 1983, pp. 29, 37.

Ruwe, Donelle R., "Weaving Stories for Food: Interview with Joy Harjo," in *Joy Harjo: The Spiral of Memory: Interviews*, edited by Laura Coltelli, University of Michigan Press, 1996, pp. 127–31, originally published in *Religion and Literature* Vol. 26, No. 1, Spring 1994.

Stever, Sharyn, "Landscape and the Place Inside: Interview with Joy Harjo," in *Joy Harjo: The Spiral of Memory: Interviews*, edited by Laura Coltelli, University of Michigan Press, 1996, pp. 79, 84, originally published in *Hayden's Ferry Review* Vol. 6, Summer 1990.

Swann, Brian, Review of *She Had Some Horses*, in *Library Journal*, February 1, 1983, p. 211.

FURTHER READING

Donovan, Kathleen M., "Dark Continent, Dark Woman: Helene Cixous and Joy Harjo," in *Feminist Readings of Native American Literature: Coming to Voice*, University of Arizona Press, 1998.

Donovan writes of the link between darkness and femaleness as explained by Toni Morrison. This female darkness is at the core of the work of Cixous and Harjo. Both seek transformation with their voices that will lead beyond polarities.

Francis, Lee, *Native Time: A Historical Time Line of Native America*, St. Martin's Press, 1996.

The book is organized with a narrative overview of Native American history by century, followed by a detailed timeline of important world events on the left-hand side of the page and parallel relevant Native American events on the right-hand side, allowing the reader to integrate the two into one larger picture.

Jahner, Elaine, "A Critical Approach to American Indian Literature," in *Studies in American Literature: Critical Essays and Course Designs*, edited by Paula Gunn Allen, Modern Language Association, 1983, pp. 211–24.

Jahner gives an overview of genres of the oral traditions and their adaptations in contemporary Native American literature.

Silko, Leslie Marmon, *Ceremony*, Viking, 1977, reprinted by Penguin, 2006.

This novel is widely read and taught as an introduction to Native American culture today. Tayo, an Indian of mixed blood, returns to the reservation for healing in the ancestral way after being held as a prisoner of war during World War II.

Smith, Patricia Clark, and Paula Gunn Allen, "Earthy Relations, Carnal Knowledge: Southwestern American Indian Women Writers and Landscape," in *The Desert Is No Lady: Southwestern Landscapes in Women's Writing and Art*, edited by Vera Norwood and Janice Monk, Yale University Press, 1987, pp.174–96.

The article on Harjo is included in a book with a cross-cultural perspective on women artists and the southwestern desert. Even though Harjo is a city poet, her home base is always Oklahoma where she was born, evident in the images of native life in the Southwest in her poetry. For her, earth is a mother.

Sonnet 75

EDMUND SPENSER

1595

Edmund Spenser's "Sonnet 75" was published in 1595 as part of the larger work, *Amoretti and Epithalamion*. *Amoretti* are small love poems, in this case, sonnets, and an *epithalamion* is a wedding song. The work as a whole was written by Spenser to his second wife, Elizabeth Boyle, whom he married in 1594. The volume of poetry was published in between Spenser's publication of the first and second parts of his epic poem *The Faerie Queene*, for which he is most famous. In "Sonnet 75," the speaker is a poetic version of Spenser and the lover to and about whom he is writing is Elizabeth. The subject of "Sonnet 75" is the immortality of love. In this sonnet, the speaker recounts his effort to immortalize Elizabeth and his love for her. Despite his lover's doubts about his ability to do this, Spenser assures his lover (and the reader) that through his poetry, her name will be remembered, and after their deaths their love will continue in a new life. In this sonnet, Spenser reveals his faith not only in the enduring nature of his love for Elizabeth but also in his faith in the power of written language and his spiritual confidence in eternal life.

The widely anthologized "Sonnet 75" is available in such collections as the fifth edition of *The Norton Anthology of English Literature* (1986). It is also available in the collection *Amoretti and Epithalamion* (2004), published by Kessinger Publishing.

Edmund Spenser

AUTHOR BIOGRAPHY

There is not a great deal known about Spenser's life. Spenser was born in London, England, most likely in 1552, and as a child attended a forward thinking grammar school, Merchant Taylors' School. He was educated there for eight years, beginning in 1561. His education was a classical one, meaning his studies centered on Latin and Greek language, philosophy, and literature. The headmaster Richard Mulcaster was considered to be a revolutionary educator at the time, as he defended the education of women. In 1569, Spenser attended college at Cambridge University's Pembroke Hall. Spenser received financial help from the university in exchange for work. He studied rhetoric, logic, philosophy, arithmetic, geometry, astronomy, and music. After receive a bachelor of arts degree in 1573, Spenser studied for his master of arts degree, which he received in 1576. Cambridge at this time was largely populated by radical Puritans, although the impact of such teachings on Spenser has been debated.

After receiving his master of arts degree, Spenser held a number of offices, working in 1578 as the secretary to the former master of Pembroke Hall, Edward Young, and in 1579 working in the household of the Earl of Leicester, uncle to Spenser's friend and fellow poet Sir Philip Sidney. Some evidence exists that in 1579 Spenser married a woman named Machabyas Childe who bore two children and died sometime before 1594. In 1580 Spenser traveled to Ireland to work as secretary to Governor Arthur Lord Grey de Wilton. During this time, England was attempting to conquer Ireland, through violence as well as by encouraging the English to settle there. Spenser was an enthusiastic participant in this effort. He served in various capacities in Ireland during the 1580s and 1590s. He was granted a large estate, Kilcolman, in 1590. From his home in Ireland, Spenser began to write in earnest, having already published a series of pastoral poems, *The Shepheardes Calendar*, in 1579. He published the first part of his famous epic poem, *The Faerie Queene*, in 1590, and the second part in 1596. Spenser married Elizabeth Boyle in 1594, and in her honor wrote the love poems and wedding song known collectively as *Amoretti and Epithalamion*, published in 1595. After being appointed to the position of High Sheriff of Cork in 1598, he was forced to return to London after rebels burned down his home at Kilcolman. Spenser died in London of unknown causes on January 13, 1599, and was buried in Westminster Abbey.

POEM TEXT

One day I wrote her name upon the strand,
But came the waves and washèd it away:
Agayne I wrote it with a second hand,
But came the tyde, and made my paynes his
   pray.
"Vayne man," sayd she, "that doest in vaineassay, 5
A mortall thing so to immortalize,
For I my selve shall lyke to this decay,
And eek my name bee wypèd out lykewise."
"Not so," quod I, "let baser thingsdevize,
To dy in dust, but you shall live by fame: 10
My verse your vertues rare shall eternize,
And in the heavens wryte your glorious name.
Where whenas death shall all the world
   subdew,
Our love shall live, and later life renew."

POEM SUMMARY

Lines 1–4

In Spenser's "Sonnet 75," the poet expresses in a straightforward manner his conviction regarding the immortal nature of his affection for his lover. With the first two lines the speaker establishes the framework for the poem. He relates how he wrote the name of his lover in the sand on the beach, only to have it washed away by the waves. In the next two lines (lines 3 and 4), he reveals that he attempted to write her name again, only to have the ocean tide once more erase his efforts. Through these lines, the speaker's diligence is revealed. Despite the fact that the waves wash away his lover's name, he repeats what is clearly a futile effort.

Lines 5–8

The next four lines of the poem (lines 5–8) reveal that the poem is not simply the speaker's expression of his feelings, but a recollection of a dialogue with his lover. He explains in these lines what his lover stated when she witnessed his actions. The lover's response to the speaker's endeavors to inscribe her name in so impermanent a medium as wet sand is gently chastising in tone. Apparently a practical woman, she tells the speaker that he exerts himself to no end. The lover goes on to compare her name written in the sand, and its being washed away by the tide, to her own existence, and its inevitable end one day by death. Her tone and her words reprimand the speaker for attempting such a prideful display. She accuses him both of being vain for making such an effort and acting in vain, for his desire to affix their love to a specific time and place is ultimately, and obviously, a fruitless one.

Lines 9–12

In lines 9–12, the speaker responds to his lover's protests. Here his idealism and the fullness of his love is revealed. He tells her that only lower, less worthy creatures will die and be reduced to dust. She, rather, will certainly live on through the fame he will create for her with his poetic verses. His poetry, he assures her, will record forever her singular virtues, thereby immortalizing her name.

Lines 13–14

In the last two lines of the poem, the speaker makes plain that not only will his lover live on forever through his poetry, but also that when death conquers the world, their love will remain and be renewed in the next life. The last lines

suggest the speaker's belief in some form of life after death, although whether he describes a bodily or spiritual existence remains unclear. In a sense, the speaker's intention to immortalize his lover through his poetry validates his lover's accusation that he is vain. His boasts about his ability to create such lasting fame for her reveals his grand opinion of his skill as a poet. Despite this vanity, however, the final lines of the poem make clear the depth of his love and his belief that the feelings they share will live on after death.

THEMES

Love and Immortality

Like most Elizabethan sonnets, Spenser's "Sonnet 75" is concerned with an amorous relationship. Often such sonnets itemize a lover's virtues or reveal the extent of a lover's passion. In this poem, rather than focusing on the qualities of his lover that inspire his admiration, the speaker explores the enduring nature of his love for the woman in question. He dismisses his lover's matter-of-fact expressions of the notion that her name, and their love, is transitory. She quite clearly states that their relationship is a mortal one. She is adamant that she will, in fact, die, and the memory of her presence on earth be extinguished, erased like her name in the sand. However, the speaker is quick to deflate her argument. Only low, base creatures are destined to die, the speaker replies

TOPICS FOR FURTHER STUDY

- Spenser's "Sonnet 75" was written in the late sixteenth century. The language and phrasing combines sixteenth century diction with the more archaic word choice of earlier English literature. Rewrite the sonnet with modern, American English. Maintain the Spenserian rhyme scheme but incorporate words and phrases that express the same sentiments in a modern fashion. Recite both Spenser's version and your own for your class. Afterwards, discuss with your classmates the level of difficulty you experienced in making this modern translation. Was it a simple word-for-word translation? Did you struggle to make the concepts addressed in the poem meaningful for a modern audience? How did you approach the translation?

- Spenser provides a general location for the setting of the poem: a beach. He also mentions the tide washing away the name he had written in the sand. Therefore, we know the beach must have been near the ocean, rather than a lake, as lakes do not cover enough area to be effected by the gravitational pull of the moon and consequently do not have tides. Using print and online resources, research the geography of England. Create a drawing or online version of a map of England in which the beaches are denoted. Also identify the other types of geographic features present in England, and its major cities.

- At the end of "Sonnet 75," Spenser references the notion of an afterlife. It is known that Spenser was a Protestant, perhaps of the more radical variety known as a Puritan. Research the beliefs of sixteenth-century Protestants regarding predestination, death, and the resurrection of the soul. How did the beliefs of Protestants of this time period differ from those of English Roman Catholics? Was this area of belief

  (the afterlife) one of the causes of friction between the two Christian groups? Which group at the time was in the minority? Create either a visual presentation (such as a Power-Point presentation) or a written report incorporating your findings.

- Lady Mary Wroth is one of the few known female English poets writing during Spenser's time. Others include Mary Sidney Herbert (Sir Philip Sidney's sister) and Queen Elizabeth I herself. Wroth is known in particular for penning the first sonnet sequence by an Englishwoman. Research Wroth's sonnets. What themes does she treat? How does her style differ from that of Spenser? How did her contemporaries regard her work? Write a research paper on Wroth and her poetry. Be sure to cite both your print and online sources.

- The Elizabethan sonnet as a genre, represented by the work of Spenser and his fellow sonneteers (Sir Philip Sidney and William Shakespeare), was inspired by the sonnets of the Italian poet Petrarch. Research the way the Elizabethan sonnet grew out of the Petrarchan tradition. What features of the Petrarchan sonnet did the Elizabethan sonneteers retain? How was the form adapted for the English language and an English audience of a later time period? Compile your findings into a written report in which you trace the development of the sonnet form from its Petrarchan roots to its Elizabethan version.

- Many books of love poems have been written using entries from teenagers. Find a book of this poetry; choose a poem to compare to "Sonnet 75" in terms of theme, style, and effect. Present your findings in an essay or an oral presentation.

to his lover. He also identifies the ways in which her immortality will be achieved. First, the speaker explains that his own written words in verse form will result in his lover being remembered for eternity. Furthermore, the speaker continues, their love will endure after death and be rekindled in the next life. Such a statement reveals the speaker's spiritual belief in an afterlife, one in which he is certain that he and his love will be reunited. The whole of the poem builds to this grand vision of their love. The initial images of the lover's name being washed away from the beach by the waves give way to the lover's acceptance of her mortality and the mortality of her relationship with the speaker. After her argument has been mounted however, it is undercut by the speaker. His argument culminates in the idea of a love that transcends physical death. The possibility of such a reunion after death hinges on the notion of an afterlife. In the Protestant tradition to which Spenser subscribed, there was a belief in the idea of an immortal soul that lived on, either in heaven or hell, after the physical death of the body.

The Power of Language

The speaker in Spenser's "Sonnet 75" displays supreme confidence in the power of his own written words. He claims that through his poetic verses he will eternalize his lover's goodness, her best qualities. Through his words, her name and her glory will be written for all time. The speaker has faith that after death their love will live on; this concept is as much related to religious faith in the nature of the immortal soul as it is to the couple's faith in the depth of their love for one another. Yet what the speaker vows to achieve through his writing is quite different than what will transpire for the faithful after the death of the body. The revival in the afterlife of the relationship between the speaker and his lover is generated by the strength of the couple's love. Yet the speaker promises that his lover's immortality on earth will be assured by the strength of his poetry alone. Mere words written by the speaker will be enough, he insists, to insure that his lover's name will never be forgotten.

The fact that the speaker makes such a promise and has such faith in the power of language is reflective of a philosophical concern of sixteenth-century writers, who often explored the nature of language and meaning. Written language was viewed as a collection of symbols, or signs, and its meaning was the intangible notion of what was signified by the symbols employed. The philosophical issues arising from

Footprints (Image copyright Roca, 2009. Used under license from Shutterstock.com)

such studies include the idea that the power of language is possibly weakened if a gap between language and its intended meaning exists. For Spenser's speaker, there is no loss of confidence in the power of language to convey his meaning. His statements regarding his ability to immortalize his lover through his writing assure the reader that language is, for Spenser, an effective and powerful tool.

STYLE

Spenserian Sonnet

Spenser, through the poems in *Amoretti and Epithalamion*, developed a style of sonnet that incorporated the use of an interlocking rhyme scheme; this became known as the Spenserian sonnet. In such a rhyme scheme, the rhyming words at the end of each line (or end rhymes) form a pattern in which each section of the poem is linked with the following section through the repetition of the rhyming words. When discussing rhyme schemes, lines are assigned a letter in order to show the repetition of the rhyme. The Spenserian sonnet rhyme scheme is: *abab bcbc cdcd ee*. (All lines with an "a" designation rhyme with one another, all lines with a "b" designation rhyme with one another and feature an end rhyme different from the "a" lines, and so on.) The effect of this rhyme scheme is a structuring of the poem into three quatrains (a section of a poem consisting of four lines of verse) and a couplet (a section consisting of two lines of verse). This physical structure relates to the poem's meaning. The first quatrain describes the speaker's actions on the beach, the second quatrain reveals the presence of the lover and her objections, the third quatrain contains the speaker's response, and the final couplet sums up the speaker's argument.

Additionally, like many Elizabethan sonnets, (written during the reign of Queen Elizabeth I, 1558–1603), Spenserian sonnets are typically written in iambic pentameter. Iambic pentameter is a type of metrical structure. Meter is a pattern of accented and unaccented syllables within a line of poetry. A line of verse written in iambic pentameter includes five accented syllables, which are each directly preceded by an unaccented syllable. Each set of unaccented and accented syllables is referred to as a metrical foot. Independent of rhyme scheme or the number of metrical feet in a line, the iambic rhythm (unaccented syllable followed by accented syllable) is viewed as a natural, common rhythm of everyday speech.

The Elizabethan sonnet as a genre was inspired by the Italian Petrarchan sonnet, a form which explored similar amorous themes. (The Petrarchan sonnet was named after the fourteenth-century Italian poet Petrarch.) The Elizabethan sonnet was popularized by poets such as Spenser and his contemporaries Sir Philip Sydney and William Shakespeare. These sonnets typically featured the musings of the speaker on the nature of love, passion, desire, or marriage, and were usually directed to a particular woman. Such sonnets often featured a first-person speaker (in which the speaker is referred to as "I") and a woman as an object to be praised, explored, and discussed. In some poems, such as Spenser's "Sonnet 75," the female figure in the poem appears as a partner in a dialogue, rather than as an object being considered and adored.

Archaic Language

Some of the language Spenser utilizes in many of his sonnets, including "Sonnet 75," is deliberately archaic (no longer used in ordinary language).

His poems are not entirely written in the style, diction, and spelling typical of sixteenth-century speech. Rather, Spenser's language harkens back to an earlier time. It has been observed that Spenser's affinity for the works of earlier English authors such as Geoffrey Chaucer, as well as his desire to create distinctively English literature, are at least part of the reasons for his usage of archaic language. The effect of such language in "Sonnet 75" is to give the poem the feel of a work that has already lasted through time. Such language supports the poet's theme of long-enduring, everlasting love.

HISTORICAL CONTEXT

Elizabethan English Protestantism

Queen Elizabeth I inherited, with the crown, a country in a state of religious turmoil. Her Protestant father, King Henry VIII, had persecuted Roman Catholics and severed ties with the Roman Catholic Church. Henry VIII's daughter (and Elizabeth's Catholic half-sister), Mary, ruled after the death of Henry's son, King Edward VI. During her reign, Mary restored relations with the Catholic Church and power to the Pope. Protestants under Mary's rule were executed or forced to flee the country. When Elizabeth became Queen of England in 1558, she restored English Protestantism. Under Elizabeth, Protestantism began to take shape as England's official religion. Parliament passed the Act of Uniformity in 1559, which established a common prayer book and instituted the basic church ceremonies. In 1563, Parliament established the Thirty-nine Articles Act, which delineated various aspects of official religious doctrine. Both acts incorporated some compromises for Catholics and more radical Protestant groups, such as Calvinists and Puritans. Calvinists believed that whether or not a person's soul is saved, or destined for heaven, is determined before the person is even born (predestination). Calvinists additionally advocated a reduced role of the clergy in the national religion. Puritans sought to purge Catholicism entirely from the Church of England.

Spenser was a Protestant, and his beliefs surface in his poetry. He was schooled with and patronized by more radical Protestants. The extent to which such teachings influenced Spenser or his later writings is a subject debated among critics. Alastair Fowler, in *Edmund Spenser*, maintains

COMPARE
&
CONTRAST

- **1590s:** After decades of religious conflict, Queen Elizabeth I takes steps to ensure that the Church of England is shaped as a primarily moderate Protestant institution, with concessions to Catholics and radical Protestants such as the Calvinists and Puritans. However, much conflict between Catholics and Protestants persists. While Queen Elizabeth I allows Catholic concerns to be voiced in Parliament, attending Catholic religious services is forbidden.

  Today: The government of the United Kingdom now insures religious freedom. The official churches are the Church of England (also known as the Anglican Church) and the Presbyterian Church of Scotland, both of which are Protestant in the basis of their beliefs, although the Church of England was influenced by Catholicism in the past. Some conflict between Catholics and Protestants persists in Northern Ireland.

- **1590s:** Queen Elizabeth I has reigned successfully for many years, but she has endured the prejudices of her society against female rulers. She has been persistently advised to marry, despite her reluctance to share her throne.

  She relies on a few loyal male advisors and keeps Parliament under her control by not allowing the houses of Parliament (Commons and Lords) to function as independent legislative bodies.

  Today: As a monarch, Queen Elizabeth II serves a primarily symbolic function in the governance of the United Kingdom. Power, rather, is decentralized in the Houses of Commons and Lords, formally presided over by the Queen Elizabeth II. The political leader of the country is Prime Minister Gordon Brown, who took office in 2007.

- **1590s:** Popular poetic forms include sonnets and epic poems. Poets such as Sir Philip Sidney and Edmund Spenser write extensively in these forms. Poet and playwright William Shakespeare achieves fame with his dramas and later solidifies his reputation as a poet with the publication of his sonnets.

  Today: Poets in the United Kingdom write in a variety of poetic forms, including traditional metrical, rhymed poems and free-verse poems. Popular British poets include Alice Oswald, Glyn Maxwell, and Andrew Motion.

---

that "Spenser emerged [from Cambridge] a moderate but fervent Protestant." However, in the introduction to *Edmund Spenser: Protestant Poet*, Anthea Hume states that there is strong evidence to suggest that Spenser "shared in the militant Protestantism of the circle in which he moved," but also concedes that "there is no clear yardstick of controversy by which we can measure whether Spenser in the 1590s retained the Puritan position of his young manhood or not." Although it cannot be accurately determined whether or not Spenser considered himself a more radical or militant Protestant, it may be conjectured that had he been truly on the fanatical, radical end of this religious spectrum, his work would perhaps contain more obvious clues than it does.

The English in Ireland

Well before Elizabeth's reign, England had cemented its presence in Ireland, intending to further colonize it and deter Irish rebellions. Spenser was known to be a staunch supporter of England's efforts in this area. In *Spenser in Ireland*, Pauline Henley studies Spenser's *View of the Present State of Ireland* (written in 1598, but not published until 1633) in order to identify the English policies toward Ireland that Spenser supported. Henley observes that Spenser, like many other Englishmen, supported a reformation of Ireland that involved the presence of armed troops to deter rebellion. He also supported such extreme notions as the banishing of

Sunrise (Image copyright S. Borisov, 2009. Used under license from Shutterstock.com)

"Irish customs, Irish dress, and the Irish language," and encouraged the prohibition of marriage between the English and Irish. Spenser's ideas regarding Irish reform, Henley observes, were not new. These harsh views were held by many of Spenser's English countrymen. Spenser fled his Irish estate in 1598 after it was attacked and burned down by a group of Irish people who rebelled against the English.

CRITICAL OVERVIEW

The sonnets in Spenser's *Amoretti* have received much critical attention over the years. According to R. M. Cummings in his introduction to *Spenser: The Critical Heritage* (1971), Spenser's work was well-received by his fellow poets but perhaps not well-known or widely read in other circles. Cummings explains, "Spenser was apparently adored by his contemporaries. But the accounts of Spenser in this period come mainly from professional poets. There is no evidence to suggest that he enjoyed a broad fame."

Most modern critics tend to look at the group of sonnets as a whole, examining individual sonnets within the context of the larger collection. The critical response has been varied, with some modern critics noting how the poems have been historically undervalued. In Prosser Hall Frye's 1908 examination of Elizabethan sonnets in *Literary Reviews and Criticisms*, the critic finds that many of the sonnets written during this time period, including Spenser's, are mediocre at best. However, Frye does point to "Sonnet 75" as one of the few Elizabethan sonnets to be singled out as quality works of poetry. In an assessment of the *Amoretti* in the essay collection *Form and Convention in the Poetry of Edmund Spenser* (1961), Louis L. Martz begins by describing the way Spenser's sonnets are often found to be disappointing and inconsistent. Yet Martz takes on these criticisms in order to demonstrate the "harmonious" nature of Spenser's efforts in the *Amoretti*. Likewise, Waldo F. McNeir, in an essay published in the 1972 *Essential Articles for the Study of Edmund Spenser*, finds that Spenser's sonnets in *Amoretti* need to be defended against past accusations of poor quality. McNeir asserts that Spenser's sonnets as a group and individually display a unity of structure. McNeir uses "Sonnet 75" as a specific example, observing the way each of the poem's quatrains "rises to a higher sphere of meaning than the preceding one." McNeir also states that this "ascent to a universal idea . . . is a feature of the *Amoretti* that gives the series one kind of unity."

In addition to these evaluations, Spenser's sonnets are also praised for the realistic relationship they portray. In an analysis of *Amoretti* in the 1930 *A Spenser Handbook*, H. S. V. Jones maintains that one of the qualities that makes Spenser's sonnets stand out among others of the time period is their intensely personal nature. Jones observes that a number of critics have found in these poems "a clearer note of personal feeling than what can be found in the usual complimentary series addressed to a poet's official mistress." Citing "Sonnet 75" in particular, Jones further finds that Spenser's habit of describing incidents that reveal Elizabeth's character produce the effect of heightening the poems' "impression of reality."

CRITICISM

Catherine Dominic

Dominic is a novelist and a freelance writer and editor. In the following essay, she maintains that despite the fact that "Sonnet 75" is part of a larger sonnet sequence, it may be fully understood on its own. She also analyzes the two personas present in the poem as characters within Spenser's vignette.

Many critics demonstrate how the individual sonnets in Edmund Spenser's sonnet sequence known as the *Amoretti* depend on one another for meaning. The sonnets are interrelated by the reappearance of the individuals presented: the poet-speaker persona representing a literary version of Spenser and the object of his love and desire, Elizabeth, who is so identified in several of the sonnets and is generally taken to represent Elizabeth Boyle. (Spenser and Boyle married in 1594.) Despite the overarching structure of the sonnet sequence as a whole, "Sonnet 75" stands on its own, and it may be read as a sonnet whose full import can be appreciated without knowledge of the relationship that develops between the speaker and his lover throughout the rest of the sequence. In "Sonnet 75," Spenser achieves the effect of creating an entire fiction, a poetic story with two characters

> DESPITE THE OVERARCHING STRUCTURE OF THE SONNET SEQUENCE AS A WHOLE, 'SONNET 75' STANDS ON ITS OWN, AND IT MAY BE READ AS A SONNET WHOSE FULL IMPORT CAN BE APPRECIATED WITHOUT KNOWLEDGE OF THE RELATIONSHIP THAT DEVELOPS BETWEEN THE SPEAKER AND HIS LOVER THROUGHOUT THE REST OF THE SEQUENCE."

engaged in a dialogue, with a distinct setting and an emotional conflict that contains grander implications.

As the poem opens, Spenser describes the setting of his story, as well as one of the main characters. The first words of the initial line invite a reading of the poem as a story or vignette (a brief descriptive account of an event), as they invoke a "once upon a time" feeling in the reader. The character whom readers first meet is the first-person speaker and he is writing a woman's name in the sand at the water's edge. The speaker describes how twice he writes her name, and twice it is washed away by the waves. In this first quatrain (a four-line section of a poem), Spenser invites his reader to immediately visualize the scene unfolding. Despite the sometimes archaic word choice and spelling, Spenser's language is ultimately straightforward as he begins to describe his day at the beach—he has set the stage for the rest of the story.

The second quatrain opens with dialogue: the words of the woman whose name the speaker has been writing. With the woman's first words, the reader is suddenly made aware that the speaker is not alone on the beach. He is accompanied and observed by his lover, who apparently thinks him rather foolish. Through her initial words to the speaker, one can intuit something of her character. She tells the speaker that he is both a vain person and that his efforts are made in vain, employing both meanings of the word in the same sentence. She is a practical woman who does not understand why the speaker would twice inscribe her name in the sand at the water's edge. When she first calls him vain, it is in the sense that he has a high

WHAT DO I READ NEXT?

- Spenser's *Amoretti and Epithalamion*, originally published in 1595 and available in a 2004 edition published by Kessinger Publishing, contains the full sonnet sequence of which "Sonnet 75" is a part.

- The epic poem *The Faerie Queene* is Spenser's best-known work. Originally published in two parts (1590 and 1596) and never completed, the allegorical poem traces the adventures of several knights, and its characters represent a variety of virtues. In the first part of the poem, Spenser uses his adaptation of the sonnet form, which later became known as the Spenserian sonnet, for the first time.

- *Fierce Wars and Faithful Loves: Book I of Edmund Spenser's "The Faerie Queene"* (1989), published by Canon Press, is a version of Spenser's *The Faerie Queene* edited by Roy Maynard for the young-adult reader. Maynard modernizes Spenser's archaic spelling and explains the poem text throughout the work.

- William Shakespeare wrote more than 150 sonnets, many of which have been highly praised among critics over the years. Like Spenser's sonnets, Shakespeare's sonnets are thought to be largely autobiographical in nature, and they feature a different adaptation of the Petrarchan structure than that which Spenser employed. Originally published in 1609, but most likely written during an earlier period, the sonnets are available in *Shakespeare's Sonnets* (Folger Shakespeare Library edition), published in 2004 by Simon & Schuster.

- *Elizabeth's London: Everyday Life in Elizabethan London* (2005), written by Liza Picard and published by St. Martin's Griffin, offers a variety of information on all aspects of daily life in London during the reign of Queen Elizabeth I, the time period within which Spenser lived and wrote.

- *American Sonnets* was written by African American poet Wanda Coleman and published in 1994 by Light and Dust Books with the Woodland Pattern Book Center. The collection features modern American versions of the sonnet form.

- *The Lady Elizabeth: A Novel* (2008), by Alison Weir, is a work of historical fiction concerning the youth of Queen Elizabeth I, the queen of England during Edmund Spenser's life. The novel, published by Ballantine Books, is aimed at high-school-level readers.

opinion of himself or his abilities. His actions are in vain, or will prove fruitless, she explains, because by writing her name in the sand, he attempts to make immortal something that is mortal. While she does not specify what this mortal thing is, she goes on to say that she herself will be eradicated from this earth, like her name in the sand, and that so too will her name be wiped away. Her words are embedded with meaning. As she completes her thought, which she uses the full quatrain to express, the reader can go back to the beginning of her statement and begin to understand why she has accused the speaker of being vain. He must have a high opinion of himself if he believes he can transform

a thing destined for death into something eternal. The mortal thing she speaks of is not only herself but also the love between her and the speaker. She speaks of her own mortality and how her name will be erased from memory. At the same time, it is likely that she understands that the speaker's action of writing her name in the sand is a representation of his love for her. Through her chastising of the speaker, she seems to suggest that their love, like her physical body, is a mortal thing that cannot become immortal simply by capturing it in writing.

The moment she speaks these words, however, the speaker contradicts her. What she describes is not true, he tells her. Only lower, base beings are destined for the type of death she discusses. He promises that through the fame he will create for her in his poetry, she will live on. For an entire quatrain, he confidently describes how his words will insure her immortality. Now the vanity that the woman accused the speaker of earlier in the poem is apparent. Writing her name in the sand was not a vain act, it was one of love. Yet what he now proposes—securing her immortality through his writing—is a boastful thing indeed. Like the woman in the poem, readers have no way of knowing what the speaker's true intentions are when he writes his lover's name in the sand. The way the speaker initially presents his actions suggests that it is simply a thing to do at the beach: he loves her, so he writes her name in the sand and they watch it disappear when the tide washes over it. At this point in the story, the speaker has not earned the woman's accusation of vanity. Yet she somehow reads the speaker's ordinary act—writing a name in the sand—as a quest for immortality. She is either presumptive by nature or possesses some knowledge of the speaker that readers do not. The poem does not offer clues to suggest why the woman makes this leap; perhaps she simply knows the speaker well enough to guess that for him, any act of writing is not as simple as it appears.

Nevertheless, her words appear to transform the speaker's intentions. It is only after she relates her interpretation of his actions—after she injects the notion of mortality and eternity into his simple act—that the speaker tells her the contrary. He exclaims that he will, in fact, make her immortal through his actions, in his poetry praising her glorious virtues. After she makes suppositions about his intentions, he becomes what she has earlier accused him of being: a vain man who thinks he can make her immortal through his poetry. Yet after her words inspire his boastfulness, the speaker further elevates their love. He asserts in the sonnet's closing couplet (a two-line section of a poem) that their love will not just become immortal through poetry. It will live on in the afterlife, he assures. In these final two lines, the speaker asserts his belief in the Christian notion of the everlasting nature of their souls and reframes their relationship into an idealized one characterized by an immortal, spiritual love. Critics such as Waldo F. McNeir (in the 1972 article "An Apology for Spenser's *Amoretti*," published in *Essential Articles for the Study of Edmund Spenser*) point out that this notion of heavenly love is one that may be characterized as Platonic in nature. (The philosopher Plato believed in the transcendent, immortal nature of love as a reflection of our perpetual yearning toward a notion he called "the Good"—or the idea of absolute harmony, goodness, and beauty.)

Through the story told within the poem, and the dialogue between the speaker and his lover, Spenser repeatedly elevates the love between the couple. The speaker initially performs a simple loving act, that of writing his lover's name in the sand. This inspires the woman to comment on the fact that she is mortal; their love will disappear with her death. Her words incite in the speaker a fervent protest, denying her claims. Rather, he insists, his poetry will preserve her name forever on earth. Finally, the speaker declares his belief in something more lasting than the earthly fame to be achieved through his writing. He insists that their souls will live on after death, and their love will then be renewed. While the speaker's vision of their love becomes more grand as the poem progresses, the story the poem tells is essentially a simple one. It is the tale of an ordinary act of love and a profession of the faith that love withstands all time.

Source: Catherine Dominic, Critical Essay on "Sonnet 75," in *Poetry for Students*, Gale, Cengage Learning, 2010.

William C. Johnson

In the following excerpt, Johnson identifies how "Sonnet 75" fits into an overarching liturgical structure in the Amoretti *sequence of poems.*

A number of years have now elapsed since Professor A. Kent Hieatt presented his controversial and revealing examination of Spenser's *Epithalamion;* quite recently, however, have critics begun to take notice of similar structural patterns in Spenser's accompanying sonnet sequence, *Amoretti*. Earlier readers who examined the sonnets as a sequence, as opposed to those, who focused only on the individual sonnets, complained of the work's diffuseness and noted such things as the "oddly indecisive" nature of the series. In general these earlier critics accepted any sequentiality only on the basis of narrative or thematic consistency rather than on structural patterns indicated by the work itself. Previous attempts at "organizing the disorder" of the *Amoretti* took various directions: some critics explained the montage of poems as sequential insofar as they represent fluctuations of the human mind on the Platonic ladder; others pointed to psychological divisions, corresponding to the stages of courtship, as being the underlying structural components. Still others, such as Professor Lever, pointed to "disproportion" in events before and after the courtship, "inconsistencies"

> THE SUBJECT OF THE SONNET, THE LOVER'S VAIN ATTEMPT TO IMMORTALIZE THE LADY, FINDS ITS LITURGICAL PARALLEL IN THE EPISTLE LESSON, I JOHN 5, THE SUBJECT OF WHICH IS THE ONLY REAL WAY OF 'OVERCOMING THE WORLD.'"

in the characterization of the heroine, and the "indecisiveness" of the ending, and attempted to explain the structural organization by the desperate expedient of eliminating some of the sonnets and rearranging others. Recently a new wave of interest in the *Amoretti* has resulted in examinations which, like Hieatt's and Professor Alastair Fowler's work on other Spenser poems, have reasserted Spenser's tightly mathematical handling of his structures—including that of the *Amoretti*. Early in 1969 Mr. Alexander Dunlop, for example, demonstrated that sonnets XXII–LXVIII correspond to the period extending from Ash Wednesday through Easter. In 1970 Professor Peter Cummings presented his narrative survey of the work, including with it a rather tightly-structured analysis of what he calls the "allegory of love" in the cycle. In the same year appeared Professor Fowler's *Triumphal Forms,* in which the *Amoretti* structure is discussed not only by itself but in its relationship to the *Epithalamion* and the intervening "Anacreontics." Most recently Professor Hieatt has argued for a numerical, structural approach to the sonnets by indicating similar patterning in *The Faerie Queene.*

These current studies have been correct in their various structural interpretations of the sonnet cycle—the numerical "facts" are not only available but visible in the sequence itself. Yet they have failed to note that in addition to providing a complexly-organized series of poems, externally asymmetrical but containing (to use Fowler's term) "inlaid symmetry," Spenser has shown us an even more intricate patterning in the internal structure of his series. Almost unnoticed Spenser put aside the old laws of courtly love and put, in their stead, a Christian outlook. Quite unexpectedly he shifted the focus from the "I" (found not only in Petrarch but in almost all the English Renaissance writers as well) to the lady, who (as

does the "ideal" in medieval works) remains throughout the poems in the foreground. Under the guise of tradition, using the rhetoric of the humanists and the language of the Petrarchan sonneteers, Spenser created his own unique version of this particular type of poem and this peculiar type of poetic organization.

Although it is no small achievement, Spenser's manipulation of the *Amoretti* sequence is not immediately apparent; however, the poet does provide readers with three clues which distinguish this sequence from similar poetic structures of the time. Taken individually each is of interest for its singularity within a poetic form where novelty is both rare and often a hindrance rather than an aid to expression. Taken collectively the three clues serve the same function as tumblers in a doorlock; when put in place, and when all are viewed as performing simultaneously, the door opens and reveals that which it had concealed. So cleverly locked, indeed so well disguised is even the "door" of the *Amoretti,* that most readers have not even noticed, until now, that it is there.

The first of the distinguishing features appears in the sequence title. When he named his series *Amoretti,* Spenser rejected the traditional practice of naming a sequence of sonnets after the lady whose virtues and beauty are therein extolled. Some sonnet ladies, such as Stella, Delia, Coelia, Hélène and Cassandre, grace not only a large number of sonnets but also the titles of their respective sequences. Some, such as Petrarch's Laura and Sidney's Stella (in addition to Scève's Délie, though in a different form of sequence) are identified by verbal play in the sonnets, or at least have their names repeated often enough in various addresses to keep the reader constantly aware of the person about whom the poems were written. Such is not the case with the lady of the *Amoretti,* whose name appears but once in the entire cycle, and then not until the seventy-fourth sonnet when the poet identifies her as one of three women named Elizabeth.

Spenser's choice to follow in the path of Dante, Ronsard and Drayton, his decision not to use his lady's name in the title of his sonnet series, is significant insofar as it reveals two things: first, the poet is not writing strictly in the English tradition but is following the more philosophically-inclined continental writers; and second, Spenser's using *Amoretti* for his title directs readers away from the lady as the subject of the poems and encourages looking elsewhere for the focus, or theme, of the sequence.

The second differentiating characteristic comes directly out of the examination of the title and the search for the theme. I refer to Spenser's concept of the *amoretti,* his loves, and the types of love he presents. A quick reading of the sequence does not suffice to give an accurate account of their author's views on the subject. Although at first glance the opposite may appear true, it is not courtly love which Spenser promotes in these poems; and although for the most part sensuality is absent in the sequence, we know from the corpus of Spenser's works that his idealized view does not reject physical love for a purely spiritual love. Recent scholarship has argued that it is also not Platonic love, although elements of it find their way into the total picture. The *amor* of the *amoretti,* while it contains some Platonic thought, is much more than a theoretical philosophy. And although Spenser employs many traditional Petrarchan courtly conceits, his "love" consists of more than a fixed decorum of expressions to be used in winning a lady. Also, while physical love does represent a part of the love described, it always takes second place to higher forms of affection.

The link by which Spenser joins the religious and philosophical, the traditional and physical concepts of love with which he was familiar, appears in the Christian concept of love. It is this which objectifies and makes practical the Neo-Platonic theories and which reinvests the worn Petrarchan conceits with a new life. And it is this same Christian concept of love fulfilled in marriage which not only distinguishes the *Amoretti* from all other sequences of the time, but which provides the second of the cycle's distinguishing marks.

From the equivocal title and the multiplistic views of love in the sonnets we may turn to the rather peculiar structure of the overall work. This provides the third of Spenser's clues, and it is particularly this one which most clearly reveals the poet's intent. In the widest sense the structural technique employed reflects the calendar structure which Spenser mentions directly several times in the series. In a more particular sense it indicates the format of one particular calendar—that of the Church—to which the poet alludes but which, when examined closely, reveals the real concern of the poems. In its most directed thematic parallel

the calendar reveals that the love of which the poet writes is not only that of a man for a woman but is, concomitantly, a metaphoric presentation of the Christian's love for Christ.

Mr. Dunlop is correct in indicating that sonnets XXII–LXVIII refer to the period from Ash Wednesday through Easter. Looking at the poems one finds that LXII corresponds to the first day of the new calendar year. The Old Style calendar which Spenser used would date this "new year's day" sonnet as March 25. Likewise, the sequence celebrates Easter day in LXVIII, six sonnets after the start of the new calendar year. The only year near the publication date of the sequence in which Easter appeared six days after Lady Day (making Easter March 31) was 1594, the year the sequence was registered and the year Spenser married. Just as the two Spring sonnets in the sequence are separated by fifty-two sonnets, and may be interpreted as possible allusions to the fifty-two weeks separating specific parts of successive years, so the six sonnets between LXII and LXVIII may be read as referring to six days between the two authenticated dates of the 1594 Lady Day and Easter.

Yet two such verified sonnet-days hardly seem proof enough for stating that Spenser intended each sonnet to represent a particular day during a particular year. We might look further into the matter by examining another key sonnet and its relation to the Easter sonnet (LXVIII). Sonnet XXII, marking "this holy season fit to fast and pray," indicates the start of the Lenten season— Ash Wednesday. By numbering the sonnets between this one and Easter we find that forty-six poems fill that space—the exact number of days in Lent (forty "fast" days plus six interpolated "feast" days). If one labels XXII Ash Wednesday (February 13, 1594), XXIII Thursday, etc., LXVIII is a Sunday—Easter, March 31, 1594....

Following the Lent-Easter sequence are another three sonnets marking Sundays in the liturgical year: LXXV, LXXXII and LXXXIX. The first of these, the famous "One day I wrote her name upon the strand" is labelled "Low Sunday" in the Church. The subject of the sonnet, the lover's vain attempt to immortalize the lady, finds its liturgical parallel in the Epistle lesson, I John 5, the subject of which is the only real way of "overcoming the world."

The second Sunday after Easter, corresponding to LXXXII, bases its Collect on I Peter 2, which praises God for the gift of His "holy son...who is both a sacrifice for sin, and also an example of

Godly life." The sonnet praises the lady for her humility in "relenting" to the lover, for uplifting him, and for inspiring him to eternal praise of her. This joyousness echoes the day's Psalm: "But let all those that seek thee be joyful and glad in thee: and let all such as delight in thy salvation, say always, the Lord be praised."

The last sonnet of the sequence, LXXXIX, corresponds to the third Sunday after Easter. The lonely lover mourns:

> Lyke as the culver on the bared bough
> Sits mourning for the absence of her mate,
> And in her songs sends many a wishfull vow
> For his returne, that seems to linger late....

The subject of this Sunday's service is, appropriately (considering the sonnet's content), constancy. Spenser uses the Gospel, John 16, for the parallel. The lesson contains Christ's assurance to His disciples that although He was to be going to heaven, He would still always be with them. This is the promise which the lover is apparently to bear in mind about the lady too; it is this which gives hope at the end of the sequence, just as the culver has hope for its mate's return. The choice of the culver—or dove—which is the common symbol of the Holy Spirit, would seem perhaps to have been used to signify both constancy and the means by which Christ intended to remain always present with His disciples.

At the very beginning of the sequence the poet had glorified the bright "starry light" of "that angels blessed looke,/ My soules long lacked food, my heavens blis." Now at the very end of the sequence the lover, in quiet meditation, mentions "blis" for the second time, only this time in a far different context: "Dark is my day, whyles her fayre light I mis,/ And dead my life that wants such lively blis."

Beginning with joy and ending with sadness at the lover's, and metaphorically Christ's absence, suffused with light at the start and filled with darkness at the end, the sequence quietly concludes. The image of the dove singing its "wishfull vows" remains; there is hope of its mate's return, just as the poet continues spending his time in expectation of the lady's return. Likewise, the Christian waits hopefully, expectantly, for Christ's second coming.

The returning of so many aspects of the sequence—the recurrence of seasons, actions, poetic images, the reassurance of love's continuance by the annual celebration of Christ's Resurrection—all underlie the notion of cyclical return. It is then but a short time until the *Epithalamion* shows that the lady's absence conforms to this pattern too, and until the various *amoretti* of the sonnets combine in that magnificent paean to the perfect consummation of earthly love in a chaste marriage. But it is here, where heavenly love is seen as the metaphoric basis for the sonnet sequence, where the pure love of the poet for his lady is paralleled by the love of the Christian for Christ, that we are prepared for the earthly love of the great marriage hymn. And it is here, where the verbal and thematic liturgical correspondencies establish the intricate patterning of sonnet-days, that we pass through the season of preparation, both of courtship and of the penitent Christian during Lent, until the years, seasons, weeks and days of the sonnets finally focus on the stanzaic hours of the *Epithalamion*. In such a way Spenser provides us with the two works which are not only "for short time an endlesse moniment," but which are, by Spenser, his narrator, and the metaphoric penitent, "vowd to eternity."

Source: William C. Johnson, "Spenser's *Amoretti* and the Art of the Liturgy," in *Studies in English Literature, 1500–1900*, Vol. 14, No. 1, Winter 1974, pp. 47–61.

SOURCES

Amir, Lydia, "Plato's Theory of Love: Rationality as Passion," in *Practical Philosophy*, Vol. 4, No. 3, November 2001, pp. 6–14.

Cummings, R. M., ed., Introduction to *Spenser: The Critical Heritage*, Routledge & Kegan Paul, 1971, pp. 1–29.

Fowler, Alastair, "Part II," and "Part IV," in *Edmund Spenser*, edited by Ian Scott-Kilvert, "Writers & Their Work" series, Longman Group, 1977, pp. 7–11, 19–25.

Frye, Prosser Hall, "The Elizabethan Sonnet," in *Literary Reviews and Criticisms*, G. P. Putnam's Sons, 1908, pp. 1–18.

Henley, Pauline, "Spenser and Political Thought," in *Spenser in Ireland*, reprint, Russell & Russell, 1969, pp.168–91.

Hume, Anthea, Introduction to *Edmund Spenser: Protestant Pope*, Cambridge University Press, 1984, pp. 1–10.

Jones, H. S. V., "Amoretti," in *A Spenser Handbook*, F. S. Crofts, 1930, pp. 335–47.

Kishlansky, Mark, "Elizabeth I," in *Microsoft Encarta Online Encyclopedia*, http://encarta.msn.com/encyclopedia_761555497/Elizabeth_I.html#s11 (accessed May 28, 2009).

Marshall, Peter, "The Estate of the Dead: The Afterlife in the Protestant Imagination," in *Beliefs and the Dead in Reformation England*, Oxford University Press, 2004, pp. 188–231.

Martz, Louis L., "The *Amoretti*: 'Most Goodly Temperature,'" in *Form and Convention in the Poetry of Edmund Spenser*, Columbia University Press, 1961, pp. 146–69.

McNeir, Waldo, F., "An Apology for Spenser's *Amoretti*," in *Essential Articles for the Study of Edmund Spenser*, edited by A. C. Hamilton, Archon Books, 1972, pp. 524–33.

"Parliament and Crown," in *United Kingdom Parliament*, http://www.parliament.uk/about/how/role/parliament_crown.cfm (accessed May 30, 2009).

Spenser, Edmund, "LXXV," in *Amoretti and Epithalamion*, Kessinger Publishing, 2004, p. 40.

———, "Sonnet 75," in *The Norton Anthology of English Literature*, Vol. 1, 5th ed., edited by M. H. Abrams, W. W. Norton, p. 770.

Streete, Adrian, "Reforming Signs: Semiotics, Calvinism and Clothing in Sixteenth-Century England," in *Literature and History*, Vol. 12, No. 1, May 2003, pp. 1–18.

"United Kingdom: International Religious Freedom Report 2002," in *U.S. Department of State*, http://www.state.gov/g/drl/rls/irf/2002/13989.htm (accessed May 30, 2009).

FURTHER READING

Dieffenthaller, Ian, *Snow on Sugarcane: The Evolution of West Indian Poetry in Britain*, Cambridge Scholars Publishing, 2009.

> Modern British poetry is influenced by the large population of immigrants from West India (a former British colony). Dieffenthaller traces the process through which traditional West Indian poetry, through British influence, became something distinct from both cultures.

Greaves, Richard L., *Society and Religion in Elizabethan England*, University of Minnesota Press, 1981.

> Greaves examines how religious beliefs permeated all aspects of social life in Elizabethan England. He explores the beliefs of the various Christian sects practicing during this time period and demonstrates the ways in which the belief in the relationship between religion and social order structured the class and legal constructs of Elizabethan society.

Hales, John W., *A Biography of Edmund Spenser*, Dodo Press, 2007.

> Hales provides an account of Spenser's life and works and includes a discussion of Spenser's harsh opinions regarding the Irish culture and his belief that it should be eradicated as part of England's colonization of Ireland.

McLaren, A. N., *Political Culture in the Reign of Elizabeth I: Queen and Commonwealth 1558–1585*, Cambridge University Press, 2000.

> McLaren provides an analysis of Queen Elizabeth I as a political ruler in the first part of her reign. Special attention is given to how the role of the English ruler and the political concepts of hierarchical and patriarchal power were transformed under the governance of a woman.

Paterson, Don, and Charles Simic, eds., *New British Poetry*, Graywolf Press, 2004.

> Paterson and Simic present an anthology of a variety of poems from thirty-five of Britain's most highly-respected and award-winning poets, including established and those emerging authors.

Success Is Counted Sweetest

EMILY DICKINSON

1878

Emily Dickinson's "Success Is Counted Sweetest" is one of the few poems Dickinson saw published in her lifetime. Although it is estimated to have been written around 1859, it was published in 1878's *A Masque of Poets*. As the poem was published anonymously, a reviewer for *Literary World* speculated that the poet was Ralph Waldo Emerson. Given Emerson's reputation then and now, the reviewer's guess is quite a compliment to the author. Dickinson admired Emerson's work and no doubt was influenced by him. In modern day, the poem appears in numerous anthologies and is usually included in sections of anthologies of Dickinson's work. It is also in the only current edition of the complete works of Dickinson, *The Complete Poems of Emily Dickinson*, published by Back Bay Books in 1976.

"Success Is Counted Sweetest" intertwines themes of longing, ambition, mortality, and war. In typical Dickinson style, the poem manages to cover these themes in a way that is brief and insightful. While many readers imagine that the dying soldier in the poem is a U.S. Civil War casualty, the specific war is unimportant for Dickinson's purposes. The poem is dated as being written in 1859, prior to the Civil War. Dickinson was more apt to write on universal truths than specific events, and here she draws the reader's attention to the moment of the soldier's death and how he feels hearing the distant sounds announcing the opposing force's victory.

Emily Dickinson (*The Library of Congress*)

AUTHOR BIOGRAPHY

Dickinson was born December 10, 1830, in Amherst, Massachusetts, to a young lawyer named Edward and his wife, Emily (Norcross) Dickinson. Dickinson had an older brother named William Austin (known as "Austin") and a younger sister named Lavinia (nicknamed "Vinnie"). Edward became a successful politician who was known to be active in his community. His father had been a major force in the founding of Amherst College, and Edward often hosted and entertained visiting guests and lecturers, including Ralph Waldo Emerson. Less is known about Dickinson's mother, but many critics agree that she retained a love of learning, particularly in the sciences, for most of her life.

The Dickinson children attended Amherst Academy after completing their studies in a local one-room school. Dickinson was an enthusiastic student, and she seized the chance to attend college-level lectures while still at Amherst Academy. Young women of the time enjoyed this educational season in their lives, where they grew their intellects and imaginations before settling into domestic lives. Dickinson certainly thrived. In addition to John Milton,

Emerson, and Henry David Thoreau, she embraced the writings of Emily and Charlotte Brontë, Robert and Elizabeth Barrett Browning, George Eliot, Charles Darwin, Nathaniel Hawthorne, Henry Wadsworth Longfellow, and Matthew Arnold. As Dickinson's friends began to marry and start their own adult lives, she delved deeper into her books.

When Dickinson completed studies at Amherst Academy, she continued her education at Mount Holyoke Female Seminary. Although Dickinson had a strong sense of self as a spiritual young woman, seminary authorities regarded her as hopeless. This was probably because some of her independent religious views challenged prevailing Calvinistic Puritan religious beliefs. Dickinson left the seminary after only a year of study, surprising her peers and instructors. Whatever the reason, she returned to her parents' home and began her slow retreat from society. She generally stayed close to home, but she entertained guests and maintained a few close relationships. At home, Dickinson had little interest in domestic work. She was content to pursue her own interests, such as writing and gardening.

Austin married Susan Gilbert, to Dickinson's delight. Susan had been a family friend since childhood, and she and Dickinson were good friends. Dickinson also corresponded with editors Samuel Bowles and Josiah Holland, literary figure Thomas Wentworth Higginson, and pastor Charles Wadsworth.

Between the late 1850s and 1865, Dickinson wrote as many as 1,100 poems. "Success Is Counted Sweetest" is placed as being written during this prolific time, and given that she pursued its publication, it was clearly one of which she was proud. In 1865, Dickinson began to have serious problems with her eyesight, which was followed by two decades of devastating loss. Her father died in 1874; her mother suffered a stroke in 1875; Wadsworth and Dickinson's mother both died in 1882; and her eight-year-old nephew whom she held especially close to her heart died from typhoid fever in 1883.

A schism that seemed already to be forming was made worse with the arrival of Mabel Loomis Todd in 1881. A friend of Susan's, Todd was married to a professor at Amherst College. Dickinson is said never to have met her in person; she hid and eavesdropped when Todd came to visit Vinnie. However, the next year, Todd began a love affair with Austin that lasted the rest of his life. Its openness created a great deal of tension among family members.

Dickinson suffered from nephritis (inflammation of the kidney) and died on May 15, 1886. Despite having published seven poems in her lifetime, she asked Vinnie to burn her writings before she died. Vinnie destroyed personal letters but preserved the poetry. It was Vinnie who pursued posthumous publication of Dickinson's poetry.

In 1890, Dickinson's first collection of poetry was published to great acclaim. The first edition (five hundred copies) sold out in only a few weeks. Remarkably, it saw eleven editions in only two years. In editing early volumes, Todd and Higginson aggressively edited Dickinson's unusual style to make it more accessible. Later publications, however, presented the poems in their original style and punctuation.

POEM SUMMARY

Stanza 1

The speaker begins with an aphorism (a brief, insightful statement of objective truth) about success. This is very typical of Dickinson's style. Here, the aphorism asserts the speaker's observation that success is valued most by those who never achieve it. The idea is that the more elusive success is, the more a person desires it and is driven to achieve it. The next two lines restate the idea with a metaphorical illustration. The speaker says that truly understanding a nectar (a sweet substance, thus referring directly back to the first line's mention of sweetness) first requires a deep, almost painful, longing. The speaker actually asserts that the person has a need for the nectar; it is not something to be dismissed as a desire or a passing fancy.

Stanza 2

In the second stanza, the speaker moves into the motif of the poem, which is battle. The purple host is the victorious army, taking the flag after winning the battle. The poet describes the army collectively when she mentions the host, and individually in the words "not one." These subtle word choices underscore her point that individual soldiers cannot fully appreciate the victory they celebrate, nor can the army as a whole. However you look at them, they are in no position to savor the victory to the degree that the

vanquished prize it. It means more to the losing army than the winning one. The third and fourth lines move right into the last stanza as the perspective transitions from the purple host and the flag to the losing side.

Stanza 3

The second stanza began with the statement that the definition of victory is more clearly understood by the dying soldier on the battlefield. The third stanza reveals this concept, as speaker describes himself as defeated before it is mentioned that he is also dying. The defeat is really more to the point of the poem, but the dying underscores the speaker's commitment to victory (or, put another way, success). The second line calls his ear forbidden, meaning that the sound of victory he hears in the distance is not really meant for him. Those celebrating are sharing an experience among those who have won, with no intention of including their fallen enemy. Still, the soldier hears the sound as he dies. The sounds burst in his ears, a final agony as he is in a unique position of best understanding the value of that victory.

Another interpretation of the poem reads the battlefield as a sports field, where the winning team's flag is flown and the crowds cheer at the end of the match. The defeated team is not literally dying; it is just exhausted and disappointed after exerting its full energy and passion into the game. The sounds of the other team celebrating and the crowd cheering bursts in their defeated ears as they reflect on how victory is precious.

THEMES

Pursuit of Success

Dickinson often states her point directly right at the beginning of her poems, and this is certainly the case with "Success Is Counted Sweetest." The first two lines state plainly that success is most valued by those who never achieve it. The suggestion is that they have tried to achieve success, but it has eluded them. Still, the pursuit of it does not lose its energy or importance, even (as the reader learns at the end of the poem) to the point of death. The stanza adds that fully understanding just how sweet success is first demands that the person longs for it. Someone to whom success comes easily can never appreciate it as the

TOPICS FOR FURTHER STUDY

- The battle between the Texans and the Mexicans at the Alamo is among history's most dramatic stories. In *The Gates of the Alamo* (2001), Stephen Harrigan presents this story and its participants as the setting for his work of historic fiction. By introducing new characters, Harrigan recreates the drama and importance of this event at both a national and personal level. Form a reading group to discuss this novel, and be sure to draw correlations between the characters' experiences and Dickinson's poem. Upon completion of the reading group, write an essay comparing the novel and Dickinson's poem and explaining how the reading group influenced your interpretation of both works.

- Toward the end of the poem, the speaker uses the word "distant." This word has more than one meaning, and Dickinson uses it intentionally. Write a blog entry on a free blog Web site, such as *Blogger.com*, *WordPress.com*, or *LiveJournal.com*, explaining this word choice and think of at least two of your own examples of how this technique can be effective in writing

brief but meaningful statements. Have at least two classmates and your teacher leave comments about your entry on your blog.

- Read Maya Angelou's poem "The Lesson." How does Angelou portray the process of dying? What is the speaker's focus, and what comments does she make about defeat? Compare this poem and its speaker to "Success Is Counted Sweetest" and its speaker. Based on your observations, what general observations can you make about the experience of dying and the individual response to it? Create a PowerPoint presentation, including visuals, and lead a class discussion comparing the two poems.

- Research Greek mythology, specifically looking for information about nectar. Why was it important, and what new reading does this information bring to the first stanza of Dickinson's poem? Prepare a brief PowerPoint presentation on allusion using the example of nectar as a springboard, incorporating images of nectar in artwork.

---

person who strives for it does. That Dickinson calls this desire a "sorest need" demonstrates that the longing is actually painful, and that the object of success is much more than a want; the person must have it. That the speaker is describing success and not, for example, food and water, indicates that Dickinson is referring here to something very personal, which has taken on a life of its own. The tone of the stanza suggests that the more elusive the success is, the more driven the person is to have it. So, not only is there a personal element to the pursuit, but there is also a psychological element.

The second and third stanzas offer an illustration of the insight of the first stanza. The setting is a battlefield, and the speaker notes that the one who truly understands victory is

not the one holding up the victory flag but instead the defeated soldier who hears the roar of victory in the distance. The sound may be of an army celebrating or perhaps a trumpet announcing victory. Regardless, it is he who has paid the greatest price in pursuit of a fruitless victory who best understands the value of that success. Dickinson emphasizes her point about elusive success by setting up this scene with opposing forces, then pointing to the one who embodies her message.

Mortality

In making a point about success and how maddeningly elusive it can be, Dickinson chooses to introduce a battle scene and a dying soldier. This image makes two main points. First, the soldier

---

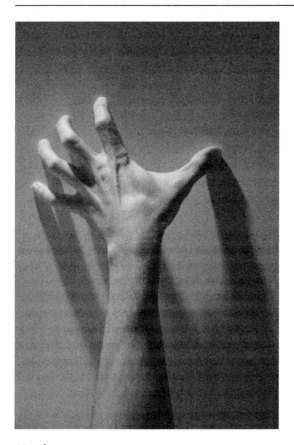

Hand *(Image copyright Jorge Pedro Barradas de Casais, 2009. Used under license from Shutterstock.com)*

in the poem never stops pursuing this success. He is dying in the poem and has knowingly and willingly given his own life for the sake of the battle. He believes in the cause so much that he is willing to sacrifice himself to the pursuit of it. Dickinson describes a very intense need to win, so much so that the person never lets up, chasing it right up to the moment of death. Second, the illustration of the soldier shows that when a person faces mortality, his or her priorities come into sharp and sudden focus. The last images the soldier's mind rests on before he dies are certainly the most important. The soldier had already made up his mind that the battle was worth taking the chance that he would never leave it alive. Then when he is lying in the field, his last conscious experience is not remembering the high points of his life, the love of a good woman, or the dreams he never fulfilled back home; in the moments of his last breaths, he fixes on the distant sound of the battle's victory because he realizes more than the victors how important and sweet the victory is. His

mortality, therefore, does not diminish the importance of the success but instead brings it into sharp focus.

STYLE

Metaphor

A metaphor is the comparison of two objects or ideas by equating one with the other, as opposed to a simile, which compares by stating that one is like the other. In "Success Is Counted Sweetest," Dickinson uses several metaphors to bring her reader deeply into her assertion that success is best understood by those who have strived for it without attaining it. In the first stanza, the speaker's comment that understanding a nectar first requires that the person desperately needs it. In the context of the stanza, the nectar is a metaphor for success. To make sure the reader makes the connection, Dickinson not only keeps the first stanza brief (consisting of only two statements), but she cleverly uses the reference to nectar to reflect back on the word "sweetest" in the first line.

The second and third stanzas focus on a metaphor as the reader is drawn into a battlefield scene. The victors take the flag while the defeated lay dying, hearing the distant sounds of victory and triumph. The battlefield is metaphorical; it could be any struggle in one's life. It represents the circumstances in which a person pursues success. In the end, one person wins and the other loses (in this case, dies). Again, this is metaphorical. The defeated soldier in the poem is actually dying, but in other situations, the person may feel despair and hopelessness. The sounds of triumph at the end of the poem represent the reward of the winner's success.

Paradox

A paradox is a statement or idea that seems inherently contradictory. The thrust of the poem, that success is best appreciated by those who never reach it, seems paradoxical. How can someone who does not have something be able to appreciate it? The apparent contradiction of the opening statement is intriguing and draws the reader in to see how the speaker is going to defend this position. Dickinson moves immediately into portraying why such an assertion is true. As the reader continues through the poem, the paradoxical statement makes sense. For most readers, the truth of the aphorism (saying) "One wants what one does not have" resonates with readers' personal experiences. The poem, after all, illuminates something about human nature, even if it does not at first make sense. The trustworthiness of the paradox is supported by the logical voice of the poem. Told in the third person, the poem lacks passion and emotion. The tone is matter-of-fact and sounds as if the speaker has thought through the idea. This reliability adds to the credibility of the paradox at the center of the poem.

Iambic Meter

Besides the brevity and insight of the poem, the meter is also typical of Dickinson's work. "Success Is Counted Sweetest" is written almost entirely in iambic trimeter. An iamb is a metrical foot, or a unit of stressed and unstressed syllables, in poetry. Iambic trimeter involves each line of poetry consisting of three iambs. Dickinson's poem maintains this meter, excluding the first two lines of the second stanza (almost the center of the poem), which add an extra foot to each line. The rhyme scheme of the poem is also characteristic of Dickinson's style, which follows an *abcb* pattern. This gives the poem a balance between freedom and structure; only half the lines are rhymed, while the other half are free verse. Like the near-standard meter of the poem, the rhyme scheme possesses enough structure to demonstrate the poet's discipline and adherence to conventions, while the unrhymed lines and occasional added metrical feet demonstrate the poet's willingness to make her own rules to convey her ideas completely.

Alliteration and Consonance

"Success Is Counted Sweetest" contains numerous examples of alliteration and consonance. Alliteration is the repetition of consonant sounds at the beginning of words, and consonance is the repetition of consonant sounds within words. Dickinson uses both literary devices, and they are best appreciated when the poem is read aloud. In the first two lines, for example, the "s" and hard "c" sounds are repeated. The hard "c" continues in the third and fourth lines but is also represented by "q" in "requires." In the second stanza, the "h" sounds tie the first two lines together. In the fourth stanza, the "d" sound repeats in the first two lines, perhaps leading into the closing idea of triumphant battle sounds. After all, the last two lines make use of the "t" sound, which, in tandem with the "d" sound creates an onomatopoetic (imitation of a sound in words) effect by sounding like drums.

HISTORICAL CONTEXT

Realistic Period in American Literature

Although the year of Dickinson's birth, 1830, was also the year that the Romantic Period in American Literature began, Dickinson is associated with the Realistic Period in American Literature, which lasted from 1865 to 1900. Where the Romantic Period yielded writing that was optimistic, exalted, hopeful, and at the time self-consciously literary, the Realistic Period emerged from a nation struggling after the Civil War and facing economic, industrial, and intellectual change. As she kept to herself and did not interact with many writers of her day, Dickinson did not set out to become a Realistic writer. She was the product of her time, place, and personality. The Realistic writers were less idealistic than their Romantic predecessors, and they were willing to both look at and write about struggle on a collective and individual level. During this time, the work of writers like Charles Darwin, Karl Marx, and Auguste Comte became more integrated in mainstream thought. Science challenged religion more directly, something that Dickinson understood well.

During the Realistic Period, literary writers transitioned to a new way of thinking, and new literary voices rose to fame. Authors, poets, and playwrights approached subjects with the intent to present them with more fidelity so that their works would be relevant to their audiences. In effect, their works leave the job of interpretation to the audience or reader. In *A Handbook to Literature*, editors William Harmon and Hugh Holman note that amidst a number of imitators of Romantic poetry during the Realistic Period were "three new and authentic poetic voices...[Walt] Whitman's, [Sidney] Lanier's, and Dickinson's." This is particularly interesting in light of the fact that one literary critic guessed that "Success Is Counted Sweetest" was written by Ralph Waldo Emerson, one of the predominant Romantic poets. Novelists in the Realistic Period wrote in style and content about growing disillusionment and cynicism. While some of the novelists were harsh and serious, others adopted the same perspective in a humorous way, most notably in the work of Mark Twain.

Women in 1860s America

In 1860s Amherst, Massachusetts, where Dickinson lived with her family, women had clearly defined roles and expectations within the home

COMPARE
&
CONTRAST

- **1859:** The issue of slavery and competing economic systems creates conflict in the United States between the North and the South. The presidential election of Abraham Lincoln is only one year away, and the outbreak of the Civil War is only two years away.

  Today: Operation Iraqi Freedom is launched in March 2003, and the Iraq War is still waging as of 2009. Although Iraqi dictator Saddam Hussein was executed for war crimes in 2006, and his regime was destroyed during George W. Bush's presidential terms, Iraq is still a war zone.

- **1859:** When a battle is won, the victory is signified by waving the victor's flag, taking the defeated army's flag, sounding a trumpet, beating drums, and shouting and singing in victory.

  Today: When a battle is won, the winning army flies its flag, soldiers shout and sing, and the media announces the victory to the world. Technology plays a critical role in alert-

ing the public to the ups and downs of a battle and its outcomes.

- **1859:** Political and social activist Susan B. Anthony and other suffragettes participate passionately in the pursuit of equal rights for women. Not only do they endeavor to succeed in their cause, but they also intend to open opportunities for other women to succeed at whatever they want to do.

  Today: The suffragettes secured the right for women to vote in 1920, and won other important rights to give women equal standing in society. Today, women vote, hold office, own property, and enjoy very similar rights as their male counterparts. In the presidential campaigns for the 2008 presidential election, Senator Hillary Rodham Clinton ran for the Democratic presidential candidacy. Although she lost to President Barack Obama, Clinton was a strong contender for the candidacy. Many women continue to organize groups that support women's efforts to advance in the United States and around the world.

and the community. They were encouraged to attend school and learn about literature, philosophy, mathematics, history, and even science, but they were not expected to build careers on their educations. During the late teen years, men's and women's educational paths diverged as men launched their careers or went to seminary, law school, or other professional schools. This was the case with the Dickinson children. While Austin advanced to law school, his sisters finished at Amherst Academy and then went to Mount Holyoke Female Seminary. The separation at this point came with the students reaching marriageable age, and they were preparing for their adult lives. Women's education was taken seriously, as is evident by the establishment of schools like Mount Holyoke. Colleges for women would be developed in the near future

at this time in U.S. history—Vassar Female College was chartered in 1861 and opened after the end of the Civil War.

Once young women completed their schooling or were married, they assumed their duties in the home. As wives and mothers, their duties included all housework, child rearing, and entertaining. The social network was vibrant and important, and hosting visitors and gatherings was part of the woman's responsibilities to her family. Women who did not marry (such as Dickinson and her sister, Vinnie) returned to their parents' homes, where they took on many of the same domestic duties as married women. They were expected to set aside their personal interests in favor of contributing to the smooth running of the house. Dickinson returned home, but she only assumed some of the traditional

Injured soldiers (© North Wind Picture Archives / Alamy)

roles expected of a woman in her position. She was less interested in socializing, hosting, and seeing suitors, and more interested in cultivating her own garden, corresponding with literary-minded people, and writing poetry. Her poetry topics were not confined to domestic matters or romance, but extended to nature, spirituality, death, and, as in "Success Is Counted Sweetest," military settings.

CRITICAL OVERVIEW

During Dickinson's life, only seven of her poems were published, one of which was "Success Is Counted Sweetest." After her death in 1886, her sister, Lavinia ("Vinnie"), set about gathering all of the poems and pursuing publication for them (even though Dickinson asked her to burn all her writings). The first volume of Dickinson's poetry was published in 1890 to great acclaim, and "Success Is Counted Sweetest" was among the selected poems. In a review from 1890, a writer for *Critic* praises

the volume as "striking and original," adding that its "main quality . . . is an extraordinary grasp and insight." Modern readers must remember how unusual Dickinson's poems were to her contemporaries, yet many critics embraced them at once. The reviewer for *Critic* concludes, "Miss Dickinson's poems, though rough and rugged, are surprisingly individual and genuinely inspired." Referring specifically to "Success Is Counted Sweetest," the same reviewer notes that it is one in which "the rare genius of Miss Dickinson is best seen," adding that it reflects the "Emersonian influence." In a review from the same year that appeared in *Nation*, a contributor states that Dickinson's poems are "simply extraordinary, and strike notes, very often, like those of some deep-toned organ."

In *Dictionary of Literary Biography*, Sarah Ann Wider observes that "Success Is Counted Sweetest" is exemplary of a theme that Dickinson revisits in various poems. Wider writes:

> "The extremes of opposition point to the bleak experience of the individual observer. Knowledge proceeds by negation. One cannot hold onto its objects. They slip from possession. One

knows something most distinctly precisely because one does not have it. Time and again Dickinson describes knowledge by its unattainable nature: 'Success is counted sweetest / By those who ne'er succeed...'"

One of the great literary critics of the 1950s was John Crowe Ransom, whose poetry and criticism is still studied today. In *Emily Dickinson: A Collection of Critical Essays* (1994), when determining Dickinson's place in the American literary tradition, Ransom not only believes that she holds a position of importance, but he also goes so far as to declare, "Whitman and Emily Dickinson were surely the greatest forces of American poetry in the nineteenth century, and both had found their proper masks." James Reeves, in *Reference Guide to American Literature* (1963), boldly states:

> "Not all poets have recognized the exceptional resources of this [English] vocabulary, but the greatest, of whom [Geoffrey] Chaucer and [William] Shakespeare are the preeminent examples, have undoubtedly done so. Dickinson, as a close reading of her poems will confirm, is to be counted among their number."

CRITICISM

Jennifer Bussey

Bussey is an independent writer specializing in literature. In the following essay, she considers Dickinson's perception of the last moments before a person dies by reading "Success Is Counted Sweetest" and "I Heard a Fly Buzz—When I Died."

Emily Dickinson's fascination with death and dying is well known, and to many readers, it is characteristic of her work. Along with themes of nature, love, and relationships, death is a topic Dickinson returns to repeatedly in her poetry. Some of her correspondence even reveals her curiosity concerning the experience of death and wanting to know what people think about, say, and feel in their final breaths. Two of her poems portray her understanding of what a person might experience at the moment of death: "Success Is Counted Sweetest" (c. 1859) and "I Heard a Fly Buzz—When I Died" (c. 1862). Although in the two poems, the speakers and their situations are very different, there are similarities between them that warrant examination.

In "Success Is Counted Sweetest," the speaker posits that success is best understood not by those who strive for and achieve it, but by those who try yet never attain it. The speaker claims that longing

WHAT DO I READ NEXT?

- Edited by Thomas Johnson, *The Complete Poems of Emily Dickinson* (1976) is the only current edition of Dickinson's poems that contains all 1,775 of her poems. Johnson is a respected Dickinson scholar, and he has arranged these poems chronologically, based on the best existing information available on the poem dates.

- *A Voice of Her Own: Becoming Emily Dickinson* by Barbara Dana (2009) is a novel about Dickinson as a teenage girl who wants to become a poet and breaks standard gender roles in mid-1800s New England.

- *Emily Dickinson: Selected Letters* (2006) is edited by Dickinson scholar Thomas Johnson. Dickinson maintained correspondence with a wide variety of people, from family members to literary experts. Her letters demonstrate her acute writing ability and her tendency to slip into poetry, even when writing prose.

- Edited by Wendy Martin, *The Cambridge Companion to Emily Dickinson* (2002) is indispensable to the high school or undergraduate student of American literature. Fourteen essays from respected scholars around the world are collected in this volume.

- Richard B. Sewall's *The Life of Emily Dickinson* (1998) is a National Book Award-winning biography. Sewall's book is very detailed and examines the heart of the woman, her poetry, and how she achieved her unique and enduring voice.

- Maria Mazziotti Gillan and Jennifer Gillan's *Unsettling America: An Anthology of Contemporary Multicultural Poetry* (1994) can be used to find comparisons and contrasts to Dickinson's feelings about the idea of success from the perspective of other Americans.

and determination uniquely enable a person to understand the value of the success that eludes him. In contrast, the successful person enjoys his success without fully appreciating its worth. To illustrate this concept, the speaker observes the battlefield on which he is dying. This setting provides the clear delineations between success and failure that Dickinson needs to proceed with her poem's central imagery.

On the battlefield, the winning army takes the flag of the defeated army and celebrates its victory. Meanwhile, a defeated soldier hears the sounds of triumph as he dies. Dickinson has craftily built the poem to move toward this moment of death; first, her speaker makes a bold assertion about the value of success and the surprising answer to the question of who best grasps it. Establishing the idea that success is sweetest to a person who has failed success, she chooses a dying soldier to illustrate this point. The figure of a battle-weary, bloodied soldier heaving his last breaths on an abandoned battlefield is dramatic, poignant, and relatable. Authors and poets have long drawn on such imagery to evoke a whole range of emotions and truths. Here, Dickinson taps into the pathos already in place to take the reader a step further—actually delving into the soldier's awareness as he dies. On what does he focus? Not his family or his evaporating dreams, nor his comrades or his own physical suffering. Instead, his senses hone in on sound. His forbidden ear (that is, the ear for which the sounds are not intended) listens intently to the sounds of triumph. We know he is listening intently because the sounds are distant (as is specified in line 11), yet they are so loud and intense that they burst clearly and agonizingly into his moment of death.

The dying soldier's experience is significant because it indicates what is most important to him at that moment. The traditional belief is that

when a person faces impending death, one's life story plays quickly in the mind. All the things that matter most are summed up in a moment; a person's entire life is distilled into a short auto-biographical filmstrip that brings to mind what is essentially the meaning of his life. In "Success Is Counted Sweetest," Dickinson portrays this distilled meaning of life in the success the soldier was unable to achieve even though he fought to the death for it. His pursuit of success was the single most important thing in his life, and as he nears his end, he focuses only on that. It is ultimately heartbreaking and pitiful as the reader is led to believe that the soldier dies with the excruciating knowledge that the thing he most wanted will never be his.

"I Heard a Fly Buzz—When I Died" is an intriguing poem whose voice is that of a person who has already died and is recalling the moment of death. The speaker remembers seeing and hearing loved ones gathered around, so weary they are almost out of tears. The speaker recalls seeing their eyes and hearing their breathing, all of which create an atmosphere of exhausted anticipation. Apparently, the speaker's deathbed vigil had been a long one, but she was fortunate enough to have family and possibly friends who loved her enough to keep that vigil. She did not die alone and unnoticed, and the reader can assume that the speaker was mourned and remembered.

The speaker remembers taking care of all of the matters of her estate, such as the will, other legal documents, and naming who should have what keepsakes. This is a very typical stage people go through when they know their time is short; but it is done by people who are dying and know it, not by people who are suddenly and tragically killed. This lets the reader know that the speaker in "I Heard a Fly Buzz—When I Died" had been dying slowly, probably of illness. She had time to prepare herself and her family and organize her affairs. Now that everything is taken care of as she wishes, the speaker is free of anxiety and worry over any worldly affairs.

Unexpectedly (to the reader and to the speaker in her memory), the presence of an ordinary fly interrupted the peaceful awareness of the speaker in her final moments. She remembers seeing it (the speaker states that it was blue and describes the light in the room) and then hearing it (its buzzing sound). The fly's clumsy, halting sounds and movement are in contrast to what had been a serene, smooth conclusion to the speaker's life. In every way, the fly is an interruption, although there is no indication that the loved ones gathered around were aware of its existence in the room at the time of the speaker's death. It is as if the speaker's attention has moved squarely off herself and the other people and onto this disruptive fly. As the poem proceeds, it becomes clear that the speaker's attention will never again move onto anything else.

Much scholarship exists concerning the significance of the fly in "I Heard a Fly Buzz—When I Died." It could represent the intrusion of the ordinary on a profound moment; death, since flies thrive on decay; or the dying person's heightened senses at the moment of death. Whatever the fly's symbolism, the poem clearly shows that the speaker focused completely on the fly as she took her last breath and closed her eyes forever. If the speaker read any meaning into its presence at her death, she does not say so. This does not rule out the fact that Dickinson intends for the reader to seek insight into its meaning, however. Yet for the speaker, the memory of the fly is the main idea and the springboard for the whole poem. She begins the poem with the memory of hearing a fly buzz when she died, and in the last stanza (when she actually dies), the fly is described in detail. So, for the speaker, the fly became the focal point at the moment of death, as surely as the sounds of military victory became the focal point for the speaker in "Success Is Counted Sweetest."

The speaker in "Success Is Counted Sweetest" and the speaker in "I Heard a Fly Buzz—When I Died" are very different people in very different situations. The first speaker is a soldier dying alone on a battlefield, struck down by mortal wounds. Although he knew he was risking his life by participating in the battle, he did not know for sure that this day would be his last day alive. His preparation leading up to his death would have been different than the second speaker's. The first speaker's purpose in life had been to succeed in war, and he failed. At the moment of death, the whole of his consciousness focuses on that matter.

The second speaker dies in a comfortable bed in her own room after having ample time to prepare thoughtfully and methodically, and she is surrounded by loved ones. Her purpose in life is not explicit, but she also finds one thing to focus on at the moment of death. The

circumstances for the speaker in "Success Is Counted Sweetest" and the speaker in "I Heard a Fly Buzz—When I Died" are completely different, as are the events that have brought them to their final moment, but there are important similarities. In both poems, death is described in terms of the senses; both speakers seem to experience heightened sensitivity to sound, especially. The reader can decide if the sound on which the speakers focus carries particular significance, but there is no argument that they pass into death with sounds in their ears. Both speakers also die peacefully. Neither is afraid of death, nor do they fight against it. They accept what is happening and do not denounce the injustice of it or state any regrets they have about their lives. Interestingly, neither contemplates what is on the other side of death. The speakers do not express doubt, fear, anticipation, relief, or exaltation about what awaits them in the afterlife. The reader can conclude that Dickinson believed that there was something awaiting her speakers because of her religious upbringing and the fact that the speaker in "I Heard a Fly Buzz—When I Died" is speaking from beyond this world. Yet it bears commenting that neither speaker considers this in the final moments of life.

Dickinson's thoughts and feelings about death were certainly complicated and, it seems, always deepening. By analyzing "Success Is Counted Sweetest" aside "I Heard a Fly Buzz—When I Died," the reader at least sees that Dickinson understood that death did not have to be horrifying and meaningless. These two poems, written around the same time, indicate that Dickinson believed that people become peaceful and focused when drawing their last breath and as life draws to a close. Her portrayal of the moment of death in these two poems is intriguing, bold, and somewhat comforting.

Source: Jennifer A. Bussey, Critical Essay on "Success Is Counted Sweetest," in *Poetry for Students*, Gale, Cengage Learning, 2010.

Coleman Hutchison

In the following excerpt, Hutchison considers "Success Is Counted Sweetest" as a manifestation of Dickinson's attitude toward Whig party politics.

During his lifetime, Edward Dickinson's name rarely appeared in print without an accompanying "Whig" rhetoric—the signifiers "Edward Dickinson" and "Whig" never straying far from one another. Edward Dickinson: a man eulogized

Emily Dickinson's house (© *James Marshall / Corbis*)

as "a grand type of a class now extinct—An Old-School-Gentleman-Whig," "a true whig in every sense of the word . . . ever ready to sacrifice personal preference to the good of principle," someone "always look[ing] toward the right, and with indomitable perseverance pursu[ing] it." Edward Dickinson: a man "well known throughout the District as an unflinching whig—one whose political principles require no chemical test to ascertain their strength, and the ardor of whose feelings is not regulated by the temperature of the weather." Edward Dickinson, who, at the Whig National Convention of 1852 gained renown for voting 53 consecutive presidential ballots for 70-year-old Whig emblem Daniel Webster; "a firm, straight Whig, a pure citizen." Edward Dickinson: a man who served as a Whig in the Massachusetts House of Representatives in 1838 and 1839; in the state senate in 1842 and 1843; and in the 33rd National Congress in 1854–1855.

Beginning here with a particularly Whiggish biography of Edward Dickinson, this essay will tell a story about the centrality of the rise and fall of the American Whig party to the poetic

projects of Emily Dickinson. Through several necessarily speculative and gestural readings, the essay charts relationships between Edward Dickinson's political poses and positions and Emily Dickinson's politico-poetic poses and positions. Though careful not to conflate Edward and Emily Dickinson's individual political investments, the essay argues that we cannot understand either Edward *or* Emily Dickinson outside of the context and discourse of latter day Whig party politics. Given a series of recurrent rhetorics that reveal "Whiggery" to be an important thematic concern in Emily Dickinson's immediate antebellum, bellum, and postbellum writing, it is time that Dickinson studies reconsider and reconceptualize the poet's complex relationship to her immediate political milieu, and, in turn, the relationship of that immediate political milieu to the coming of the American Civil War. . . .

While the paucity of extant Edward Dickinson correspondence makes a thoroughgoing comparison of father-daughter rhetoric impossible, one uncanny rhetorical convergence is worthy of attention. Cajoled into accepting the Whig nomination

> IN ADDITION, A RHETORIC OF DEFEAT
> RECURS WITH A STARTLING FREQUENCY IN EMILY
> DICKINSON'S EARLIEST VERSE—VERSE WRITTEN, WE
> THINK, DURING THE LATE 1850S, AFTER THE GRAND
> DEMISE OF THE WHIG PARTY AND EDWARD
> DICKINSON'S TWO MAJOR POLITICAL DEFEATS."

for Congressional Representative in 1855, Edward Dickinson wrote that, "My inclination would lead me to avoid the publicity of being a candidate for office." While a discourse of publicity was not uncommon for the period, it is nonetheless striking to see a rhetoric of "publicity"—and specifically a rhetoric of avoided or deferred publicity—coming from the father of Emily Dickinson, a poet too often defined by the politico-poetic poses her texts struck: for example, "Publication—is the Auction / Of the Mind of Man—" (Fr788 [1863]); "Don't tell! they'd advertise us—you know!" an alternate line from "I'm Nobody! Who are you?" (Fr260[1861]). As numerous critics note, the language of withdrawal or removal proliferate in Dickinson's poetry leading up to and during the Civil War. Consider

> Safe in their alabaster chambers
> Untouched by morning,
> And untouched by noon,
> (Fr124A [1859])

Indeed, throughout the war, the Dickinsonian text continually thinks though the ethics and efficacy of withdrawal: "We grow accustomed to the Dark—/ When Light is put away—" (Fr428 [1862]); or,

> To put this World down, like a Bundle—
> And walk steady, away,
> Requires Energy—possibly Agony—
> 'Tis the Scarlet way
> (Fr404 [1862])

When we encounter withdrawal in Emily Dickinson's poetry we understandably privilege *Emily* Dickinson's biography, conflating ever so slightly the relationships between poet, speaker, and poetic subject. Yet, such a privileging of *Emily* Dickinson's biography also limits our understanding of the texts' exploitation of

personae and polyvocalism. Could Emily Dickinson's rhetoric of withdrawal emanate from a persona roughly approximating her father? Could these verses be speaking of or to *Edward* Dickinson's experiences in and out of the political spotlight? In light of both their biographies, that by 1862 *both* Emily and Edward Dickinson had to some extent put a "World down, like a Bundle" and walked "steady away" seems a given. Emily Dickinson's poetic (or poeticized) withdrawal is profoundly timely, resonant precisely because it doubles Edward Dickinson's withdrawal from the local and national political spheres. As such, we might ask, could these poems of remove thematize a withdrawal from the political sphere (a la Edward Dickinson) just as ably as a withdrawal from "public" life (a la Emily Dickinson)? Most urgently, could these poems thematize a *shared* experience of withdrawal and remove? Such questions remind us to attend to the ironic preponderance of plural pronouns in these poems of removal and withdrawal: "we," "their," "us," "our." Though such pronoun use furthers the claims to universalism so many critic-readers of Dickinson prefer, here we might ask, in what sort of seclusion do the speakers and poetic subjects of these poems find them*selves?*

To this end, an oft-mentioned, much-interpreted poem of withdrawal from early in the war—and thus early in Edward's political seclusion—is rendered through a telling rhetoric:

> The Soul selects her own Society—
> Then—shuts the Door—
> To her divine Majority—
> Present no more—
>
> Unmoved—she notes the Chariots— pausing—
> At her low Gate—
> Unmoved—an Emperor be kneeling
> Opon her Mat—
>
> I've known her—from an ample nation—
> Choose One—
> Then—close the Valves of her attention—
> Like Stone—
> (Fr409A [1862])

Often taken to be a personal-poetic manifesto for *Emily* Dickinson, the poem couches its dramatic removal in terms of specifically national election ("divine Majority"; "from an ample nation— / Choose One") perhaps resonant with *Edward* Dickinson's withdrawal from political life. Similarly, we would do well to pay close attention to a poem like Fr115B (1859).

> Ambition cannot find him—
> Affection does'nt know
> How many leagues of nowhere
> Lie between them now!
> (Fr115B [1859])

For Edward Dickinson, the degree of his removal from political life after 1855 was profound. Once a regular on the pages of both *The Springfield Daily Republican* and *The Hampshire and Franklin Express,* Edward Dickinson (cf. "him") found himself less and less often in the pages of local periodicals, further and further away from "publicity," "ambition," and "affection," and more and more subject to the capricious winds of political change that would find one "Yesterday, undistinguished! / Eminent Today."

In addition, a rhetoric of defeat recurs with a startling frequency in Emily Dickinson's earliest verse—verse written, we think, during the late 1850s, after the grand demise of the Whig party and Edward Dickinson's two major political defeats. Some of these verses are aphoristic, deceptively trite, bootstrap-pulling affairs:

> We lose—because we win—
> Gamblers—recollecting which—
> Toss their dice again!"
> (Fr28 [1858])

or, "Best Gains—must have the Losses' test—/ To constitute them—Gains" (Fr499 [1863]). Others seem broad rationalizations of defeat:

> Success is counted sweetest
> By those who ne'er succeed.
> To comprehend a nectar
> Requires sorest need.
>
> Not one of all the purple Host
> Who took the Flag today
> Can tell the definition
> So Clear of Victory
>
> As he defeated—dying—
> On whose forbidden ear
> The distant strains of triumph
> Burst agonized and clear!
> (Fr112C [1859])

In verses such as these, defeat is experienced not in isolation but in clear view of others' victories. Might such verses be, among many things, not-so-oblique references to the experience of defeat brought on by the failures of both Edward Dickinson's election bids and his political party? In the case of "Success is counted sweetest," might the

"distant strains of triumph" evoke the political successes other political parties achieved following the failures of the Whig party?

At least one of these lyrics of defeat offers provocative resonances with such failures:

> I never lost as much but twice—
> And that was in the sod.
> Twice have I stood a beggar
> Before the door of God!
>
> Angels—twice descending
> Reimbursed my store—
> Burglar! Banker—Father!
> I am poor once more!
> (Fr39 [1858])

Edward Dickinson, perhaps apostrophized by line seven's Banker—Father! exclamation, had "never lost . . . but twice in Whig elections: once in 1854 and again in 1855, just a few years before the composition date both Johnson and Franklin have assigned the poem. One could certainly offer an aggressive reading of the rhetoric of "sod" at line two, marking perhaps a subtle intertext to the discourse of "free soil"—a discourse Edward Dickinson was intimately familiar with given his strong advocacy against the Kansas-Nebraska Act while congressional representative to the 33rd Congress. In many important ways, the issue of "free soil," the "Free-Soil" party, and the Kansas-Nebraska act's "popular sovereignty" solution did in fact spell doom for the American Whig party, and concomitantly, Edward Dickinson's political career. In a calculus perhaps too complex to limn here, Michael Holt counts the debate over and passage of the "Nebraska act" as a major cause of the downfall of the Whig Party: "The Nebraska act thus badly damaged intersectional comity in the party, although some Whigs in both sections continued to hope that it might be restored in time for the 1856 election" (957). Here then we find an example of Emily Dickinson's verse being engaged not simply with a rhetoric of defeat but with a rhetoric of defeat wholly resonant with the American Whig Party.

The following, little-read poem also arguably betrays a deep investment in Whiggery:

> Papa above!
> Regard a mouse
> O'erpowered by the Cat!
> Reserve within thy kingdom
> A 'Mansion' for the Rat!
>
> Snug in seraphic Cupboards
> To nibble all the day,

While unsuspecting Cycles
Wheel solemnly away!
(Fr151B [1860])

The poem begins emphatically with a paternal trope, as the speaker draws "father's" attention to a scene of defeat. "Regard" as a verb here is appropriately ambiguous; read as a directive to "take note of" the Mouse, the poem becomes merely a humorous revision of a religious set piece. If, however, we gloss "regard" with a bit more care, the poem opens up in intriguing ways. "Regard" also signifies "to look to, have a care of or for," "to consider, take into account," and "to take heed of." Given these additional definitions, line two's directive might be more didactic in nature: to take heed of the lessons the Mouse-cum-"Rat" offers "Papa."

In lines three and four the poem reveals its central conceit: a parody of John 14:1–3: "Reserve within thy kingdom / A "Mansion" for the Rat!" Exaggerated by the trite "Cat-Rat" rhyme at lines 3 and 5, such a perversion of religious rhetoric renders the verse sardonic, even slightly blasphemous, beginning as it does not with God-the-Father but with God-the-Papa, and suggesting that a "Rat" should have a place reserved in heaven. In turn, the stanza break after line five marks a seeming shift from the earthly to the ethereal, imagining the Rat care-free and "Snug in seraphic Cupboards."

While this poem surely offers us Dickinson at her most playful, it may also offers us Dickinson at her most political. If we concede the indeterminacy of "regard," allowing for the possibility that the directive is for something more than mere observation, then the poem can be read parabolically: something to the effect of "it is a far, far better thing the Mouse-cum-Rat does now." In particular, we must trouble over the poem's final two lines: "While unsuspecting Cycles / Wheel solemnly away!" Evoking at once images of revolution and cycles of history, progress, and fate, the lines remind the reader of the world the Mouse-cum-Rat has left behind. Tellingly, the poem does not actively mourn the fallen Mouse-cum-Rat; instead, the poem offers solace in the fact that said Mouse-cum-Rat will find peace in the afterlife, in celestial cupboards where it is able "To nibble all the day." Free of worldly concern, our Mouse-cum-Rat thus transcends that world's machines and machinations, which "solemnly," "unsuspecting[ly]" go on turning, regardless of the Mouse-cum-Rat. Reading the poem aggressively, we might suggest that as the speaker draws "Papa's" attention to the

Mouse-cum-Rat, Emily Dickinson draws her father's attention to the parable that Mouse-cum-Rat offers. As such, we can interpret this poem as a parable of the benefits of remove from a political sphere, of the peace and fulfillment to be found in the "seraphic Cupboards" of political seclusion; as an assurance that the Massachusetts political machine continues to function with or without Edward Dickinson.

"Papa above!" was written (we think) in 1860, the same year that the Bell-Everett/Constitutional Union party nominated Edward Dickinson for lieutenant governor, and, by extension, nominated Emily Dickinson for lieutenant governor's daughter. In a letter to Louise and Frances Norcross, dated mid-September 1860, the poet writes, "Won't Fanny give my respects to the 'Bell and Everett party' if she passes that organization on her way to school? I hear they wish to make me Lieu-tenant-Governor's daughter. Were they cats I would pull their tails, but as they are only patriots, I must forgo the bliss . . . / Love to Papa" (L225). The import of this letter is two-fold: first, the epistle tellingly attaches a discourse of patriotism—a particularly contested discourse during the period, one not to be used lightly—to the Bell-Everett party. Given that the Bell-Everett party was the closest political cousin to the Whig party, such a declaration of "patriotism" offers a sinewy if subtle political commentary. Second, the letter shows that Dickinson had taken to representing the Bill-Everett party as a cat in 1860. This letter enables a near allegorical interpretation of the poem/parable: having witnessed the Bell-Everett party "o'erpow-ering" a potential nominee, the speaker chides her "Papa/Father" to heed the lesson, remain out of the "unsuspecting Cycles," and stay "snug" in political repose. . . .

Source: Coleman Hutchison, "'Eastern Exiles: Dickinson, Whiggery and War," in *Emily Dickinson Journal*, Vol. 13, No. 2, Fall 2004, pp. 1–26.

Chanthana Chaichit

In the following essay, Chaichit argues that through her inner journeys and through the international popularity of such poems as "Success Is Counted Sweetest," Dickinson has ultimately transcended her self-imposed seclusion.

Emily Dickinson secluded herself from ordinary human associations, especially during the last years of her life (from approximately 1865–1886). The topic: "Emily Dickinson Abroad," with the usual meaning of "to go abroad" implying that

"

IF EMILY DICKINSON WERE STILL LIVING, CERTAINLY SHE WOULD BE SURPRISED TO KNOW THAT SHE HAD BEEN INTERNATIONALLY ACCLAIMED. SINCE DICKINSON CONSCIOUSLY SEPARATED HERSELF FROM HUMAN CONNECTIONS, THE RECOGNITION OF VARIOUS SCHOLARS ALL AROUND THE WORLD OF HER GENIUS IS PARADOXICAL IN THAT IT BELIES HER INTENTION TO WITHDRAW."

Dickinson was far away from home in foreign lands, is ironic in view of what we know about the poet's life. The attempt to explain that Emily Dickinson was or is in fact abroad, then, has to deal with her life and work in three different ways: first, Dickinson was abroad in her imagination, as revealed in her poems of travel or poems of adventure; thus, she was imaginatively abroad. Second, Dickinson is now truly abroad, since she has been internationally recognized through her poetic works and letters. Third, the fact that Dickinson is abroad, imaginatively or internationally, is a paradoxical twist to her conscious decision to withdraw from the world.

Evidence appearing in critical works on Emily Dickinson since 1890 supports the idea that, deliberately or not, Emily Dickinson withdrew from the normal world. However, despite her physical confinement, the poet used her fantastic imagination, sometimes alone but often with someone, to create adventures through levels of spiritual experiences. As the outlet for her explosive genius, many poems such as "I went to Heaven—", "I started Early—Took my Dog—", etc., can be seen as an indication of her psychic communication with the world outside her private refuge. One of these poems, "I never saw a Moor—" confirms the poet's inexperienced life and at the same time reveals her imaginative ability to see "How the Heather looks."

In Dickinson's poems concerning travel or the poems of adventure of the mind, the first way to look at "Emily Dickinson Abroad" lies in her artistic technique plus her imaginative passion in creating an inner world as a way to journey abroad. This technique covers three significant dimensions: the movement from consciousness to unconsciousness, from reality to fantasy, and from Amherst to the whole universe: heaven, death, eternity and immortality. The presumption is based on her belief that she dwells "in Possibility—;" that in spreading her "narrow Hands" she could "gather Paradise—" (P657). That Emily Dickinson is truly abroad, then, is closely associated with those three movements of her mind.

To sum up, through her imagination Emily Dickinson moves wherever she wants, as we can see in many poems such as "I took my Power in my Hand—" (P540) and "The Brain—is wider than the Sky—" (P632). Driven by her fanciful imagination, Dickinson travels back and forth between two levels of experience, with at least two subconscious motives: to display her poetic genius and to calm her psychological turmoil.

The second way in which Emily Dickinson has travelled is posthumously. Though she never set foot outside her father's home after 1865, she has now "arrived" in countries whose names she might not even have recognized. In *Emily Dickinson: An Annotated Bibliography. Writings, Scholarship, and Criticism, 1850–1968* published in 1970, Willis J. Buckingham, the editor, gathered a detailed collection of published materials relating to Emily Dickinson.

Covering more than a hundred years of Dickinson's bibliographies, Buckingham's collection presents fairly comprehensive information on the poet's recognition in foreign countries, showing that Dickinson's works are appreciated not only in democratic societies but also in former socialistic ones, including Hungary, Romania, Poland, Czechoslovakia, Croatia, and Russia. In Asia, Japan was the first country to play an important role in the study of Dickinson's life and works, starting particularly in the 1950's.

Although Buckingham supplies a great deal of useful information, the editor did not cite any translations or critical works from China, India, or Switzerland, despite the interest in those countries in Dickinson. Moreover, Buckingham does not include the work of Dickinson scholars in Austria in the list.

Besides Buckingham's collection, I would like to mention as particularly important the following compendiums:

1. *Emily Dickinson: A Bibliography 1850–1966* (1968) by Sheila T. Clendenning;

2. *Dickinson Scholarship: An Annotated Bibliography 1969–1985* (1988) by Karen Dandurand.

Also, it is important to note the excellent bibliographies published in the *Emily Dickinson Bulletin* and *Dickinson Studies* from 1974 to 1991 by George Monteiro, the late Frederick L. Morey, and William White.

The sources show that among the foreign Dickinson scholars, the Indians, Japanese, Germans, Portuguese, Spanish, Italians, and Dutch are the most active in making the poet's work accessible to speakers of their own languages.

As for Thailand, interest in Emily Dickinson became apparent in 1975. Thus far, at least two Thai scholars (Prapan Raksa in his *American Literature: An Anthology,* 1975; Chanthana Chaichit, "Emily Dickinson and Death Poems" in *The Faculty of Arts Bulletin,* 1975 and *American Literature in the Later Part of the Nineteenth Century: Historical and Analytical Approach,* 1990) have written in the Thai language about the poet. The scope of writings covers analyses in articles and parts of books of Emily Dickinson's life and works that reveal the writers' views of Dickinson's importance as the forerunner of modern American poetry along with translations of some of her poems, especially those about nature and death. Dickinson has long been taught in university level courses in Thailand. Thai students' papers definitely show their understanding of the poet's thematic viewpoint on nature, death, and the inner mind. Thai students appreciate the poems expressing the poet's individualistic attitude towards life, such as "Success is counted sweetest" (P67), "I'm Nobody! Who are you?" (P288), and "The Soul selects her own Society—." Recently, the Thai public was widely exposed to the poet when some of her lyrics were flashed on the screen during program breaks on an international cable T.V. channel. Some examples are "'Nature' is what we see—" (P668), "A word is dead" (P1212), and "Fame is the one that does not stay—" (P1475), and such quotations would be readily understood by those raised in a Buddhist culture.

If Emily Dickinson were still living, certainly she would be surprised to know that she had been internationally acclaimed. Since Dickinson consciously separated herself from human connections, the recognition of various scholars all around the world of her genius is paradoxical in that it belies her intention to withdraw.

It is an ironic, maybe even tragic, paradox that Dickinson's psychological and social life was stilted by her childhood experiences to the extent that she could taste the joys of human life only imaginatively and later felt compelled to become a recluse. Even if Dickinson's poems and letters are not completely autobiographical, we can, at least, consider that they reflect her personal life. Accordingly, in her poems of travel, it is quite ironic that she assumes a persona of one who is brave, strong, and always travelling away from home. In many cases, she travels widely to exotic places around the world, including deserts and wildernesses. Certainly, the knowledge Dickinson gained from her father's library merged well with her fancy in making what she had yearned for come true. As a recluse, Dickinson withdrew into herself in order to see with the eyes of her imagination. Consequently, her attitude towards the world is not one of complete negation.

Judging by one of her poems, "Deprived of other Banquet, / I entertained Myself—" (P773), we understand that it was necessary for Emily Dickinson to deal with something outside her routine, relatively dull life. Ecstatically, she dreamed of riches, greater than those of the Emperor ("'Tis little I—could care for Pearls—," P466); she dreamed of being away from home together with someone ("Away from Home are some and I—," P821). She dreamed of being the "Czar" of a foreign land ("I'm 'wife'—I've finished that—," P199). And she was very happy to meet "Thou" "Where Thou art—" whether in "Cashmere—or Calvary—," P725).

In another attempt to free herself from home confinement, Dickinson indulged in suffering while making imaginative excursions. "On the strangest Sea—" (P254) far from home she dreamed that she had heard beautiful music lamenting a hopeless hope. In "The Malay—took the Pearl—" (P452) she expressed her sadness at having lost what she deemed the most beloved. More than once, the Dickinson persona went up to "Heaven," which "was a small Town" but with a "unique Society—" (P374), and once she was deprived of her right to enter "Heaven" as she described in P378 "I saw no Way—The Heavens were stitched— / I felt the Columns close—."

Whether as an expression of suffering or ecstasy, poems containing the persona's fanciful movement from Amherst play an important role in Dickinson's paradoxical situation. These poems can also be considered as an outlet to release the poet's energetic creativity and fantastic imagination, both in the realm of distress and rapture.

In her imagination, Dickinson escapes from her self-imposed imprisonment; she feels free to wander around the world and can "taste a liquor never brewed" (P214). However, instinctively, she yearns to come back. The need to assume "a Life I left" (P609), then, is a sign of her willingness to return from fantasy to reality. It is also a sign that Dickinson does not totally sever herself from human concerns, as she stated in a letter dated 1862 to Higginson and in a poem of 1862 as well.

All of the poems under discussion help reveal the point where Dickinson ties her human feelings tightly to her private visions. Life, happiness, love, death, and disappointment form the core of her awareness. No matter where and how Emily Dickinson lived, her reactions towards life were without boundaries and still closely linked with universal human experiences.

Dickinson lives in opposition to her real life. Although secluded, she is not alone. In every one of life's situations, she knows how to contact and measure the world with courage and a stoic heart. Superficially, her seemingly detached personality observed by persons who did not know her well is in profound contrast to her interior attachment to the world in all its aspects.

Thus, in writing poems of travel, Emily Dickinson reveals herself as a normal human being reacting against the humdrum life. She is neither a stolid individual nor a reble with an avant-garde spirit. To a certain extent, Emily Dickinson is a victim of a lonely environment that drives her to triumphs of the imagination. This double life leads her to a realm of exotic imagination, unattainable in reality. We know that her life was full of distress and despair caused by the lack of maternal love, by the death of people for whom she deeply cared and by her ostensible failure to develop passionate relationships with the three men she is thought to have secretly loved but who were supposedly unaware of her feelings: Benjamin Newton, the Reverend Charles Wadsworth, and Samuel Bowles.

If we accept that in her life she experienced an evanescent happiness only when dealing with the dream of love in close relationships with the members of her immediate family and friends, if we accept that she was acutely estranged and isolated due to her need to express her emotions, then we must be receptive to the feelings in her poems, even though deep in our hearts we might be aware that the experiences maybe imaginary.

In addition, we have to accept that as a female poet, Emily Dickinson was not at all a timid creature in a hidden world. With absolute poetic power in her hand, Dickinson becomes an intellectual "twice as bold—" (P540), asserting herself spiritually as an independent individual in seeing that "The life we have is very great." Such a statement agrees with a confidence (as confirmed in a letter dated spring of 1850) that she shared with Jane Humphrey, one of her best friends: "I have dared to do strange things—bold things, and have asked no advice from any—." At the same time, even though her poems enable her to reach heaven and the Garden of Paradise, Dickinson is humble enough to accept the limitations of life stoically and to expound her faith in human dignity: "I deem that I—with but a Crumb— / Am Sovereign of them all—" (P791).

We can also say that in order to provide a contrast to her solitary, loveless life, Dickinson taps an inward source that allows her to face life calmly in her own unique manner. As in the teaching of Buddhism, Dickinson's theory of life is concerned with human suffering and fundamentally accepting life's reality. Knowing what suffering is, she knows how to deal with it, bravely and stoically so that she can escape being crushed. She detachs herself from unhappiness and lives serenely on the one hand, while escaping from reality through imagination on the other.

The paradox of Emily Dickinson's life is that from her seclusion, she is able to tell the world more about the truth of human love, suffering and loss than the world itself maybe aware of. Her life may be said to have been almost monastic. To follow the Lord Buddha's path in seeking the truth of life, some monks go into retreat, living their lives in a very limited world of experience.

My discussion of the paradox of Emily Dickinson's life is not the first. Other critics have analyzed her life in a similar way. (Among these critics are Henry W. Wells in his *Introduction to Emily Dickinson*, 1947; Elizabeth Phillips in her *Emily Dickinson: Personae and Performance*, 1988; and Maryanne M. Garbowsky in *The House Without the Door*, 1989.) In *The Capsule of the Mind: Chapters in the Life of Emily Dickinson* (1961), Theodora Ward also saw Dickinson's life as a paradox, concluding that "The fascination of her character is enhanced by paradoxes that continually baffle the observer" (96). In being deprived of what ordinary people have experienced, Emily Dickinson found so many of the things for which we endlessly search in her inner world.

Source: Chanthana Chaichit, "Emily Dickinson Abroad: The Paradox of Seclusion," in *Emily Dickinson Journal*, Vol. 5, No. 2, Fall 1996, pp. 162–68.

Critic

In the following anonymous review, the critic praises Dickinson's poems, pointing out "Success Is Counted Sweetest" as a particular example of her "rare genious."

Here is a volume [*Poems by Emily Dickinson*] of striking and original poems by a writer who, during the fifty years of her life, wrote much and published almost nothing. The name of Emily Dickinson is a new name in our literature, but whoever reads the striking verses in this book which her two friends, Mabel Loomis Todd and Col. T. W. Higginson, have edited, will agree that its place is established and sure to remain, associated with a collection of poems whose main quality, as is pointed out in an admirable preface, is an extraordinary grasp and insight. So clearly are the characteristics of these verses defined and so exactly does our opinion of them agree with the writer's, that we are almost tempted to quote him literally; but there are some features which he has left for others to describe—namely, the similarity between these poems and some of Emerson's (a similarity both of thought and manner of expression), and, in the poems of love, the absence of much that is essential to poems of this kind—sensuousness and symmetry and melody. It is in the other poems that the rare genius of Miss Dickinson is best seen—in those of Life, Nature, Time and Eternity. Here, for instance, is an example chosen from the verses on Life, which will show, too, what we call the Emersonian influence. The poem appeared first in *A Masque of Poets*, published at the request of the author's friend 'H. H.,' who had often urged her to print a volume. It is called 'Success.'

> Success is counted sweetest
> By those who ne'er succeed.
> To comprehend a nectar
> Requires sorest need.
> Not one of all the purple host
> Who took the flag to-day
> Can tell the definition,
> So clear, of victory,
> As he, defeated, dying,
> On whose forbidden ear

The distant strains of triumph
Break, agonized and clear.

We venture to give some of the things which have most impressed us. Many of the poems are untitled, but the first of the following is called 'The Secret':—

> Some things that fly there be,—
> Birds, hours, the bumble-bee:
> Of these no elegy.
> Some things that stay there be,—
> Grief, hills, eternity:
> Not this behooveth me.
> There are, that resting, rise.
> Can I expound the skies?
> How still the riddle lies!

It is of Nature that the poet writes best. Of the thirty-one poems under this heading, it is hard to find favorites, they are all so fine. We select the two following ["New feet within my garden go" and "Like trains of cars on tracks of plush"]:—

> New feet within my garden go,
> New fingers stir the sod;
> A troubadour upon the elm
> Betrays the solitude.
> New children play upon the green,
> New weary sleep below;
> And still the pensive spring returns,
> And still the punctual snow!
> * * *
>
> Like trains of cars on tracks of plush
> I hear the level bee:
> A jar across the flowers goes,
> Their velvet masonry
> Withstands until the sweet assault
> Their chivalry consumes,
> While he, victorious, tilts away
> To vanquish other blooms.
> . . . . .
> His labor is a chant,
> His idleness a tune;
> Oh, for a bee's experience
> Of clovers and of noon!

We must make room for this one of the poems on Life and Eternity ["If I shouldn't be alive"]:–

> If I shouldn't be alive
> When the robins come,
> Give the one in red cravat
> A memorial crumb.
> If I couldn't thank you,
> Being just asleep,
> You will know I'm trying
> With my granite lip!

Miss Dickinson's poems, though rough and rugged, are surprisingly individual and genuinely inspired.

Source: "The Poems of Emily Dickinson," in *Critic*, Vol. 14, No. 63, December 13, 1890, pp. 305–306.

SOURCES

Allison, Alexander W., ed., "Emily Dickinson," in *The Norton Anthology of Poetry*, 3rd edition, Norton, 1983, pp. 804–16.

Harmon, William, and Hugh Holman, eds., "Realistic Period in American Literature, 1865-1900," in *A Handbook to Literature*, Prentice Hall, 2003, pp. 422–23.

Hendrickson, Paula, "Dickinson and the Process of Death," in *Dickinson Studies*, Vol. 77, 1991, pp. 33–43.

Ransom, John Crowe, "Emily Dickinson: A Poet Restored," in *Emily Dickinson: A Collection of Critical Essays*, edited by Jim Kamp, St. James Press, 1994.

Reeves, James, "Emily Dickinson: Overview," in *Reference Guide to American Literature*, edited by Richard Sewall, Prentice Hall, 1963, pp. 88–100.

Review of "Poems by Emily Dickinson," in *Nation*, No. 1326, November 27, 1890, p. 423.

Review of "The Poems of Emily Dickinson," in *Critic*, Vol. 14, No. 63, December 13, 1890, pp. 305–306.

Wider, Sarah Ann, "Emily Dickinson," in *Dictionary of Literary Biography*, Vol. 243, *The American Renaissance in New England, Fourth Series*, edited by Wesley T. Mott, The Gale Group, 2001, pp. 103–28.

FURTHER READING

Bradbury, Malcolm, and Richard Ruland, *From Puritanism to Postmodernism: A History of American Literature*, Penguin, 1992.

Considered a readable overview of American history, this volume follows the patterns and reactions of literature from the earliest days of the United States up to 1990. Dickinson is given consideration in the authors' analysis.

Gladwell, Malcolm, *Outliers: The Story of Success*, Little, Brown, 2008.

Gladwell's book about success takes a surprising approach to the topic of success by examining why certain people have risen to success, while others who seem more positioned for it do not. Gladwell explains how circumstances, both personal and cultural, are a critical part of the formula for success.

Grabher, Gudrun, Roland Hagenbuchle, and Cristanne Miller, eds., *The Emily Dickinson Handbook*, University of Massachusetts Press, 1998.

In this collection of essays, leading Dickinson scholars cover topics ranging from letters to theory to visual arts. A solid introduction to the wide field of scholarship on Dickinson and her verse, this anthology guides students deeper into her work.

Zeller, Bob, *The Blue and Gray in Black and White*, Praeger Publishers, 2005.

Zeller's book collects photos from the Civil War with explanation of how the advent of photography brought the Civil War to the people. The people and events in this war were contemporary to Dickinson and best represent her generation's vision of war.

To a Sky-Lark

PERCY BYSSHE SHELLEY

1820

"To a Sky-Lark" was written by the English Romantic poet Percy Bysshe Shelley in late June, 1820. Shelley was staying in Leghorn (Italian name, Livorno) Italy, at the time, and he and his wife, Mary, were taking a stroll in the lanes on a summer evening when they heard the song of a skylark. This inspired Shelley to write the poem, which was published in his volume of poems, *Prometheus Unbound*, in the same year. The poem can be found in *Shelley: Poems*, (1993) in the Everyman's Library "Pocket Poets" series, or in any edition of the poet's work.

The skylark (Latin name *Alauda arvensis*) is a small bird found in Europe and known for its song. The skylark sings only when in flight, when it is high in the sky and often barely visible. Shelley uses the song of the skylark to suggest the creative inspiration of the poet, which often comes from a hidden, unseen source. Also, the skylark embodies for the poet a kind of transcendental joy, beyond the reach of human thought and more pure and delightful than anything the poet can compare it with.

"To a Sky-Lark" has always been one of Shelley's most popular lyrics, although only since the 1960s has it received serious attention from literary critics for the craftsmanship it displays and the subtlety of many of its images. The poem is an ideal introduction to Shelley's lifelong interest in an unorthodox transcendental philosophy and the nature of creativity.

Percy Bysshe Shelley (The Library of Congress)

AUTHOR BIOGRAPHY

Percy Bysshe Shelley is known primarily as one of the great English Romantic poets, but he was also an essayist, dramatist, translator, and pamphleteer. Shelley was born on August 4, 1792, at Field Place, near Horsham, Sussex, England, the eldest of seven children born to Sir Timothy Shelley, a landowner and a Whig member of Parliament, and Elizabeth Pilfold. At a young age Shelley was known as a highly imaginative boy with an excitable temper. When he was only twelve or thirteen he experimented with gunpowder, blowing up some of the boundary poles in the playground. From 1804 to 1810 Shelley attended Eton College, a private school (known in England as a public school), where he was known for his nonconformist beliefs. He was also frequently bullied and subjected to practical jokes by his peers.

Shelley's first published work was the Gothic novel *Zastrozzi: A Romance*, in 1810, the same year that he entered University College, Oxford. The following year Shelley and his friend Thomas Jefferson Hogg wrote a pamphlet titled *The Necessity of Atheism*, for which both men were expelled from the college. Still the rebel,

Shelley eloped with the sixteen-year-old Harriet Westbrook and they were married on August 28, 1811. In 1812 Shelley met the radical journalist William Godwin, and his highly intelligent daughter, Mary. In 1814, Shelley deserted Harriet and ran away with Mary and her stepsister Claire Clairmont. They toured Europe, and Shelley married Mary in 1816 after the suicide by drowning of Harriet Shelley. A year later, Shelley was denied custody of their two children.

In 1816, on a visit to Switzerland where Shelley and Mary spent time with his friend, the poet Lord Byron, Shelley wrote two of the lyric poems for which he is best known: "Hymn to Intellectual Beauty" and "Mont Blanc." In 1818, reviled in England for his political radicalism and professed atheism, Shelley and his family sailed to Italy, where he would live for the remainder of his life. During this year Shelley visited Venice and Rome before settling in Naples. His verse drama, *The Revolt of Islam*, was published that year.

Shelley fathered four children with Mary, three of whom died in infancy. The last child, Percy Florence, was born in 1819, the year in which the Shelleys moved from Naples to Leghorn. There, Shelley wrote a five-act tragedy, *The Cenci* (1819), The family next moved to Florence, where Shelley wrote one of his best-known poems, "Ode to the West Wind," and completed his masterpiece, the lyric drama *Prometheus Unbound*, which was published, 1820.

Also in 1820 the Shelleys moved to Pisa, and then stayed at Leghorn from June until August, where Shelley wrote "To a Sky-Lark." Later that year, at Baths of San Giuliano, he wrote "The Witch of Atlas," before returning to Pisa in October. His productivity continued in 1821, with the poem *Epipsychidion*; the essay, *A Defence of Poetry*; and the elegy, *Adonais*, a tribute to John Keats, the young English poet who had died in February of that year.

In the spring of 1822, Shelley wrote what proved to be his last poem, the unfinished "The Triumph of Life." On July 1, 1822, he and his friend Edward Williams sailed in Shelley's schooner, the *Don Juan*, to Leghorn to meet their friend, the journalist Leigh Hunt. On the return voyage on July 8, 1822, a storm came up quickly and the boat sank in the Bay of Spezia, drowning Shelley and Williams.

POEM TEXT

Hail to thee, blithe Spirit!
Bird thou never wert—
That from Heaven, or near it,
Pourest thy full heart
In profuse strains of unpremeditated art.   5

Higher still and higher
From the earth thou springest
Like a cloud of fire;
The blue deep thou wingest,
And singing still dost soar, and soaring
          ever singest.   10

In the golden lightning
Of the sunken Sun—
O'er which clouds are brightning,
Thou dost float and run;
Like an unbodied joy whose race is just begun.   15

The pale purple even
Melts around thy flight,
Like a star of Heaven
In the broad day-light
Thou art unseen,—but yet I hear thy shrill
          delight,   20

Keen as are the arrows
Of that silver sphere,
Whose intense lamp narrows
In the white dawn clear
Until we hardly see—we feel that it is there.   25

All the earth and air
With thy voice is loud,
As when Night is bare
From one lonely cloud
The moon rains out her beams—and Heaven
          is overflowed.   30

What thou art we know not;
What is most like thee?
From rainbow clouds there flow not
Drops so bright to see
As from thy presence showers a rain of melody. 35

Like a Poet hidden
In the light of thought,
Singing hymns unbidden,
Till the world is wrought
To sympathy with hopes and fears it heeded
          not: 40

Like a high-born maiden
In a palace-tower,
Soothing her love-laden
Soul in secret hour,
With music sweet as love—which overflows
          her bower: 45

Like a glow-worm golden
In a dell of dew,
Scattering unbeholden
Its aerial hue
Among the flowers and grass which screen it
          from the view: 50

Like a rose embowered
In its own green leaves—
By warm winds deflowered—
Till the scent it gives
Makes faint with too much sweet these
          heavy-winged thieves: 55

Sound of vernal showers
On the twinkling grass,
Rain-awakened flowers,
All that ever was
Joyous, and clear and fresh, thy music doth
          surpass.   60

Teach us, Sprite or Bird,
What sweet thoughts are thine;
I have never heard
Praise of love or wine
That panted forth a flood of rapture so divine: 65

Chorus Hymeneal
Or triumphal chaunt
Matched with thine would be all
But an empty vaunt,
A thing wherein we feel there is some
          hidden want.   70

What objects are the fountains
Of thy happy strain?
What fields or waves or mountains?
What shapes of sky or plain?
What love of thine own kind? what ignorance
          of pain?   75

With thy clear keen joyance
Languor cannot be—
Shadow of annoyance
Never came near thee;
Thou lovest—but ne'er knew love's sad satiety. 80

Waking or asleep,
Thou of death must deem
Things more true and deep
Than we mortals dream,
Or how could thy notes flow in such a
          chrystal stream?   85

We look before and after,
And pine for what is not—
Our sincerest laughter
With some pain is fraught—
Our sweetest songs are those that tell of
          saddest thought.   90

Yet, if we could scorn
Hate and pride and fear;
If we were things born
Not to shed a tear,
I know not how thy joy we ever should come
          near.   95

Better than all measures
Of delightful sound—
Better than all treasures
That in books are found—
Thy skill to poet were, thou Scorner
          of the ground!   100

Teach me half the gladness
That thy brain must know,
Such harmonious madness
From my lips would flow
The world should listen then—as I am
    listening now.   105

POEM SUMMARY

Stanzas 1–3

"To a Sky-Lark" consists of twenty-one stanzas of five lines each. The first six stanzas describe the skylark as observed by the poet. In the first stanza, the poet greets the bird as if it were a spirit singing from the limits of heaven. The song of the bird is so beautiful, so spontaneous, that it seems almost impossible that it comes from a real bird. In stanza 2, the bird soars even higher away from the earth; it flies in the sky, continuously singing as it ascends. The third stanza makes it clear that the bird is singing at sunset; above the sinking sun, which is sending out its last red rays for the day, are some clouds. The skylark flies and floats in the scene, with a joy that seems not to belong to or be defined by any physical form.

Stanzas 4–6

Stanza 4 continues the description of the skylark, with a sense of wonderment on the part of the poet. The poet cannot detect the physical presence of the bird in the evening sky. Even though it is still daylight, the poet says, the bird cannot be seen, just like a star cannot be seen in daylight, but the bird can certainly be heard. In stanza 5, the poet compares the skylark to Venus, which is visible at night but fades at dawn until it can barely be seen, and yet people can sense that it is still present. Stanza 6 states that the whole earth and the air is full of the loud voice of the skylark just as, at night, the moon can be seen shining from behind a cloud, seeming to fill the heavens with light.

Stanzas 7–9

Stanza 7 states that the bird seems like such an unearthly thing it cannot really be known; and the poet, in this and the following five stanzas, contemplates something with which the bird may be compared. He first considers clouds that produce rain while a rainbow shines but concludes that raindrops are not as bright as the melody that pours forth from the skylark.

In stanza 8, the skylark is compared to the mind of a poet, which also cannot be seen, but from which the poet expresses himself spontaneously in his work. The work of the poet then finds an audience, and people start to care about what the poet has expressed. In stanza 9, the skylark is compared to an aristocratic maiden, perhaps from some old romantic tale, imprisoned in a tower. The lovelorn maiden finds solace for her tormented soul through music, which flows out all around her.

Stanzas 10–12

In stanza 10, the poet continues his search to find something with which the skylark might be compared. In this stanza it is the light from a glow-worm as it nestles in the dew. No one sees it, because it is hidden by flowers and grass. In stanza 11, the comparison is between the skylark and a rose. The rose has lost its leaves due to a warm wind but still gives off a delightful scent. In stanza 12, another comparison is attempted, between the song of the skylark and rain showers that fall on the grass and encourage the flowers to bloom. But in the last two lines of this stanza, the poet admits that nothing in the world is superior to the song of the skylark.

Stanzas 13–15

Stanza 13 begins a new section of the poem, in which the poet addresses the bird directly, asking it to teach humans about the thoughts it has that produce such a happy song. Expressing himself in the first person, he says that he has never heard anyone praise love or wine in poetry—he is referring to a tradition in which poets praise love and wine in short poems—that equals the joyous song of the bird. In stanza 14, the poet says that even a wedding song or some other celebratory music would lack something if they were to be compared to the skylark's song. Stanza 15 consists of a series of rhetorical questions. A rhetorical question is one to which the speaker does not expect an answer, or which cannot be answered. In this case, the questions are about the causes of the joyous of the bird. What makes it sing so beautifully? Is it some stimulus the bird receives from land or sea or sky? Does it sing because of love for some other creature like itself, or simply because it knows no pain or suffering?

Stanzas 16–18

Stanza 16 meditates on the nature of the bird that produces such a song. The poet states that this little being cannot experience exhaustion or lack of energy; nor can it be troubled by anything. The bird knows the joy of love but has never experienced its sadness. In stanza 17, this thought is extended. Whether the bird is awake or asleep, it experiences a greater depth of truth than mortal man can even dream of. If this were not so, the poet asks, how could the skylark sing so beautifully? Stanza 18 contrasts the reality of the bird with the reality of humans. Humans think about the past and the future and want things to be different from how they are. Humans also live in a world that contains opposing emotions; they experience sorrow as well as joy. In the final line of this stanza the poet states that sad songs are somehow more satisfying than happy ones.

Stanzas 19–21

In stanza 19, the poet imagines the activation of human potential. But even if people could learn to get beyond their negative emotions, or if human nature were somehow different and did not have the capacity to experience emotional pain, even then, humans would still not be able to experience the same level of joy that the skylark does. In stanza 20, the poet states that the song of the bird is the best of all music, and also superior to all the poetry that has been published in books. In the final stanza, the poet addresses the skylark directly, asking it to teach him even half of the joy it embodies. If the skylark would do that for him, the poet would be so inspired

that he would write great verse that everyone in the world would listen to and understand, just as he is now listening to and grasping meaning from the song of the skylark.

THEMES

Transcendental Source of Joy

"To a Sky-Lark" is a philosophical or spiritual poem in the sense that the image of the skylark is used as a symbol of a higher order of reality than the one that human beings occupy. The skylark symbolizes a transcendental, nonphysical realm of life that is characterized by joy. There is nothing like this joy to be found in the human or natural world. All comparisons to it fall short, as the last two lines of stanza 12 indicate.

Stanza 1 makes it clear that the actual physical bird is not in the forefront of the poet's mind. He refers to it as a spirit and states that it never was a bird. Shelley's skylark exists in an absolute, heavenly realm, removed from the human experience of life. The last line of stanza 3 emphasizes this again, with a reference to the bird as an incorporeal, that is, nonphysical reality. That line also suggests that the bird is a symbol of the very source and origin of life as it first manifests in its most pure and joyous state.

The principle of absolute joy symbolized by the song of the skylark is beyond human comprehension and knowledge (stanza 7, line 1). It is transcendental to everything, superior even to the most beautiful or unusual phenomena in nature; for example, it is brighter than raindrops that fall when a rainbow shines. Its transcendental nature is emphasized by the simile that compares it to something that cannot be seen by the bodily eye, such as the morning star when dawn arrives. The song of the lark is also beyond the most beautiful music created by humans. Its joy is better described as emanating from some divine rather than natural source, as the last line of stanza 13 suggests. The fact that the poem is crowded with similes of comparisons to the bird is ironic in the sense that the similes only establish the indescribable nature of the skylark's song. It is in fact not like anything else. It is unique and absolute, beyond anything that can be known by the human mind or senses, existing by itself, the principle of joy. This is a joy unmixed with sorrow, which makes it different from human joy, for human experience takes place within a field of opposites; humans experience joy but they also know sorrow. Indeed, the

TOPICS FOR FURTHER STUDY

- Read "Ode to a Nightingale," by John Keats, and write an essay in which you compare it to Shelley's "To a Sky-Lark." In what ways are these two poems, written at about the same time by the two English Romantic poets, similar and how do they differ? Which poem appeals to you more, and why? Use a free blog service, such as Blogger.com, WordPress. com, or LiveJournal.com, to write about your thoughts. Ask your teacher and at least two classmates to comment on your blog entry.

- Write a short poem about an animal, or specifically a bird, in which you address the subject directly, as Shelley does in "To a Sky-Lark." Like Shelley, use the animal as a way of reflecting on your own thoughts about life, perhaps in contrast to the creature.

- Prepare to read "To a Sky-Lark" or another of Shelley's lyric poems aloud to your class. Memorize it if you can. As you practice reading the poem aloud, how does your understanding of it change and grow? How will you convey the emotions of elation and regret in your reading? Present your answers to these questions in a brief class presentation after your performance of the poem.

- Using for your research *The Romantics: English Literature in Its Historical, Cultural, and Social Contexts* by Neil King, one of five volumes in the "Backgrounds to English Literature" series published by Chelsea House (2002), give a class presentation in which you explain why "To a Sky-Lark" should be considered a Romantic poem. What characteristics does it have that make it Romantic? Topics you might want to consider include imagination, idealism, and nature. Use PowerPoint or a similar program to present your ideas to your class.

- Choose several poems from the young-adult book *I Am Phoenix: Poems for Two Voices* (1985) by Paul Fleischman. Most are arranged as duets. With a partner, select a poem that represents the same symbolism as the skylark in Shelley's poem. Perform the poem for your class and lead a discussion on the features it shares with "To a Sky-Lark."

---

presence of one emotion implies the potential of the other; they are always intermingled. Joy can become sorrow, laughter can become tears, and vice versa. For the reality symbolized by the skylark, however, nothing can alter or touch its joy, which is preexisting, uncreated. Even if humans could be taught or persuaded always to favor their better nature, they would still not come close to the joy of the skylark, which is unattainable. Humans can recognize it for what it is, become inspired by it, and may learn something from it, but they can never fully emulate it. For this reason the poem contains an element of yearning, of a striving on the part of the poet for a higher reality that will always remain out of reach.

Poetic Creativity

"To a Sky-Lark" compares the effortless, brilliant song of the skylark to the creativity of the poet. The poem suggests, by analogy to the skylark's song, that when a poet creates a poem, he or she taps into some deep source of inspiration, beyond the workings of the rational mind. This is an effortless process, taking place almost without the conscious knowledge of the poet. In stanza 1, for example, the effortlessness and spontaneity of the bird's song is emphasized, and it is referred to as art. This indication at the beginning of the poem is as much about the creative process as it is about an actual bird glimpsed on a summer evening in Italy. Just as the bird itself can barely be seen, creativity occurs in some hidden, secret place in the human mind and imagination, from where it pours out—like the skylark's song. The comparison with a poet is made explicit in stanza 8, in which a poet is presented as offering his own

Skylark *(© Mike Lane / Alamy)*

songs—poems—even though no one has asked him to do so. The poems just rush out spontaneously, and the world is changed by them. This image suggests Shelley's elevated view, stated elsewhere in his work, of the power of the poet and of poetry to transform the world. The poet draws inspiration from the song of the skylark because it encourages him to express in his work the absolute joy that exists at the heart of existence, and which humans—with their fears and strife—too often obscure.

STYLE

Rhyme Scheme and Stanza Structure

Each of the twenty-one stanzas (units of thought in a poem) follows the same rhyme scheme: line 1 rhymes with line 3, line 2 rhymes with lines 4 and 5. Such a rhyme scheme is often noted as *ababb*. Most of the rhymes are perfect rhymes (also known as full or true rhyme), but Shelley also makes use of imperfect rhyme (also called near or partial rhyme), as in stanza 1, lines 2 and 4,

and stanza 11, in which line 4 is a near rhyme to lines 1 and 5. In stanza 21, lines 2, 4, and 5, there is an example of what is called eye rhyme in which words look on the page as if they rhyme, but the vowel sounds are in fact pronounced differently. Many of the rhymes in the poem are called feminine rhymes, consisting of one stressed syllable followed by an unstressed syllable (stanzas 2, 3, 15, 21 are among those that contain feminine rhymes).

The basic meter of the poem is trochaic trimeter. A trochee is a poetic foot (the smallest unit of rhythm in a line of poetry) consisting of one heavily stressed syllable followed by a lightly stressed one. A trimeter consists of three poetic feet. A foot may consist of two or three syllables—a strongly stressed syllable and one or two weakly stressed syllables.

The last line of each stanza breaks this pattern, however, being much longer than the other four lines, extending to six feet to form an iambic hexameter. (An iambic foot is a weak stress followed by a strong stress.) This is an effective way to end each stanza, because it shows the song of the bird flowing out effortlessly and expanding until it is heard everywhere, as if the song cannot be contained in the shorter lines.

Similes

The poem contains many similes. A simile is a comparison between two different things, made in such as way as to reveal similarities between them. Similes are often introduced by the words *as* and *like*. Stanzas 2, 3, 4, and 6 all contain similes that highlight a different aspect of the skylark as perceived by the poet. The bird is likened to fire; a joy without any physical source; the planet Venus, unseen in daylight; and the light shed by the moon. In stanza 7 the poet announces directly that he is going to try to find other things that are worthy of comparison to the skylark, and stanzas 7 to 12 all contain similes, drawn from the human and natural worlds. However, as stanza 12 reveals, these similes can only go so far, since there is in truth nothing with which the skylark can be compared.

HISTORICAL CONTEXT

The Romantic Movement in England

The Romantic era in English literature began in the 1790s with the work of poet and artist William Blake (1757–1827), particularly his collection of short poems, *Songs of Innocence and of Experience* (1794). In 1798, William Wordsworth (1770–1850) and Samuel Taylor Coleridge (1772–1834) published their landmark work, *Lyrical Ballads*. These three poets were the major voices in the first period of English Romanticism. They were followed by a younger generation, in which the most important poets were George Gordon, Lord Byron (1788–1824), Shelley (1792–1822), and John Keats (1795–1821).

The Romantic period was a time of social upheaval, coinciding with the French Revolution and the Napoleonic wars. The English Romantics were at first earnest supporters of the French Revolution, believing that it heralded a new era of freedom and equality, but later they became disillusioned with the increasingly reactionary course the revolution took. The early nineteenth century was also a period of social dislocation in England caused by the Industrial Revolution, which brought wealth to some but misery to many who toiled for long hours in bad conditions in the factories that were springing up all over the country. The sudden growth of cities and the shift of the population from rural to urban areas produced many tensions and injustices, and there was growing pressure for political reform that would ease the burden on the working classes. The poets generally aligned themselves with progressive forces that favored reform.

Romanticism was a vibrant period for poetry. The writers of this period are notable for their individualism, their generally optimistic view of human potential and their interest in experimentation in a variety of poetic forms. Inspired by Wordsworth and Coleridge's *Lyrical Ballads*, the Romantics replaced the more formal poetic diction of the eighteenth century with a representation that was closer to the real language spoken by ordinary people. The Romantics in general had a deep feeling for nature, especially as they experienced nature interacting with the workings of their own minds. They valued imagination over reason, and they frequently had an interest in the supernatural and the strange, as well as in dreams and mythology. In general, the Romantic poets stressed an elevated concept of the role of the poet as a sage, the wise person in society who could see into the truth of things.

The Romantics aspired to write epic poetry to set alongside the epics *Paradise Lost* (1667) and *Paradise Regained* (1671) by John Milton (1608–1674), but in a way that would allow them to present their own themes and concerns. Blake wrote two epic poems in blank verse, *Milton* (1809) and *Jerusalem* (1820), while Wordsworth wrote *The Prelude* (published in three different versions in 1798, 1805, and 1850), an account of his own development as a poet. Keats wrote two unfinished epics, *The Fall of Hyperion* (1817) and *Hyperion* (1818).

The Romantics, especially Byron, also succeeded at the verse narratives (a novel-length work written in a poetic rather than prose fashion) and the closet drama (a dramatic lyric not intended to be produced on the stage). Byron's *Manfred* (1817) and *Cain* (1821), and Shelley's *The Revolt of Islam* (1818) are examples of this form.

By 1832 the major English Romantic poets were either dead or nonproductive, and a new era began in British society with the passing of the Great Reform Bill and the ascension of Queen Victoria to the throne in 1837. However, the literature of the early Victorian years contained much that was Romantic in tone, including the poetry of Alfred, Lord Tennyson (1809–

COMPARE
&
CONTRAST

- **1820s:** The song of the skylark is widely loved throughout Europe. The bird is also hunted and is much sought after because of its flavor. In southern and eastern England during the nineteenth century, an estimated four hundred thousand skylarks a year are brought down.

  Today: In England, the number of skylarks has fallen dramatically since the 1970s. This is due to a change in farming practices by which cereals are harvested in early summer rather than early autumn. This makes it harder for the skylark to find food in the summer. Measures are underway to improve the skylark's habitat and restore its population.

- **1820s:** In Pisa, Italy, Shelley and his expatriate English friends constitute what becomes known as the Pisan Circle. It is an unorthodox group of young people, the most prominent of whom is the poet Lord Byron. Byron is the most celebrated and widely read poet in Europe, although scandal follows him everywhere he goes. Shelley is scorned in England and lacks a readership. Along with Byron's works, the long narrative poems and novels of Sir Walter Scott are the most popular literature of the day.

  Today: Shelley's work is considered part of the literary canon; along with Byron, he has long been established as one of the six major English Romantic poets. In contemporary England, poets no longer have the notoriety the Romantics had in the early nineteenth century. Scandals are associated more with celebrities in the entertainment world than with poets, whose books sell in only very small numbers. British Poet Laureate Andrew Motion founds the *Poetry Archive* on the Internet, an electronic library which features poets reading their own work. Set up in 2006, the *Poetry Archive* now has approximately 150,000 visitors per month, which strongly suggests that an audience for poetry still exists.

- **1820s:** Shelley, who advocates freedom and political reform, follows political events in England from Italy. In the wake of the Peterloo massacre in Manchester, England, in August 1819 (in which a protest by sixty thousand working men and women was put down by a militia, resulting in eleven deaths), Shelley expects a revolution similar to the French Revolution to break out. He also thinks this will happen because economic conditions will continue to deteriorate. However, during the 1820s the British economy improves, standards of living rise, and no revolution occurs. Political reform, however, will not take place until the 1830s.

  Today: Along with most of the rest of the world, Britain faces an economic crisis. After a sixteen-year period of expansion, the recession begins in the second half of 2008. The Labour government, under British Prime Minister Gordon Brown, tries to stimulate the economy by partly nationalizing banks, cutting taxes, and increasing public spending.

1892), Robert Browning (1812–1889), and Matthew Arnold (1822–1888), as well as the novels of Charles Dickens (1812–1870).

The Romantic Lyric Poem

The English Romantic poets excelled at the lyric poem. As defined by M. H. Abrams in the fourth edition of *A Glossary of Literary Terms* (1981), a lyric poem is a "fairly short, nonnarrative poem presenting a single speaker who expresses a state of mind or a process of thought and feeling." In addition to "To a Sky-Lark," examples of the Romantic lyric include Shelley's "Ode to the West Wind," Coleridge's "The Eolian Harp" and "Frost at Midnight," Wordsworth and Coleridge's *Lyrical Ballads*, and Keats's "Ode to a Nightingale." In many of these lyric poems, the speaker meditates on a particular emotional situation, perhaps in interaction with the natural scene in which he finds himself, and eventually finds a solution—a new way of looking at the situation—that restores his peace of mind. The poem then rounds back on itself and ends where it began but with a new level of understanding. Often, but not always, the speaker may be taken to be the voice of the poet. Some of the best-known lyrics by Wordsworth and Coleridge are known as "conversation poems," because of the informal tone the speaker adopts. Keats and Shelley adopted a rather different style, often apostrophizing the object of their contemplation. (An apostrophe is a direct address to an inanimate object, absent person, nonhuman creature, or abstract quality.)

CRITICAL OVERVIEW

Prometheus Unbound, the volume of poems in which "To a Sky-Lark" first appeared, had a tiny circulation when first published in 1820. Shelley did not expect it to sell more than twenty copies. However, the book did receive some reviews in literary periodicals, and John Gibson Lockhart, in *Blackwood's Edinburgh* magazine (available in *Shelley: The Critical Heritage*, edited by James E. Barcus), comments on "To a Sky-Lark" and some of the other shorter poems as "abounding in richest melody of versification, and great tenderness of feeling." Shelley's friend Leigh Hunt, reviewing the collection in the *Examiner* (also available in *Shelley: The Critical Heritage*), quotes "To a Sky-Lark" in its entirety, commenting, "I know of nothing more beautiful than this,—more choice of tones, more natural in words, more abundant in exquisite, cordial, and most poetical associations." In the early twentieth century, Shelley's reputation was generally low, given the hostile approach to his work by F. R. Leavis, the most influential critic of the day. But in the 1950s and 1960s Shelley's critical reputation began to rise, and a number of critics devoted considerable attention to "To a Sky-Lark." David Perkins in *The Quest for Permanence: The Symbolism of Wordsworth, Shelley, and Keats*, argues that the skylark "is probably one of [Shelley's] most successful

representations of the ecstatic gladness arising in the flight to the transcendent realm." Perkins interprets the poem in the light of Shelley's Platonic metaphysics: the joy the poet experiences comes from his fleeting contact with the Platonic principle of Intellectual Beauty. Kathleen Raine in "A Defence of Shelley's Poetry," an essay that appears in her book *Defending Ancient Springs*, also interprets the poem in terms of the Platonic tradition, arguing that many of the images reveal "the flowing of the created from the uncreated."

Later critics, however, have not so willingly viewed this poem or others by Shelley in terms of Platonic ideas. For James O. Allsup in *The Magic Circle: A Study of Shelley's Concept of Love*, the skylark is a symbol of both human love and divine love, and the poem shows the transformation of the former into the latter. Judith Chernaik, in *The Lyrics of Shelley*, mounts a defense of the poem against detractors who assert that Shelley's love of poetic inspiration reveals a lack of discipline and control in his work. Chernaik concludes that the final stanza of the poem affirms "the role of the poet as mediator between nature and society, as one who, himself awakened and inspired, has the power to awaken a sleeping earth." For Angela Leighton, in *Shelley and the Sublime: An Interpretation of the Major Poems*, the poem reveals not the contact between the poet and what the bird represents but the distance between them. The poet is aware of the limitations of his art. Leighton states that Shelley uses the poem as a "mode of address to explore the distance between heaven and earth, inspiration and composition, which lies at the heart of his aesthetic of poetry." "To a Sky-Lark" does have its critics; Richard Holmes, for example, in his biography *Shelley: The Pursuit*, calls it "sentimental," expressing a longing for "the idea of escape into a world of immortal and effortless creativity." In general, however, it is favorably regarded today and remains one of Shelley's most successful lyric poems.

CRITICISM

Bryan Aubrey

Aubrey holds a Ph.D. in English. In this essay he uses the ideas expressed in Shelley's essay, A Defence of Poetry, *to shed light on "To a Sky-Lark."*

Shelley was not the only English Romantic poet to write about the skylark. In 1827, only seven years after "To a Sky-Lark" was published,

WHAT DO I READ NEXT?

- Shelley's "Ode to the West Wind" (1820; available in any edition of Shelley's work), was written about a year before "To a Sky-Lark" and, like the later poem, expresses ideas about poetic inspiration and the role of the poet in the world.

- Shelley was not the only nineteenth-century English poet who was inspired by the song of the skylark. Victorian poet George Meredith's rapturous 122-line poem "The Lark Ascending" (1895) is also a celebration of this little bird and shows many similarities to Shelley's poem. It can be found in *Selected Poems of George Meredith* (2004) or online at http://www.bartleby.com/246/680.html. Those interested in tracing connections between the works will be intrigued to know that Meredith's poem was the inspiration for "The Lark Ascending" (1914), a musical composition for violin and orchestra by twentieth-century English composer Ralph Vaughan Williams, in which the lark is represented by a solo violin.

- "Shelley's Skylark" (1887) is a wry but appreciative reflection on Shelley's poem by Thomas Hardy, a poet who most decidedly did not share Shelley's transcendental philosophical beliefs. In this poem Hardy offers some thoughts about what time has done to the real, actual bird that for Shelley was a messenger from an immortal realm. The poem can be found in *Thomas Hardy: The Complete Poems*, edited by James Gibson (2002).

- *From Totems to Hip-Hop: A Multicultural Anthology of Poetry Across the Americas 1900–2002*, edited by the poet and novelist Ishmael Reed (2002), is a unique anthology that covers many aspects of American culture and society over a period of one hundred years. Poets of all races are represented, including Sylvia Plath, Yusef Komunyakaa, Thulani Davis, Bob Holman, Jayne Cortez, Diane Glancy, Garrett Hongo, Charles Simic, Al Young, Nellie Wong, Gertrude Stein, Ai, and Tupac Shakur. The anthology reveals just how wide the range of poetry is and how far it has traveled since, for example, Shelley wrote his carefully rhymed poem about the skylark. The anthology also includes some poetic manifestos and commentaries that can be compared to Shelley's own beliefs about poetry as expressed in his "A Defence of Poetry."

- *River of Words: Young Poets and Artists on the Nature of Things* (2008), edited by Pamela Michael with an introduction by Robert Hass, is a collection of poems about water and nature by writers age six to eighteen. Including artwork as well, the book takes the best writing from the annual project of the nonprofit organization River of Words (ROW). The poems are divided into nine sections: California, Pacific Northwest, Inland West, Midwest, Southwest, Northwest, Mid Atlantic, South, and International.

- Those who are fascinated by Shelley's short, troubled, and tragic life will find much of interest in the 2008 biography of the poet *Percy Bysshe Shelley: A Biography* by James Bieri, a nearly nine-hundred-page book about Shelley's life and work. A number of reviewers expressed the view that this well-researched book may become the definitive biography of the poet.

William Wordsworth wrote a short lyric poem titled "To the Skylark." Wordsworth was familiar with Shelley's poem, and naturally enough he preferred his own. In *Shelley: The Critical Heritage*, James E. Barcus quotes a comment Wordsworth made, recorded by a contemporary observer, that "Shelley's poem on the Lark was full of imagination, but that it did not show the same observation of nature as his poem on the same bird did." Wordsworth's assessment was undoubtedly right,

> POETRY, SHELLEY SAYS, OPENS PEOPLE UP TO THE DEEPEST ASPECTS OF THEIR OWN BEING, A REALM WITHIN IN WHICH ABSOLUTE JOY, HAPPINESS, AND BLISS EXIST, EVEN THOUGH THESE FEELINGS CAN BE KNOWN IN THEIR PURITY ONLY FOR FLEETING MOMENTS."

but observing nature was not Shelley's intention. He was not a nature poet but a philosophical one. Yes, he listened to and was captivated by the song of the skylark that he heard in his walks with his wife, Mary, and their friends in the lanes and fields of Leghorn, Italy. However, his intention in "To a Sky-Lark" was not to write about a real bird but to record the elevated ideas that came to him as he listened to the bird's song. The skylark simply became a convenient symbol for Shelley to express philosophical and metaphysical ideas and notions about creativity that he had long held and expressed in other poems and prose.

When Shelley heard the skylark pouring forth its spontaneous flow of melody, it is not surprising that he immediately connected it by analogy to the way the poet draws inspiration from some unknown source and effortlessly writes a verse. This was Shelley's idea of how poetry originated. He asserts in his essay, *A Defence of Poetry* (available in *Shelley's Poetry and Prose*, selected and edited by Donald H. Reiman and Sharon B. Powers), much of which was written in 1821 but was not published until 1840 (eighteen years after his death), that no one, not even the greatest of poets, can write poetry simply by deciding to do so. Poetry does not come as the result of an act of will; it is the result of a mysterious, unbidden inspiration that the poet must try to grab hold of. The mind of the poet, in the creation process, is like "a fading coal which some invisible influence, like an inconstant wind, awakens to transitory brightness: this power arises from within, ... and the conscious portions of our natures are unprophetic either of its approach or its departure." Whole passages in *A Defence of Poetry* read almost like a commentary on "To a Sky-Lark,"

as when Shelley states that the poet can never capture the full flood of the original inspiration, the finished result being a much diluted version of the original conception. This strongly suggests the thoughts expressed in the latter part of the poem, in which the poet can never fully capture the pure joy of the skylark, symbol of creative inspiration. He can sense it and respond to it, but he cannot fully embody it, either in his person or his verse.

Shelley continues in the same paragraph to explain his idea of the effortlessness of the creative act. He states that it is "an error to assert that the finest passages of poetry are produced by labor and study. The toil and the delay recommended by critics can be justly interpreted to mean no more than a careful observation of the inspired moments." The poet, then, is like the skylark, which never has to stop to revise its song or think about what note it will sing next or look back to think it might have sung its song better. (It is, by the way, the male skylark that sings; his purpose, say ornithologists [zoologists who study birds], is to attract the female, who prefers males who sing for longer periods of time.)

Shelley's ideas about poetic inspiration as expressed in *A Defence of Poetry* were subject to fierce criticism by F. R. Leavis, one of the most influential literary critics of the mid-twentieth century. In *Revaluation* (1936; reprinted in *The English Romantics: Major Poetry and Critical Theory, with Selected Modern Critical Essays*, 1978), Leavis argued that Shelley's idea of spontaneous inspiration "demands that active intelligence shall be, as it were, switched off." According to Leavis, who attacked what he saw as the incoherence of much of Shelley's imagery, Shelley's notion of inspiration meant "surrendering to a kind of hypnotic rote of favourite images, associations and words." Leavis singled out "To a Sky-Lark" as an example of this, regarding the poem as "a mere tumbled out spate ... of poeticalities, the place of each one of which Shelley could have filled with another without the least difficulty and without making any essential difference."

Later critics have taken issue with Leavis's harsh judgment of the poem. It might be argued that in *A Defence of Poetry* Shelley seems somewhat carried away by his own vision, and the passage quoted above may give a rather distorted or exaggerated view of how he worked as a poet. For example, his revisions to the original draft of "To a Sky-Lark" are very carefully done, and he also commented in his preface to his verse drama, *The Revolt of Islam*, that he exercised a watchful and critical attitude to his work as he was writing it. Shelley may have been a poet who depended on inspiration, but he was also a craftsman who shaped his product with the aid of a discriminating intellect.

There is much more in *A Defence of Poetry* that sheds light on the underlying thought of "To a Sky-Lark." Shelley describes special moments in which the poet receives his most elevated thoughts, stimulated by a person or scene or by the spontaneous activity of the mind itself (as when Shelley listened to the skylark), and he says that such moments are inherently pleasurable, even though the feelings pass, because the mind has participated "in the nature of its object." (In the poem, the poet feels in touch with the being of the skylark, if only for a few moments.) For Shelley, such experiences represent "the interpenetration of a diviner nature through our own," and to record such moments is the purpose of poetry, so that others may know of them too. It is in this sense that poetry "makes immortal all that is best and most beautiful in the world; it. . . . redeems from decay the visitations of the divinity in man." Poetry, Shelley says, opens people up to the deepest aspects of their own being, a realm within in which absolute joy, happiness, and bliss exist, even though these feelings can be known in their purity only for fleeting moments. This is exactly the theme of "To a Sky-Lark"—the poet's opening up to joy, as symbolized by the skylark, and the attempt to give it form in poetry for the benefit of humankind.

Not many great writers have had such an elevated concept of the status and role of the poet as Shelley expresses in *A Defence of Poetry*. He defines a poet rather broadly, simply as the person who apprehends "the true and the beautiful . . . the good" and "participates in the eternal, the infinite, and the one." This definition, which is influenced by Shelley's knowledge of the philosophy of Plato (he translated several works by Plato from the Greek) includes not only those who write poems but also painters, musicians, philosophers, and lawmakers—as long as they embody one basic requirement, which is to apprehend the truth of life in its highest aspect. Shelley believed that poets, because their words embody truth and encourage others to seek it,

have a unique ability to transform the world for the better; they are, he declared in the famous phrase with which he concludes his essay, "the unacknowledged legislators of the World." Again, it is easy to see the connection to "To a Sky-Lark," which is also concerned with the status and influence of the poet. In stanza 8, for example, the poet sings his hymns (poems seen as possessing a kind of sacred purpose) and has an effect on the world at large. People start to feel "sympathy" with the emotions of others that they have not felt before.

The word sympathy is key here, because it also occurs in *A Defence of Poetry* in a rather specialized sense. Shelley draws on the eighteenth-century idea, developed by a number of British philosophers, of the sympathetic imagination. Poetry awakens the imaginative faculty, which is the aspect of the human mind that is able to identify intuitively with objects and feelings that lie beyond the individual self. Poetry thus has the power to create a sense of unity between diverse people on the basis of the sharing of high ideals and generous emotions. Poetry "transmutes all that it touches, and every form moving within the radiance of its presence is changed by wondrous sympathy to an incarnation of the spirit which it breathes." For Shelley this means that poetry has the ability to promote selfless love, which in turn strengthens the moral foundations of society and contributes to the social good. This belief lies beneath the impassioned yearning he expresses in the final stanza of "To a Sky-Lark." If only he could embody just half of the joy he hears in the skylark's song, his poetry would be so irresistible, so beautiful, and so true that the troubled world would have no option but to listen and be transformed.

Source: Bryan Aubrey, Critical Essay on "To a Sky-Lark," in *Poetry for Students*, Gale, Cengage Learning, 2010.

Prem Nath

In the following article, Nath considers how some of Shelley's poems, including "To a Sky-Lark," pay tribute to Shakespeare's Othello.

Shelley's high opinion of Shakespeare can be gauged from a rhetorical question that he posed in a letter, on Sept. 29, 1816, to Byron "What would the human race have been if Homer, or Shakespeare, had never written?" Certainly Shelley's poetry would have been different in certain ways at least if Shakespeare had never written. The purpose of this note is to show that *Othello* has left its impact on three of Shelley's famous poems, "Ode to the West Wind" (1819), "To A Skylark" (1820) and "Epipsychidion" (1812).

In the third passage of his "Ode to the West Wind," Shelley describes the moss and flowers which are "so sweet, the sense faints picturing them!" Connecting these words from "Ode to the West Wind" to lines 450–52 of "Epipsychidion," "from the moss violets and jonquils peep, / And dart their arrowy odour through the brain / Till you might faint with that delicious pain," Dennis Welland observes that they are "possibly a recollection of [Shelley's] visit to Il Prato Fiorito in July 1818 where the overpowering scent of jonquils had made him feel faint." Welland's remark is quite sound, and it is not improbable that Shelley in the "Ode to the West Wind" and "Epipsychidion" recalls his experience in Italy I wish to point out that the words that Shelley employs to give body to his experience come from *Othello*. Shelley's word-picture of the effect of the flowers and moss is nearly identical to the one that Othello draws of his beautiful but supposedly unfaithful bride "Oh thou weed / Who art so lovely fair, and smell'st so sweet, / That the Sense aches at thee" (Variorum edn IV n. 77–79, spellings modernized).

It appears that Shelley was fascinated by Othello's description of Desdemona He recalls it again in his poem "To a Skylark." In the eleventh stanza Shelley compares the Skylark to a growing rose which with "the scent it gives / Makes [the bees] faint with too much sweet."

Critics, and editors of neither Shelley (including Neville Rogers, and Ingpen and Peck), nor Shakespeare (Furness or M R. Ridley) have so far noticed these Shakespeare reverberations in Shelley. I have not found them recorded in the two scholarly essays by David L. Clark and Frederick L. Jones on Shelley and Shakespeare, or elsewhere.

Source: Prem Nath, "Shelley and Shakespeare," in *American Notes & Queries*, Vol. 21, No. 5-6, January-February 1983, p. 71.

Stewart C. Wilcox

In the following excerpt, Wilcox argues that "To a Sky-Lark" is rooted in the myth of the winged soul from Plato's Phaedrus.

The sources and influences which stimulated Shelley's imagination when he composed the "Sky-lark" are not merely significant in themselves, but also essential in understanding its meaning. In particular, his use of the myth of the soul from

> THE CONCLUDING LINE EMPHASIZES ONCE MORE THE MORAL FUNCTION OF THE POET—HERE SHELLEY HIMSELF—WHO, IF ONLY HE WERE AS DIVINELY JOYOUS (*BLITHE*) AS THE SKYLARK, WOULD GAIN THE EAR OF THE WORLD."

Plato's *Phaedrus,* a source hitherto mentioned only incidentally, needs to be elucidated. Woven into the imagery of the poem are three main threads of development: observations of nature and the skylark mainly suggested by the spot in Italy which, John Gisborne tells us, he associated with Shelley and skylarks; suggestive references to the poet's own state of mind in early summer of 1820 when he composed the poem; and philosophical ideas, principally embodied in the bird as a Platonic symbol of the ideal spirit of poetry. These three strands of meaning—natural, personal, and philosophical—Shelley so blends in his design that they bring artistic wholeness to its structure and unity to its ideas....

The heart of this discussion of sources and influences is that Shelley used Plato's myth of the winged soul in the *Phaedrus* as the philosophical basis of his symbolism of the bird in the *"Sky-lark."* If he did, it then follows that the poem should be Platonistically interpreted. Moreover, its unity—its steady progression to climax in imagery, structure, and meaning—will be clearly seen to depend upon the consistency of the ideas suggested by the skylark as a symbol.

First we should observe that Shelley read both the *Phaedrus* and the *Phaedo* during his stay at Pisa during the first half of 1820, and that during the previous two years he had translated the *Ion, Symposium, Menexenus,* parts of the *Republic,* and the notes on Socrates. Even the brief, though important, essay *"On Love"* was probably composed in 1820. Thus Shelley's mind was full of Platonic concepts and images. Perhaps the most famous and striking of all these is the myth of the charioteer in the *Phaedrus,* wherein is found the figure of the winged soul as well as observations upon the soul itself and its divine inspiration....

Shelley clearly indicates his three main divisions. The first six stanzas are the proem, which is followed by a transitional stanza apostrophising the skylark, "What is most like thee?" This stanza and the following four that answer Shelley's question in as many figures lead up to a second stanza of transition in which the skylark's music is said to surpass "All that ever was / Joyous, and clear, and fresh. . . ." Both transitional stanzas, it should be remarked, belong in division two, which is bounded by them, and both are skilfully constructed to look both forward and backward: the first effects the change from the natural, real skylark to a being apprehensible only through figurative comparisons that reveal aspects of hidden beauty; the second summarizes part two and carries us over from its comparisons to the third, philosophical part of the poem, which accomplishes the skylark's metamorphosis into a symbol representing the soul, the spirit, of the ideal poet, and the soaring spirit of poetry which is his essence. The subdivisions of this philosophical part ". . . emphasize the symbolic value of the skylark first to the poet in general, and then to the particular poet Shelley."

Indeed, the extraordinary care that Shelley took to prepare the reader for the three main as well as the lesser parts of his poem is revealed in the very first stanza. Here the skylark is both a real bird and a spiritual symbol. Yet we soon perceive that Shelley is going to begin relatively close to the ground with natural particulars. The natural skylark is not of course described. Nevertheless its spiral, evermounting flight is vividly suggested by the lilting rhythm of the line "And singing still dost soar, and soaring ever singest." The verse, as Elizabeth Nitchie has pointed out, overflows its bounds. The image of the 'flood of rapture' (1. 65), which is repeated many times in the poem, is reflected in the stanza form. The long fifth line of the stanzas, especially, gives the effect of a swift cascade of sound overflowing the rim of the quatrain, for the 'profuse strains' cannot be confined within narrow limits. They rush over into the wider space, often with no pause indicated by punctuation, or possible in the reading.

We are next given the setting (the sunset, st. 3) and its background (purple evening, st. 4). In addition the similes of these stanzas suggest the ethereal nature of the skylark, for it is like an "unbodied joy" or a " star of Heaven" but dimly seen in daylight. Stanza five, which Mr. T. S. Eliot has perhaps wilfully said he does not understand, carries us

skilfully on by its metaphor. Like Venus, the morning-star whose "intense lamp narrows" until it is hardly seen and is but *felt* still to be in the sky, so is the skylark still heard, though become invisible:

> Keen as are the arrows
> Of that silver sphere,
> Whose intense lamp narrows
> In the white dawn clear
> Until we hardly see—we feel that it is there.

This preparation, moreover, is peculiarly necessary, for Shelley is not going to appeal primarily to our sight, but to our hearing—a departure from Plato's emphasis upon our vision as the faculty through which we best apprehend essential forms and beauty. It may be remarked further that Plato's emphasis upon vision occurs in the very passage which sets forth the figure of the "feathered soul." Hence if Shelley did use the myth, he was doubtless aware of the significance of this change in sensory appeal and developed his metaphors and imagery accordingly. The next stanza, the last in part one, veritably rings with the bird's song:

> All the earth and air
> With thy voice is loud,
> As, when night is bare,
> From one lonely cloud
> The moon rains out her beams, and Heaven
>   is overflowed.

Here, then, is the reversal in order of emphasis designed to reinforce the shift from vision to hearing, for it is now the light which is in the simile. That is, instead of describing the visual, as do the early lines of the third, fourth, and fifth stanzas, the first two lines describe the aural. In succeeding stanzas a consummately handled shift from appeal to one sense to another has prepared us for part two.

The second part (sts. 7–12) begins with the first of the two transitional stanzas:

> What thou art we know not;
> What is most like thee?
> From rainbow clouds there flow not
> Drops so bright to see
> As from thy presence showers a rain of
>   melody.

Most striking here is the coalescence of the appeals to our sense perceptions. In the previous stanza the moon has rained out her beams from a cloud to overflow Heaven with light. Here, however, the liquid notes of the skylark showering a rain of music are like bright drops seen descending from a rainbow cloud. The suggestion of the colors of the spectrum, of the brilliant refraction of the raindrops, and the organic inclusion of these elements in the metaphor "rain of melody" produce a coalescent imagery of the highest order. Without mixing his sense references Shelley works his imagery forward from his comparison into the active word *showers*. Sound, color, light, all are blended into one phrase. We are now fully prepared for the similes describing the skylark, the answers to the poet's rhetorical question "What is most like thee?"

The first reply compares the skylark to the Poet, who, if he is "rightly mad" (Plato's phrase) like the skylark itself in stanza one, sings "hymns unbidden" from the divine inspiration of "unpremeditated art." In this conception of the ideal poet, who in Shelley's figure is hidden "In the light of thought," just as the bird is unseen in its airy spiral upward, is to be perceived the core of his moral philosophy. For through his imagination the poet becomes "the great instrument of moral good," a disseminator of love, "that powerful attraction towards all that we conceive, or fear, or hope beyond ourselves, when we find within our own thoughts the chasm of an insufficient void, and seek to awaken in all things that are, a community with what we experience within ourselves." (*On Love*)

The "maiden ... Soothing her love-laden / Soul in secret hour / With music sweet as love" (st. 9) arouses two trains of reflection: first that the arts of poetry and music were to Plato, as to all Greeks, practically one; second that the maiden is, figuratively, an aspect of Intellectual Beauty, Love, the soul of the type-Poet. Thus the skylark's music, which overflows Heaven, is like the maiden's, which "overflows her bower." Though the reference is hardly more than a hint, in its organic imagery it is correspondent with the development of the whole poem so far as the poem relates to Shelley's ideas on Love.

The comparison of the skylark to a glowworm in the grass, which reminds the admirer of Marvell of "The mower to the glowworms," was undoubtedly prompted by the fireflies Shelley saw among the myrtle hedges at Lehorn. External nature is again used for comparison in the next stanza, where the bird is compared to a rose. And then in the next, the last stanza of part two, the use of simile is abandoned and the previous stanzas unified. In *showers* we are reminded of the same word in the first stanza of this second

part. Here also Shelley creates organically, for the showers *sound* on the grass that is twinkling with the phosphorescent fireflies, and the flowers, in contrast to the rose with its sweet order in the stanza before, are brightly awakened by the refreshing rain. Finally, the previous images, though there seems to be no necessary order in their arrangement, are summed up in the word *All* of the last two lines:

> All that ever was
> Joyous. and clear. and fresh, thy music doth
>   surpass.

In their figures the Poet, maiden, glowworm, and rose are bidden beauty, and since to Shelley beauty was an aspect of Love, concealment becomes the mode of its suggestion. This motif is implicit, to be sure, yet that makes no less effective the use of hidden beauty as a preparation for part three, for which we are now ready.

"I have never heard," says Shelley of the skylark in the first stanza of the last part,

> Praise of love or wine
> That panted forth a rapture so divine.

This, I believe, harks back to Plato's *Symposium*, he subject of which is Love, the occasion a feast at which the wine is partly symbolical. In the succeeding stanzas the superiority of inspiration to artistry is again indicated in the comparison of the divine notes of the skylark to such lesser music, "wherein we feel there is some hidden want," as a marriage chorus or mere chant of triumph. Moreover, the objects that evoke the bird's song (st. 15) give pause for question; and unlike man, says Shelley, the bird loves its own kind and knows no pain. It would seem that the contrast is to his own worldly tribulations in 1820, bound down as he is in the earthly prison-house of his mortal form, as it is also in the next stanza, where the skylark's spirit is said to be free of weariness (*languor*) and annoyance. Nor is the skylark's ethereal spirit subject to the satiety of earthly love as is the mortal poet, who must suffer from the soul's mixture of earthly and heavenly love, knowing not the pure perfection of the beauteous forms gazed upon by nonmortals whose souls are fully winged.

In stanza seventeen the poem reaches its climax. The apotheosis of the skylark becomes complete:

> Waking or asleep
> Thou of death must deem
> Things more true and deep

Than we mortals dream
Or how could thy notes flow in such a crystal
    stream?

In the mythopoeic sense the skylark is now a symbol of spirit and as if it were a fully winged soul must be able to see behind the veil that prevents mortals from apprehending pure form. Man comes into the world "trailing clouds of glory"; but his recollections are a dim, shadowy memory. Moreover, he yearns for life-in-death, to see what the idealized skylark can see. Using Plato's poetic fable, Shelley has made the skylark a symbol of exultation and spiritual desire. Benjamin Kurtz concludes that the poem here ascends a climax to a synthesis of life-in-death, to the same "true and deep" intuition that *"The Cloud"* attains in its culmination. "I change, but I cannot die." But our realization is not purely joyous, for

We look before and after,
And pine for what is not:
Our sincerest laughter
With some pain is fraught,
Our sweetest songs are those that tell of
    saddest thought.

Significantly, the first line of this stanza is an echo of a phrase in the fragment "On Life" (1819?). There Shelley asks,

For what are we? Whence do we come? and whither do we go? Is birth the commencement, is death the conclusion of our being? What is birth and death?

The most refined abstractions of logic conduct to a view of life, which, though startling to the apprehension, is, in fact, that which the habitual sense of its repeated combinations has extinguished in us. It strips, as it were, the painted curtain from this scene of things. I confess that I am one of those who am unable to refuse my assent to the conclusions of those philosophers who assert that nothing exists but as it is perceived.

It is a decision against which all our persuasions struggle, and we must be long convicted before we can be convinced that the solid universe of external things is "such stuff as dreams are made of [*sic.*]" The shocking absurdities of the popular philosophy of mind and matter, its fatal consequences in morals, and their violent dogmatism concerning the source of all things, had early conducted me to materialism, This materialism is a seducing system to young and superficial minds. It allows its disciples to talk, and dispenses them from thinking. But I was discontented with such a view of things as it afforded; man is a being of high aspirations, "looking both before and after," whose

"thoughts wander through eternity," disclaiming alliance with transience and decay; incapable of imagining to himself annihilation; existing but in the future and the past; being, not what he is, but what he has been and shall be. Whatever may be his true and final destination, there is a spirit within him at enmity with nothingness and dissolution. This is the character of all life and being.

That man's "thoughts wander through eternity" is from Belial's harangue in *Paradise Lost* (II. 148). The previous phrase is from *Hamlet:*

Sure, He that made us with such large
    discourse,
Looking both before and after, gave us not
That capability and god-like reason
To fust in us unus'd
(IV, iv, 37)

But Shelley's use in the *"Skylark"* "large discourse [i. e., reasoning power] looking both before and after" undoubtedly goes back not only to Shakespeare but also to the foregoing argument in which man is considered "not what he is, but what he has been and shall be." Thus the central mood of yearning aspiration in the poem is fulfilled in the joy of the ideal bird. Shelley is saying that we are mortals, with the capacity, to be sure, which the bird does not have, of looking before and after, but without the ability of the bird or of the winged soul to fly straight to heaven. We merely pine for it, for what is not, and consequently sorrow and joy are blended in our human song. This paradox of pain and sadness in human pleasure he discusses in *"A Defence of Poetry":*

... from an inexplicable defect of harmony in the constitution of human nature, the pain of the inferior is frequently connected with the pleasures of the superior portions of our being. Sorrow, terror, anguish, despair itself, are often the chosen expressions of an approximation to the highest good. Our sympathy in tragic fiction depends on this principle; tragedy delights by affording a shadow of the pleasure which exists in pain. This is the source also of the melancholy which is inseparable from the sweetest melody. The pleasure that is in sorrow is sweeter than the pleasure of pleasure itself. And hence the saying, "It is better to go to the house of mourning, than to the house of mirth." Not that this highest species of pleasure is necessarily linked with pain. The delight of love and friendship, the ecstasy of the admiration of nature, the joy of the perception and still more of the creation of poetry, is often wholly unalloyed.

The production and assurance of pleasure in this highest sense is true utility. Those who produce and preserve this pleasure are poets or poetical philosophers.

Hence the *"Skylark"* reflects Shelley's keen awareness of the mixture of his personal sorrows and his yearning for the pure joy of imagination in its most exalted mood. This I think he makes clear in the next stanza:

Yet if we could scorn
Hate, and pride, and fear;
If we were things born
Not to shed a tear,
I know not how thy joy we ever should come near.

Of it Mr. Ellsworth Barnard says, "The meaning ... is somewhat obscure. Shelley may mean that even if man were not subdued by suffering, he still, in the happiest state conceivable, could not come near perfect joy of the skylark; or he may mean that by virtue of that very suffering man becomes able to experience a joy that *does* come near the skylark's." Perhaps the obscurity can be resolved by remembering what Blake said, that if it were not true that

Joy and woe are woven fine,
A clothing for the soul divine,

we could not even approach the joy of the aspiring soul, we should have no comprehension of it. There is something of a paradox, but that is not to be wondered at, for Shelley pictured man in the millenium as not free from, though master over, " labor and pain and grief":

Passionless? no: yet free from guilt or pain,
Which were, for his will made, or suffered them,
Nor yet exempt, though ruling them like slaves,
From chance, and death, and mutability,
The clogs of that which else might oversoar
The loftiest star of unascended heaven....
(*Prometheus Unbound*, III, 198–203)

Again man's longing for the perfection of the skylark-poet is emphasized in the next stanza, where Shelley suggests that the skylark's skill makes it the ideal for a poet to follow: neither the loveliest music nor the finest poetry can equal the mad ecstasy of the songbird. And finally in the last stanza Shelley appeals to the skylark for personal inspiration of divine madness. Like Coleridge in the corresponding lines of *Kubla Khan*, he is drawing upon the ancient concept of *furor poeticus*. The poem has come full turn,

> EACH POET WAS SINCERELY FACE TO FACE WITH HIS IDEAL, AND EVEN THOUGH THEIR IDEALS WERE NOT IDENTICAL, SHELLEY MAY WELL HAVE RECALLED MARVELL'S SUPREME ADMIRATION IN PHRASING HIS OWN."

Could I revive within me
Her symphony and song
To such a deep delight 'twould win me
That with music loud and long,
I would build that dome in air

. . .

And all should cry, Beware! Beware!
His flashing eyes, his floating hair!

for here too is the "unpremeditated art" of the first stanza. The concluding line emphasizes once more the moral function of the poet—here Shelley himself—who, if only he were as divinely joyous (*blithe*) as the skylark, would gain the ear of the world. . . .

Source: Stewart C. Wilcox, "The Sources, Symbolism, and Unity of Shelley's 'Skylark,'" in *Studies in Philology*, Vol. 46, No. 4, October 1949, pp. 560–76.

Irving T. Richards

In the following essay, Richards contends that Shelley found his inspiration for "To a Sky-Lark" and "The Cloud" in the writings of others, specifically Robert Herrick and Andrew Marvell, rather than purely in nature.

Mrs. Shelley in her preface to her husband's collected poems remarked:

> There are others, such as the "Ode to the Sky Lark," and "The Cloud," which, in the opinion of many critics, bear a purer poetical stamp than any other of his productions. They were written as his mind prompted, listening to the carolling of the bird, aloft in the azure sky of Italy; or marking the cloud as it sped across the heavens, while he floated in his boat on the Thames.

The implication here is obviously that the two glorious lyrics were wholly inspired by nature and are quite free from any bookish influence. This implication, in view no doubt of their nearly divine perfection, has been permitted to go unchallenged. Experience has demonstrated, however, that the greatest English literary masterpieces are rarely altogether spontaneously generated. That Shelley's two bright gems, for all their flawlessness, reflect something of a borrowed light shining from familiar sources is thought to be apparent in the following comparisons.

In writing "The Cloud," Shelly seems, whether at the time adrift in his little boat or immured in the more barren seclusion of his study, to have been vividly conscious of the qualities of Robert Herrick's little *tour de force,* "The Hag," which in consideration of its brevity, it is perhaps permissible to quote:

> The Hag is astride,
> This night for to ride;
> The Devill and shee together:
> Through thick, and through thin,
> Now out, and then in,
> Though ne'r so foule be the weather.
> A Thorn or a Burr
> She takes for a Spurre:
> With a lash of a Bramble she rides now,
> Through Brakes and through Bryars,
> O're Ditches, and Mires,
> She followes the Spirit that guides now.
> No Beast, for his food,
> Dares now range the wood;
> But husht in his laire he lies lurking:
> While mischeifs by these,
> On Land and on Seas,
> At noone of Night are a working.
> The storme will arise,
> And trouble the skies;
> This night, and more for the wonder,
> The ghost from the Tomb
> Affrighted shall come,
> Cal'd out by the clap of the Thunder.

It will be observed at once that both poets, despite obvious differences, treat the same general subject in the same general manner: an excursion through the air on the part of a definitely conceived voyager gifted with magic or supernatural powers, to whom comes a kaleidoscopic variety of experience for which the voyager is itself in some mysterious way responsible.

The meter of the two poems, it will also be observed, strikes the same norm—a norm rare, to say the least of it, in English poetry. For if Shelley's first and alternate tetrameter lines, with their internal rime, be taken as the equivalent of one of Herrick's dimeter couplets, then Herrick's six-line stanza becomes the metrical equivalent of each quatrain of Shelley's poem. When read aloud, the poems are alike in that peculiar lilting, swaying, floating measure that is so highly appropriate to their aërial journey, their metrical difference consisting merely in Shelley's arrangement of his verses (including his stanzaic grouping) and his greater freedom in departure from a normal arrangement of iambs and anapests, to which Herrick adheres quite faithfully. The metrical norm and the rime scheme of the two poems are, then, the same; and hence come their peculiar suspended, swinging movement and rich, haunting cadences, to be matched in few other English poems. This effect is greatly enhanced by the use in both poems of frequent feminine rimes and firm, full masculine ones. A rather unusual rime, "these—Seas," occurs in both poems; and Herrick's "wonder—Thunder" is echoed by Shelley's use twice of "under—thunder."

Other echoings of thought and phrase occur. Herrick's Hag "followes the Spirit that guides now," presumably that of the devil who rides with her; Shelley's Cloud carries "Lightning my pilot" and moves wherever "This pilot is guiding me," the pilot himself being lured and his movements determined by "The Spirit he loves." Each voyager, that is to say, has its movements controlled ("guided") by an accompanying "Spirit" outside itself to which it is subject, and whose representative, at any rate, rides with it. Besides the references to "seas" and to "thunder" already pointed out as entering into the rimes of both poems (where they are particularly conspicuous and particularly certain to haunt the memory, or to occur from having already haunted the memory), both poems close with the eventuality of a storm by means of which the eerie voyager is to disturb the serenity of nature. In Herrick the storm, in Shelley the Cloud, is to "arise" for this purpose; and at this point in both poems occurs, in the rimes, with almost the finality of a signature, the striking phrase "ghost from the tomb."

On the whole, since Shelley sets himself somewhat the same general task as Herrick, since in the performing it he adopts Herrick's unusual and especially appropriate metrical and rime schemes, and since he echoes both specific thoughts and specific phrases of Herrick's—the one in a guiding and an accompanying "Spirit," the presence of "thunder" and "seas," and a valedictory storm with its "ghost from the tomb," and the other notably in expressions that entered conspicuously into Herrick's rimes—it seems altogether probable that Herrick's poem had not only pleased him in the past, but was haunting his memory whenever and wherever he composed "The Cloud."

Somewhat less certain, perhaps, is another by no means improbable recollection of Shelley's in the process of composing that other superb lyric, his lines "To a Skylark." In his well-known melodious verses "On Paradise Lost," Andrew Marvell thus apostrophized Milton:

> That Majesty which through thy Work doth Reign
> Draws the Devout, deterring the Profane.
> And things divine thou treatst of in such state
> As them preserves, and Thee inviolate.
> At once delight and horrour on us seize,
> Thou singst with so much gravity and ease;
> And above humane flight dost soar aloft,
> With Plume so strong, so equal, and so soft.
> The *Bird* nam'd from that *Paradise* you sing
> So never Flags, but alwaies keeps on Wing.
> Where couldst thou Words of such a compass find?
> Whence furnish such a vast expense of Mind?
> Just Heav'n Thee, like *Tiresias,* to requite,
> Rewards with *Prophesie* thy loss of Sight.
> Well mightst thou scorn thy Readers to allure
> With tinkling Rhime, of thy own Sense secure ...

Again, as in the case of "The Cloud" and "The Hag," the general purpose of this passage and of Shelley's poem—if not this time of both poems as a whole—is the same. Though there are quite obvious differences between the poet Milton and the bird of Shelley's praise, both are treated in the passage and the poem now under consideration as consummate masters of poetic expression, whom each author envies their great gifts. Shelley, no less than Marvell, is apostrophizing his ideal poet, symbolized or typified in the bird. Thus passage and poem have at least a natural *rapprochment.*

But is it difficult, looking more closely, to find in Marvell's verses the complete outline of Shelley's poem? Milton and the Skylark both sing of "things divine," keeping themselves and their subjects alike "inviolate" and thrilling with "delight" the "Devout" listener. It is even significant that they both *sing;* Milton, apparently upon the authority of his invocation to the Muse to inspire his "song" and his expressed determination "with no middle flight ... to soar," having become for purposes of Marvell's verse himself a bird—and a bird remarkably suggestive of Shelley's! Marvell seems pretty certainly to have had in mind in his simile the popular superstitions regarding the bird of paradise, but surely the essential preëmininse of Shelley's skylark is that it "above humane flight dost soar aloft" and that it "never Flags, but alwaies keeps on Wing"—"And singing still dost soar, and soaring ever singest." And finally each poet breaks into rhetorical questions concerning the source of his ideal's inspiration—questions that he at least partially answers by a reiteration of the ideal being's full isolation from mundanity. The Skylark never felt "Shadow of annoyance"; Milton is isolated by blindness: both are rewarded with powers of prophecy and revelation. What essential thought of Shelley's poem—aside from its golden imagery, diction, and music—is not traceable in Marvell's lines?

Shelley's stanzas of course close with an Alexandrine, so that such a line as his question, "Or how could thy notes flow in such a crystal stream?," which might otherwise be reasonably equated with Marvell's line, "Where couldst thou Words of such a compass find?," is not in Marvell's pentameter. Yet because of the rapidity everywhere demanded by the ecstatic rush of Shelley's poem, his hexameters are not far from pentameter in effect. They are not the slow, summarizing Alexandrine of Spenser and his followers; their time equivalent is nearer that of such a normal pentameter line as Marvell's.

Verbal echoes are not perhaps so full or so numerous as one might wish, nor by themselves altogether convincing. Marvell refers to the "things divine" of which Milton treats; Shelley's lark pants forth "a flood of rapture so divine." Both Milton and the lark render "delight." The form "singest," which might have been drawn from Marvell's "singst," enters conspicuously into Shelley's rimes, and is there associated with the word "soar," once in the form "dost soar," which occurs in Marvell with almost the same significant juxtaposition that Shelley gave it in the line quoted above. Marvell justifies Milton's "scorn" of rime; and Shelley, first implying the wish that we might "scorn/Hate, and pride, and fear," thereafter denominates his lark a "scorner of the ground." Possibly, since we are probably investigating here a feat of memory and not a conscious, intentional use of source, it is not fantastic to suggest that the sounds of Marvell's phrase "tinkling Rhime" may lie at the bottom of Shelley's happy euphony of "twinkling grass."

More convincing than verbal parallels, however, is the general similarity of thought. Each poet is addressing in the guise of a bird that soars unrestrainedly toward heaven an ideal singer endowed with the precious gifts of perfect expression and of prophecy—a seer, a *vates,* who has found and can gloriously convey the deeper meaning of life. Each poet's admiration eventually bursts forth in rhetorical questions concerning the source of such inspiration—questions that have in each instance a simple, plaintive earnestness rare in the use of apostrophe in English, the apostrophe in English poetry usually ringing with something of bombastic inflation. Each poet was sincerely face to face with his ideal, and even though their ideals were not identical, Shelley may well have recalled Marvell's supreme admiration in phrasing his own.

Source: Irving T. Richards, "A Note on the Source Influences in Shelley's 'Cloud' and 'Skylark,'" in *PMLA*, Vol. 50, No. 2, June 1935, pp. 562–67.

SOURCES

Abrams, M. H., *A Glossary of Literary Terms*, 4th ed., Holt, Rinehart and Winston, 1981, p. 99.

Allsup, James O., *The Magic Circle: A Study of Shelley's Concept of Love*, Kennikat Press, 1976, pp. 13–19.

Barcus, James E., ed., *Shelley: The Critical Heritage*, Routledge & Kegan Paul, 1975, p. 2.

Central Intelligence Agency, "United Kingdom," in *The World Factbook*, https://www.cia.gov/library/publications/the-world-factbook/geos/uk.html (accessed March 23, 2009).

Chernaik, Judith, *The Lyrics of Shelley*, Press of Case Western Reserve University, 1972, p. 130.

Dabundo, Laura, ed., *Encyclopedia of Romanticism: Culture in Britain, 1780s–1830s*, Garland Publishing, 1992.

Holmes, Richard, *Shelley: The Pursuit*, Quartet Books, 1976, p. 599.

Hunt, Leigh, Review of *Prometheus Unbound*, in *Shelley: The Critical Heritage*, edited by James E. Barcus, Routledge, 1975, p. 327; originally published in the *Examiner*, January-June 1820.

"The Lark Ascending," *BBC Radio 4 Online*, June 5, 2006, http://www.bbc.co.uk/radio4/science/nature_20060605.shtml (accessed March 23, 2009).

Leavis, F. R., *Revaluation*, Chatto and Windus, 1936; reprinted in *The English Romantics: Major Poetry and Critical Theory, with Selected Modern Critical Essays*, edited, with introduction and notes by John L. Mahoney, D. C. Heath, 1978, pp. 769, 771.

Leighton, Angela, *Shelley and the Sublime: An Interpretation of the Major Poems*, Cambridge University Press, 1984, p. 124.

Lockhart, John Gibson, Review of *Prometheus Unbound*, in *Shelley: The Critical Heritage*, edited by James E. Barcus, Routledge, 1975, p. 239; originally published in *Blackwood's Edinburgh* magazine, September 1820.

Motion, Andrew, "Yet Once More, O Ye Laurels," in *Guardian*, March 21, 2009, http://www.guardian.co.uk/books/2009/mar/21/andrew-motion-poet-laureate (accessed March 23, 2009).

Perkins, David, *The Quest for Permanence: The Symbolism of Wordsworth, Shelley, and Keats*, Harvard University Press, 1959, p. 141.

Poetry Archive, http://www.poetryarchive.org/ (accessed March 24, 2009).

Raine, Kathleen, "A Defence of Shelley's Poetry," in *Defending Ancient Springs*, Lindisfarne Press, 1985, p. 149.

Shelley, Percy Bysshe, "A Defence of Poetry," in *Shelley's Poetry and Prose*, selected and edited by Donald H. Reiman and Sharon B. Powers, W. W. Norton, 1977, pp. 482–83, 504–505, 508.

———, Preface to "The Revolt of Islam," in *Poetical Works of Shelley: Poetical Works*, 2nd ed., edited by Thomas Hutchinson, corrected by G. M. Matthews, Oxford University Press, 1970, p. 36.

———, *Shelley: Poems*, Everyman's Library, 1993.

———, "To a Sky-Lark," in *Shelley's Poetry and Prose*, selected and edited by Donald H. Reiman and Sharon B. Powers, W. W. Norton, 1977, pp. 226–29.

FURTHER READING

Fogle, Richard Harter, *The Imagery of Keats and Shelley: A Comparative Study*, University of North Carolina Press, 1949.

This is an illuminating study of John Keats and Shelley. Fogle particularly notes the synesthetic quality of much of Shelley's imagery, in which one sensory experience is described in terms of more than one sense, that is, a color may be heard, or a sound seen.

Morton, Timothy, ed., *The Cambridge Companion to Shelley*, Cambridge University Press, 2006.

This collection of essays contains many illuminating new perspectives on the poet. The essays cover Shelley's work in all genres, as well as his translations. Shelley's life, politics, language, and philosophy are all addressed.

Rogers, Neville, *Shelley at Work*, Oxford University Press, 1967, pp. 206–210.

Using the two manuscript versions of "To a Sky-Lark," Rogers shows how and why Shelley made his revisions. The book also includes a photograph of Shelley's draft for the beginning of the poem.

Ruston, Sharon, *Romanticism*, Continuum, 2007.
This is a guide to British Romanticism from 1780 to 1820. It includes an overview of the historical, cultural, and intellectual background of the period, a survey of the developments in literary genres, and analysis of the work of William Blake, William Wordsworth, Samuel Taylor Coleridge, Keats, Shelley, Lord Byron, Mary Wollstonecraft, and Felicia Hemans. The book also includes a chronology and an annotated list of further reading.

Sibley, David Allen, *Sibley's Birding Basics*, Knopf, 2002.
This is an ideal guide for anyone starting out as a bird watcher. Sibley explains all the basics, such as how to understand feathers, spot voices, and evaluate age variations for common and rare birds. The book also includes two hundred paintings.

To Be of Use

MARGE PIERCY

1973

Much of Marge Piercy's poetry is informed by her Jewish background as well as by her sense of activism, which was cultivated during the anti-Vietnam War and women's rights movements of the 1970s. The poem "To Be of Use," which first appeared in 1973 in a volume by the same name, is often examined within the context of Piercy's Jewish identity and her role as a political and social activist. A self-described feminist, Piercy is a well-respected novelist as well as a poet, and the vivid phrasing as well as the visual vignettes of "To Be of Use" are suggestive of her storytelling abilities. In the loosely-structured poem, Piercy uses straightforward language and an informal tone to praise the value of hard work and purposeful action. Acts of common, physical labor are compared with beautiful yet utilitarian artifacts from different cultures. Piercy evokes a simpler time with her references to ancient cultures and the hand-harvesting of food, lending the poem a sense of yearning for times past. At the same time, the poem is uplifting and hopeful about the future. Piercy acknowledges her love for people who embrace this same simple, hard-working attitude of long ago, and her reverent attitude regarding such people conveys her faith in their abilities to improve the world through their efforts.

Originally published in the volume *To Be of Use*, the poem "To Be of Use" is available in the more recent collection *The Art of Blessing the Day: Poems with a Jewish Theme*. The paperback reprint was published in 2007 by Alfred A. Knopf.

Marge Piercy (The Library of Congress)

and poetry. In 1973, the volume *To Be of Use*, containing the poem by the same name, was published. The volume focused heavily on contemporary social issues. During the next several years, Piercy, now active in the women's rights movement, published a number of novels, as well as poetry collections.

Piercy and Shapiro divorced in 1980. Two years later, she married her current husband, author and publisher Ira Wood, with whom she lives in Wellfleet, Massachusetts. As a couple, they wrote a play, poetry, and the 1998 novel *Storm Tide*. Piercy has continued to prolifically write fiction and poetry since then and has taught at a number of universities, including her alma mater, the University of Michigan. Her fiction and poetry have won a number of awards, including a National Endowment for the Arts Award (1978), two Carolyn Kizer Poetry Prizes (1986, 1990), and the Golden Rose Poetry Prize (1990). In 1997, Wood and Piercy founded a small literary publishing company, Leapfrog Press. Piercy's most recent volume of poetry, *The Crooked Inheritance*, was published in 2006.

AUTHOR BIOGRAPHY

Piercy was born on March 31, 1936, in Detroit, Michigan, to working-class parents Robert Douglas Piercy and Bert Bernice Bunnin Piercy. Piercy attended public schools in Detroit and afterward attended the University of Michigan in Ann Arbor. There, Piercy won the prestigious Hopwood Awards in 1956 and 1957, first for poetry and fiction and then for poetry. She graduated with a bachelor of arts degree in 1957 and earned a master of arts degree from Northwestern University in Evanston, Illinois, in 1958. Piercy married Michel Schiff that same year. Piercy and Schiff briefly lived in France, but their marriage was short-lived. After the divorce in 1959, Piercy worked a variety of jobs, became an active participant in the civil rights movement and wrote several unpublished novels. In 1962, she married Robert Shapiro.

During the 1960s, Piercy and Shapiro became anti-Vietnam War activists. Piercy's diligent writing efforts paid off in 1968 when her first volume of poetry, *Breaking Camp*, was published; her first novel, *Going Down Fast*, was published a year later. Piercy and her husband moved to Cape Cod in 1971, and she continued to write fiction

POEM SUMMARY

Stanza 1

In the first stanza of "To Be of Use," Piercy announces her love of people who are able to embrace work without a sense of avoidance or delay. She compares such people to seals, at home in their environment and able to navigate the waters of toil with grace, strength, and confidence. The tone in this stanza is reverential, as it emphasizes the speaker's love for and admiration of individuals who gladly seek out and do the work before them. Piercy's image of seals bobbing in the water, buoyant like balls, and smooth and graceful in their appearance, conveys both a sense of innate ability as well as a sense of joy.

Stanza 2

The second stanza begins in a manner similar to the first, with the poet stating her love for people who are able to yoke themselves to the job to be done. Likening such people this time to beasts of burden, such as oxen and water buffalo, the poet describes the strength and patience of such individuals. She praises their diligence and persistence, and she acknowledges their dedication to tasks that are both necessary and repetitive.

MEDIA ADAPTATIONS

- *Louder, We Can't Hear You (Yet): The Political Poems of Marge Piercy* is an audio CD collection of thirty of Piercy's political poems, including "To Be of Use." It was published in 2004 by Leapfrog Press.

While the seals in the previous stanza bounce happily through the water, the animals that Piercy references in this second stanza are those often considered more durable, reliable, and less than carefree. The need for such animals to work in often unpleasant conditions, striving to pull their carts or plows through the mud, reveals another layer to Piercy's notion of work. While the first stanza lauds the eagerness of people who take on their work, the second stanza praises their determination in the face of adverse conditions. The work is now revealed to be not necessarily something that can always be characterized as fun or happy. The tone has shifted from pleasant to purposeful with the change in animal imagery as well as the change in scenery. Rather than the sea, the poet now describes an environment of sloppy, thick mud.

Stanza 3

In the third stanza, the poet moves away from animal imagery. She discusses her desire to surround herself with people who possess the ability to lose themselves in the task at a hand. Now using images of people at work rather than animals, Piercy explores the nature of the act of harvesting crops by hand, marveling at people's ability to work in concert with one another in a steady rhythm to accomplish a common goal. Observing that such individuals are not those who dictate orders from the comfort of a parlor, nor do they abandon their task, the poet comments on the necessity that drives their labor. She points out that they work simply because the food must be harvested.

Stanza 4

In the poem's final and longest stanza (it consists of nine lines), Piercy speaks to the universal nature of this type of practical, purposeful work. She notes that work that is not done with the proper care becomes useless, a waste of time. However, when something worth doing is done well, the results are wholly positive. Such an act has both beauty and purpose. She compares such work to objects like Greek amphoras (pitchers used for wine or oil), and vases made by Native American Hopi people to hold corn. Piercy states that such items are often found in museums as beautiful artifacts of ancient cultures. Yet she stresses that they were made for a purpose. The pitchers and vases, made lovingly and beautifully, were designed for work, and when on display, Piercy imagines them calling out to be put to use. In the final line of the poem, she connects such objects with people, emphasizing the need for each person to do meaningful work.

THEMES

Purposeful Work and Beauty

The notion of useful, purposeful action that Piercy advocates in "To Be of Use" has a social dimension that links it to the Jewish idea of *tikkun olam*, or "repair of the world." In modern Jewish philosophy, this idea has come to be seen as a call for social action to make the world a better place. This idea is at work in Piercy's poem as well. Throughout the poem, the concept of purposeful, meaningful work is linked with providing food for the community. In the second stanza, the work of oxen and water buffalo is praised. These animals have historically been used to plow fields for planting crops. In the third stanza, Piercy discusses the harvesting of fields by hand, with people side by side, working the rows, passing the bags of collected crops down the row. In the final stanza, Piercy further incorporates the idea of usefulness and its relation to food when she employs the imagery of the Greek amphora, used for wine or oil, and of vases made by the Native American Hopi people, vessels used for storing corn. The notion of usefulness that Piercy explores in this poem is related repeatedly to hard work in the service of nourishing communities. It speaks both to an individual's personal need to be engaged in work that bears tangible, beneficial results, as well as to the greater social need for people to aid one another in taking

TOPICS FOR FURTHER STUDY

- Piercy's poem "To Be of Use" is often viewed as a political poem. It is included in her audio collection that was released, at least in part, as a response to the Iraq War, despite the fact that the poem was written in 1973 at the end of the Vietnam War. African American activist, poet, and novelist Alice Walker published the illustrated poem "Why War Is Never a Good Idea" in 2007. Compare the poems. Walker's poem focuses overtly on destruction and warfare, while Piercy's centers on the opposite of war-making, that is, on positive, purposeful action for the betterment of the world. Both poems have a political message. What other similarities do they share? What techniques, language, or imagery, do the poets use to make their respective points? How do the illustrations (by Stefano Vitale) that accompany Walker's poem help shape its meaning? What would the effect of illustrations be on Piercy's poem? Consider these questions and either write a comparative essay or illustrate Piercy's poem and present your comparison of the two illustrated works to your class.

- Piercy references Native American Hopi vases and Greek amphoras in her poem. Using print and online resources, research Hopi or Greek art and culture. Find examples of the Hopi vases or Greek amphoras Piercy mentions in her poem, and find out when they were made and how they were used. What other Hopi or ancient Greek pieces are both utilitarian and artistic? How has their craftsmanship changed over time? Create a Web site or other form of visual presentation in which images of the artistic pieces you have researched are viewable and in which you discuss your findings.

- Piercy's poem "To Be of Use" reflects the Jewish philosophy of *tikkun olam*, or "repairing the world," although it makes no direct reference to this idea. Piercy's activist history, her Jewish background, and the content of the poem suggest a relationship between the poem and the notion of *tikkun olam*. Using works such as Elliot N. Dorff's *The Way into Tikkun Olam: Repairing the World* (Jewish Lights Publishing, 2007) as a guide, further research this way of thinking. In an essay, explore the ways in which this philosophy may be employed in a secular (nonreligious) way, and describe how Piercy's poem reflects the poet's interpretation of this philosophy. Consider as well the possible parallels between the Jewish idea of repairing the world with the social work of other religious groups. Are Catholic missionaries, for example, guided by a similar philosophy? Beyond religious motivations, what, in your opinion, compels people to work in the service of others?

- Two years after Piercy published "To Be of Use," she published the novel *Woman on the Edge of Time*. On the surface, the work is the story of a Mexican American woman who is unfairly placed in a mental institution. However, on a deeper level the novel explores a possible Utopian future. Read Piercy's novel and consider the future she envisions. Is it a possible one? Could it be achieved through the same type of altruistic behavior she advocates in "To Be of Use?" With these questions in mind, write your own free-verse poem in which you create a type of detailed plan to guide society from where it is now to your own vision of a utopian community. What type of behavior, action, or attitude would you encourage in people to make the world a better place in the future?

---

care of the larger world community. In *Meaning and Memory: Interviews with Fourteen Jewish Poets*, Piercy states, "I respect hard work," noting that during her formative years "pride in hard work and doing something useful was still strong."

Ploughing (© *Photolocation ltd / Alamy*)

This sense of usefulness is joined with a broad notion of beauty. Piercy accomplishes this in the first several lines of the poem's final stanza. She observes that this necessary, hard work (work that serves the purpose of sustaining communities) is as common as mud. Done incorrectly, she notes, it becomes tarnished and ruined. Yet when difficult, purposeful work is done well, the results take the shape of something with a clean, satisfying form. A purpose fulfilled, the poet seems to be saying, results in a product of great beauty, such as the Greek and Hopi objects she discusses. They exist as artworks in a museum but also serve a function that must be fulfilled if their full beauty and full potential is to be realized.

The World Community

In "To Be of Use," Piercy seems to be endorsing the notion of a worldwide community. Her images are universal and timeless, and they speak to her understanding of the world as a community that must be nurtured by all. The images that stand out from each stanza depict a vibrant, wide world: an ocean of bobbing seals, an ox pulling a cart, a water buffalo pulling a plow, a field of people at work harvesting food, ancient Greek amphoras, and vases made by the Hopi people, and still crafted today, that were originally used for storing corn. The images are of a world long past as well as of the moment. Beasts of burden were, and still are in many parts of the world, used to pull carts and plow fields. Visually, the reader can just as

easily imagine the American pioneer in an ox-drawn cart as he or she can imagine a water buffalo plowing a field of rice in Vietnam. Piercy describes the pitchers and vases as being on display in a museum but also states their need to be put to their intended uses. Again, there is the sense of universality in terms of time and place, as the Greek and Hopi cultures may be viewed as both ancient and modern. Through such images, Piercy circumscribes the people of the world into one community with a shared past and the shared purpose of nurturing that community.

STYLE

Free Verse

"To Be of Use" is an example of free-verse poetry. In free-verse poetry, there is no set structure in terms of line length, stanza length, or number of stanzas (a stanza is a grouping of lines in a poem similar to a paragraph in a work of prose), nor is there any established metrical structure. Metrical structure refers to a set pattern of stressed and unstressed syllables within a line of poetry. Free-verse poetry additionally lacks a rhyme pattern. The unstructured nature of free-verse poetry compliments Piercy's conversational tone. The lack of structure does not negate the fact that through the course of the poem, Piercy builds toward a fuller understanding of the nature of usefulness.

First-Person Poetics

Piercy inserts herself, or at least a version of herself, into the poem "To Be of Use" with the usage of a first-person figure within the poem. This figure refers to herself as "I" and appears in the first three stanzas of the poem. It is her thoughts and feelings shaping these stanzas, as she discusses the type of people whom she loves and what they do. With clear admiration, she explores the nature of their enthusiasm for hard work, their unfailing determination, and the necessity and worth of their endeavors. In the final stanza, the first-person figure does not appear. Rather, by discussing the Hopi and Greek pitchers and vases, Piercy uses the second-person figure when she states that *you* know what such things were made for, even though the pieces now appear in a museum. By transitioning from "I" to "you," Piercy transfers from the poet to the reader the sense of urgency toward action that the first-person figure had previously owned throughout the first three stanzas. In this transition, a call to

COMPARE
&
CONTRAST

- **1970s:** The Vietnam War is ending. In the last few years of the war in particular, the antiwar movement is strong. A protest turns violent at Kent State University in Kent, Ohio, in 1970, when Ohio National Guard soldiers fire on and kill four student protesters. A cease-fire agreement in Vietnam is signed in 1973.

  Today: The prolonged Iraq War, as well as the war in Afghanistan, has been compared to the Vietnam War by some critics. Troop escalations called for under President George W. Bush may be reduced by President Barack Obama.

- **1970s:** Social activists, including activist poet Marge Piercy, fight for equal rights, particularly equal-employment and reproductive rights, for women. Congress passes the Equal Rights Amendment in 1972, but the amendment is not ratified. Some progress is made, including the passage of Title IX of the 1970s Educational Amendments, which are intended to reduce gender discrimination in education and school athletic programs.

  Today: Social activists fight for equal rights for the gay and lesbian community. In particular the issue of same-sex marriage appears on state ballots across the country. In 2007, same-sex marriage is legal in only one state: Massachusetts. In 2008, Connecticut and California both legalize same-sex marriage, but California voters later ban marriage between same-sex individuals through the controversial Proposition 8. As of June 2009, gay rights activists are still protesting the measure. Additionally, women's rights organizations continue to fight for the ratification of the Equal Rights Amendment and attempt to defend past victories for women's rights. For example, the federal government passes legislation from 2000 to 2008 that threatens the gains made by Title IX.

- **1970s:** Free verse becomes a commonly used and increasingly respected poetic form. Poets writing in this form include Marge Piercy, John Ashberry, and Alice Walker. In response, a parallel movement takes shape. It is known as "new formalism," and it advocates a return to classic poetic forms and structures. The early new formalist poets include Rachel Hadas, Charles Martin, and Timothy Steele.

  Today: Free-verse poetry remains popular as it allows poets to be both accessible and experimental. Piercy, Ashberry, and Walker continue to publish successful volumes of free-verse poetry. At the same time, new formalist poetry is also thriving in the works of poets such as Dana Michael Gioia. Hadas, Martin, and Steele continue to publish new formalist poetry as well.

---

action may be understood, an insistence on utilizing one's knowledge of the notion of purposeful action.

HISTORICAL CONTEXT

Social Activism in the 1970s

During the early 1970s, two parallel social movements were advocating change in U.S. governmental policies. One of these movements was the women's rights movement, which began in the early 1960s with the publication of Betty Friedan's 1963 work *The Feminine Mystique*. Friedan criticized the fact that in middle-class America, women had very few choices or opportunities; she advocated an expansion of the roles available to women and encouraged women to seek their own identities, professionally and personally. In the 1970s, women's organizations such as the National Organization for Women (NOW), established in 1966 with the help of

Friedan, fought for the ratification of an amendment to the U.S. Constitution, the Equal Rights Amendment, that would insure equal opportunities and rights for women. It was passed by Congress in 1972 but did not have enough states' support to be ratified.

Also during this time period, the Vietnam War was coming to an end. The United States became involved in the war in 1964 in an effort to stop the spread of communism. Throughout the 1960s, the war, and the U.S. involvement in it, escalated. Antiwar protests were so fervent that in 1968, President Lyndon B. Johnson, who had until this time overseen the increase in U.S. involvement, opted to not seek another term. When President Richard Nixon took office, a slow withdrawal of U.S. troops from Vietnam was accompanied by an intense bombing campaign. War protests became more heated, and in 1970, at one demonstration at Kent State University in Kent, Ohio, National Guard troops killed four students. In 1973, the United States signed a cease-fire agreement. By the spring of 1975, the last of the U.S. troops had returned home, and North Vietnam took over control of the whole of Vietnam.

Jewish Poetry in the 1970s

Piercy was just emerging as a poet and novelist in the early 1970s. During that same time period, there was an instinct among many liberal artists and writers to disassociate themselves from the conservative elements in the government and society. The path toward this disassociation for some ethnic writers, including some Jewish writers, was clear, according to Abraham Chapman, in his introduction to the 1974 poetry anthology *Jewish American Literature: An Anthology*. Chapman states that in Jewish American fiction and poetry of the early 1970s, one can detect an "intensified ethnic consciousness and identification with non-Anglo-Saxon ancestral pasts." In this increased association among ethnic minorities, Chapman says, one sees "evidence of the desire to disaffiliate from the shames and horrors" of the American political body during the Vietnam War era. During the 1970s, therefore, the work of individual Jewish American writers gradually began to be viewed as a category of literature, as evidenced by Chapman's anthology. In the introduction to *Jewish American Poetry: Poems, Commentary, and Reflections* (2000), editors Jonathan N. Barron and Eric Murphy Selinger identify traits common among Jewish American poems, including a

Women carrying water *(© Peter Horree / Alamy)*

return to Jewish traditional texts as inspiration, the depiction of both American and Jewish personal identities within the poetry, and a desire to explore the nature and purpose of poetry in a post-Holocaust world.

CRITICAL OVERVIEW

Piercy's volume of poetry *To Be of Use* received critical praise when it was published in 1973. In a review in *Parnassus: Poetry in Review* in 1974, Marie Harris praises the fact that Piercy energetically employs the "language of the women's movement" and consequently creates, in *To Be of Use*, a "truly useful book." The title poem, Harris also states, serves to "emblemize" the whole book, transforming it into "a manual, a handbook," for purposeful, social action. The poem "To Be of Use" has subsequently appeared in other volumes of Piercy's poetry, including *Circles on the Water: Selected Poems*, published in 1982. The criticism of this volume is typical of what much of her poetry has received over the years. Her poems are characterized by energy and purpose, critics state, but the poems lack structure and rhythm. In a 1982 review for *Library Journal*, Suzanne Juhasz states that Piercy's "work is strong in images but slight in music, and her language has a flatness that is at odds with the fullness of her life." Novelist Margaret Atwood, in her 1982 review of *Circles on* the Water: Selected Poems for the *New York Times*, praises Piercy's energy and emotional range. In terms of structure and organization, Atwood states that Piercy makes use of metaphor and simile illustratively within her poems, but not as structural devices.

While critics such as Harris examine Piercy's poetry against the backdrop of the women's rights movement, others focus on the relationship of Piercy's Jewish background to her poetry. Gary Pacernick, in his 2001 collection of interviews titled *Meaning and Memory: Interviews with Fourteen Jewish Poets*, includes Piercy in his list of poets whose work reflects the poet's activism and Jewish heritage. Pacernick states that these poets, including Piercy, "might claim the radical political influence of communism and socialism... but they are also driven by their experience as Jews, who, as an oppressed minority, have always empathized with other oppressed people." Likewise, Steven J. Rubin, in his introduction to the poetry collection he edited, *Telling and Remembering: A Century of American Jewish Poetry*, finds that Piercy, in her poetry, examines "diverse aspects of her Jewish religion, heritage, and identity."

CRITICISM

Catherine Dominic

Dominic is a novelist and a freelance writer and editor. In the following essay, she examines the way Piercy's language and imagery, in their balancing of realism and hopefulness, enable the poem "To Be of Use" to be as relevant today as it was in the 1970s.

Marge Piercy's poem "To Be of Use" first appeared in the volume by the same name in 1973. Since then it has appeared in other Piercy collections: *Circles on the Water* in 1982, *The Art of Blessing the Day: Poems with a Jewish Theme* in 1999 and reprinted in paperback in 2007, and in the audio collection *Louder, We Can't Hear You: The Political Poems of Marge Piercy* in 2004. It has been studied within the light of Piercy's Jewishness, as it may be viewed as advocating the Jewish idea of *tikkun olam*, a Jewish practice in which the "repair" of the world is the goal. Written, as it was, during the Vietnam War and during Piercy's involvement in the women's rights movement, the poem has also been examined in terms of Piercy's social activism and

WHAT DO I READ NEXT?

- Piercy's poetry collection *The Crooked Inheritance*, published in 2006, is a selection of new poetry with such weighty themes as war, Jewish tradition, and Hurricane Katrina, as well as reflections on life's simple pleasures, such as cooking and gardening.

- Piercy's novel *He, She, and It*, published in 1991 by Fawcett, reflects the author's concerns regarding the environment and the social conscience of society. It depicts a futuristic, post-apocalyptic world in which cyborgs (bionic human or humanized robots) feature prominently.

- Merle Feld's *A Spiritual Life: A Jewish Feminist Journey*, published by the State University of New York Press in 1999, is a combination of memoir and poetry that explores the nature of spirituality from a viewpoint similar to Piercy's.

- Frank Waters's *The Book of the Hopi*, published by Penguin in 1977, is an exploration of the beliefs, culture, and history of the Hopi people that can be used to compare spiritual philosophies.

- In her 2002 memoir *Sleeping with Cats: A Memoir*, published by Harper Collins, Piercy offers a candid look at her difficult childhood, her marriages, and her writing career.

- Mikki Halpin's 2004 *It's Your World—If You Don't Like It, Change It: Activism for Teenagers*, published by Simon Pulse, is a guidebook for teenagers looking to make positive changes in the world. It focuses on such social issues as animal rights, women's rights, racism, and war protest, providing discussion of real-life student experiences as well as ideas on how teens can get involved in various activist movements.

antiwar activism. Whether it is regarded as a Jewish poem or an activist's call to action, the poem "To Be of Use" has a timeless quality that is evidenced by its repeated appearance in

> WHETHER REGARDED AS A JEWISH POEM OR AN ACTIVIST'S CALL TO ACTION, 'TO BE OF USE' HAS A TIMELESS QUALITY THAT IS EVIDENCED BY ITS REPEATED APPEARANCE IN PIERCY'S COLLECTIONS. ITS CONTINUED APPEAL OVER TIME IS PERHAPS DUE TO THE FACT THAT IT IS AS REALISTIC AS IT IS OPTIMISTIC."

Piercy's collections. Its continued appeal over time is perhaps due to the fact that it is as realistic as it is optimistic. Audiences today are perhaps more jaded than Piercy's original audience in 1973, when there was a fervent atmosphere of political activism in the United States. Yet whether or not the activist attitude is as strong today as it was decades ago, Piercy's evenhanded approach offers an acknowledgement of the obstacles to pursuing purposeful work, yet her tone conveys a sense of confidence that people will rise to the occasion because it is right and necessary, even though it is hard.

Piercy's language and her selection of imagery throughout the poem depicts a story in which the physical and emotional cost of hard work is not glossed over or glamorized. Rather, Piercy advocates the continued performance of such work because it is needed and it is what we are made to do. As Piercy acknowledges the challenges of doing hard work in order to benefit others, many readers may be more likely to remain open-minded to her message, rather than be turned off by an overly optimistic, "let's make the world a better place" approach. Still, this is her message. It is simply tempered with an understanding of what the task involves and what it is worth. Whether regarded as a Jewish poem or an activist's call to action, "To Be of Use" has a timeless quality that is evidenced by its repeated appearance in Piercy's collections. Its continued appeal over time is perhaps due to the fact that it is as realistic as it is optimistic.

Piercy's opening stanza begins optimistically enough, with her praise of individuals who dive into their work with great enthusiasm. Comparing such people with swimmers, she observes the way

they do not linger in the shallow water but swim confidently and with strength until they are almost out of view. They are further compared with seals, at home in their environment. The feelings conveyed by such images are ones of happiness and an eagerness to attack one's work, and Piercy confides that these are people whom she loves. In fact, by stating that they swim nearly out of view, Piercy's language imbues such people with an aura of idealism. In their vigor to tackle their work, they become almost out of reach of the rest of society.

Yet in the next stanza, this idealism is grounded in the reality of the rough, hard labor that is encompassed in the poet's notion of useful work. Piercy expresses her love for people, who, like an ox or water buffalo, strain to do the work necessary to sustain life. The stakes are higher than in the first stanza, where approaching work with an eager attitude was simply fun; it had not yet been characterized as hard and important, as it is in the second stanza. Piercy's usage of the images of the water buffalo and the ox are employed to great effect as she describes the way they strain and pull through thick, wet mud, always determined to move forward. Her imagery and word choice here emphasize that this is not just work, it is labor, and it is messy. The last line of the stanza solidifies the dreary, repetitive nature of such work, for it has to be done over and over again.

In the third stanza, Piercy is even more explicit than before in emphasizing the necessity of the hard work to be done. She talks about people crouched in rows in a field, harvesting crops by hand. Piercy also observes the way they work together in harmony toward a common purpose. If the food is not harvested, she explains using fire imagery, life will be extinguished like a flame. Also in this stanza, Piercy describes the field workers in terms of what they are not, using military terms. They are not generals or deserters, she points out, suggesting the common bond and purpose of the hardworking people. They do not issue orders from a removed position, nor do they desert the people they should be aiding. The feelings evoked by the detailed images in this stanza emphasize group effort. The harvesters are a gathering of people, rather than the singular individuals represented by the ox and the water buffalo. They work alongside one another in a row and hand the bags of collected food to one another. The workers' efforts are in tune, and they understand the vital nature of their activities—providing sustenance to their community.

Thus far, the poem has progressed from the exuberance of individuals who jump eagerly into their work, to individuals who embrace hard, repetitive, dirty, and necessary labor, to groups of individuals who work hard together to sustain their community. The tone of the poem becomes increasingly serious as the poem progresses. The final stanza is both a culmination and a turning point. Piercy encourages caring for the world as a community of people. People all over the world care for others on a small scale. She comments on how easily it is mishandled, and how, through mismanagement, efforts are wasted. The image she uses to convey this sentiment is mud. It is common, it can make us dirty, and it easily may crumble apart, becoming nothing but dust. In comparison, the same mud can be formed into clay to make useful, beautiful things, such as the Greek amphoras and Hopi vases Piercy next references. The mud imagery underscores the notion that everything possessing the potential to fall into ruin can also be formed into something purposeful. The objects the poet has specified, the Greek amphoras and Hopi vases, may be taken out of context, Piercy states, and put on display in a museum. At this significant turning point, Piercy addresses her readers. She tells them that they know that these items were intended for purposeful use, to store oil, wine, and corn. Pointing out how the pitcher yearns to carry water, to fulfill its purpose, so do people long for real, meaningful work to embrace. When the poet reveals her knowledge of individuals' complicity, she emphasizes that the amphoras and vases are purposeful things, not just artifacts. In a sense, Piercy calls out to readers to take action, to make something purposeful out of their lives. She asks this even as she has just taken great pains to demonstrate that doing something purposeful is hard, messy, monotonous labor. To accomplish it properly, we have to be in the thick of it, working alongside one another, not issuing orders from afar or giving up when the work becomes overwhelming.

In "To Be of Use," Piercy does not sugarcoat the subject matter. She knows what she is asking is difficult, but she asks it anyway. Writing as she was during a time when she fought for women's equal rights and protested the Vietnam War (a war many viewed as unnecessary), Piercy understood the nature of hard work toward a

> YOU'RE A DIFFERENT PERSON IN EVERY RELATIONSHIP. THERE ARE DIFFERENT ASPECTS OF YOU THAT ARE ALLOWED TO FLOURISH, ARE ENCOURAGED OR DISCOURAGED, ARE GIVEN ROOM OR NOT GIVEN ROOM."

larger social purpose. Given Piercy's social activism and her desire to work hard to make the world a better place, it is no surprise that "To Be of Use" was included in the 2004 audio CD collection *Louder, We Can't Hear You (Yet): The Political Poems of Marge Piercy*. A contributor to the *Leapfrog Press* Web site states that the collection was released, in part, in response to the growing opposition to the Iraq War. As a part of the 2004 collection, "To Be of Use" once again becomes a social call to action, an antiwar poem, and an example of *tikkun olam*, the Jewish effort to encourage individuals to engage in the hard work necessary to improve the world.

Source: Catherine Dominic, Critical Essay on "To Be of Use," in *Poetry for Students*, Gale, Cengage Learning, 2010.

John Rodden

In the following excerpt from an interview with Rodden, Piercy reveals how "To Be of Use" forms part of her identity as both a person and a poet.

... John Rodden: You wrote in the Introduction to Circles on the Water, *"To me it is all one vision." What also interests me is the way in which the political / personal manifests itself in your work and the interconnections among personal integrity, wholeness, and social community. Much of your poetry insists that politics and poetry are never separate.*

Marge Piercy: It's a very modern heresy that you can't have political poetry. You couldn't have told that to Pope or Shakespeare or Dryden or Catullus. It's a heresy that seems to be mainly to the advantage of people for whom political poetry means a poetry whose politics they don't agree with. Politics is interwoven throughout discourse. If the attitudes that are spoken or implied agree with those you're used to, you don't consider them political. That's just the

Harvesting *(© Roger Ressmeyer / Corbis)*

way things are. That's what all "right-thinking" people feel and think. That's the way it is, that's how you're supposed to think. If the attitudes expressed or implied are different, then it is seen as political or even polemical.

JR: Politics is obviously a crucial component of your literary and also personal identity. Are you a utopian? Is that a characterization that you embrace?

MP: No. *Woman on the Edge of Time* is consciously in the utopian tradition. But it doesn't make me a utopian. It just means that I've written in that tradition. There's also a dystopia in *Woman on the Edge of Time*. My novel *He, She, and It* also plays utopia / dystopia games. I'm very conscious of the utopian tradition. I write in it, I write against it. I situate myself in it in a critical way. I'm always playing with the received legends, stories, and myths of the culture.

JR: In your poem "If I had been called Sabrina or Anne, she said," you say that even your name "sounds like an oil can, like a bedroom slipper / like a box of baking soda, useful, plain." Once again, "to be of use" seems very much a part of your identity as a writer and as a person.

MP: Well, I was complaining about my name in that poem actually because it's such a sort of plain, working-class name.

JR: But it seems nonetheless a strong affirmation.

MP: Well, it's my name!

JR: And it seems to signify your embrace of your destiny.

MP: Yes, though the poem would have been titled something different if I had been called Sabrina or Anne. Actually, I wish that I had taken my Hebrew name: Mara. My grandmother changed my name when I almost died. I like it even more. It means bitter. My family wanted to change my Hebrew name at one point. I wouldn't let them change it. I hyphenate it now. So it's Mara-Meira.

JR: What does it mean?

MP: Mara means bitter and Meira means bringer of light.

JR: That's fascinating.

MP: Meira is the second one that I received. So I have a hyphenated Hebrew name.

JR: "Bitter Bringer of Light."

MP: Yes, they're two different names, but I hyphenate them because I won't give up the old one. As I was saying, I was given the name Mara—"bitter"—because my grandmother was afraid I was going to die, and she believed that you could fool the Angel of Death by choosing an off-putting name. I don't know what my original Hebrew name was. But it was changed so that I wouldn't die. That's a superstition in a lot of cultures. . . .

JR: All this is intriguing, given that you mention in poems that you have a lot of anger and that you feel it's quite important to express it. Your willingness to express it seems part of your journey toward light and of bringing other people to the light of day—even if that harsh light is painful. Those two names relate to your poetic work in a deep way: The bitterness, anger, and rage on one side and the will to enlightenment on the other.

MP: Yes, there is wisdom contained in those namings.

JR: Your recent poetry frequently addresses your early family life, especially your relationship to your mother. Could you comment on how that relationship has evolved since the 1980s, particularly since the poems in My Mother's Body *(1985)?*

MP: My mother died in 1981. We had had a very antagonistic relationship for much of my life. But it became much better in the last few years of her life. We were able to talk to each other in a way that I had always fantasized. I am very much my mother's daughter, and indeed my mother and my grandmother's creation. So I never had the same fear that a lot of women have of becoming their mother. I always wanted to become the best parts of her—only not to become the weakness, not to become these parts of her that exercised little choice, little control. I wanted to become those parts of her that I admired and respected.

And I've integrated her strengths in the last decade. So it's a different kind of relationship. I think it's maybe a little more like the relationship that some black women have with their mothers, where your mother has gone through hell and has had little choice and chance in life, but she had an endurance, strength, and a richness that the society never respected, never acknowledged, but which was something very beautiful. I want to celebrate all that, because it was so put down when my mother was alive.

JR: In "What remains" [in My Mother's Body*] you talk about burying her ashes, so that*

now that she'll become a rose: "I have brought | you home. Now you want to be roses."

MP: Yes, she chose to be buried, so I brought the ashes back.

JR: Did that poem reflect some new beginning in your relationship?

MP: No, the beginning occurred before that. During the last years of her life, we were much closer. I used to call her every Monday when my father was out. My father would go out on Monday and I would call her, because then she could talk to me openly.

JR: Could you discuss your relationship with your father and your Welsh identity?

MP: I know very little about that side of things. I've only been in Wales once and I didn't connect with it. I know very little about Wales and I don't know Welsh.

JR: Your poetry seems to portray your father as a difficult man.

MP: He was. We were never close.

JR: What part of him is in you?

MP: His temper. My mother, however, had a temper too. But my glaucoma comes from him.

JR: During your childhood or youth, did you have a feminist consciousness? Did it emerge even before the women's movement began?

MP: Long before. In childhood, really. In fact, I probably had less of a feminist consciousness in the middle 1960s than at any time in my life previously. I was so involved in the anti-war movement that I forgot about feminist issues for awhile. But yes, in the late 1950s I was very concerned with what they used to call "the Woman Question." The Woman Question! What a way to put it!

JR: So long before [Betty Friedan's] The Feminine Mystique *[1963] you had developed such a consciousness?*

MP: Yes. But it feels nutty when it's only you. You're regarded as insane. It isn't until there exists some kind of framework in which to hold onto the insights that it makes any sense. To be concerned with these things by yourself was, in the 1950s, to be a little crazy. It was only when other people became concerned with them that, suddenly, I wasn't crazy anymore. I was something closer to a prophet, by that time!

JR: Before you were affirmed for it, you felt very isolated and alone. How did you cope with this emerging feminist consciousness in the face of such isolation?

MP: I did try to share my feelings about it. I tried to write about it. But other people didn't like what I wrote.

JR: Didn't like the poetry? Or the fiction? Or both?

MP: The poetry was better received. The poetry got published long before the fiction did.

JR: So there were some feminist poems from the 1950s and early 1960s?

MP: I don't think any of the feminist ones got published. The feminist short stories and poems all had to wait until later to get published—after I had already been published on other subjects. Then the feminist work could get published. By that time, the world had changed enough.

JR: Let me ask you about your college and postgraduate years in the 1960s. As you reflect on your experience as an SDS organizer in the 1960s and on the revolutionary aspirations of some of your fellow radicals, how do you regard that period?

MP: I look back on those years with great fondness. I'm still very close to a lot of the people.

JR: Many historians, especially those hostile to the Left, criticize the leaders of the student movement as immature and misguided.

MP: Well, we were destroyed! I mean, come on! What did we have, up against the government, with its millions to spend on lots of agents and repression! It had the ability to crush us! I mean, come on!

JR: It's evident that your activities as an SDS organizer proved "to be of use" in your literary work. For instance, your second novel, Dance the Eagle to Sleep, *emerged from your SDS years.*

MP: Oh sure, yes, that novel expressed my desire to deal with a number of things without doing any damage to anybody. I didn't want to give the government any valuable information about the Movement. So I moved the setting and plot to a sci-fi context.

JR: Did that attempt at science fiction serve as a preliminary for the sensibility and conception of novels such as Woman on the Edge of Time *and* He, She, and It?

MP: Just in the sense that I was conscious that I was writing speculative fiction. I've always read a lot of science fiction, so I knew what I was doing. But when I wrote *Woman on the Edge of Time,* I was consciously placing myself in a particular tradition: the feminist utopian tradition.

JR: In 1971, you moved to Wellfleet. Since that time, you've written a great deal of earth and nature poetry. Love of place is now a prominent theme in your work. Could you comment on the role of the Cape?

MP: The Cape is a fragile ecosystem. You become conscious of that when you live here. It's easily injured and destroyed. And if you live near the ocean, you know how fragile in many ways the ocean is and how we've been destroying it. These are things you experience living here.

JR: How would you describe your evolution as a writer since your early days of living in Detroit?

MP: Well, I'd never much experienced the natural world before living here. I had little sense of the seasons, little sense of the lunar cycle. I had no relationship with the land. Every Jewish holiday has three dimensions: a spiritual dimension, an historical dimension, and a seasonal or agricultural dimension. That latter part was totally missing from my understanding of everything. I didn't have any relationship to the land. It's very hard to develop that in the center city of Detroit where I grew up, as well as in all the cities that I lived in after that.

JR: Has Wellfleet given you a greater sense of serenity or peace? Has it moderated the anger and the rage that you speak about in your poetry?

MP: I still get plenty angry! I don't think there's any question about that!

JR: I had a sense that you've mellowed without having lost the capacity for anger. Your anger seems to be expressed in a less direct or overt way.

MP: Don't say that! There are some direct political poems now in press [in *What Are Big Girls Made Of?*]. The title poem is quite direct. And so is "Two women who were shot to death in Brookline, Massachusetts."

JR: Let me rephrase the question: Have the last couple of decades here affected your temperament in any noticeable way?

MP: When I was in the Movement in New York, I was extremely driven—to the point of collapse. I had to learn that I was not an infinitely renewable resource, learn to love myself a little better, learn to take care of myself a little better. I had to learn to live in a healthier way.

JR: *You came here partly because of poor health.*

MP: Yes. That was a reason for the move here: to learn to live in a way less driven, less crazy, less fanatical, more rooted.

JR: *You came to Wellfleet, then, in order to respect and embrace your own fragility in this fragile ecosystem, to honor the fact that you yourself are not an infinitely renewable resource and are not indestructible.*

MP: I'm a lot less fragile now than when I moved here.

JR: *Wellfleet has renewed you?*

MP: Yes. And I mean that in physical terms. I made a decision several years ago that the current aesthetic of what women are supposed to look like had no appeal to me. I do not wish to be thin. I wish to occupy more space and I wish to be strong. I am strong. I work out regularly. I made a choice. . . . I want to be strong. I want to have muscles.

JR: *One senses that commitment in "For Strong Women," which is obviously autobiographical.*

MP: Well, that's "strong" in a different sense: emotionally strong. That's a different kind of strength.

JR: *Another work that seems to grow out of your life is* Summer People, *which is set on the Cape. Is it heavily autobiographical?*

MP: No. *Summer People* is an operetta. It's about the Cape, but it's not autobiographical.

JR: *What about* Braided Lives? *That novel seems to be about your teenage years and young adulthood.*

MP: That's the closest I've ever come to an autobiographical novel. It's not really one, but it's the closest I've ever come to one. I guess I get to exorcise my desire for autobiography in the poetry. So I don't much use the novels for autobiography. There isn't much impulse left for that when I get to the fiction. I prefer to explore other people's lives. . . .

JR: *You just mentioned that you express your autobiographical impulse in your poetry, whereas you explore the lives of other people in your fiction. Could you elaborate on the different impulses in you to which poetry and fiction give expression?*

MP: Well, fiction is narrative. It's storytelling. It is the creation of patterns through time. It's quite different from poetry. My poetry is not always direct expression, however. I'm not always writing directly at all. And you can't assume the voice in any particular poem is necessarily me. But a lot of it is my voice. A lot of the experiences come more directly out of my life into the poetry than they ever do in the fiction.

JR: *"Being Left" in* Stone, Paper, Knife *seems very personal. It's about a difficult parting between lovers, or between a husband and wife. I found this line very powerful: "What you have abandoned is not behind / but far ahead / where we shall never now arrive." It seemed like your own road not taken in response to this person that you had split from.*

MP: You're a different person in every relationship. There are different aspects of you that are allowed to flourish, are encouraged or discouraged, are given room or not given room.

JR: *Did that poem reflect any specific break-up?*

MP: My [two] divorces.

JR: *Many of your other poems also contain memorable, arresting lines that seem to sum up important experiences that most readers share. You've said, in fact, that one of your goals is to have people remember your poems and even put them up on their bathroom walls.*

MP: Or their refrigerators! Yes.

JR: *Would that also be included in your conception "to be of use"?*

MP: Yes. I write poetry that people really relate to and like to have around them. For example, "For the young who want to" [in *The Moon Is Always Female*] is a poem that a lot of writers hang over their computers or typewriters.

JR: *Yes, I also have given my students, "How Divine Is Forgiving?" [in* Available Light*]. It helps the class reflect on what forgiveness is really about.*

MP: I would classify that as a religious poem. It comes from trying to understand the notion that you have to forgive. What does it mean if you have to forgive people? How real is that? What does that really mean?

"To be of use" is another favorite poem of readers. There are also little incidental love poems that people carry around in their wallets. Even ones that surprise me. For a long time I didn't read the poem about my father, "Burial by salt," because I thought it was too nasty. And then a woman who'd been in a similar relationship with her father asked me to read it at a reading. So I did it. And a lot of people responded to it. So now I often do it, and I find that there are always people who come up afterwards and say that the poem spoke to them. So even poems you think can't possibly speak to other people—sometimes they do speak to them. People pick out what they need. They find the poems that speak directly to them.

JR: Yes, you're giving voice to their needs and aspirations.

MP: Well, that's what poetry's for....

Source: Marge Piercy and John Rodden, "A Harsh Day's Light: An Interview with Marge Piercy," in *Kenyon Review*, Vol. 20, No. 2, Spring 1998, pp. 132–43.

Edith J. Wynne

In the following excerpt, Wynne explores how Piercy characteristically employs "imagery of association" to the end that her poems will "be 'of use' to the reader."

Under the title, *Circles on the Water,* Marge Piercy published, in 1982, a collection of more than one hundred and fifty poems selected from seven of her previously published volumes. In the introduction to Circles on the Water, Piercy remarks,

> One of the oldest habits of our species, poetry is powerful in aligning the psyche. A poem can momentarily integrate the different kinds of knowing of our different and often warring levels of brain, from the reptilian part that recognizes rhythms and responds to them up through the mammalian centers of the emotions, from symbolic knowing as in dreams to analytical thinking, through rhythms and sound and imagery as well as overt meaning. A poem can momentarily heal not only the alienation of thought and feeling Eliot discussed, but can fuse the different kinds of knowing and for at least some instants weld mind back into body seamlessly.

Piercy's allusion to T. S. Eliot in her discussion of what poetry can do to integrate our ways of knowing is significant. While Piercy gives some attention to the relatively new psychological theory of opposing brain hemisphere functions, she also recalls the old debate between the functions of logic and emotion in the metaphysical poets, a group with which Piercy has some commonality in her imagistic techniques. Piercy's collected poems contain a startling array of images which, in their variety and number, in their apparently haphazard distribution, in their wide-ranging sensuousness, and in their seemingly antithetical juxtaposition of thought and feeling, create that kind of *discordia concors* so often associated with the metaphysical tradition. On the surface, Piercy's poems might aptly be described by Samuel Johnson's observation on the poet, Cowley:

> The most heterogeneous ideas are yoked by violence together; nature and art are ransacked for illustrations, comparisons, and allusions; their learning instructs, and their subtilty surprises.

Yet, Piercy's poetry does more than merely surprise and instruct. Eliot and other theorists have made commonplace the critical edict that the metaphysicals were able to express experience both emotionally and intellectually at the same instance. Piercy contends that, in her poems, the richness of thought and feeling possessed by all human beings informs her choice of images and brings a kind of unity out of chaos for us:

> That the poems may give voice to something in the experience of a life has been my intention. To find ourselves spoken for in art gives dignity to our pain, our anger, our lust, our losses.... We have few rituals that function for us in the ordinary chaos of our lives.

Piercy speaks directly to her readers in her own voice although she reminds us that the experiences she recounts are not always her own, nor are the poems confessional. She states that when she is writing she is not aware of any distinction between her own and other people's experiences, but that she is "often pushing the experience beyond realism." In this sense, Piercy creates a vortex of images which are often paradoxical but "reader-friendly." As Cleanth Brooks noted in his discussion of the language of paradox,

> The poet must work by analogies, but the metaphors do not lie in the same plane or fit neatly edge to edge. There is continual tilting of the planes; necessary overlappings, discrepancies, contradiction. Even the most direct and simple poet is forced into paradoxes far more often than we think, if we are sufficiently alive to what he is doing.

Piercy is such a direct and simple poet as Brooks describes, particularly in diction, tone, and form. She writes, she tells us, as a social animal and intends her poems not for other poets, but to be "of use" to the reader; she says, "I am not a poet who writes primarily for the approval or attention of other poets.... Poetry is too important to keep to ourselves." She admits to occasional didacticism and to conscious feminist politics; she believes that her poems "coax, lecture, lull, seduce, exhort, denounce." Her poetry reminds us in several ways of the metaphysical tradition but stripped of the intellectual pyrotechnics of that tradition.

Piercy's use of imagery is one of the major assets of her poetic technique. The title of the volume *Circles on the Water* provides a descriptive metaphor for the recurrent, intertwined, echoic use of images so characteristic of her work. A few of her poems are built upon a single, extended metaphor; among these are "A work of artifice" in which a bonsai tree is compared throughout the poem to the stunted growth of a stereotyped female, and "The best defense is offensive" in which the actions of a turkey vulture are equated with a useful political stance. Much more typical of her work, however, is a lyrical, almost free-flowing series of images, built upon emotional and psychological associations rather than upon logical paradox or metaphysical conceit. Like circles on water created when a pool's surface tension is disturbed, her images form concentric, ever-widening patterns linked only by the energy and force of the precipitating experience. Usually, we are made fully aware of the initial event, for Piercy often begins with a narrative and maintains a strong sense of time and place. The force and energy of the image patterns is, therefore, one of the most exciting and unique qualities of the poems, but a quality not easily analyzed.

One of the poems which most clearly and dramatically displays the image-by-association artistry through which Piercy constructs an organic whole is "Sign," written in 1967 and included in her first published volume, *Breaking Camp.* As in the majority of her poems, Piercy provides a dramatic narrative structure; an event in the present precipitates contemplation. In "Sign," this event is quite commonplace—the poet discovers an emblem of aging:

> The first white hair coils in my hand,
> more wire than down.
> Out of the bathroom mirror it glittered at me.
> I plucked it, feeling thirty creep in my joints,
> and found it silver. It does not melt.

This brief opening stanza contains four images which are interwoven throughout the remainder of the poem in a carefully orchestrated, psychological point counter-point. The hair itself is the focal object, but one made up of several different sense impressions. The hair has color (white, then silver), texture (more "wire" than "down"), and substance (unlike quicksilver, it does not "melt" at body warmth). Furthermore, the hair is seen in a mirror, glitters, and is "plucked." Then, the poet feels thirty "creep" in her joints.

These visual, tactile, and kinaesthetic impressions of the hair are repeated in the next stanza, but within a completely different time and place:

> My twentieth birthday lean as glass
> spring vacation I stayed in the college town
> twangling misery's electric banjo offkey.
> I wanted to inject love right into the veins
> of my thigh and wake up visible:
> to vibrate color
> like the minerals in stones under black light.
> My best friend went home without loaning
>   me money.
> Hunger was all of the time the taste of my
>   mouth.

This shift to past time is perfectly natural; finding a white hair at thirty precipitates a realistic and commonplace reaction; the subject remembers her twentieth birthday. What is not so commonplace is the subtle, almost incremental, repetition of images from the first stanza, given new meaning in this different context. The mirror in which she first sees the hair is now transformed into her body, for she is "lean as glass." She spends time "twanging" an electric banjo "offkey," as in the first stanza she "plucked" the offending wirelike hair. Both actions call up misery, an emotion. At twenty, she twangs "misery's" banjo; at thirty, she experiences the misery of awareness of aging. The hair is, in its natural state, white or silver, almost colorless; at twenty, she had wanted to "vibrate color," but as minerals do, under "black" light. In both stanzas, the parts of the body receive attention. At twenty, she wished to inject love directly into "veins" and "thigh." At thirty, age is felt creeping into her "joints." Finally, in the second stanza, a new sense impression is added to the catalogue of recurrent images; "hunger" and "taste" provide a gustatory dimension which will be repeated in the third stanza, as the poet returns to present time:

Now I am ripened and sag a little from my
　　spine.
More than most I have been the same ragged
　　self
in all colors of luck dripping and dry,
yet love has nested in me and gradually
　　eaten
those sense organs I used to feel with.
I have eaten my hunger soft and my ghost
　　grows stronger.

The love which the subject wished to inject into thigh and vein in her twentieth year, when she was lean, constantly hungry, and eager for an awakening to visible self, has now "nested" in her and gradually "eaten" her sense organs. The aging process of which she has become dramatically aware causes her spine to sag, as a parallel to the creeping of age into her joints in stanza one. The hunger of her college vacation now consumes itself, but her "ghost" grows stronger although she is the "same ragged self" with "all colors of luck" within her. The word "ghost" appears intentionally ambiguous, open to several interpretations, all of which may best be treated after examination of the final stanza which brings together again the colors, textures, and motions of the opening lines:

Gradually, I am turning to chalk,
to humus, to pages and pages of paper,
to fine silver wire like something a violin
could be strung with, or somebody garroted,
or current run through: silver truly,
this hair, shiny and purposeful as forceps
if I knew how to use it.

Once again, the color motif returns to become central to the message. Chalk and paper are white or colorless, as is the found hair. Humus is dark, as is black light, and as are youthful tresses. With these colors, attention to the ambiguity of aging is further disclosed. Darkness (or blackness) is both life-giving and death-dealing. Black light brings up colors in minerals; humus is fertile loam; dark hair is abundantly youthful growth. On the other hand, humus is soil, black soil, the earth to which we return in death. Black light is an artificial means which uncovers natural mineral beauty hidden to the naked eye, just as death perhaps transforms the soul (or "ghost"), or as a mirror brings attention to the sign of aging. White is played upon equally paradoxically. Now the subject becomes white chalk and colorless paper, inert, yet potentially productive. The coarse white hair of the opening stanza has become "fine silver

wire" strung into a violin, in sharp contrast to the wire strung into an offkey electric banjo in her twentieth year. Paradoxically, however, this same free silver wire is associated with death by garroting or by electrocution. Finally, the hair shines as purposefully and usefully as forceps, instruments commonly associated with birth rather than death. The poet ultimately perceives in the silver wire-hair a power as ambiguous as the images employed to re-tell the experience. Life or death, creativity or repression, growth or stagnation—the meaning lies not within the discovered object itself, the emblem of aging, but within the human spirit. The ghost which grows stronger within the poet may be death or life; the outcome depends upon the qualifying clause, "If I knew how to use it."

This intensive study of the images in "Sign" demonstrates the intricate networking and intertwining of seemingly disparate elements which is one of the great strengths of Piercy's poetic vision. While not every poem in her canon is so full of leit-motifs as is "Sign," patterns of psychological association appear in many other places in her work. A brief glance at three other pieces can identify the pattern. In "Erasure" from the volume *Hard Loving*, the poet's subject is the loss of a lover. Images of light, vision, and a mouse graphically convey the emotional impact of the experience. The poet moves from "blood turned grey," to a burning out of the "glittering synapses of the brain," to "stars fading in the galaxy," and on to a picture of the imaginary animal figures of the constellations that "would photograph more like a blurry mouse." Falling out of love she then defines as a "correcting vision" which nevertheless damages the optic nerve. The final lines of the poem powerfully unite all these loosely connected images:

To find you have loved a coward and a fool
is to give up the lion, the dragon, the sunburst
and take away your hands covered with
　　small festering bites
and let the mouse go in a grey blur
into the baseboard.

… What Marge Piercy accomplishes with her circling, concentric, seemingly disparate images is exciting, fresh, and flexible poetry as demanding of the reader as any metaphysical performance by Donne. With Piercy, as with Donne, we are always in touch with the human elements, body and mind, flesh and spirit. Piercy's purposeful and powerful use of images is perhaps most clearly stated in her own words. Introducing a series of poems based upon the Tarot deck, she says:

> We must break through the old roles to encounter our own meanings in the symbols we experience in dreams, in songs, in vision, in meditation.... What we use we must remake. Then only are we not playing with dead dreams but seeing ourselves more clearly, and more clearly becoming.

Piercy is, then, constructing a poetic vehicle through which old ways of seeing, old ways of knowing, are wrenched out of old contexts to be given new meaning. True to the feminist movement which she claims changed her life, she intends to break with linear, patriarchal patterns in favor of circles, moons, emotions superior to logic. These form a dialectic which teaches us, as she says in her recent poem "Digging in":

> You are learning to live in circles
> as well as straight lines

Source: Edith J. Wynne, "Imagery of Association in the Poetry of Marge Piercy," in *Publications of the Missouri Philological Association*, Vol. 10, 1985, pp. 57–63.

SOURCES

"12,000 U.S. Troops Out of Iraq by Fall, Military Says," in *Cable News Network World News Online*, http://www.cnn.com/2009/WORLD/meast/03/08/iraq.troop.withdrawal/index.html (accessed May 20, 2009).

Atwood, Margaret, "Strong Woman," in *New York Times Online*, August 8, 1982, http://www.nytimes.com/1982/08/08/books/strong-woman.html (accessed May 20, 2009).

Baer, William, "Appendix IV: The Formalist Revival," in *Writing Metrical Poetry*, Writer's Digest Books, 2006, pp. 236–40.

Barron, Jonathon N., and Eric Murphy Selinger, eds., Introduction to *Jewish American Poetry: Poems, Commentary, and Reflections*, Brandeis University Press, 2000, pp. 3–21.

"California High Court Upholds Prop 8," in *Los Angeles Times Online*, May 27, 2009, http://www.latimes.com/news/local/la-me-gay-marriage27-2009may27,0,7752874.story (accessed June 25, 2009).

Chapman, Abraham, ed., Introduction, in *Jewish American Literature: An Anthology*, New American Library, 1974, pp. xxi–lxiii.

Harris, Marie, "Let Me See that Book," in *Parnassus: Poetry in Review*, Fall-Winter 1974, pp. 149–58.

Juhasz, Suzanne, Review of *Circles on the Water: Selected Poems*, in *Library Journal*, July 1982, p. 1329.

Kremer, S. Lillian, "A Feminist Interpretation of Jewish History and Spirituality: Collision and Fusion in Marge Piercy's Later Poetry and Fiction," in *Connections and Collisions: Identities in Contemporary Jewish-American Women's Writing*, edited by Lois E. Rubin, University of Delaware Press, 2005, pp. 160–78.

Macleod, Jennifer S., "Equal Rights Amendment Still Brings Out Ranters," in *On the Issues Online*, http://www.ontheissuesmagazine.com/2009spring/2009spring_7.php (accessed May 20, 2009).

"Marge Piercy: Biography," in *Marge Piercy Home Page*, http://www.margepiercy.com/main-pages/biography.htm (accessed May 19, 2009).

"New Hampshire House Opposes Governor on Same-sex Marriage," in *Cable News Network Online*, http://www.cnn.com/2009/POLITICS/05/20/new.hampshire.same.sex.marriage (accessed May 20, 2009).

"Overview: Tikkun Olam," in *My Jewish Learning*, http://www.myjewishlearning.com/practices/Ethics/Caring_For_Others/Tikkun_Olam_Repairing_the_World_.shtml (accessed May 19, 2009).

Pacernick, Gary, Introduction to *Meaning and Memory: Interviews with Fourteen Jewish Poets*, Ohio State University Press, 2001, pp. 1–19.

Piercy, Marge, "Marge Piercy," in *Meaning and Memory: Interviews with Fourteen Jewish Poets*, Ohio State University Press, 2001, pp. 215–21.

———, "To Be of Use," in *The Art of Blessing the Day: Poems with a Jewish Theme*, Alfred A. Knopf, 2007, pp.73–4.

Potemra, Michael, "The Gioia Creation," *National Review*, Vol. 55, No. 4, March 10, 2003, p. 52.

Reviews of *Louder, We Can't Hear You (Yet): The Political Poems of Marge Piercy*, in *Leapfrog Press Web site*, http://www.leapfrogpress.com/available-books/poetry/Louder.htm (accessed May 20, 2009).

Rubin, Steven, J., ed., Introduction to *Telling and Remembering: A Century of American Jewish Poetry*, Beacon Press, 1997, pp. 1–12.

"United States History: The War in Vietnam," in *U.S. Department of State Country Studies*, http://countrystudies.us/united-states/history-124.htm (accessed May 20, 2009).

"United States History: The Women's Movement," in *U.S. Department of State Country Studies*, http://countrystudies.us/united-states/history-131.htm (accessed May 20, 2009).

"Vietnam Photography," in *Dean McCullagh Photography Web site*, http://www.mccullagh.org/photo/vietnam/water-buffalo-plowing (accessed May 20, 2009).

Walker, Sue B., "Marge Piercy," in *Dictionary of Literary Biography*, Vol. 227, *American Novelists Since World War II*, 6th ser., edited by James R. Giles and Wanda H. Giles, The Gale Group, 2000, pp. 240–50.

FURTHER READING

Belzer, Tobin, and Julie Pelc, eds., *Joining the Sisterhood: Young Jewish Women Write Their Lives*, State University of New York Press, 2003.

Belzer and Pelc have collected a variety of personal essays and essays from adolescent and teenage Jewish girls about their lives and the role of their faith and culture in their lives. The writings are grouped under such topics as "Ourselves in Relation to Others and the Environment" and "Our Emotional and Intellectual Selves."

Filreis, Alan, *Counter-Revolution of the Word: The Conservative Attack on Modern Poetry, 1945–1960*, University of North Carolina Press, 2008.

Filreis explores the history of American free-verse poetry, finding connections between the creation of free-verse poetry and political developments in the United States, such as the rise in anti-Communist sentiment in the 1950s. The work provides a framework for understanding the popularization of free verse in the 1970s.

Piercy, Marge, and Ira Wood, *So You Want to Write: How to Master the Craft of Writing Fiction and Personal Narrative*, Piatkus Books, 2003.

Piercy and her third husband, Ira Wood, collect their teachings (from the writing workshops they have conducted) on the art and craft of writing into this resource for writers. Not just a how-to book, the work also explores the authors' philosophies on the writing process and the idea of writing as both an art form and a career.

Schneir, Miriam, ed., *Feminism: The Essential Historical Writings*, Vintage, 1994.

Schneir collects in this volume significant writings on feminism from the eighteenth through the twentieth century. She provides selections by feminists of different cultural and ethnic backgrounds as well as a section devoted to male feminists.

To Lucasta, Going to the Wars

RICHARD LOVELACE

1649

"To Lucasta, Going to the Wars" (also often referred to as "To Lucasta, Going to the Warres") was written by Richard Lovelace in about 1640. The poem appeared in 1649 in Lovelace's first full-length poetry collection, *Lucasta*. Most of Lovelace's poems were addressed to the same woman, though that woman was not a real person but rather a representative ideal. The Latin roots for the name Lucasta, *lux casta*, can be translated to mean "pure light" or "chaste light." "To Lucasta, Going to the Wars" is often hailed as one of Lovelace's best and most famous poems, second only perhaps to his "To Althea, From Prison" (written circa 1642). The former poem sets forth much of Lovelace's political ideals, those that uphold honor before love. On a deeper level, this same ideal can be expressed as the need to stand up for one's beliefs even if the cost is the loss of, or separation from, that which is closest to one's heart. This idea is the crux of "To Lucasta, Going to the Wars" and one embodied by Lovelace's own life. The poet was no stranger to war and dissension; he was imprisoned for his political actions for seven weeks in 1642 and for several months from 1648 to 1649.

AUTHOR BIOGRAPHY

Lovelace was born in 1618 into an upper-class English family seated in Kent County, England. His exact birthplace is unknown, but scholars believe it may have been the Netherlands

Richard Lovelace (The Library of Congress)

(specifically Holland) or perhaps Kent. Lovelace was the eldest son of Sir William and Anne Barne Lovelace. His father was a distinguished soldier, and the family's prosperous position was largely derived from its history of military valor. As a boy, Lovelace attended the Charterhouse School in London, England, before attending Oxford University. His first play, a comedy titled *The Scholar*, was written around 1634 and subsequently performed at Oxford. Lovelace's second play, a tragedy titled *The Soldiers*, was written around 1640. Lovelace earned his master of arts degree from Oxford after only two years of study (a feat that was remarkable even then) before attending Cambridge University, where he was much hailed for his grace and good looks. He developed a reputation as a Cavalier, both for his romantic exploits and his romantic and Royalist (supporting a king or monarchy) poetry.

Lovelace studied for only a few months at Cambridge before joining the court of King Charles I in 1638. The following year he served as a soldier under Lord Goring during the Bishops' Wars. Lovelace returned to Kent in 1640, attending to local matters of little political import. (It is around this time that he is thought to have authored "To Lucasta, Going to the Wars.") By 1641, however, Lovelace had joined a group of men opposed to the cessation (end) of Episcopal rule. This move led him to travel to the House of Commons (the lower

house of the British parliament) with a petition promoting the Episcopacy (government of the church by bishops). As a result, Lovelace was imprisoned for seven weeks. It is likely that he wrote "To Althea, From Prison" at this time. The subsequent conditions of Lovelace's release from prison prevented him from any interaction with the House of Commons and also from taking part in the burgeoning English Civil War.

As the war waged on, Lovelace did his best to support King Charles I against the Parliamentarians (supporters of the parliament in opposition to the king). His open and staunch Royalist position led to his second, and far longer, imprisonment in 1648. By his release in April 1649, King Charles I had been executed and the Royalists were defeated. Throughout this period of political turmoil, Lovelace produced several poems outlining his moral, political, and spiritual beliefs. These poems were published in 1649 alongside "To Lucasta, Going to the Wars" in Lovelace's first poetry collection, *Lucasta*.

Little more is known of Lovelace's life following this time. Some sources note that by 1649, he had squandered his fortune in pursuit of his cause and lived thereafter in poverty, though this notion is contested by some scholars. Lovelace died in 1658. He is believed to have been buried in London's St. Bride's Church (which was destroyed in the Great Fire of 1666). One of Lovelace's brothers published more than one hundred of Lovelace's poems posthumously in the 1659 collection *Lucasta: Posthume Poems*.

POEM TEXT

> Tell me not, Sweet, I am unkind,
> That from the nunnery
> Of thy chaste breast and quiet mind
> To war and arms I fly.
>
> True, a new mistress now I chase,   5
> The first foe in the field;
> And with a stronger faith embrace
> A sword, a horse, a shield.
>
> Yet this inconstancy is such
> As thou too shalt adore;   10
> I could not love thee, Dear, so much,
> Loved I not Honour more.

POEM SUMMARY

"To Lucasta, Going to the Wars" is comprised of twelve lines broken into three quatrains (four-line

MEDIA ADAPTATIONS

- "To Lucasta, on Going to the Wars," recorded by Ian Bostridge and Julius Drake, is available on *The English Songbook*, EMI Classics, 1999. An MP3 audio file of the recording can be downloaded at *Amazon.com*.

- "To Lucasta, Upon Going to the Wars," recorded by Colonel Mason, is available on *Santa's Movin' In, Plus Classic Library Favorites by Colonel Mason*, Raven-Tone, 2004. An MP3 audio file of the recording can be downloaded at *Amazon.com*.

- Though no definitive album exists, several of the poems from *Lucasta* were set to music by Lovelace's contemporary, Henry Lawes (c. 1640s–1650s).

stanzas). The rhyme scheme is *abab*, meaning that each alternating line rhymes (i.e., in each stanza, the first line rhymes with the third and the second line rhymes with the fourth). The poem is additionally set forth in an alternating line pattern of eight and six syllables. In other words, the first and third lines of each quatrain consist of eight syllables and the second and fourth lines consist of six syllables. By its title, it is clear that the poem is addressed to Lucasta, the idealized lover representing chastity, purity, and light. It is also clear that the speaker is leaving her in order to join the war.

Stanza 1

In the first line of the first stanza, the speaker addresses his lover with pet names, and he admonishes her for admonishing him. He says that she should not chastise him for leaving her or accuse him of being cruel. In the second and third lines, the speaker acknowledges that he must leave the safe shelter of Lucasta's pure heart and calm demeanor. In the fourth line, he states that he leaves them (her) in order to run to war and weapons. This line also indicates a haste and eagerness

to do so, which seems incongruous given that it embodies an urgent desire to choose war over love.

Stanza 2

Though the speaker asks Lucasta not to accuse him of being inconstant, he nevertheless admits in the first line of the second stanza that he is taking a new lover. The new lover is then revealed in the second line to be that of the enemy in battle. In the following lines the speaker claims that he will take to arms with more vigor than he has taken to love. The final line of stanza 2 is a brief list of the implements of war, those most representative of battle: offensive weapons, defensive tools, and a stallion to ride. These are the objects that the speaker will now embrace with more fervor than he has ever shown his love.

Stanza 3

Still, in stanza 3, the speaker insists that his faithless behavior is not cruel, and that even Lucasta will come to understand. The speaker declares that Lucasta will do so even to the point where she will learn to love her rival. As the speaker explains in the final couplet, he could not love Lucasta at all if he did not love honor better. In the final couplet (as in the first), the speaker returns to addressing Lucasta with the sweetest of descriptions. Even more noteworthy is the fact that this final couplet is one of the most famous in English poetry, it is often quoted and recited as a justification for standing up for one's belief despite the cost. Seen from this light, the speaker rightly claims that if he did not uphold his honor and self-respect, he would be unable to, and incapable of, love.

THEMES

Love

Love in "To Lucasta, Going to the Wars" is set from the outset as a force that is in opposition to war. From the outset it is also clear that war has the upper hand. Despite the speaker's clear intentions to leave Lucasta, the poem opens and closes with him addressing her in endearing terms. She is described as chaste and calm and as offering shelter of a religious nature, as that of a monk in his cloisters (a monastery or convent). This idea is in line with the fictional mode of the idealized Lucasta, the *lux casta* of pure or chaste

TOPICS FOR FURTHER STUDY

- In light of the themes in "To Lucasta, Going to the Wars," read Marc Aronson and Patty Campbell's collection *War Is . . . Soldiers, Survivors, and Storytellers Talk About War* specifically geared toward young-adult readers. How is this assembly of the modern and ancient writings on war by those who have lived it similar to or different from the poem? Give a class presentation using PowerPoint in which you address this question.

- Given the lack of official record keeping in seventeenth-century England, exact dates related to Lovelace's life and work are unavailable. Use the Internet to research different biographies of Lovelace and do your best to determine the dates that you believe his most famous works were written. In a brief essay, discuss what led you to your conclusions and why.

- Read more about the disagreements at the heart of the English Civil War. Divide your class into those who side with the Parliamentarians and those who side with the Royalists. Stage a debate arguing each faction's core values.

- Which do you think is more important, love or honor? Write an essay in which you argue for the dominance of one or the other. Be sure to cite examples from your life, the lives of those around you, or even historical and contemporary events.

light. While the speaker admits that he is leaving his lover for the war, he also describes the war in terms of love. War is also his lover; the enemy on the battlefield is openly described as his mistress. The implements of battle are also embraced just as a lover would be.

Love is even employed as a possibility for the spurned lover. According to the speaker, Lucasta will love war (here the embodiment of honor) because without it, her lover could not love her. At the very least, she will learn to love her paramour's love for war. In every sense of the word, "To Lucasta, Going to the Wars" is a love poem; it is dedicated not to Lucasta or to war, as one might at first suspect, but rather it is dedicated ultimately to honor.

War

Much of the poem is dedicated to war. Of the twelve lines, war is mentioned directly in the final line of the first stanza and referred to throughout the entirety of the second stanza. War is the mistress that will usurp Lucasta. The bloody embrace of the enemy in battle and that of the implements of war (the stallion, weapons, and shield) are all given as much attention as Lucasta's various charms. Yet war is only a vehicle; it is ultimately the proving ground for honor. On the surface, the speaker leaves his lover for the war, and his justification for this abandonment is that he could not love Lucasta if he did not put honor ahead of her. Thus, war—the act of fighting and the participation in it—is an exhibit of the speaker's love for honor.

Honor

Though mentioned only once in the last line of the poem, honor is ultimately the most important theme in "To Lucasta, Going to the Wars." Honor is the justification used by the speaker for all that precedes it: leaving Lucasta, rushing off to war, killing the enemy, and glorifying battle. All are done in the name and service of honor. Honor is the speaker's first love and, in accordance, all other love that he is capable of stems directly from that first love.

Femininity

Though not an explicit theme in the poem, Lucasta is representative of the feminine ideal. Addressing the idealized feminine was a common poetic practice in the seventeenth century, and Lovelace's contemporaries would have been well aware of that fact. In using the ideal feminine, Lovelace underscores all of the themes in "To Lucasta, Going to the Wars." For instance, because Lucasta is not a real woman, she is not subject to real women's flaws. This makes the speaker's leaving her even more striking; he is departing from perfection of the purest light in favor of war, blood, and violence. The use of the ideal also allows for a subtle play on words. Where traditionally females were accused of being inconstant and faithless lovers, the speaker

A bearded knight caresses his lady with one hand while the other rests on his armour—a winged helmet and a shield emblazoned with a Death's Head. (© Hulton Archive / Getty Images)

instead turns these flaws on himself. Even more striking is the idea that the ideal of honor is paramount to the ideal woman. Not only is the love of honor supreme to the love of the ideal woman, but the two are essentially linked. The latter could not exist without the former.

STYLE

Rhyme Scheme

The rhyme scheme in "To Lucasta, Going to the Wars" is one of alternating rhyming lines. This is represented in the first stanza by the *abab* notation. However, the rhymes in each quatrain change, which means the second quatrain is represented by a *cdcd* rhyme scheme. The third stanza is thus represented by the *efef* rhyme scheme. Notably, the second and fourth lines in the first quatrain are a slant rhyme (the vowels or consonants of the stressed syllables match). Furthermore, many of the exact rhymes in the poem are unequal in rhythm. That is, a one-syllable rhyme is often paired with the end rhyme of a two-syllable word. This occurs in the slant line and the first and third lines of stanzas 1 and 2. This trend is then reversed in stanza 3, with the same syllabic dissonance occurring in the second and fourth lines (rather than the first and third).

Syllabic Symmetry

Despite the syllabic dissonance inherent in the poem's rhyme scheme, the poem is subject to a rigid syllabic structure. Alternating lines throughout the poem are comprised of eight and six syllables, respectively. This structure does not deviate throughout the poem, nor does the speaker's resolve to leave his lover.

Sonnet

While "To Lucasta, Going to the Wars" is not a sonnet, it shares several characteristics with the form. It sets forth a similar thematic step-by-step argument with an unexpected turn at the end (the introduction of honor as the justifying force for a man to choose war over love). The poem also shares the same traditional rhyme scheme of a sonnet. Yet because "To Lucasta, Going to the Wars" is missing a final couplet and each line does not consist of ten syllables (as a standard sonnet), it only evokes the sonnet form.

Love Poem

At first glance, "To Lucasta, Going to the Wars" is a simple love poem. It professes love to an ideal woman, one who is pure, virtuous, and calm; one who provides a safe harbor for the speaker. It becomes clear that the speaker intends to leave Lucasta. Still, the reader might continue to assume that this is a love poem, albeit one that laments loss and separation. From the title, one might assume that the speaker must go to war and does so only because it is his duty. However, it comes as a surprise that he does not regret leaving his love. In fact, the speaker will rush to war gladly; by his own words it is as if he is taking another lover. This revelation stops the reader from interpreting the work as merely a conventional love poem. This remains the case until the reader reaches the final line of the poem. There, the speaker professes that his love for war stems from his love for honor. In addition, the speaker admits that his love for Lucasta also stems from his love for honor. Thus, the idea of "To Lucasta, Going to the Wars" as a love poem is restored, but in a less conventional

COMPARE & CONTRAST

- **1600s:** Poetry is largely written in preset forms. These forms often feature rhyming couplets with equal stanzas and measured syllabic lines. Poems at this time also feature similar thematic conventions such as love, war, mortality, and friendship.

  Today: Following the popularity of free verse in the twentieth century, contemporary poets have started to return to formal verse poetry. There are no common themes under discussion, and this modern take on structured poetry is often referred to as New Formalism.

- **1600s:** Lovelace lives during a time in England where political and religious dissension can bring imprisonment and even execution.

  Today: Around the world, political and religious dissension still brings similar conse-

quences. However, England is no longer such a place, nor, for that matter, is the United States.

- **1600s:** War is a common fact of existence and almost all men are expected to participate in it or be forever branded as cowards. It is this cultural belief that largely influences "To Lucasta, Going to the Wars."

  Today: While war is still largely common, it no longer requires the vast participation it once did, and this is largely due to the mechanization of battle (e.g. warplanes, bombs, and guns). Changing social views regarding cowardliness, manliness, and the morality of war itself also make compulsory participation in battle a less culturally dominant concept.

---

sense. "To Lucasta, Going to the Wars" is a love poem dedicated to honor. More importantly, it is a meditation on the source of love.

HISTORICAL CONTEXT

The English Civil War

The best-known aspects of Lovelace's life and work pertain to his participation in the English Civil War, which raged from 1642 to 1651. Many historians actually split this period of time into three subwars. The first two occurred from 1642 to 1646 and 1648 to 1649, and the opposing sides were the Royalists (supporters of a monarch, specifically King Charles I) and the Parliamentarians (supporters of the Long Parliament). The third war, between supporters of the Rump Parliament and supporters of King Charles II, took place from 1649 to 1651. It is the first two periods of war, however, that had the most impact on England, resulting in the toppling of the crown and the establishment of the Commonwealth of England

in 1649. The war that broke out in 1642 had been developing since 1603, as the Parliament and the crown struggled for power. This struggle was also one based in religious theory. Kings and Royalists believed that the crown held an absolute power sanctioned by God (known as the theory of divine right). The Presbyterians and Puritans, who were gaining influence in the House of Commons, however, fundamentally disagreed with this interpretation. Arguments raged to such an extent by 1629 that Charles I dismissed the Parliament and ruled alone for eleven years.

On April 13, 1640, however, Charles I was forced to reconvene Parliament in order to address the Bishop's War with Scotland (the war in which Lovelace served). This session of parliament, often referred to as the Short Parliament, lasted for only three weeks. Parliament refused to assist the king unless some concessions to its own power were made. In response, Charles I quickly disbanded the governing body yet again. By November 1640, the war raged on, and Charles I was once again forced to call upon the Parliament. This session, known as the Long Parliament, made peace with Scotland. It also passed several acts to curtail the king's power and attempted to turn the Church of England into a Presbyterian institution. It was this latter effrontery that led to the formation of the Royalist faction in 1642. War broke out that August.

While the war against the king was largely spearheaded by Puritans and Presbyterians, another faction, the Independents, wished not only to topple the monarchy but also to topple organized religion as well. Led by Oliver Cromwell, this group ultimately came to the forefront of the issue. The Presbyterians, realizing the instability of their position, attempted to make peace with the king. In response, Cromwell led his New Model Army to imprison the king in 1647. Though Charles I escaped, he was soon recaptured. Cromwell, with the aid of Colonel Thomas Pride, also removed the Presbyterians from the House of Commons in 1648 (thus transforming the Long Parliament into the Rump Parliament). The following year, Pride had Charles I tried for treason and subsequently executed.

This definitive act led the Rump Parliament to pass acts abolishing the House of Lords and the crown. To further establish its power, the Rump Parliament also passed the Treasons Act, which dictated that anyone who criticized the government would be guilty of treason. On May 19, 1649, the Parliament officially established the Commonwealth of England. Though kingship ultimately returned to English governance, it never again held the power that it did before the civil war. The English Civil War led to the lasting cessation of an absolute monarchy. It also set the precedent that the monarchy must rule through Parliament, a practice that continues to this day.

Cavalier Poetry

The Cavalier poets were a group of seventeenth-century poets who supported King Charles I during the English Civil War. Lovelace, of course, was one of the more prominent Cavalier poets. Other noteworthy poets of this group were Robert Herrick, Ben Jonson, Sir John Suckling, and Thomas Carew. Despite being defined by the political affiliation of its poets, Cavalier poetry was not overtly political. Furthermore, it was not blatantly religious. This fact is even more remarkable when one considers that a major contributing factor leading to the war was that of theologically divergent views. Cavalier poetry was largely secular and somewhat

De Viris Illustribus: *Marco Forzata Capodilista*
(© The Art Archive | The Picture Desk Limited | Corbis)

informal in its structure, especially when compared with other seventeenth-century verse. The Cavaliers were best known for writing poems of a romantic or sexual nature, and their love poetry often plays on or references Roman verse. In addition, the Cavaliers managed to convey a new level of eroticism not seen before in formal English verse. This was accomplished via the use of the idealized woman, particularly in regard to her chaste and virtuous nature. Chastity in the idealized feminine lover became, in Cavalier poetry, a factor that incited desire, rather than one that quelled it. All of these classic traits of Cavalier poetry can be seen in Lovelace's "To Lucasta, Going to the Wars."

CRITICAL OVERVIEW

Richard Lovelace was a famous Cavalier poet while he was alive, and that fame has undoubtedly withstood the test of time. His work is still considered one of the foremost examples of Cavalier poetry. Of that body of work, "To Lucasta,

Going to the Wars" is often singled out as one of Lovelace's best. The poem is often discussed in tandem with Lovelace's other highly celebrated poem, "To Althea, From Prison." In fact, most critics find that these two poems are far superior to the rest of Lovelace's work. For instance, F. W. Moorman, writing in *The Cambridge History of English Literature: Cavalier and Puritan, Vol. VII* (1911), says of both poems, "there is no trace of the pedantry or prolixity, the frigid conceit and the tortured phrase, of his other poems." Moorman adds that "in their simplicity, their chivalrous feeling and their nobility of thought, they touch perfection." In an originally unsigned 1864 article published in the *North American Review*, James Russell Lowell calls "To Lucasta, Going to the Wars" "graceful, airy, and nicely finished." Noting that the poem is far greater than Lovelace's other work, Lowell quips that the poet "is to be classed with the *lucky* authors who, without great powers, have written one or two pieces so facile in thought and fortunate in phrase as to be carried lightly in the memory."

Despite the arguable quality of Lovelace's overall oeuvre (body of work), critics universally agree that "To Lucasta, Going to the Wars" is to be applauded. This is an opinion that has held for several centuries. In an 1890 *Harper's New Monthly* magazine article, Louise Imogen Guiney observes that "it might surprise Lovelace, who had but a modest opinion of himself, despite the popular adoration, to know how many bosoms have throbbed over his farewell 'To Lucasta on Going to the Wars.' Its high tenderness is very characteristic of his genius." Nearly one hundred years later, in a 1987 introduction to *Richard Lovelace: Selected Poems*, Gerald Hammond notes that "To Lucasta, Going to the Wars" embodies "the Lovelace which everyone responds to: the effortlessly lyrical statement of elegantly heroic behaviour." Hammond also states that the poem "is clever too. . . . A masculine embrace is superimposed upon a feminine one." In a 1991 overview of the poet's work in the *Reference Guide to English Literature* Walter R. Davis remarks that a "serious adjustment of love with honor in facing death at the end of the lyric is achieved within a context of tender humor . . . and reckless playfulness." Based on this idea, Davis finds that "Lovelace's is the poetry of poise—distant, judicious, open to conflict."

In a lengthy review of the poem in a 1993 edition of *Dictionary of Literary Biography*, Sharon Cadman Seelig comments that "'To Lucasta, Going to the Warres' and 'To Althea, From Prison'—reveal [Lovelace] as soldier, poet, and courtier, as an attractive and magnetic personality, but also suggest his wider intellectual and aesthetic interests." Seelig also states that "the Cavalier ideal for which Lovelace has often been taken as an exemplar is most clearly set out in 'To Lucasta, Going to the Warres,' a poem that defines the two central activities of that ideal, love and war, and articulates wittily and forcefully the relationship between them." Seelig also notes that "both the stance . . . and the rhetorical means by which it is accomplished are characteristic of Lovelace. His poem is supremely graceful, deft, and masterful."

CRITICISM

Leah Tieger

Tieger is a freelance writer and editor. In the following essay, she discusses the tensions inherent in Richard Lovelace's "To Lucasta, Going to the Wars." In addition, she explores the poem as a political declaration of the poet's Royalist sympathies before going on to discuss an alternative interpretation of the poem.

Critics often hail Richard Lovelace's "To Lucasta, Going to the Wars" as a standout work of Cavalier poetry and seventeenth-century English verse. It is often cited as an exemplary poem in Lovelace's entire body of work. These approbations largely rest on two factors. The first is the deceptive simplicity of the poem. The second is its whole-hearted embodiment of the Cavalier aesthetic and morality (most notably on account of its Royalist sentiments).

In exploring the poem's deceptive simplicity, one finds that what appears to be a simple love poem is actually a complicated treatise placing love, war, and honor in apposition and opposition. In this sense, a tension is apparent in the poem largely evinced by the relationship between being both attracted to and repelled by love. The speaker is attracted by his love to Lucasta, but he is also repelled by a love that is (at least in the opinion of the speaker) far greater (i.e., the love of honor). According to *Dictionary of Literary Biography* contributor Sharon Cadman Seelig, "the tension is heightened by making war not simply a rival activity but" a rival lover. Additional

WHAT DO I READ NEXT?

- To further your understanding of the work of Richard Lovelace, read *The Poems of Richard Lovelace: Lucasta, Etc.* This comprehensive 2007 collection presents the entirety of Lovelace's work.

- *Why Do They Hate Me? Young Lives Caught in War and Conflict,* compiled by Laurel Holliday, was published in 1999. The book features first-person accounts from young adults who have lived through war or ethnic persecution. It also provides a look at war that is far different from the honor-filled endeavor described in "To Lucasta, Going to the War."

- Lovelace's poem is a shining example of a seventeenth-century English love poem. For a markedly different cultural perspective on love poetry, read *I Hear a Symphony: African Americans Celebrate Love.* Edited by Paula L. Woods and Felix H. Liddell, the 1994 volume is geared toward young adults. The collection also features essays and artwork dedicated to the subject of love.

- The 1998 collection *Poetry and Revolution: An Anthology of British and Irish Verse 1625-1660,* edited by Peter Davidson, presents an overarching selection of seventeenth-century poetry. Among others, it features the work of such Cavalier poets as Thomas Carew and Sir John Suckling. The volume also discards the definition of Cavalier poetry, seeking instead to present more inclusive exploration of British verse in the 1600s.

- For an in-depth look at the history of the English Civil War and the establishment of the Commonwealth of England, read Peter Gaunt's *Essential Histories 58: The English Civil Wars 1642-1651.* In particular, the 2003 volume focuses on the military history surrounding the war, and it provides detailed analyses of the battles that were waged.

- Prominent Cavalier poet Thomas Carew has been hailed by critics as one of the master's of English verse. His work is largely lauded, whereas Lovelace's body of work is often dismissed but for the exception of his best poems. The 2009 collection of Carew's poems, *The Works of Thomas Carew,* provides a thorough introduction to the Cavalier poet.

---

tensions in the poem lie in the inert nature of the beloved Lucasta and the dynamic nature of the lover (i.e., the speaker). Lucasta does not speak or act in the poem; she serves as little more than a mute audience. Even the traits attributed to her (of embodying purity and spiritual shelter) are of a placid nature. The speaker, however, outlines his intentions to leave her and to participate in war, also giving a rational argument for his actions. Seelig emphasizes this dynamic: "while the poem compliments Lucasta, that chaste light, so pure as to be designated a kind of sanctuary, the poet's position is both active and definitive, while hers is static and passive."

Expanding on the tension of opposites created in the poem, Seelig finds that its argument

> depends . . . on the finessing of oppositions, so that what has appeared to be inconstancy is redefined as the highest form of faith. The lady is both sweet and dear, but Lovelace asserts that he must yield, not with regret but with adoration, to the new mistress . . . a realm in which war and love are inseparably linked.

This observation of tension and opposition is not limited to Seelig alone. For instance, A. D. Cousins, writing in *Parergon,* asserts that the "opposites, attraction and departure, are the basis of the dialectic informing the poem, for it unfolds as ... the separation, evaluation, and resolution of alternatives." Cousins also notes that "at the same time as the persona seemingly polarizes those alternatives he cunningly connects them, for it is through the very conceit which proclaims Lucasta's attractiveness that he starts to justify departure from her."

However, this tension, which drives the poem, exists only to underscore the importance of the poem's conclusion. As much as the speaker loves Lucasta, he loves honor more. In fact, without honor, the speaker would be incapable of loving Lucasta. Based on this reasoning, the speaker admonishes Lucasta not to be jealous of her rival, but rather to be grateful to it. This is an astonishing assertion, but it is far less astonishing when one considers "To Lucasta, Going to the Wars" as a Royalist poem. This fact is remarked upon by Cousins, who finds that it is this very logic that "reveals the profundity of the poem's royalism." As George Fenwick Jones points out in *Comparative Literature*, "Lovelace was a true cavalier. As a cavalier he was the heir of an unbroken military tradition.... And one would expect that he would show the idea of honor that belongs to that tradition." In addition to the politics inherent in Lovelace's elevation of honor above romantic love, the Catholic imagery in the poem further emphasizes Lovelace's Royalist sympathies. While the English Civil War was essentially political, it was also a religious war. Where the Parliamentarians were largely affiliated with the Presbyterians and Puritans, the Royalists were mainly associated with the Church of England and sympathetic to the Catholics. This connection, particularly, stems from the fact that political ideals regarding the rights of kings were largely dictated along religious and theological lines. Where both the Church of England and Catholicism promoted strict hierarchies and the divine right of kings, Presbyterianism did not.

Both the translation of the Latin roots of Lucasta's name ("pure light") and the comparison of her love to the shelter of a nunnery are two instances of overt Catholic imagery. The speaker's description of Lucasta as chaste is another example. In particular, the speaker's reference to the nunnery "indicates that [his] love for her draws him towards a stillness beyond his world's unrest," Cousins writes. "And that in turn suggests how, through those royalist categories of the nunnery conceit, Lovelace's poem defines the role that the object of

desire should, at least ideally, fulfill: she should incarnate the unchanging tranquility and integrity of a morally ordered existence, being truly one in a contradictory and various world." This is also the role that Catholics believed the papacy, the crown, and organized religion should play. "Through the quintessentially royalist principles of his lyric, Lovelace represents what love finally is," declares Cousins. It seems that the very heart of Lovelace's Royalist ideals inform the poem. Those ideals also inform the speaker's leave-taking. The "persona clearly implies that, as a man, he cannot naturally live in a private world—ideal as it may be—isolated from the demands of social and political action," Cousins remarks. In fact, the same lofty ideals that the speaker finds in Lucasta are those that drive him from her. Cousins states that "his departure actually attests to his love for Lucasta, emphasizing their spiritual unity, for he leaves her ... only to affirm and express through heroic virtue ... those ideal, privately manifested qualities that he so reverences in her."

This crux of the poem, "the warrior's choice between love and action, between shame and glory" (as Jones calls it), may in fact be more complex than it first appears. Though the speaker informs Lucasta that he cannot love her without setting his love for honor above her, he also insists that she should love him all the more for doing so. As Seelig remarks, the speaker sets forth "not the terms on which she would find him worthy of love ... but the terms on which *he* will love *her*." In fact, it is this edict that *Explicator* critic Christopher S. Nassaar identifies as the main theme in the poem. Nassaar claims that the honor that the speaker refers to is not one of religious or political affiliation, or even one related to the glory of participating in battle (i.e., standing up for one's beliefs). Instead he argues that the honor at stake is that of the speaker's masculinity, which is asserted through his demanding Lucasta's happy submission to his will. In the second stanza of the poem, the speaker claims that he is leaving Lucasta for his new lover (an enemy soldier). This "metaphor is double-edged," Nassaar explains, "for it also compares Lucasta to an enemy soldier. Such a soldier has to be defeated and subdued." Thus Nassaar finds that "honor is not to hesitate to go to war when necessary, but it is also not to be defeated in the gentle war of the sexes."

Source: Leah Tieger, Critical Essay on "To Lucasta, Going to the Wars," in *Poetry for Students*, Gale, Cengage Learning, 2010.

Woman reading *(© Gerard Terborch | The Bridgeman Art Library | Getty Images)*

Robert H. Ray

In the following essay, Ray discusses the influence of Sir Philip Sidney on Thomas Carew and Lovelace, drawing comparisons between "To Lucasta, Going to the Wars" and Sidney's Astrophil and Stella.

Two of the so-called "Cavalier Poets" of the early seventeenth century apparently held the work of Sir Philip Sidney in high esteem. His influence on the poetry of both Richard Lovelace and Thomas Carew is apparent in several hitherto unnoted allusions to Sidney's poetry. Their uses of Sidney are of the kind that assumes a recognition of his poetry, and these allusions too closely parallel Sidney's lines to be attributed to mere coincidence.

Richard Lovelace overtly alludes to Sir Philip Sidney in two poems. One is his mention of Sidney in lines 15–21 of "A Paradox":

> So from the glorious Sunne,
> Who to his height hath got,
> With what delight we runne
> To some black Cave or Grot?
> And Heav'nly *Sydney* you
> Twice read, had rather view
> Some odde *Romance*, so new!

Quite evident is Lovelace's high opinion of Sidney as being like the sun and in a heavenly

position compared to more mundane writers. In addition, another clear allusion by name occurs in lines 1–2 of "Clitophon and Lucippe Translated": "Pray Ladies breath, awhile lay by / Caelestial *Sydney's Arcady*." Again Lovelace elevates Sidney's work to the highest heavenly realm, implying his great respect for Sidney's art.

Apparently unnoted, however, are two more subtle allusions to Sidney in which his name is not overtly mentioned. These references are to *Astrophil and Stella*. The famous lines (11–12) of Lovelace's "To Lucasta, Going to the Warres" are as follows: "I could not love thee (Deare) so much, / Lov'd I not Honour more." These lines seem clearly to echo the sestet of number 62 in the *Astrophil and Stella* sequence:

> And therefore by her Love's authority,
> Willd me these tempests of vaine love to flie,
> And anchor fast my selfe on *Vertue's* shore.
> Alas, if this the only mettall be
> Of *Love,* new-coind to helpe my beggery,
> Dear, love me not, that you may love me
> more.

Especially pertinent are Lovelace's echoes of Sidney's last line, particularly with the use of *Deare* and *more*. But the context of the entire sestet is relevant, with Lovelace substituting *Honour* for *Vertue* and emphasizing his speaker's insistence on honor as the basis for a pure love, played against Astrophil's wish that Stella would not love him for virtue, but for the satisfaction of a baser love, one that rebels against the chastity insisted on by Stella in number 61. So, Lovelace's echo of Sidney here is ironic in that it delineates the difference between the honorable, mature man speaking to Lucasta and the sensually-inclined, immature Astrophil who is trying to seduce Stella. The likelihood that Lovelace is indeed alluding to Sidney's work is strongly supported, of course, by his two overt allusions (noted above).

The other interesting allusion to *Astrophil and Stella* occurs in Lovelace's "Lucasta, Taking the Waters at Tunbridge," Lines 1–2 are as follows: "Yee happy floods! That now must passe / The sacred conduicts of her Wombe." These lines deliberately echo Sidney's number 103 of *Astrophil and Stella,* lines 1–2: "O HAPPIE Tems, that didst my Stella beare, / I saw thy selfe with many a smiling line." The parallel opening phrase of three words in each poem, the middle word being *happy* in each case, takes this reference beyond coincidence. In addition, it is a body of water being addressed in each poem (the *Thames* of Sidney becomes simply *floods* in Lovelace). In each poem, the water is personified as being happy because it is in close proximity to the speaker's lady, with Lovelace's speaker imagining much more physical and intimate contact than that pictured by Sidney's speaker.

Lovelace's influences from and adaptations of Sidney's work, therefore, seem to be a bit more extensive than previously realized. Perhaps these further allusions make more credible the phrase in Francis Lenton's prefatory poem to Lovelace that praises his "seraphique Sydneyan fire."

Thomas Carew's "To My Worthy Friend Master George Sandys, on His Translation of the Psalmes" first appeared as a prefatory poem in the second edition of Sandys's *A Paraphrase upon the Divine Poems* (1638). The speaker of Carew's poem presents himself as one hitherto occupied with sensual love, mortal beauty, and writing poetry about those matters. But in the face of Sandys's divine writing, he now humbly acknowledges the unclean, unhallowed, and profane nature of his own muse. He poses the possibility that now he will be converted to search for God and immortal love, turning away from his former adoration of frivolous earthly women and concerns.

Carew's poem effectively refers to some of the repeated topics of secular poetry in the late-sixteenth and early-seventeenth centuries: earthly flames, tears wept for love, lyric feet, and efforts to achieve fame as a secular poet. But the extent to which Carew plays against Sidney's *Astrophil and Stella* seems not to have been noted in criticism. Specifically, Carew's lines 31–32 are central in his use of Sidney: "But teare those Idols from my heart, and write / What his blest Sprit, not fond Love shall indite." This couplet primarily alludes to the couplet ending the first sonnet in the *Astrophil and Stella* sequence: "Biting my trewand pen, beating myself for spite, / 'Foole,' said my Muse to me, 'looke in thy heart and write.'" Carew's rhymes (*write* and *indite*) closely parallel Sidney's (*spite* and *write*). But even more striking is the deliberate reversal of the advice: Astrophil's muse tells him to look into his own heart for his love for Stella and express it in writing, but Carew's speaker vows to eliminate such a secular idol as "fond Love" from his heart and

follow what God's spirit inspires him to write. Also relevant as a secondary allusion is the last line of Sidney's fifteenth sonnet: "Stella behold, and then begin to endite." Carew's use of "indite" parallels Sidney's "endite," but also important is that Stella is precisely the type of "Idol" to be torn out of the heart of Carew's speaker, not one to "behold" and be inspired by. Finally, also relevant in Carew's echoing of Sidney is the couplet in number 90 of *Astrophil and Stella:* "Since all my words thy beauty doth endite, / And love doth hold my hand, and makes me write." Here the rhyming words are precisely those used in Carew's couplet but in reverse order. More interesting, the argument in Sidney's lines also is reversed by Carew, again enforcing the fact that in contrast to Astrophil's feeling that his words come from Stella's beauty and love, Carew's speaker does not now want that feminine beauty as "Idol" and does not want "fond Love" inspiring his writing. Only God's spirit can now inspire his superior love and artistry.

Greater appreciation for and understanding of Carew's excellent poem to Sandys comes from perceiving his creative adaptation of Sidney. The well-read Carew certainly would expect his learned audience to recognize the references to Sidney's work and to appreciate Carew's combination of past poetic tradition and his own unique talent.

In sum, these two courtly poets felt a kinship with the ideal courtier of the Renaissance, Sir Philip Sidney. Their subtle references are quite clear to someone familiar with Sidney's *Astrophil and Stella,* and any educated person of the early seventeenth century who was interested in reading poetry—and especially those who also were writing poetry—would be thoroughly familiar with Sidney's poems and would be well equipped to perceive such allusions as those that appear in Lovelace and Carew.

Source: Robert H. Ray, "The Admiration of Sir Philip Sidney by Lovelace and Carew: New Seventeenth-Century Allusions," in *American Notes & Queries,* Vol. 18, No. 1, Winter 2005, pp. 18–21.

Christopher S. Nassaar

In the following essay, Nassaar suggests that embedded in "To Lucasta, Going to the Wars" is a battle of the sexes in which Lovelace proclaims his dominance.

Richard Lovelace's "Lucasta" poem has often been praised for its simplicity of thought and diction, and for its very effective and memorable phrasing of plain emotions. And yet Lovelace is in the line of Donne, and his poem is also full of Donne-like wit. His lady's breast is "chaste" and a "nunnery," for instance, and the word "arms" in line 4 has a double meaning. My thesis, however, is that the poem is more complex and witty than has generally been recognized and that the poet presents his relationship with his mistress in terms of a conflict in which the man should definitely triumph.

The poem is clearly the result of a difference of opinion between the poet and his mistress: Lucasta wishes her lover to remain with her while he insists on going off to war. This situation of "war" between the two lovers is best caught in the metaphor that dominates the second stanza:

> True, a new mistress now I chase,
> The first foe in the field;

By comparing the first enemy soldier he sees to a mistress, Lovelace is demonstrating how eager he is to fight for his king and country. But the metaphor is double-edged, for it also compares Lucasta to an enemy soldier. Such a soldier has to be defeated and subdued, and what Loveplace seems to be implying is that this is also true of Lucasta. Indeed, the mixing of the imagery of love and war is prominent throughout the poem, for Lovelace also flies to "arms" and "embraces" his sword, horse, and shield. The difference between Lucasta and an enemy soldier is that the former has to be subdued gently, with a sweetness that is not devoid of firmness. (Thus, part of the process of subduing her is to write a poem to her).

To allow Lucasta to rule him would be unnatural, and the poet implies this in the first line of the poem: "Tell me not, sweet, I am unkind." In the seventeenth century, the word "unkind" had its present-day meaning but also meant unnatural. For Lovelace, natural behavior is not only to fight for one's king and country, but also to remain the dominant partner in any love relationship. Had he yielded to Lucasta's plea and remained with her, his behavior would have been unnatural in a two-fold sense. Read in this way, the word "honour" in the final stanza of the poem acquires new meaning:

> Yet this inconstancy is such
> As you too shall adore;
> I could not love thee, dear, so much,
> Loved I not honour more.

Honor is not to hesitate to go to war when necessary, but it is also not to be defeated in the gentle war of the sexes. In the poem, the two are interconnected and inseparable. Had Lovelace yielded to Lucasta, he would have been disgraced both in the larger world of politics and in the smaller one of sexual love. For natural harmony in the world of love is for the woman to yield to the man. To allow the opposite to happen is to behave unnaturally and ultimately to destroy the very love one seeks to preserve. Natural behavior, on the other hand—which is also honorable—will preserve and strengthen the love bond that exists between Lovelace and Lucasta.

All this is not to say that Richard Lovelace is what would be called today a male chauvinist. His attitude toward sexual love was the normal, accepted one in the seventeenth century. We find a similar attitude, for instance, in *Paradise Lost*, when Eve says to Adam:

> "My author and disposer, what thou bid'st
> Unargued I obey; so God ordains.
> God is thy law, thou mine; to know no more
> Is woman's happiest knowledge and her
>   praise."
> (IV, 635–638)

For Milton, Eve's submission to Adam is part of the natural order of things. And if we continue to insist that Milton was a male chauvinist, there is always John Donne, who in "The Sun Rising" compares his lady to the entire world and himself to its ruler. The concept of the equality of the sexes did not achieve anything like wide acceptance before the final decades of the nineteenth century.

Source: Christpoher S. Nassaar, "Lovelace's 'To Lucasta, Going to the Wars,'" in *Explicator*, Vol. 39, No. 3, Spring 1981, p. 44–45.

Alexander C. Judson

In the following essay, Judson argues that the poems Lovelace wrote to Lucasta were directed to an imaginary individual and not to Lucy Sacheverall.

When Lovelace issued his slender volume of poems in 1649, he called it *Lucasta: Epodes, Odes, Sonnets, Songs, etc.* It contains, besides commendatory verses, fifty-five poems. Of these, seventeen are addressed to Lucasta, or at least refer in some way to her. There are also four poems to Ellinda, and one each to Gratiana, Chloe, and Althea. Ten years later, after Lovelace's death, his brother collected and published another volume of his poems, which he entitled *Lucasta: Posthume Poems of*

> **LOVELACE MAY HAVE COURTED LUCY SACHEVEREL. HE MAY HAVE LOVED HER. HE MAY EVEN HAVE NAMED HIS BOOK AFTER HER."**

Richard Lovelace, Esq. In this second volume, Lucasta's name still appears most frequently: Lucasta figures in ten poems, Laura in two, and Chloris in one. Since most writers on Lovelace have been content to repeat Anthony à Wood's casual identification of Lucasta as Lucy Sacheverel, with little or no search for corroboration in the poetry concerned, it may not be amiss to give further study to the question of Lucasta's identity.

Before turning, however, to this problem, let us consider briefly an idea about Lucasta and Lovelace which has been several times advanced, but which may, I think, be safely dismissed as sentimental conjecture. We are asked to picture Lovelace pining away because his betrothed had married another man, and finally dying miserably in London of a broken heart. Thus Rev. J. H. B. Masterman, in his *Age of Milton* (p. 98), says: "According to tradition, his death was due to despair, caused by the unfaithfulness of the lady addressed as Lucasta, who married under the impression that he was dead." Mr. Edmund Gosse similarly remarks in *Ward's English Poets* (p. 182): "It being reported that he was killed, his betrothed married another man; and after wasting all his substance in the recklessness of despair, this darling of the graces died in extreme want, and in a cellar." The late Louise I. Guiney writes in an article in the *Catholic World* (XCV, 650): "Utter affliction and discouragement, due to the loss of his love, may have disabled him from profiting by such common measure of alleviation as fell to his colleagues."

I have been able to discover no evidence whatever for the idea here advanced. Of his early biographers neither Aubrey nor Winstanley throws any light on his love affair, and Wood, who is the chief source of our knowledge of Lovelace, distinctly says that he pined away, not because of disappointment in love, but because of poverty. "After the murther of King Charles I," writes Wood, "Lovelace was set at liberty, and having by that time consumed all his estate, grew very melancholy (which brought him at length into a consumption)," etc. Wood certainly did not attribute any of Lovelace's melancholy to the loss of Lucasta.

And yet I can think of nothing except an inattentive reading of Wood that could have occasioned these statements. In the preceding paragraph, Wood describes Lovelace's departure to France in 1646 to fight under Louis XIV, his being wounded at Dunkirk, and his return to England in 1648. Upon his return he was imprisoned, says Wood, in Lord Petre's house in Aldersgate Street, and there, to quote again, "he framed his poems for the press, entitled *Lucasta . . . etc . . .* The reason why he gave that title was because, some time before, he had made his amours to a gentlewoman of great beauty and fortune, named Lucy Sacheverel, whom he usually called Lux casta; but she upon a strong report that Lovelace was dead of his wound received at Dunkirk, soon after married." He lost his betrothed. He died of melancholy. What more natural than to connect the two facts? Very likely someone's careless reading of Wood is responsible for the tradition to which Mr. Masterman refers.

Certainly the contents of the poems to Lucasta could not have given rise to such a tradition. In none is there any hint of the loss of Lucasta, or of despair arising from this or any other cause; nor in the eight elegies on Lovelace written by his friends within two years of his death is there a single reference to Lucasta's faithlessness. We may, then, I think, free Lucy Sacheverel from any responsibility—even unintentional—for Lovelace's pitiful end.

But the main problem already proposed remains, namely, whether the Lucasta of the poems really does represent the woman to whom, according to Wood, Lovelace made his amours. Thomas Seccombe in his article on Lovelace in the *Dictionary of National Biography* remarks that Lucasta was possibly an imaginary personage, after whom, in accordance with the familiar practice of the time, he called his poems. My own examination of the poems to Lucasta has, in spite of Wood's statement, convinced me that this supposition is not merely possible, but in the highest degree probable. I do not believe that these poems can have been written about any woman whom Lovelace loved and sought in marriage.

The reasons that have led me to this conclusion are as follows:

1. With two or three exceptions the poems that concern Lucasta read like frigid exercises, not genuine love poems. It is of course a commonplace that much Elizabethan and Caroline love poetry is conventional; yet even beside the conventional poetry of that day, the love poems to Lucasta seem curiously lacking in feeling. They are almost completely devoid of ardor and tenderness, and are remarkable only for the utter lack of restraint shown in their conceits. One exception is "To Lucasta: Going beyond the Seas," which contains the fine passage:

Above the highest sphere we meet
Unseen, unknown, and greet as angels greet.

This poem, however, seems to be reminiscent of Donne's famous "Valediction Forbidding Mourning," a fact that makes at least questionable whether the apparent feeling as well as the matter may not be owing to Donne. A second exception is "To Lucasta: Going to the Wars." There is a distinct note of tenderness here; yet the primary devotion shown in this poem is of course to the king and to the king's cause. The third and last exception that I find is a poem entitled "Calling Lucasta from Her Retirement." In this poem Lovelace represents himself, seconded by trees, waters, air, and fire, as summoning her from the "dire monument" of her "black room." At the end he declares she comes, and that her coming makes him forget even the tragedy of civil war:

See! she obeys! By all obeyed thus
No   storms,   heats,   colds,   no   souls
    contentious,
Nor civil war is found; I mean; to us.

Most of the poem is labored and obscure, and leaves the reader with the suspicion that Lucasta may here be no more than a symbol for the clear light of truth. Is it not odd that Lovelace, even assuming he felt no tenderness, could not have simulated it more successfully in his love poems?

It may be objected that he was one of those men not gifted with the power of expressing their feelings in verse. Yet how genuinely his lines on Charles glow when in "To Althea: From Prison" he sings of the sweetness, mercy, and majesty of his king. So, too, in his little-known poem "To Lucasta: From Prison," there throbs a splendid devotion to Charles. In this poem Lovelace turns over in his mind the various things he might love, such as Peace, War, Religion, Parliament, Liberty, Property, etc. But he finds some impediment to his loving any of these. He ends his poem thus:

Since, then, none of these can be
Fit objects for my love and me;
What then remains but th' only spring
Of all our loves and joys, the King?
He who being the whole ball
Of day on earth, lends it to all;
When seeking to eclipse his right
Blinded we stand in our own light.
And now an universal mist
Of error is spread o'er each breast,
With such a fury edged as is
Not found in th' inwards of th' abyss.
Oh, from thy glorious starry wain
Dispense on me one sacred beam
To light me where I soon may see
How to serve you, and you trust me!

The "starry wain" mentioned in the last stanza is Charlemagne's Wain, or Wagon, the seven stars forming the Great Dipper, which during the seventeenth century was associated with the name of Charles I. The poem was pretty evidently written during Lovelace's second imprisonment, at a time when events were hurrying Charles toward his execution. It is addressed to Lucasta, but there is no real love in the poem for anyone but Charles. So also in certain of his occasional verses—especially in "The Grasshopper, To My Noble Friend, Mr. Charles Cotton," "The Lady A. L., My Asylum in a Great Extremity," and "To His Dear Brother, Colonel F. L."—a clear flame of affection warms and illumines the halting, obscure lines. Lovelace was certainly not a man devoid of feeling, nor incapable of conveying that feeling into his poetry, facts that make the frigidity of his love poetry all the more noteworthy.

2. The poems to Lucasta contain no individualizing descriptive touches such as the thought of an actual woman would naturally give rise to. We do not learn whether she was fair or dark, tall or short, responsive, reserved, or proud. We do not know where she lived, for I think we may quickly dismiss as of no significance the reference to Tunbridge in the poem "Lucasta, Taking the Waters at Tunbridge," on which Hazlitt comments as follows: "From this it might be conjenctured, though the ground for doing so would be very slight, that Lucasta was a native of Kent or of one of the adjoining shires;

but against this supposition we have to set the circumstance that elsewhere this lady is called a 'northern star.'" We do, to be sure, meet some conventional praise of her charms: her eyes rival the sun in brightness; and when she steps into a pool of water, it is purified by the touch of her body. But not one simple detail, such even as Herrick gives us of his probably imaginary Julia, or Carew of his enigmatical Celia, do we find in these poems. If ever a woman was less than a shadow, that woman is Lucasta.

3. The seventeen commendatory poems in English, Latin, and Greek, written for Lovelace's 1649 volume, and the eight elegies, collected and published in 1660 by his brother, Dudley Posthumus Lovelace, and reprinted by Hazlitt, furnish no indication that their authors supposed Lucasta had any identity. In one of the commendatory poems in particular, that of Colonel John Pinchbacke, the thought seems strongly to invite a reference to Lucasta, for the Celia (most likely of Carew) and the Sacharissa of Waller are both mentioned; but there is no word of Lucasta.

4. One poem among those in the first volume of *Lucasta* argues strongly against identifying Lucasta with any real woman. It has exactly the cynicism of Donne's early poems in which he insists on variety in love. The opening phrase, "The beauteous star to which I first did bow," must surely refer to Lucasta, who again and again, in playful allusion to her name, is addressed as one of the heavenly bodies. The most significant lines of this poem (entitled "A Paradox") are as follows:

> 'Tis true the beauteous star
> To which I first did bow
> Burnt quicker, brighter far
> Than that which leads me now; ...
> So from the glorious sun
> Who to his height hath got,
> With what delight we run
> To some black cave or grot! ...
> The god that constant keeps
> Unto his deities
> Is poor in joys, and sleeps
> Imprisoned in the skies.
> This knew the wisest, who
> From Juno stole, below
> To love a bear or cow.

Can it be that Lovelace would have written in this way about a real woman whom he had loved or courted?

5. In composing witty love verses with no particular woman in mind, he would have been doing what many other poets of the age did. Cowley, for example, admits that his volume of love poems called *The Mistress* was written merely because "poets are scarce thought freemen of their company without paying some duties...to Love." So Vaughan, alluding in his poems to Amoret, assures us in the Preface that "the fire at highest is but Platonic." Recent critics feel pretty confident that classic models rather than real women inspired most of Herrick's poems to his "many dainty mistresses." There is no reason why Lovelace also should not have wished to prove himself a freeman of the company of poets by paying some duties to Love.

Perhaps no one of the arguments I have adduced would by itself be convincing. Taken together they lead me to a conclusion not indeed at variance with what Wood actually says, but at variance with the natural implication of his statement. Lovelace may have courted Lucy Sacheverel. He may have loved her. He may even have named his book after her. But that he should have consistently identified her in his own mind with the person addressed as Lucasta in his poems seems to me, in view of the poems themselves, incredible.

Source: Alexander C. Judson, "Who Was Lucasta?," in *Modern Philology*, Vol. 23, No. 1, August 1925, pp. 77–82.

SOURCES

Anselment, Raymond A., *Loyalist Resolve: Patient Fortitude in the English Civil War?*, University of Delaware Press, 1988.

Corns, Thomas N., *The Cambridge Companion to English Poetry, Donne to Marvell*, Cambridge University Press, 1993.

Cousins, A. D., "Lucasta, Gratiana, and the Amatory Wit of Lovelace," in *Parergon*, No. 6A, 1988, pp. 97–104.

Davis, Walter R., "Richard Lovelace: Overview," in *Reference Guide to English Literature*, 2nd ed., edited by D. L. Kirkpatrick, St. James Press, 1991.

Guiney, Louise Imogen, "English Lyrics under the First Charles," in *Literature Criticism from 1400 to 1800*, Vol. 24; originally published in *Harper's New Monthly* magazine, Vol. 53, No. 453, May 1890, pp. 946–59.

Hager, Alan, *The Age of Milton: An Encyclopedia of Major 17th-Century British and American Authors*, Greenwood Press, 2004.

Hammond, Gerald, Introduction, in *Richard Lovelace: Selected Poems*, Carcanet Press, 1987, pp. 7–19.

Jones, George Fenwick, "Lov'd I Not Honour More: The Durability of a Literary Motif," in *Comparative Literature*, Vol. 11, No. 2, Spring 1959, pp. 131–43.

Lovelace, Richard, "To Lucasta, Going to the Wars," in *101 Best-Loved Poems*, edited by Philip Smith, Dover Publications, 2001, pp. 21–22.

Lowell, James Russell, "Lucasta: The Poems of Richard Lovelace, Esq.," in *Literature Criticism from 1400 to 1800*, Vol. 24; originally published in the *North American Review*, Vol. 99, No. 204, July 1864, pp. 310–17.

Moorman, F. W., "Cavalier Lyrists," in *Literature Criticism from 1400 to 1800*, Vol. 24; originally published in *The Cambridge History of English Literature: Cavalier and Puritan*, Vol. 7, edited by A. W. Ward and A. R. Waller, G. P. Putnam's Sons, 1911, pp. 1–29.

Nassaar, Christopher S., "Lovelace's 'To Lucasta, Going to the Wars,'" in the *Explicator*, Vol. 30, No. 3, Spring 1981, pp. 44–5.

Norbrook, David, *Writing the English Republic: Poetry, Rhetoric and Politics, 1627-1660*, Cambridge University Press, 1999.

Purkiss, Diane, *The English Civil War: Papists, Gentlewomen, Soldiers, and Witchfinders in the Birth of Modern Britain*, Basic Books, 2007.

Russell, Conrad, *The Causes of the English Civil War (Ford Lectures)*, Oxford University Press, 1990.

Seelig, Sharon Cadman, "Richard Lovelace," in *Dictionary of Literary Biography*, Vol. 131, *Seventeenth-Century British Nondramatic Poets, Third Series*, edited by M. Thomas Hester, Gale Research, 1993, pp. 123–33.

Tilmouth, Christopher, *Passion's Triumph over Reason: A History of the Moral Imagination from Spenser to Rochester*, Oxford University Press, 2007.

FURTHER READING

Fitzmaurice, James, Carol Barash, Eugene R. Cunnar, and Nancy A. Gutierrez, eds., *Major Women Writers of Seventeenth-Century England*, University of Michigan Press, revised edition, 1997.

> This volume provides an excellent introduction to seventeenth-century English writings specifically by women. The works of Aphra Behn, Katherine Philips, Ester Sowernam, Rachel Speght, Elizabeth Cary, Margaret Cavendish, Anne Finch, Aemilia Lanyer, and Mary Wroth are included.

Kohler, Sheila, and Peter Washington, eds., *Love Poems*, Everyman's Library, 1993.

> This anthology of love poems includes verse from ancient Greece to the contemporary United States. Poets featured include Sappho, John Donne (a contemporary of Lovelace's), W. H. Auden, Edna St. Vincent Millay, e. e. cummings, Dorothy Parker, Anna Akhmatova, Robert Graves, and W. B. Yeats.

Winn, James Anderson, ed., *The Poetry of War*, Cambridge University Press, 2008.

> War poems from the world's greatest poets throughout time are included in this comprehensive anthology. These addressed include the glory of war, as well as the horror of it. Other poems, like "To Lucasta, Going to the Wars," touch upon the importance of honor. Poets featured in the volume include Homer, and the lyrics of musician Bruce Springsteen are also covered.

Wiseman, Susan, *Conspiracy and Virtue: Women, Writing, and Politics in Seventeenth-Century England*, Oxford University Press, 2007.

> In his poem, Lovelace uses his love for Lucasta as a vehicle for a political statement and for placing himself within a political continuum. Wiseman's historical exploration does the same, as she seeks to ascertain women's role and place in the politics of seventeenth-century England.

Glossary of Literary Terms

A

Abstract: Used as a noun, the term refers to a short summary or outline of a longer work. As an adjective applied to writing or literary works, abstract refers to words or phrases that name things not knowable through the five senses.

Accent: The emphasis or stress placed on a syllable in poetry. Traditional poetry commonly uses patterns of accented and unaccented syllables (known as feet) that create distinct rhythms. Much modern poetry uses less formal arrangements that create a sense of freedom and spontaneity.

Aestheticism: A literary and artistic movement of the nineteenth century. Followers of the movement believed that art should not be mixed with social, political, or moral teaching. The statement "art for art's sake" is a good summary of aestheticism. The movement had its roots in France, but it gained widespread importance in England in the last half of the nineteenth century, where it helped change the Victorian practice of including moral lessons in literature.

Affective Fallacy: An error in judging the merits or faults of a work of literature. The "error" results from stressing the importance of the work's effect upon the reader—that is, how it makes a reader "feel" emotionally, what it does as a literary work—instead of stressing its inner qualities as a created object, or what it "is."

Age of Johnson: The period in English literature between 1750 and 1798, named after the most prominent literary figure of the age, Samuel Johnson. Works written during this time are noted for their emphasis on "sensibility," or emotional quality. These works formed a transition between the rational works of the Age of Reason, or Neoclassical period, and the emphasis on individual feelings and responses of the Romantic period.

Age of Reason: See *Neoclassicism*

Age of Sensibility: See *Age of Johnson*

Agrarians: A group of Southern American writers of the 1930s and 1940s who fostered an economic and cultural program for the South based on agriculture, in opposition to the industrial society of the North. The term can refer to any group that promotes the value of farm life and agricultural society.

Alexandrine Meter: See *Meter*

Allegory: A narrative technique in which characters representing things or abstract ideas are used to convey a message or teach a lesson. Allegory is typically used to teach moral, ethical, or religious lessons but is sometimes used for satiric or political purposes.

Alliteration: A poetic device where the first consonant sounds or any vowel sounds in words or syllables are repeated.

Allusion: A reference to a familiar literary or historical person or event, used to make an idea more easily understood.

Amerind Literature: The writing and oral traditions of Native Americans. Native American literature was originally passed on by word of mouth, so it consisted largely of stories and events that were easily memorized. Amerind prose is often rhythmic like poetry because it was recited to the beat of a ceremonial drum.

Analogy: A comparison of two things made to explain something unfamiliar through its similarities to something familiar, or to prove one point based on the acceptedness of another. Similes and metaphors are types of analogies.

Anapest: See *Foot*

Angry Young Men: A group of British writers of the 1950s whose work expressed bitterness and disillusionment with society. Common to their work is an anti-hero who rebels against a corrupt social order and strives for personal integrity.

Anthropomorphism: The presentation of animals or objects in human shape or with human characteristics. The term is derived from the Greek word for "human form."

Antimasque: See *Masque*

Antithesis: The antithesis of something is its direct opposite. In literature, the use of antithesis as a figure of speech results in two statements that show a contrast through the balancing of two opposite ideas. Technically, it is the second portion of the statement that is defined as the "antithesis"; the first portion is the "thesis."

Apocrypha: Writings tentatively attributed to an author but not proven or universally accepted to be their works. The term was originally applied to certain books of the Bible that were not considered inspired and so were not included in the "sacred canon."

Apollonian and Dionysian: The two impulses believed to guide authors of dramatic tragedy. The Apollonian impulse is named after Apollo, the Greek god of light and beauty and the symbol of intellectual order. The

Dionysian impulse is named after Dionysus, the Greek god of wine and the symbol of the unrestrained forces of nature. The Apollonian impulse is to create a rational, harmonious world, while the Dionysian is to express the irrational forces of personality.

Apostrophe: A statement, question, or request addressed to an inanimate object or concept or to a nonexistent or absent person.

Archetype: The word archetype is commonly used to describe an original pattern or model from which all other things of the same kind are made. This term was introduced to literary criticism from the psychology of Carl Jung. It expresses Jung's theory that behind every person's "unconscious," or repressed memories of the past, lies the "collective unconscious" of the human race: memories of the countless typical experiences of our ancestors. These memories are said to prompt illogical associations that trigger powerful emotions in the reader. Often, the emotional process is primitive, even primordial. Archetypes are the literary images that grow out of the "collective unconscious." They appear in literature as incidents and plots that repeat basic patterns of life. They may also appear as stereotyped characters.

Argument: The argument of a work is the author's subject matter or principal idea.

Art for Art's Sake: See *Aestheticism*

Assonance: The repetition of similar vowel sounds in poetry.

Audience: The people for whom a piece of literature is written. Authors usually write with a certain audience in mind, for example, children, members of a religious or ethnic group, or colleagues in a professional field. The term "audience" also applies to the people who gather to see or hear any performance, including plays, poetry readings, speeches, and concerts.

Automatic Writing: Writing carried out without a preconceived plan in an effort to capture every random thought. Authors who engage in automatic writing typically do not revise their work, preferring instead to preserve the revealed truth and beauty of spontaneous expression.

Avant-garde: A French term meaning "vanguard." It is used in literary criticism to describe new writing that rejects traditional approaches to literature in favor of innovations in style or content.

B

Ballad: A short poem that tells a simple story and has a repeated refrain. Ballads were originally intended to be sung. Early ballads, known as folk ballads, were passed down through generations, so their authors are often unknown. Later ballads composed by known authors are called literary ballads.

Baroque: A term used in literary criticism to describe literature that is complex or ornate in style or diction. Baroque works typically express tension, anxiety, and violent emotion. The term "Baroque Age" designates a period in Western European literature beginning in the late sixteenth century and ending about one hundred years later. Works of this period often mirror the qualities of works more generally associated with the label "baroque" and sometimes feature elaborate conceits.

Baroque Age: See *Baroque*

Baroque Period: See *Baroque*

Beat Generation: See *Beat Movement*

Beat Movement: A period featuring a group of American poets and novelists of the 1950s and 1960s—including Jack Kerouac, Allen Ginsberg, Gregory Corso, William S. Burroughs, and Lawrence Ferlinghetti—who rejected established social and literary values. Using such techniques as stream of consciousness writing and jazz-influenced free verse and focusing on unusual or abnormal states of mind—generated by religious ecstasy or the use of drugs—the Beat writers aimed to create works that were unconventional in both form and subject matter.

Beat Poets: See *Beat Movement*

Beats, The: See *Beat Movement*

Belles- lettres: A French term meaning "fine letters" or "beautiful writing." It is often used as a synonym for literature, typically referring to imaginative and artistic rather than scientific or expository writing. Current usage sometimes restricts the meaning to light or humorous writing and appreciative essays about literature.

Black Aesthetic Movement: A period of artistic and literary development among African Americans in the 1960s and early 1970s. This was the first major African-American artistic movement since the Harlem Renaissance and was closely paralleled by the civil rights and black power movements. The black aesthetic writers attempted to produce works of art that would be meaningful to the black masses. Key figures in black aesthetics included one of its founders, poet and playwright Amiri Baraka, formerly known as LeRoi Jones; poet and essayist Haki R. Madhubuti, formerly Don L. Lee; poet and playwright Sonia Sanchez; and dramatist Ed Bullins.

Black Arts Movement: See *Black Aesthetic Movement*

Black Comedy: See *Black Humor*

Black Humor: Writing that places grotesque elements side by side with humorous ones in an attempt to shock the reader, forcing him or her to laugh at the horrifying reality of a disordered world.

Black Mountain School: Black Mountain College and three of its instructors—Robert Creeley, Robert Duncan, and Charles Olson—were all influential in projective verse, so poets working in projective verse are now referred to as members of the Black Mountain school.

Blank Verse: Loosely, any unrhymed poetry, but more generally, unrhymed iambic pentameter verse (composed of lines of five two-syllable feet with the first syllable accented, the second unaccented). Blank verse has been used by poets since the Renaissance for its flexibility and its graceful, dignified tone.

Bloomsbury Group: A group of English writers, artists, and intellectuals who held informal artistic and philosophical discussions in Bloomsbury, a district of London, from around 1907 to the early 1930s. The Bloomsbury Group held no uniform philosophical beliefs but did commonly express an aversion to moral prudery and a desire for greater social tolerance.

Bon Mot: A French term meaning "good word." A *bon mot* is a witty remark or clever observation.

Breath Verse: See *Projective Verse*

Burlesque: Any literary work that uses exaggeration to make its subject appear ridiculous, either by treating a trivial subject with

profound seriousness or by treating a dignified subject frivolously. The word "burlesque"
may also be used as an adjective, as in "burlesque show," to mean "striptease act."

C

Cadence: The natural rhythm of language caused
by the alternation of accented and unaccented syllables. Much modern poetry—
notably free verse—deliberately manipulates
cadence to create complex rhythmic effects.

Caesura: A pause in a line of poetry, usually
occurring near the middle. It typically corresponds to a break in the natural rhythm or
sense of the line but is sometimes shifted to
create special meanings or rhythmic effects.

Canzone: A short Italian or Provencal lyric
poem, commonly about love and often set
to music. The *canzone* has no set form but
typically contains five or six stanzas made
up of seven to twenty lines of eleven syllables
each. A shorter, five- to ten-line "envoy," or
concluding stanza, completes the poem.

Carpe Diem: A Latin term meaning "seize the
day." This is a traditional theme of poetry,
especially lyrics. A *carpe diem* poem advises
the reader or the person it addresses to live for
today and enjoy the pleasures of the moment.

Catharsis: The release or purging of unwanted
emotions—specifically fear and pity—
brought about by exposure to art. The
term was first used by the Greek philosopher
Aristotle in his *Poetics* to refer to the desired
effect of tragedy on spectators.

Celtic Renaissance: A period of Irish literary and
cultural history at the end of the nineteenth
century. Followers of the movement aimed to
create a romantic vision of Celtic myth and
legend. The most significant works of the
Celtic Renaissance typically present a dreamy,
unreal world, usually in reaction against the
reality of contemporary problems.

Celtic Twilight: See *Celtic Renaissance*

Character: Broadly speaking, a person in a literary work. The actions of characters are what
constitute the plot of a story, novel, or
poem. There are numerous types of characters, ranging from simple, stereotypical figures to intricate, multifaceted ones. In the
techniques of anthropomorphism and personification, animals—and even places or
things—can assume aspects of character.

"Characterization" is the process by which
an author creates vivid, believable characters in a work of art. This may be done in a
variety of ways, including (1) direct description of the character by the narrator; (2) the
direct presentation of the speech, thoughts,
or actions of the character; and (3) the
responses of other characters to the character. The term "character" also refers to a
form originated by the ancient Greek writer
Theophrastus that later became popular in
the seventeenth and eighteenth centuries. It
is a short essay or sketch of a person who
prominently displays a specific attribute or
quality, such as miserliness or ambition.

Characterization: See *Character*

Classical: In its strictest definition in literary
criticism, classicism refers to works of ancient
Greek or Roman literature. The term may
also be used to describe a literary work of
recognized importance (a "classic") from any
time period or literature that exhibits the
traits of classicism.

Classicism: A term used in literary criticism to
describe critical doctrines that have their
roots in ancient Greek and Roman literature, philosophy, and art. Works associated
with classicism typically exhibit restraint on
the part of the author, unity of design and
purpose, clarity, simplicity, logical organization, and respect for tradition.

Colloquialism: A word, phrase, or form of pronunciation that is acceptable in casual conversation
but not in formal, written communication.
It is considered more acceptable than slang.

Complaint: A lyric poem, popular in the Renaissance, in which the speaker expresses sorrow
about his or her condition. Typically, the
speaker's sadness is caused by an unrespon-
sive lover, but some complaints cite other
sources of unhappiness, such as poverty or
fate.

Conceit: A clever and fanciful metaphor, usually
expressed through elaborate and extended
comparison, that presents a striking parallel
between two seemingly dissimilar things—
for example, elaborately comparing a beautiful woman to an object like a garden or
the sun. The conceit was a popular device
throughout the Elizabethan Age and Baroque Age and was the principal technique of

the seventeenth-century English metaphysical poets. This usage of the word conceit is unrelated to the best-known definition of conceit as an arrogant attitude or behavior.

Concrete: Concrete is the opposite of abstract, and refers to a thing that actually exists or a description that allows the reader to experience an object or concept with the senses.

Concrete Poetry: Poetry in which visual elements play a large part in the poetic effect. Punctuation marks, letters, or words are arranged on a page to form a visual design: a cross, for example, or a bumblebee.

Confessional Poetry: A form of poetry in which the poet reveals very personal, intimate, sometimes shocking information about himself or herself.

Connotation: The impression that a word gives beyond its defined meaning. Connotations may be universally understood or may be significant only to a certain group.

Consonance: Consonance occurs in poetry when words appearing at the ends of two or more verses have similar final consonant sounds but have final vowel sounds that differ, as with "stuff" and "off."

Convention: Any widely accepted literary device, style, or form.

Corrido: A Mexican ballad.

Couplet: Two lines of poetry with the same rhyme and meter, often expressing a complete and self-contained thought.

Criticism: The systematic study and evaluation of literary works, usually based on a specific method or set of principles. An important part of literary studies since ancient times, the practice of criticism has given rise to numerous theories, methods, and "schools," sometimes producing conflicting, even contradictory, interpretations of literature in general as well as of individual works. Even such basic issues as what constitutes a poem or a novel have been the subject of much criticism over the centuries.

D

Dactyl: See *Foot*

Dadaism: A protest movement in art and literature founded by Tristan Tzara in 1916. Followers of the movement expressed their outrage at the destruction brought about by

World War I by revolting against numerous forms of social convention. The Dadaists presented works marked by calculated madness and flamboyant nonsense. They stressed total freedom of expression, commonly through primitive displays of emotion and illogical, often senseless, poetry. The movement ended shortly after the war, when it was replaced by surrealism.

Decadent: See *Decadents*

Decadents: The followers of a nineteenth-century literary movement that had its beginnings in French aestheticism. Decadent literature displays a fascination with perverse and morbid states; a search for novelty and sensation—the "new thrill"; a preoccupation with mysticism; and a belief in the senselessness of human existence. The movement is closely associated with the doctrine Art for Art's Sake. The term "decadence" is sometimes used to denote a decline in the quality of art or literature following a period of greatness.

Deconstruction: A method of literary criticism developed by Jacques Derrida and characterized by multiple conflicting interpretations of a given work. Deconstructionists consider the impact of the language of a work and suggest that the true meaning of the work is not necessarily the meaning that the author intended.

Deduction: The process of reaching a conclusion through reasoning from general premises to a specific premise.

Denotation: The definition of a word, apart from the impressions or feelings it creates in the reader.

Diction: The selection and arrangement of words in a literary work. Either or both may vary depending on the desired effect. There are four general types of diction: "formal," used in scholarly or lofty writing; "informal," used in relaxed but educated conversation; "colloquial," used in everyday speech; and "slang," containing newly coined words and other terms not accepted in formal usage.

Didactic: A term used to describe works of literature that aim to teach some moral, religious, political, or practical lesson. Although didactic elements are often found in artistically pleasing works, the term "didactic" usually refers to literature in which the message is more important than the form. The term may also be used to criticize a work that the critic finds "overly didactic," that is, heavy-handed in its delivery of a lesson.

Dimeter: See *Meter*

Dionysian: See *Apollonian and Dionysian*

Discordia concours: A Latin phrase meaning "discord in harmony." The term was coined by the eighteenth-century English writer Samuel Johnson to describe "a combination of dissimilar images or discovery of occult resemblances in things apparently unlike." Johnson created the expression by reversing a phrase by the Latin poet Horace.

Dissonance: A combination of harsh or jarring sounds, especially in poetry. Although such combinations may be accidental, poets sometimes intentionally make them to achieve particular effects. Dissonance is also sometimes used to refer to close but not identical rhymes. When this is the case, the word functions as a synonym for consonance.

Double Entendre: A corruption of a French phrase meaning "double meaning." The term is used to indicate a word or phrase that is deliberately ambiguous, especially when one of the meanings is risque or improper.

Draft: Any preliminary version of a written work. An author may write dozens of drafts which are revised to form the final work, or he or she may write only one, with few or no revisions.

Dramatic Monologue: See *Monologue*

Dramatic Poetry: Any lyric work that employs elements of drama such as dialogue, conflict, or characterization, but excluding works that are intended for stage presentation.

Dream Allegory: See *Dream Vision*

Dream Vision: A literary convention, chiefly of the Middle Ages. In a dream vision a story is presented as a literal dream of the narrator. This device was commonly used to teach moral and religious lessons.

E

Eclogue: In classical literature, a poem featuring rural themes and structured as a dialogue among shepherds. Eclogues often took specific poetic forms, such as elegies or love poems. Some were written as the soliloquy

of a shepherd. In later centuries, "eclogue" came to refer to any poem that was in the pastoral tradition or that had a dialogue or monologue structure.

Edwardian: Describes cultural conventions identified with the period of the reign of Edward VII of England (1901-1910). Writers of the Edwardian Age typically displayed a strong reaction against the propriety and conservatism of the Victorian Age. Their work often exhibits distrust of authority in religion, politics, and art and expresses strong doubts about the soundness of conventional values.

Edwardian Age: See *Edwardian*

Electra Complex: A daughter's amorous obsession with her father.

Elegy: A lyric poem that laments the death of a person or the eventual death of all people. In a conventional elegy, set in a classical world, the poet and subject are spoken of as shepherds. In modern criticism, the word elegy is often used to refer to a poem that is melancholy or mournfully contemplative.

Elizabethan Age: A period of great economic growth, religious controversy, and nationalism closely associated with the reign of Elizabeth I of England (1558-1603). The Elizabethan Age is considered a part of the general renaissance—that is, the flowering of arts and literature—that took place in Europe during the fourteenth through sixteenth centuries. The era is considered the golden age of English literature. The most important dramas in English and a great deal of lyric poetry were produced during this period, and modern English criticism began around this time.

Empathy: A sense of shared experience, including emotional and physical feelings, with someone or something other than oneself. Empathy is often used to describe the response of a reader to a literary character.

English Sonnet: See *Sonnet*

Enjambment: The running over of the sense and structure of a line of verse or a couplet into the following verse or couplet.

Enlightenment, The: An eighteenth-century philosophical movement. It began in France but had a wide impact throughout Europe and America. Thinkers of the Enlightenment valued reason and believed that both the individual and society could achieve a state of perfection. Corresponding to this essentially humanist vision was a resistance to religious authority.

Epic: A long narrative poem about the adventures of a hero of great historic or legendary importance. The setting is vast and the action is often given cosmic significance through the intervention of supernatural forces such as gods, angels, or demons. Epics are typically written in a classical style of grand simplicity with elaborate metaphors and allusions that enhance the symbolic importance of a hero's adventures.

Epic Simile: See *Homeric Simile*

Epigram: A saying that makes the speaker's point quickly and concisely.

Epilogue: A concluding statement or section of a literary work. In dramas, particularly those of the seventeenth and eighteenth centuries, the epilogue is a closing speech, often in verse, delivered by an actor at the end of a play and spoken directly to the audience.

Epiphany: A sudden revelation of truth inspired by a seemingly trivial incident.

Epitaph: An inscription on a tomb or tombstone, or a verse written on the occasion of a person's death. Epitaphs may be serious or humorous.

Epithalamion: A song or poem written to honor and commemorate a marriage ceremony.

Epithalamium: See *Epithalamion*

Epithet: A word or phrase, often disparaging or abusive, that expresses a character trait of someone or something.

Erziehungsroman: See *Bildungsroman*

Essay: A prose composition with a focused subject of discussion. The term was coined by Michel de Montaigne to describe his 1580 collection of brief, informal reflections on himself and on various topics relating to human nature. An essay can also be a long, systematic discourse.

Existentialism: A predominantly twentieth-century philosophy concerned with the nature and perception of human existence. There are two major strains of existentialist thought: atheistic and Christian. Followers of atheistic existentialism believe that the individual is alone in a godless universe and that the basic human condition is one of suffering and loneliness. Nevertheless, because there are no fixed values, individuals can create their own characters—indeed, they can shape themselves—through the exercise of free will. The atheistic strain culminates in and is popularly associated with the works of Jean-Paul Sartre. The Christian existentialists, on the other hand, believe that only in God may people find freedom from life's anguish. The two strains hold certain beliefs in common: that existence cannot be fully understood or described through empirical effort; that anguish is a universal element of life; that individuals must bear responsibility for their actions; and that there is no common standard of behavior or perception for religious and ethical matters.

Expatriates: See *Expatriatism*

Expatriatism: The practice of leaving one's country to live for an extended period in another country.

Exposition: Writing intended to explain the nature of an idea, thing, or theme. Expository writing is often combined with description, narration, or argument. In dramatic writing, the exposition is the introductory material which presents the characters, setting, and tone of the play.

Expressionism: An indistinct literary term, originally used to describe an early twentieth-century school of German painting. The term applies to almost any mode of unconventional, highly subjective writing that distorts reality in some way.

Extended Monologue: See *Monologue*

F

Feet: See *Foot*

Feminine Rhyme: See *Rhyme*

Fiction: Any story that is the product of imagination rather than a documentation of fact. Characters and events in such narratives may be based in real life but their ultimate form and configuration is a creation of the author.

Figurative Language: A technique in writing in which the author temporarily interrupts the order, construction, or meaning of the writing for a particular effect. This interruption takes the form of one or more figures of speech such as hyperbole, irony, or simile. Figurative language is the opposite of literal language, in which every word is truthful, accurate, and free of exaggeration or embellishment.

Figures of Speech: Writing that differs from customary conventions for construction, meaning, order, or significance for the purpose of a special meaning or effect. There are two major types of figures of speech: rhetorical figures, which do not make changes in the meaning of the words, and tropes, which do.

Fin de siecle: A French term meaning "end of the century." The term is used to denote the last decade of the nineteenth century, a transition period when writers and other artists abandoned old conventions and looked for new techniques and objectives.

First Person: See *Point of View*

Folk Ballad: See *Ballad*

Folklore: Traditions and myths preserved in a culture or group of people. Typically, these are passed on by word of mouth in various forms—such as legends, songs, and proverbs—or preserved in customs and ceremonies. This term was first used by W. J. Thoms in 1846.

Folktale: A story originating in oral tradition. Folktales fall into a variety of categories, including legends, ghost stories, fairy tales, fables, and anecdotes based on historical figures and events.

Foot: The smallest unit of rhythm in a line of poetry. In English-language poetry, a foot is typically one accented syllable combined with one or two unaccented syllables.

Form: The pattern or construction of a work which identifies its genre and distinguishes it from other genres.

Formalism: In literary criticism, the belief that literature should follow prescribed rules of construction, such as those that govern the sonnet form.

Fourteener Meter: See *Meter*

Free Verse: Poetry that lacks regular metrical and rhyme patterns but that tries to capture the cadences of everyday speech. The form allows a poet to exploit a variety of rhythmical effects within a single poem.

Futurism: A flamboyant literary and artistic movement that developed in France, Italy, and Russia from 1908 through the 1920s. Futurist theater and poetry abandoned traditional literary forms. In their place, followers of the movement attempted to achieve total freedom of expression through bizarre imagery and deformed or newly invented words. The Futurists were self-consciously modern artists who attempted to incorporate the appearances and sounds of modern life into their work.

G

Genre: A category of literary work. In critical theory, genre may refer to both the content of a given work—tragedy, comedy, pastoral—and to its form, such as poetry, novel, or drama.

Genteel Tradition: A term coined by critic George Santayana to describe the literary practice of certain late nineteenth-century American writers, especially New Englanders. Followers of the Genteel Tradition emphasized conventionality in social, religious, moral, and literary standards.

Georgian Age: See *Georgian Poets*

Georgian Period: See *Georgian Poets*

Georgian Poets: A loose grouping of English poets during the years 1912-1922. The Georgians reacted against certain literary schools and practices, especially Victorian wordiness, turn-of-the-century aestheticism, and contemporary urban realism. In their place, the Georgians embraced the nineteenth-century poetic practices of William Wordsworth and the other Lake Poets.

Georgic: A poem about farming and the farmer's way of life, named from Virgil's *Georgics*.

Gilded Age: A period in American history during the 1870s characterized by political corruption and materialism. A number of important novels of social and political criticism were written during this time.

Gothic: See *Gothicism*

Gothicism: In literary criticism, works characterized by a taste for the medieval or morbidly attractive. A gothic novel prominently features elements of horror, the supernatural, gloom, and violence: clanking chains, terror, charnel houses, ghosts, medieval castles, and mysteriously slamming doors. The term "gothic novel" is also applied to novels that lack elements of the traditional Gothic setting but that create a similar atmosphere of terror or dread.

Graveyard School: A group of eighteenth-century English poets who wrote long, picturesque meditations on death. Their works were designed to cause the reader to ponder immortality.

Great Chain of Being: The belief that all things and creatures in nature are organized in a hierarchy from inanimate objects at the bottom to God at the top. This system of belief was popular in the seventeenth and eighteenth centuries.

Grotesque: In literary criticism, the subject matter of a work or a style of expression characterized by exaggeration, deformity, freakishness, and disorder. The grotesque often includes an element of comic absurdity.

H

Haiku: The shortest form of Japanese poetry, constructed in three lines of five, seven, and five syllables respectively. The message of a *haiku* poem usually centers on some aspect of spirituality and provokes an emotional response in the reader.

Half Rhyme: See *Consonance*

Harlem Renaissance: The Harlem Renaissance of the 1920s is generally considered the first significant movement of black writers and artists in the United States. During this period, new and established black writers published more fiction and poetry than ever before, the first influential black literary journals were established, and black authors and artists received their first widespread recognition and serious critical appraisal. Among the major writers associated with this period are Claude McKay, Jean Toomer, Countee Cullen, Langston Hughes, Arna Bontemps, Nella Larsen, and Zora Neale Hurston.

Hellenism: Imitation of ancient Greek thought or styles. Also, an approach to life that focuses on the growth and development of the intellect. "Hellenism" is sometimes used to refer to the belief that reason can be applied to examine all human experience.

Heptameter: See *Meter*

Hero/Heroine: The principal sympathetic character (male or female) in a literary work. Heroes and heroines typically exhibit admirable traits: idealism, courage, and integrity, for example.

Heroic Couplet: A rhyming couplet written in iambic pentameter (a verse with five iambic feet).

Heroic Line: The meter and length of a line of verse in epic or heroic poetry. This varies by language and time period.

Heroine: See *Hero/Heroine*

Hexameter: See *Meter*

Historical Criticism: The study of a work based on its impact on the world of the time period in which it was written.

Hokku: See *Haiku*

Holocaust: See *Holocaust Literature*

Holocaust Literature: Literature influenced by or written about the Holocaust of World War II. Such literature includes true stories of survival in concentration camps, escape, and life after the war, as well as fictional works and poetry.

Homeric Simile: An elaborate, detailed comparison written as a simile many lines in length.

Horatian Satire: See *Satire*

Humanism: A philosophy that places faith in the dignity of humankind and rejects the medieval perception of the individual as a weak, fallen creature. "Humanists" typically believe in the perfectibility of human nature and view reason and education as the means to that end.

Humors: Mentions of the humors refer to the ancient Greek theory that a person's health and personality were determined by the balance of four basic fluids in the body: blood, phlegm, yellow bile, and black bile. A dominance of any fluid would cause extremes in behavior. An excess of blood created a sanguine person who was joyful, aggressive, and passionate; a phlegmatic person was shy, fearful, and sluggish; too much yellow bile led to a choleric temperament characterized by impatience, anger, bitterness, and stubbornness; and excessive black bile created melancholy, a state of laziness, gluttony, and lack of motivation.

Humours: See *Humors*

Hyperbole: In literary criticism, deliberate exaggeration used to achieve an effect.

I

Iamb: See *Foot*

Idiom: A word construction or verbal expression closely associated with a given language.

Image: A concrete representation of an object or sensory experience. Typically, such a representation helps evoke the feelings associated with the object or experience itself. Images are either "literal" or "figurative." Literal images are especially concrete and involve little or no extension of the obvious meaning of the words used to express them. Figurative images do not follow the literal meaning of the words exactly. Images in literature are usually visual, but the term "image" can also refer to the representation of any sensory experience.

Imagery: The array of images in a literary work. Also, figurative language.

Imagism: An English and American poetry movement that flourished between 1908 and 1917. The Imagists used precise, clearly presented images in their works. They also used common, everyday speech and aimed for conciseness, concrete imagery, and the creation of new rhythms.

In medias res: A Latin term meaning "in the middle of things." It refers to the technique of beginning a story at its midpoint and then using various flashback devices to reveal previous action.

Induction: The process of reaching a conclusion by reasoning from specific premises to form a general premise. Also, an introductory portion of a work of literature, especially a play.

Intentional Fallacy: The belief that judgments of a literary work based solely on an author's stated or implied intentions are false and misleading. Critics who believe in the concept of the intentional fallacy typically argue that the work itself is sufficient matter for interpretation, even though they may concede that an author's statement of purpose can be useful.

Interior Monologue: A narrative technique in which characters' thoughts are revealed in a way that appears to be uncontrolled by the author. The interior monologue typically aims to reveal the inner self of a character. It portrays emotional experiences as they occur at both a conscious and unconscious level. Images are often used to represent sensations or emotions.

Internal Rhyme: Rhyme that occurs within a single line of verse.

Irish Literary Renaissance: A late nineteenth- and early twentieth-century movement in Irish literature. Members of the movement aimed to reduce the influence of British culture in Ireland and create an Irish national literature.

Irony: In literary criticism, the effect of language in which the intended meaning is the opposite of what is stated.

Italian Sonnet: See *Sonnet*

J

Jacobean Age: The period of the reign of James I of England (1603-1625). The early literature of this period reflected the worldview of the Elizabethan Age, but a darker, more cynical attitude steadily grew in the art and literature of the Jacobean Age. This was an important time for English drama and poetry.

Jargon: Language that is used or understood only by a select group of people. Jargon may refer to terminology used in a certain profession, such as computer jargon, or it may refer to any nonsensical language that is not understood by most people.

Journalism: Writing intended for publication in a newspaper or magazine, or for broadcast on a radio or television program featuring news, sports, entertainment, or other timely material.

K

Knickerbocker Group: A somewhat indistinct group of New York writers of the first half of the nineteenth century. Members of the group were linked only by location and a common theme: New York life.

Kunstlerroman: See *Bildungsroman*

L

Lais: See *Lay*

Lake Poets: See *Lake School*

Lake School: These poets all lived in the Lake District of England at the turn of the nineteenth century. As a group, they followed no single "school" of thought or literary practice, although their works were uniformly disparaged by the *Edinburgh Review*.

Lay: A song or simple narrative poem. The form originated in medieval France. Early French *lais* were often based on the Celtic legends and other tales sung by Breton minstrels—thus the name of the "Breton lay." In fourteenth-century England, the term "lay" was used to describe short narratives written in imitation of the Breton lays.

Leitmotiv: See *Motif*

Literal Language: An author uses literal language when he or she writes without exaggerating or embellishing the subject matter and without any tools of figurative language.

Literary Ballad: See *Ballad*

Literature: Literature is broadly defined as any written or spoken material, but the term most often refers to creative works.

Lost Generation: A term first used by Gertrude Stein to describe the post-World War I generation of American writers: men and women haunted by a sense of betrayal and emptiness brought about by the destructiveness of the war.

Lyric Poetry: A poem expressing the subjective feelings and personal emotions of the poet. Such poetry is melodic, since it was originally accompanied by a lyre in recitals. Most Western poetry in the twentieth century may be classified as lyrical.

M

Mannerism: Exaggerated, artificial adherence to a literary manner or style. Also, a popular style of the visual arts of late sixteenth-century Europe that was marked by elongation of the human form and by intentional spatial distortion. Literary works that are self-consciously high-toned and artistic are often said to be "mannered."

Masculine Rhyme: See *Rhyme*

Measure: The foot, verse, or time sequence used in a literary work, especially a poem. Measure is often used somewhat incorrectly as a synonym for meter.

Metaphor: A figure of speech that expresses an idea through the image of another object. Metaphors suggest the essence of the first object by identifying it with certain qualities of the second object.

Metaphysical Conceit: See *Conceit*

Metaphysical Poetry: The body of poetry produced by a group of seventeenth-century English writers called the "Metaphysical Poets." The group includes John Donne and Andrew Marvell. The Metaphysical Poets made use of everyday speech, intellectual analysis, and unique imagery. They aimed to portray the ordinary conflicts and contradictions of life. Their poems often took the form of an argument, and many of them emphasize physical and religious love as well as the fleeting nature of life. Elaborate conceits are typical in metaphysical poetry.

Metaphysical Poets: See *Metaphysical Poetry*

Meter: In literary criticism, the repetition of sound patterns that creates a rhythm in poetry. The patterns are based on the number of syllables and the presence and absence of accents. The unit of rhythm in a line is called a foot. Types of meter are classified according to the number of feet in a line. These are the standard English lines: Monometer, one foot; Dimeter, two feet; Trimeter, three feet; Tetrameter, four feet; Pentameter, five feet; Hexameter, six feet (also called the Alexandrine); Heptameter, seven feet (also called the "Fourteener" when the feet are iambic).

Modernism: Modern literary practices. Also, the principles of a literary school that lasted from roughly the beginning of the twentieth century until the end of World War II. Modernism is defined by its rejection of the literary conventions of the nineteenth century and by its opposition to conventional morality, taste, traditions, and economic values.

Monologue: A composition, written or oral, by a single individual. More specifically, a speech given by a single individual in a drama or other public entertainment. It has no set length, although it is usually several or more lines long.

Monometer: See *Meter*

Mood: The prevailing emotions of a work or of the author in his or her creation of the work. The mood of a work is not always what might be expected based on its subject matter.

Motif: A theme, character type, image, metaphor, or other verbal element that recurs throughout a single work of literature or occurs in a number of different works over a period of time.

Motiv: See *Motif*

Muckrakers: An early twentieth-century group of American writers. Typically, their works exposed the wrongdoings of big business and government in the United States.

Muses: Nine Greek mythological goddesses, the daughters of Zeus and Mnemosyne (Memory). Each muse patronized a specific area of the liberal arts and sciences. Calliope presided over epic poetry, Clio over history, Erato over love poetry, Euterpe over music or lyric poetry, Melpomene over tragedy, Polyhymnia over hymns to the gods, Terpsichore over dance, Thalia over comedy, and Urania over astronomy. Poets and writers traditionally made appeals to the Muses for inspiration in their work.

Myth: An anonymous tale emerging from the traditional beliefs of a culture or social unit. Myths use supernatural explanations for natural phenomena. They may also explain cosmic issues like creation and death. Collections of myths, known as mythologies, are common to all cultures and nations, but the best-known myths belong to the Norse, Roman, and Greek mythologies.

N

Narration: The telling of a series of events, real or invented. A narration may be either a simple narrative, in which the events are recounted chronologically, or a narrative with a plot, in which the account is given in a style reflecting the author's artistic concept of the story. Narration is sometimes used as a synonym for "storyline."

Narrative: A verse or prose accounting of an event or sequence of events, real or invented. The term is also used as an adjective in the sense "method of narration." For example, in literary criticism, the expression "narrative technique" usually refers to the way the author structures and presents his or her story.

Narrative Poetry: A nondramatic poem in which the author tells a story. Such poems may be of any length or level of complexity.

Narrator: The teller of a story. The narrator may be the author or a character in the story through whom the author speaks.

Naturalism: A literary movement of the late nineteenth and early twentieth centuries. The movement's major theorist, French novelist Emile Zola, envisioned a type of fiction that would examine human life with the objectivity of scientific inquiry. The Naturalists typically viewed human beings as either the products of "biological determinism," ruled by hereditary instincts and engaged in an endless struggle for survival, or as the products of "socioeconomic determinism," ruled by social and economic forces beyond their control. In their works, the Naturalists generally ignored the highest levels of society and focused on degradation: poverty, alcoholism, prostitution, insanity, and disease.

Negritude: A literary movement based on the concept of a shared cultural bond on the part of black Africans, wherever they may be in the world. It traces its origins to the former French colonies of Africa and the Caribbean. Negritude poets, novelists, and essayists generally stress four points in their writings: One, black alienation from traditional African culture can lead to feelings of inferiority. Two, European colonialism and Western education should be resisted. Three, black Africans should seek to affirm and define their own identity. Four, African culture can and should be reclaimed. Many Negritude writers also claim that blacks can make unique contributions to the world, based on a heightened appreciation of nature, rhythm, and human emotions—aspects of life they say are not so highly valued in the materialistic and rationalistic West.

Negro Renaissance: See *Harlem Renaissance*

Neoclassical Period: See *Neoclassicism*

Neoclassicism: In literary criticism, this term refers to the revival of the attitudes and styles of expression of classical literature. It is generally used to describe a period in European history beginning in the late seventeenth century and lasting until about 1800. In its purest form, Neoclassicism marked a return to order, proportion, restraint, logic, accuracy, and decorum. In England, where Neoclassicism perhaps was most popular, it reflected the influence of seventeenth-century French writers, especially dramatists. Neoclassical writers typically reacted against the intensity and enthusiasm of the Renaissance period. They wrote works that appealed to the intellect, using elevated language and classical literary forms such as satire and the ode. Neoclassical works were often governed by the classical goal of instruction.

Neoclassicists: See *Neoclassicism*

New Criticism: A movement in literary criticism, dating from the late 1920s, that stressed close textual analysis in the interpretation of works of literature. The New Critics saw little merit in historical and biographical analysis. Rather, they aimed to examine the text alone, free from the question of how external events—biographical or otherwise—may have helped shape it.

New Journalism: A type of writing in which the journalist presents factual information in a form usually used in fiction. New journalism emphasizes description, narration, and character development to bring readers closer to the human element of the story, and is often used in personality profiles and in-depth feature articles. It is not compatible with "straight" or "hard" newswriting, which is generally composed in a brief, fact-based style.

New Journalists: See *New Journalism*

New Negro Movement: See *Harlem Renaissance*

Noble Savage: The idea that primitive man is noble and good but becomes evil and corrupted as he becomes civilized. The concept of the noble savage originated in the Renaissance period but is more closely identified with such later writers as Jean-Jacques Rousseau and Aphra Behn.

O

Objective Correlative: An outward set of objects, a situation, or a chain of events corresponding to an inward experience and evoking this experience in the reader. The term frequently appears in modern criticism in discussions of authors' intended effects on the emotional responses of readers.

Objectivity: A quality in writing characterized by the absence of the author's opinion or feeling about the subject matter. Objectivity is an important factor in criticism.

Occasional Verse: poetry written on the occasion of a significant historical or personal event. *Vers de societe* is sometimes called occasional verse although it is of a less serious nature.

Octave: A poem or stanza composed of eight lines. The term octave most often represents the first eight lines of a Petrarchan sonnet.

Ode: Name given to an extended lyric poem characterized by exalted emotion and dignified style. An ode usually concerns a single, serious theme. Most odes, but not all, are addressed to an object or individual. Odes are distinguished from other lyric poetic forms by their complex rhythmic and stanzaic patterns.

Oedipus Complex: A son's amorous obsession with his mother. The phrase is derived from the story of the ancient Theban hero Oedipus, who unknowingly killed his father and married his mother.

Omniscience: See *Point of View*

Onomatopoeia: The use of words whose sounds express or suggest their meaning. In its simplest sense, onomatopoeia may be represented by words that mimic the sounds they denote such as "hiss" or "meow." At a more subtle level, the pattern and rhythm of sounds and rhymes of a line or poem may be onomatopoeic.

Oral Tradition: See *Oral Transmission*

Oral Transmission: A process by which songs, ballads, folklore, and other material are transmitted by word of mouth. The tradition of oral transmission predates the written record systems of literate society. Oral transmission preserves material sometimes over generations, although often with variations. Memory plays a large part in the recitation and preservation of orally transmitted material.

Ottava Rima: An eight-line stanza of poetry composed in iambic pentameter (a five-foot line in which each foot consists of an unaccented syllable followed by an accented syllable), following the abababcc rhyme scheme.

Oxymoron: A phrase combining two contradictory terms. Oxymorons may be intentional or unintentional.

P

Pantheism: The idea that all things are both a manifestation or revelation of God and a part of God at the same time. Pantheism was a common attitude in the early societies of Egypt, India, and Greece—the term derives from the Greek *pan* meaning "all" and *theos* meaning "deity." It later became a significant part of the Christian faith.

Parable: A story intended to teach a moral lesson or answer an ethical question.

Paradox: A statement that appears illogical or contradictory at first, but may actually point to an underlying truth.

Parallelism: A method of comparison of two ideas in which each is developed in the same grammatical structure.

Parnassianism: A mid nineteenth-century movement in French literature. Followers of the movement stressed adherence to well-defined artistic forms as a reaction against the often chaotic expression of the artist's ego that dominated the work of the Romantics. The Parnassians also rejected the moral, ethical, and social themes exhibited in the works of French Romantics such as Victor Hugo. The aesthetic doctrines of the Parnassians strongly influenced the later symbolist and decadent movements.

Parody: In literary criticism, this term refers to an imitation of a serious literary work or the signature style of a particular author in a ridiculous manner. A typical parody adopts the style of the original and applies it to an inappropriate subject for humorous effect. Parody is a form of satire and could be considered the literary equivalent of a caricature or cartoon.

Pastoral: A term derived from the Latin word "pastor," meaning shepherd. A pastoral is a literary composition on a rural theme. The conventions of the pastoral were originated by the third-century Greek poet Theocritus, who wrote about the experiences, love affairs, and pastimes of Sicilian shepherds. In a pastoral, characters and language of a courtly nature are often placed in a simple setting. The term pastoral is also used to classify dramas, elegies, and lyrics that exhibit the use of country settings and shepherd characters.

Pathetic Fallacy: A term coined by English critic John Ruskin to identify writing that falsely endows nonhuman things with human intentions and feelings, such as "angry clouds" and "sad trees."

Pen Name: See *Pseudonym*

Pentameter: See *Meter*

Persona: A Latin term meaning "mask." *Personae* are the characters in a fictional work of literature. The *persona* generally functions as a mask through which the author tells a story in a voice other than his or her own. A *persona* is usually either a character in a story who acts as a narrator or an "implied author," a voice created by the author to act as the narrator for himself or herself.

Personae: See *Persona*

Personal Point of View: See *Point of View*

Personification: A figure of speech that gives human qualities to abstract ideas, animals, and inanimate objects.

Petrarchan Sonnet: See *Sonnet*

Phenomenology: A method of literary criticism based on the belief that things have no existence outside of human consciousness or awareness. Proponents of this theory believe that art is a process that takes place in the mind of the observer as he or she contemplates an object rather than a quality of the object itself.

Plagiarism: Claiming another person's written material as one's own. Plagiarism can take the form of direct, word-for-word copying or the theft of the substance or idea of the work.

Platonic Criticism: A form of criticism that stresses an artistic work's usefulness as an agent of social engineering rather than any quality or value of the work itself.

Platonism: The embracing of the doctrines of the philosopher Plato, popular among the poets of the Renaissance and the Romantic period. Platonism is more flexible than Aristotelian Criticism and places more emphasis on the supernatural and unknown aspects of life.

Plot: In literary criticism, this term refers to the pattern of events in a narrative or drama. In its simplest sense, the plot guides the author in composing the work and helps the reader follow the work. Typically, plots exhibit causality and unity and have a beginning, a middle, and an end. Sometimes, however, a plot may consist of a series of disconnected events, in which case it is known as an "episodic plot."

Poem: In its broadest sense, a composition utilizing rhyme, meter, concrete detail, and expressive language to create a literary experience with emotional and aesthetic appeal.

Poet: An author who writes poetry or verse. The term is also used to refer to an artist or writer who has an exceptional gift for expression, imagination, and energy in the making of art in any form.

Poete maudit: A term derived from Paul Verlaine's *Les poetes maudits* (*The Accursed Poets*), a collection of essays on the French symbolist writers Stephane Mallarme, Arthur Rimbaud, and Tristan Corbiere. In the sense intended by Verlaine, the poet is "accursed" for choosing to explore extremes of human experience outside of middle-class society.

Poetic Fallacy: See *Pathetic Fallacy*

Poetic Justice: An outcome in a literary work, not necessarily a poem, in which the good are rewarded and the evil are punished, especially in ways that particularly fit their virtues or crimes.

Poetic License: Distortions of fact and literary convention made by a writer—not always a poet—for the sake of the effect gained. Poetic license is closely related to the concept of "artistic freedom."

Poetics: This term has two closely related meanings. It denotes (1) an aesthetic theory in literary criticism about the essence of poetry or (2) rules prescribing the proper methods, content, style, or diction of poetry. The term poetics may also refer to theories about literature in general, not just poetry.

Poetry: In its broadest sense, writing that aims to present ideas and evoke an emotional experience in the reader through the use of meter, imagery, connotative and concrete words, and a carefully constructed structure based on rhythmic patterns. Poetry typically relies on words and expressions that have several layers of meaning. It also makes use of the effects of regular rhythm on the ear and may make a strong appeal to the senses through the use of imagery.

Point of View: The narrative perspective from which a literary work is presented to the reader. There are four traditional points of view. The "third person omniscient" gives the reader a "godlike" perspective, unrestricted by time or place, from which to see actions and look into the minds of characters. This allows the author to comment openly on characters and events in the work. The "third person" point of view presents the events of the story from outside of any single character's perception, much like the omniscient point of view, but the reader must understand the action as it takes place and without any special insight into characters' minds or motivations. The "first person" or "personal" point of view relates events as they are perceived by a single character. The main character "tells" the story and may offer opinions about the action and characters which differ from those of the author. Much less common than omniscient, third person, and first person is the "second person" point of view, wherein the author tells the story as if it is happening to the reader.

Polemic: A work in which the author takes a stand on a controversial subject, such as abortion or religion. Such works are often extremely argumentative or provocative.

Pornography: Writing intended to provoke feelings of lust in the reader. Such works are often condemned by critics and teachers, but those which can be shown to have literary value are viewed less harshly.

Post-Aesthetic Movement: An artistic response made by African Americans to the black aesthetic movement of the 1960s and early '70s. Writers since that time have adopted a somewhat different tone in their work, with less emphasis placed on the disparity between black and white in the United States. In the words of post-aesthetic authors such as Toni Morrison, John Edgar Wideman, and Kristin Hunter, African Americans are portrayed as looking inward for answers to their own questions, rather than always looking to the outside world.

Postmodernism: Writing from the 1960s forward characterized by experimentation and continuing to apply some of the fundamentals of modernism, which included existentialism and alienation. Postmodernists have gone a step further in the rejection of tradition begun with the modernists by also rejecting traditional forms, preferring the anti-novel over the novel and the anti-hero over the hero.

Pre-Raphaelites: A circle of writers and artists in mid nineteenth-century England. Valuing the pre-Renaissance artistic qualities of religious symbolism, lavish pictorialism, and natural sensuousness, the Pre-Raphaelites cultivated a sense of mystery and melancholy that influenced later writers associated with the Symbolist and Decadent movements.

Primitivism: The belief that primitive peoples were nobler and less flawed than civilized peoples because they had not been subjected to the tainting influence of society.

Projective Verse: A form of free verse in which the poet's breathing pattern determines the lines of the poem. Poets who advocate projective verse are against all formal structures in writing, including meter and form.

Prologue: An introductory section of a literary work. It often contains information establishing the situation of the characters or presents information about the setting, time period, or action. In drama, the prologue is spoken by a chorus or by one of the principal characters.

Prose: A literary medium that attempts to mirror the language of everyday speech. It is distinguished from poetry by its use of unmetered, unrhymed language consisting of logically related sentences. Prose is usually grouped into paragraphs that form a cohesive whole such as an essay or a novel.

Prosopopoeia: See *Personification*

Protagonist: The central character of a story who serves as a focus for its themes and incidents and as the principal rationale for its development. The protagonist is sometimes referred to in discussions of modern literature as the hero or anti-hero.

Proverb: A brief, sage saying that expresses a truth about life in a striking manner.

Pseudonym: A name assumed by a writer, most often intended to prevent his or her identification as the author of a work. Two or more authors may work together under one pseudonym, or an author may use a different name for each genre he or she publishes in. Some publishing companies maintain "house pseudonyms," under which any number of authors may write installments in a series. Some authors also choose a pseudonym over their real names the way an actor may use a stage name.

Pun: A play on words that have similar sounds but different meanings.

Pure Poetry: poetry written without instructional intent or moral purpose that aims only to please a reader by its imagery or musical flow. The term pure poetry is used as the antonym of the term "didacticism."

Q

Quatrain: A four-line stanza of a poem or an entire poem consisting of four lines.

R

Realism: A nineteenth-century European literary movement that sought to portray familiar characters, situations, and settings in a realistic manner. This was done primarily by using an objective narrative point of view and through the buildup of accurate detail. The standard for success of any realistic work depends on how faithfully it transfers common experience into fictional forms. The realistic method may be altered or extended, as in stream of consciousness writing, to record highly subjective experience.

Refrain: A phrase repeated at intervals throughout a poem. A refrain may appear at the end of each stanza or at less regular intervals. It may be altered slightly at each appearance.

Renaissance: The period in European history that marked the end of the Middle Ages. It began in Italy in the late fourteenth century. In broad terms, it is usually seen as spanning the fourteenth, fifteenth, and sixteenth centuries, although it did not reach Great Britain, for example, until the 1480s or so. The Renaissance saw an awakening in almost every sphere of human activity, especially science, philosophy, and the arts. The period is best defined by the emergence of a general philosophy that emphasized the importance of the intellect, the individual, and world affairs. It contrasts strongly with the medieval worldview, characterized by the dominant concerns of faith, the social collective, and spiritual salvation.

Repartee: Conversation featuring snappy retorts and witticisms.

Restoration: See *Restoration Age*

Restoration Age: A period in English literature beginning with the crowning of Charles II in 1660 and running to about 1700. The era, which was characterized by a reaction against Puritanism, was the first great age of the comedy of manners. The finest literature of the era is typically witty and urbane, and often lewd.

Rhetoric: In literary criticism, this term denotes the art of ethical persuasion. In its strictest sense, rhetoric adheres to various principles developed since classical times for arranging facts and ideas in a clear, persuasive, appealing manner. The term is also used to refer to effective prose in general and theories of or methods for composing effective prose.

Rhetorical Question: A question intended to provoke thought, but not an expressed answer, in the reader. It is most commonly used in oratory and other persuasive genres.

Rhyme: When used as a noun in literary criticism, this term generally refers to a poem in which words sound identical or very similar and appear in parallel positions in two or more lines. Rhymes are classified into different types according to where they fall in a line or stanza or according to the degree of similarity they exhibit in their spellings and sounds. Some major types of rhyme are "masculine" rhyme, "feminine" rhyme, and "triple" rhyme. In a masculine rhyme, the rhyming sound falls in a single accented syllable, as with "heat" and "eat." Feminine rhyme is a rhyme of two syllables, one stressed and one unstressed, as with "merry" and "tarry." Triple rhyme matches the sound of the accented syllable and the two unaccented syllables that follow: "narrative" and "declarative."

Rhyme Royal: A stanza of seven lines composed in iambic pentameter and rhymed *ababbcc*. The name is said to be a tribute to King James I of Scotland, who made much use of the form in his poetry.

Rhyme Scheme: See *Rhyme*

Rhythm: A regular pattern of sound, time intervals, or events occurring in writing, most often and most discernably in poetry. Regular, reliable rhythm is known to be soothing to humans, while interrupted, unpredictable, or rapidly changing rhythm is disturbing. These effects are known to authors, who use them to produce a desired reaction in the reader.

Rococo: A style of European architecture that flourished in the eighteenth century, especially in France. The most notable features of *rococo* are its extensive use of ornamentation and its themes of lightness, gaiety, and intimacy. In literary criticism, the term is often used disparagingly to refer to a decadent or over-ornamental style.

Romance: A broad term, usually denoting a narrative with exotic, exaggerated, often idealized characters, scenes, and themes.

Romantic Age: See *Romanticism*

Romanticism: This term has two widely accepted meanings. In historical criticism, it refers to a European intellectual and artistic movement of the late eighteenth and early nineteenth centuries that sought greater freedom of personal expression than that allowed by the strict rules of literary form and logic of the eighteenth-century neoclassicists. The Romantics preferred emotional and imaginative expression to rational analysis. They considered the individual to be at the center of all experience and so placed him or her at the center of their art. The Romantics believed that the creative imagination reveals nobler truths—unique feelings and attitudes—than those that could be discovered by logic or by scientific examination. Both the natural world and the state of childhood were important sources for revelations of "eternal truths." "Romanticism" is also used as a general term to refer to a type of sensibility found in all periods of literary history and usually considered to be in opposition to the principles of classicism. In this sense, Romanticism signifies any work or philosophy in which the exotic or dreamlike figure strongly, or that is devoted to individualistic expression, self-analysis, or a pursuit of a higher realm of knowledge than can be discovered by human reason.

Romantics: See *Romanticism*

Russian Symbolism: A Russian poetic movement, derived from French symbolism, that flourished between 1894 and 1910. While some Russian Symbolists continued in the French tradition, stressing aestheticism and the importance of suggestion above didactic intent, others saw their craft as a form of mystical worship, and themselves as mediators between the supernatural and the mundane.

S

Satire: A work that uses ridicule, humor, and wit to criticize and provoke change in human nature and institutions. There are two major types of satire: "formal" or "direct" satire speaks directly to the reader or to a character in the work; "indirect" satire relies upon the ridiculous behavior of its characters to make its point. Formal satire is further divided into two manners: the "Horatian," which ridicules gently, and the "Juvenalian," which derides its subjects harshly and bitterly.

Scansion: The analysis or "scanning" of a poem to determine its meter and often its rhyme scheme. The most common system of scansion uses accents (slanted lines drawn above syllables) to show stressed syllables, breves (curved lines drawn above syllables) to show unstressed syllables, and vertical lines to separate each foot.

Second Person: See *Point of View*

Semiotics: The study of how literary forms and conventions affect the meaning of language.

Sestet: Any six-line poem or stanza.

Setting: The time, place, and culture in which the action of a narrative takes place. The elements of setting may include geographic location, characters' physical and mental environments, prevailing cultural attitudes, or the historical time in which the action takes place.

Shakespearean Sonnet: See *Sonnet*

Signifying Monkey: A popular trickster figure in black folklore, with hundreds of tales about this character documented since the 19th century.

Simile: A comparison, usually using "like" or "as," of two essentially dissimilar things, as in "coffee as cold as ice" or "He sounded like a broken record."

Slang: A type of informal verbal communication that is generally unacceptable for formal writing. Slang words and phrases are often colorful exaggerations used to emphasize the speaker's point; they may also be shortened versions of an often-used word or phrase.

Slant Rhyme: See *Consonance*

Slave Narrative: Autobiographical accounts of American slave life as told by escaped slaves. These works first appeared during the abolition movement of the 1830s through the 1850s.

Social Realism: See *Socialist Realism*

Socialist Realism: The Socialist Realism school of literary theory was proposed by Maxim Gorky and established as a dogma by the first Soviet Congress of Writers. It demanded adherence to a communist worldview in works of literature. Its doctrines required an objective viewpoint comprehensible to the working classes and themes of social struggle featuring strong proletarian heroes.

Soliloquy: A monologue in a drama used to give the audience information and to develop the speaker's character. It is typically a projection of the speaker's innermost thoughts. Usually delivered while the speaker is alone on stage, a soliloquy is intended to present an illusion of unspoken reflection.

Sonnet: A fourteen-line poem, usually composed in iambic pentameter, employing one of several rhyme schemes. There are three major types of sonnets, upon which all other variations of the form are based: the "Petrarchan" or "Italian" sonnet, the "Shakespearean" or "English" sonnet, and the "Spenserian" sonnet. A Petrarchan sonnet consists of an octave rhymed *abbaabba* and a "sestet" rhymed either *cdecde, cdccdc,* or *cdedce.* The octave poses a question or problem, relates a narrative, or puts forth a proposition; the sestet presents a solution to the problem, comments upon the narrative, or applies the proposition put forth in the octave. The Shakespearean sonnet is divided into three quatrains and a couplet rhymed *abab cdcd efef gg.* The couplet provides an epigrammatic comment on the narrative or problem put forth in the quatrains. The Spenserian sonnet uses three quatrains and a couplet like the Shakespearean, but links their three rhyme schemes in this way: *abab bcbc cdcd ee.* The Spenserian sonnet develops its theme in two parts like the Petrarchan, its final six lines resolving a problem, analyzing a narrative, or applying a proposition put forth in its first eight lines.

Spenserian Sonnet: See *Sonnet*

Spenserian Stanza: A nine-line stanza having eight verses in iambic pentameter, its ninth verse in iambic hexameter, and the rhyme scheme ababbcbcc.

Spondee: In poetry meter, a foot consisting of two long or stressed syllables occurring together. This form is quite rare in English verse, and is usually composed of two monosyllabic words.

Sprung Rhythm: Versification using a specific number of accented syllables per line but disregarding the number of unaccented syllables that fall in each line, producing an irregular rhythm in the poem.

Stanza: A subdivision of a poem consisting of lines grouped together, often in recurring patterns of rhyme, line length, and meter.

Stanzas may also serve as units of thought in a poem much like paragraphs in prose.

Stereotype: A stereotype was originally the name for a duplication made during the printing process; this led to its modern definition as a person or thing that is (or is assumed to be) the same as all others of its type.

Stream of Consciousness: A narrative technique for rendering the inward experience of a character. This technique is designed to give the impression of an ever-changing series of thoughts, emotions, images, and memories in the spontaneous and seemingly illogical order that they occur in life.

Structuralism: A twentieth-century movement in literary criticism that examines how literary texts arrive at their meanings, rather than the meanings themselves. There are two major types of structuralist analysis: one examines the way patterns of linguistic structures unify a specific text and emphasize certain elements of that text, and the other interprets the way literary forms and conventions affect the meaning of language itself.

Structure: The form taken by a piece of literature. The structure may be made obvious for ease of understanding, as in nonfiction works, or may obscured for artistic purposes, as in some poetry or seemingly "unstructured" prose.

Sturm und Drang: A German term meaning "storm and stress." It refers to a German literary movement of the 1770s and 1780s that reacted against the order and rationalism of the enlightenment, focusing instead on the intense experience of extraordinary individuals.

Style: A writer's distinctive manner of arranging words to suit his or her ideas and purpose in writing. The unique imprint of the author's personality upon his or her writing, style is the product of an author's way of arranging ideas and his or her use of diction, different sentence structures, rhythm, figures of speech, rhetorical principles, and other elements of composition.

Subject: The person, event, or theme at the center of a work of literature. A work may have one or more subjects of each type, with shorter works tending to have fewer and longer works tending to have more.

Subjectivity: Writing that expresses the author's personal feelings about his subject, and which may or may not include factual information about the subject.

Surrealism: A term introduced to criticism by Guillaume Apollinaire and later adopted by Andre Breton. It refers to a French literary and artistic movement founded in the 1920s. The Surrealists sought to express unconscious thoughts and feelings in their works. The best-known technique used for achieving this aim was automatic writing—transcriptions of spontaneous outpourings from the unconscious. The Surrealists proposed to unify the contrary levels of conscious and unconscious, dream and reality, objectivity and subjectivity into a new level of "super-realism."

Suspense: A literary device in which the author maintains the audience's attention through the buildup of events, the outcome of which will soon be revealed.

Syllogism: A method of presenting a logical argument. In its most basic form, the syllogism consists of a major premise, a minor premise, and a conclusion.

Symbol: Something that suggests or stands for something else without losing its original identity. In literature, symbols combine their literal meaning with the suggestion of an abstract concept. Literary symbols are of two types: those that carry complex associations of meaning no matter what their contexts, and those that derive their suggestive meaning from their functions in specific literary works.

Symbolism: This term has two widely accepted meanings. In historical criticism, it denotes an early modernist literary movement initiated in France during the nineteenth century that reacted against the prevailing standards of realism. Writers in this movement aimed to evoke, indirectly and symbolically, an order of being beyond the material world of the five senses. Poetic expression of personal emotion figured strongly in the movement, typically by means of a private set of symbols uniquely identifiable with the individual poet. The principal aim of the Symbolists was to express in words the highly complex feelings that grew out of everyday contact with the world. In a broader sense, the term "symbolism" refers to the use of one object to represent another.

Symbolist: See *Symbolism*

Symbolist Movement: See *Symbolism*

Sympathetic Fallacy: See *Affective Fallacy*

T

Tanka: A form of Japanese poetry similar to *haiku*. A *tanka* is five lines long, with the lines containing five, seven, five, seven, and seven syllables respectively.

Terza Rima: A three-line stanza form in poetry in which the rhymes are made on the last word of each line in the following manner: the first and third lines of the first stanza, then the second line of the first stanza and the first and third lines of the second stanza, and so on with the middle line of any stanza rhyming with the first and third lines of the following stanza.

Tetrameter: See *Meter*

Textual Criticism: A branch of literary criticism that seeks to establish the authoritative text of a literary work. Textual critics typically compare all known manuscripts or printings of a single work in order to assess the meanings of differences and revisions. This procedure allows them to arrive at a definitive version that (supposedly) corresponds to the author's original intention.

Theme: The main point of a work of literature. The term is used interchangeably with thesis.

Thesis: A thesis is both an essay and the point argued in the essay. Thesis novels and thesis plays share the quality of containing a thesis which is supported through the action of the story.

Third Person: See *Point of View*

Tone: The author's attitude toward his or her audience may be deduced from the tone of the work. A formal tone may create distance or convey politeness, while an informal tone may encourage a friendly, intimate, or intrusive feeling in the reader. The author's attitude toward his or her subject matter may also be deduced from the tone of the words he or she uses in discussing it.

Tragedy: A drama in prose or poetry about a noble, courageous hero of excellent character who, because of some tragic character flaw or *hamartia*, brings ruin upon him- or herself. Tragedy treats its subjects in a dignified and serious manner, using poetic language to help evoke pity and fear and bring about catharsis, a purging of these emotions. The tragic form was practiced extensively by the ancient Greeks. In the Middle Ages, when classical works were virtually unknown, tragedy came to denote any works about the fall of persons from exalted to low conditions due to any reason: fate, vice, weakness, etc. According to the classical definition of tragedy, such works present the "pathetic"—that which evokes pity—rather than the tragic. The classical form of tragedy was revived in the sixteenth century; it flourished especially on the Elizabethan stage. In modern times, dramatists have attempted to adapt the form to the needs of modern society by drawing their heroes from the ranks of ordinary men and women and defining the nobility of these heroes in terms of spirit rather than exalted social standing.

Tragic Flaw: In a tragedy, the quality within the hero or heroine which leads to his or her downfall.

Transcendentalism: An American philosophical and religious movement, based in New England from around 1835 until the Civil War. Transcendentalism was a form of American romanticism that had its roots abroad in the works of Thomas Carlyle, Samuel Coleridge, and Johann Wolfgang von Goethe. The Transcendentalists stressed the importance of intuition and subjective experience in communication with God. They rejected religious dogma and texts in favor of mysticism and scientific naturalism. They pursued truths that lie beyond the "colorless" realms perceived by reason and the senses and were active social reformers in public education, women's rights, and the abolition of slavery.

Trickster: A character or figure common in Native American and African literature who uses his ingenuity to defeat enemies and escape difficult situations. Tricksters are most often animals, such as the spider, hare, or coyote, although they may take the form of humans as well.

Trimeter: See *Meter*

Triple Rhyme: See *Rhyme*

Trochee: See *Foot*

U

Understatement: See *Irony*

Unities: Strict rules of dramatic structure, formulated by Italian and French critics of the

Renaissance and based loosely on the principles of drama discussed by Aristotle in his *Poetics*. Foremost among these rules were the three unities of action, time, and place that compelled a dramatist to: (1) construct a single plot with a beginning, middle, and end that details the causal relationships of action and character; (2) restrict the action to the events of a single day; and (3) limit the scene to a single place or city. The unities were observed faithfully by continental European writers until the Romantic Age, but they were never regularly observed in English drama. Modern dramatists are typically more concerned with a unity of impression or emotional effect than with any of the classical unities.

Urban Realism: A branch of realist writing that attempts to accurately reflect the often harsh facts of modern urban existence.

Utopia: A fictional perfect place, such as "paradise" or "heaven."

Utopian: See *Utopia*

Utopianism: See *Utopia*

V

Verisimilitude: Literally, the appearance of truth. In literary criticism, the term refers to aspects of a work of literature that seem true to the reader.

Vers de societe: See *Occasional Verse*

Vers libre: See *Free Verse*

Verse: A line of metered language, a line of a poem, or any work written in verse.

Versification: The writing of verse. Versification may also refer to the meter, rhyme, and other mechanical components of a poem.

Victorian: Refers broadly to the reign of Queen Victoria of England (1837-1901) and to anything with qualities typical of that era. For example, the qualities of smug narrowmindedness, bourgeois materialism, faith in social progress, and priggish morality are often considered Victorian. This stereotype is contradicted by such dramatic intellectual developments as the theories of Charles Darwin, Karl Marx, and Sigmund Freud (which stirred strong debates in England) and the critical attitudes of serious Victorian writers like Charles Dickens and George Eliot. In literature, the Victorian Period was the great age of the English novel, and the latter part of the era saw the rise of movements such as decadence and symbolism.

Victorian Age: See *Victorian*

Victorian Period: See *Victorian*

W

Weltanschauung: A German term referring to a person's worldview or philosophy.

Weltschmerz: A German term meaning "world pain." It describes a sense of anguish about the nature of existence, usually associated with a melancholy, pessimistic attitude.

Z

Zarzuela: A type of Spanish operetta.

Zeitgeist: A German term meaning "spirit of the time." It refers to the moral and intellectual trends of a given era.

Cumulative Author/Title Index

Cumulative Nationality/Ethnicity Index

Subject/Theme Index

Russian history
    Everything Is Plundered: 36,
        38–40, 48–49
    Grudnow: 77, 79

S

Sacrifice
    Remember: 185, 189
Sadness
    *In Response to Executive Order
        9066: All Americans of Japanese
        Descent Must Report to
        Relocation Centers:* 133, 139
Seasons
    After Apple Picking: 5, 9
    *On the Grasshopper and the
        Cricket:* 170–171
Self respect
    To Lucasta, Going to the Wars: 292
Selflessness
    The Explorer: 61
Sex roles
    Success Is Counted Sweetest:
        234–236
    See also Female-male relations
Sexism
    Hanging Fire: 94–95, 105–106
Shame
    *In Response to Executive Order
        9066: All Americans of Japanese
        Descent Must Report to
        Relocation Centers:* 131
Silence
    The Explorer: 55
    The Horses: 111, 114, 120, 121
    *In Response to Executive Order
        9066: All Americans of Japanese
        Descent Must Report to
        Relocation Centers:* 130, 132,
        133
Similes
    To a Sky-Lark: 256
Simplicity
    *On the Grasshopper and the
        Cricket:* 179
    Grudnow: 85
    To Lucasta, Going to the Wars: 297
    Remember: 190
Skepticism
    Jade Flower Palace: 151
Sleep
    After Apple Picking: 9–10, 16–17
Social activism. *See* Activism
Social change
    The Explorer: 61
Social evolution
    A Black Man Talks of Reaping: 21
Social protest
    To Be of Use: 280
Society
    The Horses: 120
    To a Sky-Lark: 258

Sonnets
    *On the Grasshopper and the
        Cricket:* 159, 161, 165, 173
    To Lucasta, Going to the Wars:
        294
    Sonnet 75: 214, 216, 218–219,
        221–222, 224–227
Sorrow
    Everything Is Plundered: 35
    The Explorer: 53
    The Horses: 112
    Jade Flower Palace: 146, 147, 153
    To a Sky-Lark: 266
Spirituality
    Hanging Fire: 91
    The Horses: 114, 120, 126
    Remember: 185, 195, 198
    To a Sky-Lark: 263
Stereotypes (Psychology)
    *In Response to Executive Order
        9066: All Americans of Japanese
        Descent Must Report to
        Relocation Centers:* 138
Strength
    To Be of Use: 284
    The Horses: 108, 112, 114, 115,
        119, 120
Struggle
    *A Black Man Talks of
        Reaping:* 29
    The Explorer: 61
    Remember: 198–203, 203
Submission
    To Lucasta, Going to the Wars: 299
Success
    Success Is Counted Sweetest:
        231–232, 233, 237–238,
        242, 247
Suffering
    *A Black Man Talks of
        Reaping:* 24
    Grudnow: 79
    Hanging Fire: 94, 99
    The Horses: 112, 120
    To a Sky-Lark: 266
Supernatural
    Everything Is Plundered: 36
Surrealism
    Remember: 197
Survival
    After Apple Picking: 13
    Hanging Fire: 104
    The Horses: 114, 120
Symbolism
    After Apple Picking: 11
    *A Black Man Talks of
        Reaping:* 23
    Everything Is Plundered: 41
    The Explorer: 62
    *On the Grasshopper and the
        Cricket:* 160, 162, 163, 164,
        169, 171
    The Horses: 115, 121

    Remember: 185
    To a Sky-Lark: 253, 260, 261,
        263, 264
Sympathy
    To a Sky-Lark: 261
Synthesis. *See* Integration
    (Philosophy)

T

Taoism
    Jade Flower Palace: 152–153
Teacher-student relationships
    Remember: 186–188, 190
Technology
    After Apple Picking: 7
Tension
    The Explorer: 53
    To Lucasta, Going to the Wars:
        297–299
Time
    After Apple Picking: 9
Tradition
    After Apple Picking: 16
    *On the Grasshopper and the
        Cricket:* 164, 169
    Remember: 185, 186, 189, 190,
        191, 194, 196–197
Tragedy (Calamities)
    The Explorer: 53, 54
Tranquility. *See* Peace
Transcendence
    Sonnet 75: 224
Transcendentalism
    To a Sky-Lark: 249, 253–254
Transformation
    Remember: 197
    To a Sky-Lark: 261
Transience of life
    Jade Flower Palace: 143, 145, 147,
        151–152, 153
Translation
    Everything Is Plundered: 41–44,
        44–45, 47
    Jade Flower Palace: 148
Travel
    Success Is Counted Sweetest:
        243–247
Truth
    After Apple Picking: 9
    Remember: 188
    To a Sky-Lark: 253, 261

U

Uncertainty
    After Apple Picking: 11, 12
Unity
    To Be of Use: 285
    To Lucasta, Going to the Wars:
        299
    Remember: 186–187, 189–190,
        197

Cumulative
Index of First Lines

B

Back then, before we came (On Freedom's Ground) V12:186

Bananas ripe and green, and ginger-root (The Tropics in New York) V4:255

Be happy if the wind inside the orchard (On the Threshold) V22:128

Because I could not stop for Death— (Because I Could Not Stop for Death) V2:27

Before the indifferent beak could let her drop? (Leda and the Swan) V13:182

Before you know what kindness really is (Kindness) V24:84–85

Below long pine winds, a stream twists. (Jade Flower Palace) V32:145

Bent double, like old beggars under slacks, (Dulce et Decorum Est) V10:109

Between my finger and my thumb (Digging) V5:70

Beware of ruins: they have a treacherous charm (Beware of Ruins) V8:43

Bright star! would I were steadfast as thou art— (Bright Star! Would I Were Steadfast as Thou Art) V9:44

But perhaps God needs the longing, wherever else should it dwell, (But Perhaps God Needs the Longing) V20:41

By the rude bridge that arched the flood (Concord Hymn) V4:30

By way of a vanished bridge we cross this river (The Garden Shukkei-en) V18:107

C

Cassandra's kind of crying was (Three To's and an Oi) V24:264

Celestial choir! enthron'd in realms of light, (To His Excellency General Washington) V13:212

Come with me into those things that have felt his despair for so long— (Come with Me) V6:31

Complacencies of the peignoir, and late (Sunday Morning) V16:189

Composed in the Tower, before his execution ("More Light! More Light!") V6:119

D

Darkened by time, the masters, like our memories, mix (Black Zodiac) V10:46

Dear Sirs: (In Response to Executive Order 9066: All Americans of Japanese Descent Must Report to Relocation Centers) V32:129

Death, be not proud, though some have called thee (Holy Sonnet 10) V2:103

Devouring Time, blunt thou the lion's paws (Sonnet 19) V9:210

Disoriented, the newly dead try to turn back, (Our Side) V24:177

Do not go gentle into that good night (Do Not Go Gentle into that Good Night) V1:51

Do not weep, maiden, for war is kind (War Is Kind) V9:252

Don Arturo says: (Business) V16:2

Drink to me only with thine eyes, (Song: To Celia) V23:270–271

(Dumb, (A Grafted Tongue) V12:92

E

Each day the shadow swings (In the Land of Shinar) V7:83

Each morning the man rises from bed because the invisible (It's like This) V23:138–139

Each night she waits by the road (Bidwell Ghost) V14:2

Even when you know what people are capable of, (Knowledge) V25:113

Everything has been plundered, betrayed, sold out, (Everything Is Plundered) V32:113

F

Face of the skies (Moreover, the Moon) V20:153

Falling upon earth (Falling Upon Earth) V2:64

Far far from gusty waves these children's faces. (An Elementary School Classroom in a Slum) V23:88–89

Fast breaks. Lay ups. With Mercury's (Slam, Dunk, & Hook) V30:176–177

First, the self. Then, the observing self. (I, I, I) V26:97

Five years have past; five summers, with the length (Tintern Abbey) V2:249

Flesh is heretic. (Anorexic) V12:2

For a long time the butterfly held a prominent place in psychology (Lepidopterology) V23:171–172

For Jews, the Cossacks are always coming. (The Cossacks) V25:70

For three years, out of key with his time, (Hugh Selwyn Mauberley) V16:26

Forgive me for thinking I saw (For a New Citizen of These United States) V15:55

From my mother's sleep I fell into the State (The Death of the Ball Turret Gunner) V2:41

From the air to the air, like an empty net, (The Heights of Macchu Picchu) V28:137

G

Gardener: Sir, I encountered Death (Incident in a Rose Garden) V14:190

Gather ye Rose-buds while ye may, (To the Virgins, to Make Much of Time) V13:226

Gazelle, I killed you (Ode to a Drum) V20:172–173

Glory be to God for dappled things— (Pied Beauty) V26:161

Go down, Moses (Go Down, Moses) V11:42

God save America, (America, America) V29:2

Gray mist wolf (Four Mountain Wolves) V9:131

H

"Had he and I but met (The Man He Killed) V3:167

Had we but world enough, and time (To His Coy Mistress) V5:276

Hail to thee, blithe Spirit! (To a Sky-Lark) V32:251

Half a league, half a league (The Charge of the Light Brigade) V1:2

Having a Coke with You (Having a Coke with You) V12:105

He clasps the crag with crooked hands (The Eagle) V11:30

He was found by the Bureau of Statistics to be (The Unknown Citizen) V3:302

He was seen, surrounded by rifles, (The Crime Was in Granada) V23:55–56

Hear the sledges with the bells— (The Bells) V3:46

Heart, you bully, you punk, I'm wrecked, I'm shocked (One Is One) V24:158

Her body is not so white as (Queen-Ann's-Lace) V6:179

Her eyes the glow-worm lend thee; (The Night Piece: To Julia) V29:206

Cumulative Index of Last Lines

O Lord our Lord, how excellent is thy name in all the earth! (Psalm 8) V9:182

O Roger, Mackerel, Riley, Ned, Nellie, Chester, Lady Ghost (Names of Horses) V8:142

o, walk your body down, don't let it go it alone. (Walk Your Body Down) V26:219

Of all our joys, this must be the deepest. (Drinking Alone Beneath the Moon) V20:59–60

of blood and ignorance. (Art Thou the Thing I Wanted) V25:2–3

of gentleness (To a Sad Daughter) V8:231

of love's austere and lonely offices? (Those Winter Sundays) V1:300

of peaches (The Weight of Sweetness) V11:230

Of the camellia (Falling Upon Earth) V2:64

Of the Creator. And he waits for the world to begin (Leviathan) V5:204

of our festivities (Fragment 2) V31:63

Of what is past, or passing, or to come (Sailing to Byzantium) V2:207

Oh that was the garden of abundance, seeing you. (Seeing You) V24:244–245

Old Ryan, not yours (The Constellation Orion) V8:53

On the dark distant flurry (Angle of Geese) V2:2

on the frosty autumn air. (The Cossacks) V25:70

On the look of Death— (There's a Certain Slant of Light) V6:212

On the reef of Norman s Woe! (The Wreck of the Hesperus) V31:317

On your head like a crown (Any Human to Another) V3:2

One could do worse that be a swinger of birches. (Birches) V13:15

"Only the Lonely," trying his best to sound like Elvis. (The Women Who Loved Elvis All Their Lives) V28:274

or a loose seed. (Freeway 280) V30:62

Or does it explode? (Harlem) V1:63

Or help to half-a-crown." (The Man He Killed) V3:167

Or just some human sleep. (After Apple Picking) V32:3

or last time, we look. (In Particular) V20:125

or last time, we look. (In Particular) V20:125

Or might not have lain dormant forever. (Mastectomy) V26:123

or nothing (Queen-Ann's-Lace) V6:179

Or pleasures, seldom reached, again pursued. (A Nocturnal Reverie) V30:119–120

or the one red leaf the snow releases in March. (ThreeTimes My Life Has Opened) V16:213

ORANGE forever. (Ballad of Orange and Grape) V10:18

our every corpuscle become an elf. (Moreover, the Moon) V20:153

Our love shall live, and later life renew." (Sonnet 75) V32:215

outside. (it was New York and beautifully, snowing . . . (i was sitting in mcsorley's) V13:152

owing old (old age sticks) V3:246

P

patient in mind remembers the time. (Fading Light) V21:49

Penelope, who really cried. (An Ancient Gesture) V31:3

Perhaps he will fall. (Wilderness Gothic) V12:242

Petals on a wet, black bough (In a Station of the Metro) V2:116

Plaiting a dark red love-knot into her long black hair (The Highwayman) V4:68

Powerless, I drown. (Maternity) V21:142–143

Práise him. (Pied Beauty) V26:161

Pro patria mori. (Dulce et Decorum Est) V10:110

R

Rage, rage against the dying of the light (Do Not Go Gentle into that Good Night) V1:51

Raise it again, man. We still believe what we hear. (The Singer's House) V17:206

Remember. (Remember) V32:185

Remember the Giver fading off the lip (A Drink of Water) V8:66

Ride me. (Witness) V26:285

rise & walk away like a panther. (Ode to a Drum) V20:172–173

Rises toward her day after day, like a terrible fish (Mirror) V1:116

S

Shall be lifted—nevermore! (The Raven) V1:202

Shantih shantih shantih (The Waste Land) V20:248–252

share my shivering bed. (Chorale) V25:51

she'd miss me. (In Response to Executive Order 9066: All Americans of Japanese Descent Must Report to Relocation Centers) V32:129

Show an affirming flame. (September 1, 1939) V27:235

Shuddering with rain, coming down around me. (Omen) V22:107

Simply melted into the perfect light. (Perfect Light) V19:187

Singing of him what they could understand (Beowulf) V11:3

Singing with open mouths their strong melodious songs (I Hear America Singing) V3:152

Sister, one of those who never married. (My Grandmother's Plot in the Family Cemetery) V27:155

Sleep, fly, rest: even the sea dies! (Lament for Ignacio Sánchez Mejías) V31:128–30

slides by on grease (For the Union Dead) V7:67

Slouches towards Bethlehem to be born? (The Second Coming) V7:179

So long lives this, and this gives life to thee (Sonnet 18) V2:222

So prick my skin. (Pine) V23:223–224

Somebody loves us all. (Filling Station) V12:57

Speak through my words and my blood. (The Heights of Macchu Picchu) V28:141

spill darker kissmarks on that dark. (Ten Years after Your Deliberate Drowning) V21:240

Stand still, yet we will make him run (To His Coy Mistress) V5:277

startled into eternity (Four Mountain Wolves) V9:132

Still clinging to your shirt (My Papa's Waltz) V3:192

Stood up, coiled above his head, transforming all. (A Tall Man Executes a Jig) V12:229

strangers ask. *Originally?* And I hesitate. (Originally) V25:146–147

Surely goodness and mercy shall follow me all the days of my life: and I will dwell in the house of the Lord for ever (Psalm 23) V4:103

syllables of an old order. (A Grafted Tongue) V12:93